Degas Landscapes

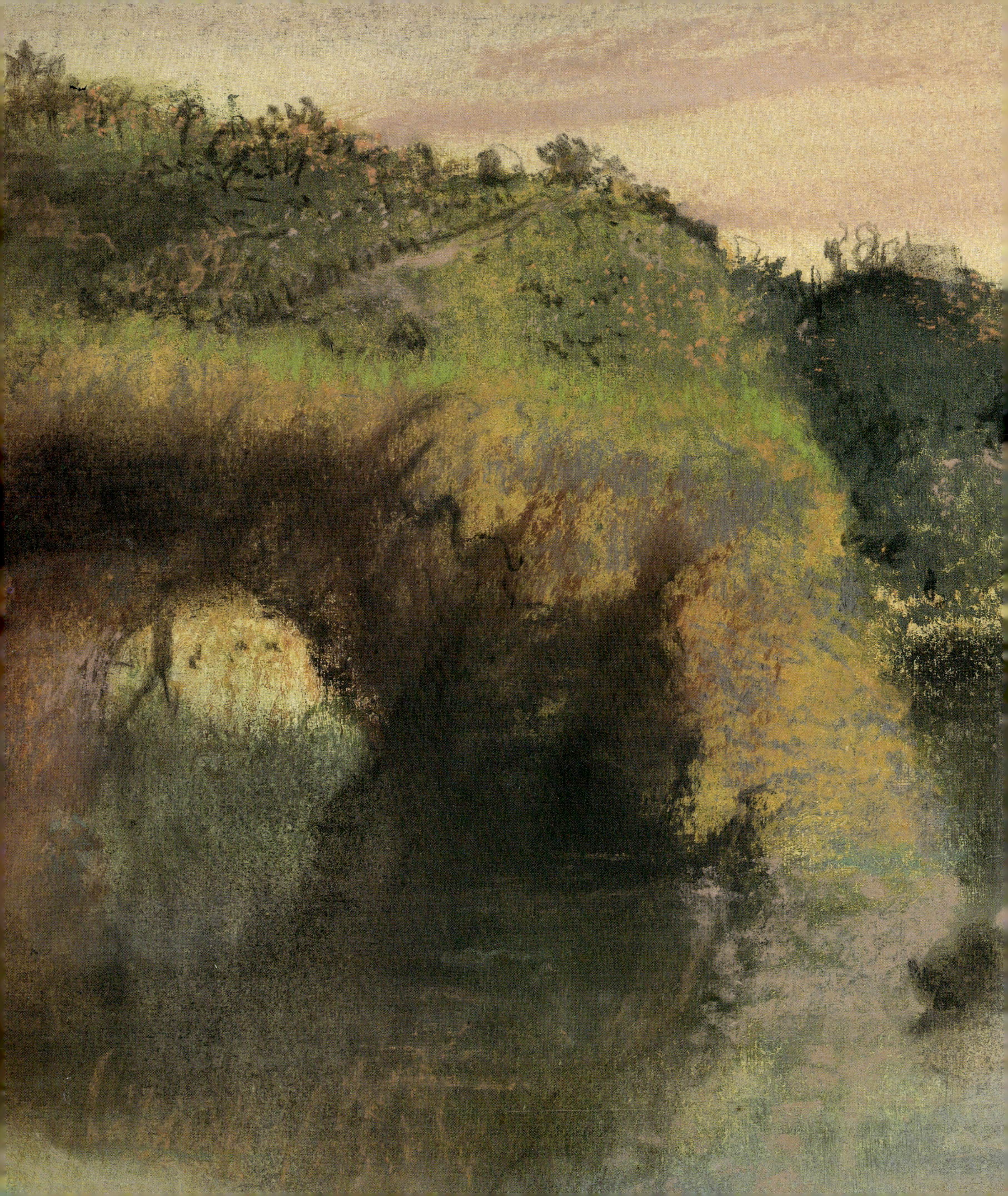

Richard Kendall

Degas Landscapes

Yale University Press, New Haven and London
in association with
The Metropolitan Museum of Art, New York
and
The Museum of Fine Arts, Houston

This book is dedicated to Mollie Sayer, and to the memory of my father.

Note on the captions to the illustrations: All works are by Edgar Degas unless otherwise stated. Measurements are in centimetres, height before width. For abbreviations used, see the Bibliography. Unless otherwise stated, photographs and transparencies have been provided by the owners or custodians of the works.

Frontispiece: Detail from *River Banks*, 1890, monotype and pastel. Private collection. See fig. 132.

Designed by Gillian Malpass
Set in Linotron Bembo by Best-set Typesetter Ltd, Hong Kong
Printed in Italy by Amilcare Pizzi, S.p.A., Milan

Library of Congress Cataloging-in-Publication Data

Kendall, Richard.
Degas landscapes/by Richard Kendall.
p. cm.
Includes bibliographical references and index.
ISBN 0-300-05837-3.—ISBN 0-300-05862-4 (paper)
1. Degas, Edgar, 1834–1917—Criticism and interpretation.
2. Landscape in art. I. Title.
N6853.D33K46 1993
760′.092—dc20 93-11554
CIP

A catalogue record for this book is available from The British Library

Contents

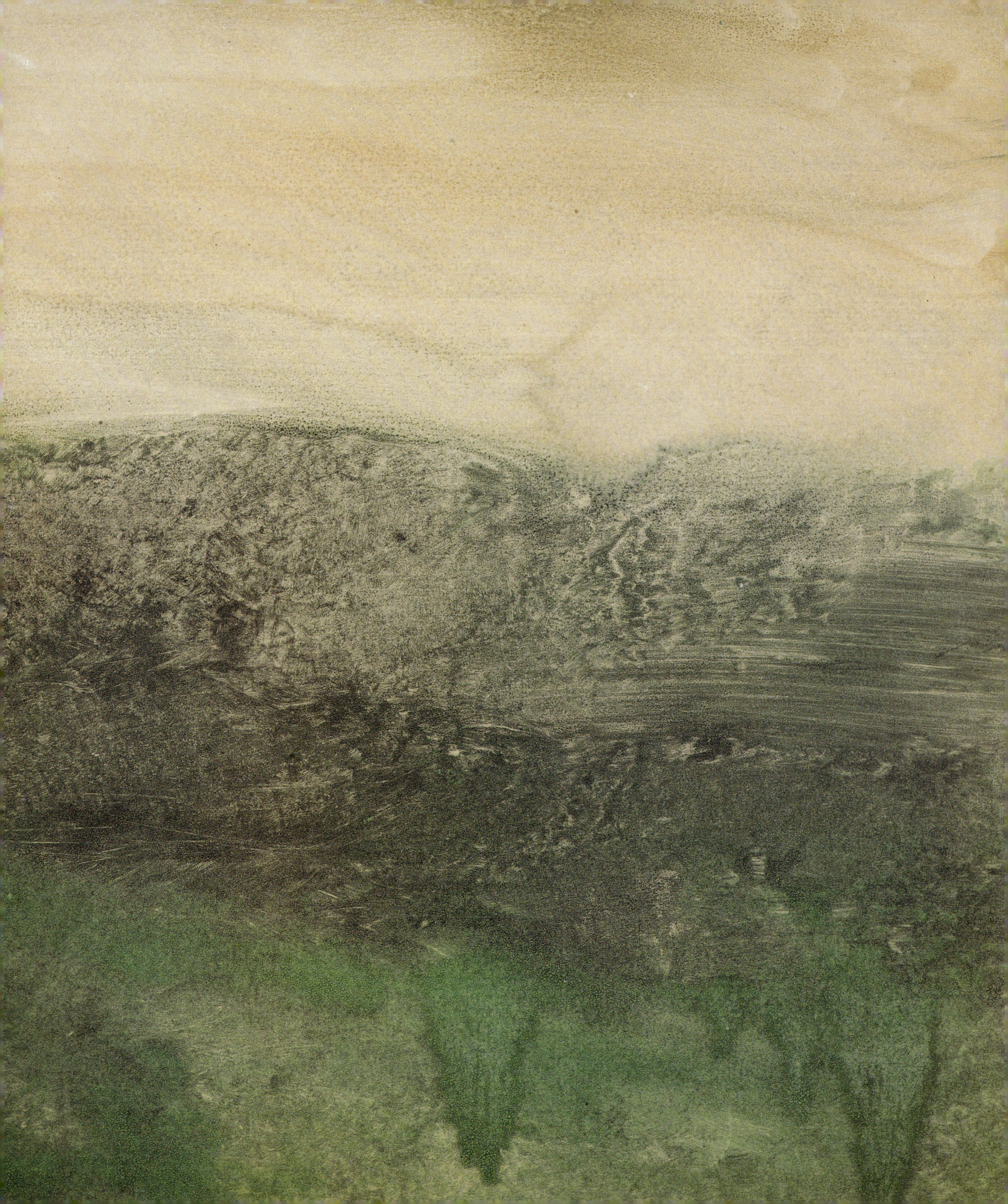

Preface

In November 1892, an exhibition of new works by Edgar Degas opened at the Galerie Durand-Ruel, on the rue Laffitte in Paris. The event was remarkable, even sensational, in at least three respects. Though Degas was approaching his sixtieth year and had already achieved considerable celebrity, the exhibition was the first 'one-man show' – in the sense it is understood today – of his long and industrious career. Technically, it was also something of a breakthrough, presenting to the art world of Paris a brand-new process of colour print-making, far exceeding in audacity and conceptual daring the experiments of his contemporaries. Most unexpected of all, however, was the subject-matter of the pictures in the Durand-Ruel show. For almost two decades, Degas had patiently built himself a reputation as the principal figure painter of the Impressionist circle, presenting his images of tired laundresses, brazen café-concert *artistes*, athletic ballerinas and closeted female nudes at seven of the group's eight exhibitions. To the surprise of some of his closest friends, and to the evident discomfort of certain admirers, his 1892 display was based on an entirely different theme, and one with which he had never before been publicly associated. All two dozen or so pictures in the Durand Ruel gallery were representations of the landscape.

The images in question came from Degas' suite of colour monotypes, most of them extended or enriched with pastel, that were begun in Burgundy in 1890 and completed some months before the Durand-Ruel show. Though they are among the most well documented of all Degas' productions, and belong with the most challenging of his mature achievements, the landscape monotypes have never been studied in detail nor the circumstances leading to their public unveiling subjected to scrutiny. Extraordinary though this neglect appears to be, it is part of a wider obliviousness to the theme of landscape in Degas' career that has curiously distorted the reception of his *oeuvre*. Otherwise reputable texts tell us that Degas was indifferent to the countryside and the beauties of nature; that he had little taste for the landscape art of his predecessors; that he kept aloof from the outdoor painting antics of his peers; and that, when landscape elements appeared in his own work, they invariably derived from his memory or imagination. Taking his reputation as 'the painter of dancers' at face value, we have tended to tidy up Degas' career, seeing him as the odd man out in a predominantly pastoral Impressionist enterprise.

To a certain extent, Degas himself was responsible for this state of affairs. Always mindful of his reputation and ready with a mischievous tongue, the artist took pleasure in satirizing the hazardous practices of his friends ('Painting is not a sport!', he told the *pleinairiste* Henri Rouart) and in advertising the superiority of pictures made in the studio. Posterity has been too quick to swallow his bait, however, and a more critical examination of Degas' travels, notebooks and unfamiliar works of art reveals an astute and sophisticated relationship with his natural surroundings. From the first months of his artistic apprenticeship to the last decade of his working life, Degas produced landscapes

2. Detail of fig. 148.

in every medium at his disposal and on almost every scale. In his early twenties, he made drawings of French and Italian scenery, graduating to watercolour, etching, oil on paper and substantial canvases of landscape *motifs*. Openly admiring Claude, Corot and the landscapes of Fromentin and Delacroix, Degas made his professional début with a group of grandiose history paintings, each set in the open air and each reflecting his experience of mountains, pasture or foliage. In the 1860s, the artist made sketches of farmland and pastels of the Normandy coast, paintings of racetracks, rivers and beach scenes, now judging himself against Boudin and Courbet, Huet and Riesener, Manet and Morisot, Fattori and Whistler. As the Impressionist project gathered momentum, Degas collaborated with Pissarro on his rustic prints, made black-and-white monotypes of picnics and moonscapes, and developed his interest in the turf. Throughout this period, there are signs of a competitive awareness of his landscape-painting colleagues, notably Monet and Cézanne, and increasingly ambitious attempts to integrate rural settings with portraits, dance subjects and studies of the nude.

It was in the decade of the 1890s, however, that Degas' diverse encounters with the landscape bore the most spectacular fruit. Apart from the 1892 exhibition of colour monotypes, this period saw his experiments with outdoor photography, his improbably rural *Russian Dancers*, his ambitious extramural *Bathers* and his greatly underrated series of Saint-Valéry oils. Many of these projects were prompted by Degas' incessant travelling and gave expression to his vivid, sometimes passionate, sometimes perverse, response to the spectacle of nature. Contrary to widespread belief, there is evidence that Degas sometimes worked in the open air and that he instructed his young followers in landscape technique, just as he occasionally contrived bizarre and erotic fantasies from the rural repertoire. In the same years, we find the artist taking note of Gauguin's scenes of Brittany, Pissarro's cityscapes, Monet's series paintings and Cézanne's outdoor nudes, and acquiring dozens of landscapes for his own collection by contemporaries and admired precursors. Set against this background, the Durand-Ruel exhibition falls suddenly into place, suggesting continuity rather than disruption, topicality rather than irrelevance.

Given the strange history of Degas' landscape production and its almost wilful omission from both specialist and popular presentations of his achievement, this book is necessarily something of an act of reclamation, even of redefinition. As many as possible of the three hundred or so pure landscape images made by the artist, as well as a large number of his landscape settings, have been located and examined, and systematically studied in the context of Degas' *oeuvre*. In this sense conventional, the book and its methodologies are also the product of their age, offering less orthodox perspectives on the period in question and an implicit critique of earlier approaches to it. Despite the monographic nature of its theme, the text shows Degas' landscapes to be in step with the picture-making practices of his contemporaries, sometimes a pace or two behind, as often striding boldly or eccentrically ahead. Similarly, the artist's utterances and known ambitions for his landscapes are found to run parallel with the literary, critical and philosophical momentum of his times, and to respond to the newest procedures and most abstruse conceptions of his circle. Whether pioneering an interest in English prints or reviving a fascination with Japanese art, whether reacting to the exhibition strategies of Monet or the printmaking expertise of Mary Cassatt, Degas found himself and his landscape activities in the vanguard of his craft. More than most of his colleagues, he also saw the landscape as a pretext for technical licence, requiring modern audiences to work hard at unaccustomed surfaces and exotic textures. In the preparation of this volume, the artist's procedures have been probed and re-evaluated, his materials and superimpositions analysed, and in certain cases, such as the colour monotypes, his studio practices unravelled for the first time. While remote from some of the theoretical gymnastics of our day, these approaches have their own unashamed radicalism, and hold out comparable hopes of fresh encounters with the art of the past, and with our ways of dealing with that past.

A subject as panoramic and a body of work as scattered as that covered by *Degas Landscapes* has demanded an exceptional degree of kindness and forbearance of a large number of individuals. Without the support of John Nicoll, Gillian Malpass and Sheila Lee, the book would never have come into being; without the exertions of George Shackelford and Colta Ives, the project would never have found its counterpart in a major exhibition of Degas' landscape art; and without the generously offered and patiently rendered help of Caroline Durand-Ruel-Godfroy, Marianne and Walter Feilchenfeldt, Henri Loyrette, Ted Reff, Anne Roquebert and Richard Thomson, many pictures would have remained undiscovered and many avenues unexplored. To Arianne Lawson, I am as grateful as ever for her translations and help with difficult texts. Particular thanks are due also to those private collectors, museum curators and auction-house officials who have allowed me to pore over their pictures, and to the archivists and librarians who have given me access to letters, photographs and texts. To these, and to the following colleagues and friends who have contributed in a hundred different ways, I offer my warmest thanks: Kathy Adler, Götz Adriani, Kate Austin, George Baer, Julian Barran, Graham Beal, Stevan Beck Beloga, Bruce Bernard, Jean Sutherland Boggs, Sylvie and Philippe Brame, Mr and Mrs Michael von Brentano, Peter and Angela Brookes, the Princesse de Broglie, Sara Campbell, Victor Carlson, Jacqueline Cartwright, Eugene Chesrow, Michael Clarke, Roger Clisby, Marjorie Cohn, Philip Conisbee, Jane Connell, Julia Collieu, William Darby, Christian Debize, Emmanuel Di-Donna, Barbara Divver, Douglas Druick, Ann and Charles Dumas, Judith Durrer, Adrian Eeles, Helga Ehret, Galerie Fischer, Lucian Freud, Kate Garmeson, John Gere, David Gol, Mr and Mrs Leonard Goldberg, Andrew and Annette Gossett, Anthony Griffiths, Gloria Groom, Vivien Hamilton, Anne Higgonet, Derek Hill, John House, Michael and Marianne Howard, Gregory Jecmen, Jeremy Johnson, Paul and Ellen Josefowitz, Sam Josefowitz, E.W. Kornfeld, Jan Krugier, Elizabeth Kujawski, Phyllis Lambert, Philippe Lanthony, Ronald S. Lauder, John Leighton, Galerie Lempertz, Elizabeth Lewyt, Peter Ludwig, Patrice Marandel, Stephen Mazoh, Sixte de Menthon, Helene Meyer, Charles Millard, Charles Moffett, Charles de Montalembert, Edward Morris, Lisa Moore, Ann Norton, Michael Pantazzi, Alfred Paquement, Merribell Parsons, Eva-Maria Preiswerk-Losel, Roy Perkinson, Maxime Préaud, Hubert Prouté, Nicole Quellet, M. and Mme A. Raoul-Duval, Bill Robinson, Galerie Römer, Robert Rothschild, Elsa Sackler, Janet Salz, Manuel Schmit, David Scrase, Barbara Shapiro, Howard and Barbara Sirak, Louise Smith, Peter Soriano, Christine Stauffer, Andrew Strauss, Patricia Tang, Christoph von Tavel, Eugene Thaw, Belinda Thomson, Gary Tinterow, Walter Tschopp, Françoise Viatte, Peter Wick, Juliet Wilson-Bareau, Jon Whiteley and Peter Zeghers. Finally, I owe the greatest debt of gratitude to Mollie Sayer, who travelled (literally) through much of this project with me; and to my ever-indulgent daughter, Ruth.

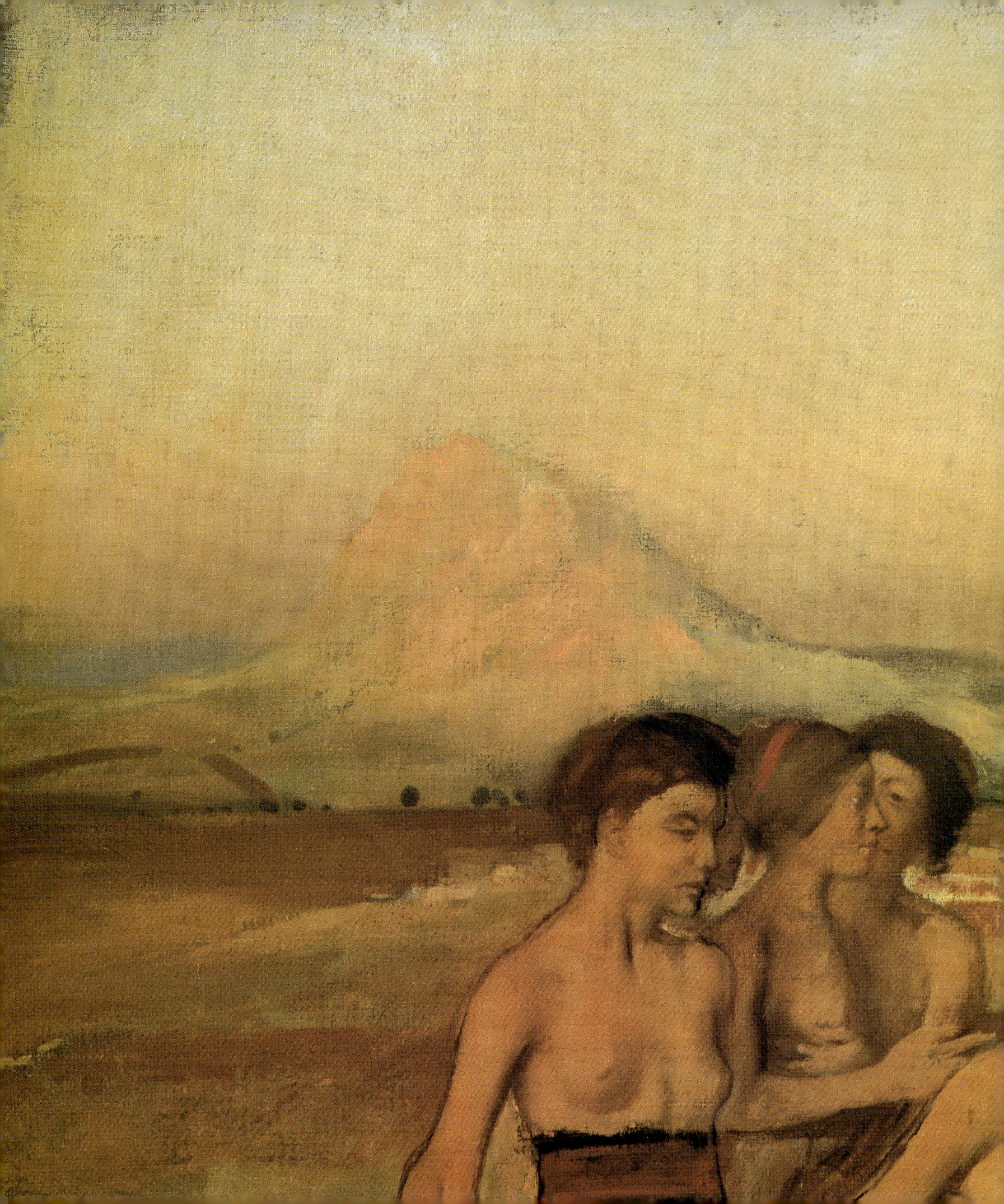

1 The Classical Landscape

'I am thinking about France, which is not as beautiful . . .'
(Degas, writing from Italy; 1858)

Degas became a painter of the landscape despite, rather than because of, his training as an artist. Nothing in his formal education predisposed him towards landscape art, while most of the decisive influences on his early years, such as the guidance of his family and the example of his teachers and mentors, encouraged him in a quite different direction. His first completed canvases were all portraits and figure studies, and much of his reputation as an artist rests on his mastery of the human form and of the draughtsmanship and compositional skills associated with it. Though he produced several hundred landscapes in the course of his working life, Degas began his career as he ended it, as an artist nurtured within the traditions of the human figure, in awe of the Old Masters and with an almost exaggerated respect for the figurative compositions of the past. Against this background, his activities as a landscapist were at best unexpected, at worst eccentric or even heretical. So pervasive were the values of Degas' early training that he never lost a sense of unease in his dealings with the landscape. Many of his most celebrated landscape images were produced in conditions of near-secrecy, and the overwhelming majority of his drawings, pastels, prints and oil paintings of the landscape remained unexhibited during his lifetime.

As a teenager growing up in Paris in the early 1850s, Degas was schooled in the most severe conceptions and practices of art the city had to offer. When he graduated from the Lycée Louis-le-Grand in 1853 at the age of eighteen, he had already learnt to draw from plaster casts of antique sculpture and to copy engravings of canonical paintings, earning commendation for his efforts if not more fulsome praise.[1] During his apprentice years, Degas continued to make copies of pictures he admired, and soon mastered the time-honoured skills of drawing from the nude model. Though his training was haphazard and abrupt by contemporary standards, it served to entrench the values of his upbringing, stressing the primacy of drawing, the centrality of the human figure and the lofty achievements of the European tradition. What little we know of Degas' father, Auguste De Gas, suggests that he played a crucial role in supporting and directing this aspect of his son's vocation. Father and son trailed round galleries, picture-dealers and private collections together, and it was Auguste who made it possible for Degas to travel to Italy and study there for almost three years.[2] Auguste's tastes appear to have been orthodox, not to say reactionary, emphasising the great figure painters and portraitists of the past and deriding the innovations of his own age. He passed on to his son his devotion to the art of the early Renaissance, more than once reminding him that 'the masters of the fifteenth century are the true, the only guides'.[3] In the letters they exchanged, Auguste praised his son's draughtsmanship and urged him towards a career in portrait painting, and there was an unspoken assumption that Degas would

3. Detail of fig. 31.

achieve greatness as a painter of the human figure, not as a master of a minor form, such as still life or landscape.[4]

Some of the most vivid evidence of Degas' formation as an artist can be found in his thirty-eight surviving notebooks, the majority compiled in the early years of his career. Unknown during his lifetime, the notebooks first came to prominence after the artist's death, when a large group was donated to the Bibliothèque Nationale in Paris by Degas' brother, René.[5] As scholars began to explore their contents, hundreds of new drawings and paintings in ink, pencil, watercolour and gouache were added to Degas' *oeuvre*, ranging from the entirely expected, such as copies from the Old Masters and working drawings for Degas' own pictures, to the less predictable genres of caricature, mild pornography and satirical verse. Most surprising of all, however, was the revelation of another, almost unknown, Degas. Paul-André Lemoisne, the curator of the Cabinet des Estampes at the Bibliothèque Nationale and later the compiler of the *catalogue raisonné* of the artist's work, was the first to write about the new discovery. In an article of 1921, Lemoisne began by describing the notebooks and summarising their contents, tantalising his audience with excerpts from the artist's written notes, many of which have subsequently become famous. He then continued:

> But one of the most curious revelations of these notebooks is Degas in his almost entirely unsuspected role as a landscape painter. We knew of a series of landscapes by him that were shown at Durand-Ruel in 1893 and seen again, with others of a similar kind, at his studio sale . . . This series of landscapes from the end of the artist's career seemed like an isolated occurrence; and indeed, except for the backgrounds of certain pictures, we knew hardly any other landscapes apart from this series; so we concluded rather hastily that Degas did not understand the landscape! On the contrary, Degas interested himself in it from his earliest years of study, and we find in his youthful notebooks several landscapes in pen and ink or pencil, still in the dry manner of d'Aligny, yet interesting in their perspective and above all in their precision of tones and spatial planes, which Degas always tried to achieve.[6]

After discussing these early landscapes, Lemoisne announced a further group of studies, made at Haras-du-Pin in Normandy in 1861:

> In these drawings, in which he described the Château du Pin with its great groves of trees, its terrace and its surroundings, a true landscapist is revealed. In a few strokes of the brush, Degas was able to present us with a landscape of a depth and vastness that astonish us in their simplicity of means and which recall Rembrandt; it is the same simplicity of execution, and above all the same sobriety, the same deliberate omission of details in order to represent only its principal lines . . . Apart from these drawings in sepia, which reveal to us Degas the unknown landscapist, numerous written notes in the pages of his earlier notebooks, jotted down during travels in Provence and Italy, finally show us the extent to which he could feel and capture the picturesqueness and beauty of a landscape.[7]

Additional examples of Degas' sensitive and unexpected response to nature followed, prompting Lemoisne to this conclusion: 'Evidently, the man who was so enthusiastic in front of nature and who knew how to see and express its beauties in this way, could have been a landscapist.'[8]

How are we to come to terms with this 'true landscapist', this clandestine maker of rural scenes that bring to mind d'Aligny and Rembrandt, this

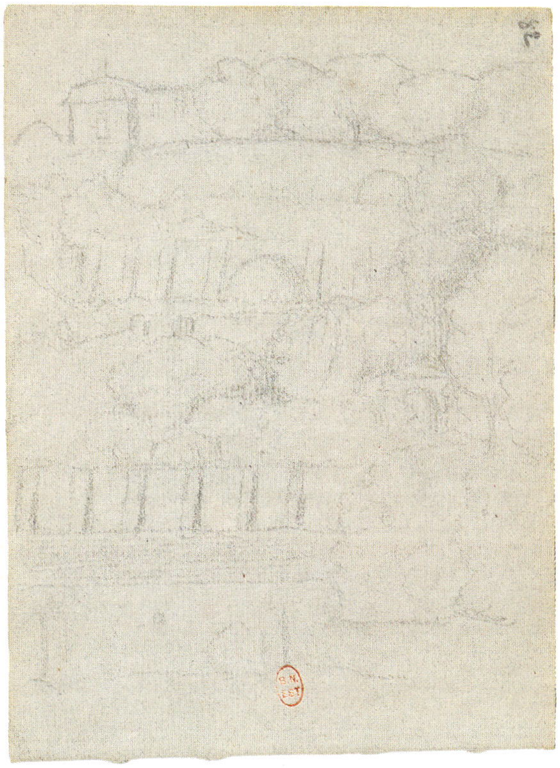

4 *Terraced Hillside*, 1855, pencil, 12.9 × 9.4. Notebook 3, page 82. Bibliothèque Nationale, Paris.

'landscape painter Degas might have been'?[9] A closer look at some of the notebooks described by Lemoisne helps to unravel the conundrum and to tease out some of the practices and achievements of Degas' formative years. Between 1853 and 1856, the year Degas left for Italy, he used six small pocket-books, filling them with notes of places visited, studies from paintings he had admired, and the first, still-timid, glimpses of his own face.[10] More than three-quarters of these drawings were directly based on the art of the past, reflecting his father's taste for such artists as Fra Angelico, Ghirlandaio and Fra Bartolommeo, his tutors' preoccupation with classical sculpture and his own aspirations towards portraiture. Of the remaining twenty-five percent, some show the first hints of a more personal, wayward sensibility, not least a group of almost forty studies of the landscape and distant buildings. All these landscape drawings are small, most are tentative or fussily detailed, and some are little more than outlines with hastily added annotations. But in the context of Degas' early formation, their existence and their considerable diversity is at least worthy of note. On this miniature scale, Degas tackled a view of Paris from Mont Valérien, several studies of the Rhône and the suburbs of Lyon, and townscapes of Avignon, Arles and Nîmes. More cautiously, he selected details from such scenes, drawing boats and river banks, trees and flowers; there is even a study of another draughtsman, apparently caught in the act of sketching the landscape.[11]

A notebook drawing such as *Terraced Hillside* (fig. 4), which measures only five inches in height, shows both the cramped technique and the bold design of many of these small-scale studies, while allowing us some mischievous speculation about their origins.[12] The scene has been identified by Theodore Reff as that of Fourvière, near Lyon, and is one of a number of sites recorded by Degas during a visit to that city in 1855.[13] The pretext for his excursion was almost certainly the presence in Lyon of Louis Lamothe, Degas' teacher, and Lamothe's own master, Hippolyte Flandrin, who were working together on the murals in the church of Saint-Martin d'Ainay.[14] Degas was clearly in the area for several days, conscientiously making drawings of pictures in the Lyon art gallery, classical casts in the Ecole des Beaux-Arts and views of prominent local buildings. An astute and deferential student with an eye to his own future might also have made studies of his teacher's work in progress, but such studies are conspicuous by their absence.[15] Apparently unimpressed by the solemn religiosity of the mural programme, Degas made almost no reference in his notebook to the labours of Flandrin and Lamothe. Instead, he took refuge in the landscape, curiously anticipating the subversive role this subject was to play in his later career. Playing truant on the outskirts of the town, he drafted out more than a dozen compositions of hillsides and wooded valleys, rocks and trees, and sketched the banks of the Rhône and the mountains beyond.[16] Nor was this an isolated example of such truancy. After leaving Lyon, Degas travelled through Provence, again drawing clusters of buildings and distant views, amongst which was the fortified town of Villeneuve-les-Avignon (fig. 5).[17]

There is a danger of exaggerating both the orthodoxy of Degas' earliest works of art and the unexpectedness of these first encounters with the landscape. Degas' notebooks are marked as much by their breadth of taste and occasional lapses of decorum as by their strict adherence to the approved canon; a study from Titian, for example, will be followed by a vignette from the heterodox Hogarth, and a crisp rendering of a naked Venus might accompany a drawing of the artist's own leg.[18] Other subjects include plants and flowers, fellow-artists standing at their easels and an early glimpse of a stage performance, while his written notes range over classical texts and lists of expenses, youthful aphorisms

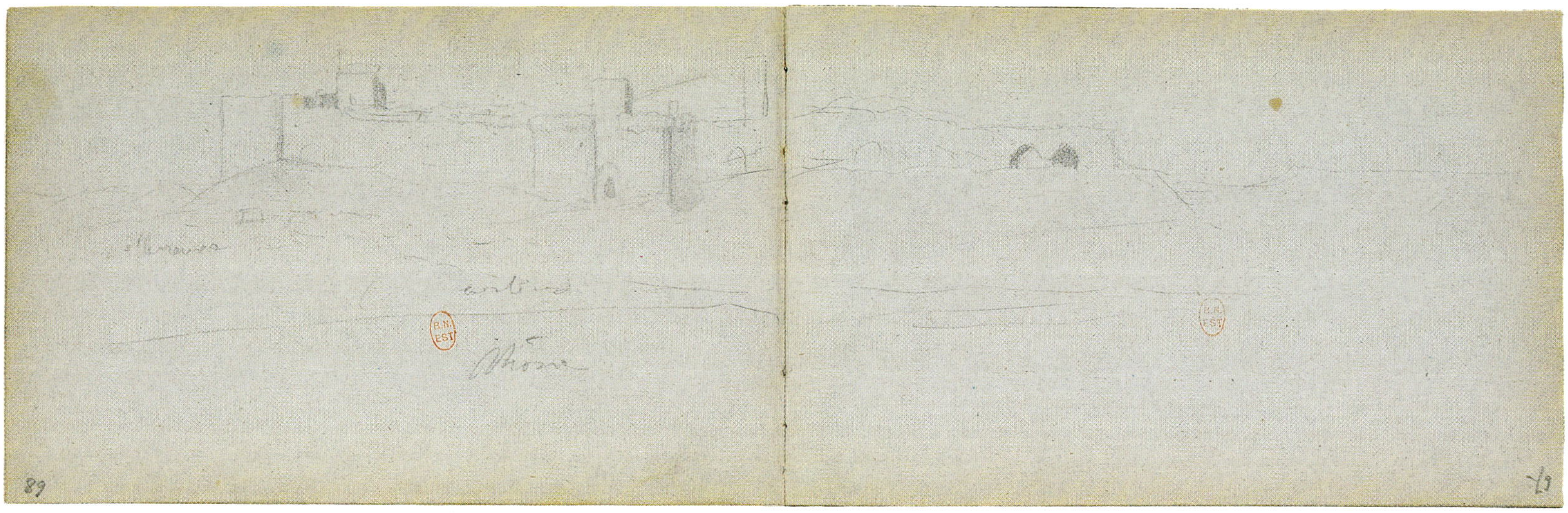

5. *View of Villeneuve-les-Avignon*, 1855, pencil, 9 × 14 (page size). Notebook 4, pages 68 and 67. Bibliothèque Nationale, Paris.

and ribald verse.[19] In this sense, the landscapes are part of a more general diversity and point to a mobile, restless curiosity on the part of the young artist. They are also typical of many comparable notebooks kept by students of Degas' generation and reflect the conventional wisdom of the day. Even under the most severe task-masters, trainee artists were encouraged to carry a pocket-book and sharpen their skills on everyday subjects, alongside their more solemn exercises in the studio and their copying activities in the Louvre.[20] For many novices, such drawings remained no more than an exercise, while for others they offered a first taste of a wider vocabulary of subject-matter and a brief engagement with skills that would dominate their later lives.

There is no evidence that Degas received formal training in landscape painting at any stage in his career. Disconcerting though this statement might appear to be, it loses much of its force when set aside the early experiences of his landscape-painting contemporaries, among them Monet, Pissarro, Sisley and Cézanne, none of whom received a systematic education in the branch of painting to which they ultimately devoted themselves. Unlike these artists, however, Degas opted for the most orthodox form of tuition then available and for a pattern of training that was at times tolerant, at others contemptuous of the forms and procedures of landscape art. While Monet and Sisley benefited from the liberal precepts of Gleyre's studio, and while Pissarro and Cézanne learnt from their colleagues, from first-hand experience and from each other, Degas committed himself to a discipline that was neither liberal nor pragmatic. In 1855, he entered the competition for places at the Ecole des Beaux-Arts in Paris, a procedure that depended entirely on the student's mastery of life drawing. After admission to the Ecole, he was registered as a pupil of Louis Lamothe, a now almost forgotten muralist and religious painter who had been trained by Flandrin, himself a celebrated pupil of Ingres. Degas' association with Lamothe was brief, and there are some indications, such as the events surrounding the Lyon excursion, that both father and son regretted their choice of mentor.[21] But there can be no doubt that Degas' decision to align himself with the school of Flandrin and, by implication, with the tradition of Ingres, was carefully deliberated and profoundly influential, not only on his artistic evolution in general but on his approach to landscape making in particular.

If a single contemporary figure can be said to preside over the early formation of Degas' art in all its aspects, it is that of Jean-Auguste-Dominique Ingres. Not

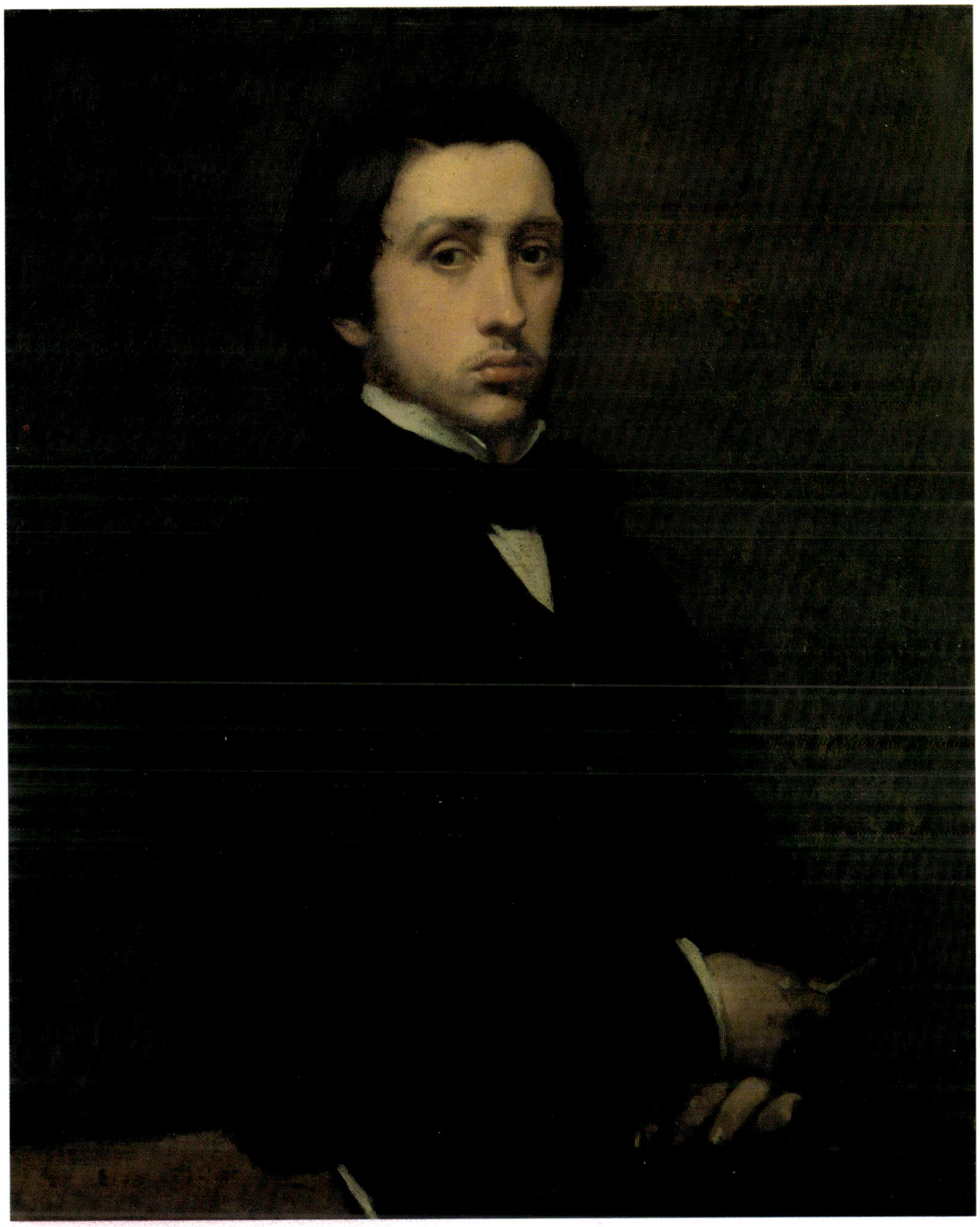

6. *Self-portrait*, 1855, oil on paper, mounted on canvas, 81 × 64 (L 5). Musée d'Orsay, Paris.

only did Degas spend a crucial period of his training under the transmitted influence of Ingres, but Degas' mature art, his conversation and even his personal life were to some extent modelled upon the older artist. In Degas' early sketchbooks there are no less than eleven partial or complete studies from the master's works, ranging from classical and religious imagery, such as the *Apotheosis of Homer* and the *Martyrdom of St Symphorien*, to the portrait of *Cherubini and his Muse* and the magnificent *Valpinçon Bather*.[22] One of Degas' first canvases, the 1855 *Self-portrait* (fig. 6), was a self-conscious variant of an image by Ingres made at about the same age, a picture than was also re-worked by Flandrin and Lamothe.[23] So great was Degas' admiration for the person and the achievement of his idol, that the timid student contrived to meet the seventy-five year-old artist, an incident he recalled solemnly and obsessively into his own old age.[24] Paintings by Ingres provided the exemplars for many of Degas' early compositions, and, as the years passed, he acquired almost twenty of Ingres' canvases for his own collection, as well as a vast number of drawings. Most famously, the mature Degas became a living repository of the master's wisdom, citing aphorisms and anecdotes as if they were articles of his own personal faith.

More than fifty years Degas' senior, Ingres was at the peak of his celebrity, a succession of major portraits and public commissions behind him and a number of large-scale murals proclaiming his achievements throughout the capital. For several decades, Ingres had also acted as standard-bearer for the most austere values of art, thundering against innovation while upholding the claims of precedent and discipline. Though he was not without powerful enemies, and indeed was driven to formulate certain of his precepts in conditions of near-paranoia, he was widely seen as, and believed himself to be, the representative of the dominant tradition in European painting. In his much-quoted maxims, many of which Degas learnt by heart, Ingres summarised the principles that had guided him throughout his career. Fundamental to these was the assertion that 'There is nothing essential to be discovered in art after Phidias and Raphael, but there is much to be done, even after them, to maintain the cult of truth and to perpetuate the tradition of the beautiful'.[25] Truth and beauty, for Ingres, resided above all in form, which was the 'foundation and condition of everything'.[26] Form, in its turn, was expressed through drawing, and 'Drawing', he notoriously declared, 'is the probity of art'; when the young Degas applied to the elderly artist for advice, he was told 'draw lines young man, draw lines!'.[27] In this, as in so much else, Ingres explicitly identified himself with the tradition of the Florentine Renaissance, opposing draughtsmanship and the rigours of form to the supposed licence of colour. 'Drawing makes up more than three-quarters of that which constitutes painting', he claimed, adding that 'Colour adds ornament to painting; but it is no more than its handmaiden, since it only makes more attractive the true perfections of art'.[28]

There is much in this rhetoric to impress a young painter, and it is evident that the foundations of Degas' art, amongst them his dedication to drawing and his attachment to tradition, were fixed by the example of Ingres. There is little here, however, to comfort the future painter of laundresses, ballet-dancers and racehorses, and even less to reassure an aspiring maker of landscapes. In the language of his age, Ingres' insistence on line and form effectively precluded the landscape as a subject for great art. Pure landscape was incompatible with history, the biblical narrative or 'elevated thoughts and noble passions', and was seen to be dependent on colour, the 'handmaiden' of painting.[29] In this, Ingres again represented a particularly obdurate faction in the contemporary establishment, albeit a faction that was steadily losing ground. Since 1816, landscape had been included amongst the subjects for the Prix de Rome, and prominent landscapists had made inroads into the Academy and its teaching practices.[30] While Ingres might pay homage to the achievements of the *paysage historique* and herald the greatness of its progenitor, Nicolas Poussin, his own priorities were clear enough. With the exception of a number of drawings and one or two miniature paintings, Ingres himself produced no landscapes in his long and wide-ranging career, and it has recently been proposed that the majority of landscape backgrounds in Ingres' own paintings were carried out by friends or paid assistants.[31] Though his collected epigrams do not denigrate the landscape, the omission of the subject from his teaching and from his *oeuvre*, as well as the unspoken assumption that the human figure formed the proper subject of art, amount to a disparagement or even a rejection of landscape by default.

It is hardly an exaggeration to claim that Ingres' teaching, as well as his personal example, excluded the landscape from the repertoire of two successive generations of young painters trained in his shadow. Artists as varied as Flandrin and Lamothe, Delaunay and Stevens, Tissot and Bracquemond were never to recover from their exposure to the superior values of line and form, and it is no coincidence that this group of painters, all of whom had been instructed by Ingres or his followers, produced not a single landscapist of distinction. More pointedly, it was James McNeill Whistler, one of the finest landscape painters of his age, who had studied with Gleyre and once called himself a pupil of Courbet, who regretted that he had *not* studied with Ingres. During a temporary crisis over his art in 1867, Whistler exclaimed, 'What a sound master he would have been – drawing! . . . Colour – its truly a vice!'[32] For Degas, the siren call of draughtsmanship was to haunt his working life, often informing his finest achievements but at times leading him into contradiction and a kind of professional schizophrenia. Both colour and landscape were presented as treacherous, at least in Degas' public utterances, though the evidence of his art magnificently contradicts such a view. Further contradiction lies in the reputation Degas acquired, and apparently encouraged, as an enemy of landscape art, even as he made drawings, etchings, monotypes and paintings of landscape subjects. Most bizarre of all was Degas' insistence that drawing was 'a more fruitful field than that of colour', made as he worked on his pyrotechnical pastels and produced what he called his 'orgies de couleur'.[33]

Simplistic though they may appear today, the polarities of colour and line, landscape and the figure, Venetian sensuality and Florentine restraint, were real enough to the young Degas and his contemporaries. Despite the laborious efforts of the painters of the *juste milieu* to reconcile the two traditions, the language of conflict and partisanship still predominated in professional debates and private introspection. When writing to his son, Auguste De Gas cautioned him against the seductiveness of Venetian colour, describing it as a 'precipice' awaiting the unwary, while in his own notebooks Degas dreamed of uniting the rigour of Mantegna with the rich hues of Veronese.[34] The rivalry between Delacroix and Ingres was, of course, another expression of the same perceived antithesis and yet again, as his horizons widened, Degas found himself tossed back and forth between these two opposing poles. In the context of landscape painting, this opposition was even more stark. Charles Baudelaire, whose Salon criticism had done much to advance the cause of Delacroix in the previous decade, summed up the dilemma:

> In general the influence of Ingrism cannot possibly produce satisfactory results in landscape. Line and style are no substitutes for light, shadow, reflections and the *colouring* atmosphere – all of which play too great a part in the poetry of Nature to allow her to submit to this method.[35]

In another review Baudelaire had been even more brutal, writing of the minor landscapist Paul Flandrin, brother of Hippolyte: 'who on earth was the weird eccentric who first took it into his head to "Ingrize" the countryside?'[36]

This, then, was the challenge that Degas and his fellow-students inherited. Trained in the doctrines of Ingres, they aspired to conquer 'line and style' and to graduate to paint the human figure, as portrait painters, muralists or interpreters of classical and national history. Though Baudelaire might eulogise the landscapes of Corot and Delacroix, and even admire a scene of cows in the forest of Fontainebleau by the former, and the 'musical seductiveness' of a painting of Morocco by the latter, the successors of Ingres were made of sterner stuff.[37] As they were aware, attempts to bring the methods of the master to bear on lesser subjects, to 'Ingrize the countryside', would lead to ridicule, and it was the lofty themes of the past that claimed their attention. If they excelled, they might spend several years in Italy as winners of the Prix de Rome, studying the great tradition at first hand and, at least in theory, ensuring the success of their careers. It is again of great significance that Degas chose this path, no doubt with the encouragement of his father but evidently, from the tone of his letters and notebook jottings, with genuine private enthusiasm. In his case, the relative prosperity of his parents allowed him to circumvent the official competition, spending three years in self-directed study alongside the Prix de Rome laureates. Amongst his later colleagues in the Impressionist group, none opted for such a profoundly conservative apprenticeship and most did not visit the classical sites until their maturity. For most of these individuals, the tyranny of the Prix de Rome procedure and the expense of the excursion were sufficient deterrents, but for those who did travel to Italy, such as Manet and Cassatt, their stay was relatively brief.

In the months immediately prior to his visit to Italy, one further element in Degas' education as a landscapist made its first appearance in his notebooks. Though not much given to first-person confidences, and even less to reflections on matters of art, Degas made the following note:

> Today, 18th January 1856, I had a long conversation with M. Soutzo. What courage there is in his studies. It is essential – one must never make bargains with nature. One certainly needs courage if one is to approach nature head-on in its grand planes and lines and it is cowardly to do it by means of facets and details.[38]

While often referred to in passing, the significance of this contact with the landscape painter Gregoire Soutzo has never been adequately pursued, nor the persistence of the older man's influence on Degas' art properly acknowledged. Documentary evidence, some of which has only recently come to light, shows that Soutzo was closely associated with Degas' career for a period of at least five years and that contact between the two was sometimes frequent. A month later, for example, Degas executed a small but meticulous copy of a landscape and inscribed it 'd'après M. Soutzo' (fig. 7), and soon afterwards recorded another 'remarkable discussion' with his friend.[39] After Degas' arrival in Rome, he continued to remember Soutzo, recalling a plaster cast owned by him and paying particular attention to works of art by Soutzo's favourite painters.[40] While Degas was abroad, Soutzo was one of the family intimates chosen by his father to comment on the drawings sent home by the young artist, and on his return to the capital it was Soutzo who offered to help Degas find a studio.[41] The extent of Degas' indebtedness to Soutzo can be even more widely demonstrated. According to the artist's brother, René, it was Soutzo who first introduced Degas to the process of etching, a suggestion that is reinforced by the distinctive landscape *motifs* of Degas' first prints.[42] Their relationship has been further elaborated by the discovery that Soutzo owned a proof of Degas' early etched *Self-portrait*, and that Degas, in his turn, acquired several works by his teacher.[43] In later life, Degas possessed at least one painting and several drawings by Soutzo and described how, since his childhood, he had felt 'an extreme admiration for his talent'.[44]

Apart from his historic contact with the young Degas, Prince Gregoire

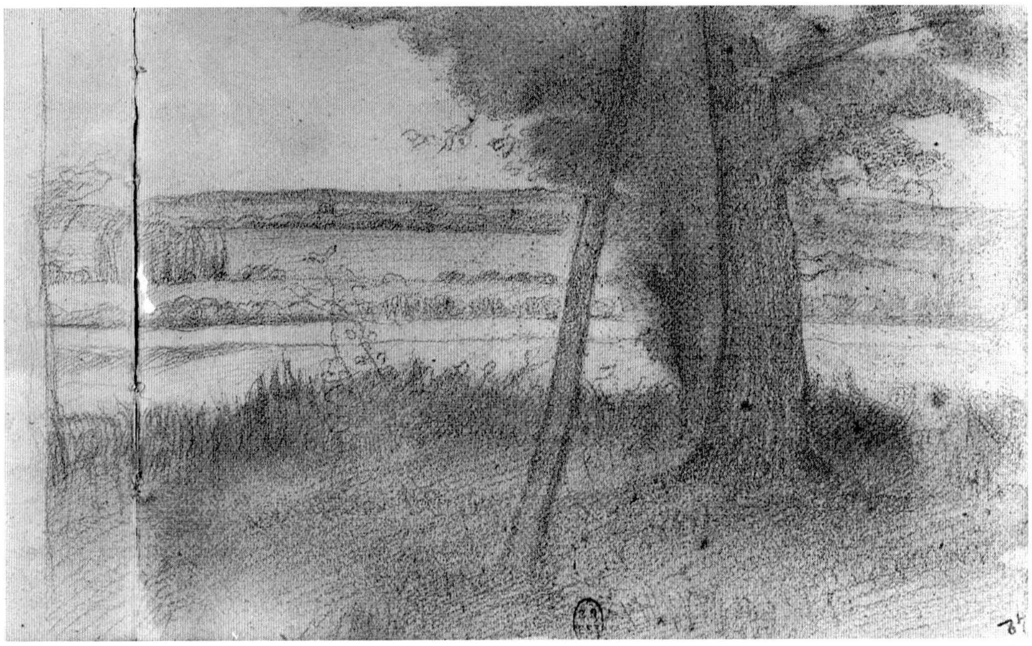

7. *Copy of a Landscape by Soutzo*, 1856, pencil, 10.5 × 13.7 (page size). Notebook 6, pages 43 and 42. Bibliothèque Nationale, Paris.

Soutzo (1815–69) has remained an obscure and somewhat exotic figure. Michael Pantazzi has shown that Soutzo came from a peripatetic Romanian family which settled first in Geneva and later in Athens.[45] Soutzo himself studied as a draughtsman with the celebrated Swiss landscape artist and caricaturist Rodolphe Töpffer, but decided to pursue his artistic career in France. By the 1850s, he was well established in Paris, on familiar terms with the Comte de Nieuwerkerke, Directeur général des Musées nationaux, and had become a close friend of Degas' father and his uncle, Henri Musson.[46] Though Soutzo is often described as an amateur artist and print-maker, the most diligent inquiries by specialists have failed to locate a single surviving work from his hand. With the exception of Degas' notebook copy, the only account of Soutzo's art is contained in a brief and previously unpublished note in an inventory of Degas' pictures, compiled by the artist himself during his old age.[47] Describing a painting entitled *View of the Acropolis at Athens*, which had been given by Soutzo to Musson, before passing into his own collection, Degas observed:

> I also have a few small drawing by him – a view of the Gulf of Geitoun, a village, fields – a little painted study of a tree – the works were given to me by M. Jacques Riso of Athens, a painter who had found them at the home of a relative of his and Soutzo's, who had left them to him – Soutzo had been our friend for a long time and ever since my youth I have always had an extreme admiration for his talent–my cousin Anna Lasserre, my Uncle Musson's daughter-in-law, has just informed me that she no longer has the view of the Temple of Theseus (painting) and an admirable little drawing (Olive trees near Athens, the Acropolis in the background) since Soutzo's daughter asked for them back, even though they belonged to her.[48]

Modest though this account may be, it adds significantly to our knowledge of Gregoire Soutzo's identity as an artist and shows the remarkable loyalty Degas still felt towards his former teacher, some fifty years after their acquaintance. Soutzo was evidently a landscape specialist, active as both draughtsman and painter in oils, and presumably as a maker of etchings.[49] The subject-matter of two of his pictures – *View of the Acropolis at Athens* and 'view of the Temple of

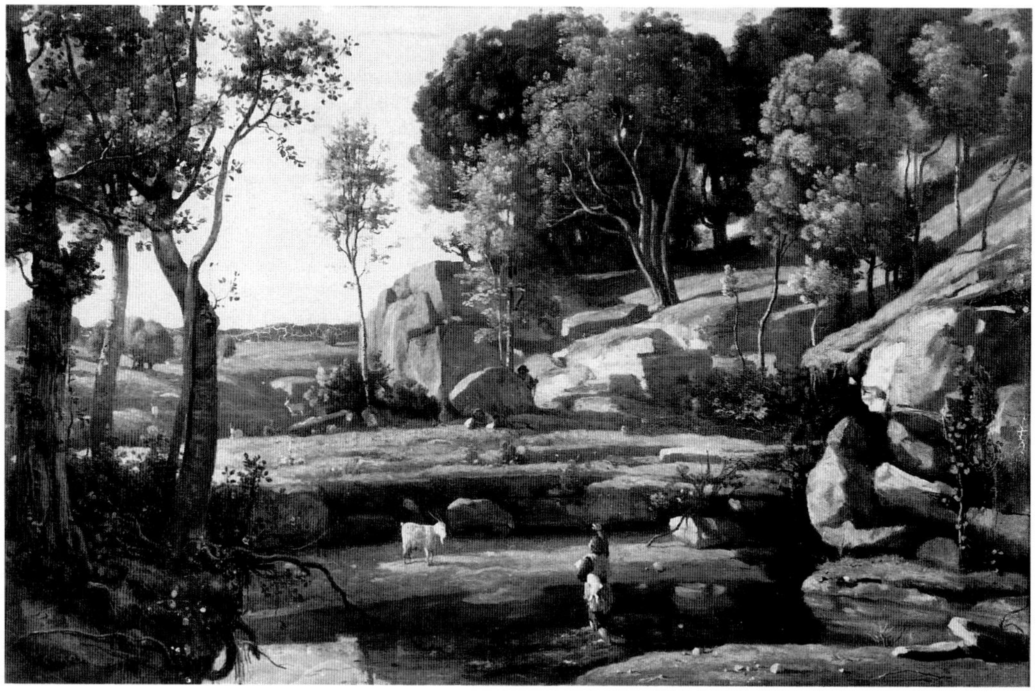

8. Camille Corot, *Italian Landscape*, 1842, oil on canvas, 90 × 135. Musée Calvet, Avignon.

Theseus' – belongs to the standard repertoire of mediterranean classicism, though the third, 'a little painted study of a tree', suggests a more informal side to his art. The title of this work reminds us also of the work copied by Degas 'd'après M. Soutzo', a pastoral scene dominated by a foreground tree. In this composition, Soutzo has clearly followed his own injunction to approach the landscape in its 'grand planes and lines', neither making 'bargains with nature' nor being distracted by her 'facets and details'. From Degas' drawing, we can see that the design was arranged around a simple equilibrium of verticals and horizontals, the prominent tree and distant pasture expressive of timeless rural tranquillity. More extraordinary is the lack of anything that might be described as picturesque in the picture; neither figures nor cattle, ruins nor quaint habitation, mountains nor remote cascades disturb the 'grand planes and lines' of Soutzo's view. In this, we can perhaps understand something of the revelation of Soutzo's art for the impressionable Degas. Accustomed to the formal complexity and the lofty ideals of Ingres and his school, and to the tortured obscurities of the *paysage historique*, Degas was understandably shocked by the 'courage' and directness of Soutzo's approach. Although the original has been lost, we can deduce from his copy that Soutzo's painting depended more on the delicacy of its tonal relationships and its finely modulated spaces than on the pretensions of its subject. As Baudelaire knew well, it was 'light, shadow . . . and the colouring atmosphere' that were at stake in such works, and it is to Degas' credit that he responded to precisely these qualities, hatching and shading his study with uncharacteristic thoroughness.

The artist who comes most naturally to mind in the company of Gregoire Soutzo is undoubtedly Camille Corot. Not only does the range of Soutzo's known subject-matter correspond closely to Corot's, especially between the latter's first trip to Italy and his Salon triumphs of the mid-century, but his precepts seem to echo Corot's aim to 'be rigorous in front of nature'.[50] The simple harmony of trees and horizon in Degas' copy is also distinctly Corot-like, recalling a favoured device in the master's compositions of the early

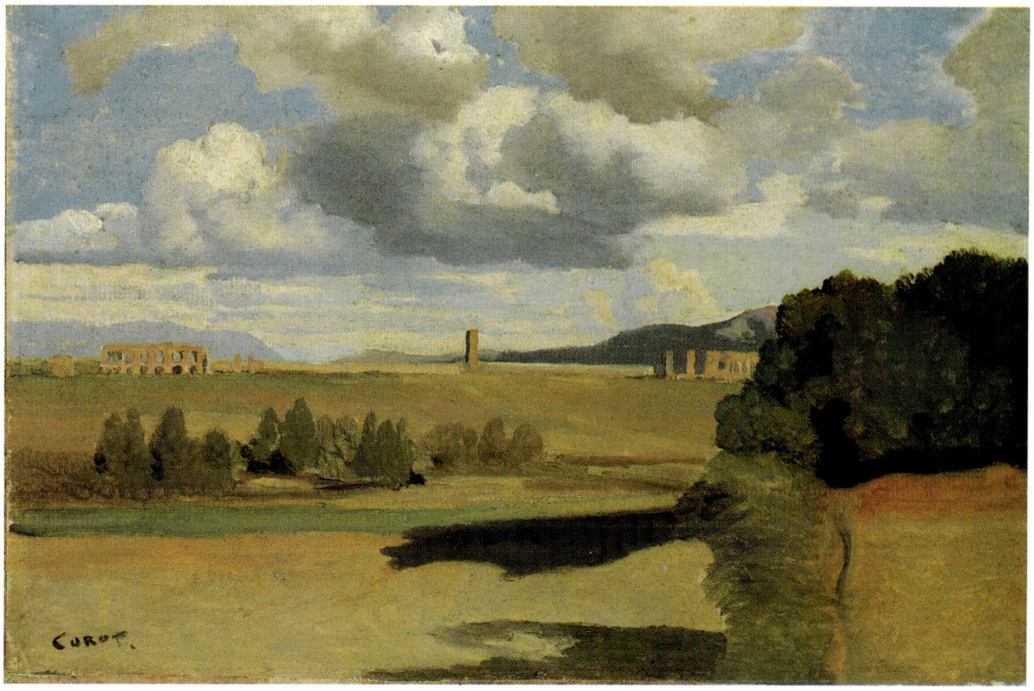

9. Camille Corot, *The Roman Campagna, with the Claudian Aqueduct*, oil on paper, mounted on canvas, 21.6 × 33. National Gallery, London.

1850s.[51] Soutzo is known to have been an admirer of Corot, owning at least one canvas by the master of an emphatically mundane scene, *Le Havre, Fishing Boat at Anchor*.[52] More intriguingly, it transpires that Degas himself linked the names of the two artists, especially when confronted by modest or unpicturesque landscape *motifs*. In a notebook entry of 1861, written as he contemplated a rain-swept stretch of Normandy countryside, Degas reflected: 'I am thinking of M. Soutzo and of Corot. Only those two would give this quietness a little interest.'[53] As early as 1855, at the time he was getting to know Soutzo, Degas made his first recorded response to Corot, noting that he had seen the artist's *Italian Landscape* (fig. 8) while on his tour of Provence.[54] This picture, which had been shown at the Salon of 1842, was one of Corot's more contrived renderings of an Italianate scene, but it is instructive that Degas took notice of it, alongside figurative works by Leonardo, Mantegna and David. Corot would hardly have been amongst the artists approved by Degas' instructors, and it seems likely that it was Soutzo who encouraged or even initiated a taste for his work, a taste that was to persist throughout Degas' lifetime. In later years, Degas often referred admiringly, if obtusely, to Corot's achievement and is even alleged to have painted an imitation Corot canvas to amuse his Impressionist colleagues.[55] He also shared with some of his closest friends the pleasure of collecting Corot's work and became the owner of several fine canvases, including the early *The Roman Campagna, with the Claudian Aqueduct* (fig. 9).[56]

Though elusive in almost every other way, Soutzo undoubtedly left his mark on the young Degas, delighting him with his frank approach to nature and opening his eyes to painters who, like Corot, made art out of the humblest materials. Recent publications have shown the dangers of over-simplifying Corot's role for the younger generation, but in Degas' youth, his work undoubtedly signalled a number of alternative conceptions of the painting process. By working extensively out of doors, by painting local and unglamorous, as opposed to distant and historically sanctioned, subjects, and by stressing the value of 'the first impression', Corot must have challenged many of the tenets of Degas' education. Neither Corot nor Soutzo were, of course, unique in this respect, and these two artists must have been among many who disturbed the tranquillity of Degas' youthful thoughts. But together their example helped to alert the twenty-year-old artist to the wider possibilities of his craft. While too much importance should not be attached to this incident, it might also be added that Soutzo's instruction to see nature 'in its grand planes and lines' and Corot's advice to capture the landscape as 'it first burst upon our view' were to linger in many of Degas' later landscape activities.

In at least two other respects, Soutzo appears to have been a formative influence on Degas prior to his Italian journey: as a collector of art and as a maker of etchings. Soutzo's collection was dominated by prints and was remarkable both for its breadth of taste and for the inclusion of works by both celebrated and less prominent artists. Most of the great etchers and engravers from the past were represented, from Marcantonio, Dürer and Goltzius to Van Dyck, Claude Lorrain and Rembrandt, though a preponderance of northern European masters gave the collection an untypical emphasis.[57] We can surely see Soutzo's example behind Degas' interest in many of these individuals, most transparently in notebook lists of works by Marcantonio and Dürer, and in his youthful admiration for the landscape prints of Claude Lorrain.[58] Further, we might suspect Soutzo's complicity in Degas' discovery of Rembrandt, an artist specifically excluded from the Ingresque canon, but one whose etchings inspired an early copy and a number of respectful paraphrases among Degas' first prints.[59] This broadening of Degas' taste took on a different form in his introduction to etching, which appears to have taken place shortly before he left for Italy. Using the kitchen of Auguste De Gas' Paris apartment as an impromptu workshop, Soutzo conducted his pupil through the preparation of the copper plates and their controlled immersion in a bath of acid, filling the room with such a powerful odour that Degas' brother claimed to recall it fifty years later.[60] Though only two or three small etched images emerged from this process, we may once again detect in them the mark of Soutzo, both as an authority on the history of prints and as a practising artist.

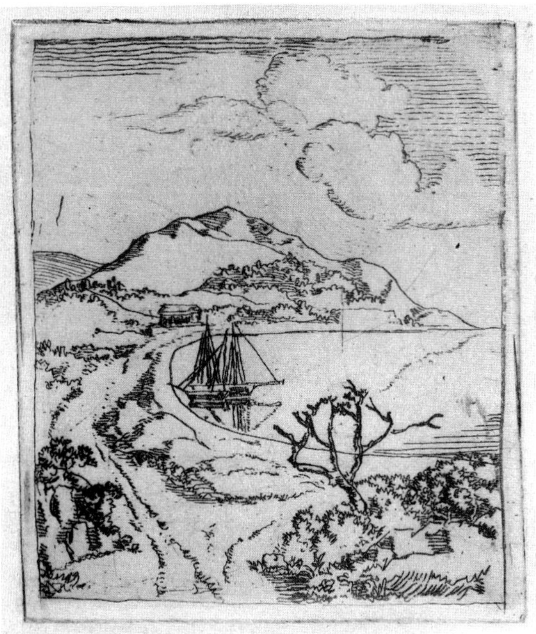

10. *Greek Landscape*, 1856, etching, 8 × 6.6 (RS 1). Private collection.

11. *Mountain Landscape*, 1856, etching (first state), 13.2 × 9.1 (RS 2). Bibliothèque Nationale, Paris.

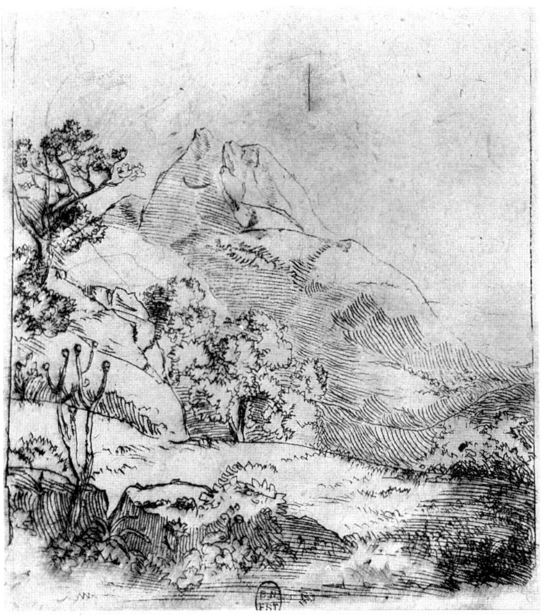

Limited though they are in size and technical complexity, Degas' first experiments in etching are remarkable in that they are all depictions of the landscape. *Greek Landscape* (fig. 10), probably Degas' earliest print, shows a schematic and somewhat improbable mediterranean scene of a kind familiar from contemporary illustrated books.[61] Its juxtaposition of trees, a remote classical building and a mountainous vista may also recall Soutzo's own imagery, such as the 'Olive trees near Athens, the Acropolis in the background' mentioned by Degas in his inventory. *Mountain Landscape* (fig. 11), on the other hand, suggests more northern or even alpine terrain, an association made explicit in Degas' addition of a church and spire to certain proofs.[62] Both are essentially linear images, as we might expect from a novice, consisting of sharply incised contours and regular, furrow-like passages of hatching. *Greek Landscape* shows some of the angularity and imprecision of a first attempt, but *Mountain Landscape* already hints at a more fluent, even Claude-like, sensuousness of touch. It is also notable that this second plate, small as it is, went through a number of revisions and embellishments, in a way that curiously foreshadows the tormented print-making practices of Degas' maturity. Degas re-worked the image with dry-point and at least one further exposure to acid, modified the shape of the plate itself and sketched in trees, buildings and a shepherd with his flock on the resulting proofs.[63] The third early print, *Sportsman Mounting his Horse* (fig. 12), is technically less complex, though some uncertainty surrounds the date of its execution. On the basis of its resemblance to the two landscape prints, Reed and Shapiro are surely right in placing it before Degas' visit to Italy and the great advance in print-making technique represented by the 1857 *Self-portrait* etching. Still extraordinary, however, is the subject of this tiny, rapidly drawn print, appearing to demonstrate an early taste for the English steeplechase lithograph and representing the first truly equestrian subject in Degas' entire *oeuvre*.[64]

Degas sailed for Italy in July 1856, arriving in Naples just two days before his twenty-second birthday. Unlike the laureates of the Prix de Rome, Degas was not required to present himself at the Villa Medici in Rome, and chose instead to spend three months in Naples, living at the home of his paternal grandfather, Hilaire Degas. For the young artist, one of the attractions of Italy was the presence in Naples and Florence of members of his father's family, who not only provided hospitality but also encouraged his ambitions as a portraitist by posing for a number of drawings and paintings. Moving between Naples, Florence and Rome, Degas spent almost three years on his idiosyncratic grand tour, financed and advised at a distance by his father but ultimately able to choose his own itinerary. In effect, Degas appointed himself to the Prix de Rome, enjoying many of the privileges of the *pensionnaires* but enduring none of their obligations. He toured the great cities and hillside towns, blind to their architecture but enchanted by the 'adorable fresco painters of the fifteenth century', as his father called them.[65] In churches and art galleries, he copied portraits, fragmentary figures and entire compositions, while in the privacy of his rooms he drafted out his own precocious canvases. During an extended visit to Rome, Degas was able to renew his acquaintance with the life class, informally mixing with his compatriots at the Villa Medici and resuming the education he had left behind in Paris. As he travelled, he was also to discover the delights of Italy itself and, perhaps for the first time in his art, to 'approach nature head-on in its grand planes and lines'.

Dutiful and earnest though Degas undoubtedly was, his visit to Italy did as much to challenge as to confirm the precepts of his earlier training. Even as he paid homage to the achievements of the Florentine draughstmen and copied the works of Giotto, Ghirlandaio and Signorelli, his attention was distracted by other traditions and by less sanctioned artists. Pictures by the masters of the Venetian school accounted for some of his most enthusiastic copies, while even more questionable individuals, such as Parmigianino and Giulio Romano, and the Flemish Snyders, were to attract him briefly.[66] Some of these new enthusiasms were undoubtedly the result of encounters in galleries visited for the first time, such as the Naples Museum, the Uffizi in Florence and the collections of the Vatican, while others were suggested by the changed milieu in which Degas found himself. In the cosmopolitan atmosphere of the Villa Medici, and later in the Caffé Michelangiolo in Florence, Degas met French, English and Italian artists, with widely varying inclinations and previous experience, united in their ambition but at odds in their taste and notions of art. In Bonnat, Delaunay, Chapu and Clère, he met artists from rival Paris studios, and in the landscape painter Félix Lionnet he encountered a pupil of Corot; in the engraver Joseph Tourny he befriended a fellow-enthusiast for the etchings of Rembrandt (and must have remembered Soutzo); he was acquainted briefly with an English watercolourist, John Bland, and appears to have come across the innovative Italian landscapists, the Macchiaioli;[67] and in the person of Gustave Moreau, he found both a confidant and an artistic mentor.

12. *Sportsman Mounting his Horse*, 1856, etching (second state), 8.3 × 7.5 (RS 3). Bibliothèque Nationale, Paris.

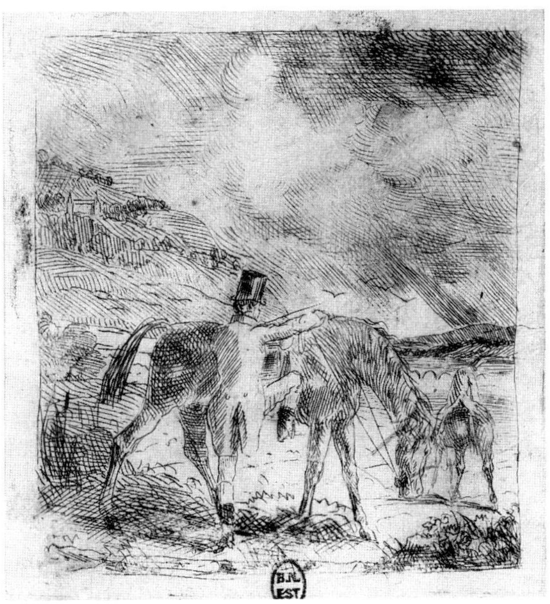

As so often in Degas' early career, it was his informal works of art, such as notebook pages and small-scale studies, that first registered these threats to his equilibrium. After his arrival in Italy, the tight, faintly modelled drawings of his first student phase gave way to a bewildering variety of strokes and flourishes, from spidery outlines in pen and ink to alarmingly superimposed studies in pencil, wash and crayon. He discovered and soon mastered the techniques of watercolour, and learnt to imitate the marks of the engraver and the mannerisms of other artists. Copies from the art of the past still predominated, but these might be overlaid with casual doodles or sketches made in the street. A similar turbulence was reflected in Degas' literary activity, preserved in notebook jottings and in hurried accounts of travels, personal encounters and moments of reflection. Amongst this wealth of visual and verbal imagery, there were also subjects new to Degas' repertoire, from vagabonds and street hawkers to themes of more far-reaching consequence, such as dancers, musicians and artists at work. Side by side with these studies, and scattered throughout his notebooks and portfolios, there was also the first substantial body of landscapes to appear in Degas' *oeuvre*.

Degas' years in Italy accounted for more than sixty images of the landscape, varying greatly in their scale and their degree of resolution, and in media as different as watercolur, pencil, ink, gouache, and oil on canvas and paper. None of them compared in ambition with his concurrent portraits and figure studies, though many show great technical accomplishment and a startling maturity of vision. While barely significant beside the production in similar circumstances of an artist like Corot, Degas' Italian landscapes showed the extent to which an aspiring figure painter could nurture an affinity with other genres, and explore that affinity in the wider interests of his art. In conjunction with his written notes, the landscapes also allow us to glimpse something of Degas' working procedures, and to challenge some of the legends that have become inseparable from his later career. We discover, for example, a Degas who waxed lyrical over a setting sun or a panorama of mountains, who would find extravagant metaphors for his sensations of the landscape, and would scribble down the colours of nature as he travelled through the countryside. The same artist kept a record of landscape paintings he had seen and could be found working *en plein air*, hurrying to capture the fugitive effects of daylight and expressing his frustration with nature's mutability. There are even signs of a more complex dialogue with his subject, as Degas questioned himself about his attachment to nature and mused on the problems of its representation.

13. *Sketches of Sorrento*, 1856, pencil and watercolour, 24.7 × 17.7. Notebook 7, page 4, Musée du Louvre, Paris.

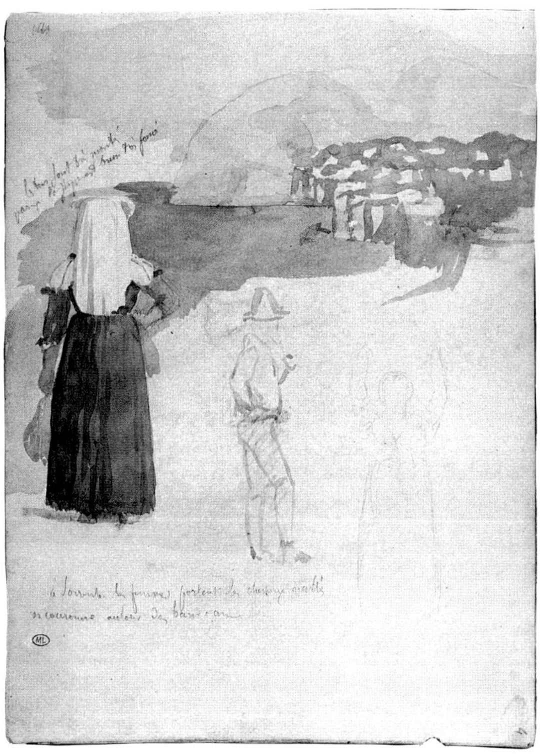

The day after his arrival in Italy in 1856, Degas wrote punctiliously on the first page of a large new sketchbook, 'Naples 18 Juillet'.[68] He remained in Naples until October and returned for a two-month stay the following year, on each occasion visiting the antiquities and paintings in the city museum, making excursions into the surrounding countryside and working at portraits of his extended family. The progress of these visits and the diversity of his interests can be traced in notebook drawings, though their decipherment is often hindered by a palimpsest-like accretion of material from his later stay in Rome. On the second page of this new sketchbook, for example, classical busts are drawn beside sketches of the artist's own hand, while on the verso of page three a faint copy of a *Bacchante with Flowers*, a Roman painting in the Naples Museum, can be made out. Soon afterwards, Degas appears to have made a trip round the bay of Naples to Sorrento, where he used the fourth page to record costumes of local dancers and to try out his watercolours on the coast itself (fig. 13). Page five reverts to classical themes, while pages six and seven are again concerned with a landscape motif, this time a brilliantly lit view seen through an

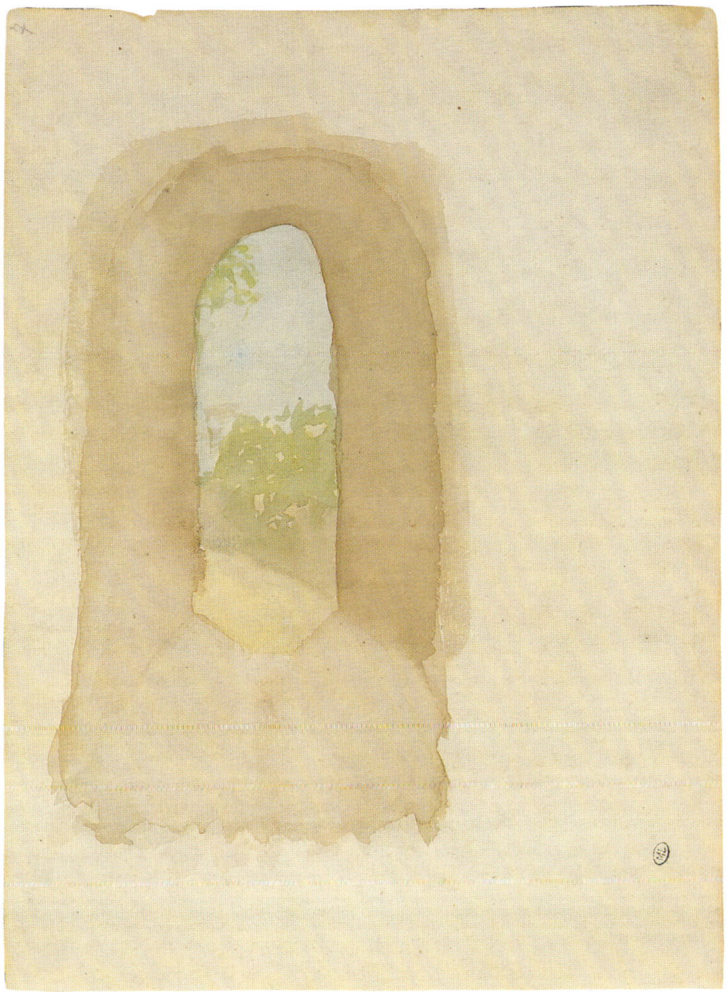

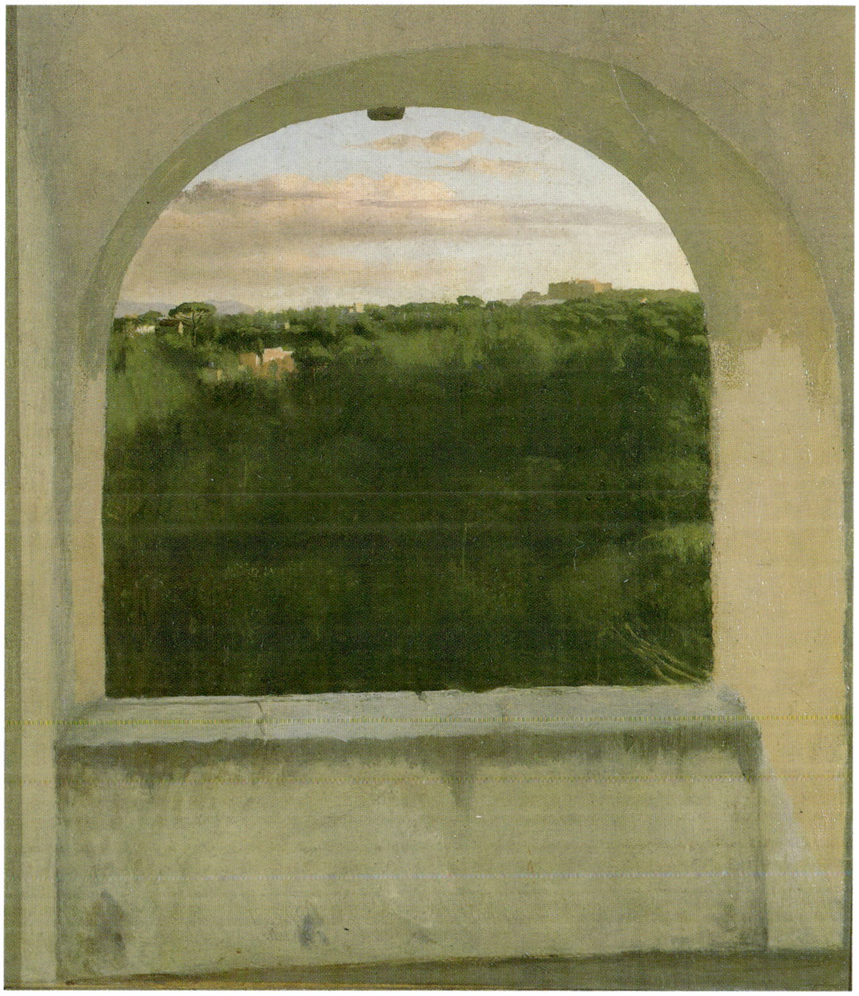

14. *View through a Window*, 1856, watercolour, 24.7 × 17.7. Notebook 7, page 7. Musée du Louvre, Paris.

15. *Italian Landscape Seen through an Arch*, 1856, oil on paper, mounted on canvas, 37 × 32 (L 48). Private collection.

arched window, rendered in washes of green, umber and eggshell blue (fig. 14). Subsequent pages return to the same range of *motifs*, and also include a striking self-portrait, an interior with musicians and lovers, and studies of mountains, a rural valley and a hillside fort.[69]

If nothing else had survived from Degas' early months in Italy, the Naples notebook would encapsulate much of the orthodoxy, enthusiasm and occasional waywardness of this multifarious young artist. In the context of landscape painting, it would also remind us of the subsidiary role this activity played in Degas' art, even as it revealed the freshness and immediacy of his response to his surroundings. Drawing and painting the landscape were part of Degas' protracted dialogue with Italy, and an essential component of his wider technical self-education. A striking example of this is a group of three notebook studies for his painting *Italian Landscape Seen through an Arch* (fig. 15). The starting point was the burst of sunlight recorded on pages six and seven of the notebook, initially shown as a glimpse through a narrow window or door, revealing foliage and a pathway beyond. In the finished work, the *motif* has been expanded and formalised, and now leads us to a densely wooded hillside and hints of architecture beyond. At the far right, the fortress of Capodimonte (visible from Hilaire Degas' villa) can be seen, derived from a razor-sharp pencil drawing on page nineteen of the same sketchbook.[70] Such an orchestration of preparatory studies and materials says much about Degas' versatility and self-confidence, but

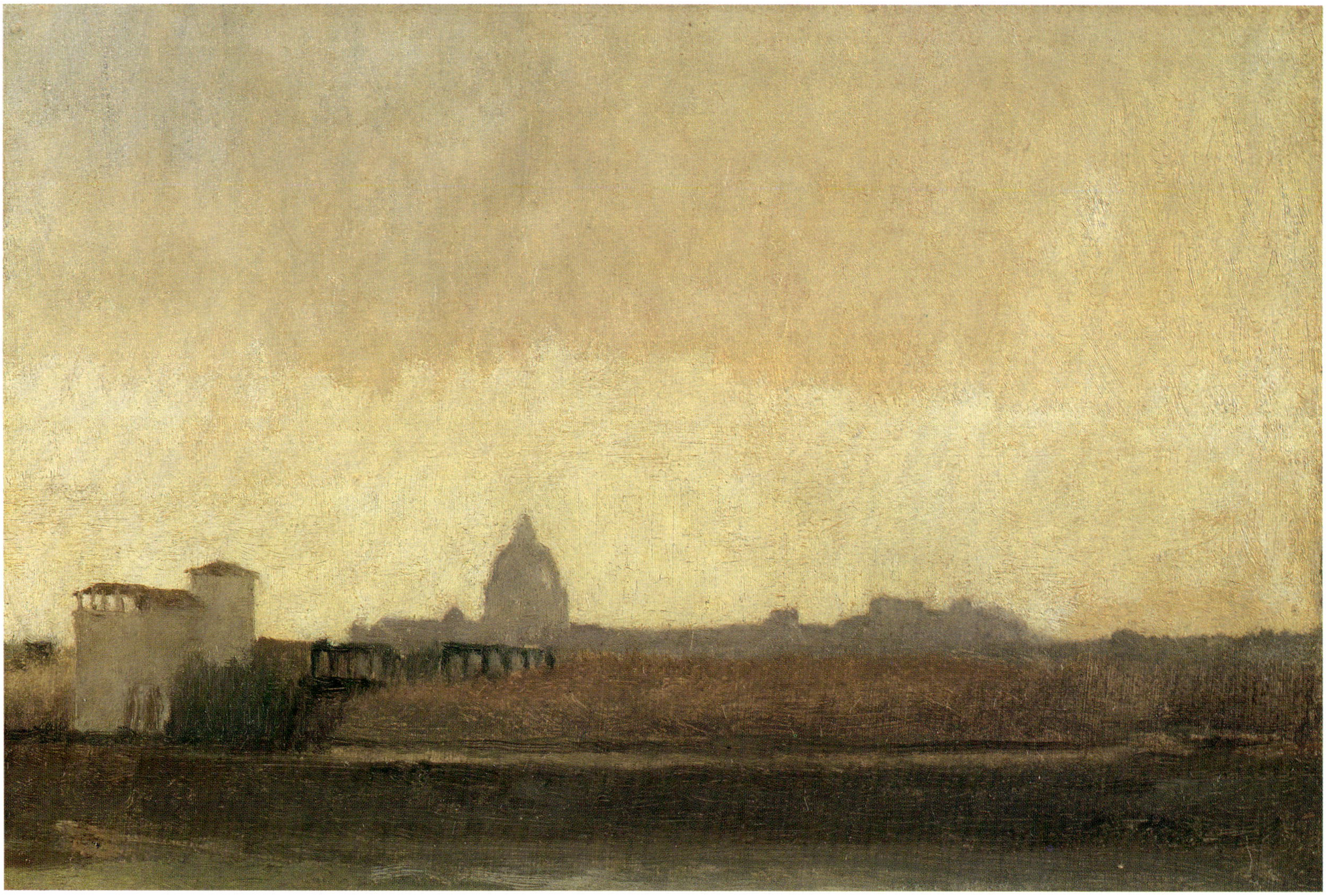

16. *View of Rome from the Banks of the Tiber*, *c.*1858, oil on paper, mounted on canvas, 18 × 26 (BR 20). Stiftung Langmatt, Baden.

as yet little of his pictorial audacity. In a brilliant analysis of the painting, Roy McMullen has written of its perverse combination of 'the past, the present, the artificial, and the real' and noted its challenging perspective and prophetically high vantage point.[71] To this should be added Degas' precocious mastery of a medium and an idiom still quite new to him. Executed in oil on paper, the picture is one of his earliest fully fledged landscape paintings and probably the first of a sequence of remarkable studies in this technique carried out during his Italian stay.

The use of oil paint on paper in *Italian Landscape Seen through an Arch* introduces us to one of the least-known and historically most resonant groups of Degas' early landscapes. More than a dozen such pictures have been linked with this period, most of similar dimensions and many showing identifiable Italian subjects, such as *View of Rome from the Banks of the Tiber* (fig. 16) and the *Convent of Santa Trinita dei Monti Seen from a Tower of the Villa Medici* (fig. 17).[72] None of the works is signed or dated, though the majority can be traced back through collectors or members of Degas' family to the *atelier* sales held after his death.[73] Given the widespread practice of oil painting on paper amongst students and professional artists, some caution in attribution is justified, but several of the pictures can be associated with Degas' works in other media and

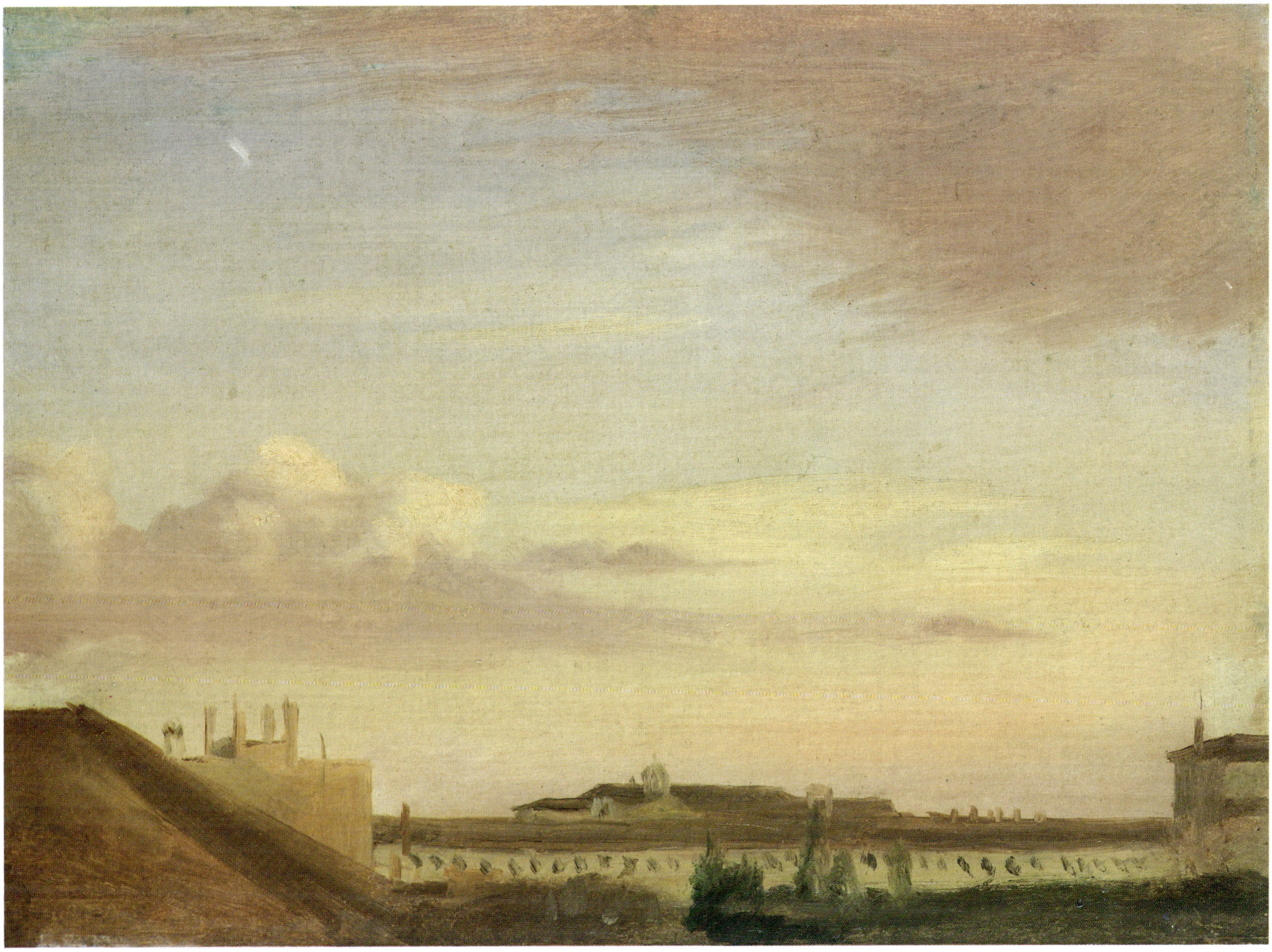

17. *The Convent of Santa Trinita dei Monti Seen from a Tower of the Villa Medici*, *c.*1858, oil on paper, mounted on canvas, 21.4 × 28.2 (L 47 *bis*). Private collection.

with the known itinerary of his Italian tour. Most decisive here is a series of painted views of Naples, each of which has a direct counterpart in the artist's notebooks or in a known canvas. In addition to *Italian Landscape Seen through an Arch*, a striking study entitled *Italian Landscape* (location unknown; BR 16) shows precisely the same view of the fortress at Capodimonte as the notebook drawing already discussed, and another Neapolitan subject, *Castello dell'Ovo* (fig. 18) depicts a site he returned to in a later sketchbook.[74]

In adopting the medium of thinned oil paint applied to prepared paper or card, Degas chose a technique he had mastered in Paris, where he used it in student exercises and in the grandiose *Self-portrait* of 1855 (fig. 6).[75] Of more significance is his application of this combination of materials to the landscape. In so doing, Degas aligned himself with the long-established tradition of outdoor landscape painting in Italy, exemplified in the late eighteenth century by Pierre-Henri de Valenciennes and Thomas Jones, and in more recent times by Corot himself. The history of this practice has been prejudiced by its informal and private character, and by the tendency for its adherents to conceal,

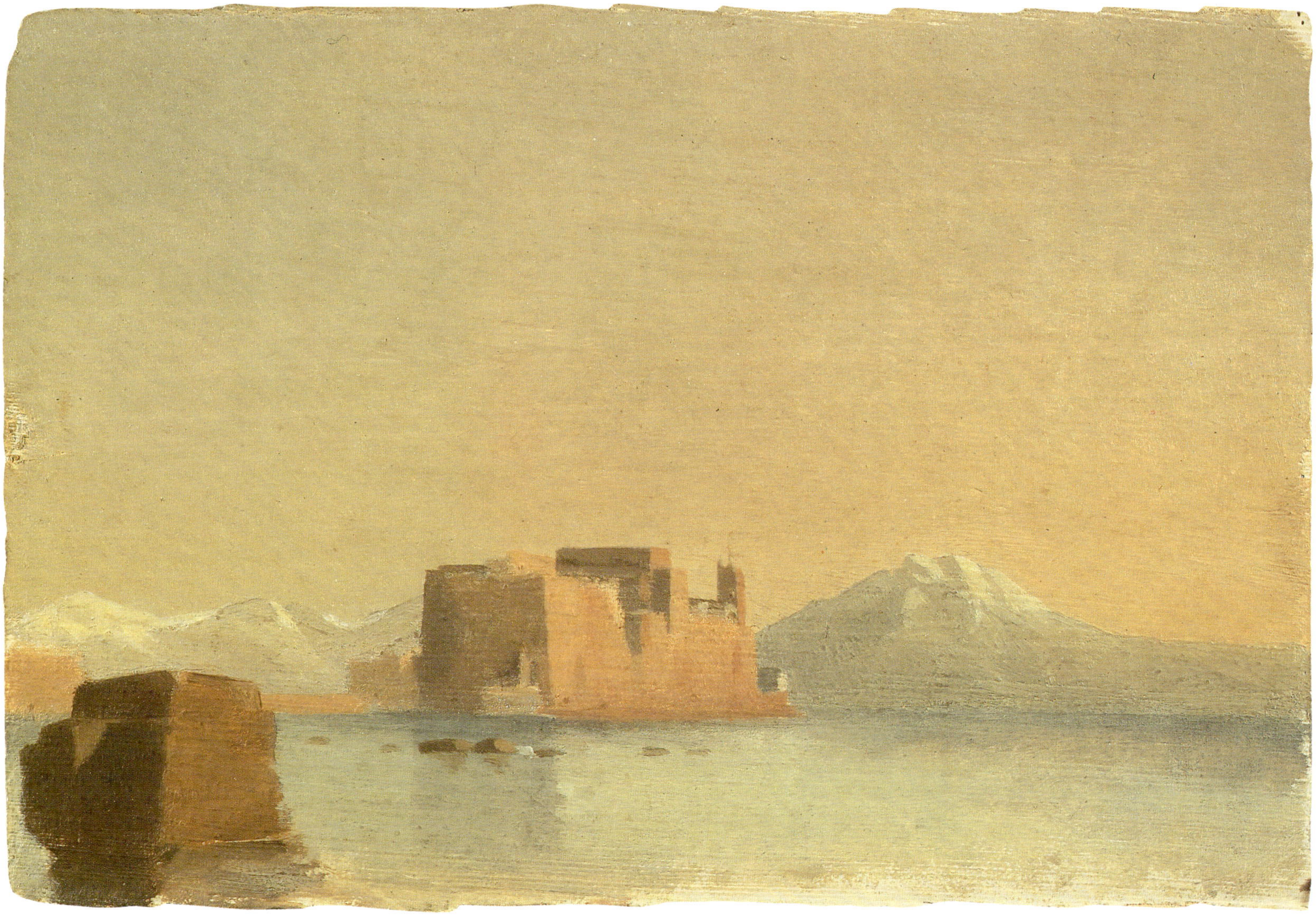

18. *The Castello dell'Ovo*, *c.*1858–9, oil on cardboard, 18 × 27 (BR). Stiftung Langmatt, Baden.

or even deny the existence of, their improvised oil sketches. Recently, Peter Galassi has revealed the extent to which the technique was in use amongst French, British, German and Scandinavian artists in the early and mid-century, and the scintillating achievements of some of its finest practitioners. Responding to the fluidity and luminance of the medium, artists were able to record rapidly changing skies, fleeting effects of shadow and the intense hues of brickwork, foliage and sun-baked earth. Colour and improvised execution were at a premium, while drawing was minimised and the complexities of composition were held in check. Though still regarded as a form of exercise, to be worked up later into grander and more finished canvases, such studies offered a historic alternative to the rigidities of studio practice.[76]

In his published guide to young artists, which first appeared in 1800 but was still current in Degas' youth, Valenciennes set out in some detail his guiding principles and the practical methods for achieving them.[77] Encouraging his pupil to work directly in oils while out of doors and 'to make studies that may serve him later in composing pictures', Valenciennes urged the advantages of 'sketches made in haste, seizing nature in its actuality'.[78] Elsewhere he recommends painting 'the same view at different hours of the day in order to observe the

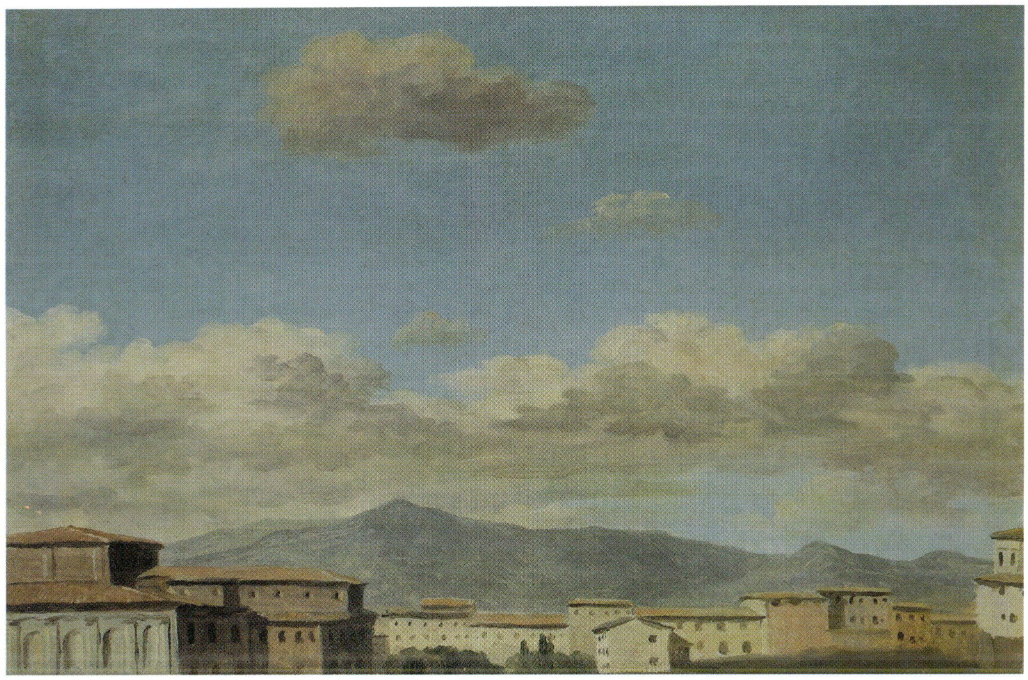

19. Pierre-Henri de Valenciennes, *Cloud Study on the Quirinal Hill, Rome*, *c.*1782–4, oil on paper, mounted on cardboard, 25.6 × 38.1. Musée du Louvre, Paris.

differences that light produces' and emphasised that 'the effect of totality in the painting depends on the colour of the sky'.[79] Valenciennes' concern that the student 'should begin his work with the sky, which gives the colour of the background, then move to those planes closely related to the sky, then work progressively towards the foreground' is evident in his own surviving oil sketches of clouds and light-filled vistas, such as *Cloud Study on the Quirinal Hill, Rome* (fig. 21), but it also appears to have been heeded, some fifty years later, by

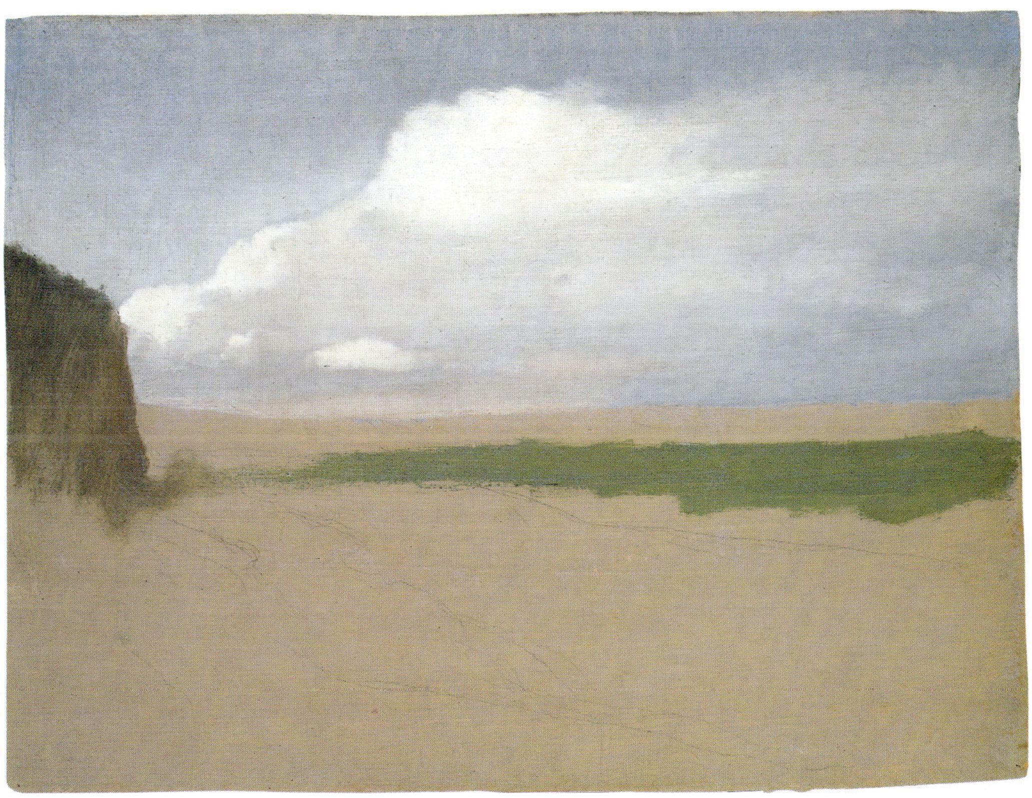

20. *Italian Landscape*, *c.*1857–8, oil on paper, 22.8 × 31.1 (BR 18). Browse & Darby, London.

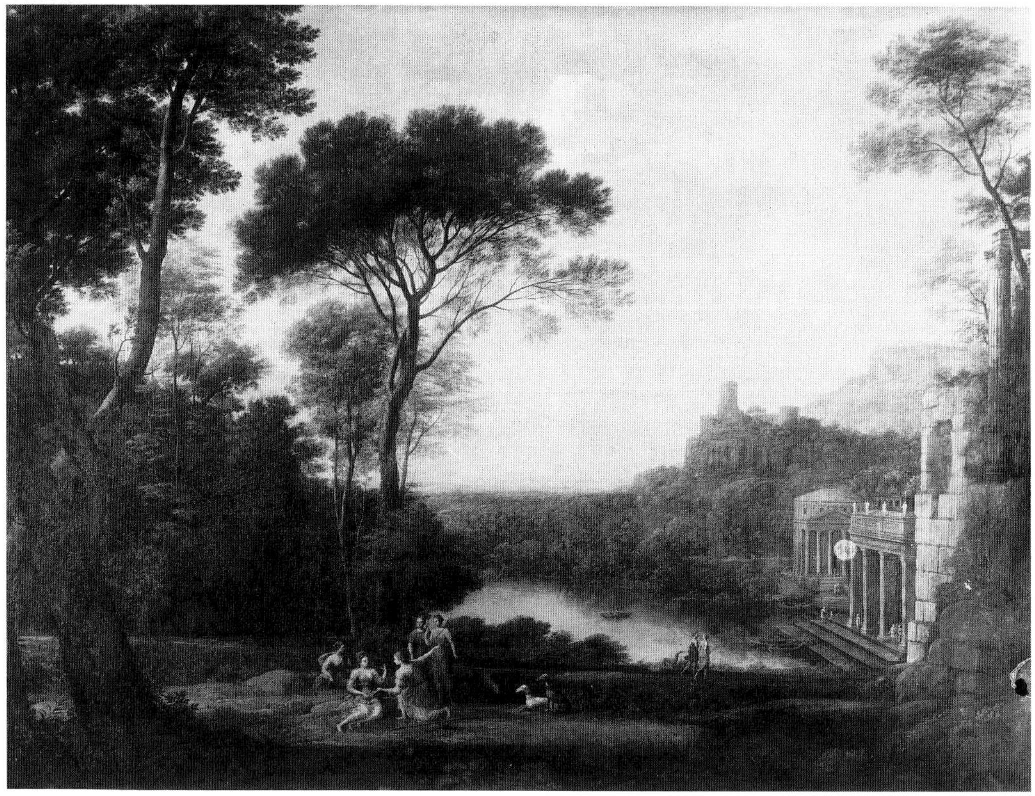

21. Claude Lorrain, *Landscape with the Nymph Egeria Mourning over Numa*, 1669, oil on canvas, 157 × 199. Museo e Galleria Nazionali di Capodimonte, Naples.

the young Degas.[80] Whether Degas read Valenciennes' text or absorbed it at second hand from fellow-students, his own oil-on-paper studies follow closely his predecessor's advice. All of them are painted freshly and rapidly, sacrificing detail to the tonal character of the whole; they are far less particularised, for example, than Corot's Italian oil sketches, with which they have sometimes been compared.[81] Many of them engage with transient light effects, such as dawn and dusk, and almost every one is dominated by a broad expanse of luminous, subtly hued sky. In the unfinished *Italian Landscape* (fig. 20), we can even observe Valenciennes' procedures at work, caught, as it were, in mid-sentence; here, Degas has established the tones of the sky on a prepared pink paper, then moved 'to those planes closely related to the sky', but was evidently interrupted as he worked 'progressively towards the foreground'.[82]

Apart from their association with the tradition of Valenciennes, Degas' first oil-on-paper landscapes had a more local resonance. For more than two centuries, Naples had attracted some of the finest landscape painters of France, Britain and Italy, and its landmarks and surrounding countryside had become fixtures on the Grand Tourist's itinerary. In the 1630s, Claude Lorrain had worked in the city, recalling its monuments and distinctive shoreline in his later harbour scenes, while other resident and visiting landscapists had included his contemporary Salvator Rosa; Hubert Robert, Richard Wilson and Thomas Jones in the eighteenth century; and Valenciennes and Corot some decades before Degas' arrival. That Degas was conscious of this precedent we cannot doubt. Within days of his first visit to the city, he recorded an encounter with 'the most beautiful Claude you could possibly see. The sky is like silver and the shadows seem to speak.'[83] The painting in question, *Landscape with the Nymph Egeria Mourning over Numa* (fig. 21), presented the young artist with a vast recapitulation of the classical-landscape vocabulary, complete with hazy vistas, space-defining ruins and finely disposed narrative groups. Given the nature of

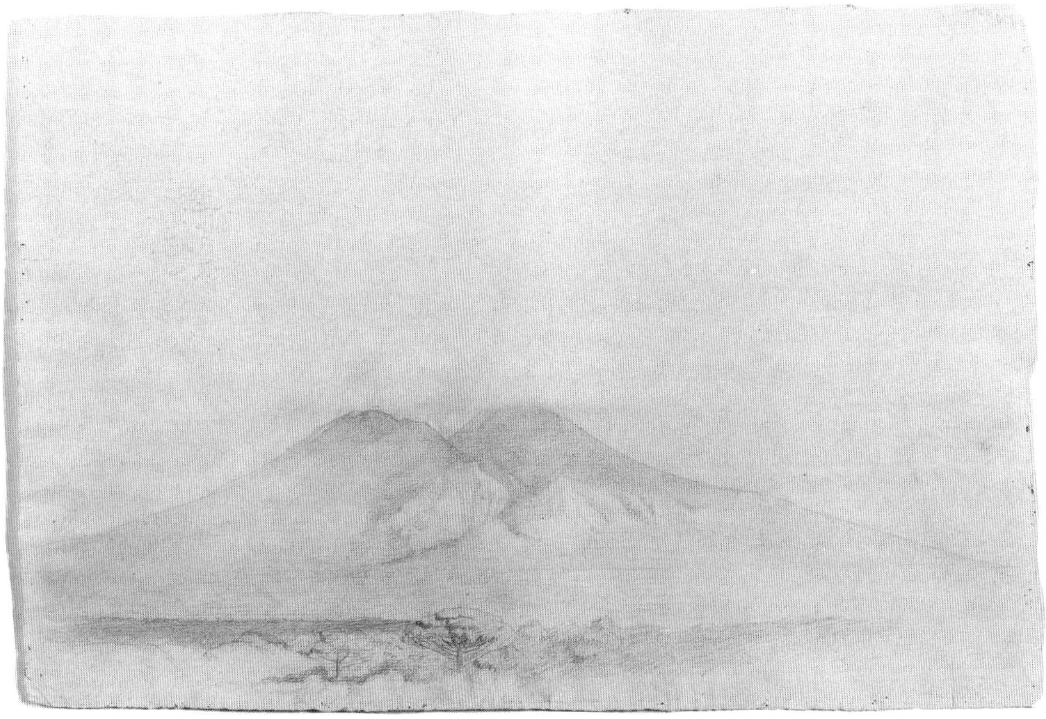

22. *View of Mount Vesuvius*, *c.*1856, pencil, 26 × 36.8. Curtis O. Baer Collection.

his training, we might suspect that Degas' admiration for the work was no more than dutiful, but a more patient examination of the notebooks and documents of this period shows that it reflects a persistent enthusiasm for Claude and his achievement.

One of Degas' earliest portrait drawings, that of René de Gas (Art Institute of Chicago) made in 1855, is catalogued as having 'an extremely faint landscape sketch on the verso'.[84] This landscape sketch is just sufficiently visible to be identified as a perfunctory copy of Claude's *Landscape with Paris and Oenone*, a canvas in the Louvre that was presumably studied at first hand before Degas left for Italy.[85] The drawing is consequently among the first of Degas' landscape studies and stands at the beginning of a long line of copies, both perfunctory and painstaking, from the art of the past. His response to the Claude on arrival in Naples follows this pattern, while his enthusiasm for the artist's work elsewhere in Italy develops and extends it. After his move to Rome, Degas continued to seek out the master's works, making enthusiastic notes about two landscapes in the Doria-Pamphilii Gallery alongside much briefer responses to portraits by Raphael in the same collection.[86] A year later, he listed a group of Claude etchings seen at the Corsini Gallery, adding written descriptions of certain plates and comments such as 'l'arbre est sublime et c'est de l'air ça', which surely go beyond routine approval.[87] Degas would already have encountered the etchings of Claude in Paris, at the home of Gregoire Soutzo, and in this context it comes as no surprise to find Degas applying their lessons to his own art. In the same notebook, he made the first of a group of small Claude-like sketches of his own, recalling from life or from memory the distinctive *motifs* of his seventeenth-century predecessor.[88]

Further gestures towards the Italianate tradition can be found in the landscapes of Degas' own Grand Tour. On his visit to Naples of either 1856 or 1857, he paid homage to that most Neapolitan of vistas, the summit of Vesuvius, invoking an entire sub-genre of imagery that included works by Valenciennes, Corot and, in a rare excursion into untamed nature, Ingres himself.[89] In Degas' pencil drawing *View of Mount Vesuvius* (fig. 22), he adopted an unusually delicate tonal manner, exercising his skill in description within the well-defined conventions of academic draughtsmanship.[90] Complete in itself, the drawing was not part of a painting or watercolour project, though its subject was to echo down the years into the last decades of Degas' career. Perhaps out of nostalgia for his early attempts at landscape, or possibly as a recollection of family associations with the city, Degas was to collect several images of Vesuvius by other artists, among them Corot and Giuseppe de Nittis, and to dedicate one of his most topographically precise monotypes to the subject almost forty years later (fig. 181).[91]

After his brief but productive stay in Naples, Degas left his grandfather's house and travelled to Rome, arriving there in early October, 1856. With the exception of a summer spent in Naples in 1857, the artist was to remain in Rome for almost two years, venturing out of the city only to visit Tivoli and other notable and picturesque sites. By all accounts, Degas' stay in Rome was a period of intense industry and self-conscious personal advancement. His notebooks teem with copies, vignettes of café and street life, and plans for more pictures than he had time to paint. Building on earlier experiences of print-making, he worked at his most ambitious etching plates to date, now graduating to the human form and producing the delicately reflective *Self-portrait* of 1857 and a copy after Rembrandt.[92] Few canvases were completed, but such works as the *Roman Beggar Woman* (Birmingham City Museum and Art Gallery; L 28) marked his accomplishment as a painter in oils, as well as his alertness to local subject-matter and pictorial traditions. From a briefer stay in Florence, Degas' first surviving letters add immeasurably to our knowledge of his activities and aspirations. Writing to his friend Gustave Moreau, the artist emerged as a lucid, often solemn, occasionally effusive young man who could be elated and discouraged by turns. His announcement that 'the best I can do is to study my craft' was soon followed by the confession 'I am starting to despair a little', while a month later he reported 'I am busy with a portrait of my aunt and my two little cousins . . . I have an inordinate desire to fill canvases'.[93]

Once settled in Rome, Degas presented his credentials at the Villa Medici and become a regular participant in the evening life classes held there, making highly finished pencil or black-chalk studies in the Ecole des Beaux-Arts manner. Degas excelled in this exercise, though it is instructive to compare his drawings with those of his colleagues, such as Elie Delaunay and Gustave Moreau, and to be reminded of the homogeneity of their skills and graphic mannerisms.[94] Such classes served as a continuation of the studio practice these artists had experienced in Paris, as well as a reaffirmation of the values and assumptions associated with it. Life drawing was a fundamental discipline for all students, whether prospective history painters or portraitists, specialists in the *paysage historique* or the arts of engraving. In the tradition of a former director of the Villa Medici, Jean-Dominique Ingres, the values of line, form and tone were still pre-eminent, while certain poses of the model were chosen to recall the classical imagery that was everywhere in evidence. Under its current incumbent, Jean-Victor Schnetz, a somewhat more liberal regime had come into being, allowing non-*pensionnaires* like Moreau, Lionnet and Degas to join in some of their activities and encouraging students to respond to a greater diversity of subject-matter. Schnetz appears to have left his mark in at least two other respects, both of which found some sympathy with Degas. On the one hand, he was a keen advocate of the fourteenth century painters who had already made an appearance in Degas' notebooks; at the other extreme, he produced oil paintings of

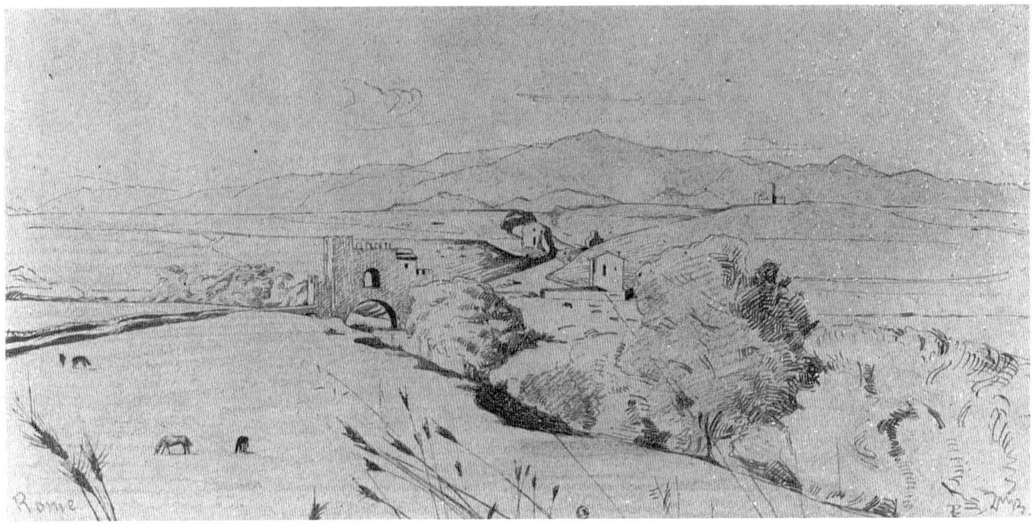

23. Léon Bonnat, *View of the Roman Campagna*, 1858, ink and black crayon, 15.3 × 30.1. Musée Bonnat, Bayonne.

contemporary Roman 'types' and may have inspired Degas' pictures of mendicants and tavern life. Under his directorship his charges also felt free to work outdoors, drawing in the streets of Rome and venturing out with paints and easels into the surrounding landscape.

In keeping with his early training, all the landscape painters with whom Degas has been identified were, in the broadest sense, representatives of the classical tradition. Claude, Valenciennes, Corot and even Gregoire Soutzo owed their different allegiances to the mediterranean vista and the antique narrative, and all worked for a significant period of their lives south of the Alps. If we add to this list the figure of Nicolas Poussin, whose letters Degas appears to have read while in Rome and one of whose paintings he later copied on a spectacular scale, the pantheon is almost complete.[95] For a young artist with such tastes, a long sojourn in Italy carried with it a number of detailed and potentially onerous associations, surrounded as he was by legendary buildings and panoramas, and even pathways and individual trees, closely identified with the great masters of the past. Above all, the monuments of Rome and the landscapes of the Roman Campagna had become some of the most visited and painted places on earth. Both Poussin and Claude had worked here for much of their lives and countless admirers had retraced their steps and repainted their *motifs*. The techniques of Valenciennes, another former resident, were widely associated with the city and were still pursued by some of its shifting community of painters. In his turn, Corot had painted the surrounding terrain, not least in his *The Roman Campagna, with the Claudian Aqueduct* (fig. 9) and the canvas of *Tivoli, Villa d'Este*, both of which Degas was ultimately to own.[96]

During their years in Rome, Degas and most of his colleagues attempted to respond to this formidable precedent, in landscape studies that ranged from the dull and the scrupulous to the occasionally inspired. Both Delaunay and Chapu recorded the streets of the city and surrounding towns, showing a patient skill and a mastery of complex perspective.[97] Gustave Moreau used pen, ink, wash and body colour to evoke the grandeur of ruins and vegetation, hinting at mysteries unsuspected by his peers.[98] With casual ease, the future portraitist Léon Bonnat drew monuments and fortifications, river views and rural scenes, such as *View of the Roman Campagna* (fig. 23), developing at least one of his subjects as a finished oil painting.[99] Though not lacking in accomplishment, most of these studies were conceived as exercises, as acts of homage to the past

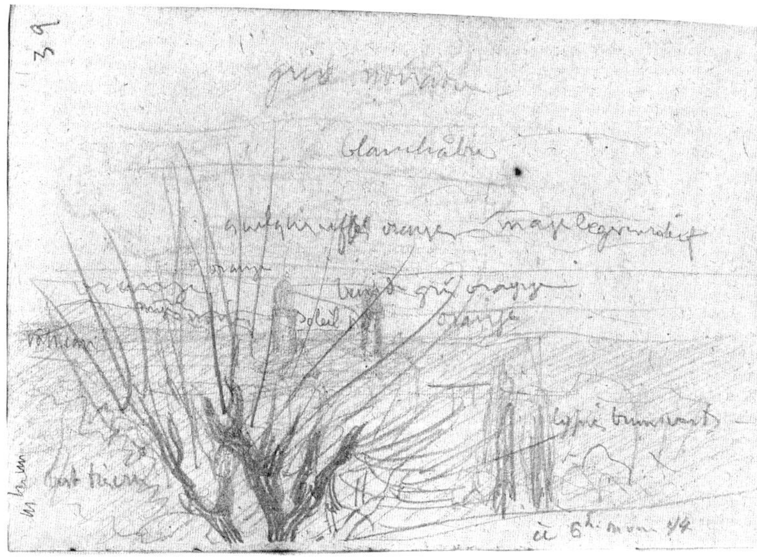

24. *Landscape Sketch*, *c.*1856–7, pencil, 8.8 × 11.8. Notebook 8, page 39. The Pierpont-Morgan Library, New York, 1985.47, f. 39. Purchased by the Board of Trustees in honor of Mr. and Mrs. Eugene Victor Thaw.

or, conceivably, as accumulations of material for later studio-based works. Only the obscure landscapist Félix Lionnet, following in the footsteps of his master, Corot, was to look back to these excursions as the foundation of his career. Immortalised in a drawing by Delaunay as he sat in the Villa Medici life class, Lionnet is referred to in one of Degas' notebooks and in his correspondance with Moreau.[100] He followed a similar itinerary to Degas, working in Naples, Rome and Florence before returning to an undistinguished career in France, exhibiting works based on his Italian studies, like the *View of the Forum* shown at the Salon of 1864 and the atmospheric *Landscape* (fig. 25).[101]

Working side-by-side with his contemporaries, Degas naturally took note of the same *motifs* and experimented with similar drawing conventions and technical practices. The sheer variety of his approach, however, and the occasional intensity and freshness of his imagery, come as a surprise. Four months after his arrival in the city, Degas made a sequence of three rapidly notated studies of Rome under the snow, recording in his sketchbook that they were drawn from the Borghese gardens and the Villa Medici. In the first (fig. 24), he jotted down the colours of the sky directly onto his drawing: 'blackish grey', 'some orange reflections', 'orange sun', adding that the study was done at

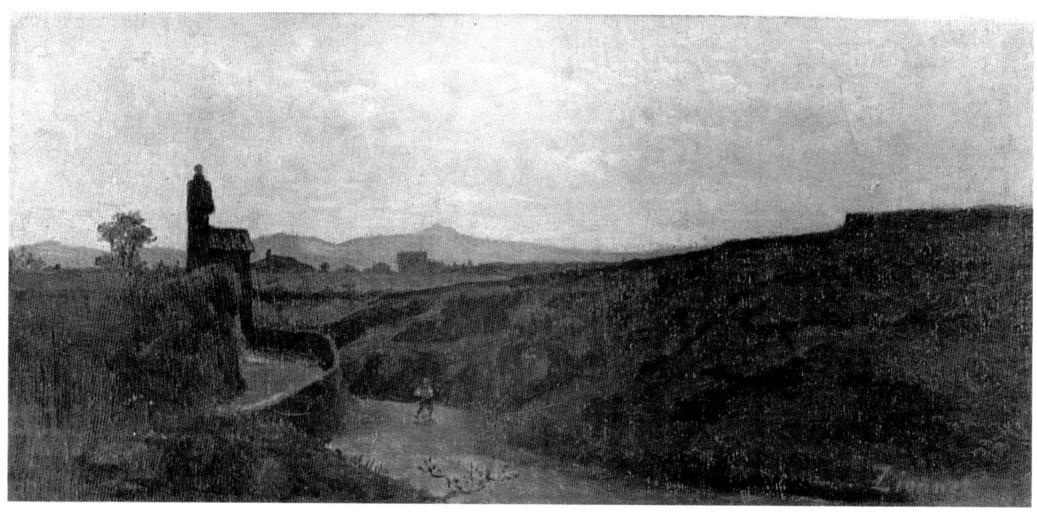

25. Félix Lionnet, *Landscape*, oil on canvas, 18 × 35. Musée Bonnat, Bayonne.

26 (facing page). Detail of fig. 28.

'a quarter to six'.[102] Almost immediately, he began a second drawing, observing amongst other things that the sky was now 'a very tender blue', with 'beautiful pinkish lights and violet shadows'.[103] Minutes later, he wrote on a third sketch that the colours included an 'uncertain blue' and a 'faded green', with 'all the countryside in a half-light', on this occasion writing 'six o'clock' in the margin.[104] Implicit in this modest sequence are a number of far-reaching truths. In the first place, Degas had responded directly, almost excitedly to his brute sensations of nature, and acknowledged that it was part of his business as an artist to engage with such sensations. Second, it was the colours of the scene that occupied him, not its historic resonance or its noble disposition. Finally, while echoing Valenciennes' advice to make studies 'in haste, seizing nature in its actuality', Degas has gone beyond the constraints of the oil sketch towards the limits of his craft. As the sun rose, the colours of the sky and the city changed as fast as he could perceive and articulate them, and even faster than his watercolours, pastels or oils could have committed them to paper.

Significantly perhaps, Degas did not attempt a painting based on this experience, though he soon made studies in oil on paper of comparable *motifs*. In the warmer light of summer, two views were painted from much the same site, the *Convent of Santa Trinita dei Monti Seen from a Tower of the Villa Medici* (fig. 17) and *View of Rome from the Banks of the Tiber* (fig. 16). Both were records of the fleeting colours of the sky, and both were executed in the rapid, fluent manner associated with their highly mobile medium. Like their apparent precursors, the oil sketches of Valenciennes, each has only a rudimentary composition, allowing the artist the maximum freedom to explore effects of light, tone and spaciousness. Other oil studies from this period develop these lines of inquiry. A painting of sky and clouds recalls sketches made by Constable, who also noted down the time and date of his observations;[105] glimpses of foliage and penumbrous hillsides remind us of Degas' morning vigil at the Villa Borghese;[106] and further views of Rome return us to the classical context.[107] On an excursion into the Roman Campagna, oil on paper was chosen for a previously unpublished study that has been associated with Degas, *A River Scene* (fig. 27), showing a view of the Tiber that was also painted by both Flandrin and Bonnat.[108] Another view of similar terrain, *Roman Landscape* (fig. 28) was executed in pencil and represents the more domestic, pastoral character of the landscape, and can again be compared with such works by Bonnat as his *View of the Roman Campagna*.[109] Notebook drawings help to document other visits in the hinterland, among them an outing to Tivoli in

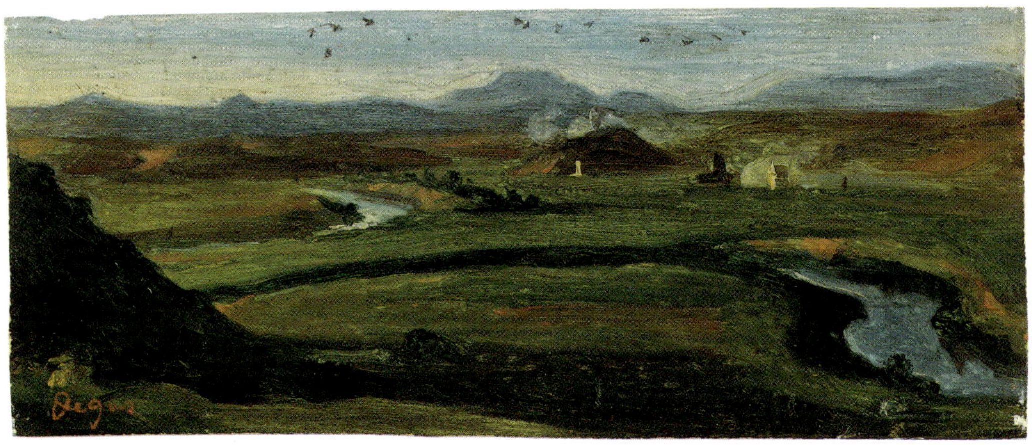

27. Attributed to Degas, *A River Scene*, oil on paper, mounted on canvas, 10.5 × 23.5. Private collection.

November 1857 which resulted in a drawing touched with chalk or pastel, arguably the first of its kind in the artist's career.[110]

Disparate though these works are, they leave us in no doubt about Degas' alertness to the natural world, his fluency with the materials of the landsape painter, and his awareness of the tradition that was visible on every side. Still small in scale and number, his landscape studies were scattered evenly amongst his grander projects and sometimes contrasted favourably with them in freshness and daring. Such qualities were also evident in Degas' written notebook commentaries, which became increasingly prolix as the months passed and often accompanied, or even overshadowed, drawings made on his travels. A vivid example concerns the trip to Tivoli of 1857, which resulted in one finished drawing and two hasty sketches, but several pages of description and colour notes.[111] Once more recording the time of day, Degas attempted to describe the elusive tints of sky and mountains, distinguishing between 'silver grey' and 'pinkish grey', and between the 'pale blue', 'blackish blue' and 'tender blue-green' of the scene before him. In such circumstances, words again came more easily to hand than paints or pastels, and gradually the artist learnt to summarise his sensations in terse, almost telegraphic prose. Journeying from Rome to Florence by carriage in 1858, he filled page after page with accounts of places visited and works of art seen, but also with notes of storms and sunsets, dazzling views and startling colours:

28. *Roman Landscape*, 1857, pencil, 27 × 43.8. Museum of Fine Arts, Houston, museum purchase with funds provided by the Sarah Campbell Blaffer Foundation.

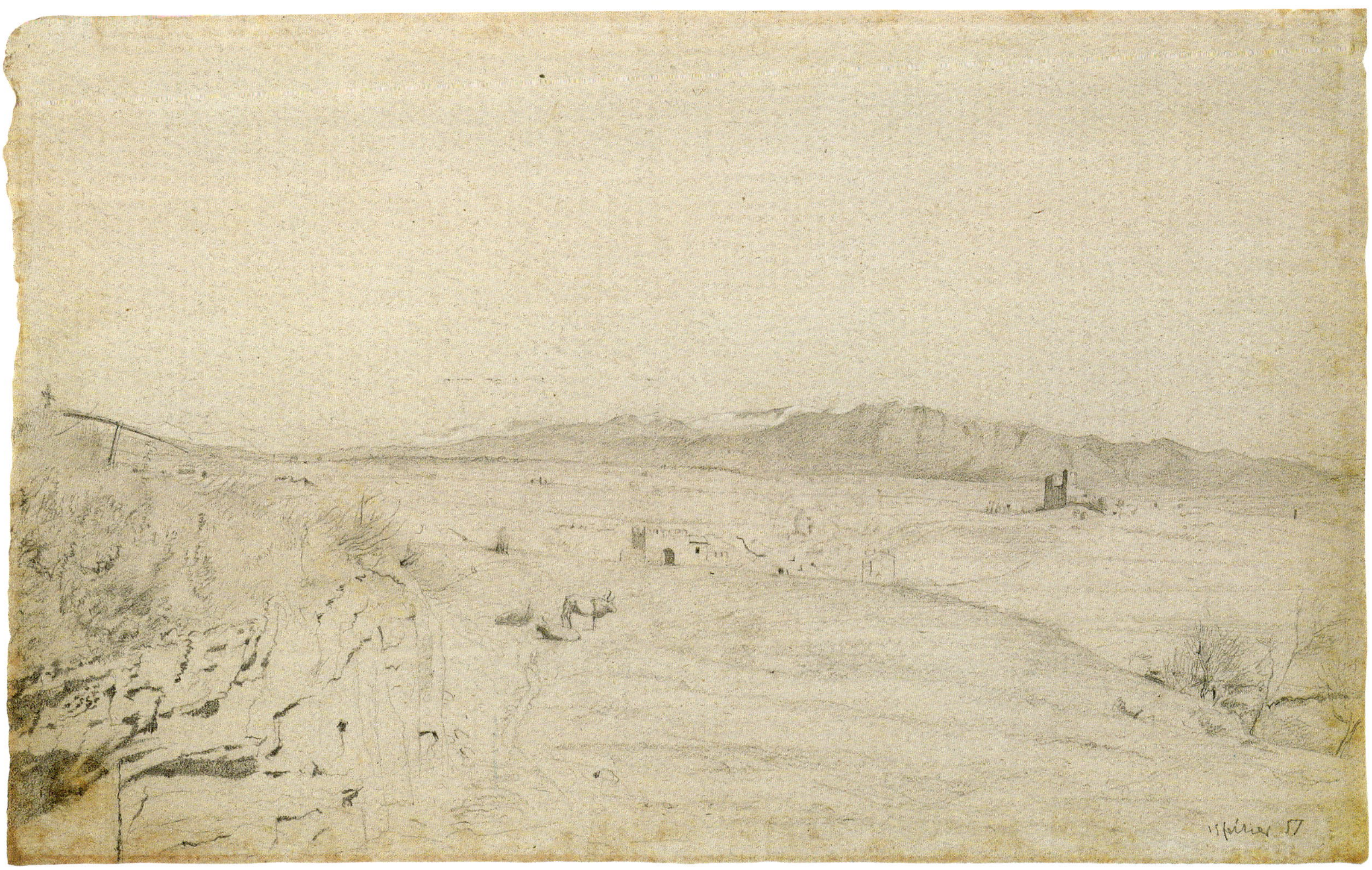

> 24 July, I leave Rome 6.45 arriving at a height beyond Ponte Molle – superb plain, the Italy of our dreams! Yellow plain, corn cut – mountains grey with night falling at their feet, hazy mountains truly azure blue . . . 7.30 – All is grey except the foreground – yellow. Very tiring night. I can make out volcanic terrain, rocks with clusters of trees . . .[112]

During his stay in Orvieto, where he admired paintings by Signorelli and Fra Angelico, Degas took an evening walk on the ramparts, apparently carrying his notebook with him and writing as he went:

> Near the Well I look down on the plain – superb spectacle to be remembered for a lifetime. The dried-out Tiber and the sun setting over the road to Florence – all these beautiful ranges of mountains. What moment of the day could be more beautiful? I am thinking about France which is not as beautiful . . .[113]

Even as he gloried in these sights, Degas was assailed by doubt, as if the words of his teachers still haunted him: 'I don't feel like going out to draw from nature. Luca Signorelli fascinates me. I must think about figures above all else . . . Boredom soon overcomes me when I am contemplating nature.'[114] On another occasion, he recorded his difficulties in responding to such fleeting sensations and anticipated the practical concerns of his later landscape-making activity: 'I would rather do anything than a rough sketch . . . my memories will do better;'[115] and, almost in despair: 'I gave up making the slightest sketch. So many changes in the landscape in such a short time'.[116]

The turbulence and self-doubt expressed in many of Degas' letters and notebook jottings are part of a wider reconsideration of his art that took place in the later phases of his Italian tour. Arriving as a timid and rather straight-laced student, Degas had developed a sense of himself as a rising young professional, free to pursue his own interests and resist the wisdom of those, like his father, whose tastes he now felt able to question. While preparing his début in grandiose projects such as *Alexander and Bucephalus* (private collection; L 91) and the *Bellelli Family* (Musée d'Orsay, Paris; L 79), Degas discovered less containable passions: for scenes of violence and fantasy, for the spectacle of the chase and for the urban landscape, and even for caricature and low comedy. Amongst many factors in this transformation, his contact with Gustave Moreau at the Villa Medici appears to have been critical.[117] Not only did Moreau offer access to artists past and present who lay beyond Degas' experience, but he encouraged in his fellow-students new habits of looking, thinking about and practising painting. In his letters to Moreau from 1858, Degas hardly mentioned the idols of his youth, preferring to enthuse about Giorgione and Carpaccio, Veronese and Rembrandt, Velázquez and Van Dyck.[118] He wrote about 'the sadness which is the lot of those involved with art', but was equally frank about the passion and delight he had discovered in the processes of painting.[119] Most tellingly, he discussed colour, searching for a reconciliation between the disciplines of his youth and the exhilaration of his widening horizons: 'It is true, isn't it, my dear Moreau, that there is a way of making light, beauty, feeling, line and colour out of a lot of love for what one does . . . ?'[120]

The debate between line and colour was as alive and real in that far-flung outpost of French culture, the Villa Medici, as in the studios, galleries and academies of Paris. From the letters of Georges Bizet, a music laureate during Degas' visit, to the fictionalised account by the Goncourt brothers in *Manette Salamon*, contemporaries bear witness to the intense exchanges that took place

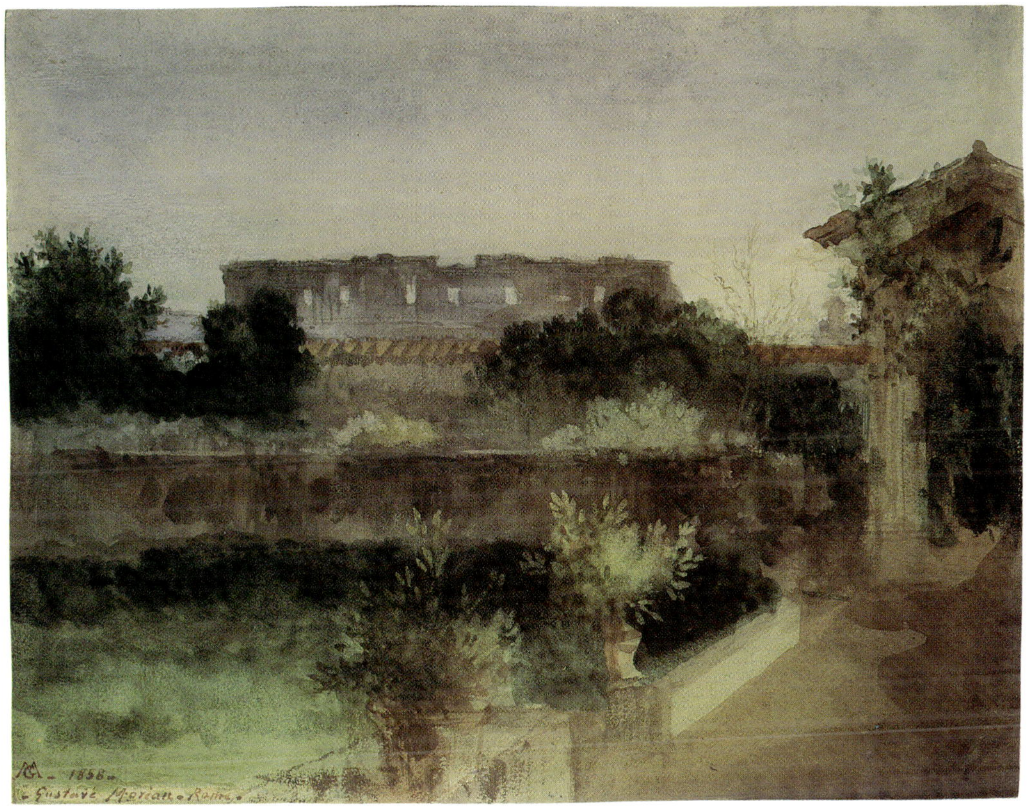

29. Gustave Moreau, *Landscape*, 1858, watercolour, 22.5 × 28.5. Musée Gustave Moreau, Paris.

under its roof.[121] Moreau was at the centre of many of them, respected for his first-hand acquaintance with such colourists as Chasseriau and Fromentin, as well as with Delacroix himself, and leading by example in his accomplished drawings and watercolours. Like Degas, many of Moreau's studies were based on the frescoes and panel paintings of the Italian masters, but more even than his younger admirer, Moreau had spread his net wide and cast it idiosyncratically. As his notebooks and portfolios show, Moreau's taste embraced the antique and the decorative, the carefully observed and the fluently invented. He drew voraciously from nature, recording animals and flowers as well as views of his Italian surroundings, including studies of Naples, Florence and Rome in a wide variety of media, among them *Landscape* (fig. 29).[122] The suggestion that Moreau introduced Degas to the use of pastel is probably mistaken, but the older artist's appetite for art of all kinds seems to have left its mark.[123] An energetic copyist, Moreau shared Degas' love for the painters of the fourteenth and fifteenth centuries, but equally directed his attention to artists who had barely featured in Degas' earlier itineraries, such as the Venetian painters Bellini and Carpaccio.

The most marked shift in Degas' allegiances during the period spent with Moreau was his discovery of, or perhaps his capitulation to, the art of Venice. Writing from Florence in September 1858, Degas proudly announced to his mentor: 'I have finished my sketch of the Giorgione; it took me nearly three weeks. I have made a virtual copy of Veronese's angel from his sketch and I have started Giorgione's landscape (Judgement of Solomon) the same size; I might put in the figures.'[124] Two months later, he wrote: 'Delaunay talked to me at length about Venice, Carpaccio, you, and a very little bit about Veronese.'[125] Degas was obliged to write, rather than speak, to Moreau because the latter had taken his enthusiasm to its logical conclusion, travelling to Venice in the company of Delaunay, Lionnet and others to study the revered masters at first hand.[126] Unwilling or unable to leave Florence, Degas tried to compensate by making copies of the Venetian paintings in the Uffizi, while corresponding with his absent friends and devouring the painted studies they brought back with them.[127] Gaining in confidence, he wrote to his father about these new activities, only to receive some cautionary advice from Auguste. Acknowledging the appeal of the Venetians, Degas' father reminded him that the 'admirable colours' of an artist like Giorgione were 'accompanied by draughtsmanship that is so beautiful, so elegant' and warned him against the 'over-hot' tones that might lead to his undoing.[128] Another letter makes clear that Auguste associated Moreau with these dangerous developments and that Degas was now expected to bring his labours to an end and return to Paris.[129]

Though some of Degas' copies from this period have been lost, a substantial number of documented examples bear out the extent and the particularity of his conversion to the Venetian cause. Contrary to the impression sometimes given, there are remarkably few painted studies after the approved models of Degas' early years, such as Raphael and Michelangelo. On the other hand, a sudden concentration of quite different copies can be identified in his last months in Italy, and in the phase soon after, the majority of them based on works by the Venetian masters. During this time, Degas made elaborate copies in oil on canvas of the two pictures by Giorgione mentioned in his letter, the *Judgement of Solomon* and the less certainly identified *Trial of Moses*; he faithfully reproduced Giovanni Bellini's *Sacred Allegory* and 'made a virtual copy of Veronese's angel', presumably from the latter's *Annunciation*; and he may have chosen this moment to paint his version of *St Anthony Reviving a Woman Killed by her Husband* by Titian.[130] In his sketchbooks, Degas studied figures and poses from other works by Bellini and Titian, a practice he continued on his return to France.[131] Now plundering the Louvre and provincial museums, the artist made further painted studies from Bellini, Veronese, Tintoretto, Giorgione and Sebastiano del Piombo, and recorded his admiration for Carpaccio and other painters associated with Venice, such as Mantegna.[132] Though some of these copies were partial or reduced in scale, others were patiently detailed and approached the dimensions of their originals. As Degas' letters make clear, such exercises required a prodigious investment of time and energy, marking the milestones of his own self-education and the limits of his developing taste.

Degas' extensive copies from Venetian painting in the late 1850s represent a decisive shift in the polarities of his art. Such shifts are easily exaggerated, and in Degas' case these events form part of a life-long vacillation between two symbolically powerful traditions. But, as Auguste De Gas was aware, the opulent colours and dense, tactile brushwork of painters like Veronese exerted a considerable power over the young painters of the day, and seemed to lead naturally to other values and painterly possibilities. Not the least of these was the landscape, a subject nurtured in fifteenth-century Venice and achieving virtual autonomy in such pictures as Giovanni Bellini's depictions of St Jerome and Giorgione's celebrated *Tempesta*. Venetian religious and secular subjects were typically painted in landscape settings, often closely observed from the local countryside and at times threatening to take precedence over the narratives they ostensibly supported. Several of the pictures chosen by Degas for his copies fell into this latter category and suggest a marked fascination for this aspect of the Venetian achievement. In the letter to Moreau describing his copy of Giorgione's *Judgement of Solomon*, a picture in which almost two-thirds of the

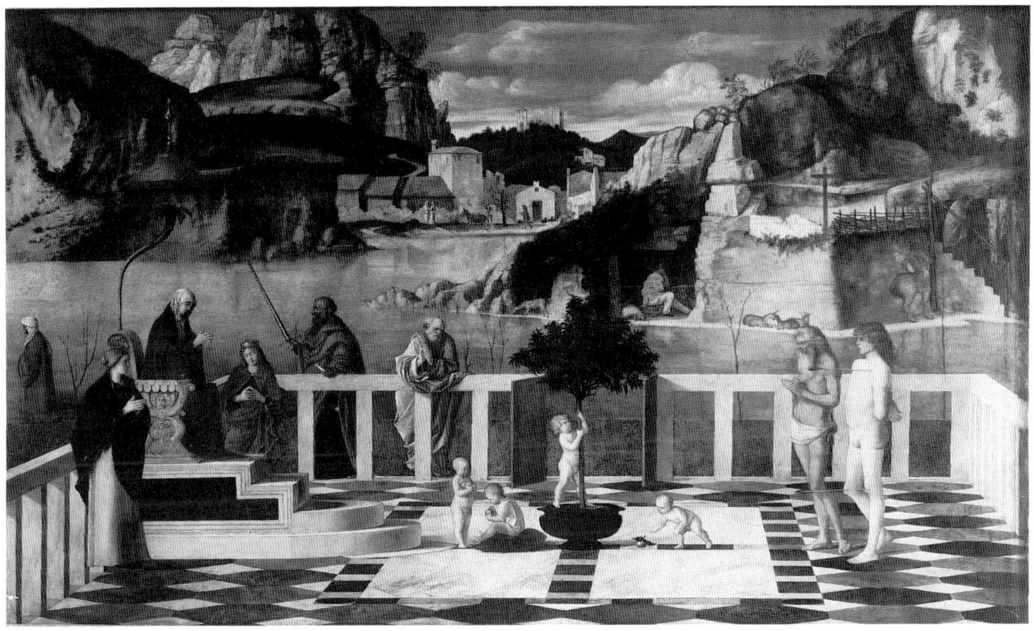

30. Giovanni Bellini, *Sacred Allegory*, oil on canvas. Uffizi, Florence.

canvas is taken up by a pastoral scene, Degas specifies that he has 'started Giorgione's landscape' and adds, almost as an afterthought, 'I might put in the figures'. Lucid though his motives are, they are even more transparent in another copy, this time from Giovanni Bellini's *Sacred Allegory* (fig. 30), a painting also studied by Moreau.[133] Here Degas has singled out one of Bellini's most sparsely populated paintings, in which a magnificent rocky landscape, a meandering lake and a mass of rural detail almost engulf the slender forms of the foreground saints. In both works, it is difficult to resist the implication that Degas has chosen them for their pastoral settings, concentrating his efforts on their backgrounds and even referring to the *Judgement of Solomon* as 'Giorgione's landscape'. By a curious paradox, such paintings seem to have offered a model for Degas' grandest aspirations, fostering his love for the landscape while allowing him to venerate the figurative masters of the past.

We might reasonably speculate about this last-minute encounter with Bellini, Giorgione and Veronese, not least in the context of Degas' burgeoning career.[134] It is clear from his correspondence that Degas was anticipating an imminent return to France and was anxious to complete the business he had in hand.[135] We could go further and guess that the paintings he copied in his last months in Florence represented a summary of his current thinking, as well as a point of departure for his impending professional career. If we look closely at the pictures in question, particularly in the light of Degas' original compositions of the period, a consistency of purpose begins to emerge. As we have seen, many of Degas' Venetian copies were based on figure-and-landscape subjects, where a complex equilibrium has been established between human and pastoral elements. In such works, the setting is not simply a painted backdrop, but a protagonist in the drama, with its own rhythms and textures which interweave with the figurative narrative. If a dominant theme can be said to link Degas' picture projects at this period, it is just such an equilibrium of elements. In his earlier canvases, such as *John the Baptist and the Angel* and *Dante and Virgil*, a modest indication of scenery surrounds his dramatis personae, who are relatively large in terms of the picture rectangle. As later subjects emerged, figures tended to be reduced in scale and landscape considerations became more prominent. In the several versions of *Alexander and Bucephalus*, for example, a towering range of hills or mountains occupies the upper half of the scene, while trees and buildings dwarf many of the human and animal actors. Even more revealing is the fact that Degas has made extensive, detailed drawings for this landscape, indicating on one of them: 'greyish-pink mountains', 'silver sky' and 'a milky tone as in Veronese'.[136]

This progression towards the figure-and-landscape composition can be seen as a partial resolution of one of the fundamental dilemmas facing the young artist. On the one hand, it enabled him to explore an alternative to the dominant figurative tradition, represented in his youth by Ingres and amongst his peers by Delaunay and Bonnat; on the other, it appeared to offer greater intellectual challenges and more public esteem than either the pure landscape, or the increasingly discredited *paysage historique*. Any doubts we might have about Degas' direction are emphatically dispelled by the most ambitious productions to emerge from his Italian phase: the history paintings executed in the months and years after his return to Paris. Each of these large canvases depends on a dialogue between the human form and a distinctive outdoor setting. In their different ways, each can also be traced to Degas' Italian experience, through its subject-matter, its incidental details or its overt references to artists he had copied and admired. The *Young Spartans* (fig. 31) of 1860 presents us with an explicitly classical subject and an identifiably mediterranean context, which once featured trees, a river and more insistent mountains.[137] While painting *The Daughter of Jephtha* (fig. 41), Degas reminded himself in his notebooks of the colours of Veronese, while in the final work he opted for a lush, rural background that recalled his contemporary visits to Normandy.[138] By 1865, when *Scene of War in the Middle Ages* (fig. 46) was accepted at the Salon, Degas' dependence on the historical set piece had almost come to an end, though his involvement in the landscape had, conversely, reached a new peak. In this masterly panorama, we are also reminded that scenes of horses and riders, now dressed in racing silks and hunting pink, had already taken root in Degas' repertory and would soon offer a topical alternative to his antique figure-in-the-landscape *motifs*.

In the months before he finally left Florence, Degas busied himself with a characteristic variety of projects, many of which seem intended to pave the way for his return to Paris. By far the grandest, the studies for the *Bellelli Family*, were designed to display his skills as a portraitist and presumably to take the Salon by storm.[139] Severe and formal, the picture has often been linked with Degas' grounding in draughtsmanship and associated with the imagery of Holbein, Ingres and even the early portraits of Bonnat.[140] Intriguingly, one of the preparatory drawings for the picture shares the page with the only known sketch for his copy of Bellini's *Sacred Allegory*, suggesting that Degas might have linked the two pictures in some way, or conceivably seen them as representative of his principal artistic concerns. The portrait, the Old Master copy and the figure-in-the-landscape account for the great majority of his Italian activities and continued to preoccupy him after his return to Paris. Landscape was never far from his thoughts, though often expressed in a minor medium or as a subsidiary theme. Interleaved with notebook studies for the *Bellelli Family*, we find drawings of trees and rocks, the River Arno and the roof-tops of Siena.[141] A dramatic gouache of a boat at sea (fig. 32) may be a souvenir of his travels, while a number of more imaginative, even nightmarish, scenes hint at the continuing influence of Moreau.[142] Nothing quite prepares us, however, for another canvas from Degas' Florentine sojourn, the *Wild Boar* (private

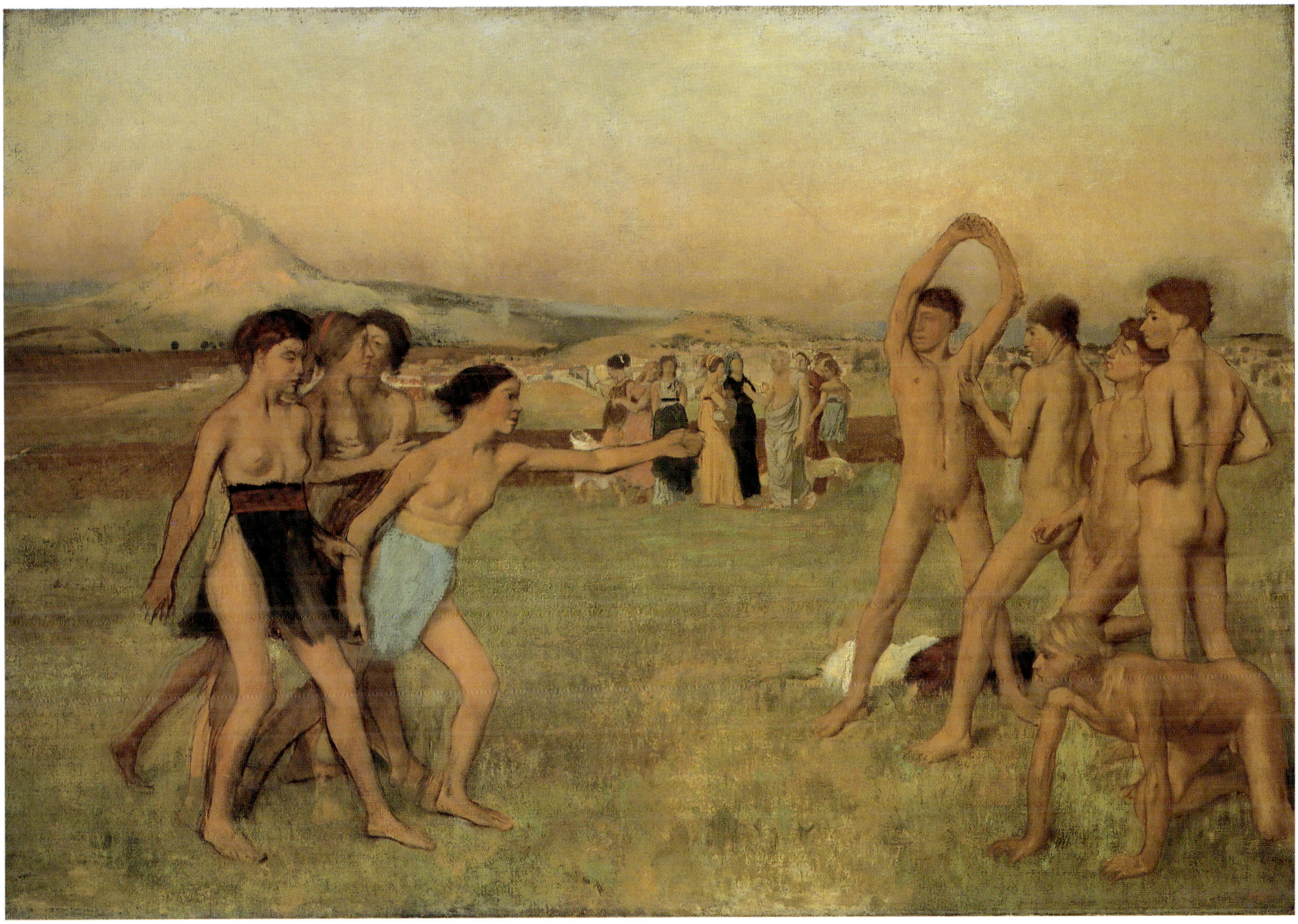

31. *Young Spartans*, 1860, oil on canvas, 109 × 154 (L 70). National Gallery, London.

collection; L 123). This substantial composition shows a heavily wooded valley occupied by a large and disgruntled boar, whose features are derived from a painting attributed to Frans Snyders in the Uffizi.[143] Degas evolved this picture in notebook studies and small sketches, eliminating most of the other figures and background features of Snyders' painting and developing his own, perhaps fanciful, setting.[144] Exceeding even the most precocious of his Venetian copies, on this occasion Degas chose an artist beyond the pale of all but the most advanced contemporary taste. Such a choice of model was at best irregular, at worst indicative of a new high-handedness towards the values he had brought with him to Italy only three years earlier.

Degas' affinity with the mundane and the rural was already apparent in his later Italian notebooks and clearly preceded his rediscovery of the artistic climate of France. Any reading of the evidence is complicated by the continuous usage of his notebooks and a lack of clear demarcation between Florentine and Parisian phases within them, but their message is clear. Before he left Italy, Degas had begun to record the everyday life of streets and cafés, and the posturings of sailors and soldiers, dandies and vagabonds. Outside the city, studies were made

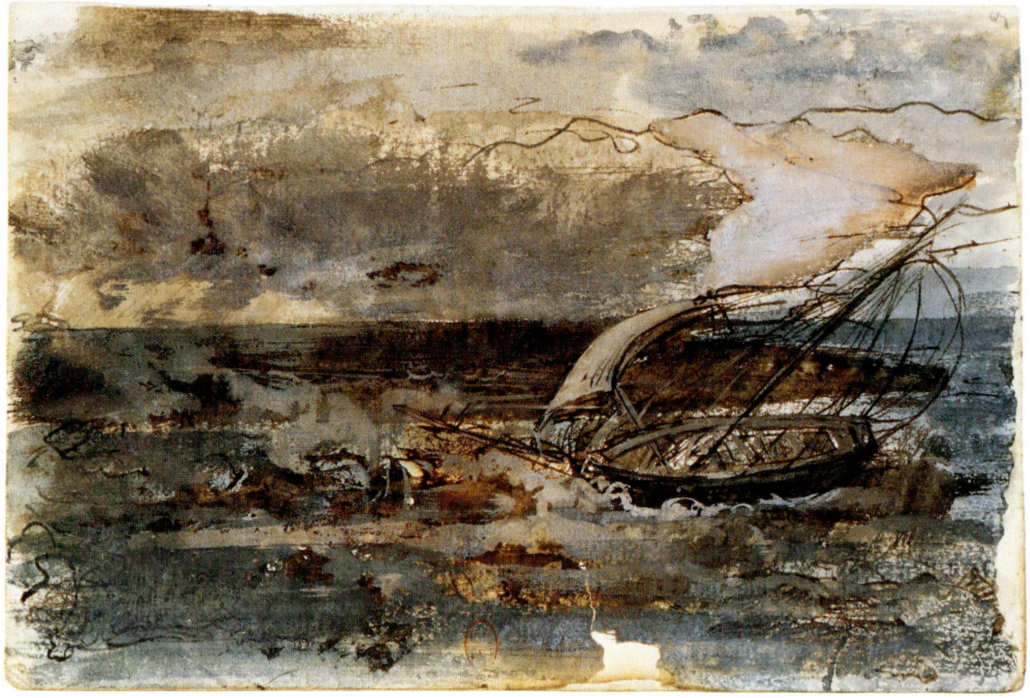

32. *A Boat at Sea*, *c.*1858–60, gouache and ink, 9.8 × 14.5. Notebook 13, page 5. Bibliothèque Nationale, Paris.

of oxen, cows and dogs, but above all of horses of every conceivable variety. A sudden and remarkable eruption of cart-horses, thoroughbreds and rearing steeds enlivens the notebooks of 1858 and 1859, and was soon to invade both history paintings and genre subjects. Some of these horses have an ancient pedigree and can be traced back to Castagno or Van Dyck, but others are unashamedly modern, pulling carriages, leaping fences and even awaiting starter's orders. As we shall see, such equestrian subjects were to contribute to one of Degas' most important groups of landscapes in the following decade and were to announce the first truly contemporary theme of the artist's career. For all the high-mindedness of his grander projects, there can be little doubt that Degas planned his first paintings of horses before he left Italy and saw them as a transition between the old and the new phases of his activity. Notebooks begun in Florence, continued on the homeward journey and taken up again on his return home show this process vividly. Studies of racehorses overlap with copies of *condottieri*, sketches after Alfred de Dreux and Géricault are followed by horses drawn from the life, and fragmentary sketches of draught animals foreshadow his own early equestrian compositions.[145]

When Degas arrived back in Paris in the spring of 1859, he carried with him a cultural baggage as assorted as that of any of his returning compatriots. Rolled up canvases and folios of drawings bore witness to three years of assiduous and conventional study, while hundreds of sketchbook pages proclaimed a catholic taste and a questioning intelligence. There were superb life drawings made at the Villa Medici to reassure those, like Degas' father, who looked for discipline and a mastery of form, and copies large and small to advertise his erudition. His studies from Venetian art demonstrated a broadening sensibility as well as the influence of his peers, while exercises in pastel, watercolour and gouache hinted at the technical gymnastics of his later career. Like many of his fellow-students, Degas was able to show a familiarity with landscape art, though few of them could boast pastels and oil-on-paper studies, notebook sketches and pencil drawings, original canvases and partial copies such as that from Snyders' *Wild*

Boar. There is no suggestion that Degas conceived of himself as a landscape painter, at this or any other period of his life, but it is striking how often this subject found a place in his activities. Having left France a virtual innocent in its practices, Degas returned home both accomplished and substantially informed in the landscapist's art.

The extent to which Degas was aware of the artistic context to which he was returning is difficult to assess. New arrivals at the Villa Medici undoubtedly brought stories of Salon triumphs and scandals, and it is clear from the correspondence of Degas, Moreau and others that information of this kind was exchanged with acquaintances at home.[146] Another, more indirect, source of news was the artistic community of Italy itself. Circumstantial evidence shows that Degas and his colleagues came into contact with a number of native-born painters, notably at the Caffé Michelangiolo in Florence, where the group known as the Macchiaioli habitually gathered.[147] Leading figures among the Macchiaioli, such as Telemaco Signorini and Giovanni Fattori, had already become familiar with a wide but haphazard range of contemporary French art and may, paradoxically, have developed more progressive tastes than their French counterparts. Works by Delacroix, Decamps, Meissonier and Rosa Bonheur were accessible in local collections, perhaps stimulating the high-toned palettes and modern-life *motifs* of the Florentine group.[148] Similarly, landscapes by Isabey, Bonington, Troyon and Daubigny offered encouragement to their direct observations of nature and may have prompted their distinctive scenes of pastureland and dunes.[149] It has been argued that Degas, among others, was sufficiently impressed by this brief encounter with the Macchiaioli to carry forward some of their innovations into his work of the next decade.[150] What is beyond dispute is that Degas renewed his acquaintance with certain of the Macchiaioli artists on future trips to Florence and enjoyed lasting friendships with some of their associates, notably Giovanni Boldini and Diego Martelli.[151]

Two brief but revealing codas must be added to the saga of Degas' Italian

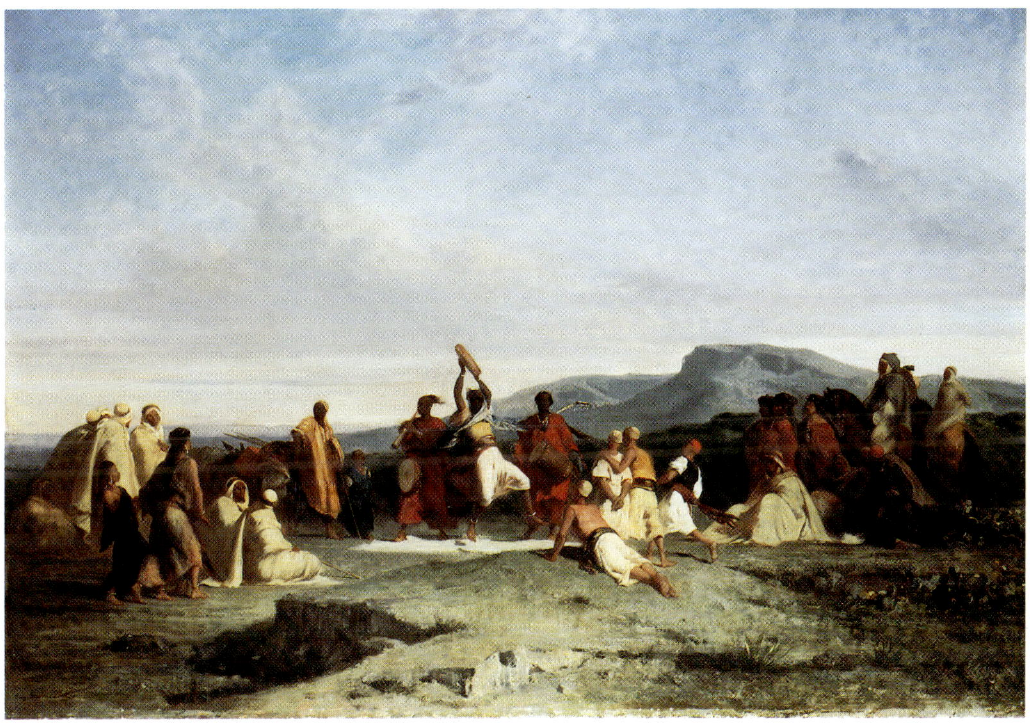

33. Eugène Fromentin, *Negro Tumblers with their Tribe*, 1859, oil on canvas, 96 × 137.5. Mathaf Gallery, photo courtesy Sotheby's.

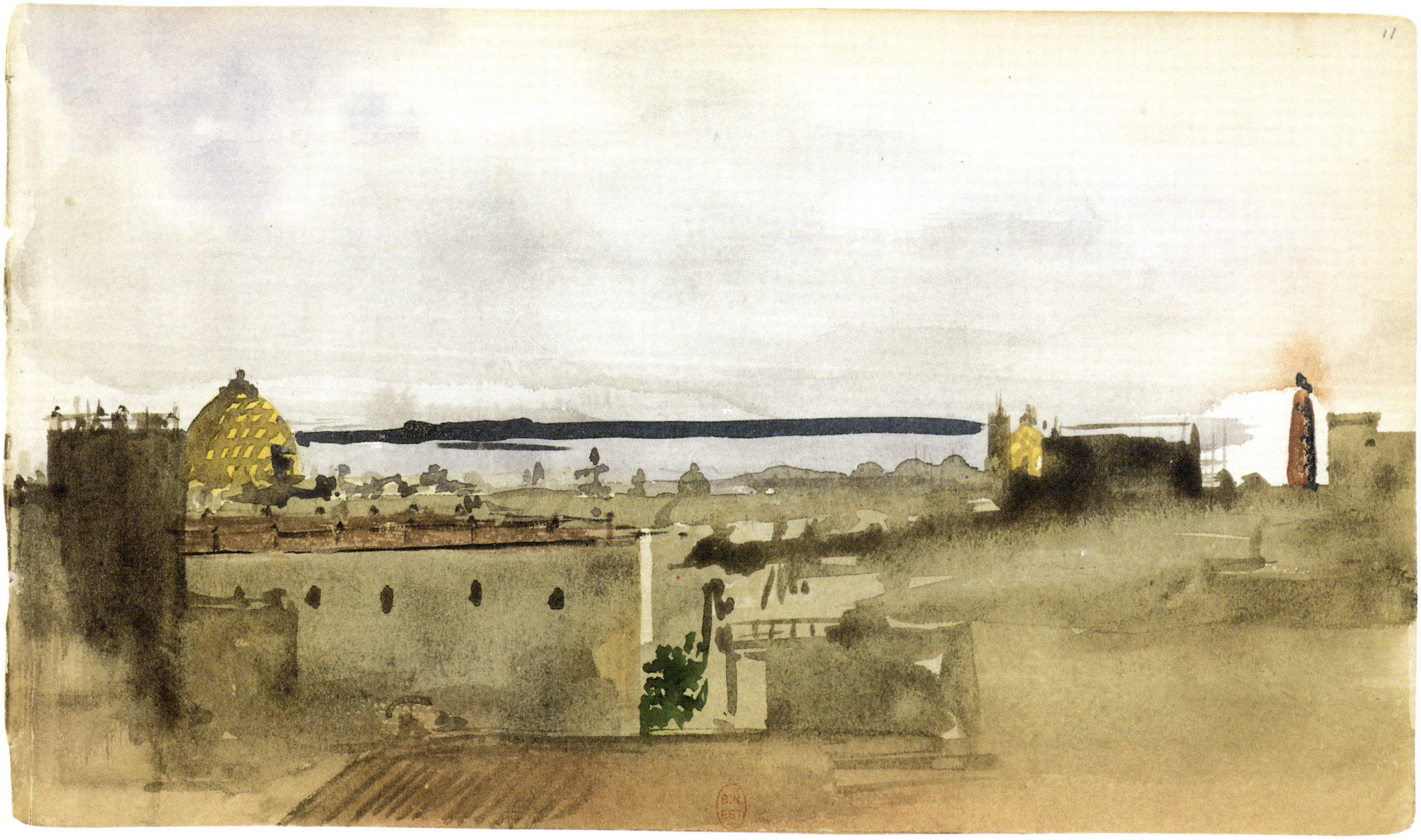

34. *View of Naples*, 1860, watercolour, 12.5 × 21.5. Notebook 19, page 11. Bibliothèque Nationale, Paris.

adventure. The first concerns the artist's response to the 1859 Paris Salon, which he visited within a few days of his return to the city. According to the accounts of his companions, Degas expressed doubts about the Ingresque portraits of Hippolyte Flandrin, but defended all the pictures submitted by Delacroix, even in the face of considerable opposition from his friends.[152] More remarkable is a note written to Moreau soon after this visit, in which Degas announced, 'I think Fromentin almost has pride of place in the Exhibition . . . There is a *Negro Tumblers with their Tribe* and an *Edge of the Oasis during the Sirocco*, both masterpieces. Next to them, everything else seems like brown sauce.'[153] Further evidence of Degas' reaction can be found in a current notebook, where he made two brief drawings from the first of Fromentin's pictures, *Negro Tumblers with their Tribe* (fig. 33).[154] The significance of his choice, the only picture from the Salon he singled out in this way, hardly needs to be underlined. After three years in Italy, Degas had chosen a work that was neither Italianate nor historical, neither concerned with Ingres' 'cult of truth' not his 'tradition of the beautiful'. Painted by a leading orientalist and associate of Delacroix's, this painting was described in Baudelaire's review of the exhibition as having 'that expert and innate understanding of colour, which is so rare among us'.[155] Combining colour with naturalism, figures with the landscape, and poised somewhere between a pastoral and a modern-life subject, *Negro Tumblers with their Tribe* was seen by the fledgling artist Degas as exemplary, and perhaps as offering a way forward in his own assault on the Paris art world.

The last echo of Degas' Grand Tour was felt in the following year, 1860, when he decided on a brief return visit to Italy. The purpose of his trip is not entirely clear, though we might note that portraiture, in the form of further studies for the *Bellelli Family*, and landscape, expressed in watercolour, drawing and written notes, were the principal beneficiaries. On this occasion, his increased maturity and sense of purpose are unmistakable. In the Naples Museum, where he had formerly admired the paintings of Claude, Degas now gloried in the colours of the Roman mosaics, likening them to Veronese and regretting that he had not brought his pastels with him to 'learn a lesson . . . which would last me a lifetime'.[156] As he looked across the city, he made more watercolours of its harbours and monuments, including one of the finest of his early career (fig. 34) which was later used in the background of his aunt's portrait.[157] A similar fluency characterises the delightful oil-on-paper study of the Castello dell'Ovo (fig. 18), where a snow-capped Vesuvius reminds us of the wintery conditions of Degas' visit. Such landscape studies were incorporated into some of his fist equestrian canvases, presumably painted after he had again returned to Paris, and sketchbook pages continued to combine visual with verbal description. He noted that the sea at Civita Vecchia was 'apple green with a few touches of indigo at the horizon', which sounds more like Delacroix than Degas, and continued:

> the boat leaves behind it a foaming trace in the middle of which is a wake of bronze. The Pontine Marshes stretch out reddish-brown, behind them the Appenines with their snow-capped peaks. This reddish-brown is just like a little branch of dead pine laid in the sunshine. Far away on the horizon, a line of small lateen-sailed boats look like a flight of seagulls, in tone and in shape. As we progress, whitish intervals like cliffs separate the reddish line of the Pontine Marshes from the sea. The outline of the Apennines is very sinuous and the lines interweave as in a basket. The foam which marks the ship's wake is like that made by a woman washing in running water, layered in little steps. Beneath the foam it looks like bubbling snow: the intervals have a greenish-blue depth which makes one giddy.[158]

In another sketchbook, Degas recorded the colours of Vesuvius and the Castel dell'Ovo, remembered a seascape by Delacroix and brought to mind 'the effect of English marine paintings'.[159] As in his description of the Apennines, his notes teem with metaphors and allusions, his vivid prose and skeletal drawings fusing to encapsulate the scene. However else we might characterise this omnivorous twenty-five year-old, and amidst his passions for things antique and modern, we must surely allow for an artist with a raw and original sense of colour, and a literate, ambitious and often poetic alertness to the landscape.

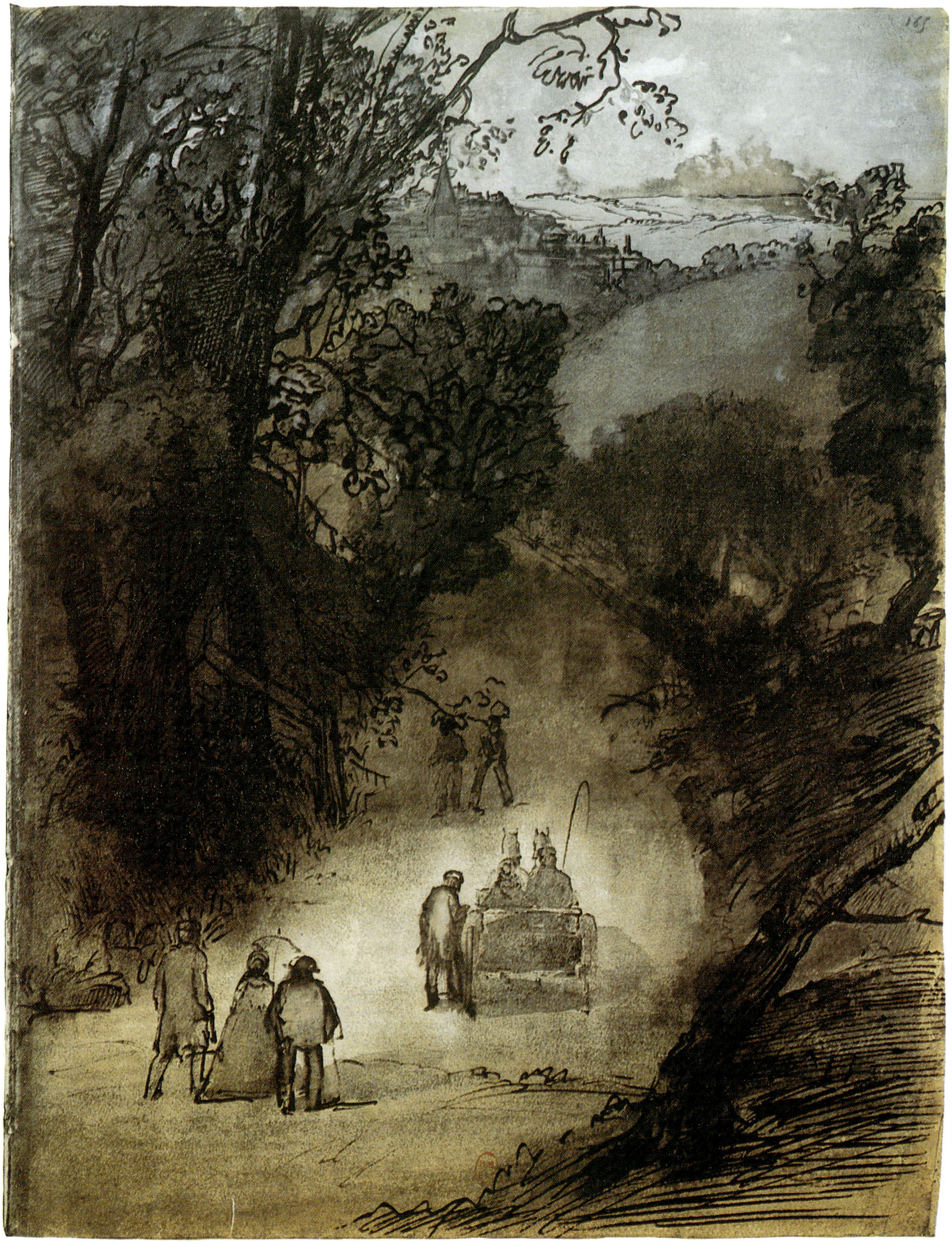

2 The Return to France

'There is only one country, it is ours, Monsieur . . .'
(Degas, in a letter of 1890)

In the autumn of 1861, Degas made the first of many visits to the village of Ménil-Hubert in Normandy, the home of his former school-friend Paul Valpinçon.[1] The Valpinçon château and grounds, both of which became the subject of pastels and photographs by Degas, are some forty miles inland from the coastal resort of Trouville, set amongst country lanes, scattered copses and rich agricultural land.[2] Almost annually, for the next two or three decades, Degas would retreat to Ménil-Hubert for a week or two in the summer months, combining his stay with experiments in portraiture, studies in landscape and even an occasional excursion into sculpture. Curiously, it is the first of these visits that is the most well-documented. According to the artist's own account, he and Paul Valpinçon undertook a prodigious walk across the rain-sodden landscape, heading towards the neighbouring village of Exmes and on to Haras-du-Pin, then as now the home of the French National Stud. In a large notebook that Degas appears to have carried with him, he evoked his surroundings and recorded a kind of inner monologue, using much the same fragmented, heightened prose he had relied on in Italy:

> . . . left the road to Argentan and headed with Paul straight for Exmes. Exactly like England. Small and large meadows, all closed in by fences. Damp paths, ponds. Green and umber. It is completely new to me; at Saint-Valéry the countryside seems to me a lot less rich and leafy than here.
>
> Continually going up and down over green hillocks. Arrived at a road nearly flooded over. A track temporarily closed on the hillside. I remember the backgrounds in those pictures of English genius, such as *The Gate* or *The Rider's Shadow*, *The Wolf and the Lamb* etc. Everywhere there are woods. Passed by some small farms. Arrived at M. Leriche's estate. At the moment I am reading *Tom Jones* and nothing would make a better background setting for its characters. Going up towards Exmes.
>
> It is really a typical clean market town with its church and its brick houses. Down below, meadows in the foreground. I am thinking of M. Soutzo and of Corot. Only these two would give this quietness a little interest.
>
> Exmes, old church – how can anybody live here? Along steep and woody paths – after half an hour suddenly emerge into an avenue in a park, with gates. Beginning of the autumn, dead leaves cry out underfoot. We wait for the appearance of the horses.
>
> Suddenly we arrive in a great avenue which leads to the château – it is the avenue of Maisons-Laffitte. The Haras dates from Louis XV. In front two main buildings like the stables at Versailles. From the terrace at the back of the château, a view over the countryside just like the ones in English coloured prints of racing or hunting scenes.[3]

35. *Sketch of a Landscape*, 1861, ink and white gouache, 25.4 × 19.2. Notebook 18, page 165. Bibliothèque Nationale, Paris.

Though the style of this account is familiar from his earlier notebooks, the subject-matter could hardly be more different. Here Degas, the young city-bred artist, responds to the landscape of his native country, fastidiously picking his way through French puddles and deploring the remoteness of provincial life. Even as he does so, the faculties that had become sharpened in Italy record the colours and sounds of a northern-European autumn, reaching for metaphors and artistic precedents to give form to his experience. The sense of immediacy is inescapable, captured in the staccato rhythms of his prose and the urgency of the accompanying drawings. Hasty pen sketches of Exmes literally interrupt the text, words run into damp patches of colour and ghostly studies of paths and meadows stain the pages. Unwittingly, Degas offers us a summary of his modes of thought and his preoccupations at the beginning of the decade. He refers several times to England, a country he had yet to visit, and to the English paintings he had encountered, such as William Collins's *Rustic Civility* (familiar in France as *The Rider's Shadow*) (fig. 36).[4] The very English subject of the horse, which may have prompted the pilgrimage to Haras-du-Pin, had already featured in Degas' own repertoire and was soon to take on a pervasive significance in his professional life. Characteristically, Degas also reflected on his prosaic surroundings, wondering how such unpromising materials might be turned into art. As he was to do so often in the coming decade, the artist found himself brooding on the northern landscape and coming to terms with the singular and contingent nature of his circumstances.

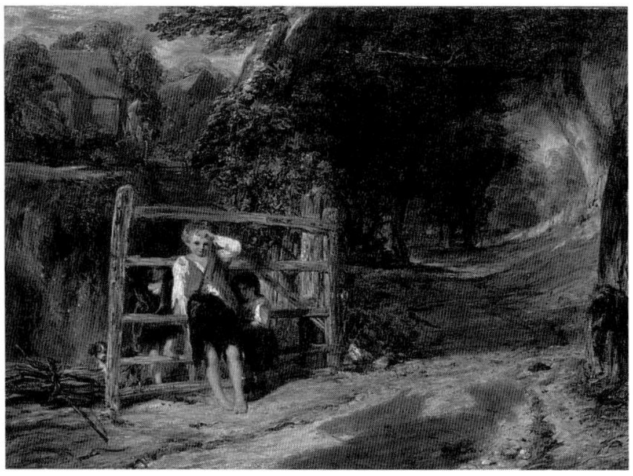

36. William Collins, *Rustic Civility*, 1833, oil on panel, 45.6 × 61. Victoria and Albert Museum, London.

Covering more than a dozen large sketchbook pages, Degas' sepia-and-wash pictures of the 1861 walk constitute some of the most remarkable landscapes of his early career. After the pellucid Italian skyscapes and Claudian vistas, these gloomy, mud-coloured hillsides seem like the work of another hand or another sensibility. In most of them, the horizon is high or blocked out by ill-kempt, entirely un-Claudian trees; looming foregrounds discourage progression into depth and concentrate our minds on texture, shadow and humidity; even the manner of their execution seems ungracious, appropriate to flooded roads and 'steep and woody paths' rather than to classical prospects. In a series of views from the terrace at Haras-du-Pin (fig. 37), Degas' technique reveals itself in progressive stages. In the upper levels, thin washes of ink summarise clouds and pasture, while darker tones establish areas of shadow. In the lower drawing, successive layers of colour have been laid over still-wet ink, encouraging random blots and stain-like veils of tone. The most heavily worked of all the studies (fig. 35) carries this process further. Warm brown and cool grey inks suggest closer and more distant planes, and the addition of cool white pigment to the sky and tree-tops emphasises their remoteness. Flurries of hatching and drifts of tone agitate the surface of the paper, relieved only by a central area of watery sunshine where colour has been wiped by hand from the sheet. Even the inscrutable line of figures, almost lost in their rain-soaked surroundings, seem expressive of the general gloom, the perfect fusion of subject and painterly means.

Other drawings from the Haras-du-Pin sequence remind us of the catholic nature of Degas' taste, as well as the imminence of his professional début. Several studies of the 'great avenue that leads to the château', a series of vast oaks that are even vaster today, show a more orthodox, symmetrical approach to composition.[5] At least three views of Exmes are artfully arranged in a horizontal format, as if in readiness for transfer to canvas.[6] Degas' recollection of Gregoire Soutzo seems to have informed yet another study, which echoes the copy the young artist made before departing for Italy.[7] Reminiscences of Corot

37. *Two Landscape Sketches*, 1861, ink, 25.4 × 19.2. Notebook 18, page 163. Bibliothèque Nationale, Paris.

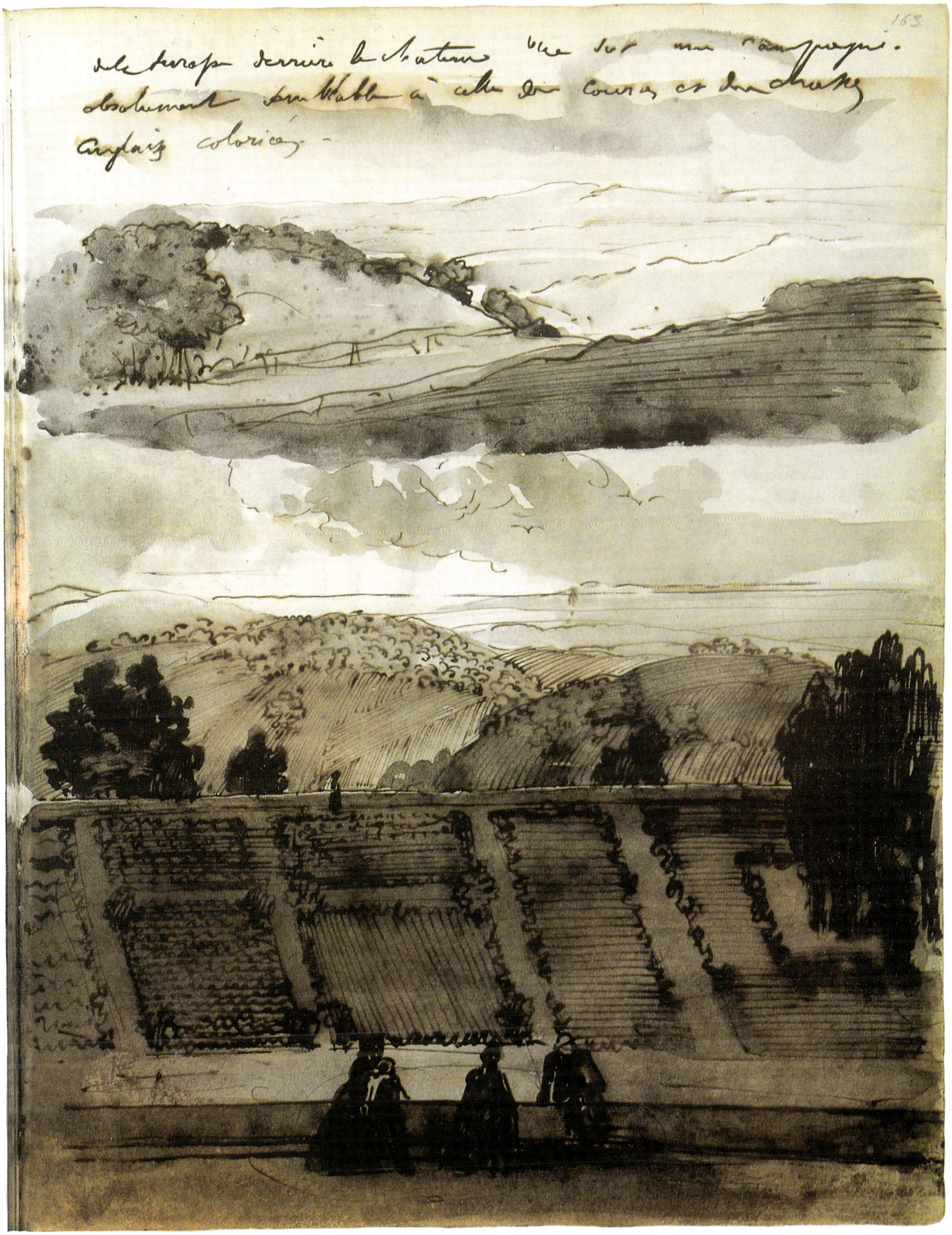
163
de la terrasse derrière la Nature vue sur une campagne.
absolument semblable à celles des courses et des chasses
anglaises coloriées.

can also be found, as well as hints of influence from further afield. The pen-and-wash technique used with such flair at Haras-du-Pin, however, has few precedents in his Italian notebooks, where a pencil contour was generally used for landscape subjects, and tonal effects were often modest. Some of the artists Degas admired, among them Delacroix and Moreau, used ink and wash freely, but none showed the vigorous, almost gestural application of the liquid medium that is such a feature of Degas' studies. Certain painters associated with Barbizon, such as Diaz and Harpignies, also showed considerable fluency in their pen drawings, but there is no reason to believe that Degas knew or admired their works at this date. Paradoxically, it was once again the Italianate masters, Poussin and Claude, who provided the best precedent. Poussin's *Undergrowth* (fig. 38) or Claude's *Tree*, both in the national collections during Degas' lifetime, show a similar breadth of handling and rich tonality, even suggesting a deliberate imitation on Degas' part of works he had seen.[8]

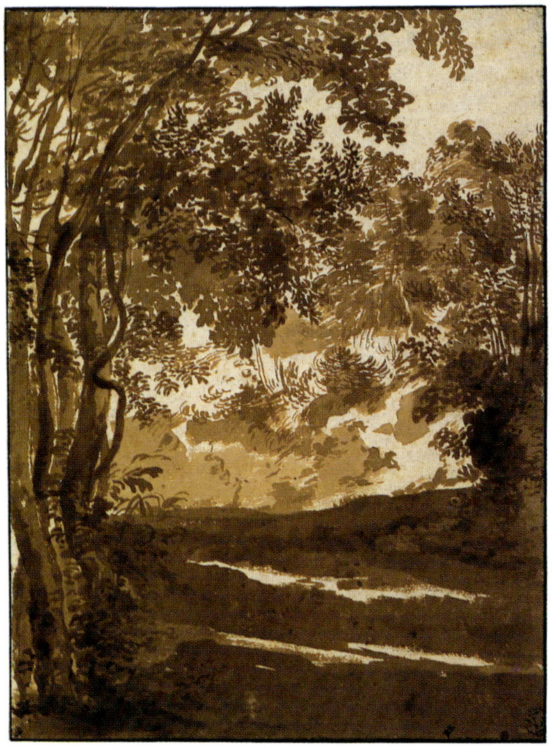

38. Nicolas Poussin, *Undergrowth*, ink. Musée du Louvre, Paris.

Throughout the early 1860s, this straddling of the old and the new, this linking of new-found erudition with the immediacy of experience, was to haunt Degas' art. Returning from Ménil-Hubert to his Paris studio in the autumn of 1861, Degas confronted the enormous and still unresolved canvas of *The Daughter of Jephtha*, and perhaps used his recent acquaintance with the landscape to repaint parts of its background.[9] He would also have found smaller and more tentative paintings, dealing with quite different subjects in a range of exploratory styles. Alongside studies of the landscape and the racetrack, there were genre scenes and portraits, including one of Paul Valpinçon.[10] Even more radical images could be found in his notebooks, where copies from the Old Masters were now outnumbered by drawings of street scenes and carriage-rides, the boxing-ring and the dance-hall, theatre productions and social gatherings.[11] Though they had yet to graduate to their own canvases, many of these subjects were to resurface later in the decade and were to define Degas' contribution to the nascent Impressionist cause. At this stage, they marked his first encounters with a new kind of art, glimpsed in occasional exhibitions and at dealers' galleries, and increasingly in the studios of friends. According to tradition, it was in the following year, 1862, that he first met Edouard Manet, appropriately enough in front of a Velázquez in the Louvre that Degas was copying.[12] Again according to received wisdom, it was this meeting that transformed Degas' approach to his subject-matter, though, as we shall see, the evidence is rather less straightforward.

Despite the radical upheavals in Degas' career during these years, there is no reason to believe that his principal ambition, to become a painter of major figure compositions in the manner of Veronese, Poussin or Ingres, had substantially changed. Whether from continuing parental pressure, financial necessity or genuine inclination on the artist's part, portraiture continued to represent a major aspect of this ambition and was to account for several of his successful entries to the Salon.[13] The history paintings formed the other strand of his public enterprise, their vast and troublesome canvases demanding endless preparation and subsequent revision. Following the experiments of his last months in Italy, many of their subjects engaged with the diverse traditions and dialects of pictorial language, ranging from the antique to the medieval and from the pageant to the pastoral. Common to them all, however, were the pronounced and insistent landscape settings that had so attracted Degas while copying in Florence. Like the subjects of the paintings themselves, a number of these landscapes seem to have had a contemporary resonance, echoing the countryside Degas knew at first hand, such as the hillsides of Normandy, or the urban vistas of his Paris home.[14] At another remove, their cumbersome subjects found a more manageable counterpart in Degas' first equestrian canvases, where ranks of jockeys and thoroughbreds took the place of the classical procession and the biblical frieze.

Pure landscape featured modestly during much of this decade, confined to sudden flurries of activity associated with Degas' travels. The superb but small-scale watercolours made on the visit to Naples in 1860 remind us of the continuity of his Italian interests, while establishing links with portraiture and equestrian works in other media. The lugubrious pen-and-wash studies of Normandy made in the following year hint at expressive resources still unfathomed, just as other sketchbook drawings point to landscape encounters and technical possibilities scarcely explored. Later in the decade, the sequence of pastels of the Channel coast moved into new conceptual territory, introducing us to Degas' most sustained engagement with the landscape to date. Though each of these groups of works might seem self-contained, they can equally be seen as symptomatic of the broader transformation of Degas' art. At the beginning of the period, the artist was painting Neapolitan vistas and still 'thinking of M. Soutzo and of Corot'. By the time of the 1869 pastels, he had turned his attention to seaside villas and working harbours, and judged his efforts beside those of Manet and Morisot, Courbet and Whistler.

The shifts in Degas' personal and professional circumstances in the 1860s were as profound as at any period in his career. As his letters and notebooks show, after the return from Italy he briefly maintained his acquaintance with the artists he had met in Florence and Rome, visiting the Salon with friends from the Villa Medici and noting down the Paris addresses of others.[15] While preserving his connections with Bonnat long enough to paint his portrait, Degas seems to have rejected Bonnat's narrow, if lucrative, vocation, just as he was unimpressed by Emile Lévy's early success as an official muralist.[16] Now openly scornful of Lamothe and Flandrin, Degas was as likely to side with Fromentin and Delacroix as with the successors of Ingres, and was perhaps more inclined than ever to step beyond their much-rehearsed rivalry. Though documentation is scarce, it is clear that by mid-decade Degas was mixing with the circle around Manet, copying a work by Whistler, recording the addresses of Fantin-Latour and Tissot, and establishing his long-lasting friendship with the Realist critic Edmond Duranty.[17] Soon afterwards, the names of Pissarro, Renoir and Bazille made their first appearances in his notebooks, and contemporary accounts described Degas' attendance at their regular meeting-places, such as the Café Guerbois.[18]

Along with many of these artists, Degas began to seek official recognition for his efforts by submitting his canvases to the Salon, measuring himself against his contemporaries and against their esteemed elders. Like them, he endured the whims of the jury and the neglect of the critics, and like them he suffered his own work to be seen against the broadest currents of contemporary painting. In the decade that witnessed the deaths of Delacroix and Ingres, the public scandals generated by Courbet and Manet, and the Salon incursions of Monet and Pissarro, Degas was obliged to define himself in terms of their example. We find evidence of rivalry with Manet and a passing fascination for Courbet, and a shift in Degas' subject-matter towards his colleagues of the Café Guerbois. The high-keyed, contemporary landscape became the obligatory setting for his outdoor scenes, whether horse-race or rural portrait, beach composition or family outing. As Degas discovered, many of his new acquaintances, unlike the companions of his early years, were equally at home with the landscape and the figure subject, and at this stage in their careers, Monet, Bazille and Renoir all appear to have shared Degas' ambition to combine the two genres.[19] Lesser objects of Degas' admiration, such as the paintings of de Dreux and John Lewis Brown, were consistent with this interest and remind us of how far and how widely Degas' tastes ranged during these years.

Throughout this period, Degas' loyalty to the idol of his youth, Ingres, seems to have remained intact, despite the doubts he expressed about the master's pupils and followers. Beneath many of Degas' experimental canvases, there remained a firm commitment to line and form, and his history paintings and portraits were founded upon some of the most elegant drawings of his career. At the same time, in a balancing act that tells us much about his art and his complex sensibility, Degas was able to nurture an equal admiration for the art of Ingres' historic rival, Eugène Delacroix. Several commentators have explored the shifting fortunes of these two artists in Degas' work of the 1860s, and there is general agreement that their conflicting claims can be traced back to the end of the previous decade, and perhaps to the encounter with Moreau in Rome in 1858.[20] What is certain is that Degas mentioned Delacroix in at least one of his letters to his father from Florence and that he began to make copies of Delacroix's paintings immediately after his return to Paris in 1859.[21] On his brief visit to Naples in 1860, he recalled Delacroix's *Demosthenes Calming the Waters* in a notebook and referred to his predecessor's colours as he made preliminary studies for *The Daughter of Jephtha*.[22] During the 1860s, Delacroix's example appears to have been in the ascendant, resulting in further copies, the quotation of specific *motifs* and sustained contact with several of Delacroix's pupils.[23]

Though the importance for Degas of Delacroix's colour has been widely acknowledged, the significance of his subject-matter in Degas' evolving *oeuvre* has yet to be defined. In the context of Degas' landscapes, such an analysis produces quite unexpected results. The complete catalogue of Delacroix's oil paintings includes only a small percentage in which landscape plays a major role, and a mere handful of works with landscape as their principal *motif*.[24] While Degas paid homage to several Delacroix compositions in the early 1860s, it is remarkable that three of his early copies were of landscape-dominated pictures: *Christ on the Lake of Genesareth*, *Ovid among the Scythians* and *Demosthenes Calming the Waters*.[25] It might be argued that Degas was simply responding to the appearance on the Paris art market or in public exhibitions of an unusual number of Delacroix landscapes, but there is reason to believe otherwise. Indeed, several factors point to a pronounced and persistent taste on Degas' part for this uncelebrated feature of Delacroix's *oeuvre*. When he first brought to mind the latter's image of Demosthenes, for example, it was to refer to its landscape setting and to compare it with a view of the Bay of Naples; observing that 'the grey was not the cold grey of the Channel but rather that of a pigeon's breast', he added, 'Just as the sea in the Demosthenes by Delacroix is true in tone. It comes to my mind as I look at this one.'[26]

An even more persuasive demonstration of Degas' interest is his copy of *Ovid among the Scythians* (fig. 39). Drawn at the time of the 1859 Salon, when Delacroix's painting was also singled out by Baudelaire, Degas' study is amongst the most detailed and complete of all his notebook copies.[27] Like the paintings by Fromentin in the same exhibition, already admired by Degas on his first visit, *Ovid among the Scythians* is an extensive landscape with a relatively small-scale foreground narrative. As such, it offered another exemplar for Degas' own works in progress, and coincided with that ambition to paint

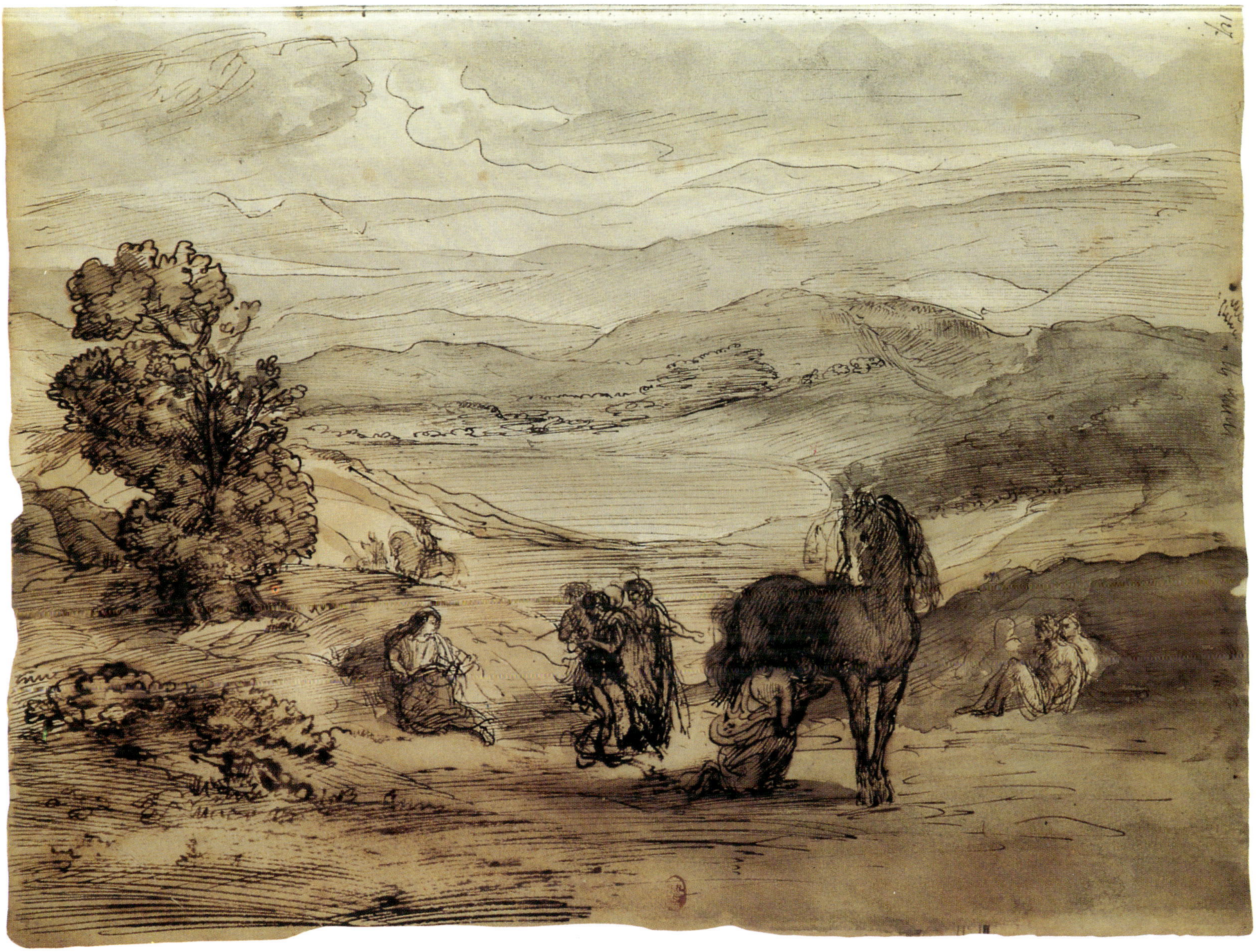

39. *Copy of Delacroix's 'Ovid among the Scythians'*, 1859, ink, 19.2 × 25.4. Notebook 18, page 127. Bibliothèque Nationale, Paris.

landscape-and-figure compositions that had begun during his years in Italy. Soon after this encounter, several features of Delacroix's picture were to reappear in Degas' own canvases, and the work may well have become a paradigm, almost a talisman, for his later landscape projects. Executed in pen and wash in the same notebook as the Haras-du-Pin studies, Degas' copy seems to bridge the two worlds of the Salon and the 'damp lanes' of Normandy. The solitary horse and troubled, mountainous landscape found their way into a number of equestrian scenes and continued to haunt Degas' views of the racetrack and the countryside. As if to reinforce this attachment, at some unknown date he acquired one of the preparatory drawings for *Ovid among the Scythians*, adding it to his remarkable collection of the artist's work.[28]

Here again, amongst the hundreds of drawings, watercolours, pastels and oil paintings eventually owned by Degas, we find an emphatic taste for Delacroix's landscape imagery. At the first sale of Degas' collection, more than a third of the seventy or so works by Delacroix had either landscape or equestrian subjects.[29] The second sale included an even greater number of lots by his predecessor, but the high proportion of landscape-based subjects persisted. Almost every medium and variety of *motif* was represented, from a *Marine* in ink on paper to an oil-on-canvas *Cheval au pâturage*.[30] Subjects included an exotic *Marss el Kebir (côte d'Afrique)* and a *Site marocain*, as well as a more homely *Pêcheurs de Dieppe*.[31] Certain pictures had their private associations for Degas, among them a drawing, *Cliffs in Normandy*, and a pair of watercolours, *Cliffs at Etretat*, while others, such as the pastel studies of skies and seashores, had a close kinship with his own landscape subjects.[32] Most telling of all, perhaps, among the fifty landscapes and related subjects acquired by Degas, was one of the very few oil paintings by Delacroix dedicated to an unpopulated rural scene. This work, *Landscape, Sunset; Champrosay* (private collection), is an understated depiction of trees, sky and dense vegetation, but its acquisition by Degas brings home the gravity of his estimation for Delacroix's landscape art.[33]

That Degas associated the painting of the landscape with the work of Delacroix we can no longer doubt. That he identified certain values and aspirations in landscape art with Delacroix's example must also be considered. In his review of the 1859 Salon, Delacroix's greatest apologist, Charles Baudelaire, attempted to put into words the salient features of Delacroix's achievement; selecting *Ovid among the Scythians* for special consideration, just as Degas had done, Baudelaire described it as 'one of those wonderful works such as Delacroix alone can conceive and paint . . . The mind sinks into it with a slow and appreciative rapture'.[34] Endeavouring to 'extract some formula which may properly express Eugène Delacroix's *speciality*', Baudelaire claimed: 'he is an excellent draughtsman, a prodigious colourist, an eager and resourceful composer', and then went on to emphasise his mastery of 'the *wonderful* aspect of things'.[35] In *Ovid among the Scythians*, Baudelaire found the embodiment of these virtues, and perhaps a model for painters of the contemporary landscape. Though his criticism of landscape art was not without its paradoxes, Baudelaire repeatedly harangued his contemporaries for their failure to engage with the imaginative in nature, and their preference for the skilful but pedantic representation of 'things as they are'.[36] Under this banner, artists as varied as Troyon, Millet and Corot were chastised for their excessive finish or over-refinement, while pictures that evoked 'memory', 'reverie' or 'the poetic' were diligently admired.[37]

Baudelaire's special venom was reserved, however, for the *paysage historique*: 'it is neither free fantasy, nor has it any connection with the admirable slavishness of the naturalists: it is ethics applied to nature'.[38] After a scathing comparison with the moribund conventions of the tragic theatre, Baudelaire described the 'tragic landscape' as

> an arrangement of master-patterns of trees, fountains, tombs and funeral urns. The dogs are cut out of some sort of historical dog-pattern . . . Every *immoral* tree that has allowed itself to grow up on its own, and in its own way, is, of necessity, cut down . . . And if ever a historical landscape-painter feels remorse for some natural peccadillo or other, he imagines his Hell in the guise of a *real* landscape, a pure sky, a free and rich vegetation . . .[39]

This invocation of the 'real landscape' as the antithesis of the *paysage historique* is illuminating in the present context. To a modern audience, *Ovid among the Scythians* may appear to be a kind of *paysage historique*, but to Baudelaire it would have differed in at least three fundamental respects: the absence from the picture of antique properties, such as 'fountains, tombs and funerary urns', delivered it from historicism; the lack of detail in its execution lent itself to 'reverie' and 'the poetic', rather than to pedantic narrative; and, most importantly, the landscape itself was actual and believable. The 'real landscape' in *Ovid among the Scythians* is unusually free of the clichés of mediterranean classicism. Historically, Ovid was banished to a town on the Black Sea, and it seems that Delacroix has pointedly created a lowering, deep-hued terrain to correspond to the poet's location and predicament. The facile representation of classical sites, based on 'a preconceived idea of these places', was often satirised by Baudelaire, as frequently as he commended those artists who responded to their own, northern landscape. After noting the affinity of Théodore Rousseau with Delacroix, Baudelaire had announced in an earlier review:

> M. Rousseau is a northern landscape-painter. His paintings breathe a great sigh of melancholy. He loves nature in her *bluish* moments – twilight effects – strange and moisture-laden sunsets – massive, breeze-haunted shades – great plays of light and shadow. His colour is magnificent, but not dazzling. The fleecy softness of his skies is incomparable. Think of certain landscapes by Rubens and Rembrandt; add a few memories of English painting, and assume a deep and serious love of nature dominating and ordering it all – and then perhaps you will be able to form some idea of the magic of his pictures. Like Delacroix, he adds much of his soul to the mixture; he is a naturalist ceaselessly swept towards the ideal.[40]

Degas certainly became familiar with some of Baudelaire's writings in the 1860s, and it is not impossible that he read the poet's reviews of the Salon after visiting the exhibition in 1859.[41] Whether he knew these lines or not, what is startlingly evident is the general and sometimes detailed affinity between Degas' landscapes and the imagery proposed by Baudelaire. If we turn again to the ink-and-wash studies made at Haras-du-Pin, it is difficult not to see them through Baudelaire's eyes. In every case, 'the tedious love of detail' deplored by Baudelaire has been held in check, at times by literally erasing areas of fine pen-work or brushing over passages of description. This is the terrain of 'free and rich vegetation', as well as 'twilight effects, strange and moisture-laden sunsets, massive, breeze-haunted shades' and 'great plays of light and shadow'. If there are no 'immense mountains' and 'crenellated abbeys', as Baudelaire specified elsewhere in his essay, there are certainly spire-topped churches and distant hills, and just the kind of ancient château that the poet demanded.[42] Glimpsed vistas and shadowy lanes offer food for thought, while unexplained human presences, a rarity in Degas' early landscapes, hint at dramas and assignations. Occurring in his sketchbook only pages after the copy of *Ovid among the Scythians*, these Normandy studies seem to aspire to a similar sense of 'the wonderful aspect of things', a 'rich and fertile drift of reverie' that is at once suggestive and melancholy.

Restricted though they are in scale, the Ménil-Hubert studies are Degas' first substantial response to the landscape of his native country. Not only are they French in their choice of terrain, but they seem to celebrate all that Baudelaire considered to be northern European, as distinct from mediterranean, in their atmosphere and tonality. That Ménil-Hubert reminded Degas of England, and that Rousseau's painting seemed to Baudelaire to contain 'a few memories of English painting', is quite consistent with this. Here are the rain-filled skies and inky hues of the north, as well as its distinctive forms and topography. In place of the gilded plains of the Roman Campagna, we find abrupt valleys and densely wooded hillsides, unkempt country lanes and dismal thickets. Even the formal vocabulary and technical means of these pictures seems remote from the classical tradition. Where a receding vista has been established, as in the heavily worked study of a road (fig. 35), it is rudely interrupted by an almost formless tree, and where spaces might be expected to flow into each other, they tend to halt or lose direction. Though a passing resemblance to the pen drawings of Claude and Poussin has been noted, the sheer physical exuberance of these works has few precedents. Ink is splashed and dribbled at their margins, suggesting haste in execution and perhaps an improvised, on-the-spot, manipulation of materials. If he had consciously sought for an equivalent to Baudelaire's 'strange and moisture-laden sunsets', Degas could hardly have found a more sympathetic medium.

At the time of his first visit of Ménil-Hubert, Degas was probably more familiar with the landscape of central Italy than that of his native France. Apart from a journey through Provence in 1855 and family holidays at Saint-Valéry-sur-Somme, the artist had travelled little in the country of his birth and was still able to find the landscape of Normandy 'completely new'.[43] In later years, he was to become an habitual, even an obsessive, maker of journeys. At different phases of his life, he would travel to see the Valpinçon family each year and visit the Halévys at La Queue-en-Brie almost as frequently. He took several holidays on the Channel coast and made a number of trips to England, and went annually, as his health deteriorated, to the Pyrenean spa town of Cauterets. In 1872, Degas crossed the Atlantic to spend five months with members of his family in Louisiana, and some years later journeyed to Spain and North Africa in the company of the painter Giovanni Boldini (in a letter from Tangiers he wrote: 'I tell you this because Delacroix passed here').[44] When his brother, René, settled in Geneva, Degas took the train on half a dozen occasions to stay with him and continued to visit Naples and Florence in pursuit of family matters. Rather surprisingly, none of these later excursions to Italy reawakened his youthful interest in painting the mediterranean countryside. To be exact, after his return from Naples in 1860, not one of the journeys taken outside France resulted in significant or identifiable landscapes. Tantalising though the prospect of a Degas drawing of New Orleans, a watercolour of Tangiers or a pastel of London might be, his passage through these places went entirely unrecorded.

For reasons of convenience, sentiment or straightforward patriotism, Degas' activities as a mature landscapist were confined to subjects that became familiar to him, such as the coastline of Normandy and Picardy, or areas associated with friends, such as Jeanniot's Burgundy. Broadly speaking, Degas' preference for native *motifs* also belongs to a more general groundswell of concern for national identity, and a resistance to the forms and traditions of other cultures. At its simplest, the change in Degas' priorities can be summarised in his own words. During his 1858 visit to Orvieto, the young artist had written while gazing at the Tiber: 'I am thinking about France which is not as beautiful'; three decades later, as he crossed the Seine on his trip through Burgundy, Degas announced to a friend: 'There is only one country, it is ours, Monsieur'.[45] As we shall see, Degas' loyalty to his colleagues and to his country were to have a detailed significance for his landscape production, but in these early years such commitments were part of a wider and sometimes contradictory state of affairs. While he struggled through the mud at Exmes and Haras-du-Pin, Degas still found himself thinking of Corot and Soutzo, and the pen-and-ink drawings he made on the same visit relied on Poussin as much as on Delacroix.

Both the profusion and the uncertainty of Degas' youthful engagement with the landscape are strikingly evident in the pages of the sketchbook used at Haras-

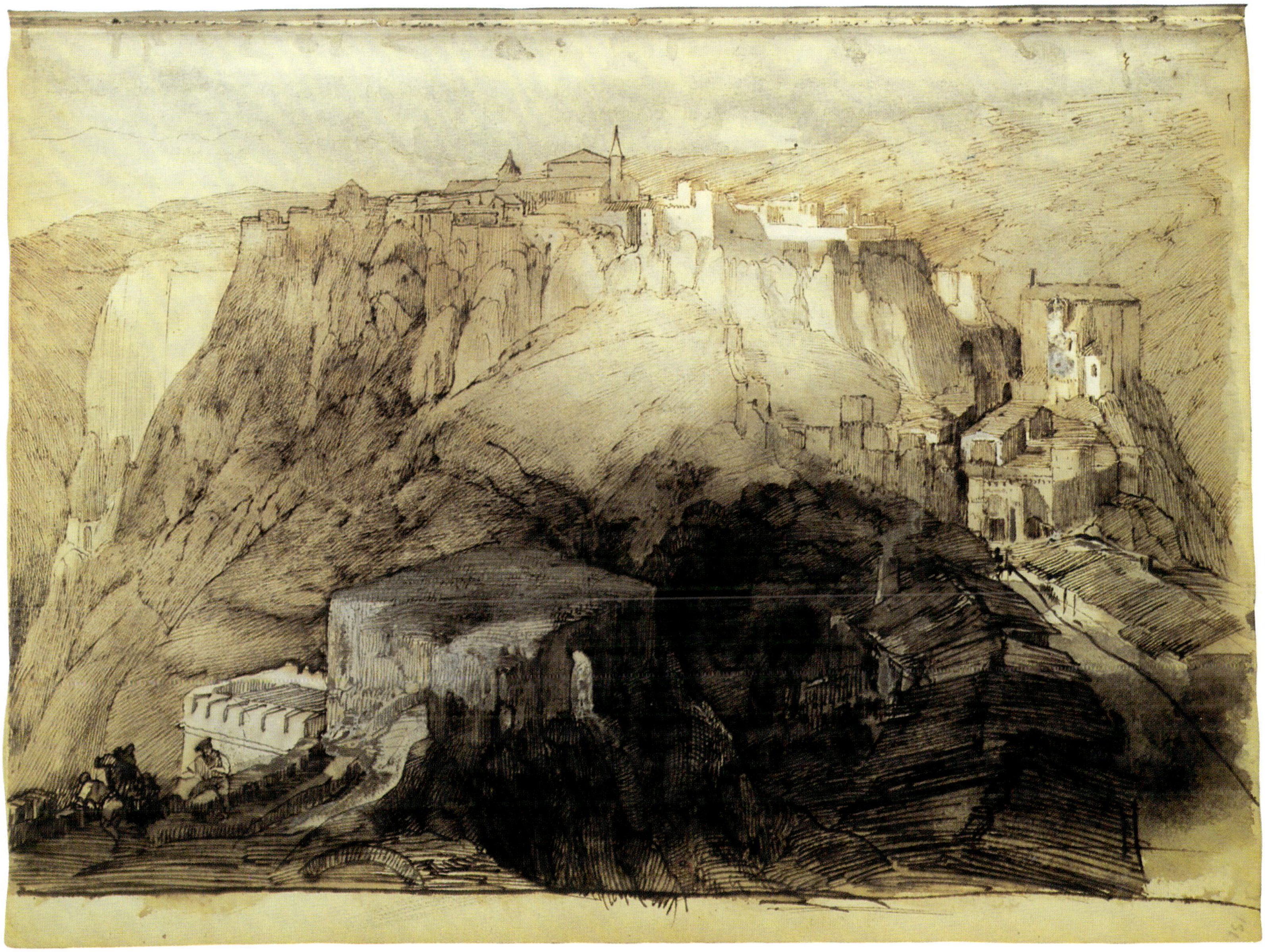

40. *Copy of David Roberts's 'Ronda'*, *c.*1859–61, ink and white gouache, 19.2 × 25.4. Notebook 18, page 131. Bibliothèque Nationale, Paris.

du-Pin. The largest of all the known sketchbooks, it comprises more than a hundred pages of pencil drawings, pen-and-ink studies, written text and pasted-in materials, with some of these functions combined on a single sheet and occasionally on both sides of the page.[46] Begun shortly after Degas' return from Italy in 1859, the notebook was used most intensively in the early 1860s and shows traces of most of his major projects from this period. Over a third of the drawings in the notebook are landscape images, and the diversity of their subject-matter is almost matched by the virtuosity of their execution. At his most familiar, Degas made pencil or ink studies of trees and distant hillsides, where written notations of colours and effects of light suggest first-hand experience of the *motif*.[47] Also reminiscent of earlier notebooks is Degas' habit of copying the landscapes of other artists, ranging from unidentified works and photographs to the magnificent and subtle rendering in ink, wash and gouache of the view of Ronda (fig. 40) by the Scottish artist David Roberts.[48] Other subjects have a more uncertain status and may combine observation with free invention, discipline with technical licence.[49] A scene of a carriage at a country

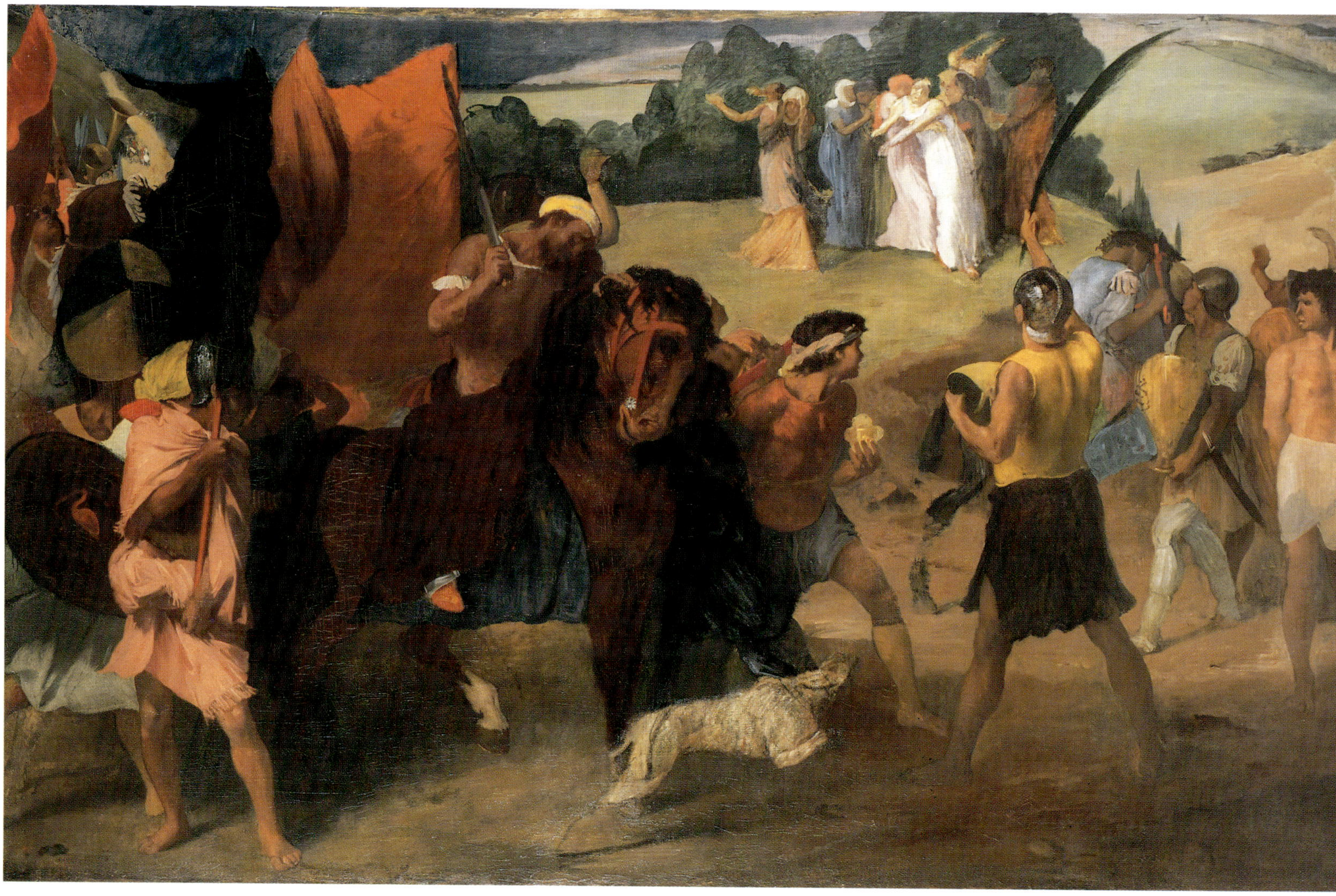

41. *The Daughter of Jephtha*, *c.*1859–61, oil on canvas, 195.5 × 293.5 (L 94). Smith College Museum of Art, Northampton, Mass. Purchased, Drayton Hillier Fund, 1933.

inn reminds us of Degas' commitment to topical themes, while glimpses of riders and their mounts establish links with current equestrian canvases.[50]

The most unexpected feature of the notebooks' landscape imagery, however, is the element of the fantastic. Walled cities and turreted castles share the page with outlandish, and dubiously identified, beasts, and a cast of be-wimpled maidens and pike-wielding varlets swashbuckle their way across ramparts and dungeons.[51] More exotically, a scene with a Chinese pagoda, a view of a Pacific jungle and a study of an African warrior make their appearance, accompanied by figures and accessories from Java, India and ancient Egypt.[52] Though some of these images were gathered in preparation for Degas' history paintings, studies for which are frequently found in these pages, most are distinct in both detail and character from the artist's known canvases. Rather, they seem to be part of a more searching exploration by Degas into the realms of his imagination, a faculty that is conspicuous by its absence in his earlier, pre-Italian notebooks. Whether under the influence of Moreau and Delacroix, or inspired by the writings of Baudelaire (who called imagination the 'Queen of the faculties'), Degas seems to have envisaged a series of fabulous or whimsical projects for his own painting.[53] From the oriental splendours of a Mughal miniature to the humbler dramas of the countryside, these subjects all aspire to that 'wonderful aspect of things' identified by the poet as the essence of Delacroix's genius.

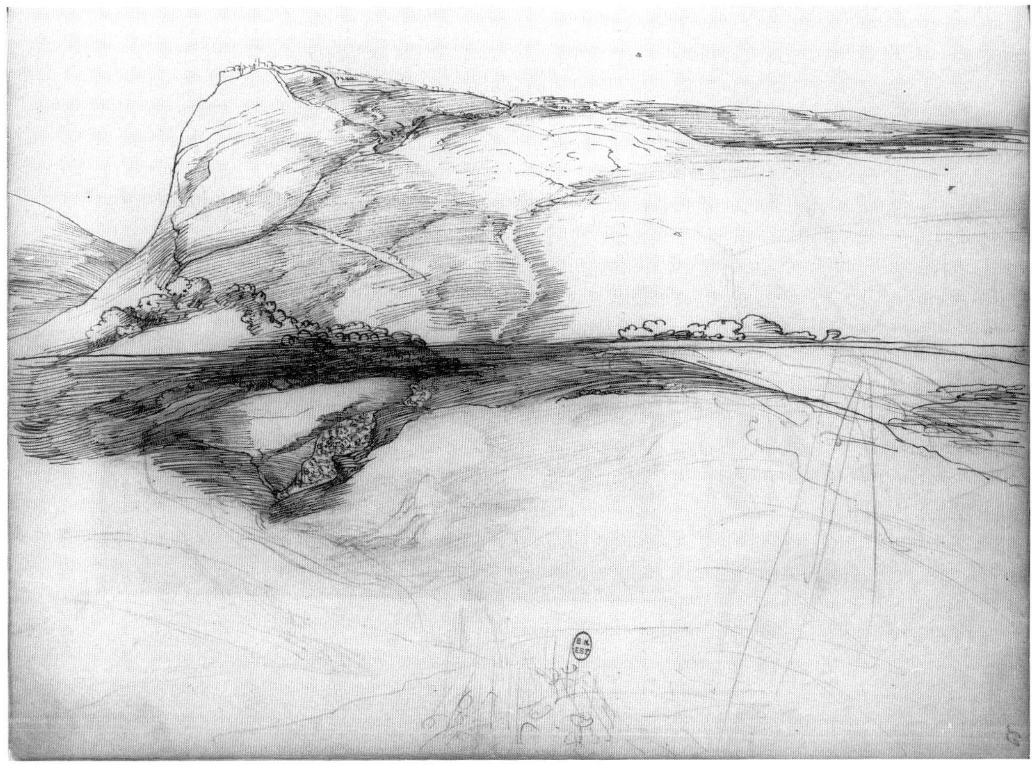

42. *Landscape Study for 'The Daughter of Jephtha'*, *c.*1859–61, ink, 19.2 × 25.4. Notebook 18, page 59. Bibliothèque Nationale, Paris.

Surely not coincidentally, many of Degas' themes have a known or implicit literary source; visual references to the Old Testament, Homer and Dante litter these pages, and written notes include the names of George Sand, Henry Fielding and other authors both ancient and modern.[54]

When seen in this context, the Haras-du-Pin studies might seem relatively prosaic, but Degas' imaginative investment in them becomes more comprehensible. For reasons that are unclear, however, neither these studies nor the majority of landscape images in the notebook were developed as independent works. Whatever lay behind Degas' flirtation with the imaginative landscape, he seems to have been content to introduce it discreetly into other subjects, or absorb it into the exoticism of his history paintings.[55] As we have seen, each of these large-scale pictures took the form of an animated landscape, in which a rural or exotically urban background set the scene, while human and animal protagonists responded to their rhythms. *The Daughter of Jephtha* (fig. 41) is played out against a verdant and doom-laden hillside, whose high horizon excludes both light and hope. In *Semiramis Building Babylon* (Musée d'Orsay, Paris; L 82), more than half the canvas is taken up with a sweeping view across the city, complete with shimmering river and crepuscular sky. Each of the versions of the *Young Spartans* is set on a luxuriant greensward, where a distant temple and sun-gilded mountain provide the setting for adolescent rituals.[56] Finally, *Scene of War in the Middle Ages* brings us closest to the fanciful pageantry of Degas' notebooks, with its nightmarish drama set in a war-torn, recognisably northern-European landscape.

Degas' integration of human and landscape elements in his history paintings is perfectly spelt out in the preparations for *The Daughter of Jephtha*, the most well documented of this sequence of works. In more than a hundred notebook drawings, watercolours and studies in oil on paper and canvas, as well as in numerous written notes, we can trace the history of the composition and the shifting fortunes of its landscape background. Initially, in a study that may have been made in Florence, Degas planned an Italianate vista, with distant poplars, a fortified town and an expanse of blue sky that the artist planned to fill with 'cottony white clouds'.[57] Next, he experimented with rocky outcrops and grim ravines, turning to the reference collection of such subjects in the pages of his notebooks.[58] Some of these drawings appear to have been done from life, while others seem to echo works of art he had copied, such as David Roberts's *Ronda*. A particularly revealing example is a pen study towards the beginning of the Haras-du-Pin notebook (fig. 42), which might be taken for a sketch of a cliff or a promontory in the French countryside.[59] Closer examination shows a walled town on top of this cliff, a common feature of many of the early *Jephtha* studies, and a series of lightly drawn pencil marks in the foreground of the drawing. As Theodore Reff has pointed out, these marks indicate the positions of figures from *The Daughter of Jephtha* and show that Degas, at this stage in its evolution, was planning a quite different setting for the picture from the one he finally chose.[60]

As the painting progressed, new combinations of hillsides and foreground narratives were explored, and new ideas for their colours were noted down:

> A grey-blue sky of such a tone that the lights can be picked out in light colours and the shadows simply black. For the red of Jephtha's gown, I must remember the orange-red tones of the old man in Delacroix's picture. The hillside with its dull and blue-green tones. Reduce much of the landscape to patches.[61]

Given the ever-present example of Delacroix, it is perhaps not surprising that the landscape in Degas' drawing should resemble the distant mountainscape of *Ovid among the Scythians*, or that Jephtha's horse should echo the gigantic mare in Delacroix's picture. Perhaps more striking is the way that Degas engaged with all these issues simultaneously, balancing colours against landscape forms, expanses of sky against groupings of figures, memories of other paintings with plans for his own. At each stage, the dynamics of the setting were adjusted to the nuances of the human confrontation, and new significances were generated by the interaction of the two elements. Sensing perhaps that the blue sky and spacious vistas of his earlier scheme would be inappropriate for so grim a story, Degas finally closed down the landscape and compressed his drama. Rocks, fortified city and 'cottony white clouds' disappeared, while fields and thickets were allowed to block out the horizon. Curiously, this new terrain looks more like the pastures of France than the semi-desert of the Holy Land; like Delacroix, Degas seems to have wrenched his subject away from its mediterranean roots and transposed it, however incongruously, to northern latitudes.

In this and his other history paintings, Degas' approach to the landscape context was inventive, self-critical and, on occasion, technically perilous. With one exception, the settings went through a long process of refinement and revision and, as with *The Daughter of Jephtha*, ended in a final overpainting of a rather violent nature.[62] While some of these revisions may have been the result of re-working later in his career, there are signs that Degas experienced difficulty in reconciling the rival elements of his large-scale rural backgrounds. Aiming to keep faith with the past and to respond to landscapes he had seen at first hand, the artist also aspired to choose subjects that mirrored the tensions of his own age.[63] True to the demands of the genre, however, these scenes were acted out in historical trappings, leaving the artist free to situate them in surroundings of his own choice. A conflict between the dramatis personae and

43. Detail of fig. 41.

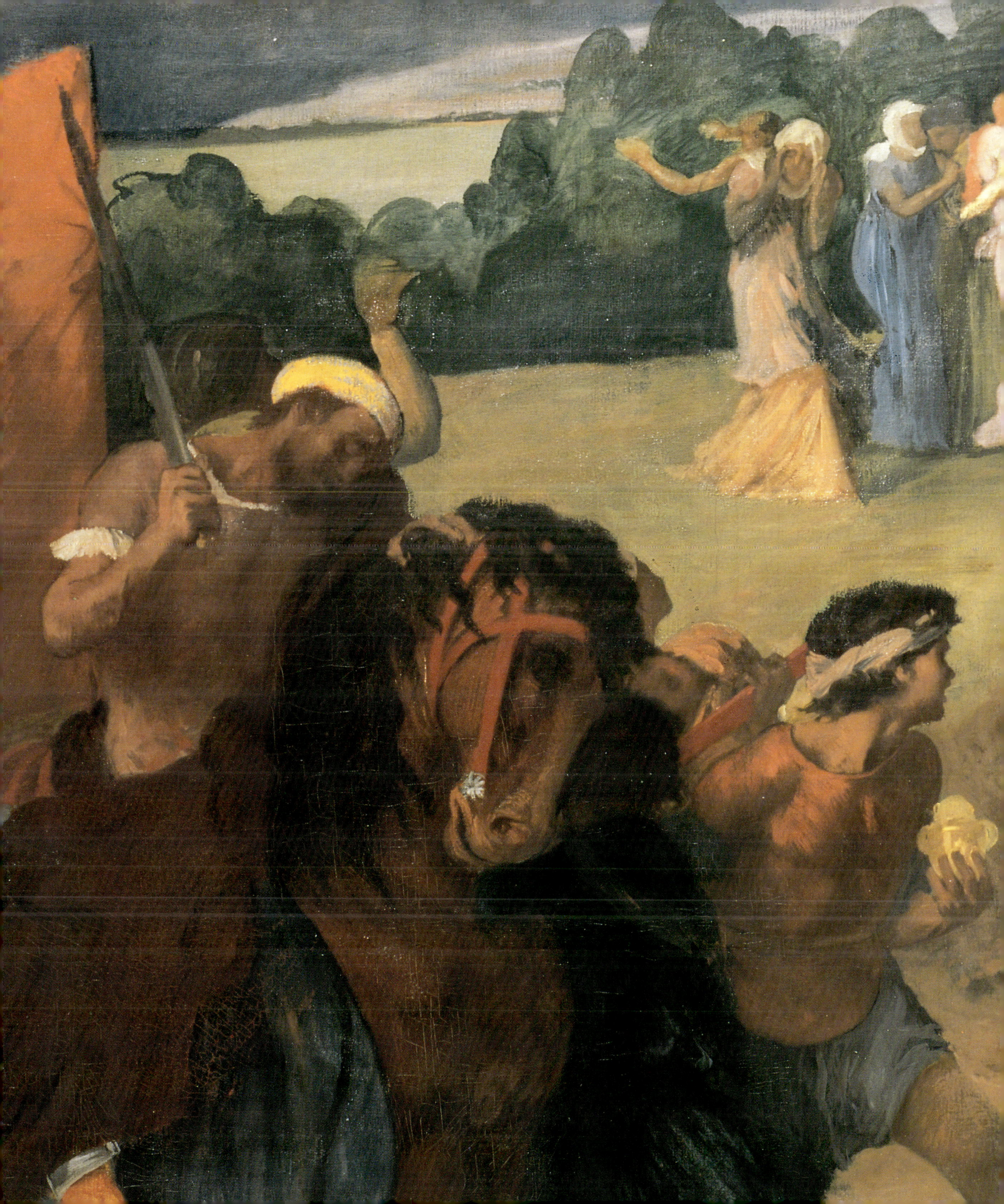

their setting often ensued, with Degas consistently nudging his compositions closer to the modern context. In several of his canvases, the figure groupings were established at an early stage, while background details and even major features were endlessly re-thought. The impression of a static group of actors holding their poses against constantly shifting scenery is unavoidable, and is well exemplified in the early stages of both the *Young Spartans* and *Semiramis Building Babylon*. In the latter, sub-tropical vegetation surrounds the young queen as she makes her first appearance in Degas' sketches, while exotic costumes and architecture compete for our attention. At a later date, much of this detail was expunged, encouraging the resemblances between Babylon and the newly rebuilt city of Paris. During the painting of the *Young Spartans*, a grove of trees, a centrally place temple and a scattering of antique accessories were similarly swept away, and even the figures were eventually remodelled as what Lemoisne called 'types montmartrois'.[64]

The research for these settings took Degas in several characteristic directions: to the Old Masters, to contemporary engravings and photographs, to memories of landscapes seen on his travels, and to the first-hand study of nature. An exquisite product of the first of these encounters was a tiny painting in oil on paper, subsequently entitled *The Stage* (fig. 44) on the basis of its resemblance to a stage-set. Previously unpublished, this picture has recently been shown to derive from part of Veronese's *Supper at Emmaus* in the Louvre, from which Degas isolated and modified a section of its mountainous background.[65] The painting can also be traced to a pencil study with written colour notes from the same picture, made soon after Degas' return from Italy and in a notebook largely taken up with drawings for *The Daughter of Jephtha*.[66] Curiously, Degas has disregarded the central human drama of Veronese's composition, singling out a small corner of the vast canvas and rearranging it to form an independent landscape *motif*. Emphasising the 'sky like old greenish-pink marble' and the 'town with its pink-grey and bluish masses', Degas recalled both the oil-on-paper sketches of his Italian sojourn and the urban landscapes of his current experience. As with the studies for his history paintings, the artist felt free to edit and decontextualise this image, subjecting all his concerns to the demands of his painterly creation. In this fascinating fragment, several worlds collide: recollections of his youth, hints of a continuing but restless *rapport* with the masters of the Louvre, glimpses of city life, and, quite unwittingly, intimations of a theatrical *oeuvre* still to come.

In a different sense, Degas turned for further assistance with his history paintings to natural forms, studying clouds and trees, hillsides and boulders, rivers and birds.[67] While working on *Alexander and Bucephalus*, for example, he made a delicate pencil drawing of a sapling, and chose watercolour for the astonishingly subtle *Four Willow Trees* (fig. 45), used in painting the landscape of *Scene of War in the Middle Ages* (fig. 46).[68] Studies of mountains and rocky outcrops from a number of sources reappear in the *Young Spartans* and *The Daughter of Jephtha*, and records of assorted foliage are common to both notebooks and canvases.[69] Generalised resemblances can be noted between two of the history pictures and the drawings made by Degas in Normandy in 1861. As we have seen, Degas returned from Ménil-Hubert in the autumn of that year to his still unfinished canvas of *The Daughter of Jephtha*. In two of his notebooks, sketches of this painting and of the Normandy countryside can be found in close proximity and his struggles with the background of the large canvas must surely have brought to mind his recent rural excursion. No detailed borrowings have been identified, but the rounded hillocks and hedge-lined contours of some of

44. *Landscape Study from Veronese* (formerly *The Stage*), *c.*1859–60, oil on paper, mounted on canvas, 25.5 × 18.5. Private collection, courtesy Galerie Schmit, Paris.

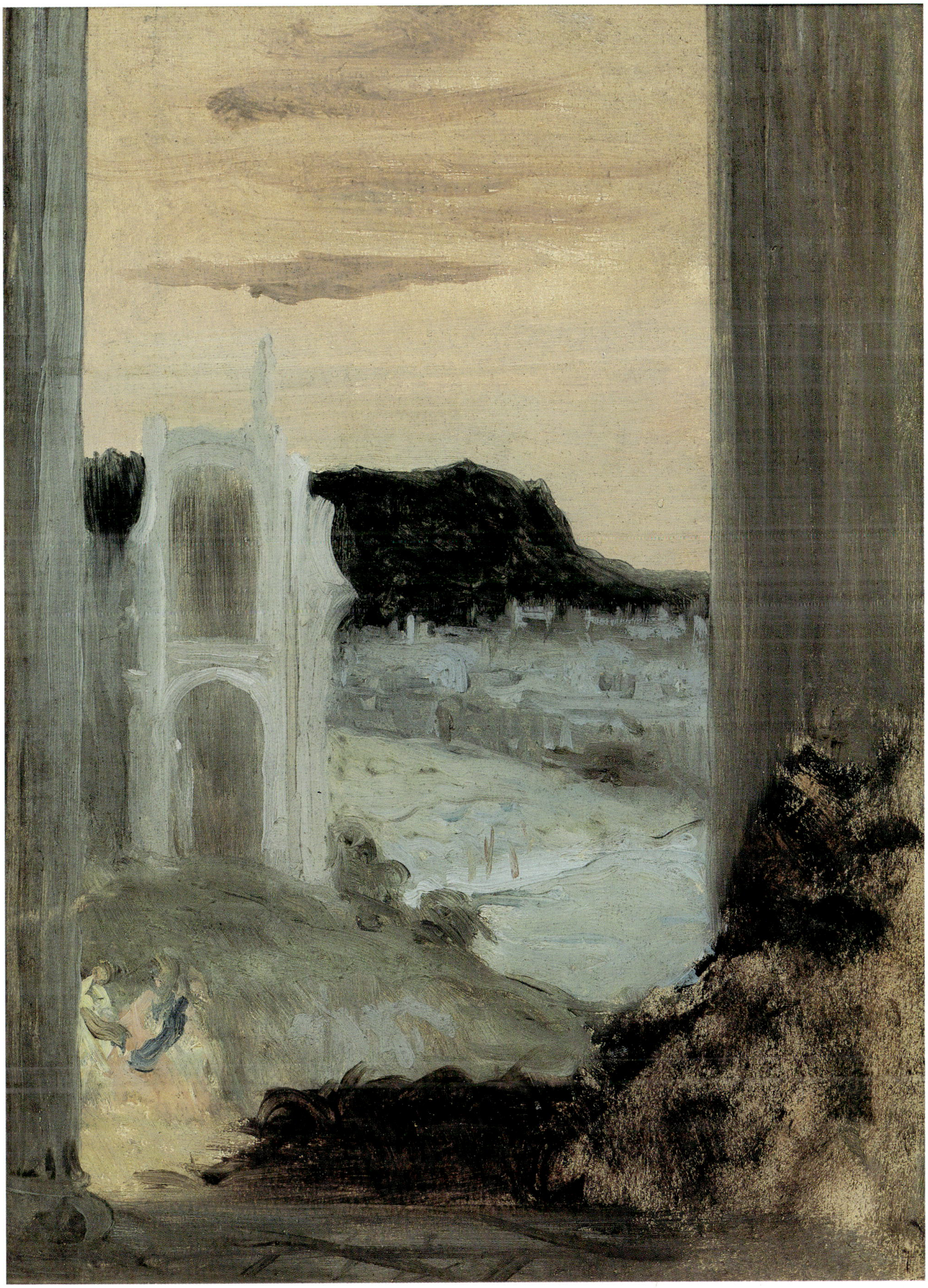

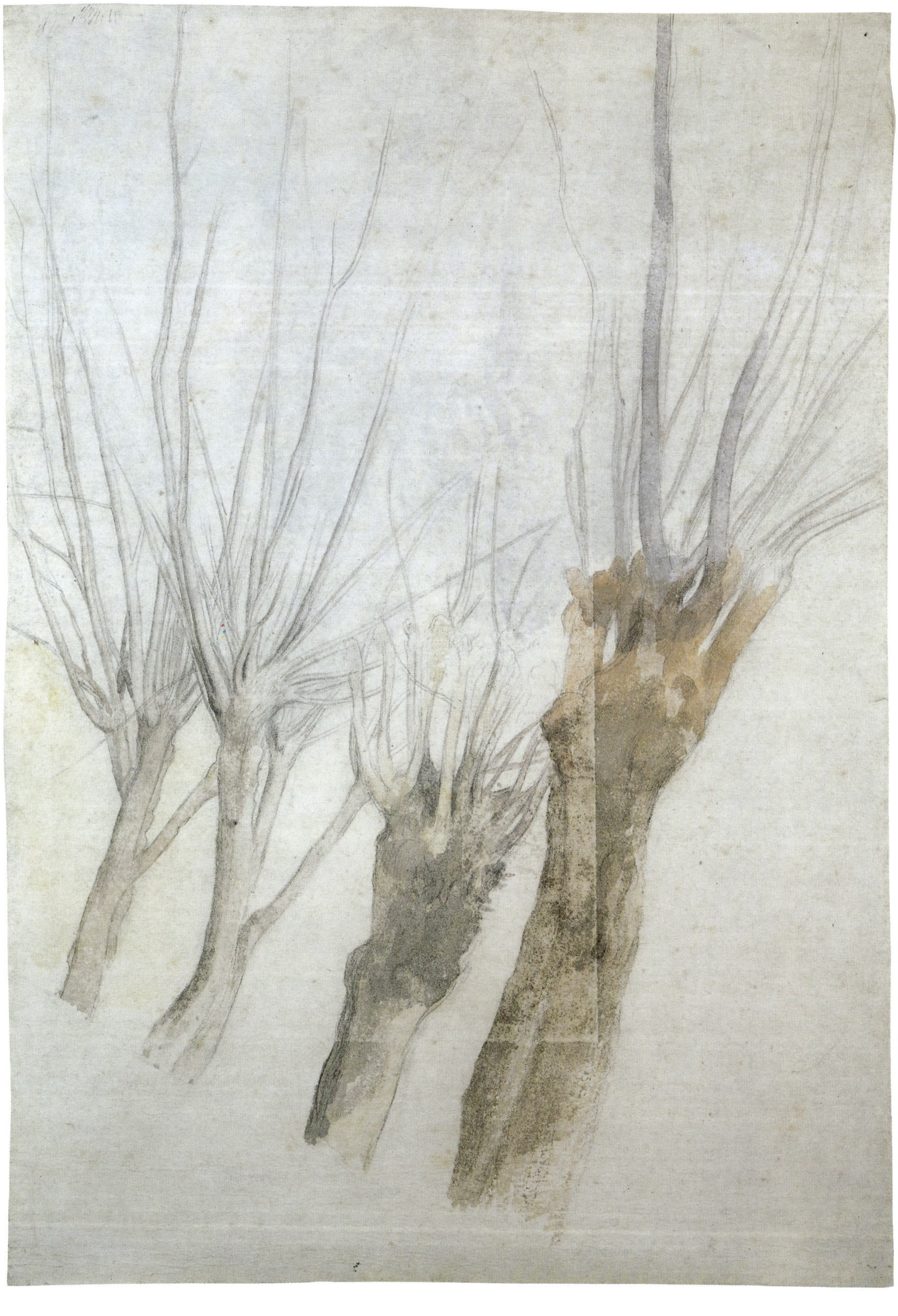

45. *Four Willow Trees*, *c.*1863–5, pencil and watercolour, 38 × 26. Private collection.

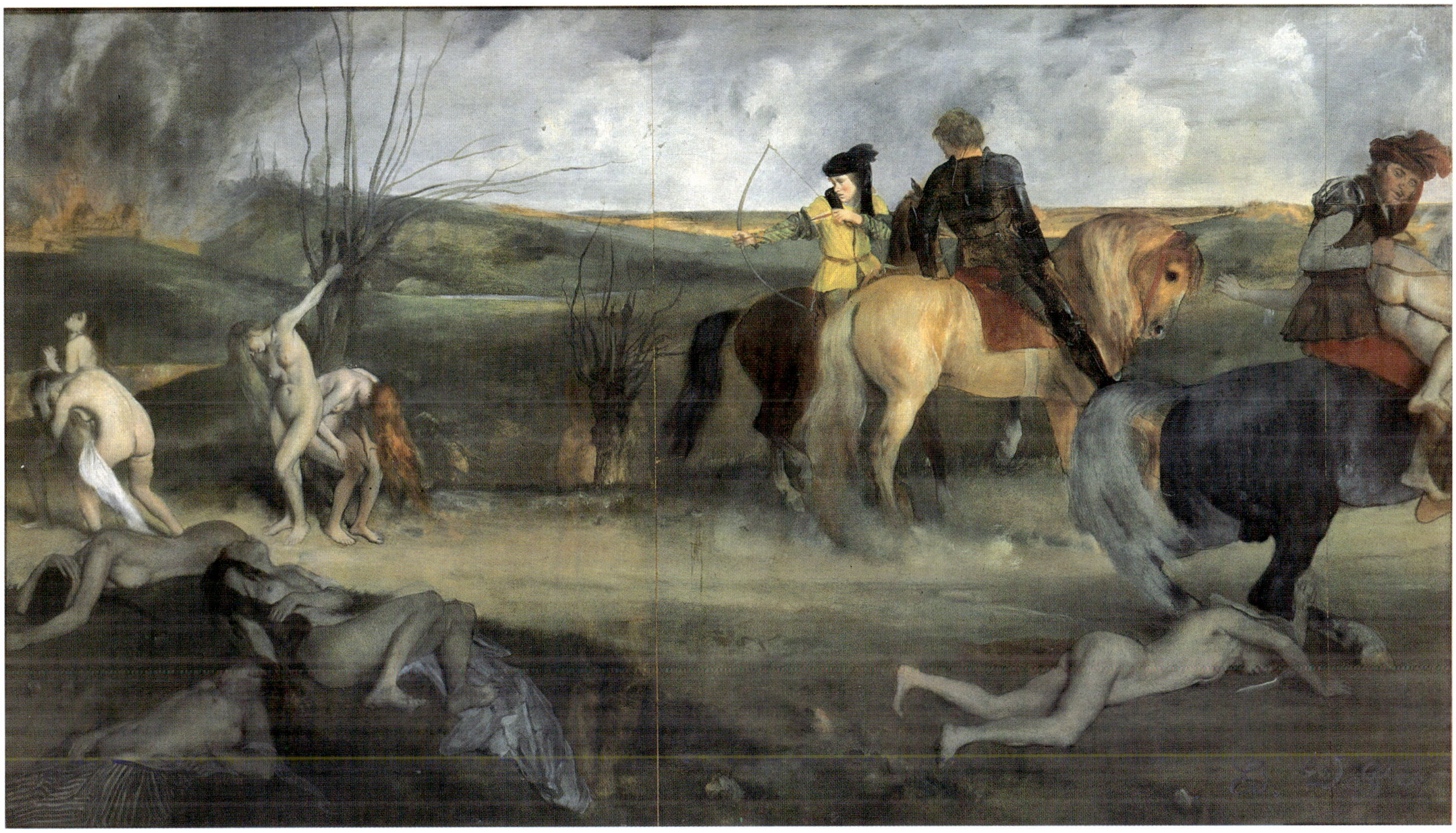

46. *Scene of War in the Middle Ages*, 1863–5, oil on paper, mounted on canvas, 81 × 147 (L 124). Musée d'Orsay, Paris.

the Haras-du-Pin studies seem to have been transposed, somewhat improbably, into the re-worked painting. To this can be added an ink-and-wash view of the village of Exmes, which is uncannily close to part of the backdrop to *Scene of War in the Middle Ages*.[70] This painting was shown at the Salon of 1865 and became the last of Degas' adventures into the pageantry of the past.[71] Strange and horrific though its subject is, the picture also represents the penultimate stage in the modernisation of Degas' figure-and-landscape project. Despite their theatrical trappings, the horsemen and their victims play out a recognisable and transparent human encounter, in a wintery setting that evokes the colours, atmosphere and topography of northern Europe. Utterly remote from their mediterranean counterparts in *Alexander and Bucephalus* and the *Young Spartans*, these figures belong to the history and landscape of France.

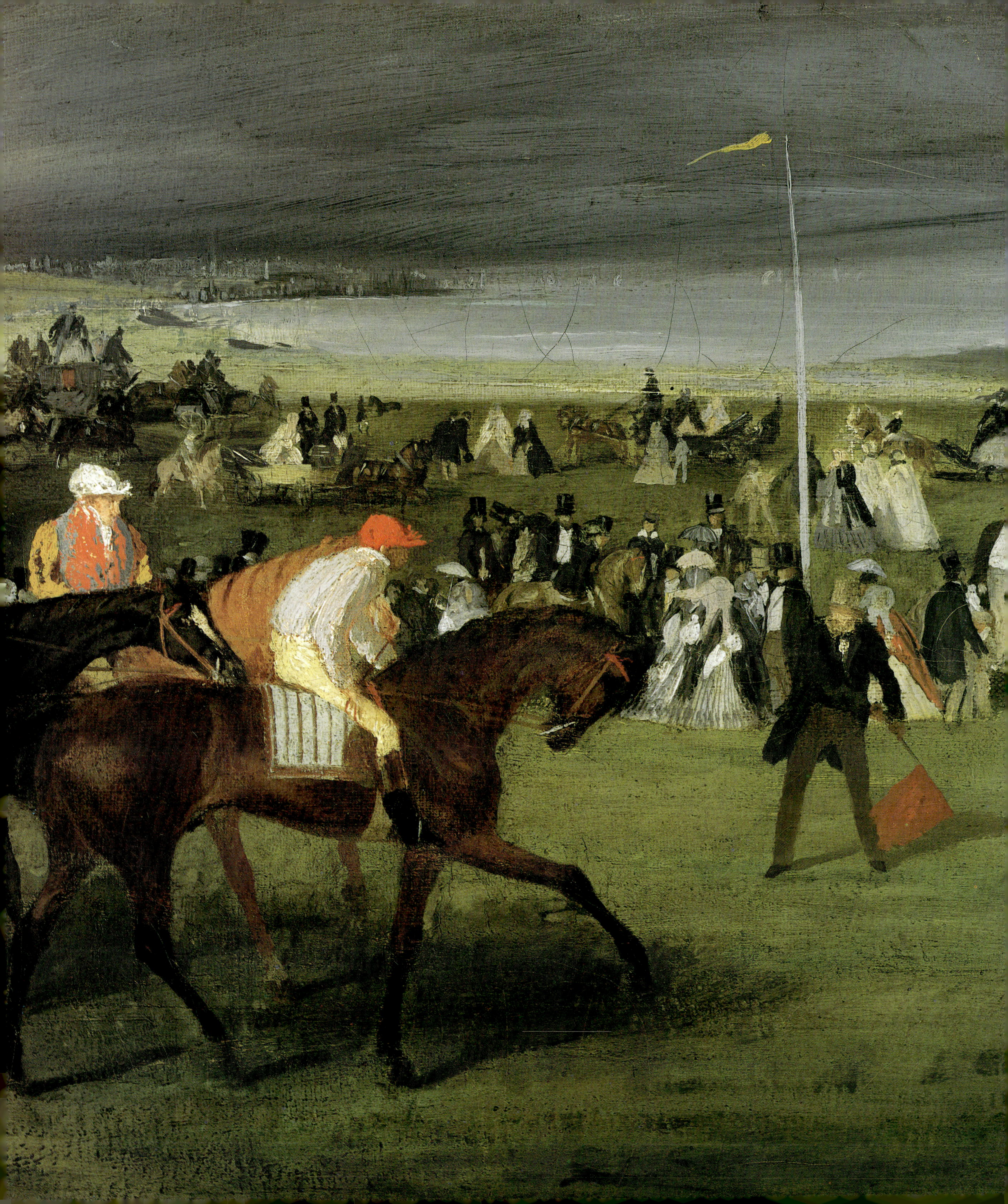

3 The First Equestrian Landscapes

'. . . a view over the countryside just like the ones in English coloured prints of racing or hunting scenes'.
(Degas at Haras du Pin, 1861)

If Degas' history paintings can be understood as a false start to his professional career, they can also be seen as an early testing ground for some of the most distinctive *motifs* of his maturity. Here, for the first time, we encounter large-scale female nudes, some fixed in postures they were still to hold two or three decades later.[1] Here, too, are figures in vigorous action, lunging forward, lifting burdens and pirouetting through crowds of fancifully dressed colleagues. Striking physiognomies, such as that of Queen Semiramis, remind us of Degas' skills as a portraitist, while anticipating a hundred later studies of charismatic modern women. In almost all these history pictures, another theme presents itself, and arguably one that most immediately bridges the void between his youthful and mature careers. Four out of five of the Salon-scale canvases give prominence to the subject of the horse, while one, *Alexander and Bucephalus*, is based on an epic tale of equestrianism. In each of these pictures, horses and their riders or attendants occupy dominant positions, some drawing attention to themselves at the expense of the narrative. Jephtha's great steed marks the centre of the drama, the horse echoing its master's pose and, implicitly, his grief. The magnificent pony in *Semiramis Building Babylon* takes up more than a third of the canvas, though here it is a decorative adjunct rather than a force to be reckoned with. Though well off-centre, the three chargers in *Scene of War in the Middle Ages* (fig. 46) are crucial to the action, their muscularity and bulk expressive of the picture's savagery.

Amongst their myriad other significances, these elaborate pictures are what might be called equestrian landscapes, presenting horses in a variety of outdoor settings and in contrasted social contexts. To Degas and his contemporaries, many of these contexts were still familiar, or at least had topical equivalents. Semiramis' urban pony, for example, was the archetype of the docile carriage horse; Jephtha's shying charger could be found in a thousand battle-scenes and civic monuments; and the massive stallions in *Scene of War in the Middle Ages* might be modern draft animals or steeplechase mounts. That Degas saw his equestrian subjects in this way is evident in his current notebooks, where historic and contemporary images of the horse frequently rub shoulders.[2] More revealingly, certain *motifs* will 'escape' from one context to another, as if the artist took their continuity for granted: a frieze-like classical composition might reappear as a family outing at the races, while a truncated thoroughbred will resurface as a medieval battlehorse.[3] At times knowing and at others playful, this intermingling of past and present did much to invigorate Degas' historical repertoire, just as it offered a way forward for his complex painterly ambitions.

In the course of the 1860s, Degas produced more than twenty canvases of the modern equestrian landscape, ranging from scenes of open parkland and the

47. Detail of fig. 53.

family outing to panoramas of the racetrack and the seashore. Some were painted side-by-side with his history paintings, while others can be shown to have preceded these pictures by months or even years. Yet others appear to carry the imagery of the history pictures into the surroundings of Degas' own age, seeking out equivalents for their compositions, if not their tormented subjects. Degas himself seems to have accepted their role as a transitional form. His earliest horse pictures were small and inconspicuous, and remained subordinate to his more public enterprises. In the middle of the decade, the last of his historical canvases were quickly followed by the first major equestrian work, *The Steeplechase* (fig. 64) shown at the 1866 Salon. Within a short time, Degas' name had become associated with racecourse imagery and he chose to be represented by such paintings at a number of current exhibitions. In more than one sense, the equestrian landscape provided a perfect vehicle for Degas' evolving career. Requiring considerable skills in draughtsmanship, as well as an affinity with colour and the moods of nature, such subjects were a natural outlet for his figure-in-the-landscape aspirations, now transposed to a contemporary milieu. As a theme, it could be as up-to-date as Manet's urban strollers or Monet's scenes of the picnic and could engage with both rural recreation and the suburban spectacle. Fashion and the market-place may well have played their part. Throughout the 1860s, horse-racing took on the status of a cult among wealthy Parisians and Degas may have been in pursuit of patronage as well as new *motifs*. Above all, the equestrian subject allowed Degas to stand abreast with, or even ahead of, his more forward-looking colleagues, while retaining a characteristic foothold in the art of the past.

There is modest evidence of an interest in equestrian imagery from the very beginnings of Degas' career. Even before his first visit to Italy, the artist had made drawings of horses from classical reliefs and medieval and Renaissance sources, though apparently none from life.[4] As his training advanced, a marked quickening of his involvement with such subjects became evident. During his years in Rome and Florence, he made studies from battle scenes and equestrian portraits, processional Magi and mounted *condottieri*, and even from lithographs of horse subjects.[5] Indeed, it is hardly an exaggeration to claim that Degas developed an obsession with the great images of horsemanship from the Western tradition.[6] In the course of his stay, he copied Uccello's *Battle of San Romano*, Gozzoli's *Journey of the Magi* and Raphael's *St George and the Dragon*, as well as a number of less well-known works from the Italian school; while still in Italy, he made further copies from Rubens' *Henri IV at the Battle of Ivry* and Van Dyck's equestrian portrait of Charles V, and from Géricault's celebrated equine *Ecorché*.[7] So pronounced was his fascination that we might deduce that the artist was already planning his own equestrian subjects, though it was not until his return to Paris that such ambitions bore fruit. In addition to the masterful drawings of horses for the *Daughter of Jephtha*, *Semiramis Building Babylon* and *Alexander and Bucephalus*, Degas drafted out a number of small-scale designs of mounted figures, obscure processions and scenes of the hunt.[8] Gaining confidence from his contemporaries, he copied equestrian subjects from Delacroix and Géricault, as well as details from the works of de Dreux and Meissonier.[9] Surprisingly late in the process, he began to draw horses from direct observation, in every conceivable pose and in unprecedented profusion.

There can be little doubt that, in the 1860s, Degas saw the equestrian landscape as a major element in his professional advancement. His notebooks, his portfolios and his copying activities show the systematic accumulation of materials appropriate to this ambition, and even his recreations, like the visit to

Haras-du-Pin, seem to conform such an aim. Despite its importance, the development of his equestrian imagery still awaits the detailed study it undoubtedly deserves.[10] Degas' relationship to the English tradition; to the art of his contemporaries, such as Manet, Fattori and John Lewis Brown; and to the arcane culture of the steeplechase and the race meeting, have yet to be fully explored. In particular, his earliest experiments are largely undated and undocumented, and are often obscured by partial or complete re-painting from the artist's own hand. Broadly speaking, Degas' equestrian pictures of the 1860s appear to have been made in three successive phases. The first group dates from the years immediately after his return from Italy and consists of small canvases of country riders and rural races.[11] Technically precocious, these pictures are also the most dependent on existing forms and the most schematic in their colouring. In mid-decade, Degas produced a second series of canvases that are diverse in both scale, treatment and subject-matter. Clustered loosely around the *Steeplechase* of 1866, these paintings range over the domestic excursion and the coastal gallop, and pitch us headlong into the rigours of the ride.[12] Finally, at the end of the decade, a third sequence returns us to the racetrack, exploring the tranquil rituals before and after the event and the spacious surroundings of the tracks themselves.[13]

The earliest of Degas' groups of horse paintings can be linked with studies made while he was visiting Italy. At least one canvas is clearly set in the Italian countryside and a number of notebooks, rather confusingly, show racehorses and jockeys on pages used by the artist in Florence.[14] Some of these drawings were undoubtedly copied from published sources, while others may have been inspired by the work of his current companions, such as Giovanni Fattori and Gustave Moreau.[15] But the evidence, however scattered, points to a marked interest in modern equestrian *motifs* before his return to France, and an immediate engagement with such *motifs* on his arrival in Paris. The most intriguing demonstration of this transitional phase is to be found in a pair of small canvases that have baffled or eluded scholars in the past. The first of these, *Promenade beside the Sea* (fig. 48), is similar in scale and tonality to the oil-on-paper studies made by Degas in Italy and may represent a first step in developing such studies into marketable works. Similar also is the fluid, sketch-like application of thinned paint and the urgency of its execution, as if time or the vagaries of the weather demanded haste.

A further connection with Italy is provided by the landscape setting of *Promenade beside the Sea*, which can now be identified as part of the Bay of Naples. On his first visit to this area, Degas had made several oil studies of the Castello San Elmo and the Castello dell'Ovo, both prominent features of the bay, and on his brief passage through the city in 1860 he returned to draw the same site.[16] One of the notebook drawings from this later excursion (fig. 49) depicts the Castello San Elmo perched on a central hill, the narrow isthmus leading to the Castello dell'Ovo at the extreme right and, just visible behind it, the lower slopes of Vesuvius. It was this setting that the artist re-used for *Promenade beside the Sea*, though here he has truncated the volcano and suppressed much of the detail of Naples itself. The references to the city, we might say, have become a private matter, rather than the proud, rhetorical gesture of his earlier studies. Unobtrusive and chromatically muted, the landscape establishes a deep spatial arena and reminds us of Degas' schooling in Claude and Corot. All the more shocking, therefore, is the explosive entry into the picture of the two dark-suited riders, who thunder across the foreground and are about to gallop off into the distance. One of the most dramatic

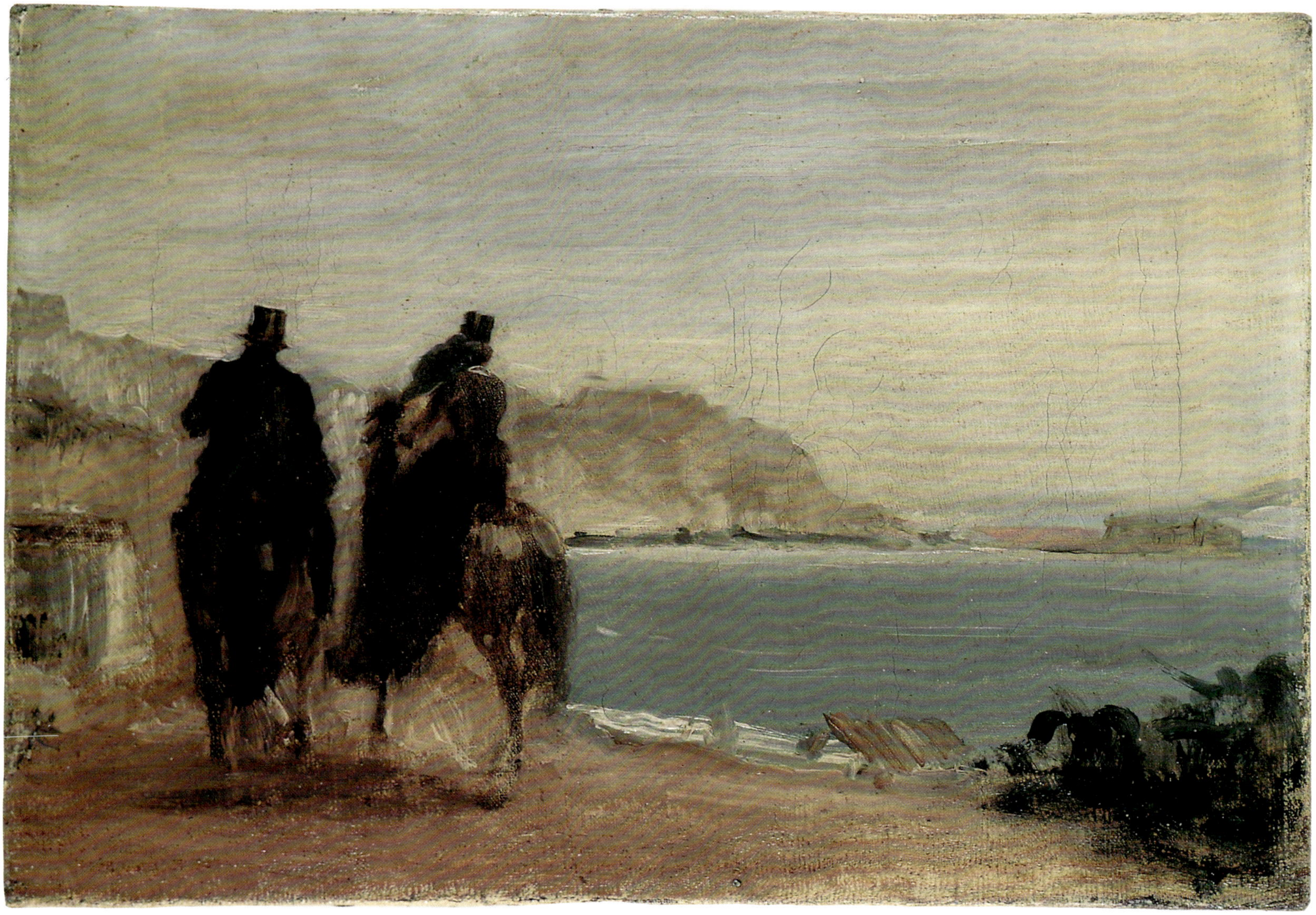

48. *Promenade beside the Sea*, *c*.1860, oil on canvas, 22.5 × 32.5 (BR 38). Private collection.

49. *View of Naples*, 1860, pencil, 12.5 × 21.5 (page size). Notebook 19, pages 6 and 7. Bibliothèque Nationale, Paris.

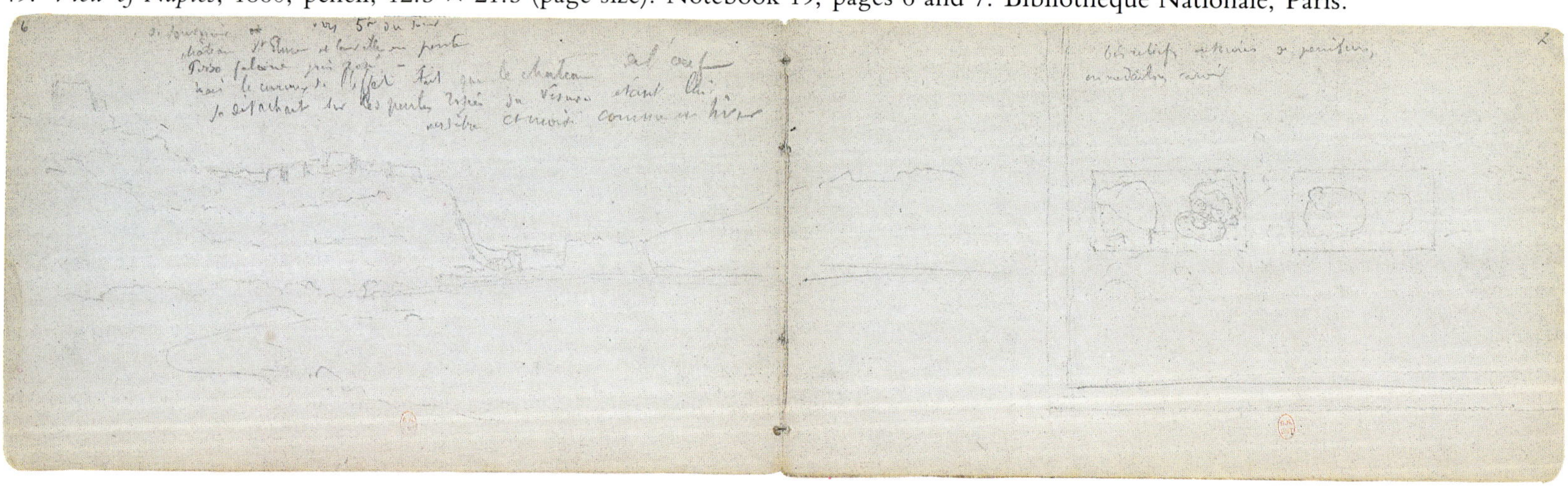

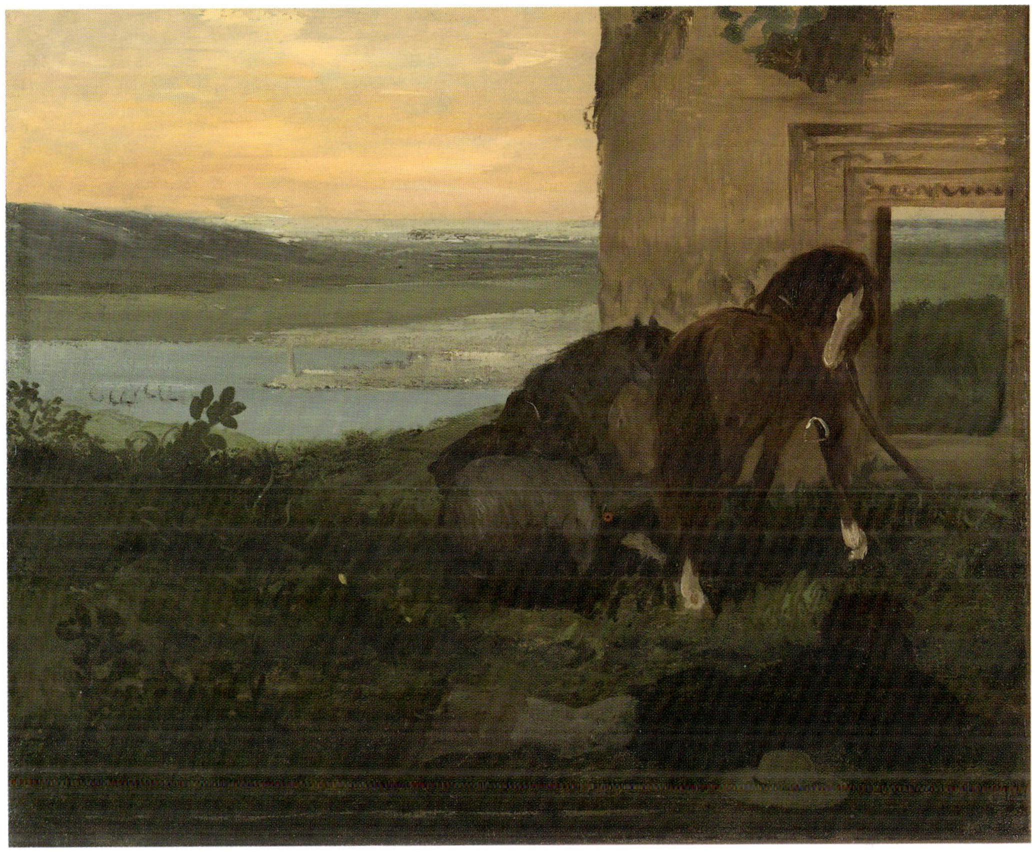

50. *Horses in a Landscape*, *c.*1860, oil on canvas, 54 × 64 (L 50). Kunstmuseum, Bern.

inventions of Degas' early career, this faceless and rather sinister group dispels in an instant the symmetry of the scene, shattering the calm of its surface and briskly announcing its contemporary credentials.

In the weeks before his second visit to Naples, Degas had visited an exhibition of paintings on the boulevard des Italiens in Paris, where he had copied and made colour notes from one of Delacroix's rare seascapes, *Christ on the Lake of Genesareth.*[17] While looking out over the Bay of Naples soon afterwards, his thoughts again turned to Delacroix, but this time to the vividly remembered tones of his *Demosthenes Calming the Waters.*[18] It is in this context that another of Degas' early equestrian canvas, *Horses in a Landscape* (fig. 50) should be seen. Painted during or soon after his Neapolitan excursion, this underestimated work is one of the most conspicuous of all Degas' acts of homage towards Delacroix. Not only do its rich tones and vigorous brushwork recall the older painter's manner, but the composition includes important elements from at least two pictures that Degas had recently seen and copied. More than any of his other early projects, *Horses in a Landscape* recalls the panoramic setting of *Ovid among the Scythians*, a work admired by Degas in the 1859 Salon and paraphrased in a notebook copy. In both pictures, a high horizon separates a warm and overcast sky from a range of gloomy, rather ominous hills. In both, a curving bay suggests distant spaces, while the elevated foreground is crowded with animals and figures. A shadowy tone predominates, allowing pools of light to pick out details and landscape features, and casting a melancholy aura over each scene. Though their subjects differ, the protagonists in the two pictures mirror each others' attributes. Degas' standing horse reflects the coyly arched neck of Delacroix's mare, while pale muzzles and fetlocks are common to both. Even the reclining figure in Degas' landscape, apparently engaged in outdoor sketching, seems to echo the recumbent Ovid, caught in the act of composition.

Before the addition of the curiously intrusive architecture, which appears to have been painted in at the last moment, the resemblance between *Horses in a Landscape* and Delacroix's seminal work must have been compelling, just as the act of deference by the younger artist must have been transparent.[19] Though the authenticity of Degas' canvas has been doubted, the forms of the two horses are clearly based on drawings in the notebook used in Naples in 1860, and its affinity with *Promenade beside the Sea* suggests that it was produced in similar circumstances.[20] Its association with Italy and with Delacroix is underlined by two further observations. First, the drawings for *Horses in a Landscape* occur only pages before several studies for *The Daughter of Jephtha*, a picture probably conceived in Degas' last months in Italy.[21] A sketch of a horse's head in these same pages, though identified as a study for *Alexander and Bucephalus* by Theodore Reff, might also have served for the principal animal in both *The Daughter of Jephtha* and *Horses in a Landscape*.[22] Second, the distant landscape in *Horses in a Landscape*, with its sunlit promontory and shadowy hills, has a marked resemblance to the background of Delacroix's *Entry of the Crusaders into Constantinople*, a picture Degas copied in oil between 1859 and 1860.[23] Though in each case Degas has cast off the historical paraphernalia of his predecessor's work, there can be no doubting his awareness of such precedents, nor his determination to find contemporary equivalents for Delacroix's imagery.

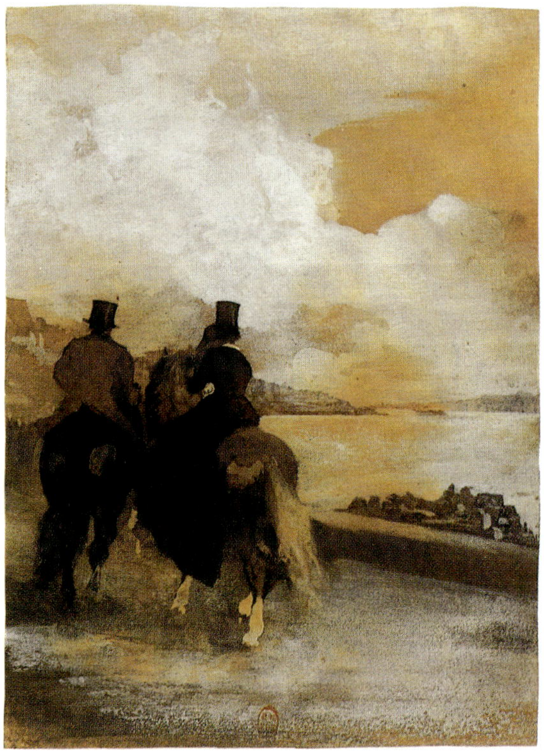

51. *Two Figures on Horseback*, *c*.1860, ink and white gouache, 25.4 × 19.2. Notebook 18, page 55. Bibliothèque Nationale, Paris.

Degas' two earliest equestrian landscapes pose as many questions as they seem to answer. Were they painted in Italy, during Degas' second visit to Naples? Were they executed wholly or partly in the open air, in front of the *motif*, as the prone figure of the artist in *Horses in a Landscape* might suggest?[24] What do they tell us about Degas' working practice, and about his landscape-painting activities in particular? The brevity of Degas' 1860 stay in Naples, and the fleeting nature of this second trip to Italy, make it unlikely that he carried oil-painting equipment or embarked on such works *in situ*.[25] More precisely, the existence of preparatory studies for both pictures indicates a pondered, studio-based approach to their production, while emphasising the role of first-hand observation in their early stages. The majority of these studies are simple pencil drawings of horses or landscape features, but the most dramatic of them all is a pen-and-wash draft for *Promenade beside the Sea* (fig. 51), made in the same notebook as the Haras-du-Pin sketches. Unexpectedly turned into a vertical format, this elaborate image is otherwise very close to the finished canvas and even incorporates additional detail in certain areas, such as the figures of the riders. What is apparent, however, is that Degas has taken considerable liberties in both the setting and the atmosphere of the two pictures. In the study, references to the Neapolitan shoreline have been suppressed, and a billowing cloudscape hints at rain or a gathering storm. Now suggesting a placid sky and a more spacious landscape, the background in the oil painting makes room for the distinctive structures of the city and emphasises the sweep of its celebrated bay.

It is clear that Degas was constrained neither by topographical exactitude nor by the imperatives of memory in these Italian scenes, and perhaps in any of his early equestrian subjects. While a painting like *Promenade beside the Sea* may well have originated in first-hand experience, the use of the same elements in different contexts points to an act of synthesis and the re-ordering of sensations. At one level, this indicates a rather arbitrary approach to the landscape, or at least the elevation of the foreground subject at the expense of its setting. At another, the practice reminds us of the god-like powers of the landscapist, who

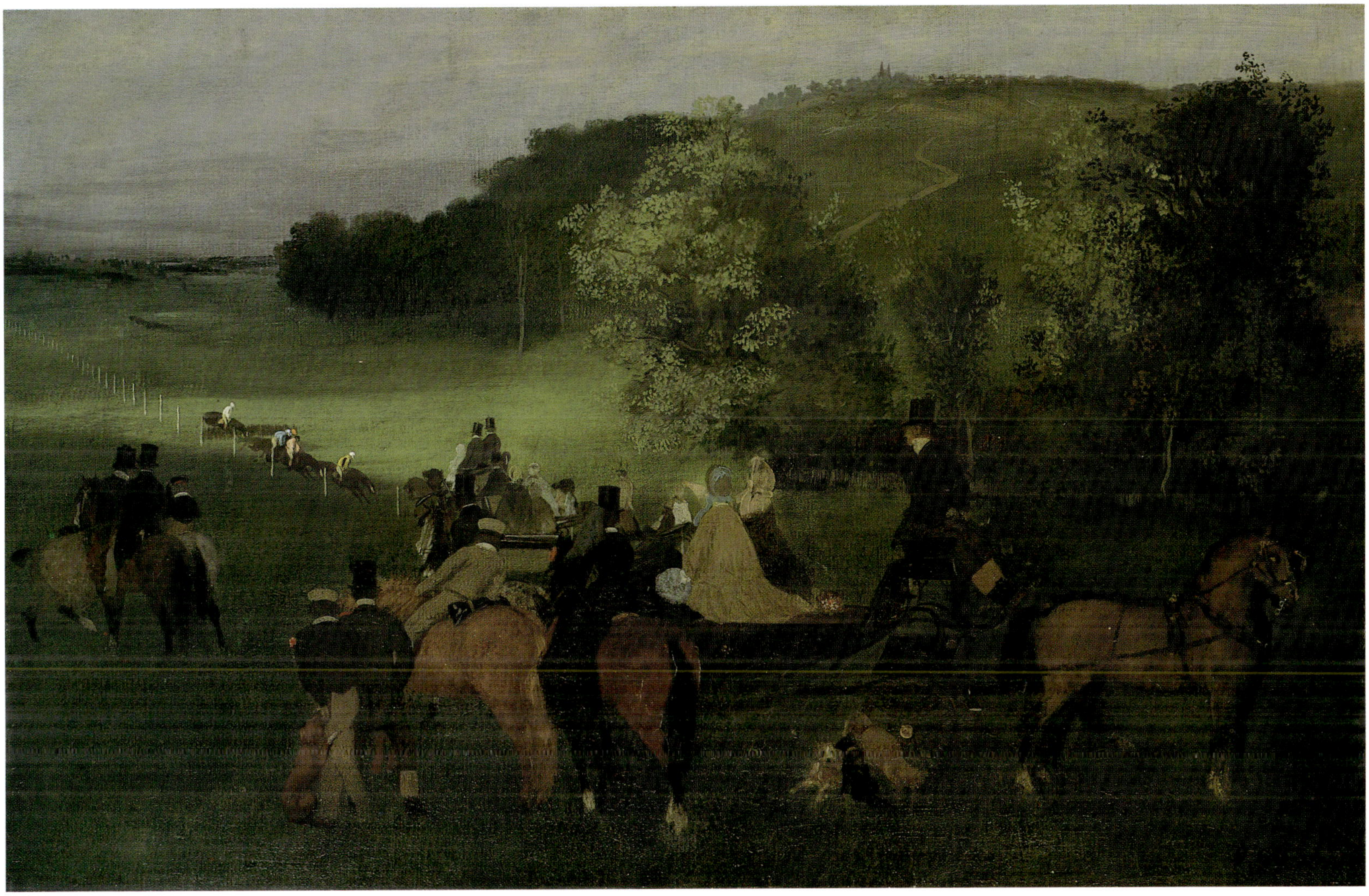

52. *On the Racecourse*, *c.*1861, oil on canvas, 43 × 65.5 (L 77). Oeffentliche Kunstsammlung, Basel.

conjures up sunlight and storms, uproots trees and rearranges coastlines, and disposes his dramatis personae according to pictorial whim. In later life, Degas was to exploit such licence to an unparalleled degree, not only in his landscapes but, more famously, in the endlessly redistributed staffage of his ballet scenes. There are few more precocious examples of this tendency, however, than the fate of the female rider in *Promenade beside the Sea*. Appearing without warning in the oil painting and related sketchbook study, this soberly clad *amazone* shows us her back, her voluminous skirts and her blue-tinted veil blowing in the breeze. For reasons best known to himself, Degas then lifted her from her Neapolitan surroundings and set her down in Normandy, placing her at the centre of his painting *On the Racecourse* (fig. 52). Unmistakably the same figure, she now gazes at a steeplechase in the gloomiest of northern landscapes, her top-hatted companion replaced by a restless stable-boy.[26]

Such wholesale transpositions of figures and their environments, as well as the integration of elements from other artists' works, seem to distinguish many of Degas' pioneering racing scenes. The most celebrated of these is *At the Races: The Start* (fig. 53), though *Jockeys at Epsom* (private collection; L 75) and the much overpainted *Gentlemen's Race: Before the Start* (Musée d'Orsay, Paris; L 101) share many of its qualities. All the pictures are small and rather crowded in composition, and each originally showed an attention to detail that was unusual

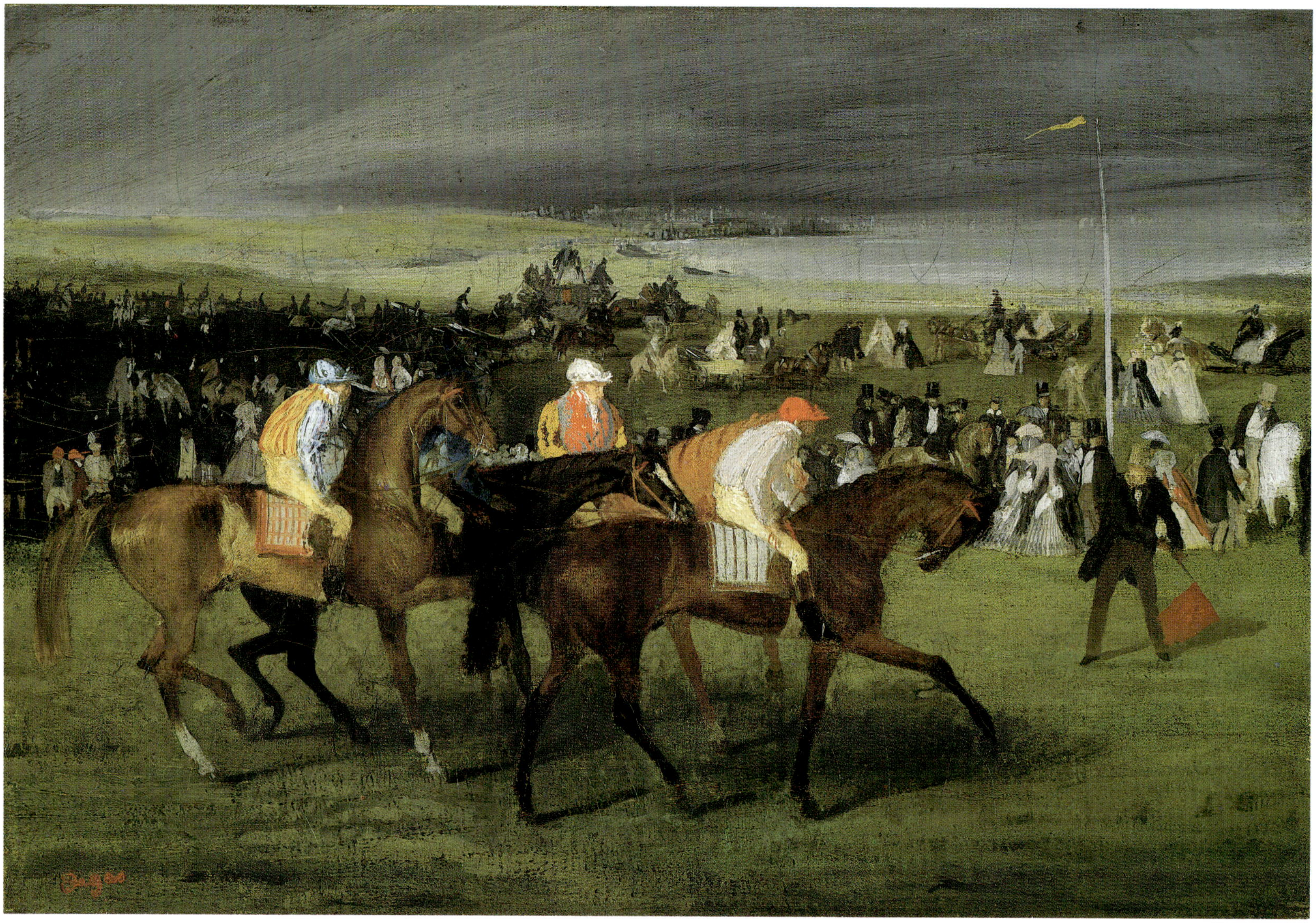

53. *At the Races: The Start*, *c.*1860–2, oil on canvas, 32 × 46 (L 76). Fogg Art Museum, Harvard University, Cambridge, Mass., Bequest of Annie Swan Coburn.

at this or any other point in Degas' career. In *At the Races: The Start*, which was painted in 1861 or 1862, an orderly procession of horses moves across the foreground, while behind them a line of spectators stands parallel to the racetrack.[27] Deeper into space, ranks of carriages continue this horizontal stratification and beyond them a deserted plain merges into a band of stormy sky and a rather improbable lake or bay. From foreground to horizon, detail is sharply focused, allowing the artist to dwell on racing silks and harnesses, parasols and top hats, and even on the faces of the distant crowd. For all its particularity, however, the scene is curiously remote, especially when compared with the Neapolitan paintings, and we might sense the use of a set of conventions, rather than first-hand observation. Described by Lemoisne as 'courses anglaises, probablement à Epsom', there is no reason to believe that Degas intended such a context and no tell-tale sketchbook drawing to reveal a youthful excursion to England.[28] There is overwhelming evidence, on the other hand, that such pictures grew out of Degas' vicarious interest in English art and that its subject and some of its detailed vocabulary were derived from 'the English coloured prints of racing or hunting scenes' he had remembered in Normandy.

The left-to-right parade of jockeys, the parallel ranks of onlookers, the bland

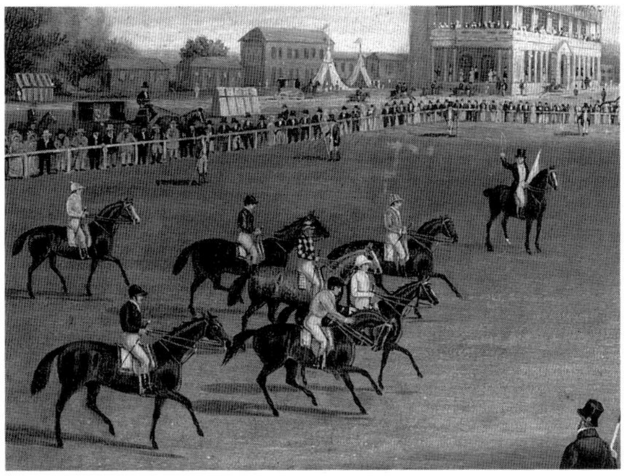

54. James Pollard, *Doncaster Races* (detail), oil on canvas, 49.5 × 75. Private collection, photo courtesy Sotheby's.

rural setting and even the polished, high-stepping ponies of *At the Races: The Start* were the stock-in-trade of an entire school of English sporting painters and print-makers. James Pollard, Henry Alken, J. F. Herring and many others had been admired and collected in France for more than a generation and painters as varied as Géricault and Manet had quoted knowingly from their repertoire.[29] Famed for their stylised views of the racecourse and their relentlessly detailed scenes of the steeplechase, these artists also benefited from a taste for English sports and English fashions under the Second Empire. Though there has been a tendency to over-simplify their artistic achievement, which could be both more inventive and more dramatic than its stereotype allows, they undoubtedly provided a ready-made equestrian vocabulary for artists of mid-nineteenth-century France. In Degas' case, we can go further, and identify specific English prints that featured in his work and even a favoured artist, James Pollard, whose pictures of the hunt and the racetrack were clearly known to him. Widely distributed as lithographic reproductions, Pollard's paintings appear to have been the source of many of the features in *At the Races: The Start*: similarly posturing jockeys and their mounts occur in Pollard's *Doncaster Races* (fig. 54); comparable lines of spectators appear in his *Epsom Races: The Betting Post* and *The Start of the Derby Stakes*; and identically posed horses can be found in *Preparing to Start*.[30]

The possibility that Degas' earliest racing scenes were pure studio confections, remote from, or even innocent of, first-hand experience, must be considered, Relying on his knowledge of Géricault, de Dreux and Guys, as well as of James Pollard and the English school, Degas may well have put together these experimental canvases without visiting the racetrack.[31] The extent of his artifice, even at this early stage in his career, is difficult to underestimate, and is carried to further extremes in this same group of paintings. More than one writer has shown the indebtedness of the equestrian subjects to copies made while Degas was in Italy, notably from the Parthenon frieze and from Benozzo Gozzoli's *Journey of the Magi*.[32] A delicate pencil drawing entitled *At the Races* (Sterling and Francine Clark Art Institute, Williamstown) seems to act as a link between Gozzoli's imagery and Degas' own age, retaining the formality of a relief or fresco, while introducing modern costumes and accessories.[33] In composition, the drawing is closest to the original appearance of *The Gentlemen's Race: Before the Start*, though a close examination of this much-altered painting shows that it, too, once featured finely detailed crowds and a rather blank landscape in the English manner. Significantly, the Williamstown drawing shows only the most rudimentary background, and, in the absence of other appropriate landscape studies, we must presume that Degas improvised his settings for these pictures, or adapted them from English models.

Combining glimpses of Italy with the heart of the northern countryside, and the conventions of the classical relief with a day at the races, Degas broke new ground in every sense with *On the Racecourse* (fig. 52). Here, the open spaces of the racetrack have been usurped by a towering, densely thicketed hill which seems to threaten the stability of the scene beneath. With unprecedented daring, Degas has thrown the entire landscape into shadow, allowing only a glimmer of sunshine to illuminate the remote event of the race. Most audaciously of all, he has set the frieze-like ranks of foreground spectators against a plunging, spatially disruptive line of carriages that runs directly into the picture space. Beginning with the back of the *amazone* from *Promenade beside the Sea*, our eyes follow a sequence of hats and averted heads that tapers off into the distance, meeting up with the line of jockeys and thus with the ostensible focus of the painting. Some of these devices can be found in Degas' English sources: the procession of horses, landaus and hangers-on across the front of the picture, for example, is present in James Pollard's *Epsom Races: The Betting Post* and in other similar works, and such stylised racehorses were a commonplace.[34] Even the orthogonal line of carriages has its precedents, but none of these older works juxtaposes so many and such contradictory structures in a context of the present kind.[35] Degas' boldest stroke has been to transpose his race-meeting into an idiosyncratic and yet entirely believable landscape. In place of the stylised countryside of the English school or the remote strands of Italy, the gloomy atmosphere and rain-drenched tones of *On the Racecourse* speak irresistibly of a personal encounter, just as its pictorial disruptions suggest urgency and immediate discomfort.

What was the motivation behind Degas' painting of *On the Racecourse*? This dramatic departure from his earlier racing scenes, as well as from the stock settings of the English lithographers, surely coincides with his own discovery of the French countryside. These lush hillsides and shadowy pastures correspond in every particular with the artist's 1861 description of Normandy and suggest that this painting was set in the landscape around Ménil-Hubert. Many details of that excursion support such a view. Normandy was famed as a horse-rearing and horse-racing area, and the nearby countryside boasted its own racecourse, as well as the stables at Haras-du-Pin. Later in the decade, Degas attended the local races with the Valpinçon family, and there is reason to believe that his painting marked an early, perhaps a first, visit to such a spectacle.[36] One of the few drawings that can be directly related to *On the Racecourse* occurs on a notebook page immediately following a study of the château of Haras-du-Pin.[37] Less precisely, but no less persuasively, the hill-top village in the painting, with its modest spire and clustered houses, brings to mind the village of Exmes, as represented in several of Degas' ink-and-wash sketches.[38] If a single picture can be said to correspond in mood and staffage, if not in the details of its composition, to *On the Racecourse*, it must be that sombre view of the approach to Exmes, with a receding line of figures and a rear view of a carriage (fig. 35). Here again, we find the darkened landscape and the single glimpse of sunshine; here are the trees heavy with rain and the paths winding into the distance; and it was here, as we remember from his notebook, that Degas thought of 'those pictures of English genius'.

Degas' attempt to make a modern equestrian landscape that corresponded to the clamorous experience of the racetrack, painted from the viewpoint of the spectator and, later, of the riders themselves, announced one of the major projects of his first professional decade. As yet lacking a reference collection of his own drawings, he naturally turned to available source materials, and as an artist obsessed by tradition, he could never entirely resist the knowing paraphrase or the historic pun. Looking around him, Degas registered the achievement of certain of his horse-painting contemporaries, such as Meissonier, John Lewis Brown and Giovanni Fattori, and was not ashamed to learn from, and occasionally borrow, their imagery. But for all their eclecticism, the twenty or so horse-and-rider pictures of the 1860s remained one of his most original achievements and the surest sign of his shifting ambition. Spatially ingenious and often audacious in their depiction of atmosphere and social exchange, this diverse sequence of paintings reminds us how far and how quickly Degas had advanced in his newly chosen repertoire. Against this background, it is hardly surprising that Manet turned to Degas' example when evolving his first

55. Detail of fig. 52.

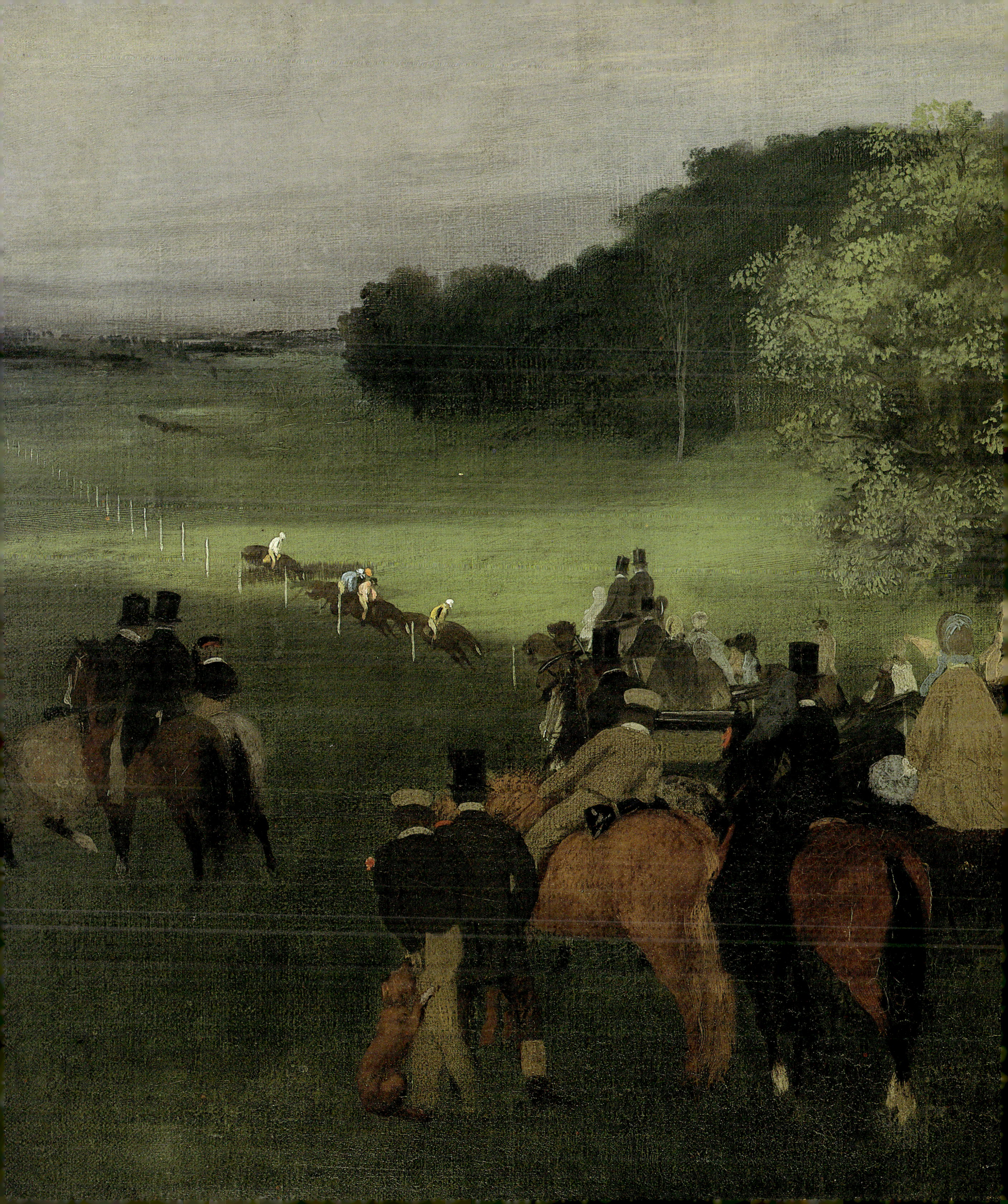

equestrian subjects, or that Degas chose the grandest of his series, the *Steeplechase*, for his first topical submission to the Salon.

At this point, however, we might stand back from the equestrian theme and question its role in Degas' developing *oeuvre*. From its inception, the diversity of the artist's treatment of the subject suggested a casting about for a personal idiom and perhaps a corresponding search for markets, dealers and collectors. In this sense, the pictures appear to have been an immediate failure. As far as is known, none of the equestrian landscapes of the 1860s found a buyer at the time, and only one, the 1866 *Steeplechase*, was placed on public exhibition. Though several of these canvases were sold when the artist achieved a certain celebrity, the majority remained in his studio and did not become known until after Degas' death. At a superficial level, therefore, the series of paintings might be seen as an abortive attempt to capitalise on a new and highly fashionable market. The closer we look at the pictures, the less plausible such an analysis becomes. In almost every case, Degas took up the subject of horses and riders, and the conventions of their representation, only to disrupt or obscure them. In *On the Racecourse*, a healthy outdoor spectacle was transformed into a dismal provincial mêlée; in *The Gentlemen's Race: Before the Start*, horses slide out of the stabilising rectangle of the picture or are truncated by its frame; and in the *Steeplechase*, a single colossal thoroughbred bisects the canvas, its jockey lying unconscious on the turf. Time after time, riders and their mounts mill about at random, oblivious to the glamour of the race-meeting or the proprieties of the hunt. To add further to their confusion, even the status of these canvases remains ambiguous. Are they paintings of the landscape, of conventionalised social ritual or simply of horses? Seen in this way, Degas' pictures might better be described as anti-racetrack scenes, designed to extend, subvert or even ridicule the vocabulary of an existing genre. By extension, they would be intended not for the orthodox tastes of the Jockey Club, but for the more discerning and independent collectors of contemporary art.[39] As much as pictures of the turf, these are paintings about visual language, the mechanics of perception and the abrasiveness of modern experience.

Such terms of reference bring us inexorably to the work of Edouard Manet, and to the meeting of these two artists in the early 1860s, when Degas was painting his first group of equestrian canvases. The complex friendship, mutual influence and knowing rivalry of Manet and Degas has yet to be studied in detail, and the significance of their much quoted banter remains only partially understood. In later years, Manet was to claim, 'When Degas was painting Semiramis, I was painting modern Paris', a view that has been almost universally accepted ever since.[40] Though precedence is only one small part of their relationship, it has been insufficiently acknowledged that it was Degas, rather than Manet, who first tackled the modern horse-race *motif* and that some of Degas' imagery was used directly by Manet in his early attempts at the subject. The most vivid example of this priority can be found in Degas' *On the Racecourse*, painted in late 1861 or early 1862, and the group of studies clustered around Manet's *View of a Race in the Bois de Boulogne* (fig. 56), dated some three or four years later.[41] Manet's study is a few centimetres narrower than Degas' canvas, but both pictures depict a sweeping, panoramic view of a racing scene backed by a distant hill and sober green foliage. Manet, like Degas, has emphasised the foreground plane by means of a stationary horse seen in profile, while a group of elegant onlookers draw our attention to the centre of both pictures. At the left-hand edge, a vignette of ponies and grooms is common to the two works, but it is the central procession of carriages that dominates each

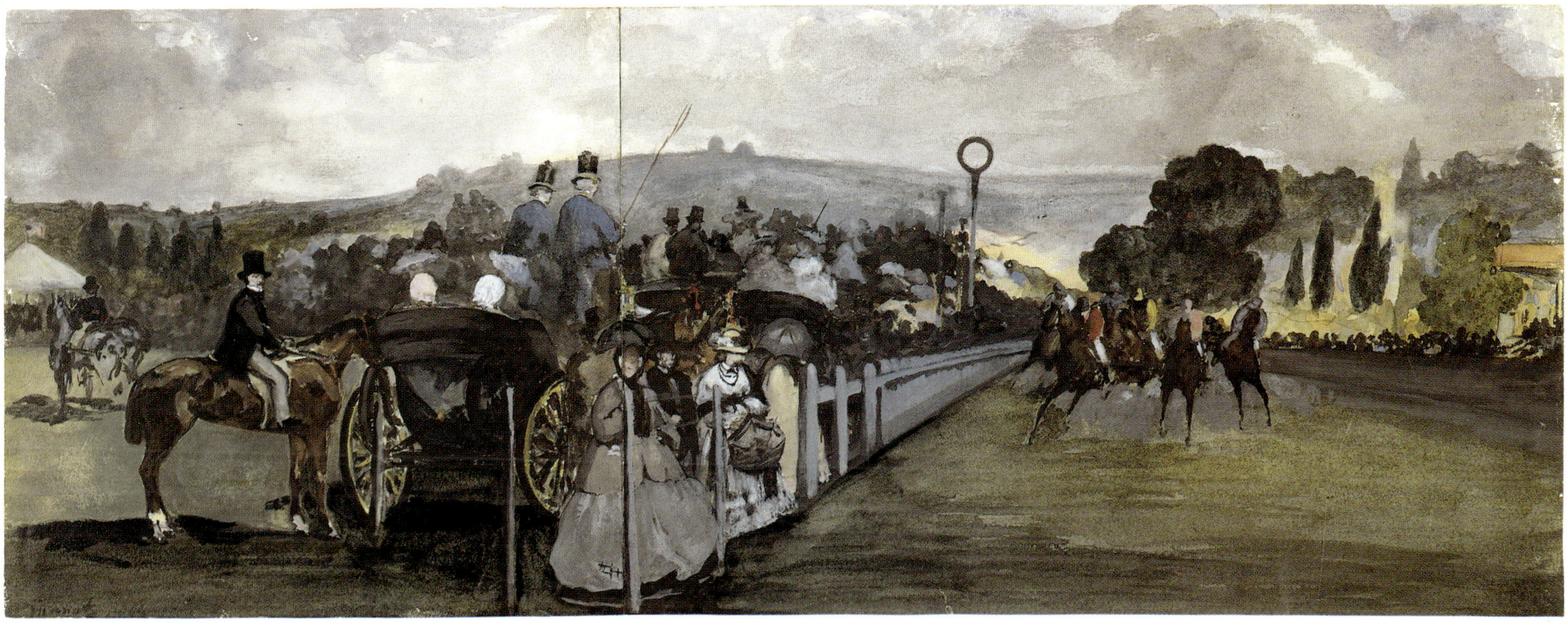

56. Edouard Manet, *View of a Race in the Bois de Boulogne*, 1864, watercolour, 22.3 × 56.5. Fogg Art Museum, Harvard University, Cambridge, Mass., Bequest of Grenville L. Winthrop.

composition. In the Manet, a veritable traffic jam of coachmen and spectators, hats and bonnets carries the viewer obliquely into space, the mirror-image of Degas' plunging diagonal. Though Manet has turned his racehorses to face the viewer, with a boldness that even he seems to have regretted, it is difficult not to see the essential structures of his composition as a re-working of, or perhaps a gesture of respect towards, his newly acquired friend.[42]

The visual radicalism of Degas' racing scenes was carried further, and into new thematic teritory, in his next group of equestrian landscapes, which span the middle years of the decade. During this period, he painted more than ten substantial horse-and-rider pictures, the largest of which was the six-foot canvas of the *Steeplechase*. Varying greatly in scale, subject-matter and technical refinement, these pictures share certain family resemblances which point to a continuity of execution and a consistency of intent. With one or two exceptions, our attention is shifted away from the formality of the racetrack and towards the individual or domestic experience of the ride. Less constrained in such themes, perhaps, by established convention, Degas also took liberties with his composition that would have been unthinkable at the beginning of the decade, exploring close-ups and high vantage points, discontinuous spaces and opaque narratives. If there is a unifying concern in these works, it is the sensations of the riders themselves, as they hurtle across obstacles or plunge down embankments, delighting in open terrain and the hazards of the chase. As in his first series, landscape plays a varying role, at times almost overshadowing the human and animal participants, at others recalling Degas' own rural excursions.

A link between Degas' first experiments with the equestrian landscape and his work of the mid-decade is suggested by the painting *Leaving for the Hunt* (fig. 57). Some confusion surrounds the dating of this picture, which has been placed as far apart as 1864 and 1873 by different authorities.[43] What has not been emphasised is the evidence that the canvas has been re-worked and that Degas himself returned to the picture some years after its inception, just as he did with *The Gentlemen's Race: Before the Start*.[44] The most dramatic sign of its early origins is, bizarrely enough, its signature, a large and flamboyant *E. De Gas* that follows exactly the pattern used in *Scene of War in the Middle Ages*, which was

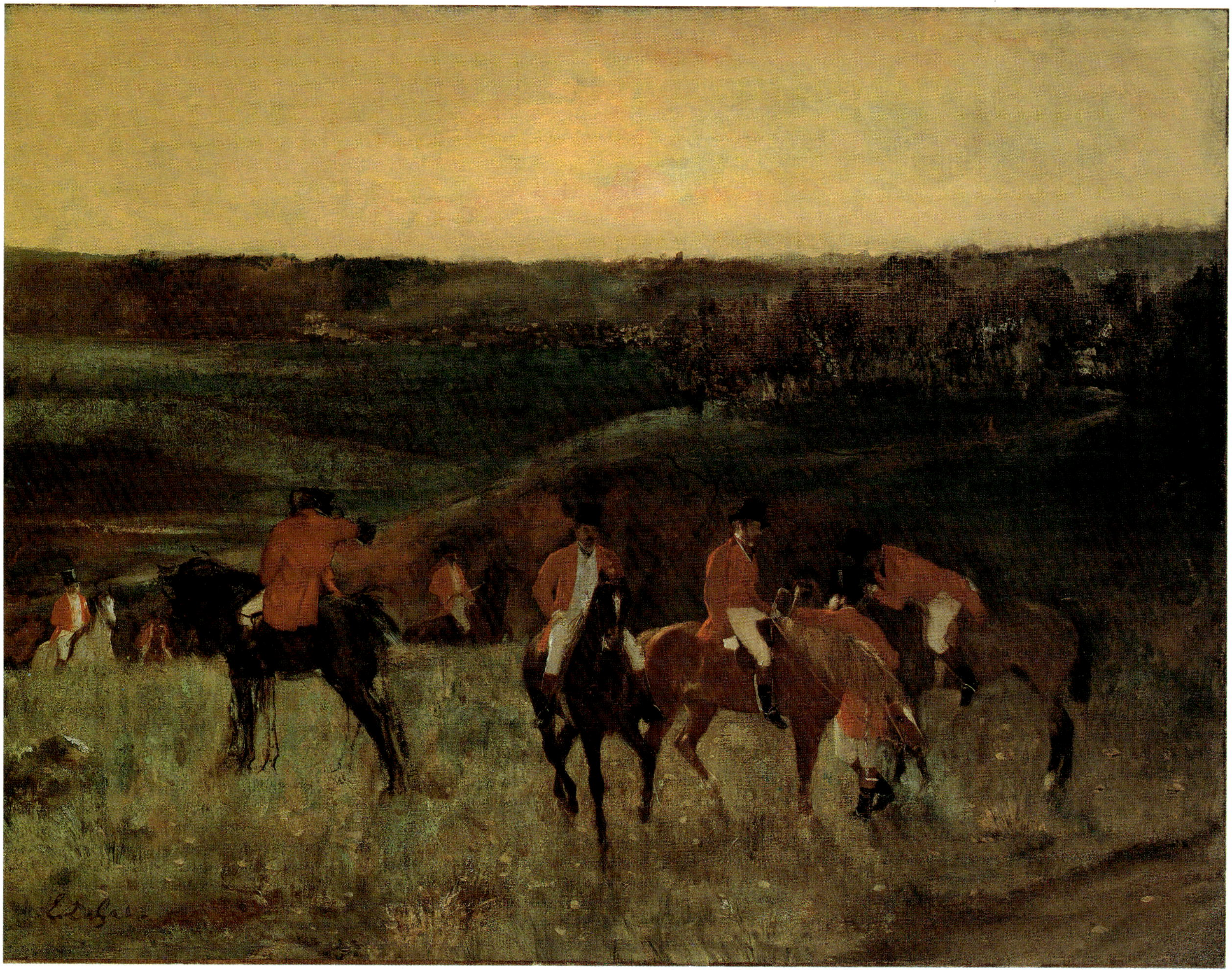

57. *Leaving for the Hunt*, *c.*1863–5 and 1873, oil on canvas, 69 × 88.5 (L 119). Private collection, courtesy Galerie Schmit, Paris.

painted about 1863 and shown at the Salon of 1865.[45] Immediately after he completed this work, Degas abandoned the aristocratic form of his family name, simultaneously putting behind him the pretensions of youth and the grandeur of *peinture historique*. Its presence on *Leaving for the Hunt* is entirely consistent with the earliest phase of work on the canvas, which resembles the technique of equestrian pictures made between 1861 and 1862.[46] Again consistent with this shift is our sense that *Leaving for the Hunt* is a modern-dress counterpart of *Scene of War in the Middle Ages*, complete with scattered male riders, undulating countryside and sombre, autumnal light. More precise affinities with both history paintings and contemporary *motifs* suggest themselves. On the one hand, the high foreground and dipping middle-distance in *Leaving for the Hunt* seem like a final recollection, however remote, of Delacroix's *Ovid among the Scythians*, just as the half-concealed riders mounting the hill are common to both works; on the other, the misty trees and signs of distant habitation in *Leaving for*

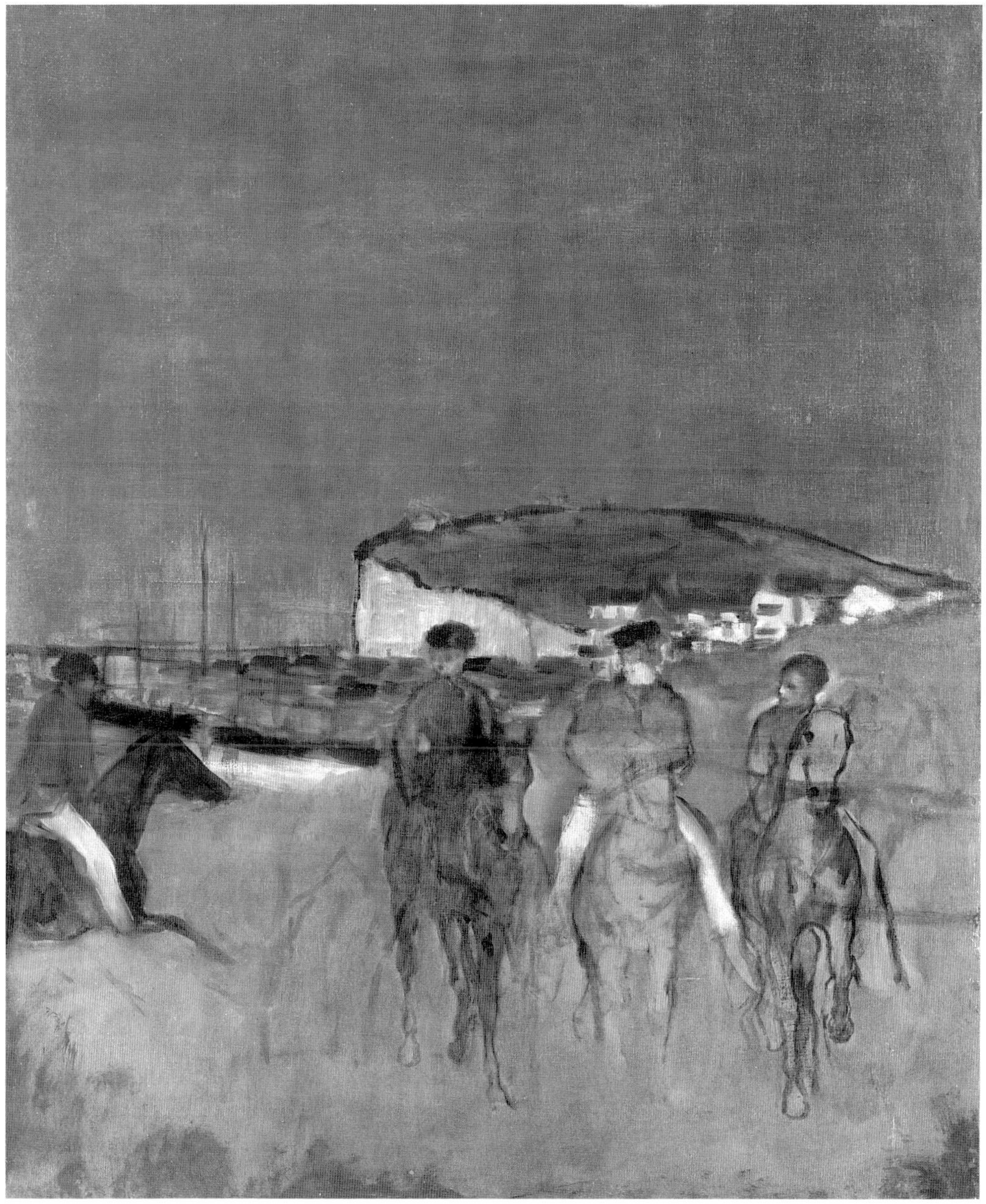

58. *The Morning Ride*, 1865–8, oil on canvas, 81 × 65 (L 118). Detroit Institute of Arts, Founders' Society Purchase, Ralph Harman Booth Bequest Fund.

the Hunt belong to Degas' own recollections and specifically to the landscape of Ménil-Hubert.

What is perhaps most unexpected about *Leaving for the Hunt* is its frank informality, both as a composition and as a narrative. Riders face to left and right, into the picture and out of it. While some seem ready to canter off into the landscape, others stand and chatter to their neighbours. Hints of a similar aimlessness can be found in earlier works, such as *On the Racecourse*, but here it becomes an animating principle, opposing rural lassitude to urban constraint, the open fields to the regulated turf. Despite it apparent licence, precedents for such an approach can still be found amongst English sporting prints, and it may be that Degas had recourse to such works as Henry Alken's *The Field Arriving at the Meet*, a chaotic confection of horses and hunters, truncated mounts and irregular hillsides. Pursuing the more casual possibilities of equestrianism, Degas borrowed the central figure from *Leaving for the Hunt* and used it no less than twice in another canvas, *The Morning Ride* (fig. 58).[47] This time, the riders make no pretence at hunting, but advance along a cliff-top in leisurely formation, while another spirited pony sprints past them in the opposite direction. Clearly a family occasion, the unfinished and technically experimental painting of *The Morning Ride* mixes male and female riders in a recognisable context, suggesting one of Degas' own excursions to the Normandy coast in the company of his friends the Valpinçons.[48]

Such paintings of amateur riders and family groups encourage us to imagine ourselves, and originally the artist, on horseback, participating in similar countryside excursions. Pictures like *The Morning Ride* and *The Promenade on Horseback* (fig. 59), are less a spectacle, more a projection of the experience of riding, as nearby ponies race ahead or fall behind, and as landscape formations loom up in the spectator's path. In the latter canvas, the family cluster at the left gallops directly into pictorial space, bringing to mind the disruptive equestrians in such early scenes as *Promenade beside the Sea*. Above them, a second and more inscrutable narrative unfolds. Imperturbably mounted on his chestnut pony, a child gazes back towards the advancing trio, and yet another group of riders disappears from sight, racing towards an indistinct horizon. Lurching from group to group, our eyes follow their unequal progress, while the rise and fall of the landscape evokes the horses' motion. Above them all, the first tints of a colourful sunset urge the riders homeward and, again through purely visual means, offer a key to their mysterious predicament.[49]

Like so many canvases of this period, *The Promenade on Horseback* was carefully rehearsed in drawings and sketchbook studies, and some of its forms reappeared in the larger family of works. The bounding pony, for example, became a recurrent *motif*, leaping across cliff-tops, along avenues and even through an elaborate flower-bed.[50] The painting itself had its origin in drawings of individual figures, a compositional sketch and a number of notebook pages, all of which suggest a date of around 1867 for the project.[51] Following Degas' established practice, these drawings concern themselves largely with horses and their riders, indicating only the most rudimentary landscape settings. By now making regular visits to Normandy and familiar with its terrain, Degas appears to have worked up the backgrounds of his pictures from memory, perhaps using a borrowed studio on his vacation or finishing the pictures after his return to Paris. Characteristically, this procedure allowed a dialogue between drawing and colour, the former fixed in the Ingresque lines of his sketchbook, the latter emanating from that 'Queen of the faculties', imagination. In the circumstances, Degas showed both confidence and accomplishment in his depictions of the landscape, tackling open fields and harbour scenes, forest clearings and gloomy lanes. Only rarely do these settings seem contrived, and more often they record the particularity of countryside freshly perceived and known at first hand.

Not the least remarkable feature of the pictures surrounding *The Promenade on Horseback* is their emphasis on women and children, and the domestic context of horse-riding. These are rural, rather than metropolitan, scenes, in which pot-bellied ponies struggle with primly dressed infants and where mothers lead the family excursion as often as their occasional male companions. Their social informality is once more reflected in their mobile structures, and in the inventive and sometimes bizarre nature of their proceedings. In *Children and Ponies in a Park* (private collection; L 171), for example, the artist has chosen the high vantage point appropriate to an adult's view of the world, looking down on a grid of lawns and pathways, and across towards a dense screen of trees. His

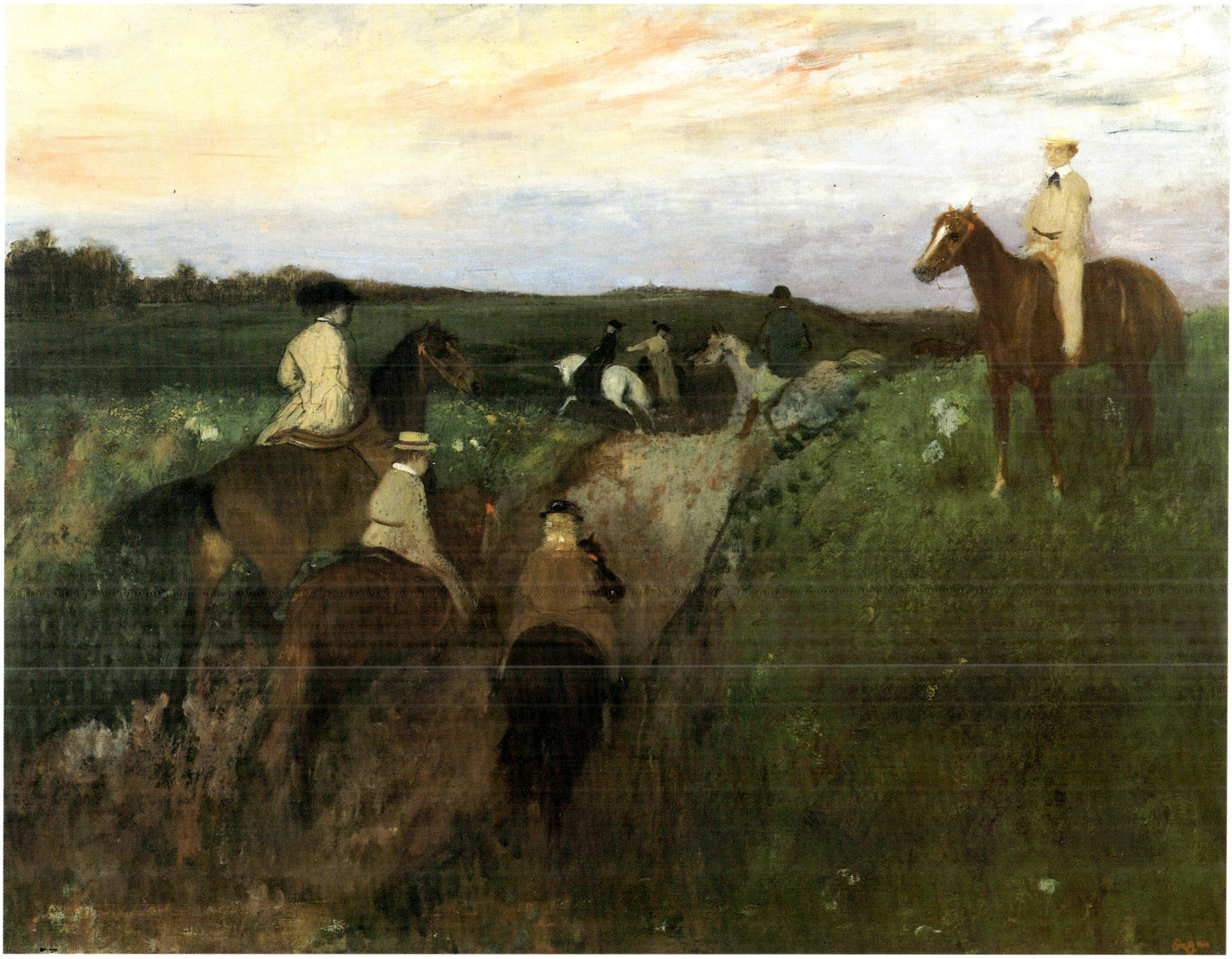

59. *The Promenade on Horseback*, *c.*1867, oil on canvas, 71 × 90 (L 117). Hiroshima Museum of Art.

elegant actresses, three young girls in straw hats and riding costumes, meet in an extraordinary collision of diagonals, as they leap through shrubbery and strain at their ill-assorted mounts.[52] There are distant echoes here of the tradition of outdoor family portraiture, such as Alfred de Dreux's *M. and Mme Mosselman and their Two Daughters* (Musée du Petit Palais, Paris), shown at the Salon of 1848.[53] As in his horse-race pictures, however, Degas recalls these conventions only to disrupt them, offering us childish mayhem in place of de Dreux's complacent stasis.

The liberties taken by Degas in his country scenes have few contemporary parallels. Manet's disreputable picnic-makers, Bazille's rural athletes and Cézanne's extraordinary cast of saints and sinners may suggest points of contact, though each had their own ambitions or social semaphores. In Degas' pictures, we watch the middle classes at play, or rather engaged in those country pursuits thought appropriate to estate-owners and holiday guests. Confident *bourgeois*

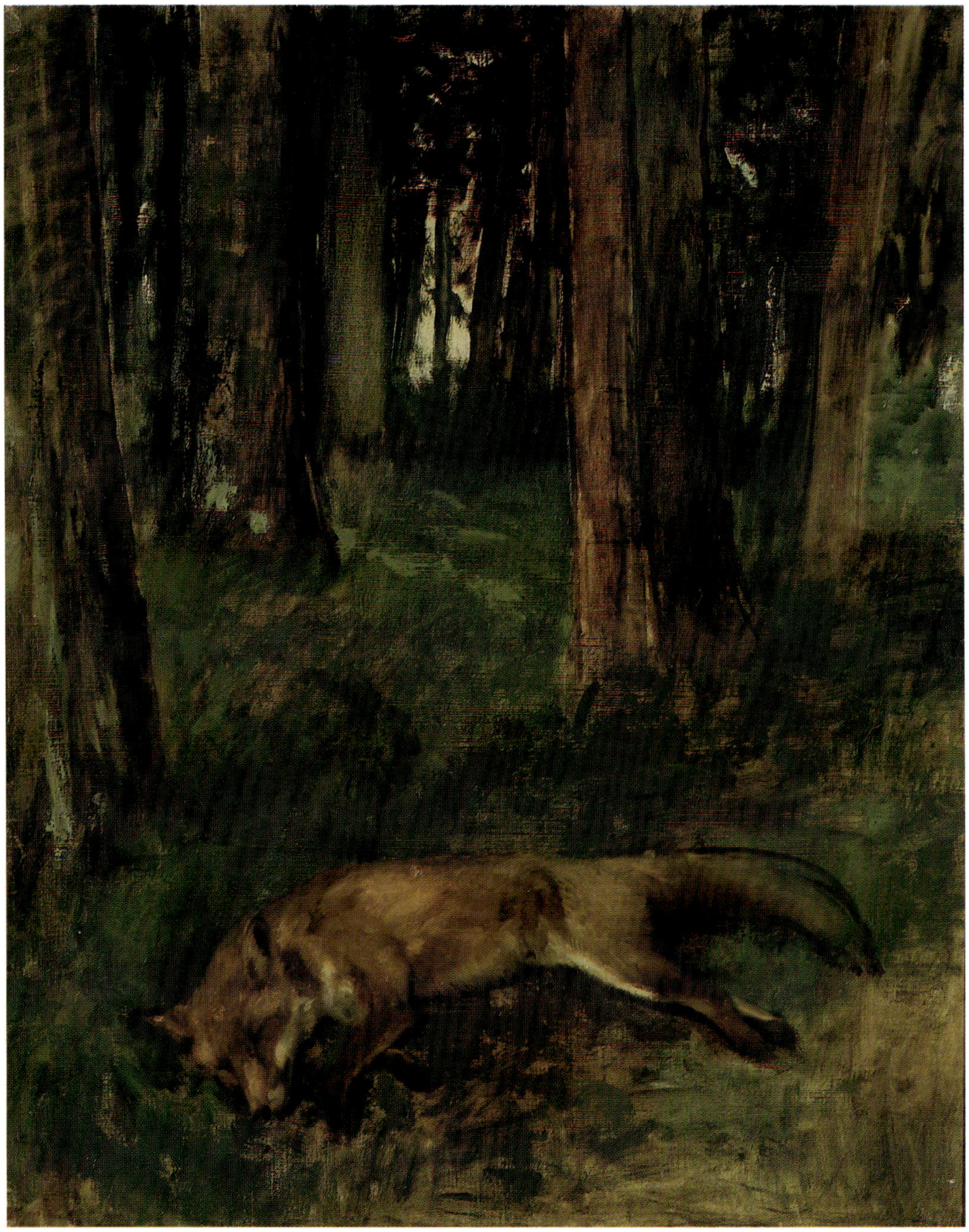

60. *Dead Fox in a Wood*, *c.*1867, oil on canvas, 92 × 73 (L 120). Musée des Beaux-Arts, Rouen.

and their smartly dressed children take their leisure in muddy landscapes, their normal codes of conduct challenged and thrown into relief by their surroundings. When seen in this way, a number of analogies come to mind in the work of a radically different artist, but one whom Degas clearly admired at this period; Gustave Courbet. Several of Degas' canvases of the late 1860s show him experimenting with Courbet's colour, brushwork and palette-knife technique, while others indicate an informed awareness of the older artist's subject-matter. Though there is no record of contact between the two painters, Courbet's celebrations of rural sport, his pictures of riders on their far-from-pedigree nags, and his frequent juxtaposition of town and country manners may well have given encouragement to Degas in his exploration of similar topics.

More pointed acts of homage to Courbet are evident in a group of little-known works from this highly eclectic phase. One of the most impressive, *Dead Fox in a Wood* (fig. 60), is evidently related to the hunt and shows a subject widely associated with Courbet. In this picture, Degas has presumptuously combined two familiar Courbet images, *Fox in the Snow* (Dallas Museum of Art) and the *Dead Deer* (private collection), both of which he could have seen during this decade.[54] In his habitual fashion, Degas laid the foundation for his painting in a masterly drawing of the principal subject, then brushed in the leafy background with considerably greater abandon.[55] On the canvas, the contrast between the delicate, almost transparent, brushwork of the animal's fur and the vigorous strokes of the foliage is unusually poignant, and remind us of Degas' increasing command of the medium. Touches of palette-knife work among the trees also bring us back to the source of his inspiration, while suggesting links with other Courbet-like paintings of the later 1860s. Two of Degas' more obscure landscape studies of this period depict a forest glade and a rock-strewn stream respectively, the latter showing dense crusts of paint and unmistakable traces of the knife.[56] A further pair of paintings, this time in watercolour on paper, are dedicated to one of Courbet's favourite *motifs*, the craggy rock-face. *Rocks in a Wood at Bagnoles-de-l'Orne* (fig. 62) and *Rocks and Trees at Bagnoles-de-l'Orne* (fig. 63) are both noteworthy for their confident handling of a subject new to the artist, in a medium he had hardly touched for a decade.[57] Lightly handled and delicately tinted, each tackles a somewhat intractable subject and brings articulation and vigour to a confusion of boulders, fissures and attendant foliage. If, as seems likely, they were carried out in preparation for the setting of his *Mlle Fiocre in the Ballet 'La Source'* (fig. 61), they also present us with those rarest of phenomena, background studies for Degas' own paintings.[58]

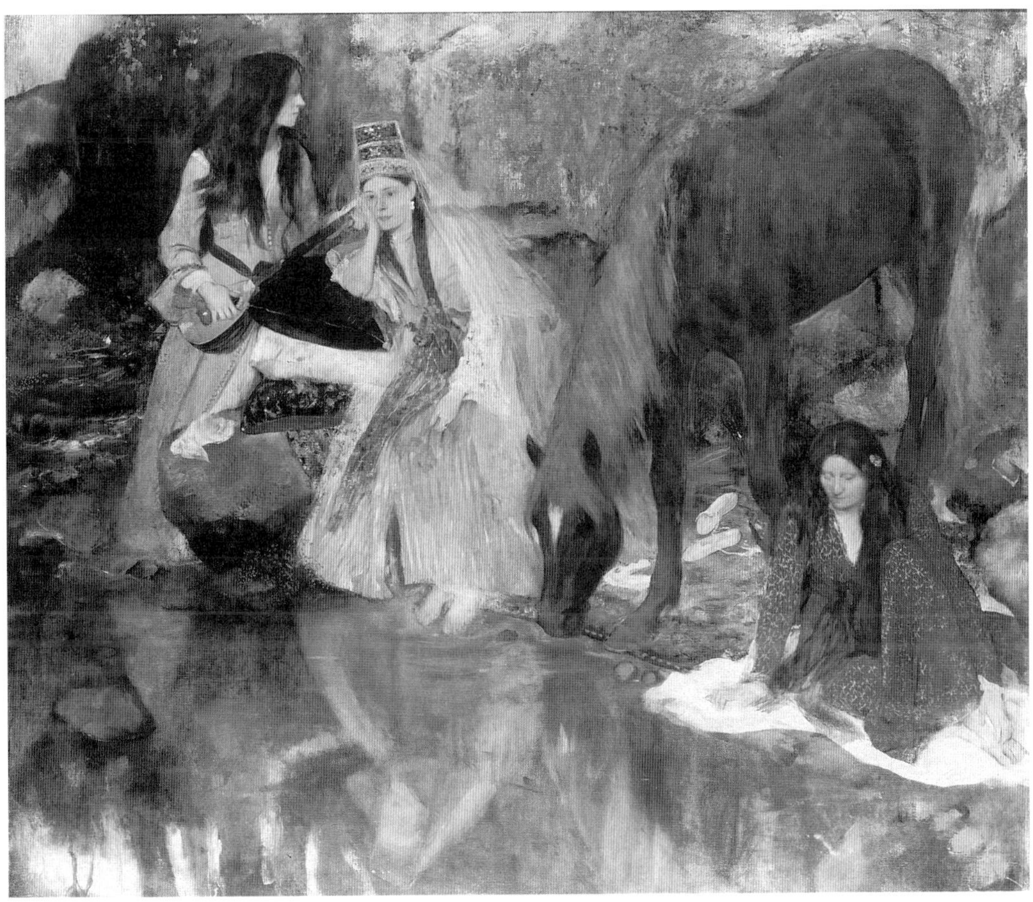

61. *Mlle Fiocre in the Ballet 'La Source'*, 130 × 145 (L 146), The Brooklyn Museum.

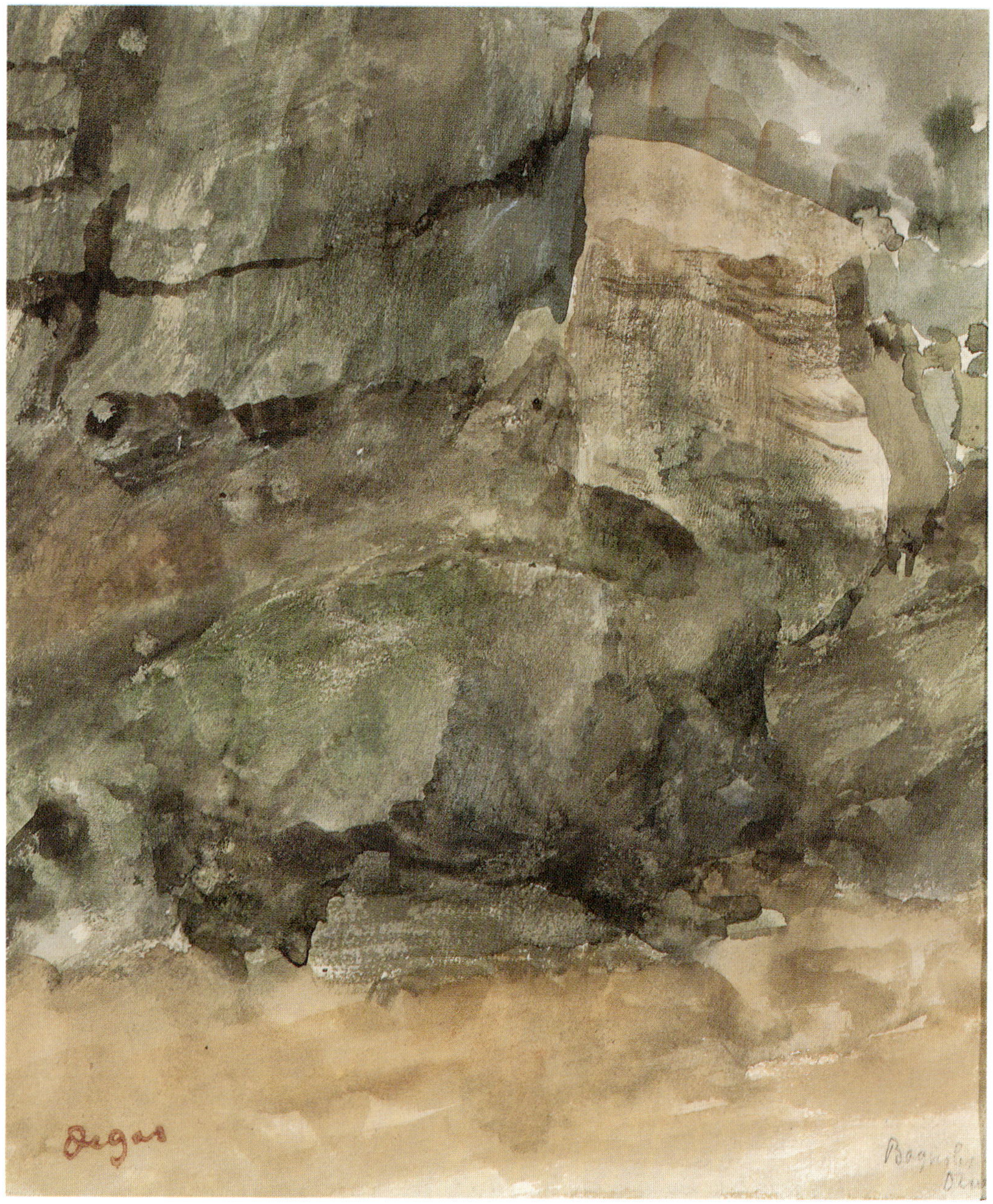

62. *Rocks in a Wood at Bagnoles-de-l'Orne*, *c.*1867, watercolour, 22 × 19 (L 191). Musée du Louvre, Département des Arts Graphiques, Fonds du Musée d'Orsay, Paris.

Among the most knowingly artificial of all his landscapes, Degas' *Mlle Fiocre in the Ballet 'La Source'* brings together and barely contains several of the great obsessions of his career. Part equestrian scene, part ballet subject, this celebration of exotic femininity is set against a rugged cliff or ravine, while a stream and a mirror-like pool extend towards the viewer. More than one admirer has noted its affinity with Courbet, not least in the rich hues and encrusted surfaces of its much-revised background.[59] The picture was based on a documented production of 1866, which featured real horses and flowing water on stage, but Degas has carefully suspended his image between naturalism and fantasy, the mundane and the chimerical. By choosing the picture for submission to the 1868 Salon, two years after *The Steeplechase*, he also suggested an element of continuity in his subject-matter, as well as a broadening of his imaginative range. At the time of the Salon, Emile Zola noted the picture with approval, admiring its refinement of detail and its precision of effect, while

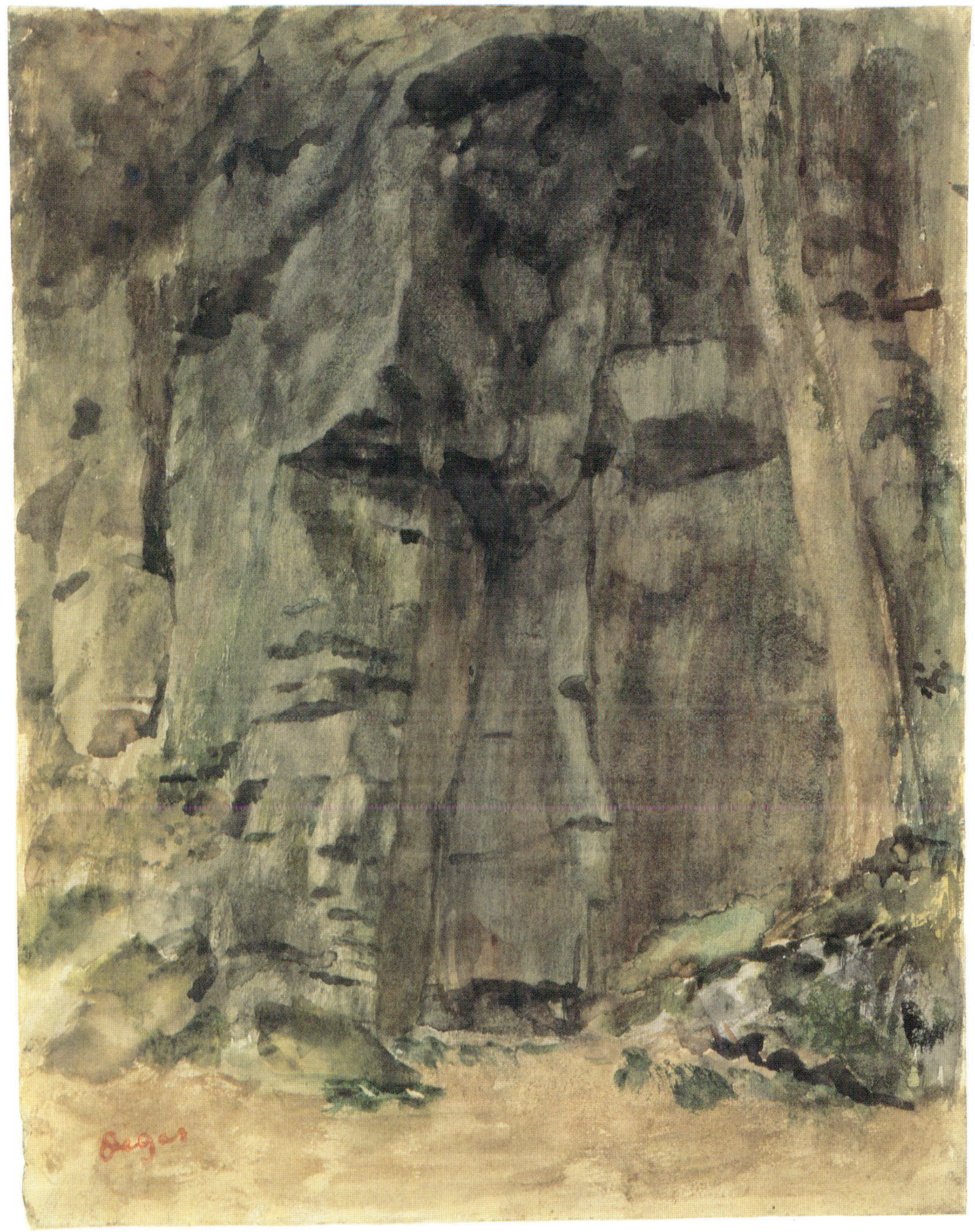

63. *Rocks and Trees at Bagnoles-de-l'Orne*, *c.*1867, watercolour, 25 × 20 (L 192). Fitzwilliam Museum, Cambridge.

comparing it, somewhat unexpectedly, to Japanese prints.[60] In the same review, Zola held forth at length about the current state of French art in general and of landscape painting in particular. Reiterating a number of earlier opinions, he welcomed those younger painters, like Pissarro and Monet, who, he believed, held out hope for the future. Like many other critics, Zola felt that Courbet's best days were past, though he continued to champion the qualities that had attracted him to Courbet's work in former times. In a resounding passage that might have been directed at Degas, Zola exclaimed:

> The classical landscape is dead, killed by life and truth. Nobody today would dare to say that nature needs to be idealised, that skies and water are vulgar, or that it is necessary to make skylines harmonious and correct if one wants to

paint beautiful pictures. We accepted naturalism without much of a fight, because nearly half a century of literature and personal judgement had prepared us to accept it. Later, I am convinced, the crowd will accept the truth about the human body, pictures of figures rendered in all their reality, just as it has already accepted the truth of the countryside, landscapes with real houses and real trees.[61]

As he made clear elsewhere in his review, Zola's naturalism was not to be confused with mere description, but could be found in those paintings where 'one quickly perceives that the artist has seen and felt, that he has painted as a man, with an energetic or delicate temperament, looking at nature and interpreting it in a personal way'.[62] Here the emphasis is on perception and sensation, as distinct from 'the poetic' or 'the wonderful aspect of things' that Baudelaire had advocated almost a decade earlier, when he had dreamt of 'immense mountains' and 'crenellated abbeys'. The divergence between the two writers cannot, of course, be summarised so starkly, and a degree of sympathy with Baudelaire, or perhaps of confusion, is evident in Zola's claim that he admired a painting of Millet's 'for its true poetry . . . its poetry that is made of nothing but reality'.[63] But in Zola's criticism, which Degas much surely have read, it was the poetry of the quotidian that was the basis of great art; pictures were described as 'powerful' or 'living' if they met with his approval, and commended for their expression of 'breadth' and 'truth'. Unhappily, Zola's remarks on *Mlle Fiocre in the Ballet 'La Source'* come from one of his few professional encounters with Degas' art and do little to elucidate the convoluted relationship between painter and critic. In the late 1860s, however, Zola's views on painting were often strikingly close to Degas' imagery and practice, a convergence of interest that was directly signalled in Degas' *oeuvre*.[64]

In the present context, the most regrettable omission in Zola's art criticism was his failure to comment on Degas' painting *The Steeplechase* (fig. 64) in his review of the 1866 Salon. His oversight is all the more frustrating since Degas' large and forceful canvas was designed to draw attention to itself, and to its still-unknown artist, in a crowded and over-hung gallery. The grandest of all Degas' outdoor scenes, *The Steeplechase* was extensively re-worked in the early 1880s and today bears little resemblance to the picture first shown in 1866.[65] On the basis of surviving drawings and a second version of the composition, it has been possible to show that the original work was, if anything, even more dramatic than it appears today.[66] Bounding diagonally across the centre of a largely empty landscape, a massive and solitary horse once filled the spectator's field of vision, its extremities clipped by the canvas edges. 'Powerful' and 'living', 'broad' and 'true', the picture thrusts us against the harsh realities of the race, positioning the viewer amongst the front ranks of spectators, or perhaps with the horses and jockeys themselves. Beneath the horse, an injured rider lies awkwardly on the turf, his proximity to the animal's hooves arousing our fears and further engaging our imaginative sympathies.

It has been pointed out that Degas' spectacular composition owes something to the precedent of the English sporting print, though little has been done to evaluate this source.[67] Images of fallen jockeys and riderless mounts were a commonplace in the English tradition and were often shown in comical or ludicrous predicaments. One such print, by Degas' favourite among this school, James Pollard, depicts the events at the end of the hunt and appears to have been copied by the artist in a hasty sketch.[68] Typically, the figures in question are mere details in a broader panorama, tumbling over distant ditches and providing

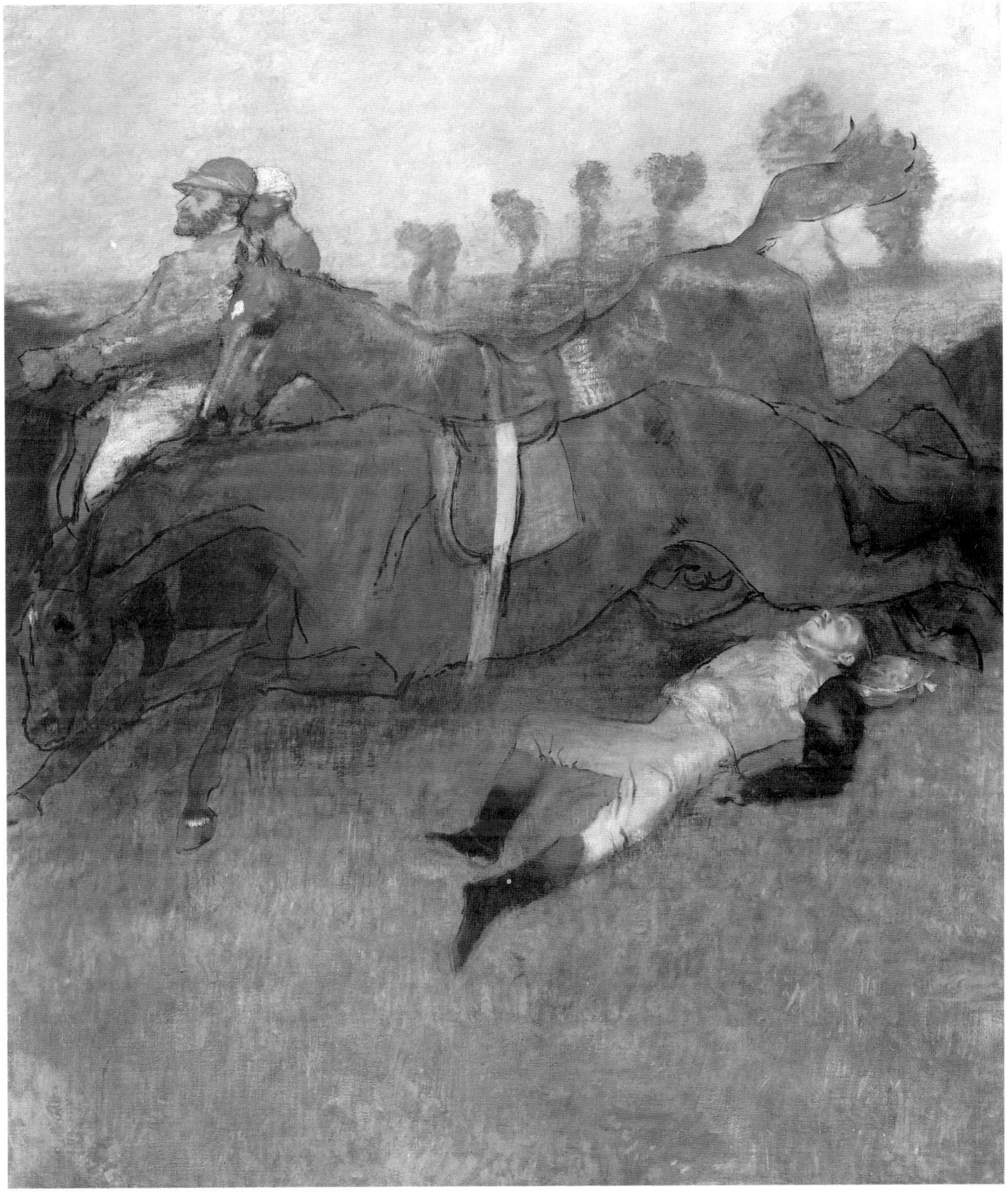

64. *The Steeplechase*, 1866, oil on canvas, 180 × 152 (L 140). Collection of Mr. and Mrs. Paul Mellon, Upperville, Virginia.

light relief from the foreground subject. While acknowledging this convention in drawings and studies, Degas has pointedly rejected most of its trappings. In *The Steeplechase*, all anecdotal matter has been swept away, taking with it the setting, the explanatory context and the narrative justification of events. The fallen jockey, once a risible extra in the drama, now takes centre stage and is seen in deadly earnest, though his relationship to the riderless horses remains unclear. As before, Degas has invoked a familiar visual vocabulary only to edit it, invert its meanings and give it contemporary resonance. By stripping away the context, he introduced uncertainty, even a sense of panic; by highlighting one individual, he stressed subjectivity and imaginative engagement; and by stressing speed, proximity and pain, he offered to critics like Zola the 'truth about the human body' they demanded.

The Steeplechase was arguably the most radical and assertive composition of Degas' early career, combining simplicity of conception with brazen modernity of subject. On the other hand, everything we know about its convoluted history tells us that the picture was laboriously put together in the studio, researched in preliminary studies and detailed drawings, and derived from a number of earlier traditions. At precisely the time Degas was working on this project, Claude Monet was notoriously engaged in the open-air painting of an even larger canvas, his *Women in the Garden* (Musée d'Orsay, Paris). There is no suggestion, however, that Degas, who almost certainly knew Monet by this date, was tempted to follow his example. Both landscape and figures were conceived and executed indoors, the rural setting apparently based on the exigencies of the composition and on improvised sketches.[69] For practical reasons, the horse and jockey could hardly have been studied at first hand and, characteristically, Degas turned to the art of the past for assistance. Apart from English lithographs, a previously overlooked prototype can be found in the work of his artistic idol of this decade, Eugène Delacroix. Delacroix's *Scene from the War between the Turks and the Greeks* (Oscar Reinhardt Collection, Winterthur) is centred on a similarly monumental horse, its legs outstretched as it leaps across the body of a fallen warrior.[70] As with his earlier borrowings, Degas has domesticated Delacroix's *motif*, excising its rhetoric and its exoticism while turning its formal structures to his own purposes. A similar process was undertaken in an even less well-known project of this period, in which Degas planned a female version of the jockey subject. Following a pattern established by Géricault, Moreau and others, he made several considered drawings of an *amazone* and her horse leaping across open terrain, a thoroughly modern image that regrettably failed to find expression in a large-scale canvas.[71]

Almost a decade after his return from Italy, pictures like *The Steeplechase* and *Mlle Fiocre in the Ballet 'La Source'* marked the launch of Degas' career as a painter of modern-life subjects, and began the public definition of his visual repertoire. Other subjects, such as portraiture and scenes of the orchestra, showed his increasing deftness in composition and his responsiveness to new visual languages, such as that of the Japanese print. At the end of the decade, a final group of horse-race pictures coincided with Degas' abandonment of the Salon, when he turned instead to the subtle effects and modest dimensions of paintings intended for dealers and private collectors. During this period, pencil, charcoal, *essence* and pastel studies proliferated, not least in the eruption of landscape studies made on the Channel coast in 1869. Now mixing with Manet and Tissot, Berthe Morisot and Fantin-Latour, Pissarro and Whistler, Degas found himself caught up in exhibition proposals and plans for secession, to say nothing of impending war and national upheaval. Before examining this extraordinary transition, one final event that confirms and illuminates the earlier phase must be noted. In 1867, along with millions of the French population and a great influx of visitors from abroad, Degas visited the Exposition Universelle on the Champ de Mars, in the centre of Paris. We know nothing of his response to the vast halls of machinery and the parades of military might, and there is no evidence that Degas, like Manet and Morisot, was inspired to paint the exhibition itself. More surprisingly, his reactions to the enormous displays of painting and sculpture, which included the private pavilions of Manet and Courbet, are barely recorded.

The only light cast on his visit emanates from the pages of one of Degas' contemporary sketchbooks. Among studies for *The Steeplechase*, *Mlle Fiocre in the Ballet 'La Source'* and *The Promenade on Horseback*, the artist wrote down a list of ten paintings he had seen and admired.[72] Two characteristics unite the pictures listed: all of them were landscapes, and all were seen in the pavilion devoted to the art of the British school. From the successful James Clarke Hook, associate of Whistler and exhibitor of *Sea Urchins* (fig. 96), to the entirely obscure Charles Lewis and his *Pièce d'orge Compte de Berkshire*, Degas' list ranged over oils and watercolours, the grand and the miniature.[73] He noted Alfred William Hunt's *Snowdon après la grêle* and one of Arthur Severn's distinctive seascapes, *Waves by Moonlight*, as well as scenes of the harvest, of fishing and of the changing seasons. Degas' selection was eccentric on several counts. Faced with a display of British painting considered 'singularly deficient' by a writer in the *Art Journal*, Degas avoided the work of such senior artists as Linnell, Roberts and Landseer in favour of their less celebrated peers;[74] and in an exhibition dominated by figure-painters, which contained 'some of the most famous pictures known in the English school', he omitted to notice such icons as Wallis's *Death of Chatterton* and Martineau's *Last Day in the Old Home*.[75] For reasons that may become clear in the next chapter, Degas reacted in an entirely idiosyncratic way, paying attention to works that ran parallel to his interests and, conceivably, with his marketing plans. On this occasion at least, we can say that Degas visited the exhibition as an active and concerned painter of landscapes.

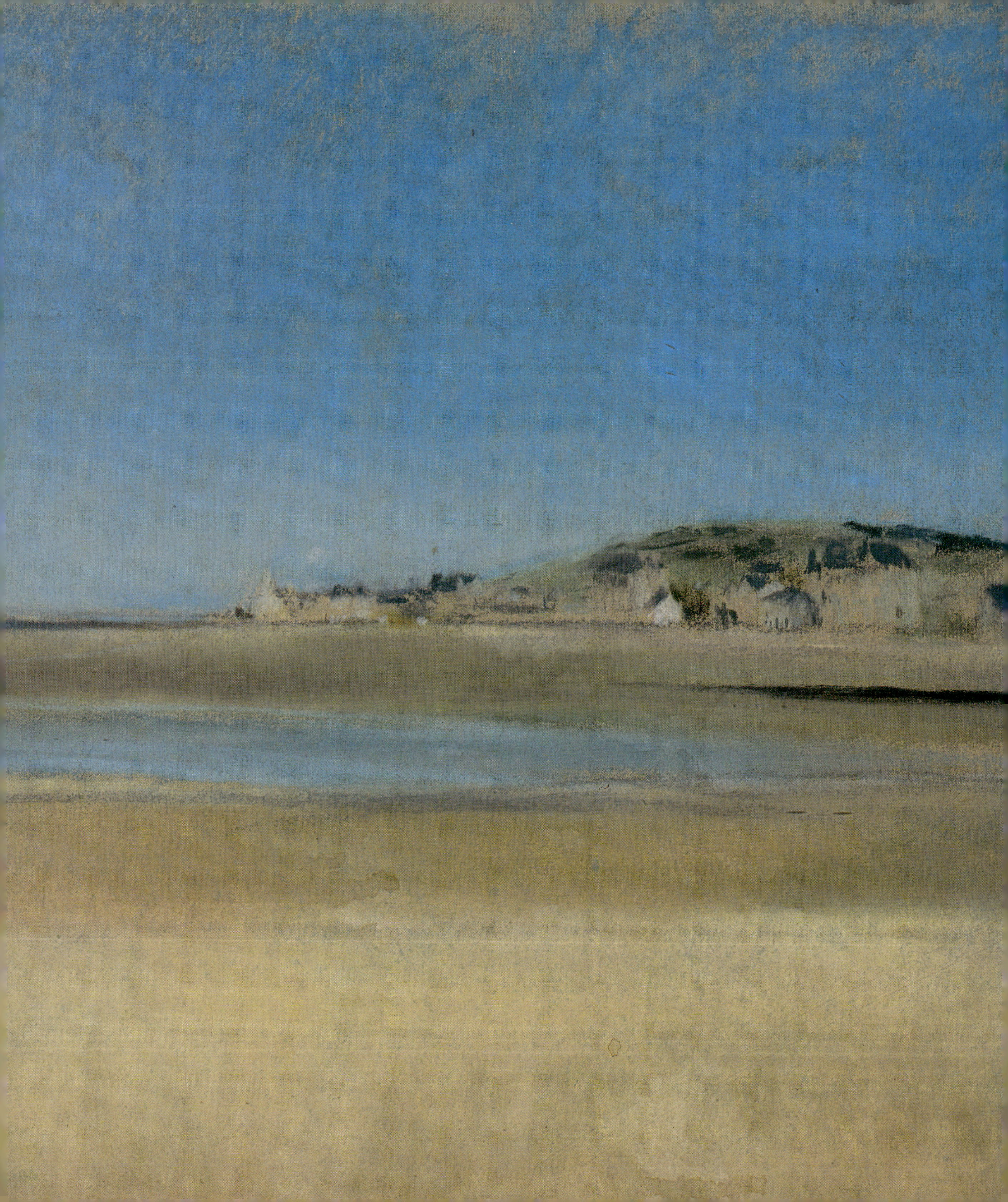

4 The 1869 Pastels

'the mysterious mingling of land and water . . .'
(Degas; letter to Tissot of 1872)

One of the surest signs of the transformation of Degas' career was the company he kept. In the early 1860s, we still find a lingering association with friends from the Villa Medici, epitomised in the small oil painting of his former mentor, Gustave Moreau.[1] By mid-decade, Degas had graduated to the circle around Manet, and we discover him paying court to Berthe Morisot and her sisters, attending the Stevenses *soirées* and exhibiting at the Salon alongside Fantin-Latour, Bracquemond and Bazille.[2] Drawings in his notebooks show a familiarity with the work of Whistler and Tissot, and contemporaries report an even broader acquaintance.[3] According to Rivière and others, Degas was a regular customer at the Café Guerbois in the later 1860s, already displaying his ferocious wit and independence of judgement in the company of Monet, Pissarro, Renoir and Manet.[4] In common with these artists, he developed a professional, if not a personal, involvement with senior colleagues such as Courbet and Boudin, exploring their technical procedures and appropriating certain of their *motifs*. Whether discussing a trip to England with Manet, painting an audacious study of Tissot, or noting down the addresses of Pissarro, Boudin and Bazille, Degas was breathing new air and contemplating fresh artistic horizons.[5]

Preoccupied as our age has become by the history of Impressionism, it is difficult to approach the late 1860s as anything other than the formative era of that movement, the inevitable matrix out of which the new art sprang fully formed. We have learned to notice the lightening of artists' palettes, the fracturing of their brushstrokes and, above all, their encounters with new kinds of landscapes, courageously begun, and often obstinately completed, out of doors. Closer study, it need hardly be said, reveals a more contradictory set of circumstances, not least as far as subject-matter is concerned. Monet, for example, worked as an occasional portraitist and chose to work on enormous compositions of the human figure in preparation for the Salon. At about the same time, Cézanne submitted a now-lost painting of a nude and a full-length portrait to the Salon jury, and devoted much of the remaining decade to allegories, bathers and narrative scenes.[6] Typically, artists such as Renoir, Bazille and Morisot pursued a variety of genres, painting portraits both urban and rural, still lifes overlapping with luncheon scenes, and landscapes with and without the human figure. In this sense, Degas' work of the later 1860s seems entirely consistent with that of his new colleagues. Like Manet, Tissot and Renoir, he had graduated from exercises in the pastoral-historic mode to panoramas of France in the Second Empire, often carrying poses and preoccupations from one mode to the other; like Monet, Morisot and Bazille, Degas had learnt to integrate the modern figure with its surrounding landscape, depicting the middle classes at recreation and at rest; and, less familiarly, Degas

65. Detail of fig. 72.

had begun to work from nature, studying *en plein air* in a way that still surprises his admirers.

Perhaps the most striking, as well as the most frequently misrepresented, evidence of Degas' atunement to the work of his contemporaries is the series of more than forty landscape pastels made in the autumn of 1869. Never exhibited as a group and still generally unknown, these pastels can be counted among the seminal achievements of his pre-Impressionist years. When mentioned at all, the pictures have been described as 'having no topographical value' or presented as 'works of the imagination', and a number of partial truths about their genesis have gained currency.[7] We are told, for example, that the series was made in Boulogne, though there is no documentary support for this view, and even that the drawings were carried out in the company of Manet, which is equally without foundation.[8] More symptomatically, it has been asserted that all the pastels were drawn indoors and, curiously, that Degas waited until his return to 'the calm of his Paris studio', after a supposedly inactive vacation, before embarking on the pictures.[9] The lack of serious attention to these works can partly be explained by their small scale, their scattered or elusive locations and, more fundamentally, the threat they pose to the orthodox view of Degas' achievement. Not for the first time, retrospective habits of thought have obscured our approach to a conceptually remarkable group of Degas' images, and only a patient scrutiny of the works themselves and the circumstances in which they were made can restore something of their original clarity.

Our first insight into the character of the pastel landscapes is the discovery that Degas himself regarded a number of them as finished, exhibitable works. The presence of his signature on nine of the sheets, and the date 1869 on eight of them, inscribed at a time when Degas rarely signed and dated works on paper, is the clearest indication of their status in the artist's eyes.[10] Despite their modest proportions and relative lack of finish, we must therefore assume that the signed works were prepared for public exhibition or offered to dealers as marketable objects, perhaps through the lucrative London trade that Degas, Manet, Tissot and Whistler were cultivating at this time.[11] Such an interpretation is consistent with Degas' ambitions and career strategies, and with his known partisanship of the exhibited drawing. Immediately before his departure for the Channel coast in 1869, for example, he had completed his first major portrait in pastel, which he submitted to the following Salon as one of his two documented exhibits. With this picture, *Mme Théodore Gobillard, née Yves Morisot* (Metropolitan Museum, New York; L 214), pastel became publicly associated with Degas' name for the first time, establishing a precedent that was to dominate much of his subsequent career.[12] On the same occasion, he wrote an open letter to the Salon jury, criticising the traditional installation of pictures and proposing detailed modifications for the forthcoming display. Among these was the suggestion that screens should be set up, 'like the English had at the Exposition Universelle', to accommodate works on paper, ensuring that 'the drawings are . . . mixed with the paintings, which they deserve'.[13] Given that Degas had particularly admired the English landscape watercolours and smaller paintings at the exhibition in question, we might go further and speculate that he, too, planned to submit his new landscapes to hang on these still-hypothetical screens.

If we look closely at one of the dated landscapes, such as *Beside the Sea* (fig. 57), the radical implications of Degas' stance become apparent. Its composition is one of almost irreducible simplicity: broad stripes or ribbons of colour cross the picture from side to side, like some ill-focused banner or a vaporous

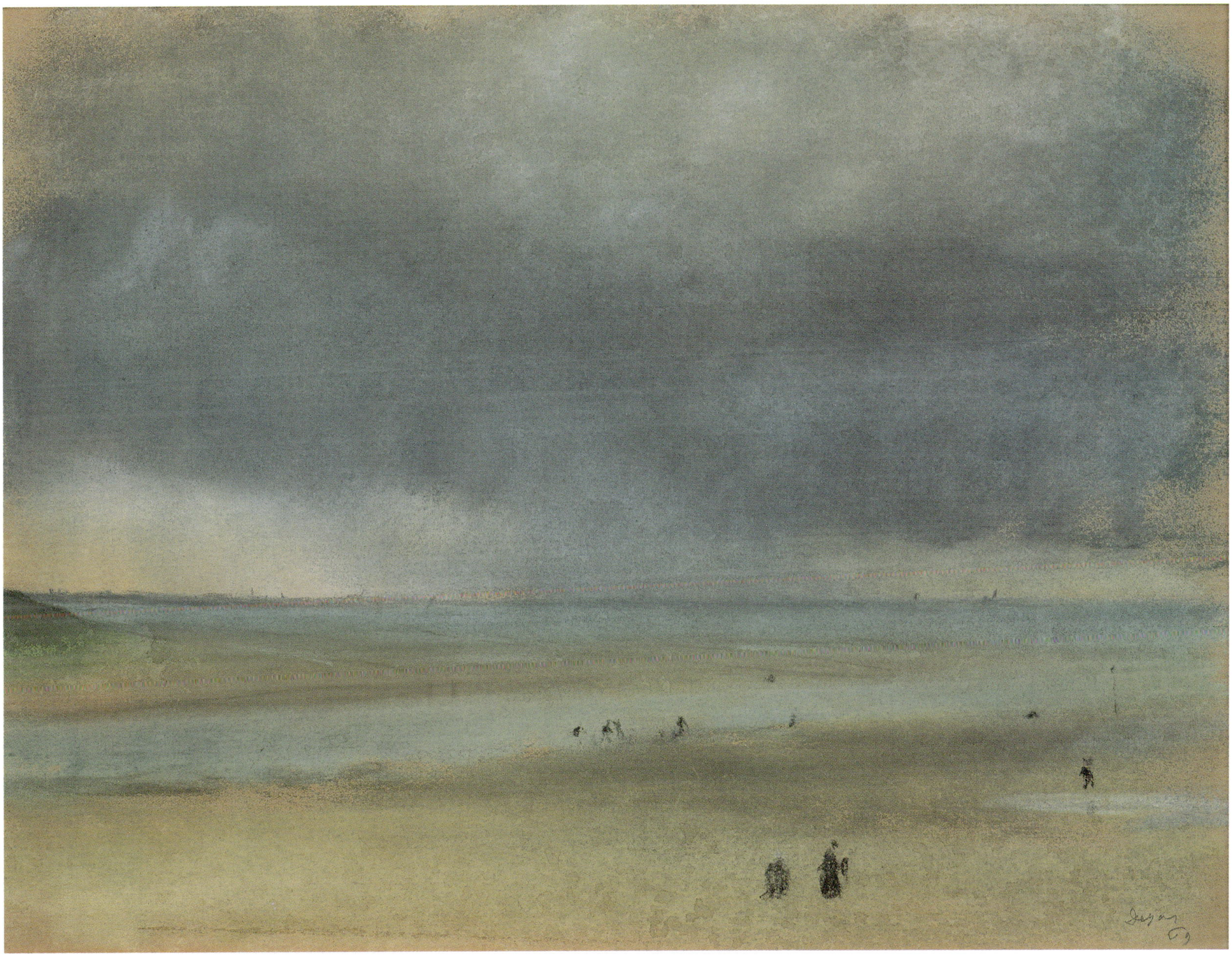

66. *Beside the Sea*, 1869, pastel, 24 × 31 (L 205). Private collection, courtesy Galerie Schmit, Paris.

latter-day abstraction. Few clearly defined forms interrupt the symmetry, even monotony, of the scene. At the left, a vestigial spur of land is sufficient to anchor the subject among cliffs and dunes, while a speckling of distant figures establishes scale, hinting at remoteness and depth. Nowhere do we find the familiar conceits and trickery of the conventional landscape painter: trees do not frame our field of view, nor do pathways and avenues indicate recession; beetling cliffs and ominous ruins are not in evidence, and industrious mariners offer no uplifting narrative. The image might almost be defined by such absences, were it not for the spaces that are opened up and the expressive potential generated. In this understated world, simple oppositions of colours evoke weather and light, atmosphere and gravity. Lightly inflected pastel describes the elemental forms of land and water, and gentle transitions of tone suggest their recession and intermingling. It is a world without anecdote, without emphasis and almost without a coherent subject. Seen in this way,

Beside the Sea and the twenty or so pastels with similar, horizontally banded compositions appear at odds with almost all Degas' earlier achievement. Even the act of drawing, so fundamental to his training and to his grand conception of art, seems lost in these tinted mists and dissolving forms. What can have persuaded Degas to make such subject-less, unhistorical works of art? What technical significance should we attach to them? And how and where did they come into being?

The origins of the 1869 pastels deserve patient examination. In late June of that year, Degas was much occupied in Paris, paying regular visits to the house of the Morisot family to make studies for his portrait of their daughter Yves.[14] 'Do you know that Monsieur Degas is mad about Yves' face, and that he is doing a sketch of her?' wrote Mme Morisot. 'He is going to transfer on to the canvas the drawing that he is doing in his sketchbook. A peculiar way of doing a portrait!'[15] His attention to the household was not entirely disinterested. The accounts of Mme Morisot and the letters of her daughters describe Degas' boisterous, even flirtatious, behaviour, and there was much talk of conquests being made and rivalries being pursued.[16] Two of the sisters, Edma and Yves, were already married, and the third, Berthe, was cautiously intrigued by Degas' advances. Whatever the significance of these manoeuvres, a month later the family had dispersed and Berthe found herself alone in Paris, where 'last Wednesday there was nobody at the Stevenses except Monsieur Degas'.[17] On 7 August, a letter from Mme Morisot noted that Degas had finally fled the capital, and for the rest of the summer the artist disappeared from their private correspondence.

Further details are difficult to establish from the fragmentary and often undated family letters, but there can be no doubt that Degas' connection with the Morisots had a number of implications for his landscape art.[18] Both Edma and Berthe had studied with Corot, the hero of Degas' youth, and later with Corot's pupil, Oudinot. By the time Degas met them, the two sisters had become accustomed to painting in the open air, using watercolour, pastel and oil on canvas to precocious effect.[19] Family holidays were spent in the Normandy village of Beuzeval, near modern-day Houlgate, where Edma and Berthe studied local *motifs* and planned their first pictures for the Salon. In 1865, Edma showed her *Cliffs at Houlgate, Calvados* (location unknown) and later made a painting of nearby Dives-sur-Mer, while Berthe produced her *Cottage in Normandy* (private collection, Paris).[20] Four years later, a visit to Brittany resulted in Berthe's magnificent *Harbour at l'Orient* (National Gallery of Art, Washington), a work already marked by the spacious and blond-hued manner of her maturity. Though their letters remain unclear on the point, some members of the Morisot family may also have revisited the Beuzeval region in the summer of 1869.[21] What is beyond doubt is that it was to this very resort, and at precisely this time, that Degas set out after leaving Paris, and it was here that he began his landscape pastels.

The reasons for the Morisot family's association with Beuzeval, and perhaps for Degas' visit in 1869, were partly personal, partly artistic. Since 1864, the Morisots had been taking holidays at an old mill belonging to Léon Riesener, cousin of Delacroix and painter of portraits, official murals and landscapes. The two families were on the friendliest of terms, Berthe painting a portrait of Rosalie Riesener in 1866 and recording an encounter with the ageing artist at the Salon of 1869, soon after she had been 'forsaken' in the crowd by Degas.[22] Riesener often stayed at the Beuzeval mill, describing in his letters the beauties of the rural landscape and the delights and frustrations of the shifting sea.[23] His

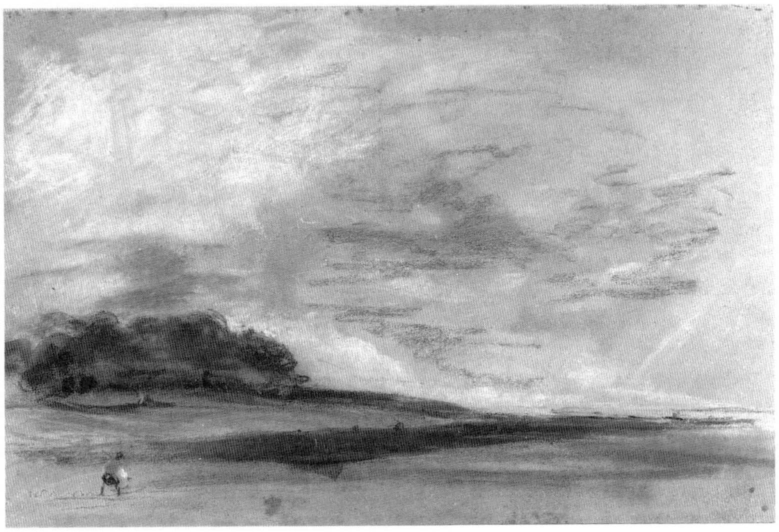

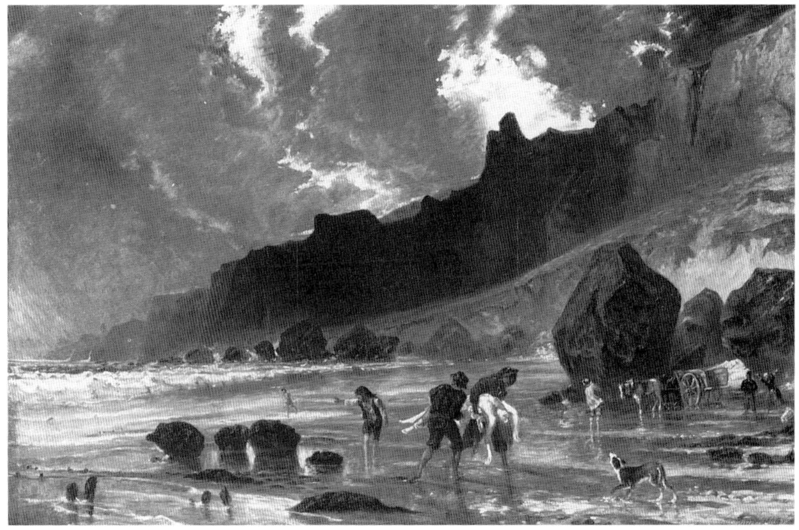

67. Léon Riesener, *Figure in a Landscape: Plain beneath a Cloudy Sky*, pastel, 28 × 42. Musée du Louvre, Paris.

68. Paul Huet, *View of the Cliffs at Houlgate*, 1863, oil on canvas, 157 × 227. Musée des Beaux-Arts, Bordeaux.

watercolours of the coastal region are of an unaffected simplicity, while his pastels of inland subjects, such as *Woman Reading in the Open Air: Landscape at Beuzeval*, suggest Delacroix at his most tranquil.[24] Some of his studies have an exceptional lightness of touch, and his pastel *Figure in a Landscape: Plain beneath a Cloudy Sky* (fig. 58), which was once attributed to Delacroix, might well have appealed to Degas at this time. A remark of Riesener's in a letter to Berthe, however, makes clear his disapproval of Degas and the other 'intransigeants', insisting that their pictures were no more than sketches or preparatory drafts, lacking the 'poetry of the ideal'.[25] Whether Degas met him at Beuzeval is not known, but some degree of familiarity with the artist and his work can be assumed, not least from the acquisition at Riesener's posthumous sale of more than seventy works for Degas' collection, including several landscape studies.[26]

An even more telling connection with Beuzeval is that of Paul Huet, close friend of both Delacroix and Riesener, and lifelong enthusiast for the Normandy coastline. For several decades, Huet had frequented the beaches and cliffs between Trouville and Houlgate, making watercolours, pastels and oil studies that were sometimes worked up into more grandiose canvases.[27] Some of these works, such as *View of the Cliffs at Houlgate* (fig. 68) are unashamedly Romantic in spirit, celebrating tempestuous seas and perilous human encounters against a background of local topography.[28] Other, like *Sea at Beuzeval* (Salon of 1861; location unknown) are daringly understated, offering only a bold strip of sky and a parallel expanse of empty waterway, interrupted by solitary figures or forlorn rocks.[29] It is pictures like these, in conjunction with their preparatory drawings, that provide the most immediate and localised precedent for Degas' works made on the Channel coast. Huet's broad, unpopulated beaches and towering skies, his first-hand observation and his use of pastel, and even his response to local landmarks, such as the cliffs at Villers known as *les vaches noires*, are closely mirrored in Degas' studies.[30] Tantalisingly, there is evidence that Huet was present in Beuzeval in 1869, but none that he made contact with Degas.[31] Their mutual familiarity with Riesener and the Morisot family, however, raises such a possibility, and a study of their informal landscapes suggests more than a coincidental affinity.

In two notebook entries that refer to his 1869 excursion, Degas wrote down addresses in the seaside resort of Villers-sur-Mer, two miles to the east of Beuzeval and Houlgate, and Etretat, some thirty-five miles further north.[32]

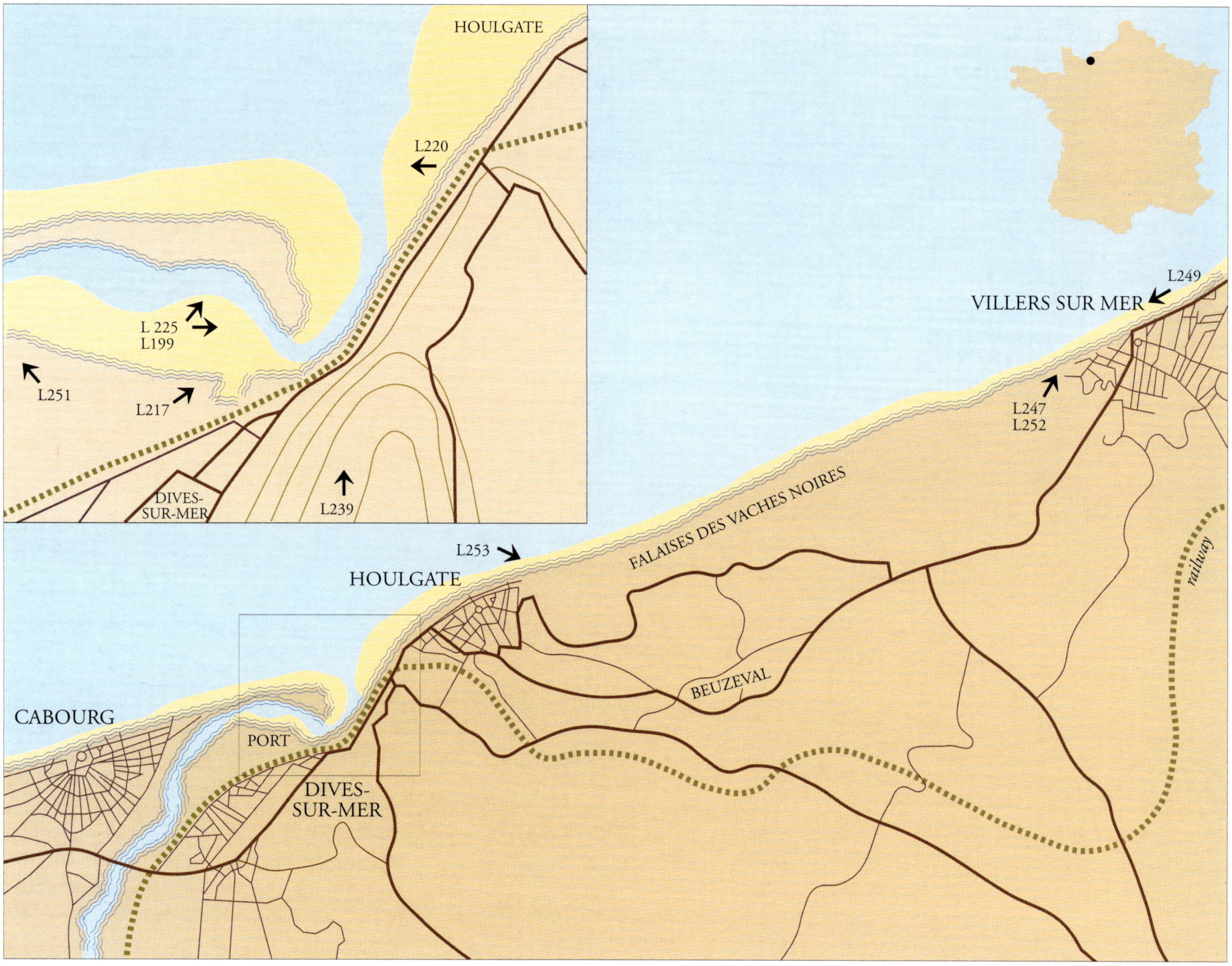

69. Map of the Normandy coast near Houlgate. Degas' pictures are identified by Lemoisne catalogue numbers, and arrows indicate their sites or vantage points.

There is no further indication that Degas travelled to Etretat, and it appears that his entire visit was spent on the short stretch of coast between Villers and Houlgate, and immediately beyond at Dives-sur-Mer (fig. 69). Crucially, it is the pastels themselves that provide the best testimony of Degas' stay. Far from being topographically vague or imaginary, approximately one third of the series are precise representations of *motifs* in the Houlgate area, many of them still clearly recognisable. Not only is the general lie of the land reflected in Degas' pictures, but the fine detail of its cliffs, estuaries, jetties and even buildings is faithfully transcribed. Of the remaining two-thirds of Degas' pastels, the majority, like *Beside the Sea*, present broad vistas of sea, sky and foreshore and thus preclude exact localisation. In these works, the glimpses of landscape are still consistent with the same stretch of coastline, but where specific features appear the pastels of the Normandy coast can be shown to be descriptive, factual and particularised.

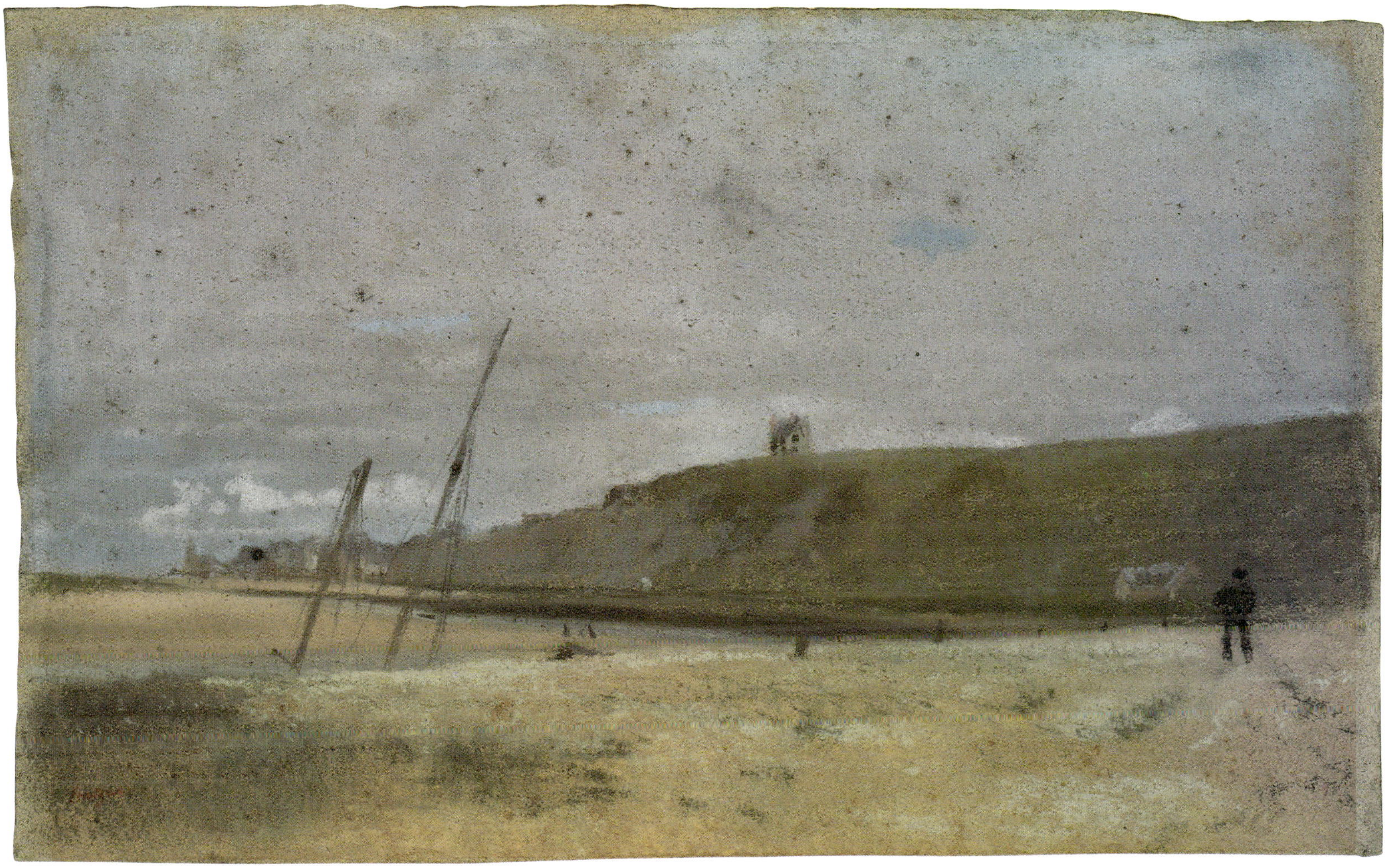

70. *Cliffs on the Edge of the Sea*, 1869, pastel, 29 × 46 (L 217). Museum of Fine Arts, Boston, Gift of Lydia Pope Tuttle and Isabel Pope Conant in memory of their father, Herbert Pope.

71. Postcard view of Dives-sur-Mer. Private collection.

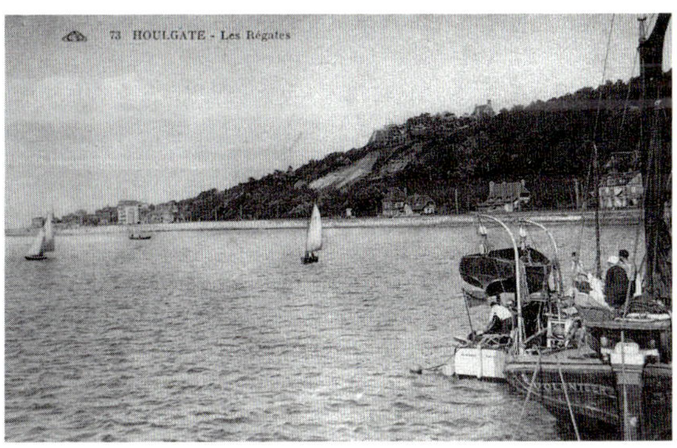

Cliffs on the Edge of the Sea (fig. 70) depicts the stretch of coast running from the harbour-front at Dives-sur-Mer (clearly visible in the foreground) to the holiday resort of Houlgate, seen as a cluster of hotels, roof-tops and a distant spire. A turn-of-the-century postcard (fig. 71) shows much the same view and underlines the documentary precision of Degas' drawing. In both images, the harsh line of the causeway connecting the two towns, which carries both road and railway links, forms a sharp horizontal division, and individual buildings, such as the gabled house on the cliff-top, bear close comparison. Where discrepancies exist, as in the greater number of harbour-side structures and more extensive tree-cover in the postcard, they are accounted for by the time lapse between pastel and photograph, and only serve to emphasise the site-specific nature of Degas' study. A second pastel of the same subject, *Houses beside the Sea* (fig. 72) was evidently studied from a more distant vantage point, and one further to the west of the harbour at Dives. As Degas confronted them more squarely, the buildings at Houlgate spread out along the waterfront, but the pale line of the causeway and the dark streak of sandbank remain as distinct as ever.

Though they once belonged to the same private collection and now hang together in the Musée d'Orsay, it has not previously been noted that *Houses beside the Sea* and a second work, *Cliffs beside the Sea* (fig. 74) form a pair.[33] When placed edge to edge, the two pictures offer a continuous panorama of estuary and cliffs, linked by the sharp accent of the causeway and the flowing silhouette of the headland. The scale of Degas' ambition and the veracity of his

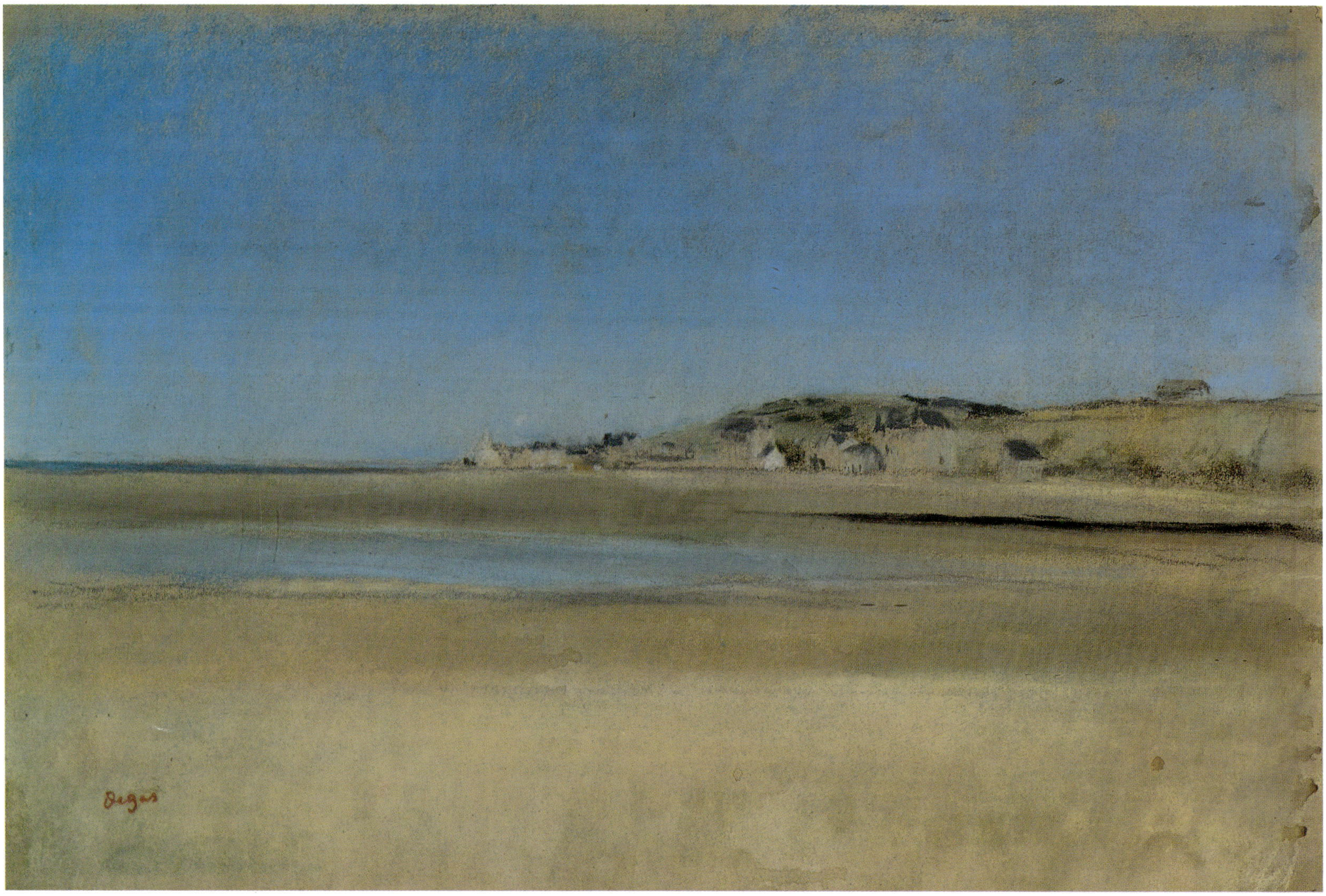

72. *Houses beside the Sea*, 1869, pastel, 32 × 46 (L 225). Musée d'Orsay, Paris.

73. View of Houlgate from Dives-sur-Mer (taken by the author).

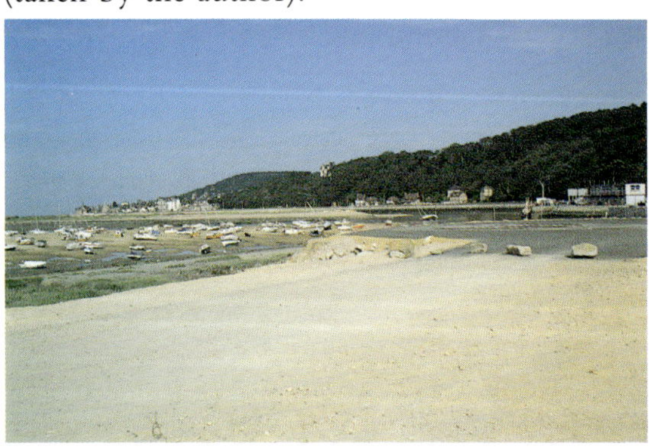

composite image can be judged from a modern photograph of the site (fig. 73). Such a comparison also draws attention to the shifts of tonality and atmosphere between the first and second pastel image; in the former, a canopy of brilliant blue is stretched over the landscape and golden highlights in the sand suggest morning or mid-day light; in its companion, cloud has covered the sky, softening the contours and deepening the colours of the promontory. That Degas should have made such exact, almost pedantic drawings of the local terrain is remarkable enough; that he should have chosen, at this point in his career, to combine two fragments of a single *motif* into a diptych-like composition, is intriguing; but that he should have recorded the actual and inconvenient appearance of sea and sky in each work, rather than a modified tonal scheme common to both, suggests a literalness in the face of nature that is rarely associated with this artist.

From his chosen site at Dives-sur-Mer, Degas could study the fishing boats as they used the harbour, the comings and goings of the tide, and the distant views of estuary and surrounding countryside. A number of pastels were clearly based on such perceptions: *Marine* (location unknown; L 203) and *Fishing Boats Moored at the Entrance to a Port* (fig. 75) represent nearby jetties and boats at anchor, while at least three works show vessels beached on the shore;[34] one of the latter,

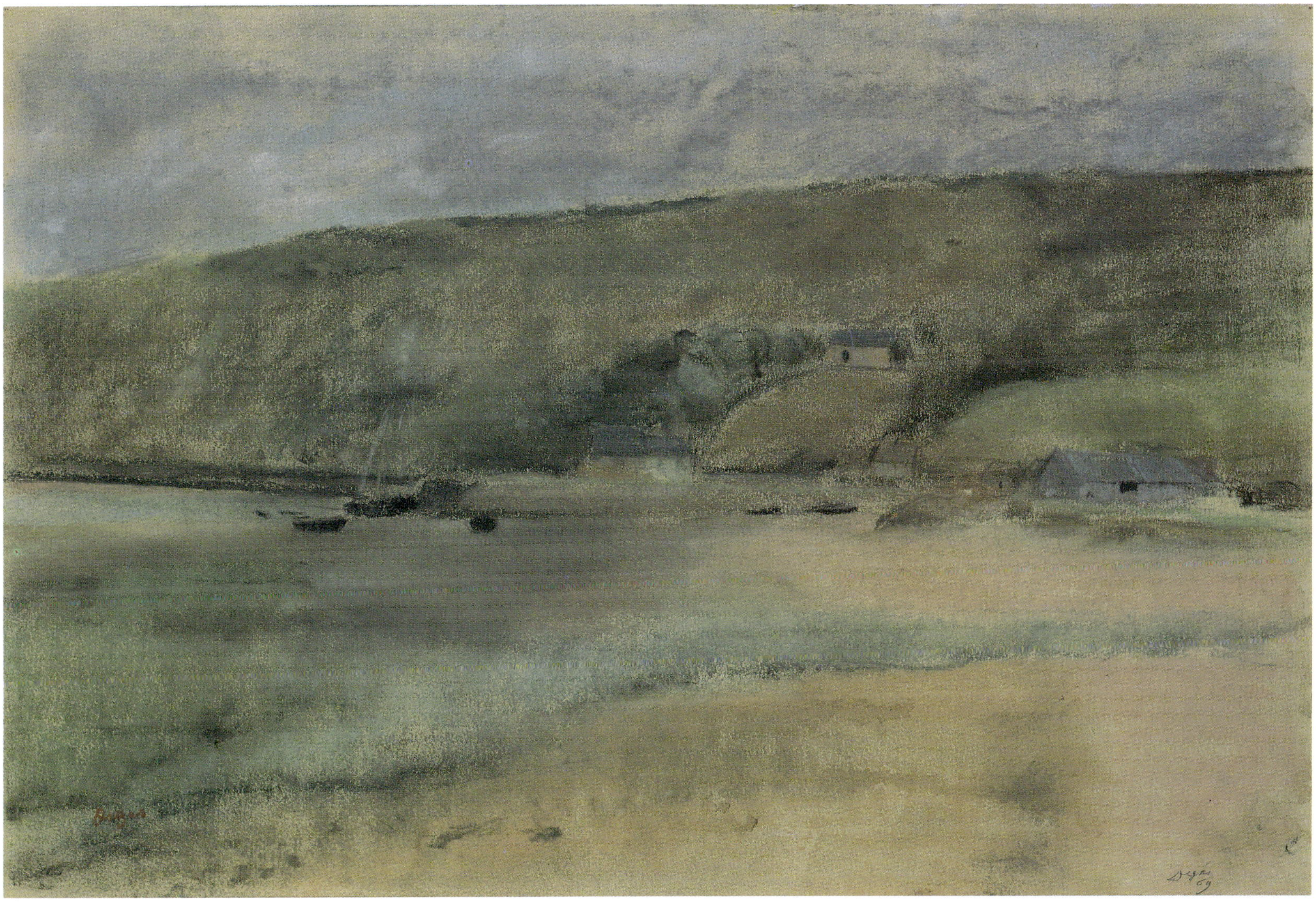

74. *Cliffs beside the Sea*, 1869, pastel, 32 × 46 (L 199). Musée d'Orsay, Paris.

Fishing Boat at the Entrance to the Port of Dives (location unknown; L 246), carries the name of the harbour in an inscription by the artist along its lower edge. Further afield, Degas made studies of dunes and beaches, glimpses of neighbouring resorts, such as Cabourg, and a number of inland *motifs*, apparently based on farms and open country along the cliff-tops.[35] One of these, *The Meadow* (location unknown; L 238) was signed by Degas and reminds us that he, like Riesener, Huet, Boudin and others, valued the coastline for its rural, as well as its marine, settings.

Another cliff-top subject, *On the Cliff* (fig. 76) is among the most simple but arresting of all Degas' Normandy images. As in his pictures of Dives, we are presented with an unexceptional corner of the landscape, but one which has been patiently scrutinised and rendered in all its modest individuality. Smudges of green and pink-brown pastel in the foreground, and occasional passages of detail in foliage and flowers, articulate an amorphous stretch of hillside, while a faintly sketched path leads us to the hill's summit. Here, an artfully disposed line of holidaymakers hint at distances covered and recreations pursued, while a dense membrane of sky announces the afternoon heat. This is the summery,

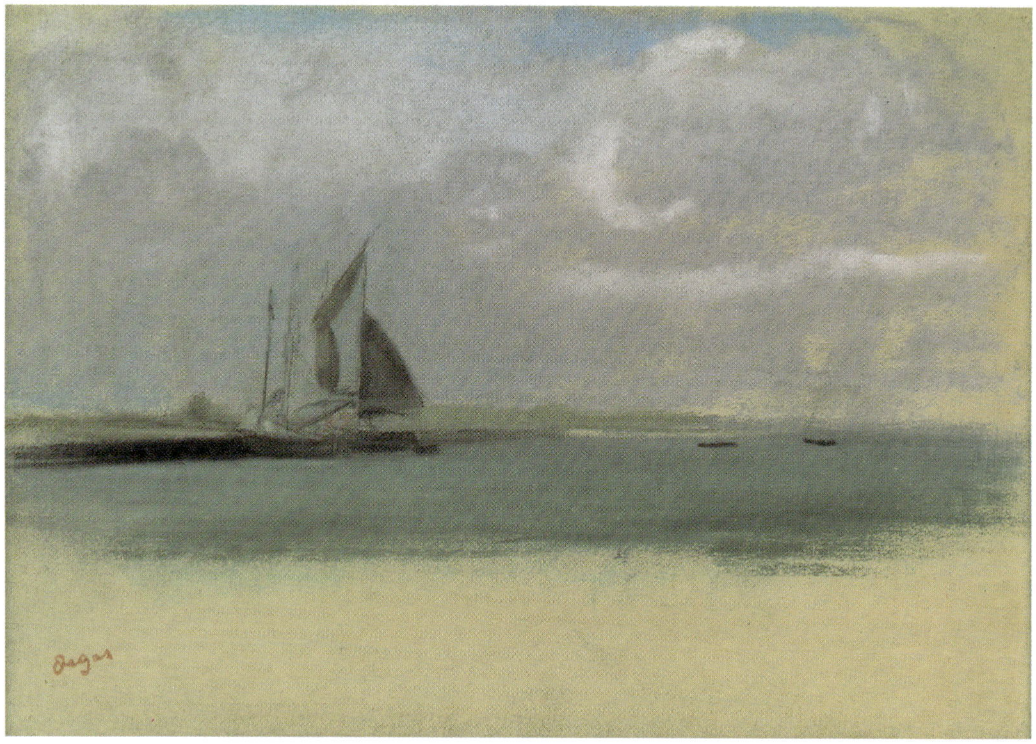

75. *Fishing Boats Moored at the Entrance to a Port*, 1869, pastel, 23 × 33 (L 251). Private collection.

carefree world of Monet's poppy fields and Renoir's boating parties, tackled by Degas with every sign of assurance. Unlike his fellow-painters, Degas has played down the possibilities for bravura display on the one hand and sentimental dalliance on the other. The fragmented mark-making and rainbow-hued colour of both artists' contemporary *La Grenouillère* canvases, for example, have no equivalent in Degas' controlled facture, and his party of walkers are kept firmly in the middle-distance.[36] Relying on local colour and inscrutable staffage, Degas has constructed an image of leisure that is at once factual, suggestive and curiously mute.

On the Cliff is drawn as if from below, the artist gazing up towards the skyline and the dense blues of the sky beyond. During his stay in the Houlgate area, Degas reversed this procedure on several occasions, installing himself high on the cliffs and peering down towards beaches, waves and the evidence of human settlement; in one of his current notebooks, he even reminded himself, 'on peut voir de haut'.[37] Immediately above Dives, the artist climbed to the crest of the very headland he had portrayed in *Cliffs on the Edge of the Sea*, to make the highly original study known as *Cliffs beside the Sea* (fig. 77). From his bird's-eye view, Degas looked down the lightly wooded face of the cliff towards the causeway linking Dives with Houlgate, following its serpentine course around the cliff and along the fringes of the estuary. Novel though this conception is, not least in its anticipation of later cliff-top pictures by Monet, Morisot and Renoir, the pastel contains a further understated surprise. At the centre of the composition, the black smudge of a railway locomotive and its distinctive plume of smoke can clearly be seen, inching their way across the causeway towards Houlgate. Diminutive and self-effacing, this is still the first image of a train in Degas' *oeuvre*, and one of the earliest in the long history of the *motif* to be found in the work of his Impressionist colleagues.[38]

It has long been a commonplace to link the growth of the railways with that of popular seaside leisure, and with the corresponding expansion of resorts such

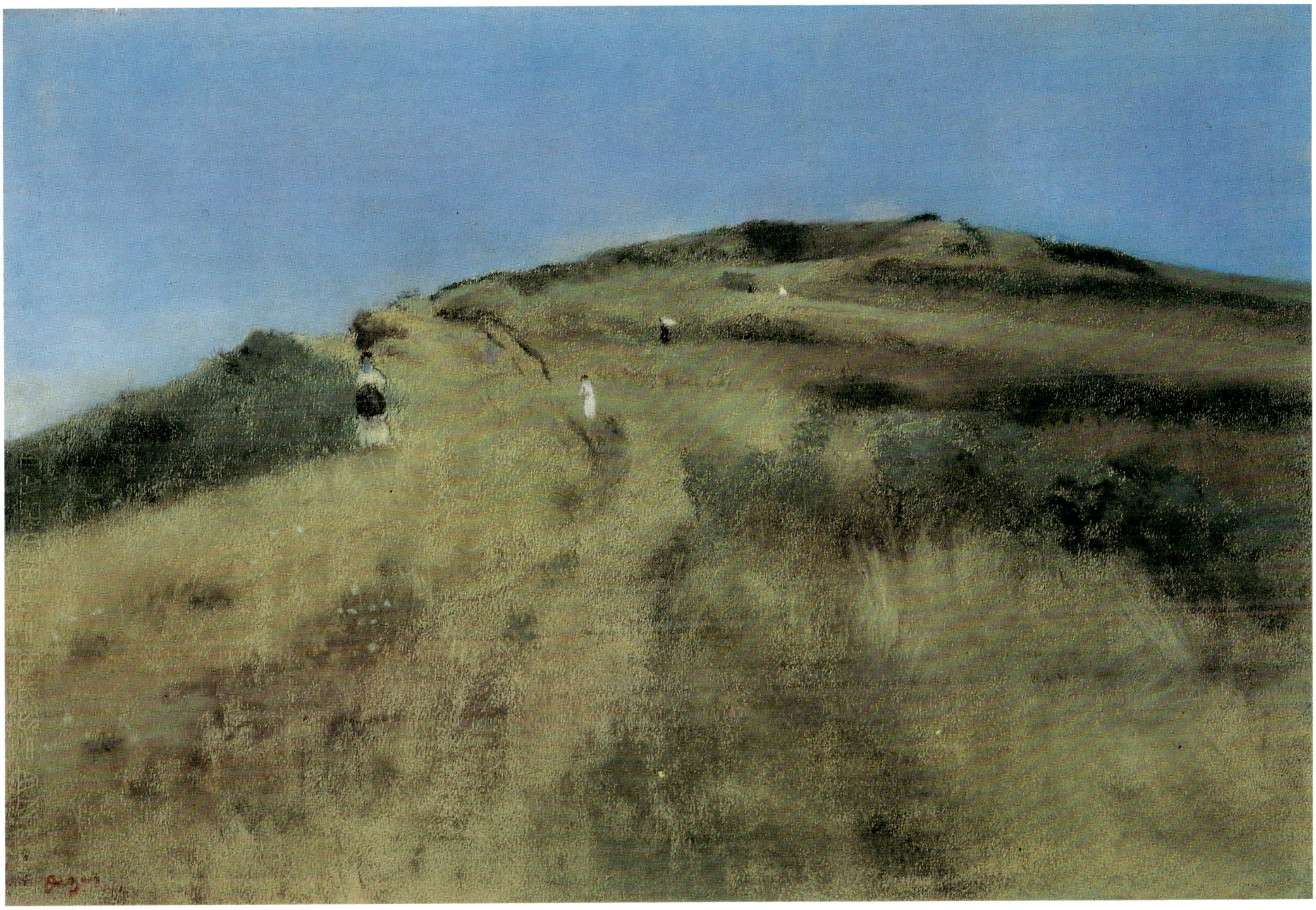

76. *On the Cliff*, 1869, pastel, 33 × 46 (L 232). Private collection.

as those visited by Degas on the Channel coast. Houlgate and Beuzeval were prime examples of this tendency, relying for much of their traffic on a line that meandered from Cabourg to Villers-sur-Mer locally, and beyond to Trouville and ultimately to Paris.[39] Degas himself presumably arrived and left by this route, and may have travelled from one site to another by train during his stay. A number of his 1869 pastels show the consequences of the railway's encroachment. Some three miles to the east of Houlgate, the station at Villers-sur-Mer had encouraged the development of its beaches and promenades, and resulted in a rash of flamboyant villas which was currently spreading along the sea-front (fig. 78). The pastel entitled *Beach at Low Tide* (fig. 79) shows the view from Villers towards the neighbouring cliff, *les vaches noires,* with one such villa perched uncertainly on its summit. Two further studies are based on views from this same cliff, looking back towards the beach and the town: *Houses on a Cliff* (fig. 80) shows the plunging descent from a group of new houses to the curving bay, while *Houses on Cliffs Surrounding a Bay* (fig. 81) describes individual gables, chimney-stacks and turrets. In both works, buildings are sharply individualised and the distinctive site, with its disrupted spaces and abrupt transitions of scale, is firmly characterised. Both also include the coastline as it sweeps round towards Trouville, a view painted several times by Caillebotte

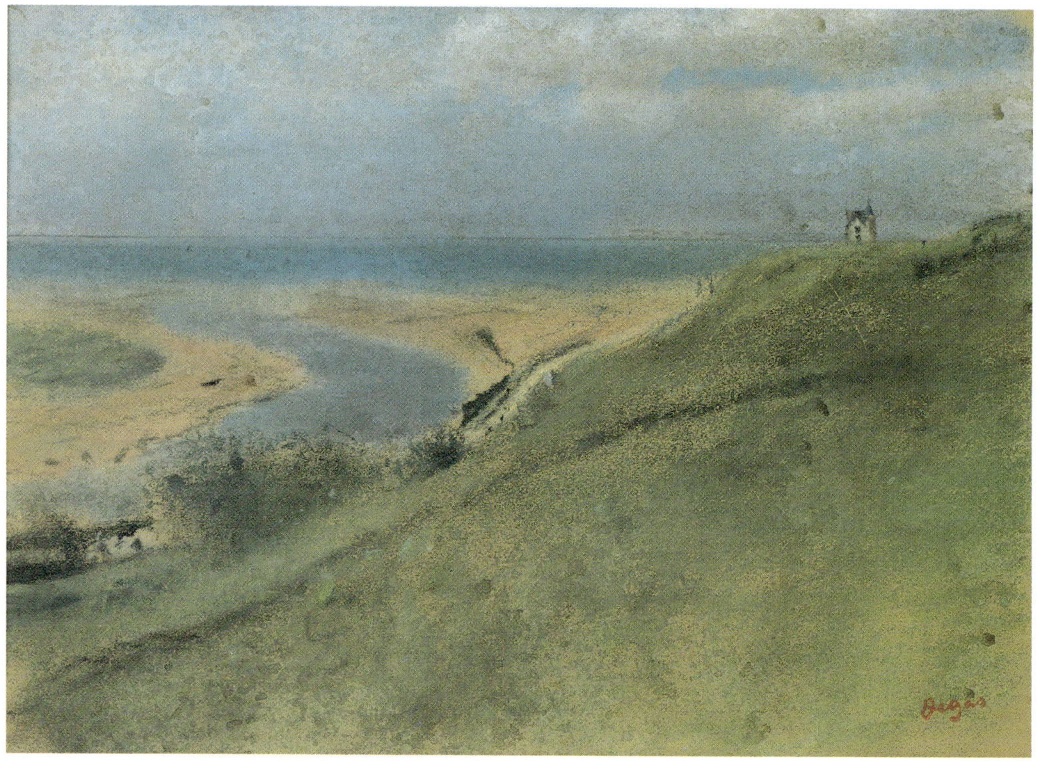

77. *Cliffs beside the Sea*, 1869, pastel, 23 × 31 (L 239). Private collection, courtesy Galerie Schmit, Paris.

two decades later, though with more emphasis on the foreground development of Villers itself.[40]

Before attempting to assess the significance of the 1869 pastels, further consideration must be given to Degas' choice of locations and *motifs*, his angles of view and points of departure. At the time of the artist's visit, the area between Dives and Villers-sur-Mer was known for its modest resorts and limited range of attractions. In contrast, the grand hotels of nearby Cabourg, which were later to be adopted by Marcel Proust, were the epitome of fashion, and the more distant towns of Tourgeville, Deauville and Trouville were both larger and more generally frequented. From contemporary guidebooks, it is clear that each of these locations had its own identity and its own distinctive clientele. Cabourg is described as 'one of the resorts most frequented today by the bourgeoisie, by tourists, by men of letters and dramatic authors'.[41] Villers and Houlgate, only recently established as holiday towns, were clearly more exclusive, Villers offering 'straight roads, bordered by pavements, embellished with beautiful houses, chalets and hotels', while we are told that 'the bathing clientele at Houlgate is not as noisy, loud or worldly as that of Trouville and Deauville; it is more aristocratic . . . Houlgate is the Faubourg Saint-Germain of the Calvados resorts.'[42]

Such accounts go some way towards explaining the preference shown by the Morisot family and Degas himself for the Houlgate and Beuzeval area, but do little to illuminate the subjects of Degas' pastels. With a perversity of orientation that was to distinguish many of his landscape activities, Degas seems to have turned his back on the fine roads and architecture, the 'aristocratic' visitors and the discreet bathers of these resorts. By comparison with Boudin, for example, who spent the summer of 1869 at Trouville, painting elegant gatherings on the sand and sparkling studies of the waterfront, Degas' repertoire seems reclusive, almost misanthropic. Even more surprising is his predilection for Dives-sur-

78. Postcard view of Villers-sur-Mer. Private collection.

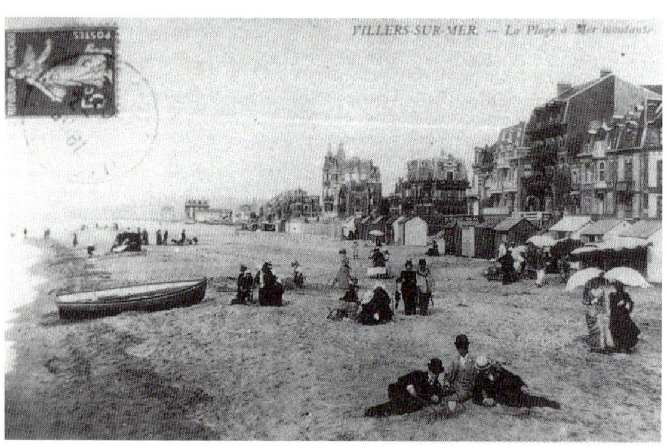

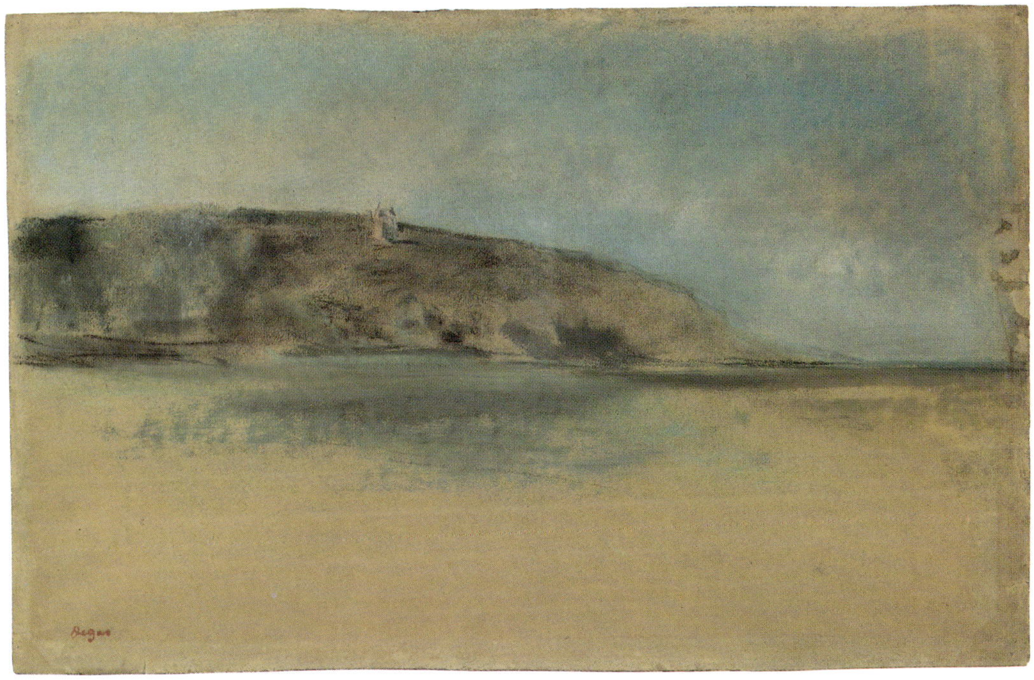

79. *Beach at Low Tide*, 1869, pastel, 30 × 46 (L 249). Von der Heydt-Museum, Wuppertal.

Mer, the site of at least ten of his identifiable pastel studies. Based on a medieval settlement and claiming (along with a dozen other towns in this area) to be the port from which William the Conqueror sailed, Dives had traditionally earned its livelihood from its harbour and fishing fleet. When the local economy began to change, the town developed as a provision centre for the grander resorts nearby, gradually attracting industry and exploiting its railway links to expand a number of commercial concerns.[43] Profoundly unfashionable, its facilities could be dismissed by the compiler of the regional guide as 'neither casino nor sea-bathing; the beach is covered with pebbles'.[44]

By neglecting the boulevards of Cabourg and Houlgate, Degas may simply have exercised his right to solitude; by disregarding the landmarks and the natural features of the area, such as the cliffs at Houlgate painted by Huet, Riesener and Morisot, he detached himself from a localised painting tradition; but by opting for the harbour-front at Dives, Degas chose the least glamorous and the least tractable material from a celebrated stretch of coastline. Admittedly, he did not turn inland and confront the factories and railway-sidings of the Dives valley; it was to be some years before artists like Monet, Pissarro and Caillebotte felt able to tackle such subjects with confidence.[45] But, in positioning himself at Dives and observing its traffic, by emphasising the unlovely and the quotidian, and by avoiding the *chic* of the promenades, Degas distanced himself from many of the assumptions and practices of his day. His pictures of fishing boats, deserted jetties and provincial railway tracks remind us of his independence of vision, just as his views of empty beaches hint at a temperamental distinction from many of his peers. Modesty may have played its part; in effect, these were the first pastel landscapes of his career and Degas may well have preferred to experiment in isolation. But, before long, his bird's-eye views and sequential scenes would achieve currency in other guises, and his taste for the neglected side of the landscape, and for its unstudied and unsung poetry, would find other forms of expression.

Almost half the forty or so pastels made on the Normandy coastline lack any recognisable land mass and thus resist our best efforts to find their locations.

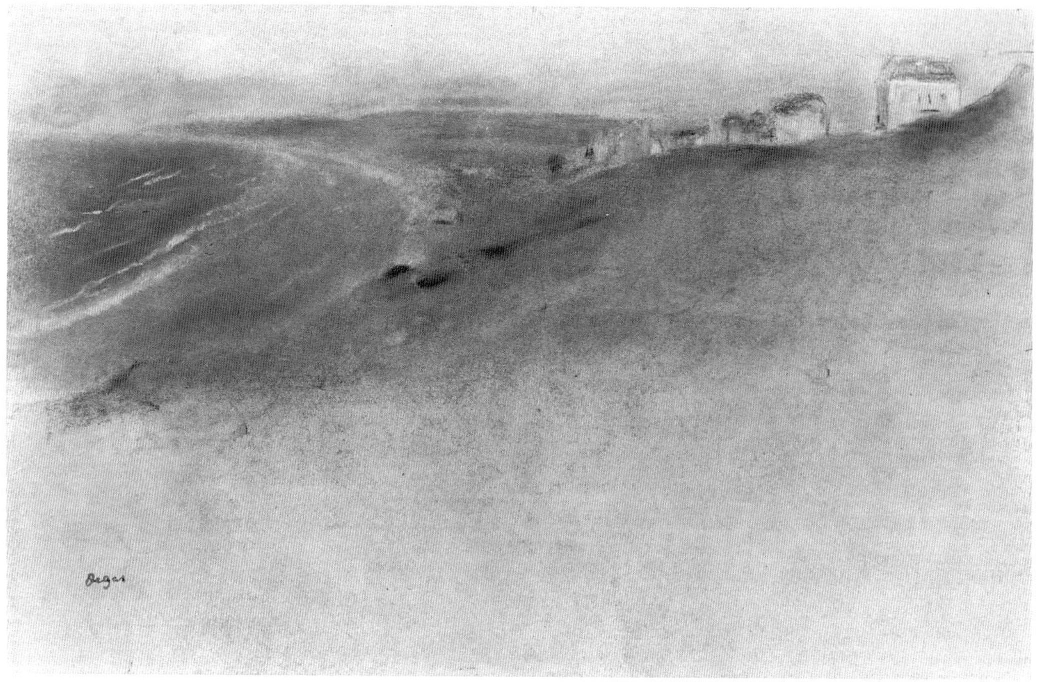

80. *Houses on a Cliff*, 1869, pastel, 31 × 47 (L 247). Wadsworth Atheneum, Hartford, Conn., Bequest of Anne Parrish Titzell.

These works, such as *Beach at Low Tide* (fig. 82), *Beside the Sea* (fig. 83) and *Seascape at Sunset* (fig. 85), present broad expanses of beach, sky and sea, relieved only by the play of clouds and the ant-like activity of distant figures. More than any other pictures of this period, such pastels have been seen as the fanciful outpourings of Degas' imagination, the products of his studio rather than of direct encounters with nature. Following our identification of many of the Dives and Villers scenes, this assumption can no longer be sustained. Given that Degas expended so much ingenuity on the transcription of local subject-matter, from estuaries to harbours and from cliffs to newly built villas, it seems improbable, to say the least, that he would have adopted a separate set of procedures when confronted by a beach or a cloudscape. In scale, technique and finish, the sea studies are interchangeable with the rest of the series, and there is every reason to believe they were carried out in the same circumstances and with similar intentions.[46]

Some indication of Degas' aims in producing these pictures can be found in a sequence of annotations made by the artist, both in the pages of his notebook and on the drawings themselves. In a little-quoted passage, he wrote:

> Villers-sur-Mer, sun-set, cold and dull orange-pink, whitish green, neutral, sea like a sardine's back and clearer than the sky. Line of the seashore brown, the first pools of water reflecting the orange, the second reflecting the upper sky; in front, coffee-coloured sand, rather sombre.[47]

On the lower edges of at least two drawings, Degas added similarly suggestive notes of colours and tonal relationships, and on the reverse of *Beach at Low Tide* he reminded himself that

> The hillocks within the large grey-green clouds are outlined one against the other and stand out against the clear areas much more sharply; the line of the sea sharper and the colour more silvery-green.[48]

These are not the words of an artist indifferent to landscape, still less of a painter

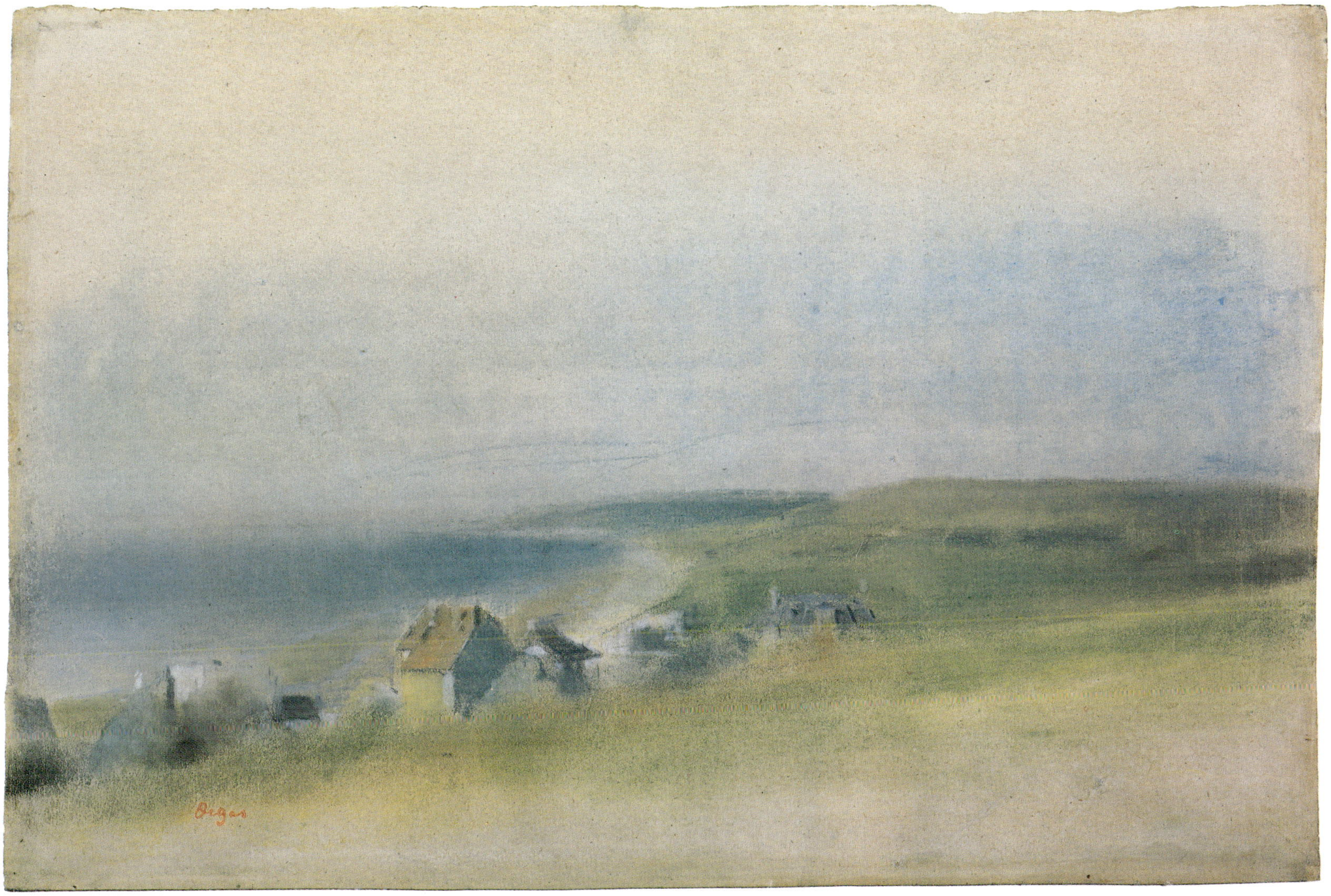

81. *Houses on Cliffs Surrounding a Bay*, 1869, pastel, 32 × 48 (L 252). Private collection.

planning 'nebulous studies' on his return to a distant Paris studio.[49] In the same way that his responses to the scenery of Italy a decade earlier had captured the intensity of that confrontation, these words seem to bridge the divide between observation and picture-making. In the late 1850s, Degas had struggled with pencil, ink and watercolour to translate his perceptions into two-dimensional imagery, adding vividly written summaries of changing light and weather conditions. Now, he could use the medium of pastel, combining the effects of colour, line and tone in a single process that almost kept pace with his perceptions. With pastel, he could scatter powdery hues across the paper to indicate coffee-coloured sand or silvery-green sea, and touch in the fine detail of a roof-top or ship's sail. With pastel, too, he could respond to the finest nuances of the atmosphere, working rapidly as weather and wind began to change. Here, it is notable that almost all the seascapes and beach scenes are depicted under cloudy, overcast skies. None of them, however, is generalised, and each proposes a subtle variation on the theme of sea mist, sun-lit haze or impending rain. Seen in this way, the pastels are as much part of Degas' documentary project as his land-based *motifs*, and even at their most vaporous must be seen as particularised accounts of local circumstances, rather than as the efflorescences of a city-dweller's mind.

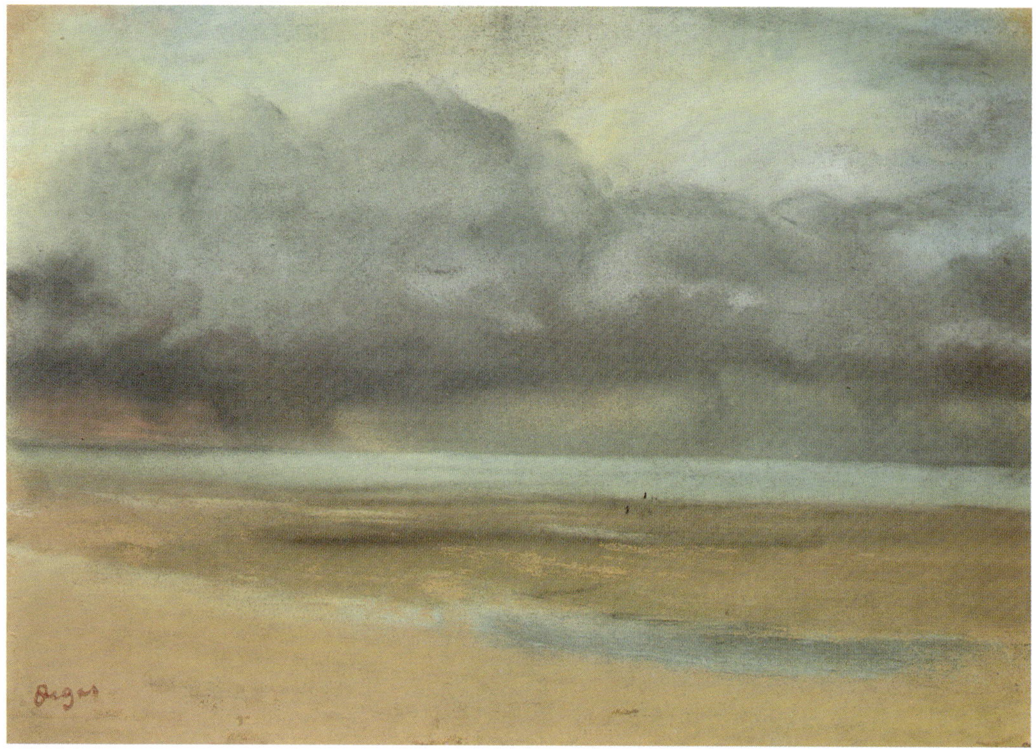

82. *Beach at Low Tide*, 1869, pastel, 22 × 31 (L 234). Private collection.

Finely observed and largely descriptive though they may be, Degas' pastel seascapes remain among his most uncharacteristic productions. The sheer *emptiness* of these scenes, devoid of central focus and even of nameable subject-matter, would be disconcerting in the output of most artists, but in the work of Degas, successor to Ingres and legendary scourge of the landscapist, they demand explanation. Much, if not quite all, their strangeness can be dispelled by returning them to the context in which they were made. As the earlier chapters of this book have shown, Degas was continuously and fruitfully in contact with the landscape painters of his day, and alert to historic precedent in his choice of both *motif* and procedure. In his formative years, he tried his hand at most of the categories of landscape then current, from the late-romantic idylls of Delacroix and the steeplechase scenes of Pollard to the craggy rocks of Courbet and the marines of Edouard Manet. A further theme of the period, though one that as yet lacks a name, seems to have found a place in Degas' repertoire. This might be called the 'subject-less' landscape, a celebration of emptiness, space and the echoing void that pervades the art of the 1860s. Characterised by towering skies and uneventful foregrounds, this virtual non-*motif* approached the numinous on the one hand, the meteorologically exact on the other. Found in Chintreuil and Huet, Delacroix and Courbet, Boudin and Jongkind, Whistler and Zandomeneghi, such a narrative-free view of nature appears to offer a lineage and a syntax for Degas' 1869 pastels.

The amorphous, significantly empty landscape has its ultimate origins in the 'tinted steam' of Turner and the soulful expanses of Caspar David Friedrich, but its definitive mid-century statement was in Courbet's beach and sky scenes.[50] In *Low Tide at Trouville* (fig. 84), for example, one of a group of about thirty similar canvases made in 1865, Courbet has stripped away all the traditional properties of the marine *tour de force*, creating his picture 'from nothing or almost nothing', as a contemporary wit remarked.[51] No picture of Courbet's era, nor perhaps of any other, is entirely free of matter, but it is clear that

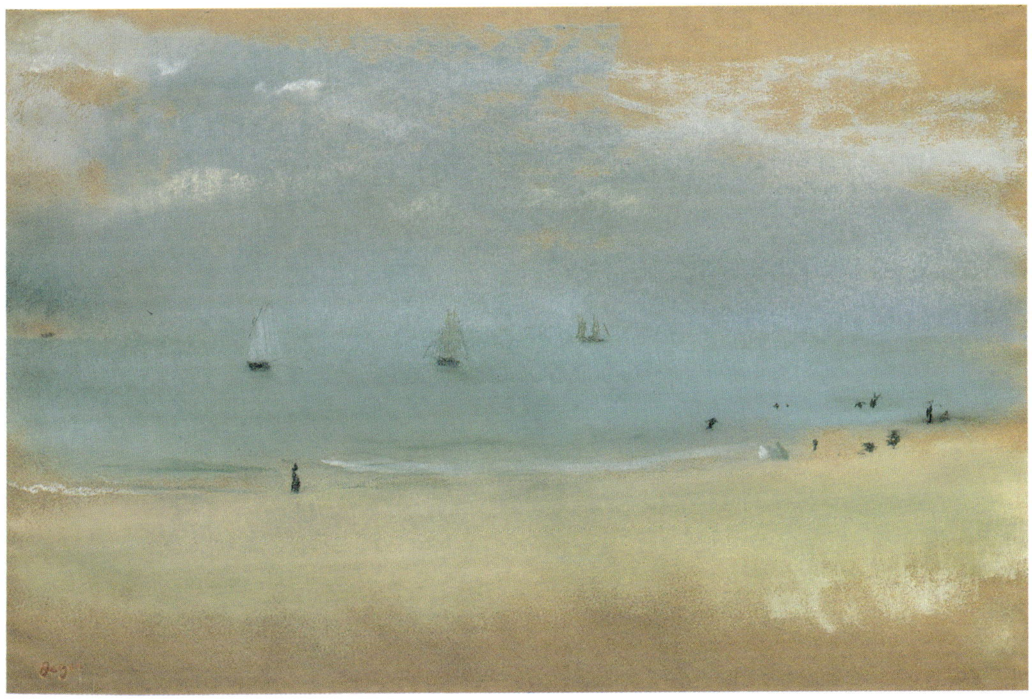

83. *Beside the Sea*, 1869, pastel, 30 × 46 (L 242). Musée d'Orsay, Paris.

neither than the low tide of the title nor the resort of Trouville are the true focus of our attention. Though Courbet has lifted the traditional burdens of the landscape, he has perhaps imposed others, each more radical and indeterminate than the last. Here the subject might be Nature, abstracted and elemental, or images 'of reverie and space', as Courbet described them in a letter.[52] Conversely, it could be the artist himself, Gustave Courbet, whose magnificent sensibility we are asked to admire and whose visual field we momentarily share. Yet again, the subject might be the very act of painting, made evident in crusts of pigment and anxious flurries of brushwork, to say nothing of the scrapings and trowellings of the knife.

Among Courbet's precursors, admirers and acolytes, a remarkable number of individuals arrived at, or made variations upon, such disembodied visions of the landscape. In almost every case, we know that Degas was familiar with the works in question and must have positioned himself with respect to their achievement. One of Delacroix's few unpopulated marines, *The Sea at Dieppe* (Louvre, Paris) was exhibited twice in 1864, at a time when Degas was much in awe of the artist, and may have provided a touchstone for his later seascapes, just as *Ovid among the Scythians* had haunted his equestrian scenes.[53] Tellingly, Delacroix's image of a deserted, wind-ruffled expanse of sea includes, in its foreground, the prow of a beached boat. Though hardly emphasised, it is sufficient to suggest a narrative or even an explicitly tragic reading of the scene, just as Courbet's occasional beach-side figures hint at the heroic. Variations of this device can be found in the watery vastnesses painted by Antoine Chintreuil, where remote and solitary fishing boats accentuate the loneliness of the ocean. Titles such as *L'Espace* (Musée d'Orsay, Paris) spell out the expressive aims of such scenes, encouraging the kind of response we find in Champfleury's 1866 essay on the artist; 'One does not describe a landscape by Chintreuil; it is an emotion.'[54]

84. Gustave Courbet, *Low Tide at Trouville*, 1865, oil on canvas, 59.6 × 72.6. Walker Art Gallery, Liverpool.

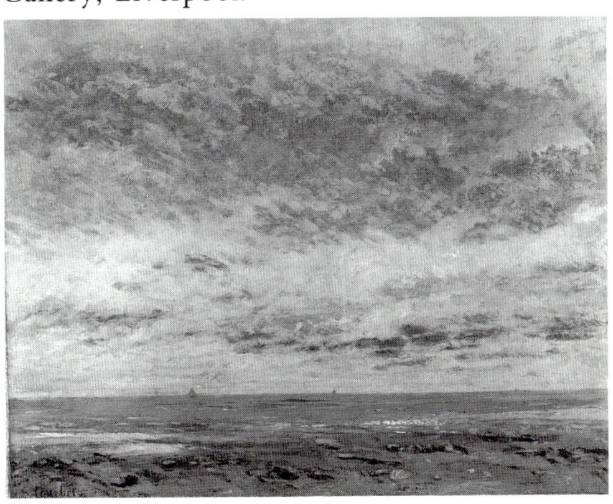

While distancing himself from such flights of fancy, James McNeill Whistler made the non-subject into his personal and anarchic speciality. In the early

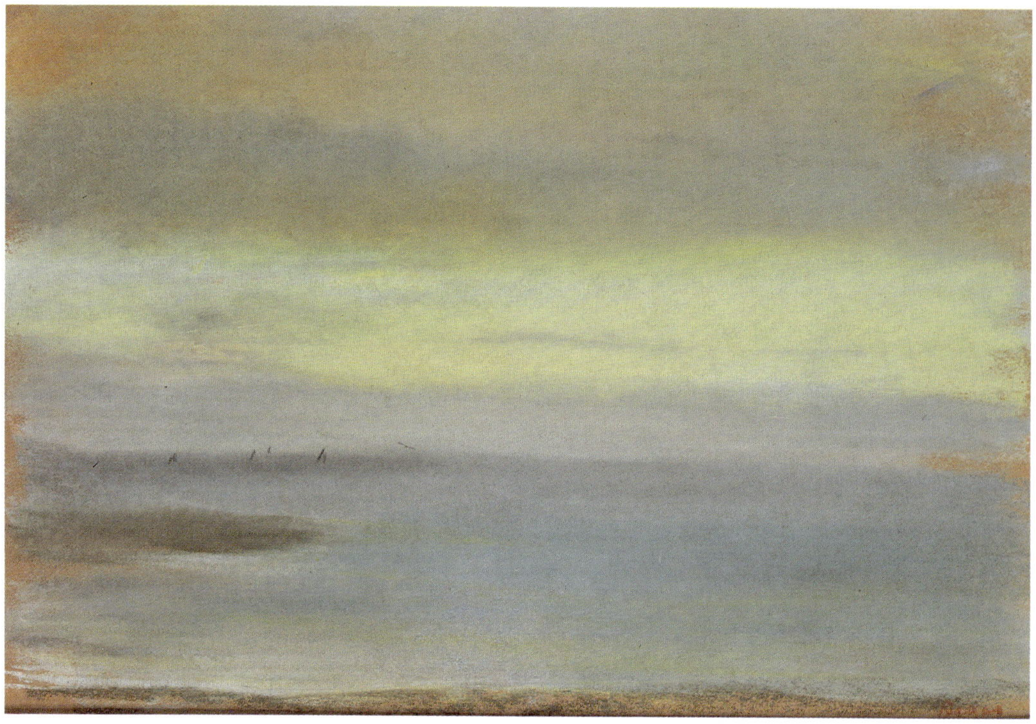

85. *Seascape at Sunset*, 1869, pastel, 24 × 31 (L 240). Dr. and Mrs. John Robertson.

1860s, his broadly stated seascapes tended to centre on a majestic wave or a poignant foreground figure, but by the middle of the decade he had put such pretexts behind him. His bluntly titled oil painting *Sea and Rain* (Museum of Art, University of Michigan) was executed at Trouville in the company of Courbet, and like the work of his mentor concerns itself with the grandest effects and the simplest of means. Responding to the picture in 1867, a British critic summarised it as 'Earth, air, and sea repeated by three splashes on the canvas, a splash to an element', while another writer claimed, 'we wish to describe Mr Whistler's picture, but the difficulty is that there is so little to describe'.[55] Contrary to the assumptions of many writers, Whistler does not seem to have reached a similar economy of manner in his pastel landscapes until the following decade. Indeed, pastel itself only took on significance in his output, as it did in Degas', in the late 1860s.[56] Despite the close involvement of Whistler and Degas at this period, it seems unlikely that Whistler's example stimulated Degas' Normandy seascapes and more probable, if influence occurred, that it proceeded in the opposite direction.

Shortly before he embarked on his own expansive and largely unpopulated landscapes, Degas had a number of opportunities to see the work of those artists who had preceeded him in the genre. At the 1867 Exposition Universelle, he took note of several marine painters admired by Whistler, such as Arthur Severn and James Clarke Hook, who both favoured broad vistas and subdued tonality.[57] On the same occasion, he must have visited Courbet's independent show at the Rond Pont d'Alma, where at least ten of the artist's Trouville waterscapes were on view.[58] Nearby, a marine by Manet was included in his own private pavilion, while two atmospheric harbour scenes by Whistler could be seen in the Salon display.[59] Two years later, at the Salon of 1869, Chintreuil's *L'Espace* was shown to the public. For all his apparent familiarity with such works, however, and in spite of his demonstrable participation in their choice of theme, Degas' Normandy series stands apart from their achievement. Unlike each of these artists, Degas chose to work in pastel and to respond in a matter of minutes, rather than hours or days, to the subjects he encountered. His views of Dives and Villers, though made on precisely the same stretch of coast as that frequented by his peers, are conspicuously lacking in gilded sunsets and meaningfully isolated barques. To a remarkable extent, Degas' pastels are free of the latter-day Romanticism of Courbet's generation and equally unmarked by the nascent aestheticism of Whistler's. His skies are generally blank or untroubled, and such boats and figures as appear in his compositions seem haphazard rather than poignant. Like any other landscapist, of course, Degas was at the mercy of the weather that prevailed during his stay; unlike most of them, however, he seems to have accepted, even welcomed, the banality of the atmosphere and the uneventfulness of the seashore. His pastels are neither metaphysical nor exquisite, but essentially matter-of-fact.

An alternative response to the same set of *motifs* and circumstances, and one that was arguably closer to Degas' own, is represented by the work of Eugène Boudin. Exactly ten years older than Degas, Boudin had been painting the resorts of the Channel coast for almost two decades, making oil and pastel studies in the open air but submitting more extended, polished works to exhibitions in Paris, Le Havre and elsewhere. As early as 1859, Baudelaire had made a historic visit to Boudin's studio and admired 'several hundred pastel-studies, improvised in front of the sea and the sky', observing that the artist recorded the date, time and wind direction in the margin of each drawing.[60] Baudelaire also noted, with obvious approval, that Boudin 'knows quite well that all this will have to be turned into a picture, by means of the poetic impression recalled at will; and he lays no claim to be offering his notes as pictures'.[61] It is difficult to imagine that the paintings later produced in such numbers by Boudin, with their dogged representation of beaches, holiday-makers and cloudy skies, continued to fulfil Baudelaire's expectations, and it is instructive that Boudin's later champions tended to admire the prosaic honesty and literalness, rather than the poetry, of his work. During the 1860s, painters like Monet and Whistler learnt much from the practical example of Boudin, while a new generation of critics, among them Chesneau and Zola, applauded his manifest sincerity. A cryptic note in a sketchbook suggests that Degas met Boudin early in the decade, and it can confidently be assumed that he, like the rest of his colleagues, was familiar with the older man's achievement.[62] Though their dates of acquisition are not known, Degas' collection included two pastels by Boudin of precisely the kind that Baudelaire had praised, among them the vigorous *Seashore in Normandy* (fig. 86).

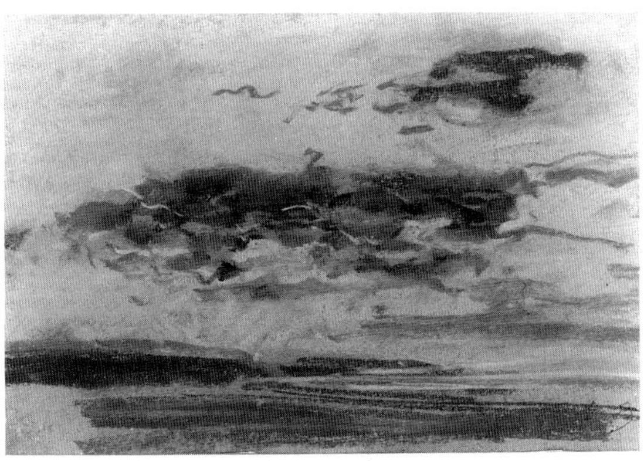

86. Eugène Boudin, *Seashore in Normandy*, *c.*1860–4, pastel, 14 × 20. Private collection, courtesy Galerie Schmit, Paris.

In the years immediately preceding Degas' Channel coast visit, Boudin was generously represented in public exhibitions and frequently discussed by contemporary critics. Writing of the 1868 Salon, Zola welcomed a new generation of landscape artists, including Pissarro and Monet, who scorned to paint 'flowers in Spring, moonlight, sunrises and sunsets' and preferred such qualities as 'exactitude', 'gravity' and 'a disdain for display'.[63] Discussing Boudin's *Jetty at Le Havre* in similar terms, Zola drew attention to his 'exquisite originality, his vast silvery-grey skies, his tiny figures with such a fine and spiritual touch. There is a rare correctness of observation in the marks, in the attitudes of these figures grouped on the brink of such vastness.'[64] In rejecting the 'sunrises and sunsets' of latter-day Romanticism, and celebrating the simple pleasures of Boudin's 'silvery-grey skies', Zola expressed in rudimentary terms one of the central tenets of pictorial Realism: that experience that was mundane and local, as opposed to exceptional and historic, could form the basis of great art. Repeatedly, Zola applauded the choice of the commonplace *motif*, rendered in all its banality and without recourse to 'piquant touches' and the 'facility of the hand'.[65] For Zola, such ordinariness was raised to the level of art by the painter's 'individuality'. When discussing Pissarro, he admired the artist's 'temperament'; in his account of Monet, he wrote of his search for the painter's 'personality'; and in responding to Boudin, he balanced his 'correctness of observation' with an emphasis on his 'exquisite originality'.[66]

In Zola's terms, Degas' landscapes of the late 1860s are curiously resistant to definition. If Zola had seen the pastels made at Dives and Villers in 1869, just as Baudelaire had discovered Boudin's studies a decade earlier, he might have found in them many qualities that corresponded with his own published views. It would have been evident, for example, that Degas was not 'one of those official painters of seascapes who are unable to paint a wave without exploding a firework' and that Degas preferred to show waves 'like those he had seen, dull blue-green and dirty'.[67] The critic would also have approved of Degas' 'correctness of observation', just as he had in Boudin, and admired the same 'sympathy towards modern subjects' that he found in Monet.[68] In this and other contexts, we sense an affinity between Degas and Zola, an affinity made more palpable in their mutual acquaintance at this time with artists such as Manet and writers like Edmond Duranty.[69] What the critic may have found lacking, however, is that conspicuous originality of temperament he extolled in Degas' peers. In comparison with the vigorous pastel flourishes and brush-marks of Boudin, Degas' facture seems detached, almost anonymous; beside the 'frankness' and 'ruggedness' of Monet, he can appear effete; and in contrast to the 'maladroitness' Zola so valued in Pissarro, his educated hand verged on the suave.[70]

In the last analysis, Degas' 1869 pastels should perhaps be located at some metaphorical crossroads, where several strands of current landscape activity converged. Looking backwards, he had acknowledged the expansive, non-narrative tradition of Romanticism, exploiting its freedoms while rejecting the more grandiose of its aspirations. With many of his colleagues, he had also travelled along the path of Realism, engaging with the commonplace rather than the picturesque. Aware of parallel developments in Britain, Degas had advanced towards a more direct, intensely rendered view of the landscape, often on a small scale and in unconventional media. And, side-by-side with these same artists, he had sensed a new way forward, towards a self-justifying immediacy of perception and execution, and a self-consciously modern mode of representation. Though apparently peripheral to his *oeuvre*, the Dives pastels were exceptionally close to the mainstream of contemporary landscape art, and serve as a reminder of Degas' conceptual and even literal proximity to his peers. In the summer of 1869, for example, Degas was part of a virtual stampede of artists towards the beaches and resorts of the Channel coast. Courbet had installed himself at Etretat, at the home of Guy de Maupassant's uncle, where he entertained Alexandre Dumas and the young Claude Monet.[71] Further up the coast, Chintreuil was working at Boulogne and, according to some sources, may have been joined there by Manet.[72] Closer to Degas' chosen site, both Boudin and Daubigny spent the season at Trouville, Huet appears to have stayed in Beuzeval, while Berthe Morisot had travelled westwards, to paint in Brittany.[73] A pastel such as *The Beached Boat* (fig. 87) is resonant with echoes of many of these artists, both in its informal technique and in its subject-matter, and might be taken as a homage to their shared ancestry in Corot and Delacroix. Far from being the Odd Man Out, Degas seems to have included himself in, at

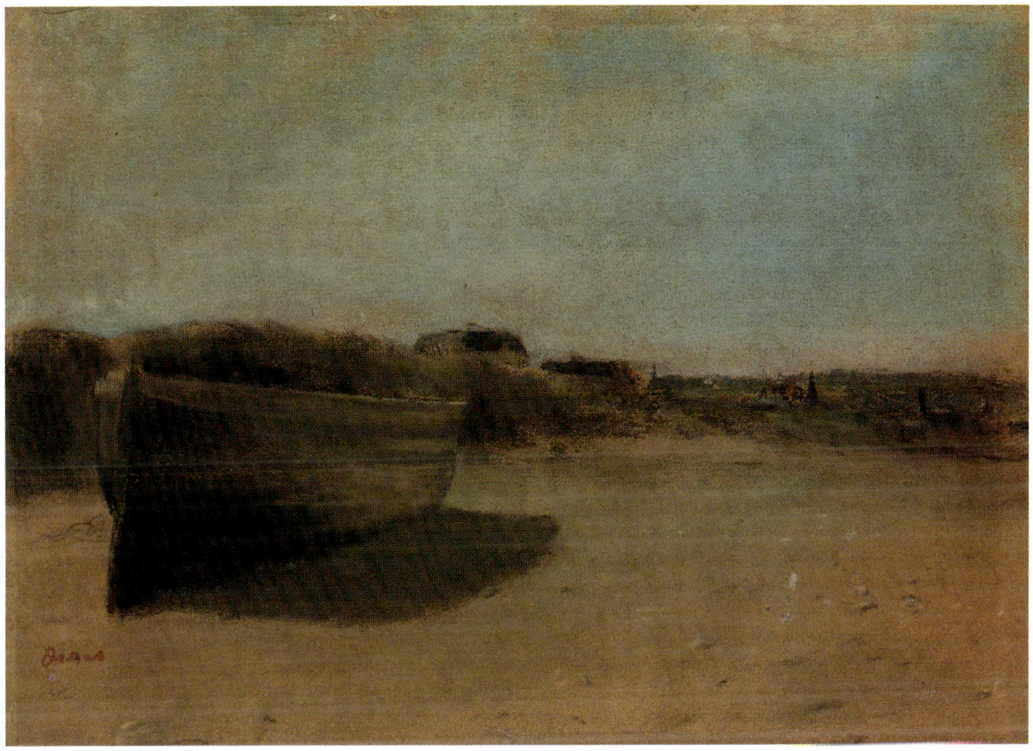

87. *The Beached Boat*, *c.*1869, pastel, 23 × 32 (L 250). Private collection.

least on this occasion, identifying himself with the routines and recreations of his landscape-painting peers.[74]

One issue at the centre of this still-remarkable episode remains to be considered: how exactly were the 1869 pastels made? Were they, as legend tells us, executed from memory in a hotel room? Were these scenes preserved in Degas' recollection for weeks, even months, and only later set down on paper, after the artist's return to his Paris studio? Or were they, as common sense and established practice might suggest, made in the open air, directly in front of the *motif*? The documentary and technical evidence surrounding these works is inconclusive, but the balance of probability favours the latter explanation, or perhaps some combination of all three. As we have seen in earlier chapters, Degas was no stranger to working *en plein air*, having already made studies from nature in pencil, watercolour, oil on paper and pen and ink, at locations as far apart as Rome and Paris, Naples and Normandy. His violent antipathy to outdoor painting, which has become one of the most familiar legends of the Impressionist era, was essentially an affectation of Degas' later years and is flatly contradicted by the artist's own accounts of his youthful career. On-the-spot notes of colour and light conditions, the use of portable media, such as watercolour and pastel, and even direct references in Degas' letters to working outdoors, all confirm his fluency in the direct notation of natural effects.[75] None of these factors precludes the completion of his drawings in an impromptu studio, but all of them strengthen the sense that the 1869 pastels are the product of a direct engagement with the scene in front of him, briskly and vividly set down with a minimum of revision.

In his maturity, Degas was celebrated for his exceptional visual memory, but even this faculty can hardly account for the extreme precision of some of the Dives-sur-Mer pastels. The careful transcription of roof-tops, steeples and hotel façades, the detailed accuracy of which can be confirmed today, could be the result only of first-hand interrogation, or, conceivably, the use of contemporary photographs. There is no evidence that Degas had access to photographs of the sites in question or that he himself experimented with landscape photography at this stage in his career. Paradoxically, where photographs of comparable subjects exist, such as Gustave Le Gray's studies of the Channel or Henri Le Secq's prints of Dieppe, they tend to favour a dramatic, pseudo-painterly view of their subject-matter.[76] Neither are there indications that Degas worked from preparatory drawings, developed later into more finished works of art. Given his known working practices, such an approach might have been expected, but no such drawings have been found. One or two lightly sketched outlines are present in notebooks of this period, accompanied by written accounts of weather effects, but none corresponds to the surviving pastels. On the contrary, many of the pastels appear to have been improvised freely on the paper in broad areas of tone and hue, their contours and formal components modified as the composition progressed. Where line is used, it is either a generalised, subordinate laying-in of principal forms, or a final sharpening of detail, executed with the edge of the pastel stick. In either case, Degas' technique represents the antithesis of the Ingresque tradition, a shameless and temporary triumph of colour over line which had no equal in his *oeuvre* until the landscape monotypes of the 1890s.

Technically, the 1869 suite of pastels are remarkably consistent, pointing to a sustained burst of activity rather than a cycle of interrupted experiments. Though the duration of Degas' visit to Normandy is not known, there is every reason to believe that a group of forty modestly scaled drawings, none of which is highly detailed or finely finished, could have been completed during an extended vacation.[77] The sizes, surfaces and colours of the papers used also point to such continuity, while the physical characteristics of the pastels increase the possibility that they were executed, at least in part, outdoors.[78] Several sheets have pin-holes at their corners, suggesting that they were fixed to a drawing board or sketching easel, though the presence of more than one set of such holes may indicate later work in the studio.[79] Unexpectedly, Degas used broad washes of water in the initial stages of some of these pastels, spreading colour across the sheet and allowing dribbles and splashes to recall the spontaneous effects of watercolour.[80] Extemporised or not, the application of the pastel is generally very restrained, not only in comparison with his later technique but in contrast to the pastellists he is known to have admired. Delacroix's works in the medium can be flamboyant in both colour and execution, while at their most vivid, Boudin's studies were described by Baudelaire as 'these immensities of green and pink . . . these firmaments of black or purple satin, crumpled, rolled or torn'.[81] In their sombre tonality, Degas' landscapes are perhaps closest to Boudin at his most subdued, or to certain works by Whistler made in parallel with, or soon after, Degas' own.

The simplest explanation of the Normandy pastels may be the most satisfactory. Prompted by the example of his senior contemporaries and encouraged by his recent experience with the portrait of Yves Morisot, Degas left for the coast in late July or early August 1869, armed with his box of pastels and a folder of suitable papers. Clearly he planned to make some landscapes, possibly in emulation of certain of his peers, conceivably in anticipation of large-scale or rurally sited images of his own. It may be that he visited Etretat, but he certainly lingered in the Houlgate area, making studies of his immediate surroundings and using portable colours to note down effects of atmosphere, dispositions of terrain and localised textures. Returning to his lodgings, he might well have tidied up or embellished his field-work, subsequently signing a limited number for sale or presentation to friends. In spirit and in execution, the pastels tend towards the literal and are neither achingly portentous nor blandly photographic. When he looks down from a cliff-top, it is to show us the familiar from an unfamiliar vantage point, and when he conjures up mists and sea-frets, he confronts the simple, unglamorous facts of the ocean. In these works, Degas threw himself into the project of Realism, reporting on his surroundings without facile emphasis, stalking his subject-matter without conspicuous drama. If we see in their empty beaches some reflection of a private melancholy, we might recall that these pastels were made at a moment of transition, when Degas had good reason to seek out personal and professional solitude.

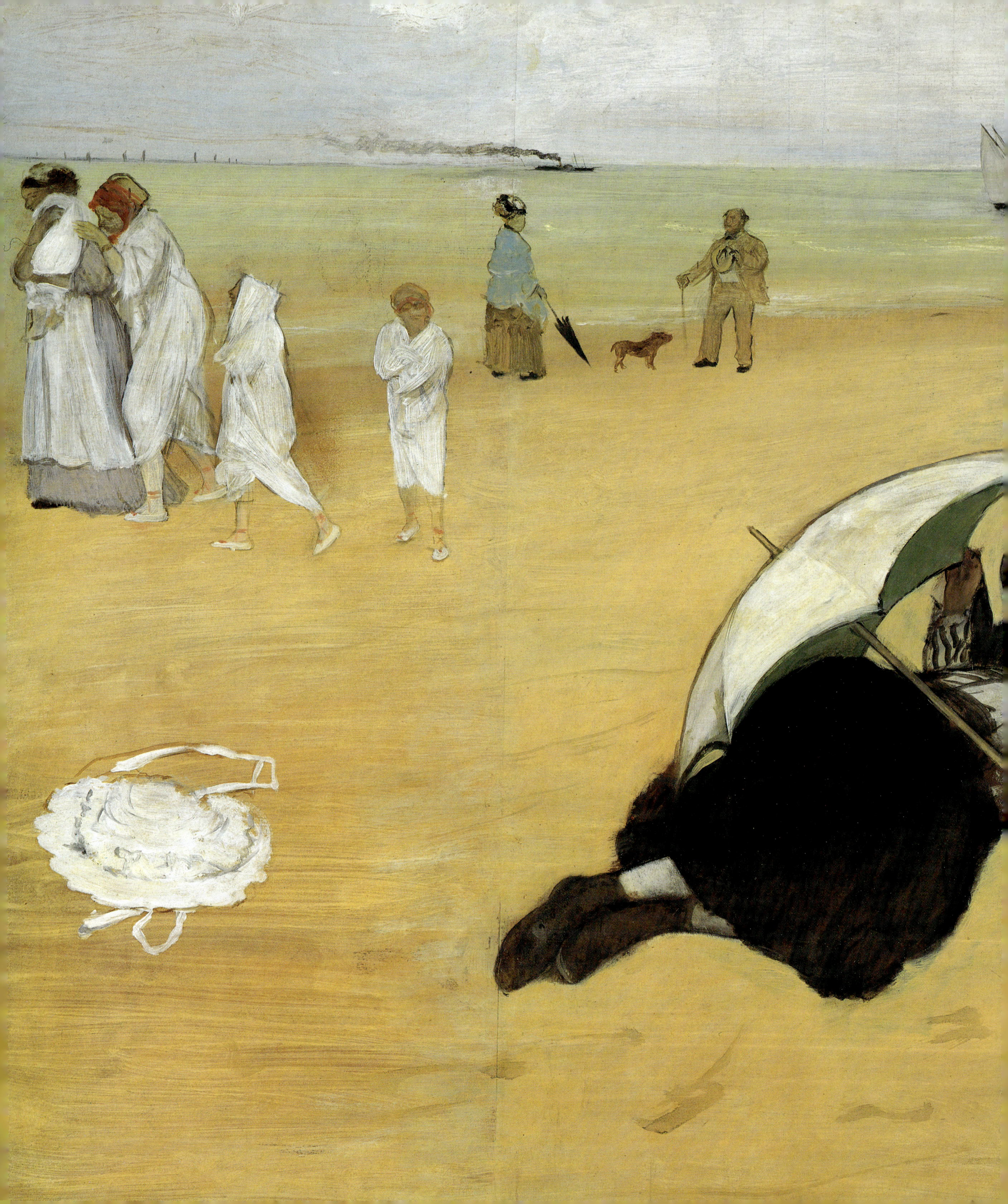

5 Degas and the Impressionist Landscape

'The air you breathe in a picture is not necessarily the same as the air out of doors.'
(Degas, recorded by Vollard)

Shot through with paradoxes though it appears to be, Degas' career as a landscapist was never more paradoxical than during the years of Impressionism. Between the first Impressionist exhibition of 1874 and the final group show of 1886, Degas was amongst the most tireless of their organisers and advocates, displaying his work in considerable numbers at seven of the eight public showings.[1] It was at these exhibitions that he unveiled many of his most distinctive *motifs*, such as the *Laundresses* in 1876 and the *Cafés-concerts* in 1877, and it was here that his reputation as 'the painter of dancers' was launched. Recent commentators have emphasised the diversity of the Impressionist shows, which encompassed the work of rising professionals and rank amateurs, makers of pottery and decorators of fans, painters of portraits and engravers of the still life. Statistically speaking, however, the exhibitions were dominated by landscape subjects, and many of Degas' celebrated colleagues, such as Monet, Sisley, Pissarro and Guillaumin, were represented almost exclusively as landscape artists. As we shall see, Degas established the most surprising relationships with some of these individuals, buying their landscape paintings, collaborating with them in practical research and maintaining personal ties with lesser-known practitioners, such as Tillot, Rouart and Lepic. But his association with the Impressionist enterprise was often oblique and sometimes abrasive, and created considerable confusion in the minds of critics and public. On occasion, and presumably to his own discomfort, Degas even found himself linked with ambitions that were at odds with his self-proclaimed practice, as when the critic Ernest Chesneau included his name in an 1874 account of the 'école du plein air'.[2]

Rather than encouraging Degas in his affinity with the landscape, however, this identification with Impressionism appears to have turned him against it. During the decade or so of the Impressionist era, Degas produced fewer exercises in pure landscape than in any other comparable phase of his career. Nor does this period feature those sudden and wilful bursts of landscape activity that punctuated the rest of his professional life. The paradox is deepened by the fact that this same phase was immediately preceded and as abruptly followed by two of the most important groups of landscape images from the artist's *oeuvre*: the 1869 Normandy pastels on the one hand, and the monotype landscapes of the early 1890s on the other. But, despite a number of notebook studies, print-making experiments and memorable landscape backgrounds; despite the proliferation of scenes of the paddock and the racetrack; and despite the continued invocation of Corot and Delacroix, Millet and Whistler, Boudin and Pissarro, the Impressionist years were a time of consolidation and retrenchment, and of thematic redefinition, for Degas the independent landscapist.

88. Detail of fig. 94.

How can we exlain this seeming reversal in Degas' youthful appetites? As modern scholars have increasingly emphasised, the Impressionist exhibitions were distinguished by factionalism and competing self-interest as much as by heroic idealism, and the divergent trajectories of individual careers tended to direct the collective enterprise. Degas was at the centre of much of this posturing, advancing the causes of his followers, insisting on details of publicity and determining the extent and appearance of his own installations. His submissions to each show were chosen with great deliberation, often giving prominence to those subjects, like the ballet, the laundress and the café-concert, to which he wished to lay claim, or presenting a new sequence of works to the public, such as the 'suite of nudes' unveiled in 1886. Some of this was mere salesmanship, a response to the need for novelty, even of theatricality, in the presentation of his wares. At a deeper level, Degas was also engaged in defining himself, not only against his fellow-exhibitors but specifically against his own earlier persona. As he matured artistically, he needed a new repertoire of subject-matter that was recognisably of its time, yet one that was distinctive and thus marketable. After the extraordinary breadth of his earlier years, where his work veered from history painting to portraiture and from landscape to the bourgeois interior, Degas needed to specialise.

Other artists were naturally involved in the same sequence of manoeuvres. In the first Impressionist shows, Monet identified himself with the sea and the river, then the railway station and the shunting yard.[3] Pissarro, already labelled the painter of 'the modern countryside', made the kitchen garden his own, while declaring his allegiance to landscapes of frost and snow.[4] From the beginning, Degas announced himself as the pre-eminent figure painter of the group. At the 1874 exhibition, his ten submissions were made up of images of dancers and laundresses, jockeys and a female bather.[5] In subsequent shows, he added portraits and studies of milliners, performers at cafés-concerts and audiences at the theatre, and such curiosities as a billiard scene and a wax statuette of a ballerina. But of the hundred or so exhibits he showed on seven occasions, none lacked a human presence, and the great majority revolved around the male or female, and occasionally animal, form. Amongst his well-known colleagues, few approached Degas' fixation with the human subject. Cézanne, who exhibited only twice, showed nudes and portraits, but alongside an equal number of still lifes and landscapes.[6] Both Morisot and Renoir ranged widely across the repertoire, and even Mary Cassatt, who joined the enterprise in 1879, showed a few pastel landscapes alongside her portraits and nudes.[7] So pronounced was Degas' specialisation that a number of critics singled him out for special attention, either doubting his allegiance to the group or praising his mastery of draughtsmanship, in contrast to the 'ineptitude' of his friends.[8] Zola summarised this view of Degas in 1876, when he described him as a painter who preferred 'l'actualité, la vie intérieure et ses types quotidiens'.[9]

Typically, Degas seems to have enjoyed the situation and turned it to his advantage. As the years went by, he publicly distanced himself from the practices of his landscape-painting colleagues, developing a rhetoric of censure that still clings to his reputation today. Principal among his targets was *pleinairisme*, a procedure based on improvisation and direct engagement with the subject, carried out away from the studio and without preparatory drawing. In time, Degas seems conveniently to have forgotten his own earlier experiments at Haras-du-Pin, Dives-sur-Mer and elsewhere, mocking his friend Henri Rouart for painting a landscape 'on the edge of a cliff' and reminding him that 'Painting is not a sport . . . !'[10] Later, he would regale his long-suffering friends

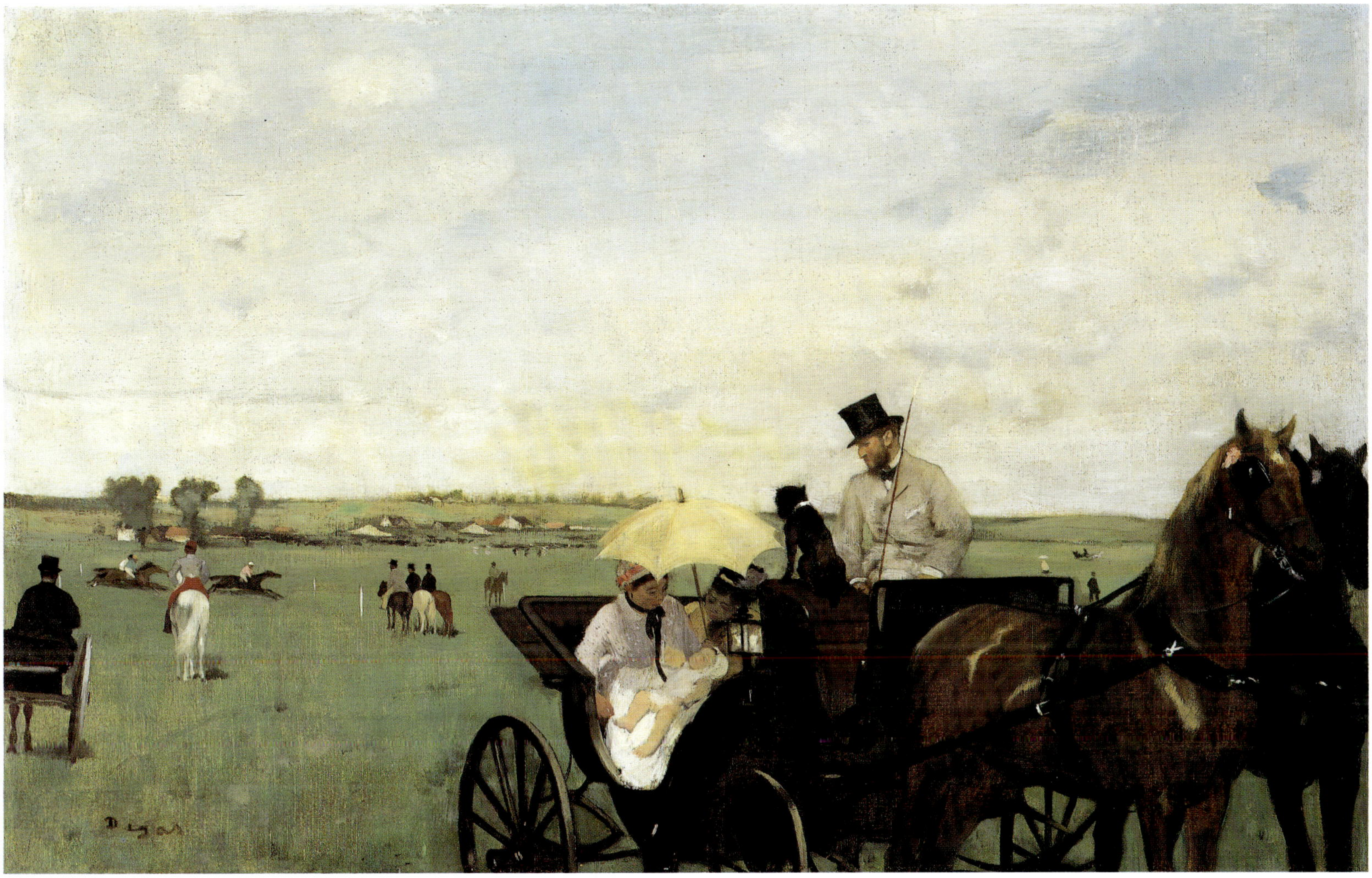

89. *At the Races in the Countryside*, 1869, oil on canvas, 36.5 × 55.9 (L 281). Museum of Fine Arts, Boston, 1931 Purchase Fund.

with variants on the same theme, telling André Gide that there should be a special detachment of police to arrest outdoor painters and repeating to Vollard that 'a little dose of bird-shot now and then' would do them no harm.[11] Today, no book on Degas is complete without one or more of these aphorisms, but the misunderstandings they have created are legion. Most importantly, few authors have noted that these accounts belong to the later years of Degas' career, and that the legend of Degas as the scourge of *plein-air* painters post-dates the Impressionist era.[12] Just as pervasively, Degas' scorn for *pleinairisme* has been taken as a dismissal of landscape painting in general, despite the overwhelming evidence of his own *oeuvre*. Several hundred landscape studies by the artist himself, in every medium and from almost every phase of his working life, including some manifestly executed *sur le motif*, prove the inadequacy of this tradition. Add to this his activities as a collector of many dozens of landscape drawings, paintings and prints by artists past and present; his documented delight in the landscapes of his peers, from Cézanne to Pissarro and from Morisot to Monet; his choice of landscape for his own exhibition in 1892 at the Durand-Ruel gallery; and gradually a less caricatural and more plausibly complex view of Degas' relationship with the genre begins to emerge.

In the years immediately preceding the 1874 Impressionist exhibition, Degas appears to have placed his own art under the broad and still-flourishing banner of Realism. The portraits he submitted to the Salon in the late 1860s, the first studies of ballet-dancers from the same period, and the pastel landscapes made on the Normandy coast, were all contemporary in their subject-matter and essentially descriptive in their technique. At their simplest, they were visual inventories of Degas' world; at their most subtle, they evoked and artfully encapsulated the manners of the age. Realism, as Degas' acquaintance shows, came in many guises and could lead to a variety of contradictory conclusions. Manet's brash confrontations with urban life set the pattern for much of his generation, including the young Degas in his formative years, though his bravura technique was rarely imitated. Contrarily, Degas was only briefly attracted to the ruralism of Courbet, though his sombre hues and textured canvases made themselves felt in one or two experimental works, such as *Dead Fox in a Wood* (fig. 61) and his portrait of Eugénie Fiocre.[13] Throughout this period, Degas was equally drawn to a literal and almost photographic view of Realism, exemplified in the obsessive detail of Bracquemond and the refinement of Fantin-Latour, and carried to an extreme in his own *Portraits in an Office (New Orleans)* (Musée des Beaux-Arts, Pau; L 320). Tissot, too, offered highly polished glimpses of the modern world, of a kind that Degas cheerfully included within his conception of the new school. After welcoming Bracquemond as 'an excellent recruit' to the cause, Degas tried to enlist Tissot: 'The realist movement no longer needs to fight with the others, it already *is*, it *exists*, it must show itself as *something distinct*, there must be a *salon of realists*', he wrote in a letter of 1874.[14]

One of the pictures Degas chose to show in the first Impressionist exhibition, and one that presumably took to the field under the colours of Realism, was *At the Races in the Countryside* (fig. 89), a work completed several years before, perhaps as early as 1869. Henri Loyrette has argued that the painting represents the Valpinçon family on an excursion near Ménil-Hubert, and that Degas conceived and may have executed the work while staying with his friends on his return from Villers-sur-Mer and Houlgate.[15] What is certain is that, in this canvas and a number of associated works, the lessons Degas learned on the beaches of Normandy have borne remarkable fruit. Using the same elemental divisions of earth and sky, and a similarly matter-of-fact execution, the artist has once more explored the prosaic beauties of emptiness. On this occasion, the audacious counterweight of carriage, horses and family group relieves the expanse of barely inflected sky, but it is the spareness and banality of the view that fixes itself in our attention.[16] In a smaller picture painted soon afterwards, *Before the Race* (fig. 90), this disproportion between sky and terrestrial narrative is even more startling, while Degas' handling of its mundane cloudscape is equally cool and masterly.[17] The soft, milky light that pervades so many of the 1869 pastels also illuminates *Horses in the Meadow* (fig. 91). Reminiscent of the Dives-sur-Mer studies in its unpicturesque scenery, this picture continues their explicit depiction of working boats and waterside industry.[18] If the needle-sharp execution of *At the Races in the Countryside* recalls the finish of Tissot, the more open brush-work of *Horses in the Meadow* hints at other allegiances, and may represent one of Degas' earliest attempts to translate the effects of pastel into oil paint.

90. *Before the Race*, *c.*1872, oil on canvas, 26 × 34 (L 317). National Gallery of Art, Washington, D.C., Widener Collection.

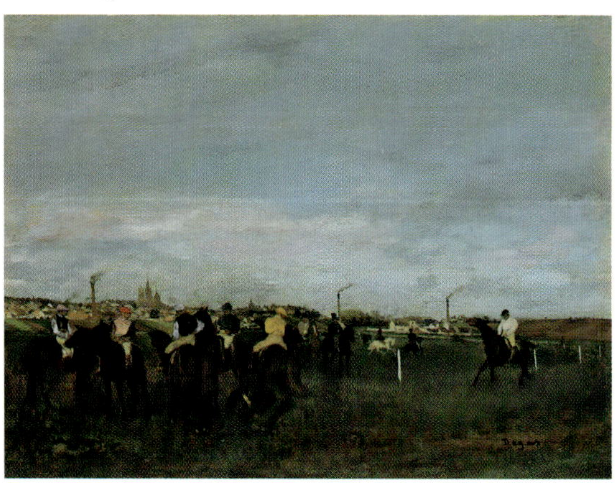

The importance Degas attached to these equestrian pictures, and to his burgeoning career as a painter of Realist scenes, can be judged from their historical record. Unlike his earlier studies of the racetrack, each of the three canvases was signed and put on public display, and each found a buyer almost immediately (James Tissot was the first owner of *Horses in the Meadow*).[19] Two

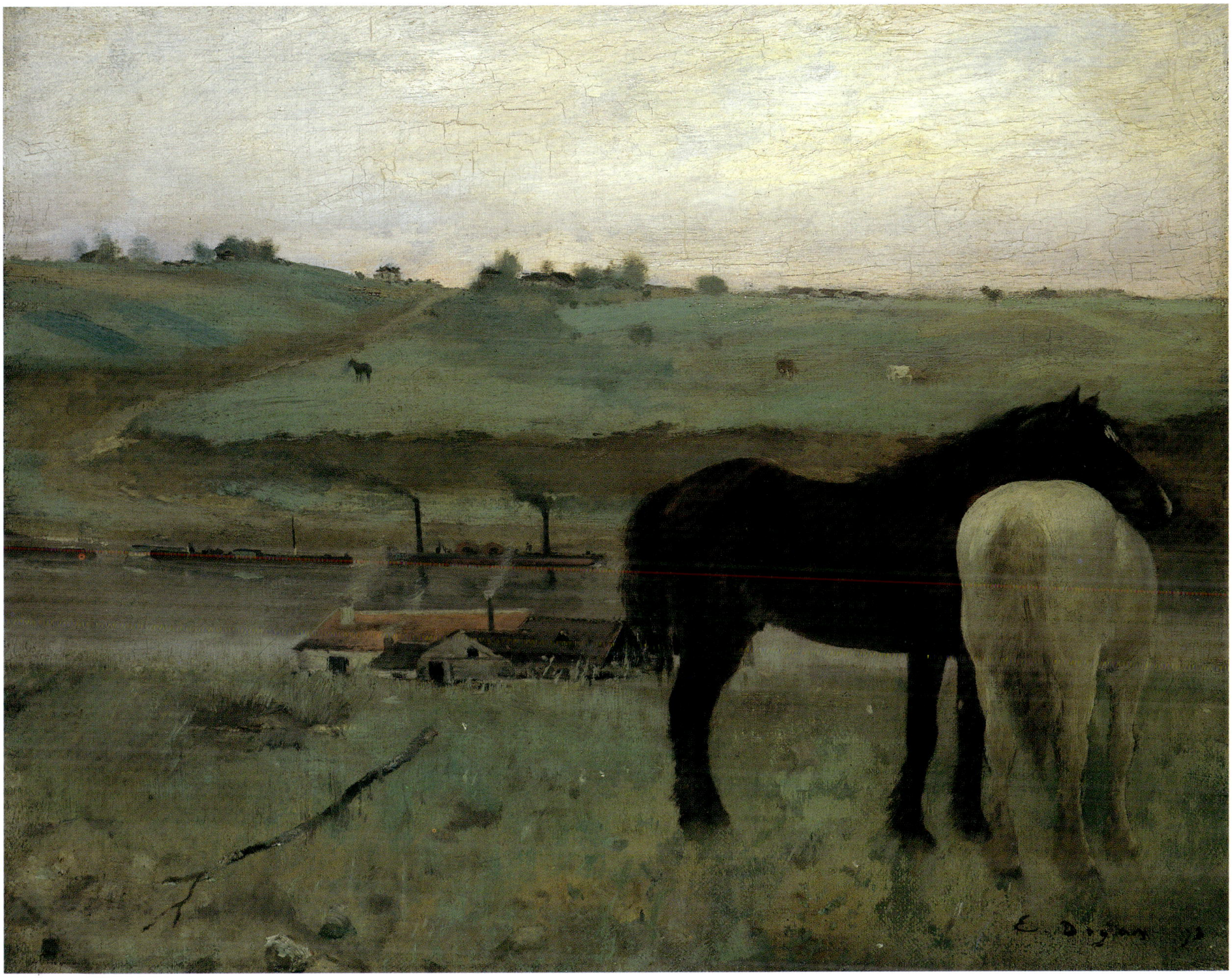

91. *Horses in the Meadow*, 1871, oil on canvas, 32 × 40 (L 289). Janet Traeger Salz.

of the paintings became the subject of prints, one supervised by the artist himself, and *At the Races in the Countryside* was chosen for exhibition in London prior to its inclusion in the 1874 Impressionist show.[20] A less well-documented but no less accomplished work, *Racehorses at Longchamp* (fig. 93), shows a similiarly confident handling of light, colour and uncertain weather. Here again, a broad expanse of beach-like terrain carries us towards an indistinct horizon, and a veil of cloud softens the evening brightness. The distant hillside is recognisably that of Mont Valérien, an urban eminence rising behind the Longchamp racecourse which had already featured in the equestrian scenes of Manet.[21] Though this picture appears to have remained in Degas' studio until later in his career, two other scenes of the track are known to have been included in the 1874 Impressionist exhibition.[22] In every known case, these paintings incorporate details of buildings, landscape features and even

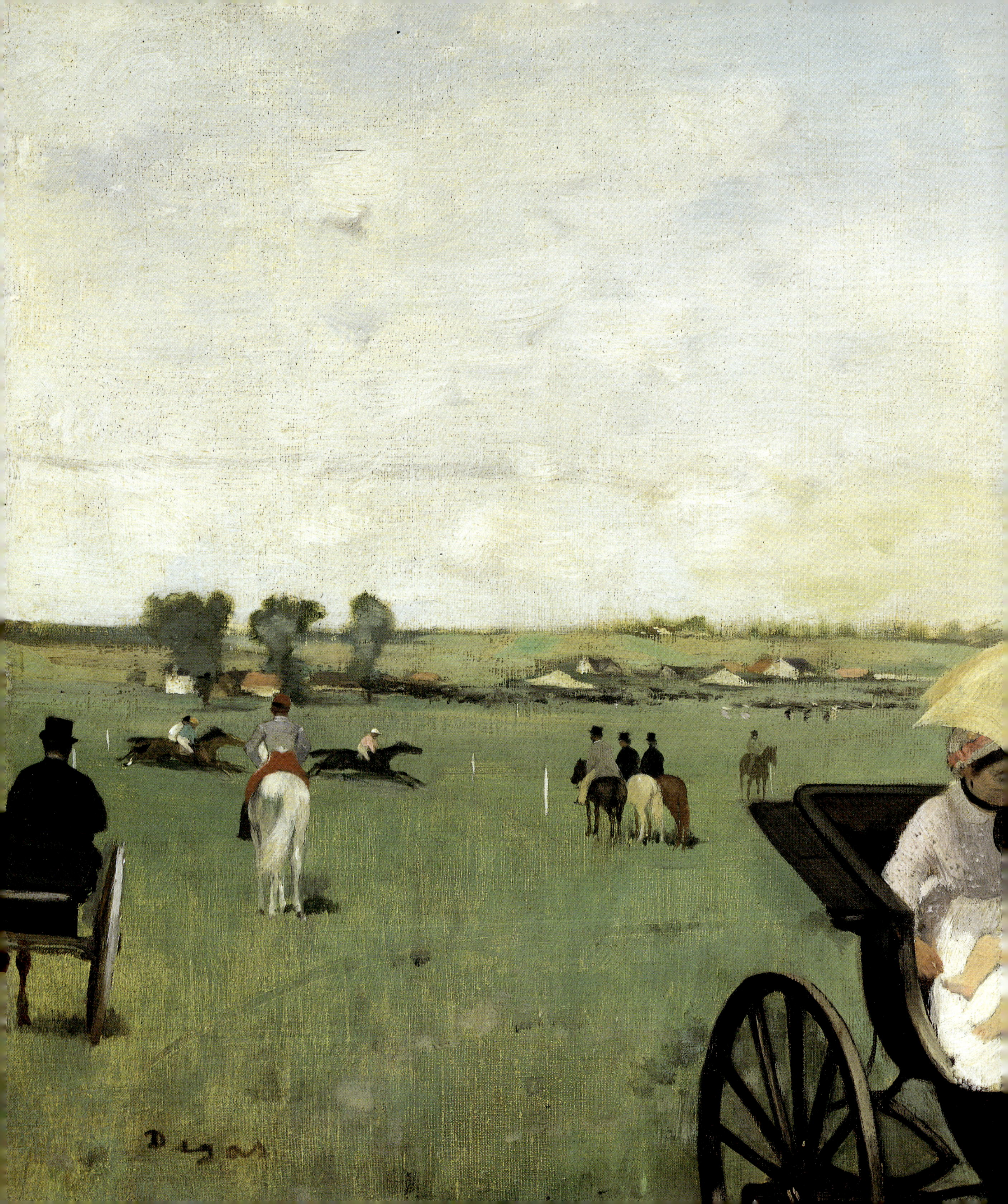

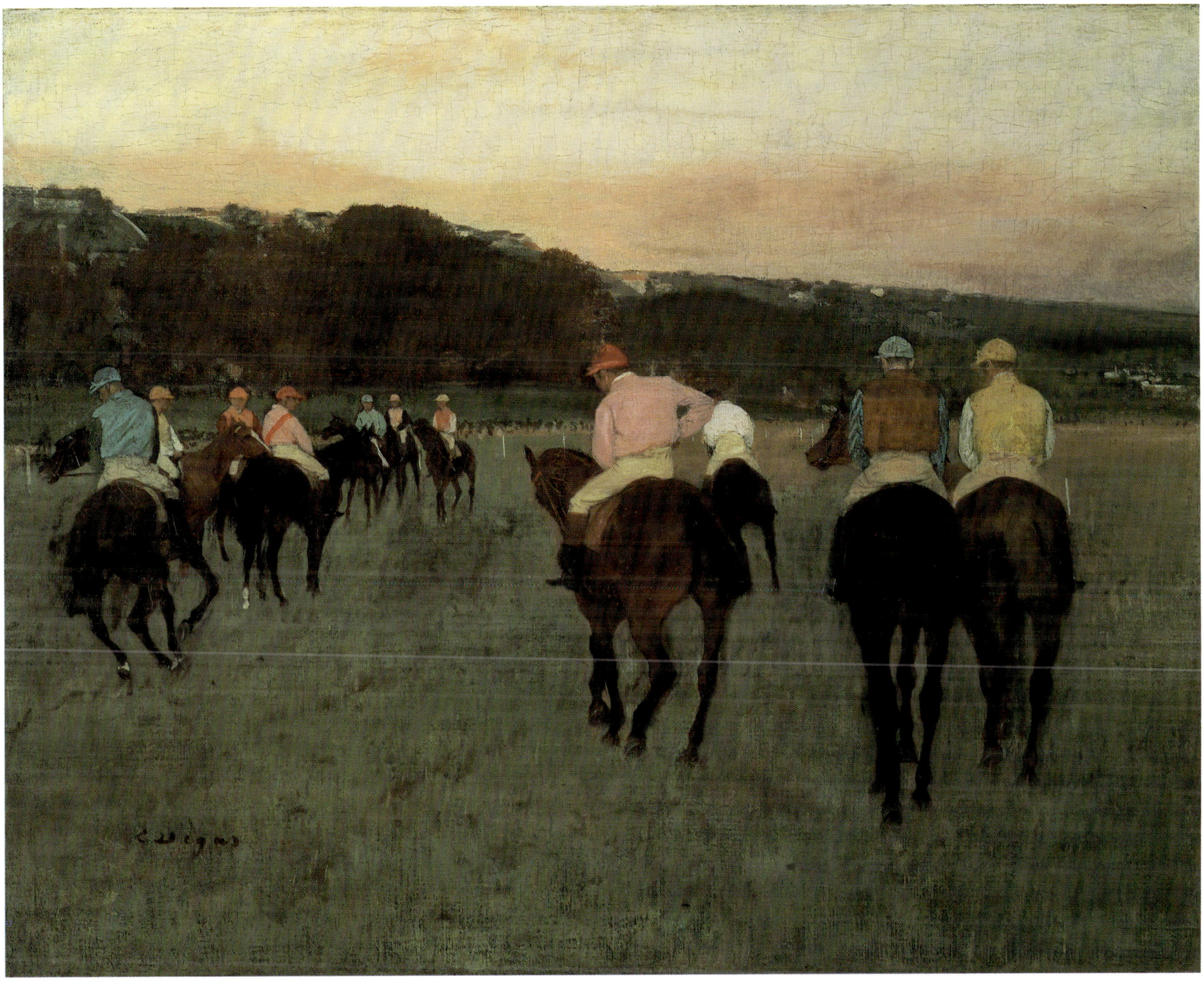

93. *Racehorses at Longchamp*, *c.*1871–4, oil on canvas, 34.1 × 41.8 (L 334). Museum of Fine Arts, Boston, S.A. Denio Collection.

identifiable individuals from Degas' milieu, reminding us of the documentary and site-specific nature of his current project. Significantly, several of their innocent-looking backgrounds also reveal chimney-stacks and factories, hinting at an industrial as well as a suburban dimension to Degas' realism.[23]

Arguably the most challenging group of works produced in the aftermath of the 1869 pastels, and again one with implications for the early Impressionist shows, is Degas' series of beach scenes. Four such scenes survive, either painted in oil on canvas or *essence* on paper: *Peasant Girls Bathing in the Sea toward Evening* (fig. 97), exhibited at the second or third Impressionist exhibition;[24] *Women Combing their Hair* (Phillips Collection, Washington, D.C.; L 376), bought by the painter Henri Lerolle in 1878;[25] *Beach Scene* (fig. 94), shown at the 1877 exhibition;[26] and *Nursemaids on the Beach* (Norton Simon Collection, Pasadena; L 374), a partially completed study in *essence*.[27] Each picture represents

92. Detail of fig. 89.

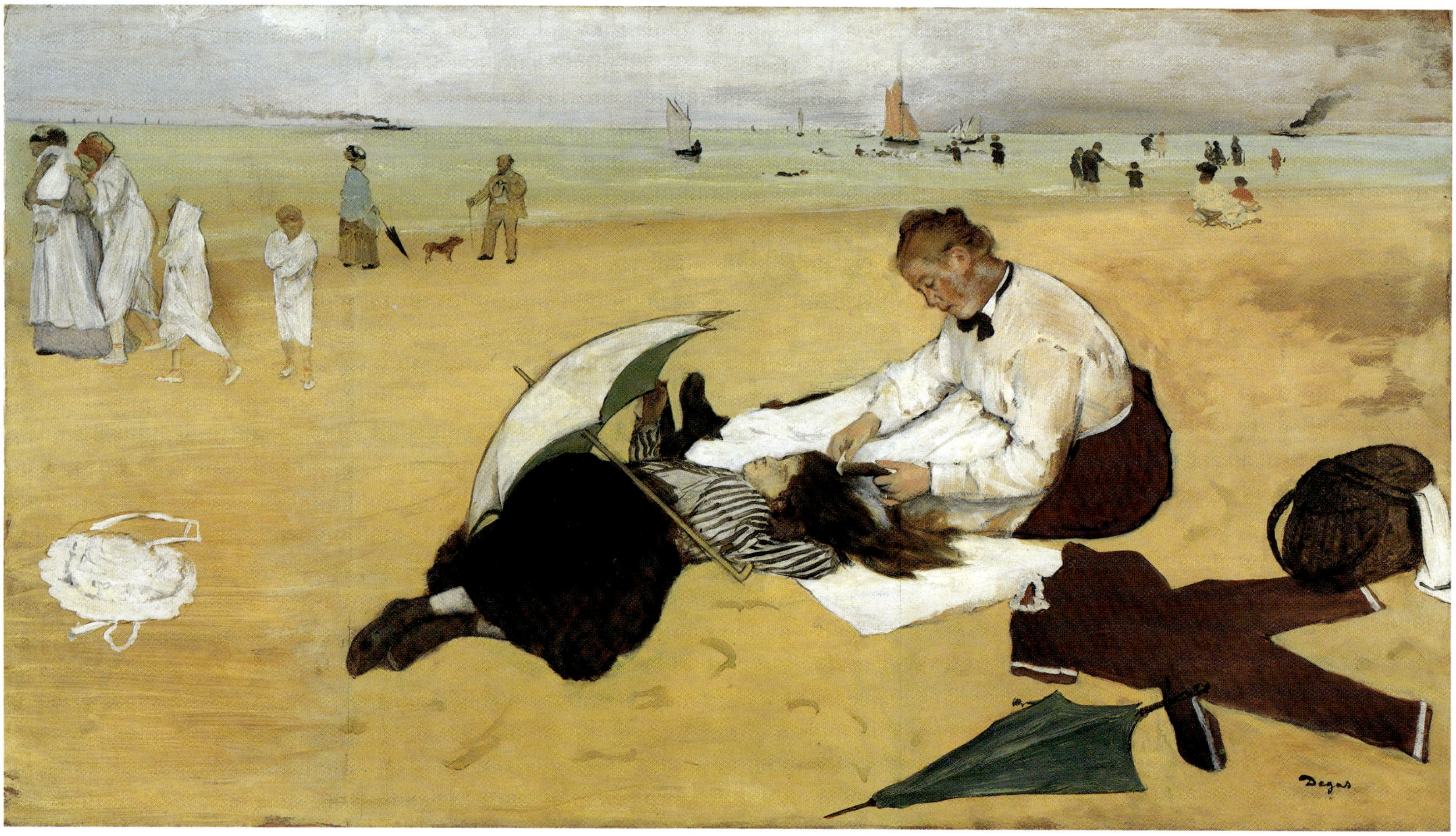

94. *Beach Scene*, *c*.1869, oil on paper, mounted on canvas, 46 × 81 (L 406). National Gallery, London.

young women beside the sea, bathing, attending to their hair or resting after their exertions. As such, they belong to a well-established repertoire that embraced popular illustration on the one hand, and the work of several painters in Degas' 'Salon of Realists' on the other. Boudin's 1868 *Beach at Trouville* (private collection), for example, has many points of similarity with Degas' *Beach Scene*, though Boudin's picture is based on a more distant viewpoint and a more decorous vision of seaside life.[28] In his less formal works, notably in drawings and sheets of watercolours, Boudin set a clearer precedent for Degas' imagery, while in certain oil studies, such as *Trouville: The Governess* (private collection), he could approach Degas' unbuttoned candour.[29]

Boudin's former pupil, Claude Monet, also engaged with the beach *motif* in a number of small canvases of this period, among them *The Beach at Trouville* (National Gallery, London). Here Monet, like Degas, explored the subject of the bather and the seaside chaperon, though Monet is known to have set up his easel on the sands and largely completed his composition *en plein air*.[30] The most persuasive analogy for Degas' series, however, is found in Manet's *Beach at Boulogne* (fig. 95), a picture recently redated to 1868.[31] Not only do we find young women involved in similar seaside activities, but precise resemblances in format, colour and local incident between this work and Degas' *Beach Scene* point to a clear historical link. So great are the similarities that Manet's canvas can seem like a pattern-book or catalogue of maritime vignettes, from which Degas has chosen and rearranged his own panorama. Both artists began with a horizontally striped rectangle of ochre sand, grey sky and opalescent sea, more

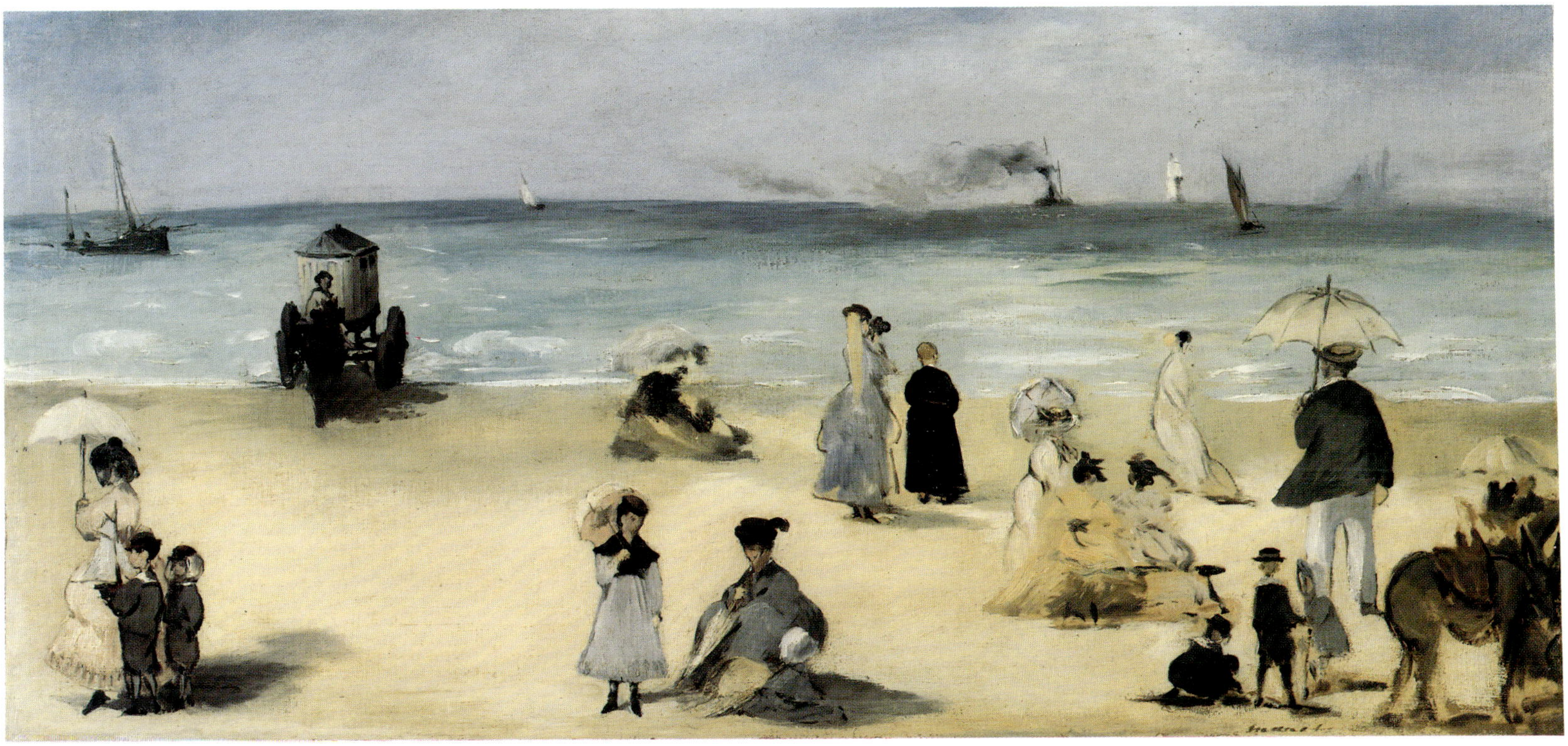

95. Edouard Manet, *Beach at Boulogne*, 1868, oil on canvas, 32 × 65. Museum of Fine Arts, Richmond, Virginia. Collection of Mr. and Mrs. Paul Mellon.

96. James Clarke Hook, *Sea Urchins*, 1861, oil on canvas, 51 × 84. Guildhall Art Gallery, London.

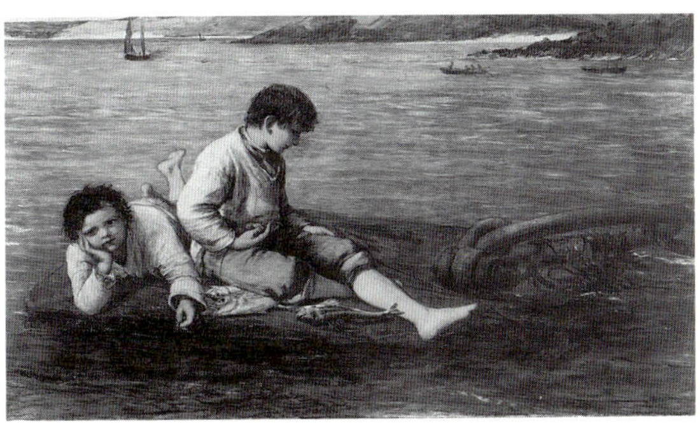

than a little reminiscent of Degas' Normandy pastels. In the distance, they then distributed sailing boats and smokestacks, and at the water's edge an ungainly bathing-machine (Degas subsequently painted his out).[32] On the beach, a scattering of bathers in white towels and ambling promenaders was added, followed by a central figure of a girl with attendant adult. Differences exist, of course, principally in the scale of the *Beach Scene*'s leading protagonists; but rarely, if ever, did Degas help himself with such frankness, even impertinence, to Manet's vocabulary of forms.

Like the equestrian pictures already discussed, Degas' beach scenes were a bold initiative in the early Impressionist market-place and a significant milestone in his professional advancement. The three finished works either found immediate buyers or were displayed in group exhibitions, and each inaugurated a theme, such as the combing of the hair or the nude bather, that was to persist into his later imagery.[33] Though two of the pictures were signed by the artist, none was dated, leaving considerable uncertainty as to their origins and the circumstances of their conception. It has been generally assumed that the series was carried out in the mid-1870s, shortly before the inclusion of one, or possibly two, of their number in the 1877 Impressionist exhibition.[34] Several arguments can be mobilised against this assumption, not least Degas' habit of exhibiting pictures that were made years, even decades, before the date of the show in question.[35] In the case of the seaside pictures, we must also account for their manifest resemblance to the pastels of 1869, and the striking similarity between Degas' *Beach Scene* and works by Boudin, Monet and Manet painted eight or nine years earlier. The debate is of more than academic interest, since in unravelling Degas' borrowings and inventions, we cast light on his continuing self-definition, and on the role of landscape in this transitional process.

What are we to make of the ironic, reverberant echo of Manet's *Beach at Boulogne* in Degas' *Beach Scene?* Is it conceivable that Degas, who had seen his own steeplechase scenes quoted by Manet within a short time of their appearance, would have waited almost a decade before responding to Manet's 1868 painting? During the 1860s, the competitive relationship between the two artists had quickened, resulting in several pairs of pictures that jostled for priority, or made witty reference to the other's achievement.[36] On the visual evidence alone, there is a strong case for regarding *Beach at Boulogne* and *Beach Scene* as another such pairing, this time with Manet taking the lead. When stylistic and technical factors are taken into account, the argument for redating Degas' picture to the period around 1869 becomes almost overwhelming. Physically, the picture has much in common with a group of studies made by Degas in the late 1860s, most of which are related to the racetrack. Like *Beach Scene*, they are painted in *essence*, or thinned oil paint, directly on to paper, and even their dimensions suggest a family resemblance.[37] Certain distinctive effects, like the exquisite black-and-white striping of the girl's blouse and the patterning of the racing silks in *Two Jockeys* (private collection; L 154), are also common to both.[38] As exercises in painting, the entire series exploits the contrast between lightly washed, almost watercolour-like areas of tone and much denser passages of fine detail. In terms of composition, the more finished works, such as the *essence* painting *Racehorses before the Stands* (Musée d'Orsay, Paris; L 262) juxtapose foreground forms with distant incident, favouring the empty middle-ground that characterises *Beach Scene* and *Women Combing their Hair*.[39]

Given all these factors, we might reasonably conclude that Degas travelled to the Channel coast in 1869 with Manet's recent picture in mind, embarking on his pastel landscapes, at least in part, as exercises or location studies for a planned rejoinder. Aware of the recently exhibited beach scenes of Boudin and Morisot, as well as Manet's continuing success in attracting patronage, Degas may also have hoped to exploit a currently fashionable subject. Degas' enthusiasm for finding customers for his work was already well known. In a letter written from Boulogne in the summer of 1868, while he was working on his marine subjects, Manet announced to his friend and rival Degas: 'I'm planning to make a little trip to London, tempted by the low cost of the journey; do you want to come along? . . . I think we should explore the terrain over there since it could provide an outlet for our products.'[40] In his own correspondence, Degas refers several times to the English market, and there is reason to believe that he associated small, crisply detailed pictures with current English taste.[41] His fascination with the landscapes of Alfred William Hunt, Charles Lewis and Brittan Willis at the 1867 Exposition Universelle is consistent with this, while his interest in James Clarke Hook's *Sea-Urchins* (fig. 96) suggests a more calculated gathering of materials.[42] In addition to its sharp focus, Hook's painting sets distant boats, a high horizon and a largely empty middle-distance against a prominent foreground group, all depicted under an overcast sky. All these features recur in *Beach Scene*, where the squatting and reclining urchins have become a correctly attired chaperon and her charge, and it is tempting to believe that the figures in Hook's picture provided the extra ingredient in Degas' re-working of Manet's slightly earlier scene. That such subjects were on Degas' mind during his 1869 excursion is demonstrated by a terse notebook entry, reminding the artist to 'make large-scale groups in silhouette, at twilight'.[43] Though this ambition hardly applies to *Beach Scene*, it may well lie behind one of the other seashore studies, *Peasant Girls Bathing in the Sea toward Evening* (fig. 97), and encourages us to believe that the entire group was executed at that time.[44]

When Degas was asked, many years after the event, how he had managed to

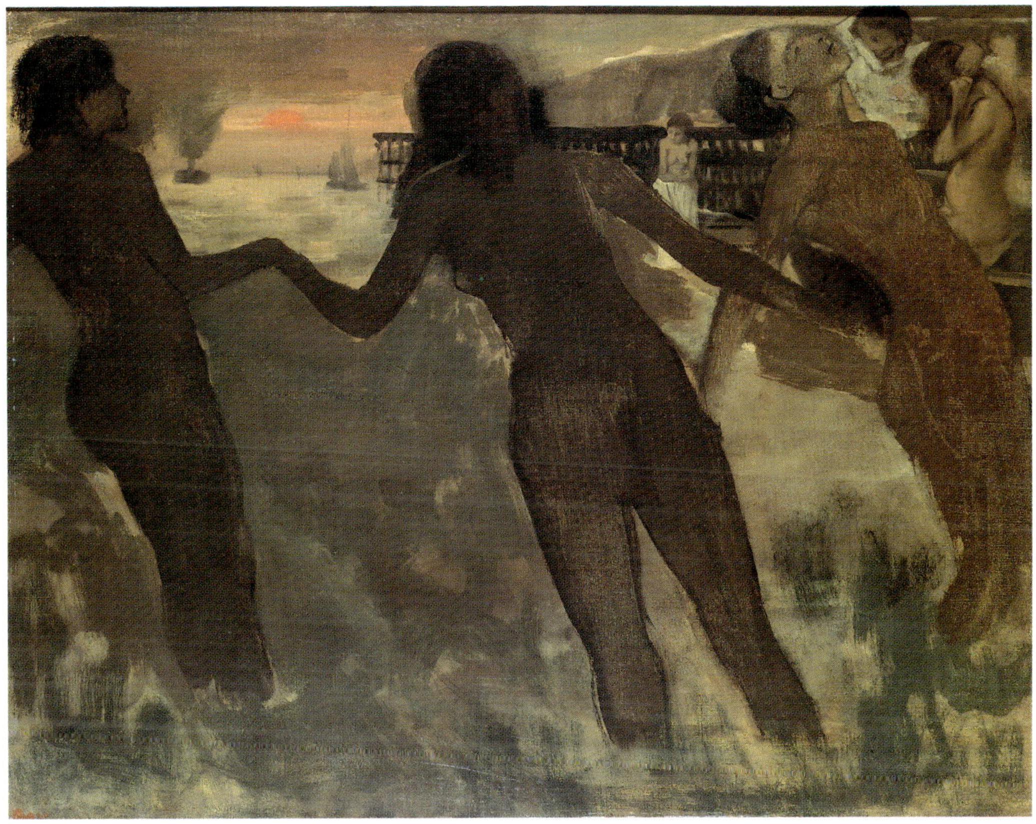

97. *Peasant Girls Bathing in the Sea toward Evening*, *c.*1869, oil on canvas, 65 × 81 (L 377). Private collection.

97*bis*. *Women Combing their Hair*, *c.*1875, oil on paper mounted on canvas, 32.3 × 46. The Phillips Collection, Washington, D.C.

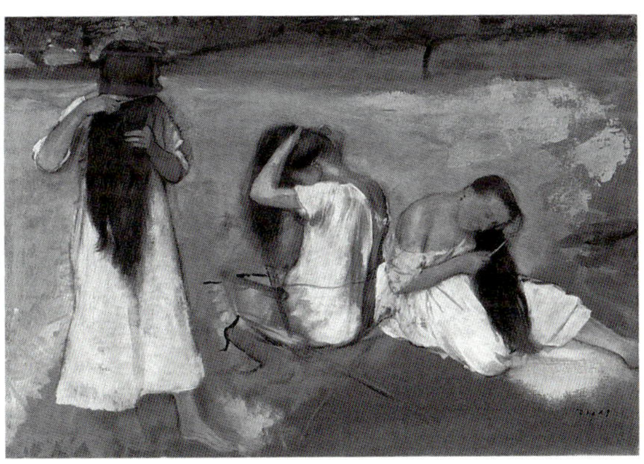

paint the *Beach Scene*, he is said to have replied: 'It was quite simple. I spread my flannel vest on the floor of the studio and had the model sit on it. You see, the air you breathe in a picture is not necessarily the same as the air out of doors.'[45] This much-quoted remark is one of very few generalisations about landscape painting to have survived in something like Degas' own words. It obliges us, therefore, to confront the question of Degas' working practices and to compare them, as he surely meant us to, with those of his Impressionist colleagues. As applied to the *Beach Scene*, it reminds us that such intricate and artful images are not the result of hasty improvisation, and that the methods of the *pleinairiste* were ill-suited to Degas' figure-in-the-landscape ambitions. From practical and temperamental necessity, Degas' equestrian scenes, outdoor portraits and bathing subjects were all executed in the studio, where lighting and composition could be carefully controlled. Degas always insisted that he approached his pictures through the artifice of drawing, still true to his Ingriste beginnings in defining each figure on a separate sheet, then bringing them together against a previously recorded or improvised background. His reiteration of such claims in later life was largely habitual, if not neurotic, but is not always borne out by existing documentation. Significantly, many of the exceptions belong to the context of landscape, where Degas can be found working from the *motif* or shamelessly allowing colour to take precedence over line. The early bather series forms another, and more unexpected, curiosity, since only one of the group has been shown to derive from even the most modest figure sketch.[46] The surfaces of the pictures suggest, on the contrary, that they evolved in an informal manner, with tentative pencil- or brush-marks locating the figures, and alterations being made to limbs, tone and colour.[47] While not casting doubt on Degas' account of their genesis, such features go further towards associating the

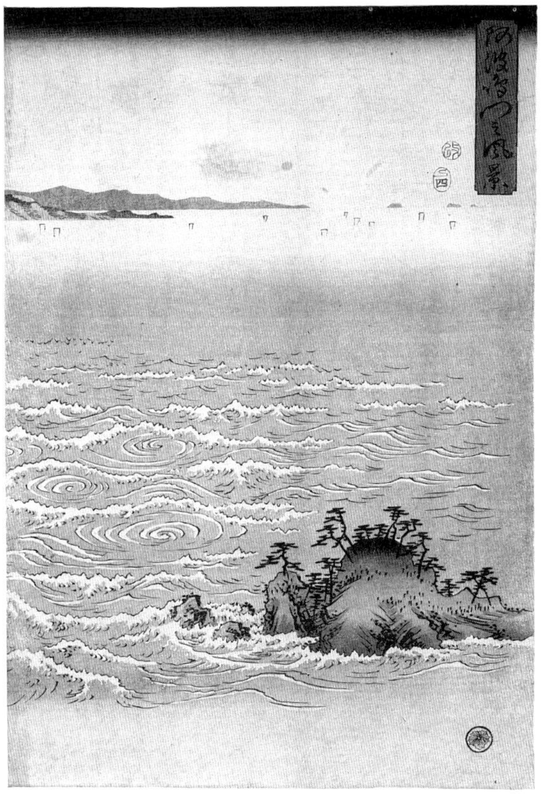

98. Ando Hiroshige, *View of Awa No Naruto*, 1857, woodblock triptych (right-hand panel), 37 × 25. British Museum, London.

99. Nishikawa Sukenobu, *Critical Studies of One Hundred Women*, 1723, woodblock, 28.5 × 19.5 (page size). British Museum, London.

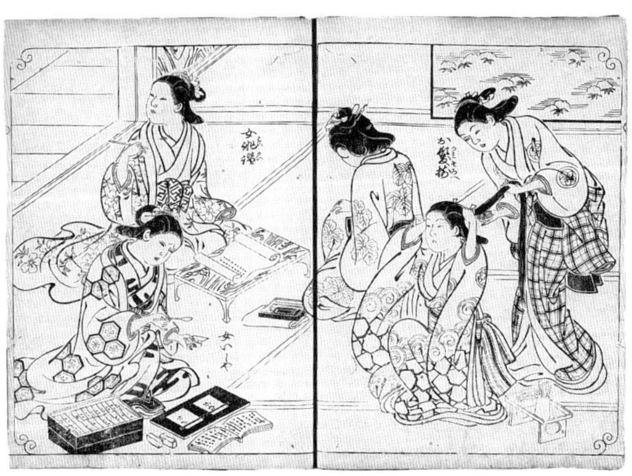

bather pictures with the 1869 pastels, as well as with Manet's known techniques at this point in his career.[48]

Degas' assertion that the air in a picture is not the same as that of the everyday world, though once again recorded towards the end of his life, was one of the most characteristic refrains of his career. He expressed similar thoughts in a number of guises: 'Art is the same word as artifice, that is to say, something deceitful. It must succeed in giving the impression of nature by false means, but it has to look true,' and 'One gives the idea of the truth by means of the false.'[49] Common to all these statements is the conviction that the artist's business is to represent the external world, in a way that is somehow 'truthful'. Equally evident is Degas' concern for what we might call the fiction of art, and for the structural and conceptual intricacies of its language. For Degas, such concerns showed themselves in the humblest aspects of his craft, such as the choice of a pose or a colour, and in the grandest flights of his historical reverie. When he drew his model in the studio for *Beach Scene*, he knew himself to be following in the footsteps of Ingres and Poussin, while simultaneously pursuing entirely modern perceptions. This teasing conjunction of artifice and realism often makes itself visible, at times uncomfortably, in Degas' imagery. The three figures in the Phillips Collection's *Women Combing their Hair*, for example, are individually plausible as depictions of the *toilette*, but in conjunction suggest a trio of instructive postures set against a pattern-book landscape. Though more naturalistically located, in a setting that once again recalls Dives-sur-Mer, the protagonists in *Peasant Girls Bathing in the Sea toward Evening* are almost as mannered, while the principal figures in *Beach Scene* are a triumph of both observation and design.

Alert to the deceits of art and fascinated by the language of veracity, Degas and his colleagues from the 'Salon of Realists' had long since fallen under the spell of that most exquisite and inventive of art forms, the Japanese wood-block print. From the early 1860s, Bracquemond, Manet, Moreau, Tillot and Whistler had acquired examples of Ukiyo-e prints, some in considerable numbers, and had emulated and frankly plagiarised their brightly coloured designs.[50] Degas' own collection of such prints was briefly itemised at the time of his death, but little is known of the dates or circumstances of their purchase.[51] What can clearly be demonstrated, however, is that a number of his paintings from this period, including his excursions into the landscape, show a lively response to Japanese art and even a preference for certain Japanese print-makers. Ando Hiroshige, claimed as the 'leading landscapist of the Ukiyo-e school', appears to have been Degas' favourite, accounting for more than forty landscapes in his private collection.[52] Amongst Hiroshige's specialities was the spacious panorama, sometimes interrupted by stark foreground forms but as often animated by little more than waves, rocks and distant sailing vessels. His print *Takanawa Ushimachi* shows a broad waterway truncated by the form of a harbour wall, much like that in Degas' *Cliffs on the Edge of the Sea*, and the spacious and expansive panels of his marine triptych *View of Awa No Naruto* (fig. 98) offer further comparisons with the landscape pastels.[53] In such works, Hiroshige addresses the vastness of the ocean and the emptiness of the shore, using tone, colour and local detail with an economy that was full of significance for Degas and his peers in the late 1860s.[54]

Other Japanese artists, again represented in Degas' collection, seem to lie behind his *Beach Scene*. The motif of the woman combing her hair, or having it combed by a friend or maid, first appears in Degas' work at this time, apparently in this picture. Though it is common in the Japanese repertoire, it

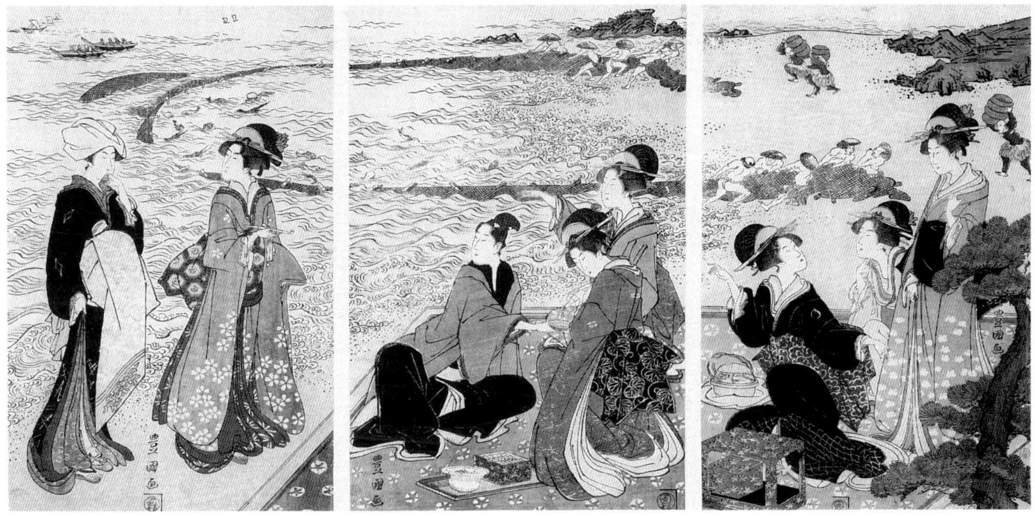

100. Utagawa Toyokuni, *A Picnic on the Beach*, *c.*1795–1800, woodblock triptych, 37 × 24 (sheet size). British Museum, London.

may have been initially suggested to Degas by an image from Sukenobu's *Critical Studies of One Hundred Women* (fig. 99), a copy of which he is known to have owned.[55] In addition, the unusual horizontal format of *Beach Scene*, with its three vertical sheets of paper mounted side-by-side, seems like a witty echo of the Japanese wood-block triptych. This echo becomes insistent as further comparisons are made. A three-panel work like *A Picnic on the Beach* (fig. 100) by Toyokuni, another print-maker whom Degas admired, offers a compelling precedent for the subject, format and even peripheral details of Degas' painting.[56] Toyokuni's beach group is more populous, but it depends on a similar opposition between flat, stylised figures and fabrics in the lower half, and remote, small-scale fishermen and boats in its distant landscape. Such works were widely known in Degas' circle, offering not only an alternative vocabulary of fashionable *motifs*, but a radical new approach to one of the pictorial problems of their generation: the integration of casual, yet artfully posed, figures into a landscape setting that remained ultimately believable.[57]

The evidence that *Beach Scene*, and by extension most of his landscape-based pictures from the Impressionist era, was painted in Degas' studio, has another, more sombre, significance. In the early 1870s, the first allusions to eye trouble appear in the artist's letters and in witness accounts by his friends, often in circumstances that suggest an advanced stage of debility.[58] A study of Degas' condition has shown that he suffered for much of his life from not just one, but several eye complaints, some of which would have made themselves felt in the early decades of his career.[59] Prominent among his symptoms was an intolerance of bright light, a condition known as photophobia, which was experienced in both natural daylight and the artificial surroundings of theatres and even domestic interiors. The possibility arises, therefore, that from the beginning of his working life, some of Degas' practices and inclinations as an artist were conditioned by the state of his eyes. Excursions into the landscape, such as those to Haras-du-Pin, Houlgate and the racetrack of the Bois de Boulogne, would have exposed him to discomfort and may well have contributed to his unease with *pleinairisme* in general. Conversely, such experiences would have recommended to Degas the stable conditions of a studio, where bright light could be avoided and his relationship with his subject controlled. In such surroundings, Degas' luminous pastels and oil paintings of outdoor subjects could be confected at leisure, though visitors report that they were produced behind the grimiest of windows and in conditions of wilful gloom.[60]

Soon after the Siege of Paris in 1871, an event in which Degas was involved and which may have exacerbated his eye complaints, the artist wrote to Tissot:

> I have just had and still have a spot of weakness and trouble in may eyes. It caught me at Chatou by the edge of the water in full sunlight whilst I was doing a watercolour and it made me lose nearly three weeks, being unable to read or work or go out much, trembling all the time lest I should remain like that.[61]

This passage is remarkable on a number of counts. In the first instance, it offers one of the earliest and most poignant accounts of Degas' eye condition and leaves us in no doubt as to its severity. Almost as dramatically, it describes Degas at work as a *plein-air* painter, carrying out a study in broad daylight in one of the landscapist's exemplary media, watercolour. Vivid as the account is, it has not been possible to identify the painting with certainty, though at least two existing studies suggest themselves as candidates.[62] Finally, Degas' letter hints at something like desperation, as he acknowledges the constraints on his painting activities and concedes that blindness may bring them to an end.

A year later, during a long excursion to America to see his brother, René, in New Orleans, Degas described in another letter to Tissot the colourful flowers, trees and streets he had seen, adding 'that is a bit of local colour if you want some, with a brilliant light at which my eyes complain'.[63] The possibility of painting such outdoor scenes was still clearly in Degas' mind, though the condition of his eyes conspired against him. Before returning to Paris, he wrote again: 'What lovely things I could have done, and done rapidly, if the bright daylight was less unbearable for me.'[64] From this period onwards, Degas spoke regularly of his visual disability, providing us with sufficient detail to identify a number of recognisable eye conditions.[65] Each of these would, quite literally, have affected his view of the world, and each had the potential to intrude on his artistic practice. None of them, however, proved debilitating, and Degas found some relief in visits to doctors and ophthalmologists, and in the wearing of dark glasses and specially prescribed eye shields.[66] As his career progressed, the artist also developed routines that minimised the inconvenience of his condition, preferring familiar surroundings and a structured relationship to his model.[67] It can even be argued that Degas' weakness was turned into strength, heightening his awareness of vision and presenting him with subversive perceptions that became part of his works of art.[68] Whatever its implications, the condition of Degas' eyes can never be entirely forgotten when approaching his landscape *oeuvre*, and it is evident that the artist himself often linked his visual problems to encounters with outdoor subjects.[69]

In the event, Degas travelled back from America in 1873 with a group of indoor portraits but, tantalisingly, no studies of the landscapes he had seen and described.[70] Within months, he had thrown himself into preparations for the first Impressionist exhibition, which took place the following spring. Hindered by his disabilities and fearful for the future of his eyesight, Degas nevertheless emerged as one of the driving forces behind the enterprise and, with ten submissions of his own, a more conspicuous exhibitor than Cézanne, Monet, Morisot, Pissarro, Renoir or Sisley.[71] As we have seen, in an exhibition dominated by landscape imagery, Degas' pictures were mistaken for *plein-air* studies by some critics and singled out by others as exceptions to this deplorable practice. Paul Mantz, for example, was soon to announce that 'Degas may be

101. Detail of fig. 91.

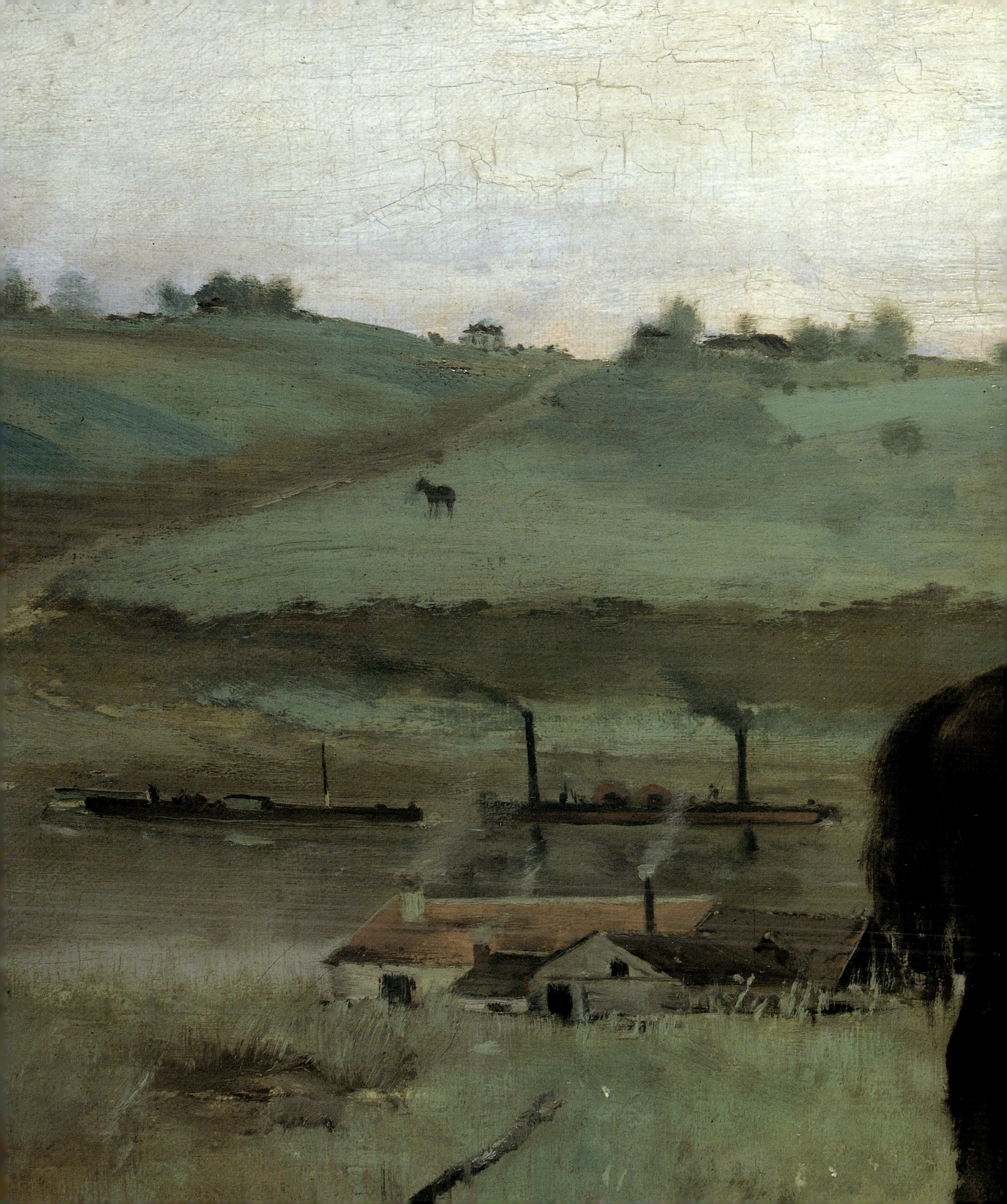

exhibiting near Pissarro and Sisley, Cézanne and Claude Monet, but he does not belong to the family', while Marius Chaumelin regretted that Degas had made 'concessions to the school of spots'.[72] The reality is, if anything, even more complex. In the 1874 show, Degas included neither pastels nor oil paintings of pure landscape subjects. On the other hand, three of his submissions were of equestrian scenes, amongst which *At the Races in the Countryside* was conspicuously based on an airy and high-keyed rural setting. When the links between this painting and Degas' outdoor pastels of 1869 are taken into account, a more subtle affinity with his fellow-exhibitors becomes apparent. In the second Impressionist exhibition of 1876, for example, Degas showed a portrait of Eugène Manet posed in the open air, a courtyard scene from New Orleans and his coastal scene of *Peasant Girls Bathing in the Sea*;[73] at the third exhibition of 1877, he included an outdoor portrait of Henri Rouart and another work associated with the Normandy pastels, the *Beach Scene*;[74] and in 1879, at the fourth exhibition, he showed the last of his equestrian scenes to be presented in this way.[75]

Broadly speaking, then, we can find a clear identification with landscape-based *motifs* in Degas' early Impressionist displays, followed by a steady decline and a final abandonment of such subjects in later exhibitions. In this sense, his first submissions were a natural extension of the versatility of the 1860s, when portraiture, racing subjects, genre scenes and landscape vied for his attention, and when his final destination as an artist was far from clear. In the years immediately before the 1874 show, Degas had produced a group of equestrian pictures and a sequence of outdoor bathing scenes, both manifestly dependent on the *plein-air* pastels of Dives-sur-Mer and Houlgate. It was natural that he should reflect this interest in his first public exhibitions, and just as natural that he should move away from such subjects as his self-presentation changed. During the 1870s, Degas became increasingly associated with subjects such as the café-concert and the laundress, and above all with the ballet, a reputation that was based largely on his Impressionist submissions. As the most emphatic figure painter of the group, he acquired a sharply defined artistic persona and a corresponding following of critics and collectors. Such specialisation had its dangers, as both Degas and his colleagues discovered. More than one was accused of repetitiveness or the exploitation of former successes, and Degas was described by Emile Zola in 1880 as having 'shut himself up in his specialities'.[76]

Despite Degas' public abandonment of landscape as one of his preferred subjects, his personal sympathy for the subject, and for its exponents both celebrated and obscure, remained undiminished. Indeed, the roll-call of landscape painters who formed part of his entourage, enjoyed his friendship or whose work he pointedly collected, reads like a directory of current practitioners of the genre. Some of them, such as Biard, Levert and Rossano, were minor figures by any standards;[77] others, like Tillot, Vignon and Cazin, moved in and out of his acquaintance and made their careers outside the Impressionist camp.[78] Ludovic Lepic, landscapist and print-maker, was a key figure in the evolution of Degas' monotypes, while Henri Rouart, who exhibited in seven of the eight Impressionist shows, was an unrepentant *pleinairiste* and life-long friend.[79] In the Italian circles frequented by Degas, de Nittis, Boldini and Zandomeneghi all worked as successful landscapists, though each was more renowned for their figure-based repertoire.[80] Among his associates from the previous decade, Boudin, Morisot and Whistler continued to play a part, if a somewhat reduced one, in his life.[81] And with each of the painters who put their conspicuous stamp on the Impressionist landscape,

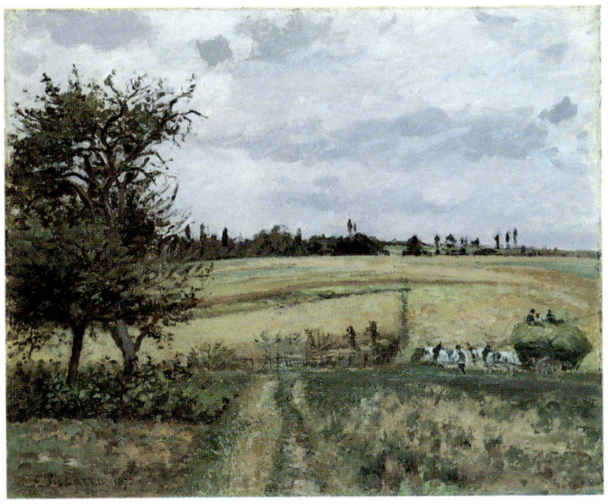

102. Camille Pissarro, *Landscape*, 1872, oil on canvas, 46 × 55. Ashmolean Museum, Oxford.

notably Pissarro, Monet and Cézanne, Degas evolved his variously productive rapport.

Of the latter three artists, Degas undoubtedly enjoyed the longest friendship and the closest professional intimacy with Camille Pissarro. They probably met in the circles of the Café Guerbois in the late 1860s, or perhaps even earlier, and exhibited together more often than any of the other prominent Impressionists.[82] Around 1880, the two artists collaborated on a projected print journal, *Le Jour et la nuit*, and their letters of this period, in one of which Degas complimented his friend on 'the art of your vegetable gardens', show them exploring new processes and exchanging recent proofs.[83] The irony of this situation was not hard to find and was certainly not lost on their contemporaries. That Degas, the scion of minor French aristocracy, should find common cause with the Jewish anarchist of Pontoise was extraordinary enough, but that 'le peintre du high-life' should share his studio with a specialist in vegetables was a sign of the changing times.[84] In spite of their differences and occasional misunderstandings, the lasting respect of these two painters for each other's achievement is well documented. When his son Lucien began to train as an artist, Pissarro went to Degas for advice and practical guidance, describing Degas as 'certainly the greatest artist of our times'.[85] Degas, in his turn, expressed his admiration by acquiring an extensive collection of Pissarro's works of every kind; his inventories include three oil paintings from the early 1870s, of which *Landscape* (fig. 102) is perhaps the finest, a gouache and a pen drawing, and more than thirty prints of Pissarro's etchings of rural and agricultural subject-matter.[86]

Our knowledge of Degas' estimation of his Impressionist colleagues is based partly on gossip, partly on the more remote, but no less eloquent, witness of his private collection. Though thoroughly documented at the time of his death, the dates of acquisition of very few of Degas' pictures are known and it has been assumed that the majority were accumulated in his later career. Two of the Pissarro canvases owned by Degas offer an illuminating exception to this rule. The first, *Terrains labourés près d'Osny*, was bought at auction in 1873 and its companion, *Sur la Seine à l'entrée de Bougival*, was purchased the following year.[87] Both pictures show Pissarro's rustic themes at their most uncompromising, and both demonstrate the 'crude tones' and 'coarse surfaces' that so irritated his critics.[88] Whatever their personal affinities, it is difficult not to see these purchases as a mark of approval and support from one artist to another, and of Degas' practical sympathy for the ambitions of his landscape-painting colleagues. Such a sympathy is repeatedly encountered in Degas' private holdings, which embraced the work of painters of all persuasions from the Impressionist enterprise. An oil-on-canvas *Inondation* by Sisley and a *Tahitian Landscape* by Gauguin; a seaside *motif* by Morisot and an outdoor bather by Cézanne; and landscape canvases, watercolours and prints by Piette, Cazin, Levert and Lepic among others, all attest to Degas' catholicity of taste.[89]

One name that is conspicuously absent from Degas' inventories is that of Claude Monet. Like Pissarro, Monet seems to have come into contact with Degas some years before the Impressionist venture and to have later worked beside him as organiser and publicist.[90] From the beginning, however, there was a coolness between the two men, exacerbated perhaps by informal rivalry within the group and by a common perception that they represented the opposing tendencies of the movement.[91] When a writer in 1876 suggested that 'Degas will take the place that Ingres holds now, while that of Delacroix is saved for Claude Monet, the colourist of the group', he hit on a raw nerve, at least as far as Degas was concerned.[92] Both artists were currently involved in a process of professional self-definition, and both may have used the example of the other to demarcate their territory. As Robert Gordon has argued, Degas appears to have set himself against Monet, gleefully inverting many of his colleague's priorities and mocking his identification with the excesses of the *plein-air* school.[93] On a visit to Etretat in 1882, Degas described the weather as 'More Monet than my eyes can stand', and on another occasion reportedly turned up his collar against the draught at a Monet exhibition.[94] According to other witnesses, Degas followed his rival's career closely and once expressed his envy for Monet's 'aplomb', contrasting it with his own laboriousness.[95] Monet himself left no comparable observations, but his acquisition of Degas' pastel *Woman at her Toilette* (Norton Simon Collection, Pasadena; L 890) and the evidence of his letters leave us in no doubt of his admiration for Degas' talent.[96]

A more fully documented case is that of Degas' relationship with the art and the person of Paul Cézanne. What we know of their private exchanges suggests an antipathy between individuals of contrasting origins, temperament and social sophistication.[97] As we look at their careers, however, a number of striking parallels emerge, not least in their relationship to the ideals associated with the Impressionist group. Though Cézanne remained broadly faithful to *plein-air* practice, both artists distrusted the rapid impression seized from nature, and both insisted on the disciplined character of their craft. Like Degas, Cézanne continued in his emulation of the Old Masters, exercising his right to paint portraits and genre studies, nude compositions as well as landscapes.[98] More specific conjunctions of taste can be identified in their exhibited work. At the first and third Impressionist exhibitions (the only two in which Cézanne participated), both artists showed representations of bathers and male or female nudes, subjects otherwise absent from the submissions of their colleagues.[99] Degas' alertness to this coincidence – and our first evidence of his fascination with his contemporary – is shown in a notebook drawing, where he recorded the outline of a figure from Cézanne's *Bathers*, shown in 1877.[100] Later in their careers the tables were turned, Cézanne admitting to Gustave Geffroy that his portrait of the critic was based on Degas' earlier portrait of Edmond Duranty, a work shown in the 1879 exhibition.[101] Degas' admiration was less equivocal in his role as collector, where he ultimately accumulated nine works by Cézanne: a drawing, a watercolour and seven oils.[102] Most are small, and all were acquired late in Degas' life, but the majority are characteristic of Cézanne's art of the 1870s and 1880s. Dominated by four still lifes, the group included also an uncompromising self-portrait (Reinhardt Collection, Winterthur) and *Venus and Cupid* (fig. 215), a work with curious intimations of Degas' own pastoral imagery.[103]

In the years of Degas' close association with the artists of the Impressionist group, two further factors contributed to his complicity in their landscape concerns: first, an increasing and even obsessive delight in travel, whether to visit friends, retreat from the city or make journeys for their own sake; and, second, a tenacious interest in landscape as background material, in his depictions of horses, portraits, dancers and, occasionally, nudes. Degas' travels were prodigious, by the standards of his own and almost any other age. With the possible exception of Monet, Degas was the most itinerant of the Impressionists, visiting Belgium, Spain, North Africa and America, and making several excursions each to Italy, Switzerland and Great Britain. Within his native country, Degas' journeyings were frequent and fearless, taking him from the Channel coast to the Pyrenees, from watering-places like Cauterets and Le Mont-Dore to the depths of Burgundy, and from Montauban to see the Ingres

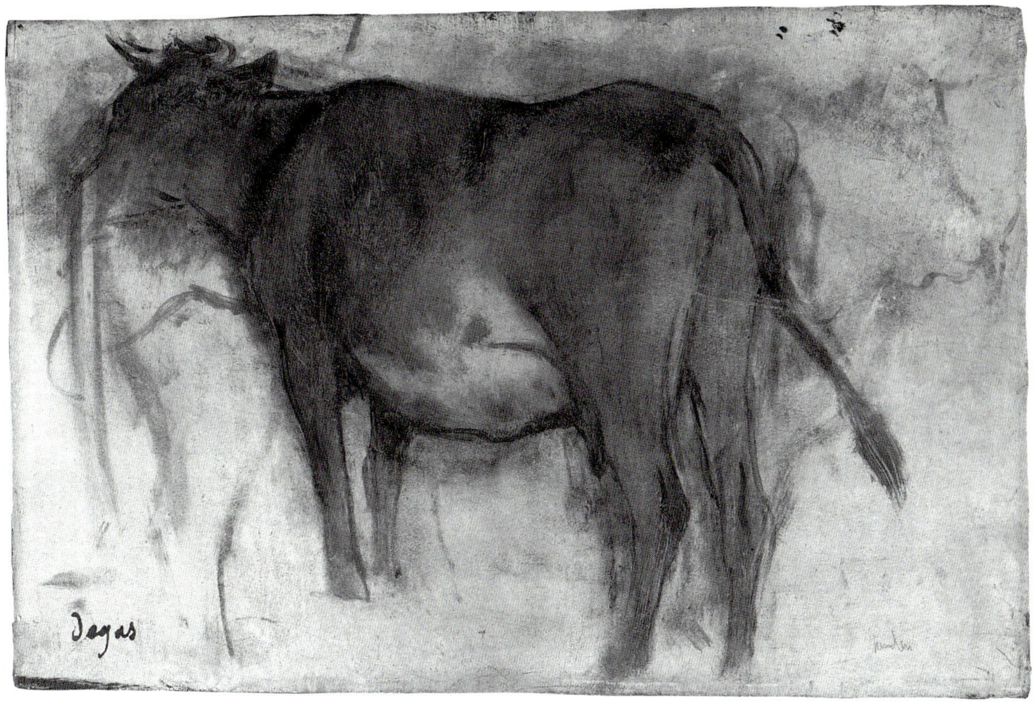

103. *Sketch of a Cow*, *c.*1876, oil on panel, 20.2 × 29.5 (L 510). Philadelphia Museum of Art: The John G. Johnson Collection.

drawings to Ménil-Hubert and Sucy-en-Brie for almost annual vacations with friends. Unlike Monet, however, Degas rarely travelled in order to paint. Typically, he regarded his peregrinations as an escape from studio routine or from personal and health worries, or as a means of sustaining geographically distant friendships. More often than is generally realised, however, Degas embarked on these visits with pastels or drawing equipment in his baggage and would explore both his surroundings and the pictorial challenges they posed. In 1873, for instance, we find him writing to Henri Rouart to tell him that he is

> considering walking to Rouen, along the banks of the Seine, of boarding pinnaces or a train if it happens to pass. So I rather fancy myself a stick in one hand but no parasol, studying values, the curves in the road . . . It is *nature*. I am expecting less delirious happiness from it than you, but just a little good for my eyes and a little relaxation for the rest of me.[104]

Subsequent letters refer to excursions of a similar kind, to the charms of the landscape and, teasingly, to a number of drawings and studies he may or may not have completed.[105] From Dieppe, he announced in 1884, 'What lovely country. Every day we go for walks in the surroundings, which will finish up by turning me into a landscapist. But my unfortunate eyes would reject such a transformation.'[106] A number of scattered and diverse landscapes exist that may have been produced on these outings. Apart from a group of pastels produced in the late 1880s, which seem to prepare the way for the coloured monotypes of the next decade, there are drawings, watercolours and works in oil on canvas and board. In Lemoisne's catalogue, we find studies of forest clearings and fields, oil paintings of Normandy-like countryside, and, unforgettably, the handsome sketch of a cow (fig. 103).[107] As a group, these pictures illustrate Degas' growing confidence, not to say virtuosity, with rural *motifs* and an increasing willingness to tackle the most humble of themes. By this stage in his career, he had reduced his reliance on notebooks, but a few glimpses of the landscape, such as the view of Etretat made in 1882 (fig. 104) and a drawing of

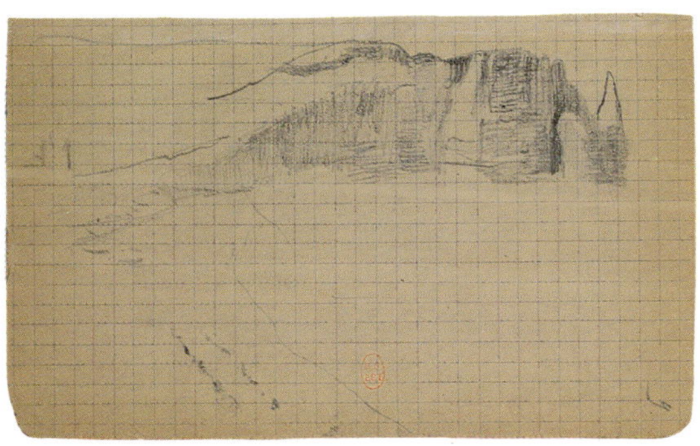

104. *View of Etretat*, 1882, pencil, 13.5 × 8.6. Notebook 35, page 9. Bibliothèque Nationale, Paris.

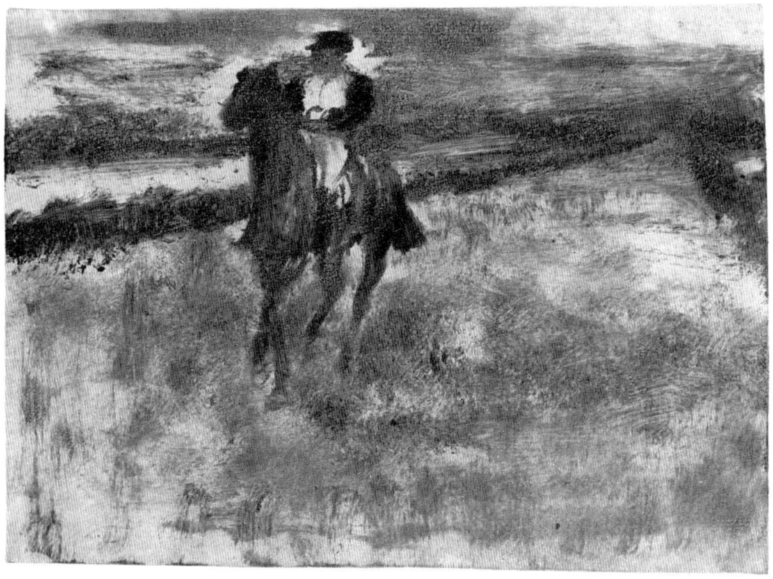

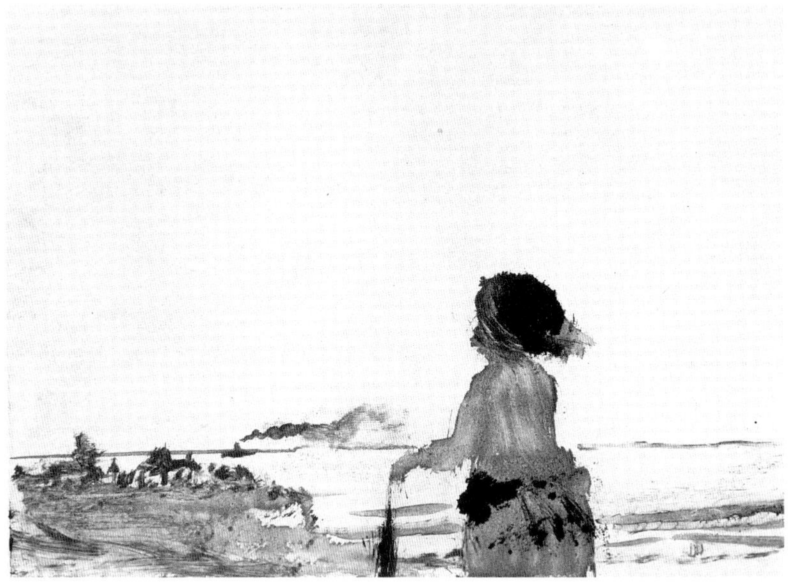

105. *The Jockey*, *c.*1877–9, monotype, 12 × 16 (J 261). Sterling and Francine Clark Art Institute, Williamstown, Mass.

106. *Beside the Sea*, *c.*1877–9, monotype, 12 × 15.8 (J 264). Private collection.

a colourful skyscape, record the progress of his travels.[108] Another study, inscribed 'August 1885' and entitled *Houses at Mont-Saint-Michel*, reinforces the impression that Degas made drawings as part of his holiday ritual and is linked with a documented visit of that year.[109] Whatever else they may signify, these varied responses to his surroundings do not result from an aversion to the open air, nor to an under-valuation of the landscapist's art. Not for the first time, we find Degas registering his satisfaction with a number of the works in question by signing them and releasing them to friends or on to the contemporary market.[110]

Historically and technically, the most resonant group of landscapes to have emerged from Degas' rural rides are his black-and-white monotypes. Paradoxically, they also seem to contradict many of the practices most widely associated with Impressionism. All the dozen or so monotypes are small, with one or two approaching postage-stamp scale; each is printed in black or brown ink; and none is coloured with pastel, unlike their contemporary equivalents showing ballet and cabaret themes. Necessarily, each monotype was made in the studio, away from the *motif* and from the moment of perception.[111] To complete their singularity, none appears to have been exhibited during Degas' lifetime, thus removing them from the disputes and critical debates that surrounded the Impressionist project. Despite their obscurity, the monotypes provide a crucial link between the landscape imagery of Degas' earlier career and the dramatic blossoming of this technique in the early 1890s. Some of the prints hark back almost pedantically to the opening phases of his career: *The Jockey* (fig. 105) recalls the equestrian imagery of the 1860s; the delightfully economical *Beside the Sea* (fig. 106) echoes the landscape pastels of 1869 and, with the *Bathers* (private collection; L 262), the beach scenes of the same period. Other subjects show the extent to which, regardless of their intimate scale and lack of colour, these works share something of the contemporaneity of Renoir, Manet and Caillebotte. The *Avenue du Bois de Boulogne* (fig. 106*bis*) is one of Degas' very few street scenes, while *Factory Smoke* (fig. 107) brings rather wittily to mind the industrial *motifs* of Monet and Pissarro, as well as Degas' much-quoted ambition to make pictures of 'smoke from locomotives, from tall factory chimneys, from steamboats'.[112]

106*bis*. *Avenue du Bois de Boulogne*, *c.*1878, monotype, 12.1 × 15.9. The Fitzwilliam Museum, Cambridge.

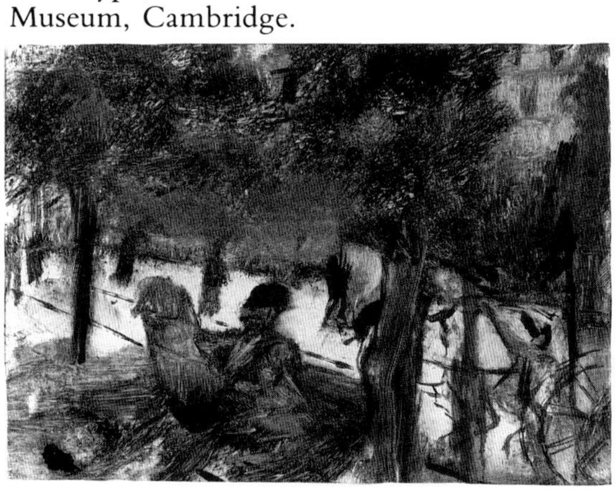

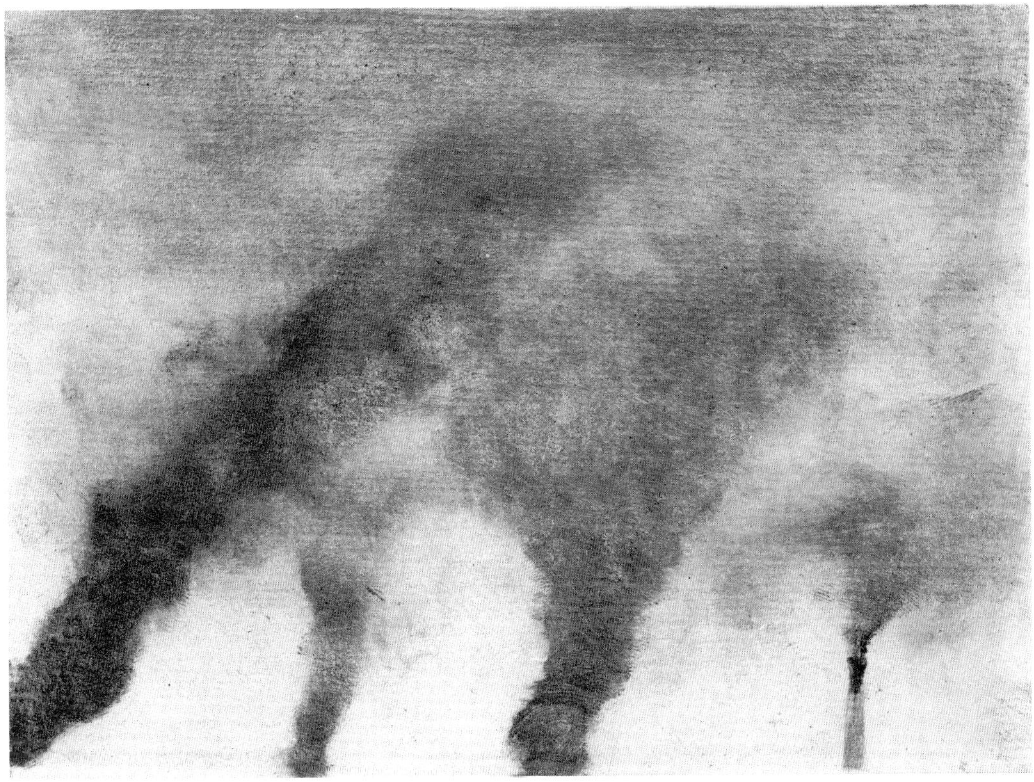

107. *Factory Smoke*, *c.*1877–9, monotype, 11.9 × 16 (J 269). The Metropolitan Museum of Art, New York, The Elisha Whittelsey Collection, The Elisha Whittelsey Fund, 1982.

Another subject widely associated with Impressionism, the picnic or rural excursion, finds its monochromatic, miniaturised expression in two of Degas' prints. *A Family out Walking* (fig. 109) and *Rest in the Field* (fig. 108) seem like two phases of the same expedition, the first more purposeful and clearly defined, the latter more provisional, even breathless. The range of their techniques, from the hasty smear to the precise, needle-sharp detail, also reminds us of their proximity to those other modern-life sequences, the brothel monotypes and the *Famille Cardinale* prints, all datable to the late 1870s.[113] In 1877, Degas had announced in the catalogue of the third Impressionist exhibition the inclusion of a number of 'Drawings made in oily ink and then printed', thus unveiling a technique he had experimented with privately the previous year.[114] His submissions included three framed groups of such works, probably with more than one image per frame, as well as other individual monotypes he had reworked in pastel. Critical response to the pictures was slight and has proved insufficient to identify the works in question, though it has always been assumed that figurative, rather than landscape, subjects were shown. Irrespective of their imagery, each of the prints was made by a process at once simple and far-reaching in its consequences. With the initial encouragement of Ludovic Lepic, who had shown his own landscapes in 1874 and 1876, Degas had learnt to manipulate ink on the surface of a copper plate, then print it directly on to a sheet of dampened paper. Whether depicting a landscape or a brothel scene, the artist could preserve the sketch-like vitality of a scene like *Landscape with House, Figures and Fountain* (fig. 107*bis*) or retain his monochrome prints for further embellishment.

107*bis*. *Landscape with House, Figures and Fountain*, *c.*1878, monotype, 17.8 × 22.2. British Museum, London.

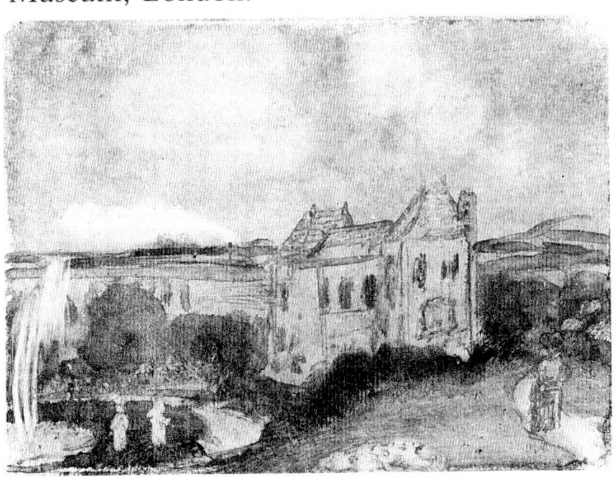

The challenge and the appeal of the monotype technique for Degas were immediate. Involving none of the protracted deliberations of etching, the monotype process encouraged spontaneity, suggesting new kinds of marks to be made with brushes, fingers and rags, and prompting bold and unrehearsed

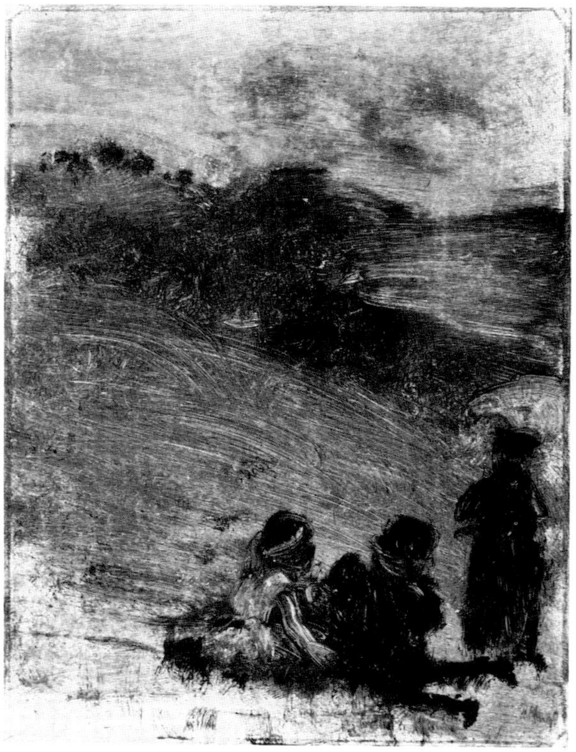

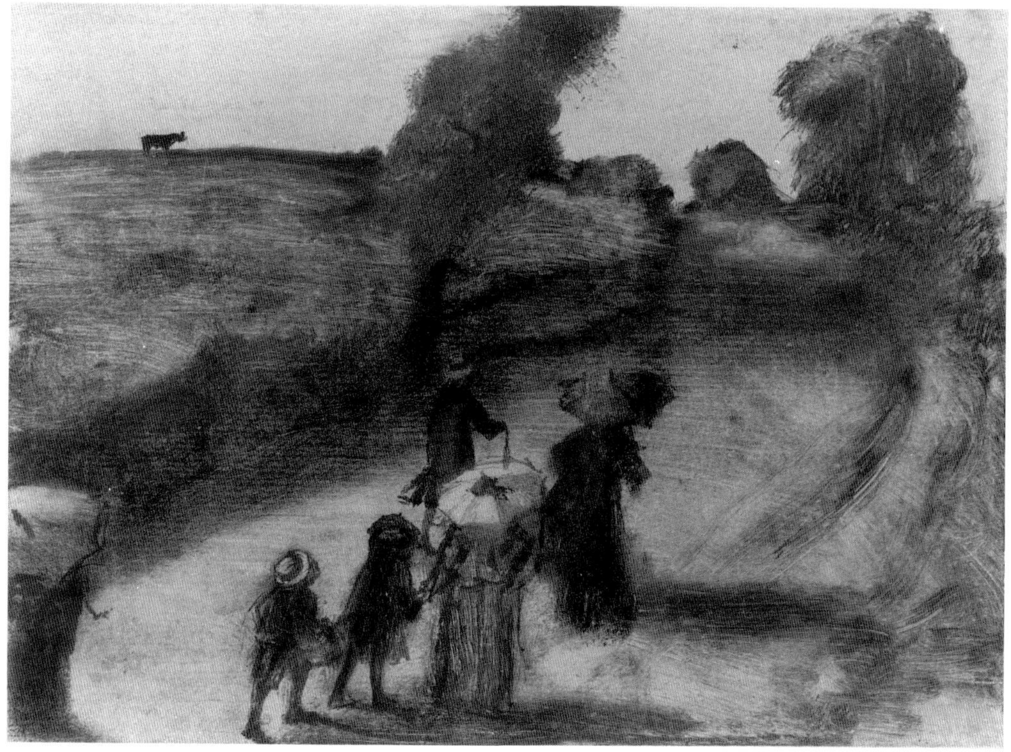

108. *Rest in the Field*, *c.*1877–9, monotype, 21.2 × 16 (J 265). Sterling and Francine Clark Art Institute, Williamstown, Mass.

109. *A Family out Walking*, *c.*1877–9, monotype, 15.8 × 21.3 (J 263). Private collection.

effects of chiaroscuro. At the same time, and in a sense that was fraught with particular significance for Degas, the new process fell somewhere between drawing and painting, separating out the need for form and structure from the requirements of colour. Up to the moment of printing, the black or brown ink on the plate remained pliant, allowing the artist to inscribe lines and adjust contours until his image fell into place. Once printed, this image resembled an *ébauche*, or tonal preparation, as used in traditional painting practice to form the basis for a final glazing in colour. Like his predecessors, Degas could choose to leave this image in its initial state, delighting in the play of tones and the subtle evocation of other monochromatic media, such as relief carving, etching and photography. Like his predecessors also, he could advance to the next stage, superimposing on his neutral groundwork the glories of oil paint, gouache or pastel. For reasons that have never been explained, Degas used this process selectively, applying colour with something like abandon to his monotypes of the ballet and the cabaret, and preferring to leave most of his brothel subjects in their muted tones. Surprisingly, the landscape prints of the late 1870s were also left in their original condition and never developed with the tints and hues of nature. It was to be more than a decade before the artist pursued his own technique to this conclusion, both initiating and completing the Burgundy monotypes of 1890 in some of the most spectacular colours of his career.

The principal limitation of the monotype process, then as now, is that only one true print of each image can be made. During the printing, most of the ink is transferred from the plate to the paper, and subsequent attempts to print from the residue will produce, at best, only one or two ghostly echoes of the original subject. These secondary proofs, or cognates, were habitually used by Degas to generate pastel variants of his initial composition, often becoming lost beneath swathes and crusts of brilliant colour.[115] But, in its essentials, monotype is a procedure for transferring a unique drawing from one surface to another,

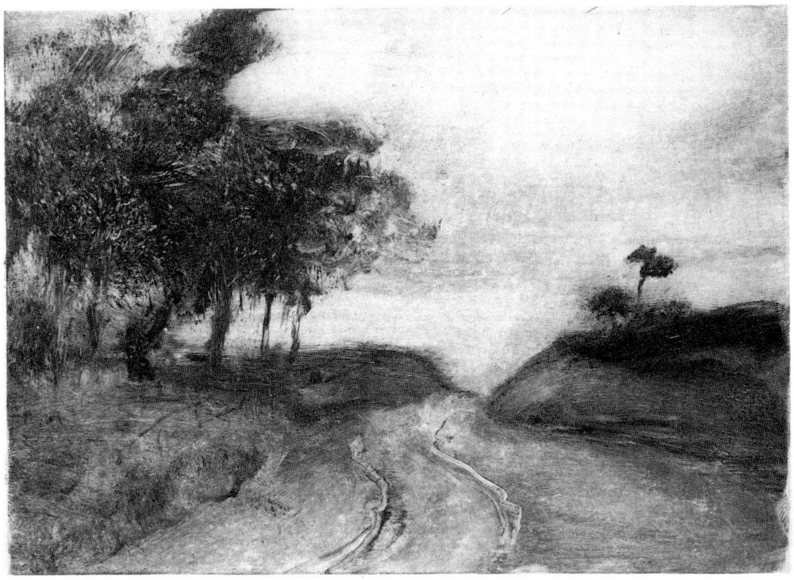

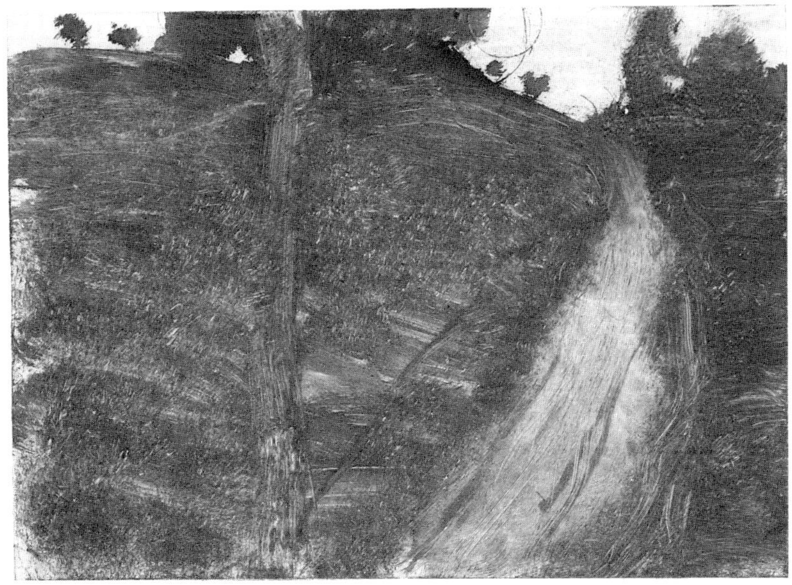

110. *The Road*, *c.*1877–9, monotype, 11.8 × 16.1 (J 266). National Gallery of Art, Washington, D.C., Rosenwald Collection.

111. *The Rising Road*, *c.*1877–9, monotype, 11.7 × 16 (J 267). Museum of Fine Arts, Boston, Horatio Greenough Curtis Fund.

112. *Moonrise*, *c.*1877–9, monotype, 11.9 × 16.1 (J 270). Sterling and Francine Clark Art Institute, Williamstown, Mass.

113. *The River*, *c.*1877–9, monotype, 8.9 × 17.3 (J 272). Museum of Fine Arts, Boston, Katherine Bullard Fund.

allowing the artist maximum freedom to add to, or subtract from, the fluid membrane of ink on the plate surface, then presenting him with the finality of a printed image. The challenge of the technique is to seize this moment, even to communicate something of its immediate and hazardous urgency. From the beginning, Degas seems to have grasped its potential, exploiting chance effects and nuances of surface on the one hand, and finely controlled draughtsmanship on the other. In *A Family out Walking*, for example, Degas spelled out the precise gait, the distinctive apparel and the accessories of half a dozen individuals, all with fine strokes of the brush and within the confines of a postcard-size rectangle. In the very different *Rest in the Field*, a few flourishes of ink were enough to summarise hills and sky, and other brushings and wipings suggest, but hardly describe, a family group. Some of these marks were clearly made with Degas' hands rather than with brushes, and it is instructive to note the use of fingerprints, even at this early stage, as part of the modelling process.

The dexterity and technical licence of the series is at its most uninhibited in the small group of pure landscapes, devoid of promenaders, factory chimneys and narrative devices of all kinds. *The Road* (fig. 110) is a *tour de force* of mark-making, offering us dabs and striations, soft hazes of tone and stark

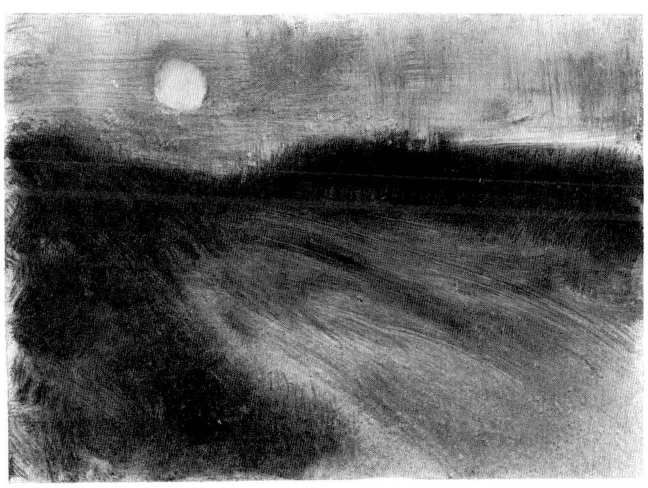

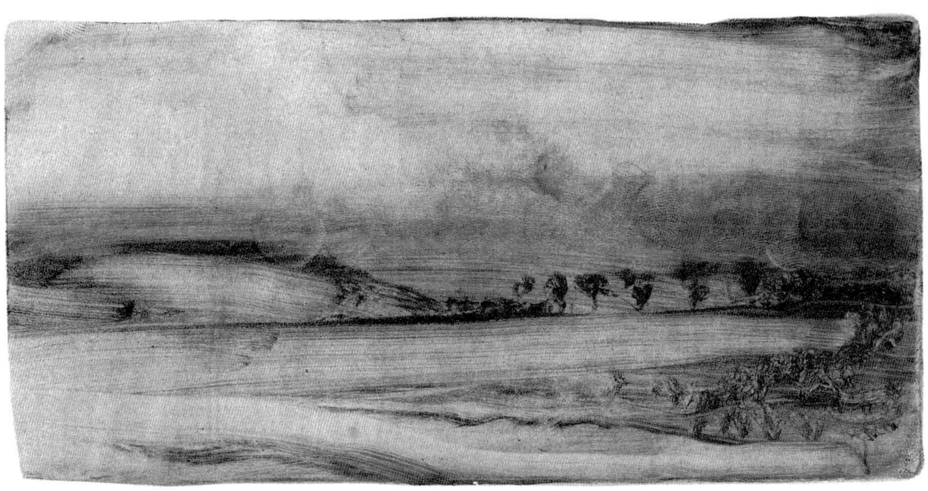

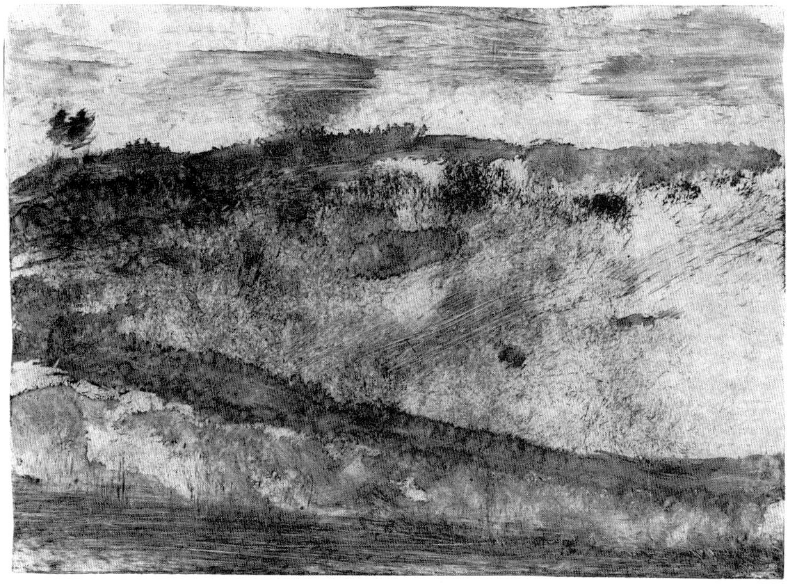

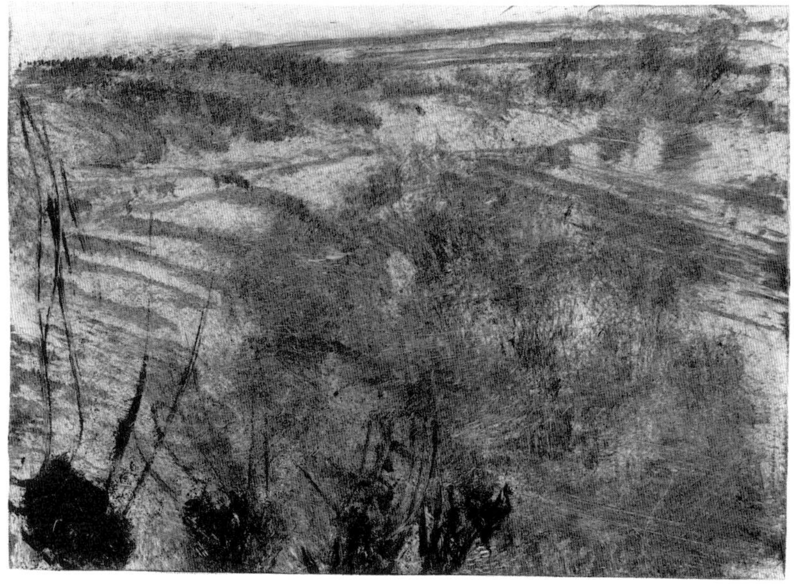

114. *The Little Valley*, *c.*1877–9, monotype, 11.9 × 16. Bibliothèque Nationale, Paris.

115. *The Valley*, *c.*1877–9, monotype, 11.9 × 16. Bibliothèque Nationale, Paris.

bristlings of foliage, finely painted trees and lightly scratched wheel-ruts. Streaks of ink make up virtually the entire composition of the *Rising Road* (fig. 94), one of Degas' most densely-textured and uncompromising monotypes. Forcing the horizon up to the top of the picture, Degas seems to tip the landscape towards us, flattening the hillside and drawing attention to his lattice-work of brushmarks. A similar, almost abstract, structure is adopted in *Moonrise* (fig. 112), though here it is used to more obviously dramatic effect. Few prints are as slender in their means as *The River* (fig. 113), where three or four liquid, almost random, sweeps of an inky finger have established sky, hills and waterway. Minimal though they are, such works illustrate with unusual clarity the interplay of medium and *motif*, of subject and substance in Degas' most daring monotypes. At another extreme, a pair of monotypes recently acquired by the Bibliothèque Nationale, Paris, shows the patient accumulation of marks and the detailed decription of landscape features. In both *The Little Valley* (fig. 114) and *The Valley* (fig. 115) a persuasive particularity is achieved, while their sweeping forms and confrontational masses prepare the way for the colour monotypes of later years.[116] Though nothing is known of the circumstances in which these monochrome prints were made, everything points to a conjunction of visual experience and studio experiment, with remembered imagery directing the artist's improvisation and haphazard textures recalling familiar scenes.

In parallel with, and sometimes dependent upon, such glimpses of the countryside, Degas extended the use of the landscape into other areas of his repertoire. Like so many of his co-exhibitors at the Impressionist shows, he made telling advances in the outdoor portrait, depicting friends and models in a variety of rural and metropolitan contexts. At about the time he was introducing Degas to the monotype process, Vicomte Ludovic Lepic was painted as he crossed the place de la Concorde in Paris, and in *Henri Rouart in front of his Factory* (Carnegie Museum of Art, Pittsburgh; L 373), Degas' landscape-painting friend was shown against railway lines, chimneys and industrial smoke.[117] Other canvases represent children in parks and girls in gardens, subjects of both sexes posed in open fields, and a small army of women leaning against gates and fences.[118] Isolated in this company, a single female nude became the subject of a magnificent pastel, *Girl Drying Herself* (fig. 116), where she stands unselfconsciously in the open air, flanked by a grassy bank and a distant copse. Shown at the 1886 Impressionist exhibition as part of Degas' 'suite of nudes', this work has often been passed over in silence, perhaps because it contradicts so emphatically the assumption that the entire series was based on images of prostitution.[119] In reality, it belongs to a vigorous line of pastoral compositions that runs throughout Degas' *oeuvre*, leading back to the beach scenes of the early Impressionist era and forward to the Poussinesque rural bathers of the 1890s. It is also a powerful example of Degas' use of landscape to define context and meaning in a picture, rather than merely to fill in a background. Here, figure and setting illuminate each other, the nude bringing animation to her surroundings, while her own flesh is 'infinitely shaded by the ambient atmosphere', as one contemporary critic put it.[120]

The significance of painted backgrounds, whether of outdoor or domestic subjects, had been explicitly addressed in one of the founding texts of Impressionism, Edmond Duranty's 1876 essay *The New Painting*. Duranty, a close friend of Degas and the subject of one of his most forceful portraits, insisted on the dynamic, documentary function of painted settings, arguing that

> a person never appears against neutral or vague backgrounds, Instead, surrounding him and behind him are the furniture, fireplaces, curtains and walls that indicate his financial position, class and profession . . . He might be avoiding carriages as he crosses the street or glancing at his watch as he hurries across the square.[121]

116. *Girl Drying Herself*, 1885, pastel, 80.1 × 51.2 (BR 113). National Gallery of Art, Washington, D.C., Gift of the W. Averell Harriman Foundation in memory of Marie N. Harriman.

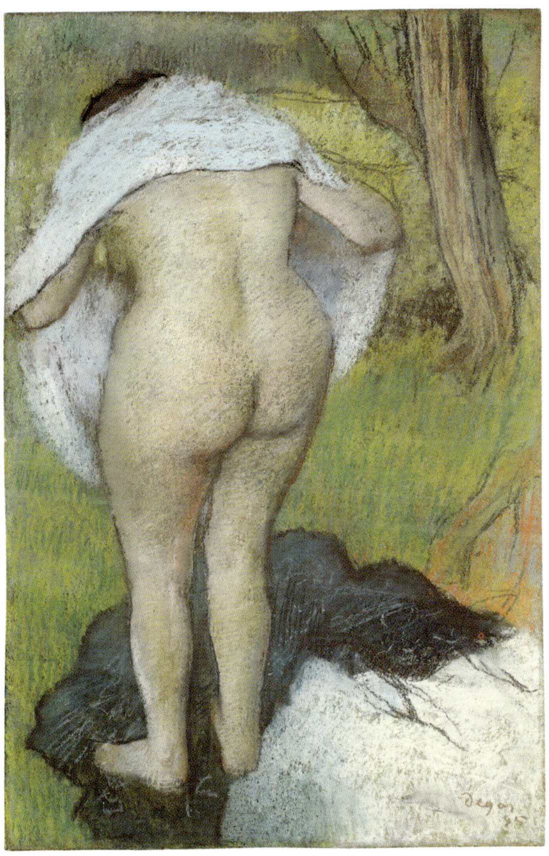

Degas' pictures were clearly in Duranty's mind, and certain of his portraits of the mid-1870s, such as *Henri Rouart in front of his Factory*, may well have helped to articulate Duranty's ideas. Another group of Degas' paintings, the racecourse scenes, shows the application of similar principles to an exclusively open-air subject, as well as the gradual erosion of these principles with the passing of time. Some of these images, such as *Horses before the Stands* (Musée d'Orsay, Paris; L 262), must have delighted Duranty and his fellow-Realists, showing in loving detail the distant spectators, pavilions and enclosures that provided the visual and social backdrop to the event, and hints of the industrial landscape beyond.[122] Already in the 1870s, however, Degas' attention was shifting to the horses themselves, and to the arabesques they performed in more neutral settings. Buildings and crowds disappeared, replaced by rural paddocks or uncluttered exercise fields, and soon the horse-race was little more than a memory. In a picture such as *Before the Race* (fig. 117), jockeys and their mounts wander aimlessly against a featureless landscape, telling us much about Degas' mastery of form and movement, little about the realities of the turf.

This shift from background seen as a detailed, socially descriptive inventory to background as an expressive arena is well exemplified in the equestrian pictures of the 1880s. In literally hundreds of drawings, pastels and oil paintings, elegant thoroughbreds are depicted at rest and at play, waiting in line or nervously prancing. Some of the pictures were made in series, notably a group of frieze-like compositions in oil and pastel that seem like contributions to a decorative scheme.[123] *Racehorses* (fig. 118), for example, is animated by a kind of musical notation, leading the eye across the picture surface from one cluster of forms or moment of rest to another. The stave-like horizon encourages this forward progress, while trees and hedges provide accents and inflections, and gently enrich the chromatic ensemble. In this work and its companions, landscape appears mutely to reassert itself, not as a narrative element but as a spatial and dynamic force. This tendency is carried to extremes in a number of later studies, where diminutive jockeys are dwarfed by empty vistas and

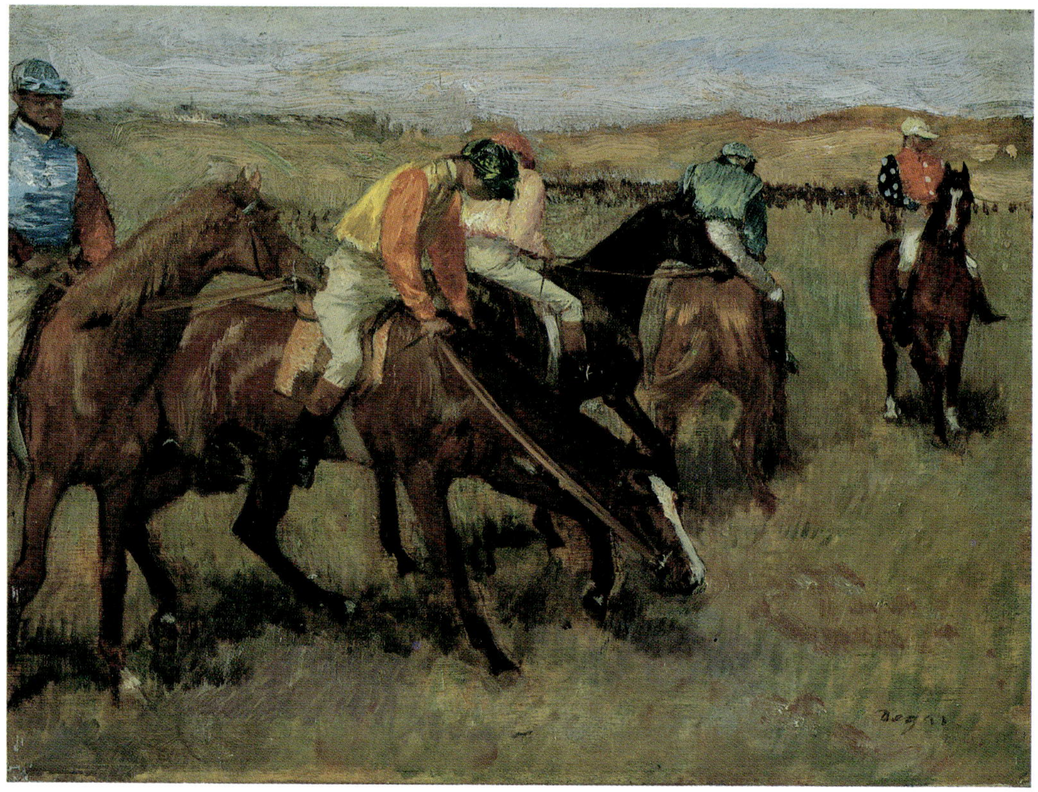

117. *Before the Race*, 1882, oil on panel, 26.5 × 34.9 (L 702). Sterling and Francine Clark Art Institute, Williamstown, Mass.

118. *Racehorses*, *c.*1885, pastel, 37 × 87 (BR 111). Carnegie Museum of Art, Pittsburgh.

towering hillsides. The real subject of *Racehorses in a Landscape* (fig. 207), it might be argued, is the blazing, coral-pink sunset, not the indecisive group of men and animals beneath.

Rather surprisingly, none of Degas' horse and jockey pictures of the 1880s was shown in the Impressionist exhibitions of that decade. Still anxious,

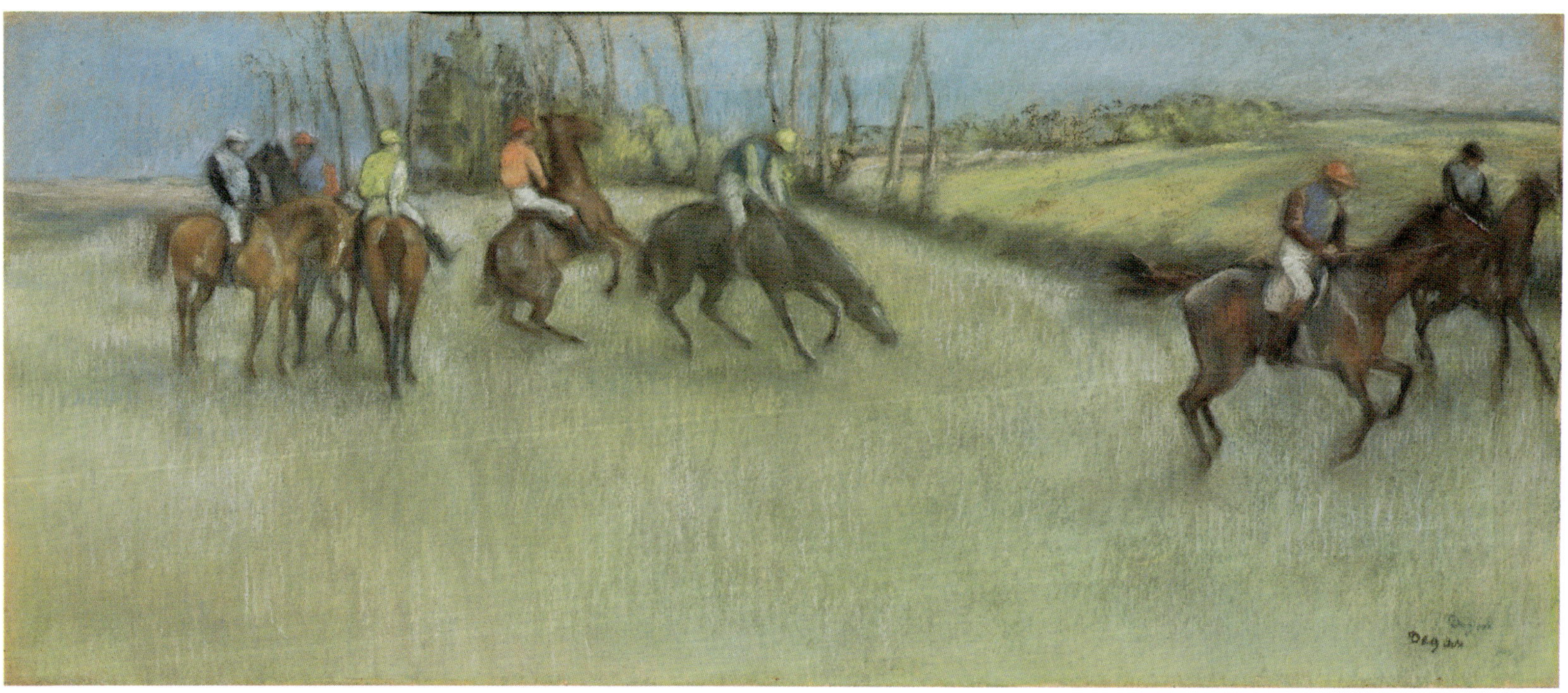

perhaps, to assert his reputation as the leading figure artist of the group, Degas continued to select portraits and theatre scenes, female nudes and the occasional laundress for public display. Equally, Degas may have been content with the brisk trade in his equestrian scenes that already existed, and with the prominence these pictures had achieved on the open market. Many of the pastels and oils sold straight from the studio, to be resold by dealers like Durand-Ruel or Theo van Gogh and acquired by the distinguished collectors of the day. *Before the Race*, for example, was bought in 1883 by Henri Lerolle, artist and patron of Renoir and Gauguin, who displayed it in his Paris apartment and presumably encouraged its inclusion in the background of Renoir's *Yvonne and Christine Lerolle at the Piano*.[124] A similar work passed through Boussod et Valadon five years later, another was sold to Mary Cassatt's brother, while *Racehorses* appeared in a New York auction as early as 1887.[125] In this sense, Degas was almost as celebrated as the artist of the turf as he was in his role as 'the painter of dancers', a reputation he soon began to regret.[126] By chance and by intention, his equestrian pictures were among the most popular of his products and have remained the only well-known landscapes of his middle years.

In what circumstances were the equestrian landscapes made? Though the historical record is scant, almost everything we know about Degas' working practice suggests that drawing or painting outdoors, using mobile animal and human models, would have been out of the question. By the same token, his preference for making pictures from memory, and for building up compositions from preparatory studies, is well documented and is amply borne out by the surviving evidence. In dozens of drawings, sculptures and even photographs, poses known from his racecourse pictures can be found, sometimes alone and sometimes in new and less familiar permutations.[127] These studies themselves, of course, may have originated in first-hand observation, but in almost every case the finished *ensemble* of a painting or pastel appears to be a confection, a synthetic re-combination of existing parts. Just as Degas had claimed that the figures in his earlier *Beach Scene* were arranged in the privacy of his studio, so the protagonists of *Before the Race* can be shown to derive from models and sketches, all manipulated at the artist's discretion.[128] The jockey who leans forward over his horse's head, for instance, makes another appearance at the centre of *Racehorses* and continues to reappear in pastels and related oil paintings. Similarly, the horse riding away into the distance, sometimes rearing up on its hind legs, becomes a virtual fixture in Degas' equine vocabulary.

Writing to the singer and collector Faure in 1886, Degas announced that he was working on a painting of the horse-race, but added 'I shall have to go and see some real racing again and I do not know if there will be any after the Grand Prix.'[129] Though he was flagrantly trying to win time from his patron, Degas' letter hints at an entirely characteristic need for contact with his source material, a need that remains consistent with the artificiality of his studio practices. However contrived they may have been, his equestrian scenes aspired to plausibility and needed continual refreshment, either from imagination or from the first-hand encounters of the track. Not the least of these needs was for landscape backgrounds, whether reticent or imposing. In contrast to the figures of horses and jockeys, almost no studies have survived for the paddocks and pastures, hedgerows and spinneys that make up their surroundings.[130] Furthermore, drawings of the riders and their mounts tend to lack even the most rudimentary settings, as if in preparation for the demands that would be put upon them. Using recollection and ingenuity, Degas conjured up his later racecourses at whim, hinting at vistas and suppressing spaces as the composition demanded. In the circumstances, we must often marvel at his mastery of the natural scene, while reminding ourselves that 'the air you breathe in a picture is not necessarily the same as the air out of doors'.

The role of artifice in Degas' landscape settings is turned on its head in that most synthetic of all contexts, the ballet. Here, the starting point is one of contrivance, of the suspension of disbelief amongst cardboard forests and gas-lit glades. In representing the ballet, the artist can choose to subscribe to this illusion, transporting his dancers to ethereal realms and taking for real that which is mainfestly bogus. Alternatively, he can mock the pretence, bringing us down to earth with glimpses of stage machinery and showing the dancers for what they are, tired, fallible operatives. Broadly speaking, Degas opted for the latter course, though rarely without humour and often with an uninhibited delight in the glamour, the extravagance and the visual fictions of the stage. As a painter of scenery, he was something of a virtuoso. His pastels, tempera paintings and oils embrace tropical beaches and snow-capped peaks, coconut palms and alpine lakes, bosky glades and fantastic grottoes. But even as he depicted these chimerical scenes, he rarely failed to subvert his own skills, interposing a glimpse of the orchestra or hinting at the practicalities of back-stage life.

True to his view of himself as a member of a 'Salon of Realists', Degas' first ballet scenes were matter-of-fact, almost documentary in intent. In the pioneering trio of pictures based on the *Ballet Rehearsal on Stage*, shown variously in the early Impressionist exhibitions, the artist described the proscenium and the wings, the orchestra pit and boxes, the scenery flats and their lurking male attendants.[131] Here, the landscape setting is reduced to an absurdity, a series of crudely painted cut-outs without benefit of lighting, music or the mysterious alchemy of performance. By contrast, in the pastel over monotype *The Star* (fig. 119), which was exhibited in 1877, we witness a ballerina in full flight, her frothy elegance made more insubstantial by the glare of the footlights. Typically, Degas reveals the background to be a sham, an all-purpose amalgam of trees, foliage and hills that provides cover for waiting dancers and *abonnés*. Two years later, at the 1879 exhibition, the artist included his monumental *Aria after the Ballet* (fig. 120), presenting the latest fruits of his research into theatrical contrivance.[132] In this pastel, the artist has moved closer to the action and views the dancers frontally, thus precluding any sideways glances into the wings. Momentarily, we can believe ourselves on a mountainside, enjoying the company of our brightly dressed companions and gazing at the spectacular forests and peaks beyond. The illusion, of course, is brief, and through the agency of the footlights, the monstrous double-bass scrolls and the sheer extravagance of the *ensemble*, the artist brings us firmly back to earth.

119. *The Star*, *c.*1876–7, pastel over monotype, 58 × 42 (L 491). Musée d'Orsay, Paris.

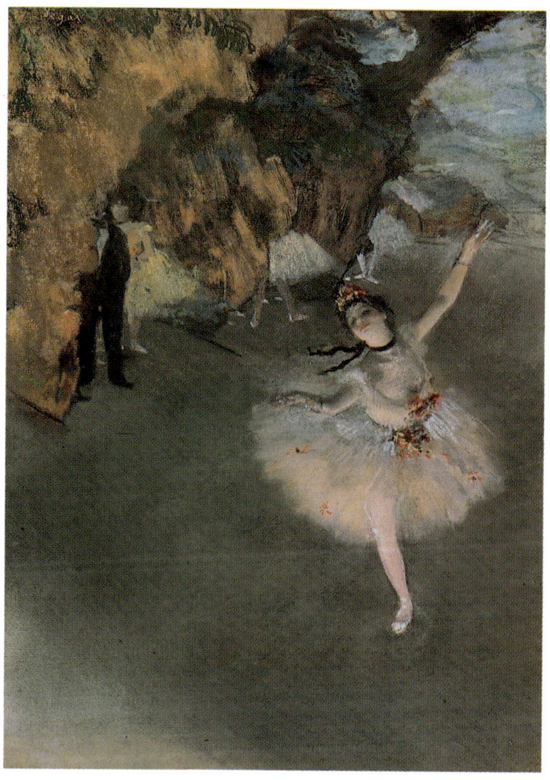

Several of Degas' dance scenes have been identified with specific ballets and documented productions, but in most cases we cannot be sure of their historical significance.[133] Degas was certainly an avid, and at times fanatical, visitor to the Paris Opéra, where ballet performances were held, attending certain productions more than a dozen times.[134] On the other hand, not a single detailed drawing of theatrical décor has been preserved, either in the artist's notebooks or in the backgrounds of his dancer studies. As with the equestrian series, we are obliged to assume that the painted backdrops of hills, skies and forests were made from memory and from the accumulated experience of a practised spectator. Again, we should note in passing the virtuosity of Degas' talents, as he reconstructed a setting in his distant studio or freely invented a mossy bank or a forlorn

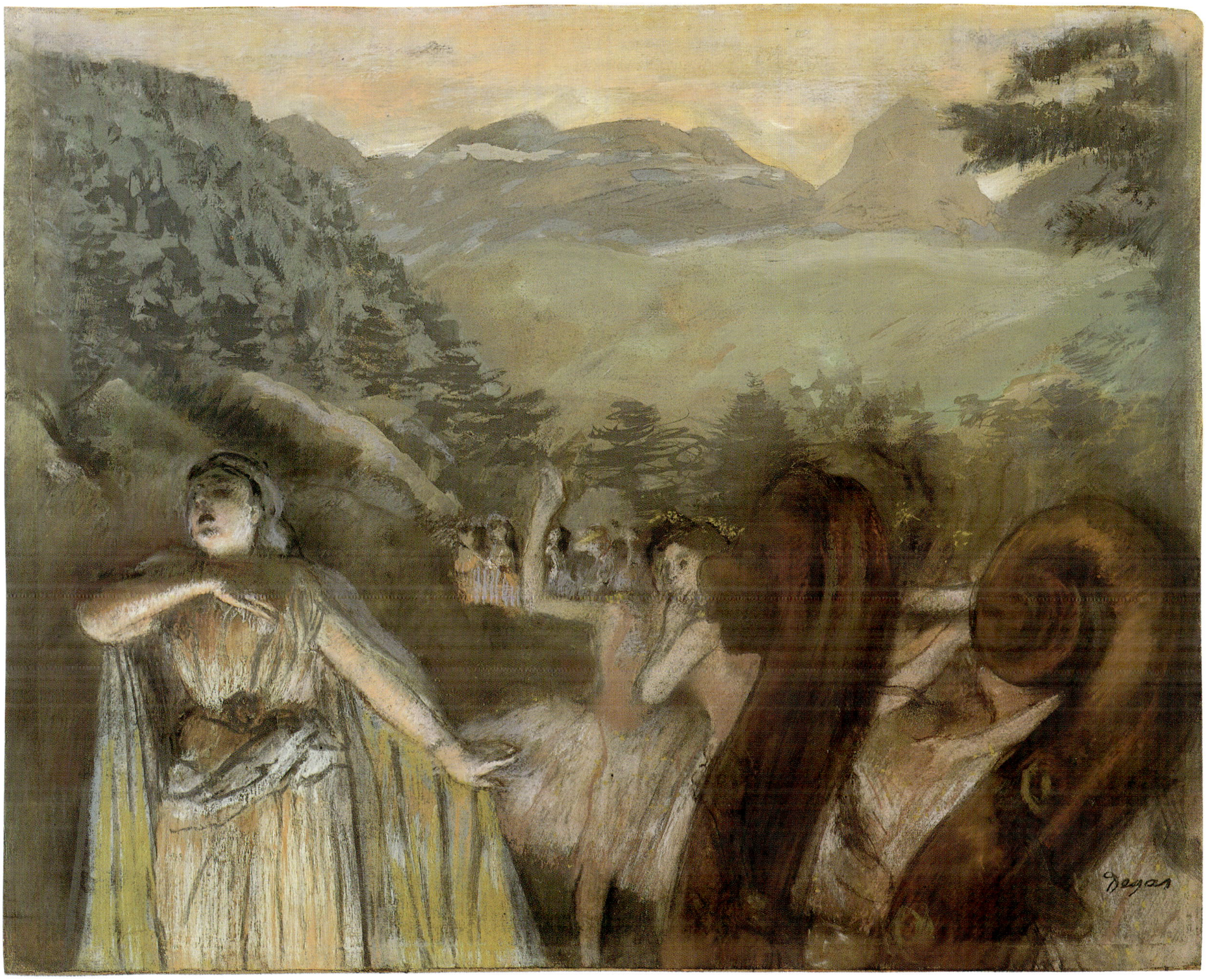

120. *Aria after the Ballet*, *c*.1879, pastel over *peinture à l'essence*, 59.7 × 75 (L 521). Dallas Museum of Art, Wendy and Emery Reves Collection.

seashore. At times, he seems to capitulate to the theatre's magic, revelling in the preposterous and the fairy-like as much as the banal. Some of his fan paintings, for example, use the same irridescent colours and cheap gilding as the décor itself, and more than one suggest an underwater world of coral reefs and glittering, balletic fish. Over the years, this fascination with the ambiguous and the suggestive became dominant, replacing the artist's insistence on the mechanics of stage life. A figure such as that in *Dancer* (Museum of Fine Arts, Boston; L 484), made perhaps in the late 1880s, seems at one with her tapestry-like surroundings, which are both dense and ill-defined. By suppressing the paraphernalia of the theatre, Degas has lifted the performer and her audience to an indeterminate realm, neither entirely prosaic nor strictly poetical. Does this dancer curtsy on stage, or in some exotic, twilit moonscape?

The transition in Degas' landscape settings from the localised and descriptive to the expressively indeterminate can be traced in his ballet pictures, his racecourse scenes and his other outdoor subjects. It can also be seen as symptomatic of a deeper upheaval in his art, and even of a broader shift in the concerns of his contemporaries. While such generalisations are by their nature hazardous, shifts of this and other kinds within the unfolding Impressionist enterprise have been energetically mapped in recent years. Though often regarded as peripheral to the group's evolving interests, historically Degas was at their centre, and his pervasive achievement was acknowledged, if sometimes idiosyncratically, in the writings of contemporary critics. In the 1870s, Duranty had linked Degas with the heroism of modern experience, and with the depiction of 'the walk, movement and hustle and bustle of passersby . . . the trembling of leaves, the shimmer of water, and the vibration of the sun-drenched air'.[135] At the end of the decade, his works were still seen as 'accurate' and 'truthful', culminating in Paul de Charry's description of the *Little Dancer Age Fourteen* as 'extraordinarily real'.[136] By the early 1880s, both Degas' pictures and the critical terminology used to discuss them were undergoing a transition. His ballet scenes, Octave Mirbeau proclaimed in 1884, were 'not just simple paintings or studies, but meditations on the dance'.[137] With some insight, Mirbeau went on to note that the horserace paintings had 'a sort of kinship with the dancers', and suggested that both had a 'violent and cruel synthetic character'.[138]

The new vocabulary of criticism, ritually invoking such concepts as 'synthesis', 'abstraction' and 'artificiality', was increasingly applied to Degas' imagery in the 1880s, and frequently by critics associated with the Symbolist movement.[139] Qualities such as colour and line would be discussed without reference to their subjects, and analogies with emotional states and correspondences with other art forms would be rehearsed. In separate articles, Mirbeau proposed that the paintings of Monet and those of Degas might be compared to music, and developed the idea of a series of images as musical variations, not in the context of Monet's pictures, but of those of Degas.[140] Such critical conceits, of course, tell us as much about the latest bee in the writer's bonnet as about the paintings in question, but there is reason to believe that the two artists shared Mirbeau's concerns, or at least his terms of reference. In their letters and conversations, Monet and Degas would both discuss a *motif* as though colour were its principal feature, and both were engaged in developing suites or serial representations of their subjects. When he unveiled his pastels of bathers at the eighth and final Impressionist exhibition of 1886, Degas invited his audience to see them as a 'suite of nudes', and in Monet's later shows of poplars and haystacks, admirers were encouraged to use the musical analogy.[141] Such easy comparisons, however, do little justice to the complexities and contradictions of the decade, and we search in vain for a critical or theoretical consensus. What is significant in the present context is the perception of change within Degas' work, and of a certain affinity between Degas' pictures and the developing sensibilities of his colleagues, and former colleagues, in the Impressionist circle.

Before taking our leave of the Impressionist decades, one small and almost entirely overlooked group of Degas' landscapes demands to be considered. Though none is dated, all offer links with the artist's output in the 1880s, and several point towards the radical experimentation of the following decade. Strictly speaking, the group consists of a number of pairs or clusters of works, each cluster demonstrating a new technical departure or a brief contact with a new theme or historic precedent. The majority are studies in pastel and were

121. Detail of fig. 120.

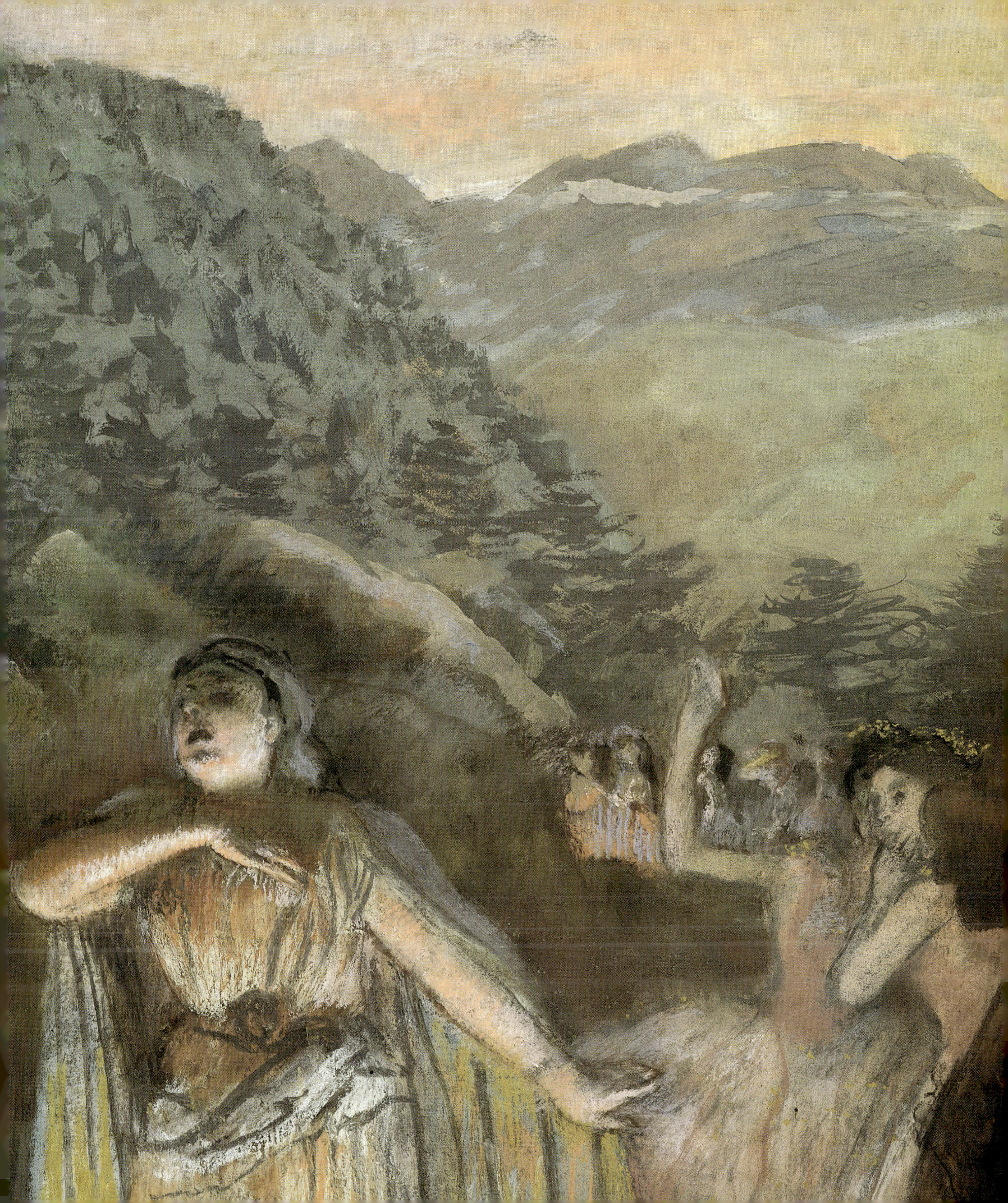

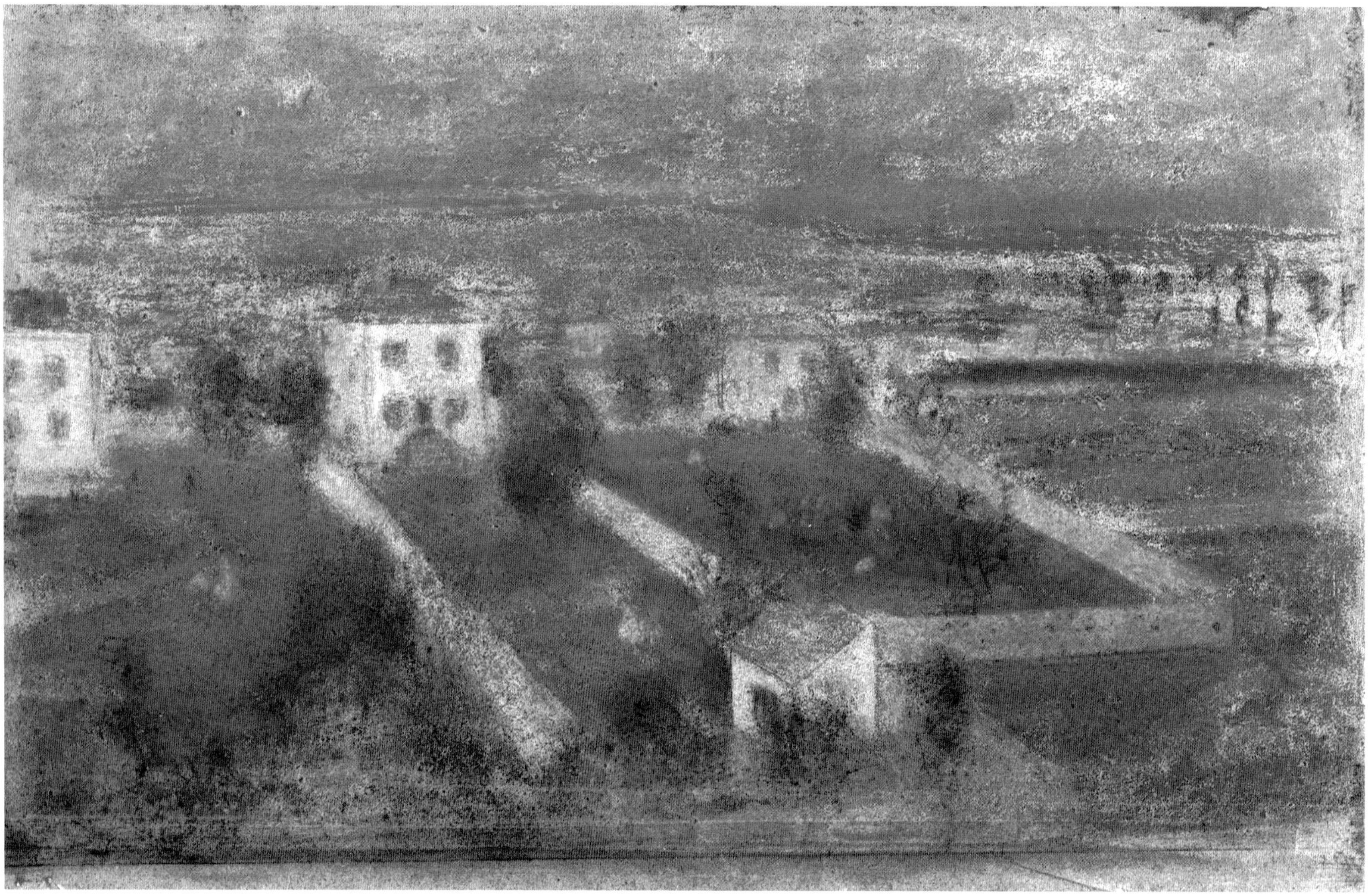

122. *Landscape at Louveciennes*, *c.*1885, pastel, 29 × 44. Private collection.

probably made on visits to the countryside, while their handling recalls the landscape backgrounds of current ballet and racecourse scenes. As drawings, they remind us of Degas' continuing engagement with the rival qualities of line and colour, which are often expressed in competing lattice-works of contours, cross-hatching and brightly tinted pigment. Still haunted by the disciplines of his youth, Degas drew sustenance from his seniors and his peers, and even in mid-career could respond to the innovations of the younger generation, such as Gauguin and Redon. His drawings of the 1880s show many of these factors at work, and, limited in size and extent though they are, reveal the restless and original maker of landscapes of earlier decades.[142]

Landscape at Louveciennes (fig. 122) is a previously unpublished and entirely unexpected image that has few precedents in Degas' career.[143] Starkly suburban in subject, it appears to depict newly constructed houses with crisp, geometric garden walls, built at the margin where town and country intersect. As in the rest of this family of images, Degas has established a high horizon and exploited the broad, pattern-making qualities of the subject. The *motif* itself reminds us forcibly of the work of Caillebotte or Pissarro; the latter's *House of Père Gallien, Pontoise* (Ipswich Museums and Galleries) has an almost identical range of architecture, though seen from ground level, while his *View from my Window, Overcast Weather* (Ashmolean Museum, Oxford), which was shown in the 1886

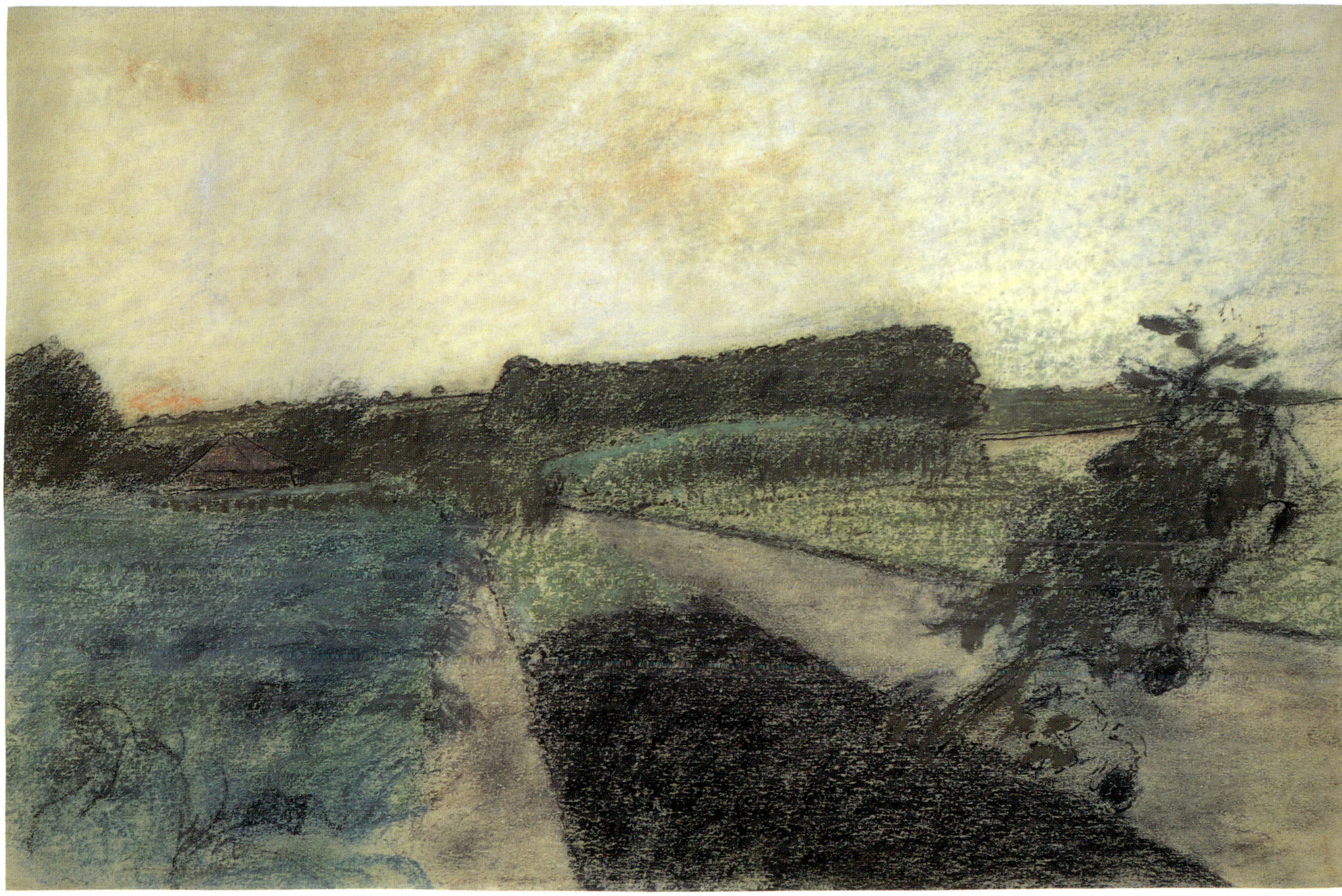

123. *Landscape in the Orne*, *c.*1885, pastel, 27 × 41 (BR 103). Private collection.

Impressionist exhibition, uses a similarly high viewpoint and angular structure.[144] Technically, Degas' drawing shows an immediate kinship with a small group of studies from this decade, exploiting the contact between rubbed, granular pastel and coarse, cheaply produced paper.[145] A somewhat similar pastel describes the Château de Ménil-Hubert (private collection, Paris; BR 102), the Normandy home of the Valpinçon family and recognisably the backdrop for some of the artist's later photographs.[146] Though the analogy should be used with caution, such pastels recall the uses of the snapshot photograph, made perhaps as souvenirs of a visit to a fellow-artist, such as Pissarro, or of a holiday with childhood friends.

Another sequence of pastels that derives from Degas' sojourns at Ménil-Hubert is represented by *Landscape in the Orne* (fig. 123), which was first owned by the Valpinçon family.[147] Two features of this work, one prominent and the other obscured, are of particular significance. First, it is a landscape without a dominant centre, and almost without a subject in the familiar sense of that word. It thus belongs to a seam of imagery that runs quietly through Degas' landscape *oeuvre*, from the Channel coast pastels of 1869 to the 1892 monotypes and beyond. Arguably, *Landscape in the Orne* is an extreme case in point, presenting us with little beyond blocks of texture, passages of tone and muted flurries of colour. Despite plunging orthogonals in road and flower-bed, we return repeatedly to the surface and its broadly stated patternings, as well as to its graphic agitation. The second characteristic of the drawing is both technical and historical. Recent examination has shown that the pastel was applied over a linear, monochromatic drawing, as so often in Degas' works in this medium. Most unusually, however, this underdrawing was made with a fine pen and dark-brown ink, rather than with Degas' customary charcoal.[148] Hesitant, almost awkward pen lines run around the boundaries of fields and groups of trees, while a curiously dotted, stitch-like contour defines the softer forms. At least two other works from the group under review exhibit the same characteristics, with finely incised lines visible beneath a rich upper layer of pastel.[149] In addition, a pair of related but unfinished drawings show us the same process at an earlier stage. This pair were left in the form of pen-and-ink studies, with starkly traced landscape forms and intermittent passages of dotting that come close to carelessness, suggesting that later reworking was envisaged.[150] One of the pair, *Landscape with Fence in the Foreground* (fig. 124), represents a subject not unlike *Landscape in the Orne* and must indicate something of the pastel's original appearance.[151]

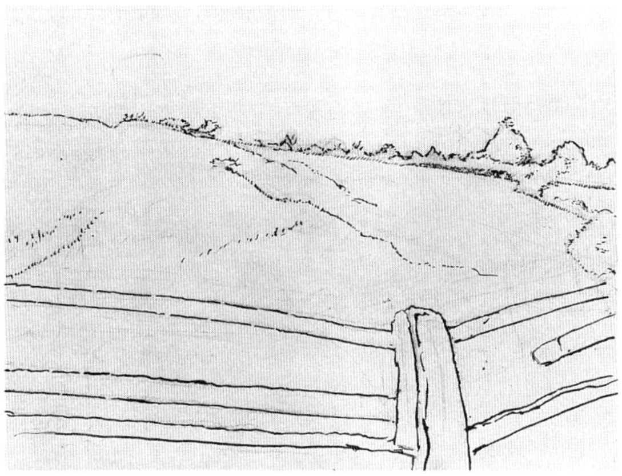

124. *Landscape with Fence in the Foreground*, *c.*1885, ink, 19 × 25. Ashmolean Museum, Oxford.

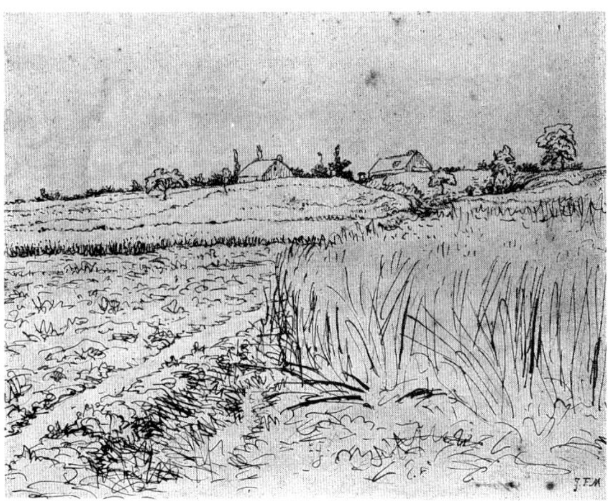

125. Jean-François Millet, *Farm on the Heights of Vichy*, 1866, ink, 21.7 × 25.5. Kunsthalle, Bremen.

Why did Degas choose pen and ink, one of the media least favoured in his maturity, to make the underdrawings for these pictures? The answer seems to lie in the work of Jean-François Millet, a painter, pastellist and draughtsman much admired by Degas in later life. According to Sickert, Degas' 'wholehearted admiration seemed, among the moderns, to be given to Millet, to Ingres and to the earlier Corot', a claim at least partially borne out by Degas' own collection.[152] Millet was a habitual and inventive user of the pen, making fine ink drawings not only of figures but of simple, boldly patterned landscapes of the kind favoured by Degas. Typically, these drawings consisted of wiry outlines and lightly hatched shadows, often accompanied by lines of staccato dots like those in Degas' *Landscape in the Orne.*[153] In Millet's pen drawing *Farm on the Heights of Vichy* (fig. 125), these elements can be seen clearly, with distant paths indicated by trails of stippling and a field of corn by bristling, erratic strokes of the nib. The same drawing shows Millet's propensity for high horizons, empty foregrounds and spare, geometric construction, and further elucidates his appeal for Degas. Typical also was Millet's habit of working up such drawings in colour, often overlaying his ink contours with watercolour and occasionally with pastel or wax crayon. Here, the resemblance to Degas' experimental studies seems even closer, and the historic link between the two artists becomes complete.

The 1880s was a period of widespread enthusiasm for Millet's work, culminating in a retrospective of his pictures at the Ecole des Beaux-Arts in 1887. Since his death in 1875, Millet had been admired and collected by many individuals in Degas' circle, amongst them the financier Ernest May, who had been painted by Degas; the painter Tillot, former intimate of Millet himself; and Degas' dealer, Paul Durand-Ruel, who exhibited Millet's work in his gallery.[154] Most prominent in this context, however, was Degas' close friend Henri Rouart, who amassed a substantial group of Millet's drawings, one of which was depicted in the background of Degas' painting of his daughter, Hélène Rouart.[155] Many of the drawings in question were carried out in Millet's distinctive pen-and-ink technique, and a number of sheets formerly in the Rouart collection, such as *Farmland near Vichy* (private collection, Paris), were finished with a final layer of colour.[156] There can be no doubt, then, that Degas was familiar with such works and that he encountered them frequently at the homes of friends.[157] By the same token, he may also have been aware that

Millet produced sequences of these drawings, choosing a single *motif* and manipulating its components at will. *Farm on the Heights of Vichy*, for example, is one of at least seven drawings of the same site, in which paths find themselves realigned, foregrounds are reinvented and details such as cottages and trees are redisposed with casual ease.[158] This degree of licence was, of course, familiar to Degas in the context of his ballet and equestrian pictures, but as yet had no true equivalent in his landscape *oeuvre*.

Degas' brief engagement with the work of Millet in the 1880s was yet another of his occasional and sometimes eccentric contacts with the landscape art of his own century.[159] Even his links with Impressionism, and his preference for the company of *pleinairistes* like Rouart over that of major practitioners like Monet, were defined by something approaching perversity. In the early days of the movement, Degas clung to his long-standing associations, such as those with Tissot, Fattori and Bracquemond, resisting the startling colours and impetuous outdoor facture of his newer colleagues. Typically, he aligned himself for a time with the obscure Lepic, who revealed to him the secrets of that most uncanonical of processes, the black-and-white monotype. While his friends painted in Pontoise and Argenteuil, Degas travelled to America, Switzerland, Spain and Tangiers, bringing back pictures of none of these of places. Soon, however, in the crepuscular light of his studio, he conjured up oriental sunshine and African snowscapes, twilights full of dancers and glades astir with nymphs. Ill at ease in the open air, Degas learnt to rely on memory and improvisation, deriding those who clung to cliff-edges in search of sincerity. Countless jockeys and horses were put together from his reserves of drawings, some already a decade or more old, then arranged against sparkling pastures and plausible but fictitious racetracks. Contrary to the end, Degas never ceased his journeyings, often making secretive forays into rural imagery while visiting far-flung colleagues. Throughout these years, landscape served as a private challenge in an otherwise public career, stimulating him to experiment and keeping him discreetly abreast of his contemporaries. In its contrariness, it seems to follow the uncertainties of earlier decades and perhaps hints at a continuing unease with the claims of the genre. After the last Impressionist exhibition of 1886, when the group finally dispersed in disarray, we might have expected a shift in Degas' attitudes, or at least a change in their complexion. Nothing, however, prepares us for the radical about-turn in his practice, or for the single most dramatic phase in his landscape-making history.

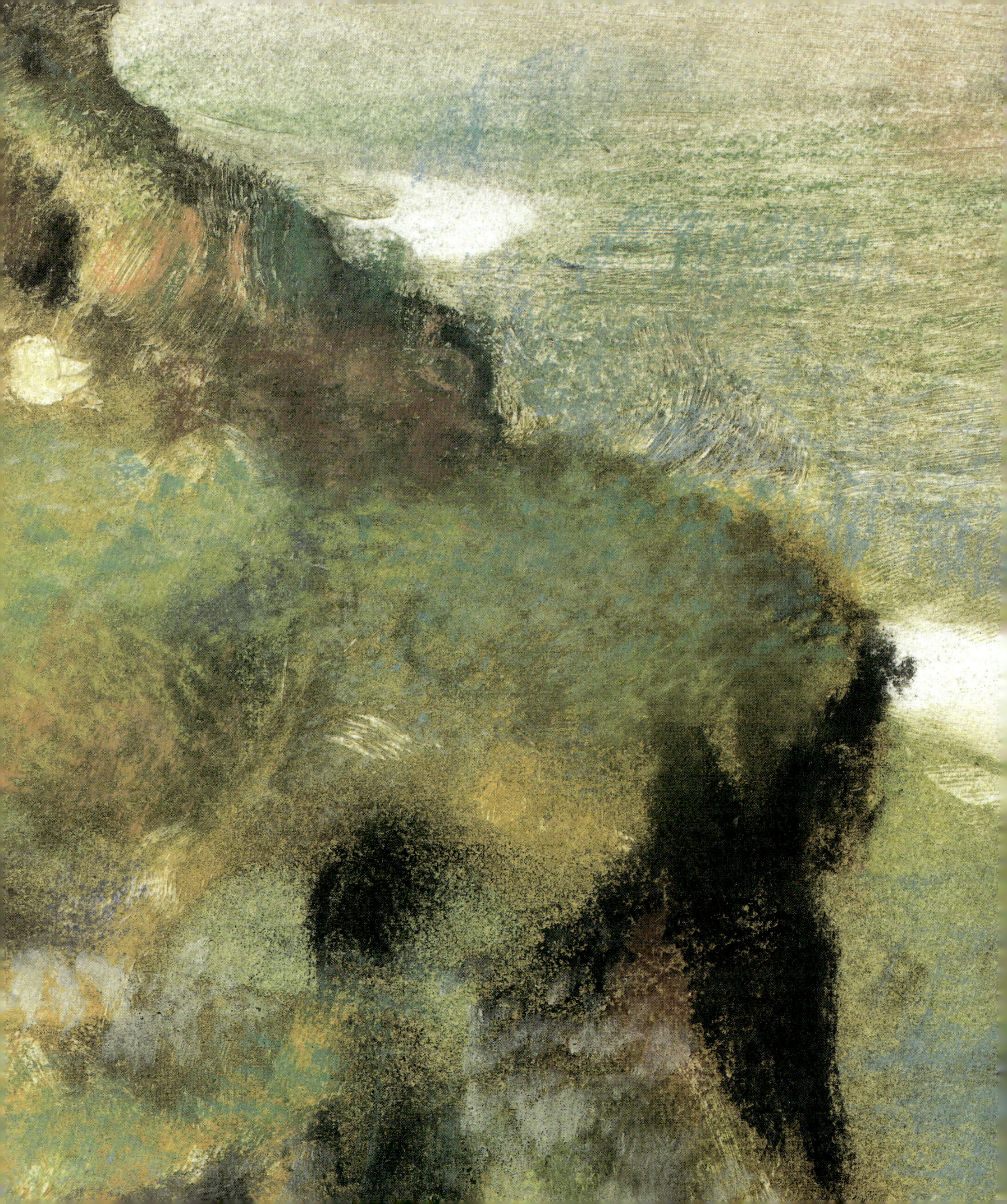

6 The Visit to Diénay

'One needs to have been sad and serious for a long time to enjoy oneself so much'
(Degas, in a letter of 1890)

In September 1890, Degas the inveterate traveller, loyal friend and stubborn landscapist set out on another journey, this time in the company of the sculptor Paul-Albert Bartholomé (fig. 128).[1] It was a journey fraught with the usual paradoxes, not least a sense of initial aimlessness followed by a burst of intense, utterly radical creativity. After hiring a two-wheeled horse-drawn carriage known as a tilbury, the two men left Paris in a south-easterly direction, following the course of the Seine towards Melun and the forest of Fontainebleau. Their plan was to travel for about a week, advancing in easy stages and staying overnight at local inns, resting their horse and sampling the local fare. They hoped eventually to reach Burgundy, where their younger friend Georges Jeanniot owned a modest château in the village of Diénay, some twenty miles north of Dijon. Here Jeanniot spent part of each year, working on his book illustrations, painting the surrounding terrain and entertaining local celebrities and itinerant colleagues.[2] He was an assiduous and enthusiastic host, but the visit of Degas and Bartholomé was clearly among the high points of his residency. Many years later, Jeanniot still preserved momentoes of their stay and wrote a detailed account of the event in his *Souvenirs de Degas*, published in 1933.[3] Though parts of his story have often been retold, it is worth reconsidering for at least two reasons. In the first instance, Jeanniot described in some detail the experience of watching Degas at work, almost the only such description to have survived and one that carries the authority of an artist and fellow-practitioner. Additionally, Jeanniot's account refers to the creation of a group of landscapes, and specifically to the first of the colour monotypes that have so dominated Degas' landscape-making reputation.

After recounting the preparations made by Degas and Bartholomé before they began their journey, Jeanniot summarised the mock-heroic welcome laid on when the tilbury arrived at Diénay. Friends and neighbours turned out to greet the visitors, some dressed as local officials to offer the keys of the village, while young girls 'advanced with their flowers, with which they covered the horse and the travellers'.[4] According to Jeanniot, 'Degas was in raptures over the journey', demanding to start work as soon as their welcoming meal was over:

> 'And now, take me to your studio,' Degas said to me as we were leaving the table. As he walked in, an expression of pleasure and well-being appeared on his face. And yet this country studio, installed in the garret of our house, really was very simple. In short, an attic with a few antique chairs, two or three easels, a settee with cushions, an etching press, a stove and everything necessary for making prints.
>
> 'That's the spirit!' he cried out, 'we are going to be able to work in your Swiss clockmaker's workshop, you have paper, ink, the printer's brush with

126. Detail of fig. 138.

> your initials on! Heavens! Then it is serious. This pad is superb and fits well in one's hand. Let's get on! Have you a smock?'
>
> 'Yes, and it is a printer's smock, brand new.'
>
> 'Your press must be hard work, but we have muscles!'
>
> 'Your studio is charming.'
>
> I put the smock on him, he had taken off his jacket and rolled up his sleeves.
>
> 'Do you have copper or zinc plates?'
>
> 'Here you are . . .'
>
> 'Perfect! I will ask you for a piece of cloth to make a pad for my own use; I have been wanting for so long to make a series of monotypes!'
>
> Once supplied with everything he needed, without waiting, without allowing himself to be distracted from his idea, he started. With his strong but beautifully-shaped fingers, his hand grasped the objects, the tools of his genius, handling them with a strange skill and little by little one could see emerging on the metal surface a small valley, a sky, white houses, fruit trees with black branches, birches and oaks, ruts full of water after the recent downpour, orangey clouds dispersing in an animated sky, above the red and green earth.
>
> All this fell into place, coming together, the tones setting each other off and the handle of the brush traced clear shapes in the fresh colour.
>
> These lovely things seemed to be created without the slightest effort, as if the model was in front of him.
>
> Bartholomé could recognise the places they had gone through, following the gait of the trotting white horse.
>
> After half an hour, no more, Degas' voice suggested:
>
> 'If you don't mind, we'll print this proof. Is the paper wet? Have you got the sponge? You know that semi-sized paper is the best?'
>
> 'Calm down, I have some strong Chinese . . .'
>
> 'He has got some Chinese! Let us see this Chinese . . .'
>
> I put down an imposing roll on the corner of the table. When every thing was ready, the plate laid on the press, the paper on the plate, Degas said: 'What an anxious moment! Roll, roll!' It was an antique press with heavy cross-shaped spars. Once the proof was obtained, it was hung on lines to dry. We would do three or four in a morning.
>
> Then, he would ask for some pastels to finish off the prints and it is here, even more than in the making of the proof, that I would admire his taste, his imagination and the freshness of his memories. He would remember the variety of shapes, the construction of the landscape, the unexpected oppositions and contrasts; it was delightful![5]

Even allowing for the licence of hindsight and for Jeanniot's near-reverential respect for the master, this is a forceful story and one with the kind of technical and incidental detail that often signals authenticity. More importantly, it tallies in almost every particular with other accounts of the visit and with the works of art produced during Degas' stay. As we shall see, all the landscape features described by Jeanniot can be found in prints made at this period, while his account of 'ruts full of water after the recent downpour, orangey clouds dispersing in an animated sky, above the red and green earth' could hardly be bettered as a description of *Burgundy Landscape* (fig. 127). This monotype, which carries a dedication to Bartholomé and was presumably given to him at the time of their journey, is one of the most intense and full-blooded of all the landscape prints.[6] Other works in the series are as pale and gossamer-like as *Burgundy*

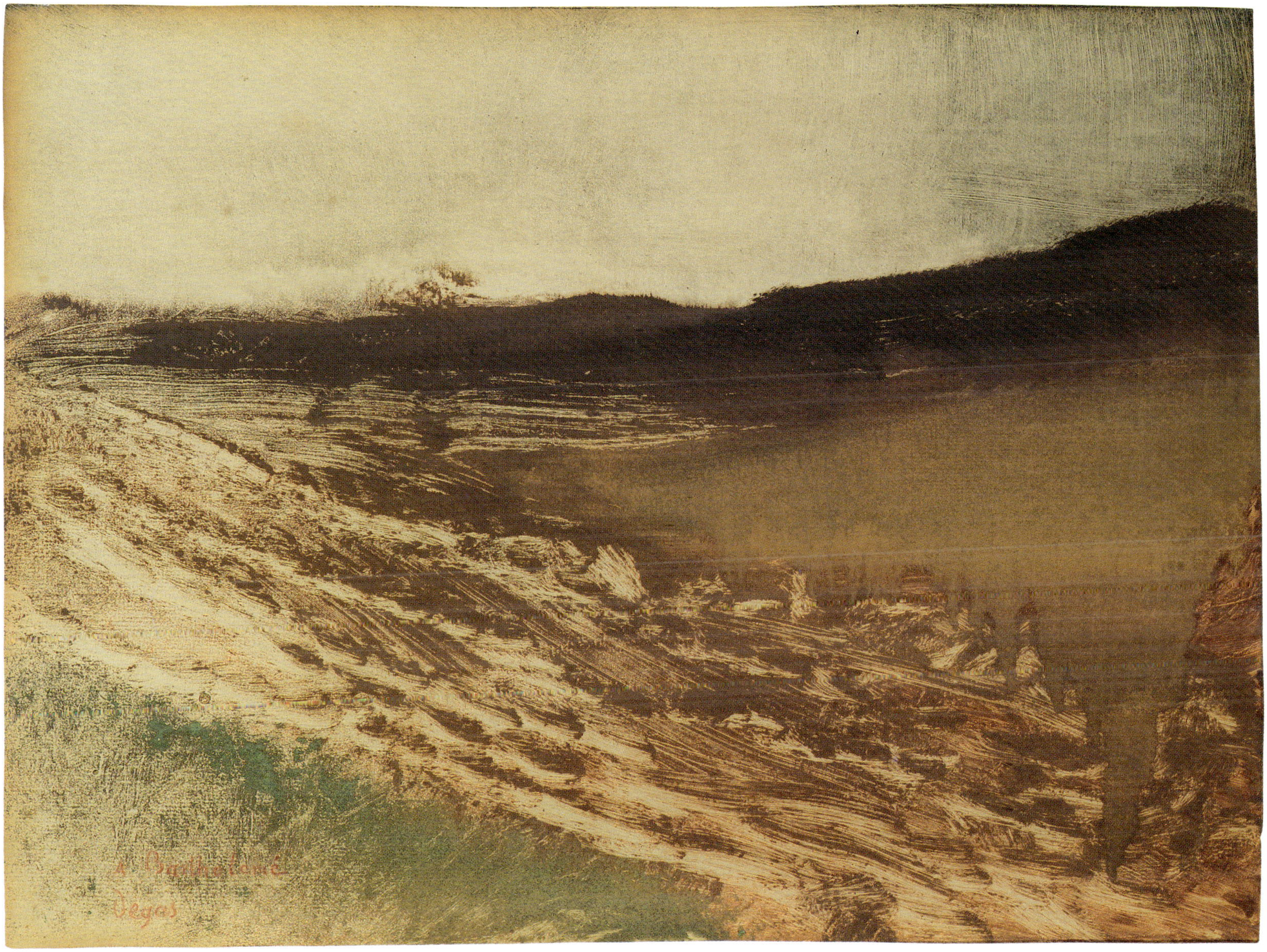

127. *Burgundy Landscape*, 1890, monotype, 30 × 40 (K 3). Musée du Louvre, Paris.

Landscape is thunderous, but all share the immediacy, the sense of a vivid exchange between artist and medium, that so fascinated Jeanniot. Even with this impressive pedigree, however, the colour monotypes leave many questions unanswered. Were they really made from memory, as Jeanniot's story seems to imply? Was the entire series of fifty or so prints made in the same way, and on the same occasion? Why had Degas 'been wanting so long to make a series of monotypes' and what prompted this unexpected excursion into improvised, anarchic colour?

By a happy series of coincidences, the landscape monotypes are amongst the most well-documented of all Degas' works of art. Apart from Jeanniot's breathless testimony and subsequent references in his correspondence, there survives a long sequence of letters written by Degas and Bartholomé before, during and after their visit to Diénay. Other corroborative material ranges from photographs (figs 128 and 129), drawings and a map of the route, to a pastel study of the two travellers in their tilbury by a mutual friend, Michel Manzi.[7] As the next chapter makes clear, some of the prints were also chosen by Degas

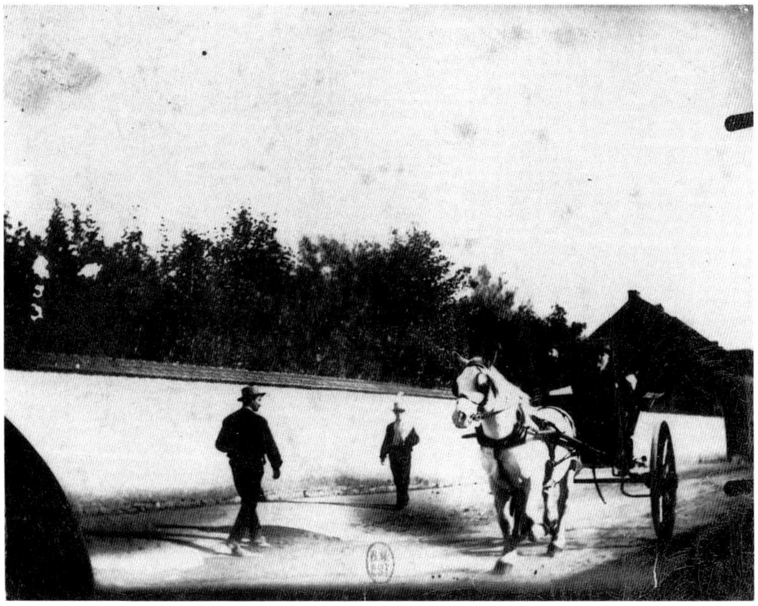 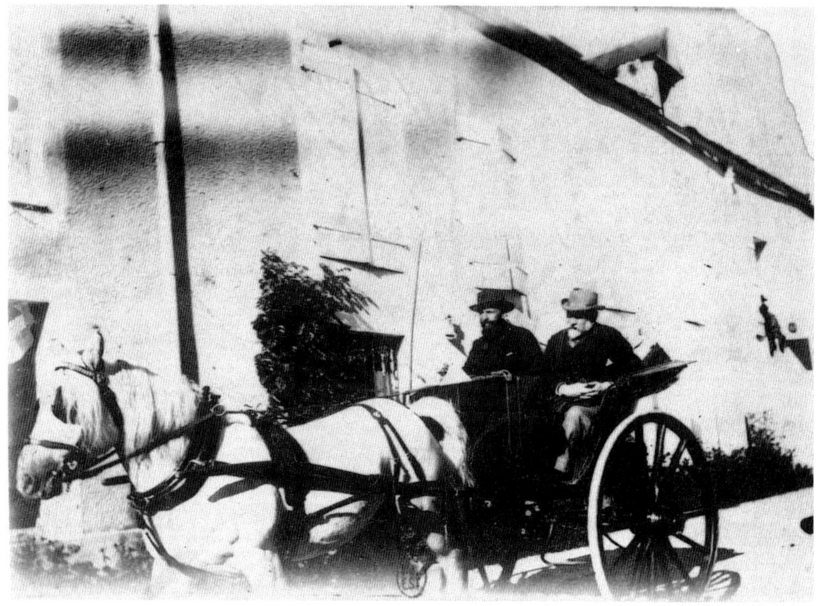

128. Anon. (Charles de Meixmoron?), *Degas and his Friend Bartholomé on a Journey*, 1890, photograph, Bibliothèque Nationale, Paris.

129. Anon. (Charles de Meixmoron?), *Degas and his Friend Bartholomé on a Journey*, 1890, photograph, Bibliothèque Nationale, Paris.

for his extraordinary 1892 exhibition at Durand-Ruel's gallery, where they were noticed by contemporaries and eulogised by a number of critics. Despite all this evidence, however, and despite their manifest importance in Degas' career, the colour landscapes have been shamefully neglected. They feature only obliquely in the major monographs, and their significance as the principal exhibited works of Degas' maturity has never been scrutinised. It is only in the last two decades, in the catalogues of Eugenia Janis, Jean Adhémar and Françoise Cachin, and in the more recent research of Howard Lay, Jean Sutherland Boggs and Michael Pantazzi, that the situation has begun to change.[8] Our knowledge of the pictures' whereabouts and of the circumstances of their exhibition has been greatly extended, though the prints themselves and their sensuous, pyrotechnical and encoded imagery remain largely mute.

Distinctive though they are, the making of the colour monotypes followed the pattern of landscape production that has been traced from the beginning of Degas' career. After a period of virtual abstinence from the subject, a flurry of activity resulted in a cluster of dense and sequentially related works, followed by an effective abandonment of the process by which they were made. Technically, they had their roots in the artist's earlier manipulations, and even in the sub-soil of the distant past, while pushing out branches and erupting in blossoms of the most unfamiliar kind. In relation to his other projects and imagery, the landscapes can seem like a diversion, or perhaps a pretext for risk-taking and conceptual licence. As with most of his landscape phases, colour took on a dominant role, obscuring and even rendering obsolete the skills of draughtsmanship that represented the legacy of his youth. There was even a hint of therapy, both personal and artistic, in these excursions. Whether visiting Ménil-Hubert, Houlgate or Burgundy, Degas escaped the disciplines of his craft and the burdens of his public role, as well as his worries over health and impending blindness. During their stay at Diénay, Bartholomé confided to a friend that Degas 'dreams of nothing but journeys. He appears to have developed a horror of work', and Degas himself wrote on the same occasion, 'One needs to have been sad and serious for a long time to enjoy oneself so much.[9]

Degas' visit to Diénay occurred during a crescendo of journeying, which gathered pace in the late 1880s and lost momentum in the following decade. In addition to annual outings to friends such as the Valpinçons, Rouarts and Halévys in Normandy and Brie, Degas increasingly ventured further afield.[10] He crossed France to see Paul Lafond, his future biographer, at Pau in the Pyrenees; to visit the spa town of Cauterets for rest-cures; or to spend time with the elderly Evariste de Valernes, former pupil of Delacroix, in Carpentras. Most years saw him travelling abroad, with trips to Naples in 1886, Spain in 1889, Belgium and Switzerland in 1890, and Switzerland again in 1892 and 1893. Some of these excursions lasted several weeks and would be linked together in improvised sequences. In July 1890, for example, immediately prior to the pilgrimage to Diénay, Degas wrote from his retreat in Normandy: 'I believe I shall dash to Carpentras, to return through Geneva and Dijon', casually sketching out a round-trip of some fifteen hundred miles.[11] In the event, he went even further, spending more than two weeks at Cauterets (where he shared a hotel with Sarah Bernhardt) and several days with Lafond and their mutual acquaintance Cherfils. Degas completed the circuit by visiting his brother, René, in Geneva, then returned to Paris via Dijon, from where he made a first, exploratory detour to nearby Diénay.[12]

Innocent in intent, Degas' peregrinations were rarely dissociated from matters of art. Most of the friends he visited were painters or collectors, whose studios he knew and whose pictures he later recalled.[13] At the hotel in Cauterets, he enjoyed the company of the landscapist Tillot and the portrait painter Carolus-Duran, and at Pau he stayed with the director of the Musée des Beaux-Arts, Paul Lafond.[14] He travelled to Madrid to see the Prado, always paid homage to a favourite Corot when in Geneva, and more than once diverted to Montauban, home of the Musée Ingres.[15] Surprisingly often, these excursions were linked to his own documented or speculative works of art: apart from the Burgundy landscapes, some of the pastels of the 1880s were manifestly made at Ménil-Hubert;[16] letters from Cauterets described his intention of drawing the surrounding scenery;[17] and his sojourns at Le Mont-Dore were later occupied with the making of photographs.[18] Inseparable from Degas' travelling was the promise of visual refreshment and the maintenance of contact with professional colleagues. In his correspondence, he made clear his pleasure in the voyage itself, bubbling over with whimsical itineraries and projected forays, and delighting in traveller's tales and boyish puns. After his initial visit to Diénay, he wrote of the 'pitch of travelling excitement' he had reached and, while on the road with Bartholomé, regaled his friends by post with daily witticisms, mock-biblical epigrams and the mildest of improprieties.[19]

The context of travel is crucial for Degas' landscape monotypes in both a practical and a conceptual sense. Though more than one account of their genesis has been recorded, all records agree that the prints emerged from the incessant journeying that marked the artist's activities in the early 1890s.[20] At its simplest, this means that they were begun at a distance from Degas' Paris studio, and at a metaphorical remove from its disciplines; that they represented territory largely unfamiliar to him; and that they were initiated in haste, and perhaps completed in that spirit. Taken further, we should note that Degas' imagery was perceived *en route*, while he was in the process of travel, and not scrutinised at leisure on arrival. Both Jeanniot and Bartholomé are clear on this point, insisting that Degas 'didn't once stop . . . to take a closer look' and marvelling at his 'astonishing memory' and his skill in reconstructing landscapes, 'as if they were still in front of his eyes'.[21] These, then, are pictures based on fleeting experience, fragmentary scenes glimpsed in a few seconds by a moving observer and never revisited. As such, they represent the antithesis of the orthodox relationship between artist and subject, and of the fundamental disciplines of observation. Where once the eye of the painter had been fixed on a posed model or a static landscape, often for hours or days at a time, here all is transient, remote and unstable.

While allowing for the fact that, on this occasion at least, Degas was travelling by carriage rather than by train, we must also weave his excursion into the wider fabric of the age. Travel was the obsession and the delight of Degas' society, permeating its art and entertainment, transforming its trade and class relations, and invading its language and patterns of thought. The railways allowed Monet to visit Italy and Holland, loaded down with crates of canvases; they encouraged Cézanne to shuttle between Provence and Paris, and Pissarro to commute from city to suburb. For the same artists, and occasionally for Degas himself, travel also offered new subject-matter, from smoke-filled engine sheds to provincial trains and paddle-steamers. In earlier decades, such subjects had also invigorated the new literature, providing metaphors of change and models for experimentation. When Champfleury called for paintings to be hung in railway stations and when Emma Bovary undertook her own epic carriage-rides, mobility was seen as the essence of the modern condition.[22] Both Zola and Maupassant evoked the train compartment and the speeding tram, each modulating their prose to the rhythms of the new vernacular.[23] In bad-tempered old age, Degas railed against this preoccupation with speed, mocking the telephone and the perils of modern transport, even as he sent his telegrams and mounted his trams.[24] For much of his life, however, he was a child of his age, as much at a 'pitch of travelling excitement' as his peers.

Journeying by train, tram and carriage, escaping from and then returning to his Paris studio, Degas conceived and executed more than fifty landscape monotypes between his 1890 trip to Diénay and the 1892 exhibition at the Galerie Durand-Ruel. Shortly before the opening of this exhibition, Degas spent the evening at the home of the Halévy family, announcing that he intended to buy an expensive new English edition of *The Arabian Nights*. According to Daniel Halévy's account, when asked how he would afford this extravagance, Degas replied:

> 'I can pay for them. I have twenty-one landscapes.' We all cried out: 'Twenty-one landscapes?' Degas had never done any; 'Twenty-one landscapes?'
>
> 'Why, yes! Twenty-one landscapes'
>
> 'But what does this mean?'
>
> 'The fruits of my journeys this summer. I stood at the door of the railway carriage, and looked around vaguely. That gave me the idea of doing the landscapes. There are twenty-one of them.'
>
> 'What? Very vague things?'
>
> 'Perhaps'.
>
> 'States of mind?' said my father. 'Amiel has said "A landscape is a state of mind." Do you like the phrase?'
>
> 'States of eyes', replied Degas. 'We do not use such pretentious language'.[25]

Apart from showing how secretive a landscapist Degas could be, even with close friends, this conversation appears to offer an alternative version of events from that recorded by Jeanniot. In reality, it is part of a consistent description of the landscape monotypes, here applied to the second and later stage of their

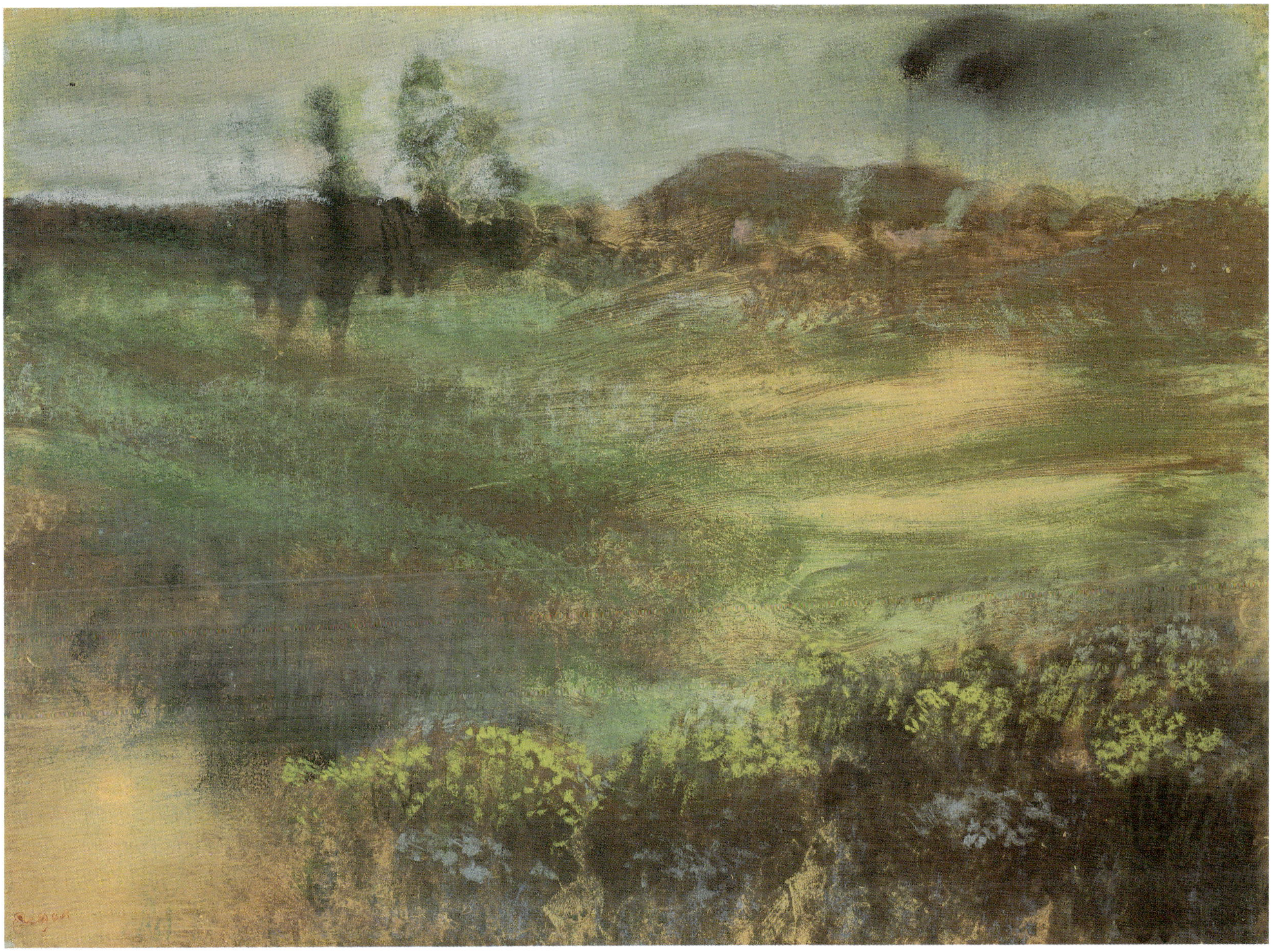

130. *Landscape with Smokestacks*, 1890, monotype and pastel, 28 × 40 (J 277). Mr. and Mrs. Daniel Searle.

evolution. Almost every writer on the monotypes has assumed that the fifty or so prints were made at the same moment, rendering either Jeanniot's or Halévy's account unsound. As our later examination of the works makes clear, both writers can be trusted and both appear to have referred to separate, but intimately related, suites of pictures.[26] What is beyond dispute, however, is that Halévy coincides with Jeanniot in associating the monotypes with Degas' mobility, and with the sensations of speed and dislocation. Crucially, also, Halévy links the event with Degas' perception, and not just with the terrain through which he passed. In an important and perhaps new sense, the subject of these works might be the artist's sensibility, his experience of travel and his anxious sense of his own identity.

Two of the more richly developed monotypes allow us to examine these propositions in practice. *Landscape with Smokestacks* (fig. 130) depicts the no man's land between open country and local industry that Degas would have encountered on many of his known itineraries.[27] While the subject is self-evident, the degree of definition and visual exposition is remarkably slight.

Forms are blurred or partly erased, detail is restricted, and entire passages, such as the hillside on the left, are spatially imprecise. The sense of engagement with a real site, however, and of masses and hues registered in all their immediacy, is intense. We are given every reason to believe that Degas saw a vista of this kind, but none that he lingered in its presence. *River Banks* (fig. 132) is less evidently fleeting, but just as emphatic in its bold composition and pronounced tonality. On this occasion, Degas allowed himself more latitude in the recollection of detail and in the generation of nuances of light and texture, but ambiguities still remain. Is this a lake, a river or a stretch of seashore? Is the viewer on a bank or beach, or perhaps in a boat? Most intriguingly, is the ponderous and smokily defined form at the left a 'pierced rock', as earlier commentators assumed, or a ruined bridge, such as the structure still visible at Pont-sur-Yonne, on Degas' route through Burgundy (fig. 131)?[28]

In both these images, it is the sweeping colour and blunt divisions of sky, earth and water that command our attention. Refinements of effect are kept in check, or are designed to be overlooked on first encounter. In this respect, they resemble scenery glimpsed by a speeding traveller, who registers the *ensemble* in all its vividness, but not the fine detail of its constituent parts. Where detail exists, as in the Millet-like black dots and flickers on the horizon of *River Banks*, it turns out to be generalised and inventive, rather than descriptive of precise topographic events. Another analogy is with a blurred photograph or snapshot, where the imperfections of the image appear to enhance our awareness of its hurried inception. In both cases, much is left to our imagination, and we are encouraged to fill in missing details or puzzle at uncertain forms. Similarly, our sense of the recorded moment, of the fallibility of the process and of the intervention of the artist or photographer is intensified. Such partial glimpses bring us back to the act of perception as much as to the thing perceived. This interpretation of the landscape monotypes is amplified in a second, and much less well-known, description of their origins by Daniel Halévy:

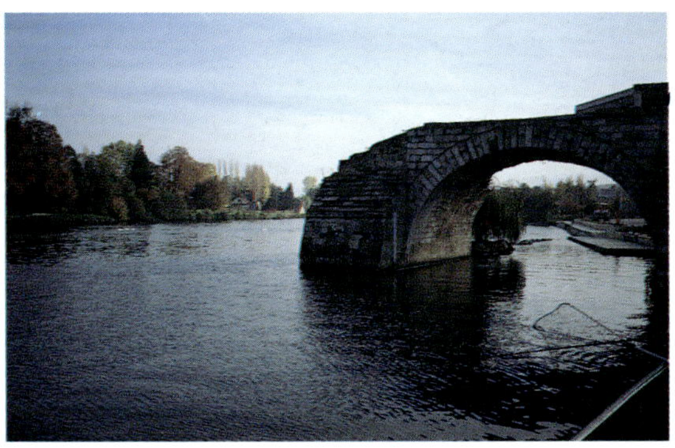

131. Bridge at Pont-sur-Yonne (taken by the author).

> I remember the autumn when he became a landscapist. The temptation had presented itself to him in the summer, on long train journeys during which he tried to rest his eyes. Sitting in the corner of a carriage and continually looking, looking as well as he could – how could he *not* look? the entire occupation of his life was in the spoils of his looking – he had glimpsed, guessed at, perceived valleys, trees, rocks, plains, and back in our own Montmartre, dreaming of everything that had taken his fancy, he had taken up his boards, his pastels, working in secret and successfully fixing his memories.[29]

While it is not necessary to see each of the monotypes as a literal record of such an excursion, their relation to Degas' imperfect vision, to his frequent peregrinations and to the operations of his memory is amply and touchingly documented.

If we now return to the autumn of 1890, and to the occasion described by Jeanniot when the first coloured monotypes were made, we can reconstruct their beginnings with some precision. After trips to Belgium and Normandy earlier in the year, Degas had embarked on his month-long tour to Carpentras, the Pyrenees and Switzerland. Writing from Cauterets in early September, at the end of a tedious and uncomfortable rest-cure, he complained to Henri Rouart: 'I have seen some very beautiful things through my anger, and what consoles me a little, is that through my anger I do not stop looking.'[30] Earlier, he had written to Bartholomé to alert him to a possible return via Dijon, and in

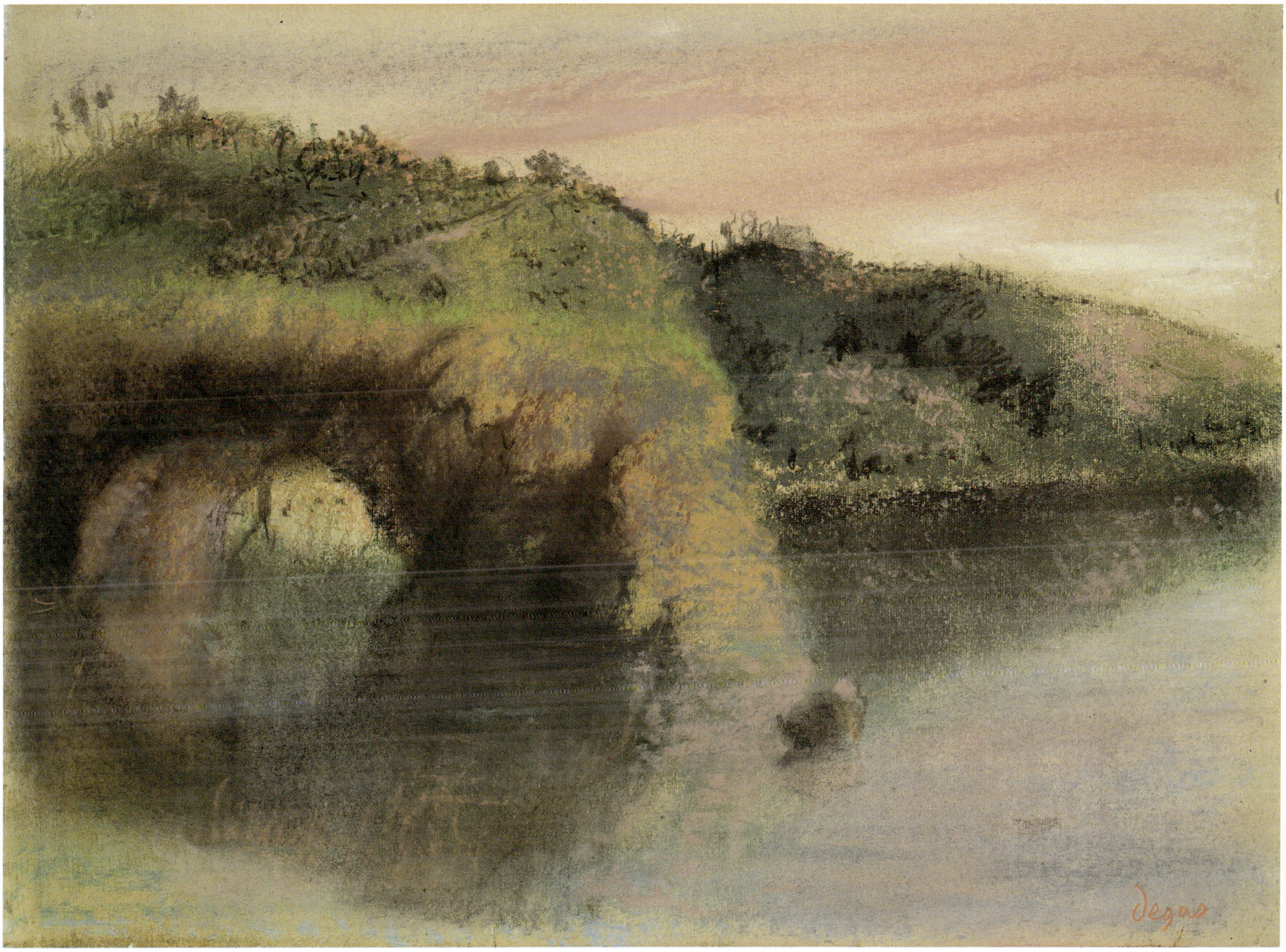

132. *River Banks*, 1890, monotype and pastel, 30 × 40 (J 281). Private collection.

due course the two friends made their first brief call at Diénay, the home of the Jeanniots.[31] To continue in Degas' own words:

> After having left them and once back again in Paris, the memory of the pleasure of this spot and the desire to see more of this admirable Burgundy, brought me to such a pitch of travelling excitement that I persuaded my good comrade to share my folly.
>
> And this folly, now classified by us and by the others as an act of particular wisdom, could only be appeased by the hiring of a tilbury and a white horse, and by traversing in twenty days, five of which were days of rest at Diénay, more than six hundred kilometres, that is one hundred and fifty leagues.[32]

As well as emphasising that the tilbury ride was a return to terrain previously encountered, this passage illustrates something of the *bonhomie* and even facetiousness of the trip. From the day of their departure, 30 September, to the final announcement of their return, on 19 October, Degas and his companion joked with their correspondents, gorged themselves with gherkins, sheeps' feet and sausage, and indulged in outlandish practical jokes. The stamina and state of digestion of the white horse, christened 'Plumer' by Bartholomé, was solemnly reported, and on one occasion the animal was painted with zebra stripes and paraded before the astonished locals.[33]

The high spirits of most of Degas' letters offer only a partial picture of the excursion. On the return journey, Degas mentioned that Bartholomé's hand was bandaged and swollen, and revealed that he himself had been taking 'bismuth and doses of laudanum' for an unspecified illness.[34] A note from the artist to Paul Lafond insists that he is 'almost sick and very agitated in spirit', to which he added with emphasis: 'I do not feel quite right in the head'.[35] Whether this was a side-effect of his alarming medication or the result of an unfamiliar régime we cannot be sure, but it certainly led to a period of 'immobility' at Diénay itself.[36] Such accounts are not always easy to reconcile with the jocularity of Degas' letters and remind us of the incompleteness of our source material. A further reminder comes in the absence of any written commentary on his surroundings, or descriptions of the 'admirable Burgundy' that had first prompted his visit. Though he was clearly enamoured of the countryside, and returned to Diénay on at least four occasions, Degas was characteristically silent about its beauties.[37] Despite their similarities in many other ways, no equivalent of the minute-by-minute record of his youthful carriage journeys in Tuscany, when he drove through from Siena to Rome more than thirty years previously, has survived. Instead, we have a few laconic remarks about 'a sunset like in pictures' or the weather ('rain all night, but we were in bed'), and a roll-call of towns and villages through which the unlikely cavalcade passed.[38]

Thanks to the detailed, hand-drawn map usually ascribed to Bartholomé (fig. 133), it is still possible to retrace the route taken by the two travellers, and consequently to put to the test Jeanniot's account of the monotypes and their origins. If Jeanniot is to be relied on, we would expect to find 'small valleys', 'white houses, fruit trees with black branches, beeches and oaks' surrounded by 'red and green earth', as well as other details that appear regularly in this group of prints. Admittedly, such features are widely found in rural France, but we might also anticipate that the general lie of the land, and the presence or absence of distinctive landscape elements, would correspond to Degas' imagery. Here, it is noticeable that the grander kind of topography, such as mountain ranges, prodigious vistas and elegant lakes, are largely missing from Degas' repertoire, as are fine châteaux and distant cities. This is entirely consistent with the countryside traversed by the two artists, which is both modest in scale and largely agricultural in usage. Initially, the route leaves Paris through flat or gently undulating terrain, along the path of the modern N6 road to Montgeron and Melun. Later, it follows the river valleys of the Seine and the Yonne towards Sens, then accompanies the Armançon as far as Tonnerre. At this point, the landscape changes, becoming hilly and more densely forested, the uneven roadway passing farms and smallholdings before descending steeply to picturesque villages or mills. Rocky outcrops occur, and certain areas are distinguished by their white, chalky roads (fig. 135), while towards Diénay the soil favours a red-brown hue, turning almost purple in the rain.

Among the group of monotypes associated with this visit, the subjects of the great majority can be accounted for by landscapes and *motifs* still visible on this route.[39] Indeed, certain local peculiarities, such as its pale and meandering roads, seem to have caught Degas' imagination and prompted entire sequences of prints. At least ten works make visual capital out of this feature, amongst them the dramatic and serpentine *Pathway in a Field* (fig. 134).[40] In this pastel over

133. Anon. (Bartholomé and de Meixmoron?), *Degas' Journey from Paris to Diénay*, 1890, map and photographs. Bibliothèque Nationale, Paris.

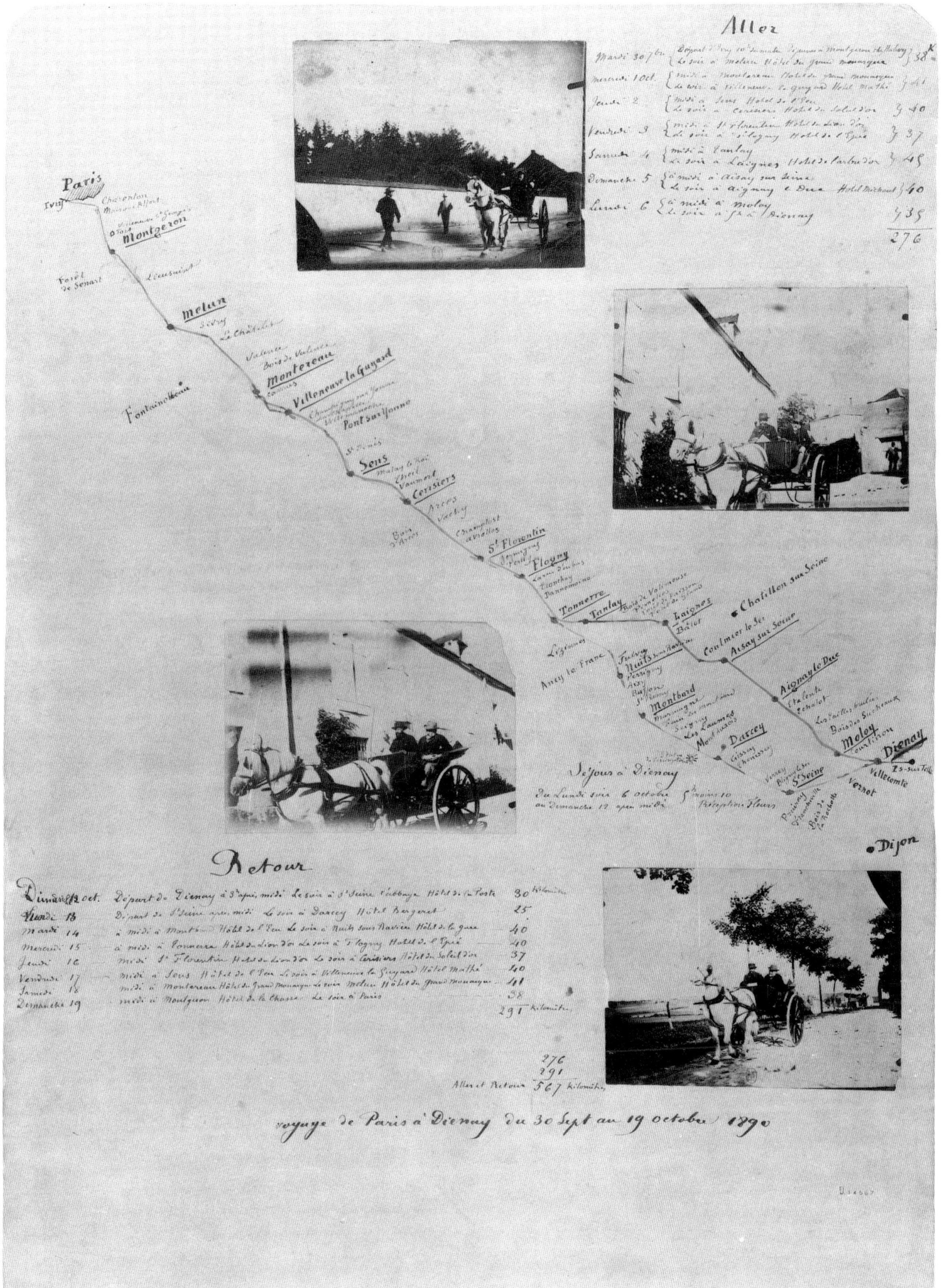

Aller
Paris
Montgeron
Melun
Montereau
Villeneuve la Guyard
Pont sur Yonne
Sens
Cerisiers
St Florentin
Flogny
Tonnerre
Tanlay
Laignes
Chatillon sur Seine
Aisay sur Seine
Aignay le Duc
Montbard
Darcey
Moloy
Dienay
St Seine
Dijon
Séjour à Dienay
Retour
276
291
567
voyage de Paris à Dienay du 30 Sept au 19 octobre 1890

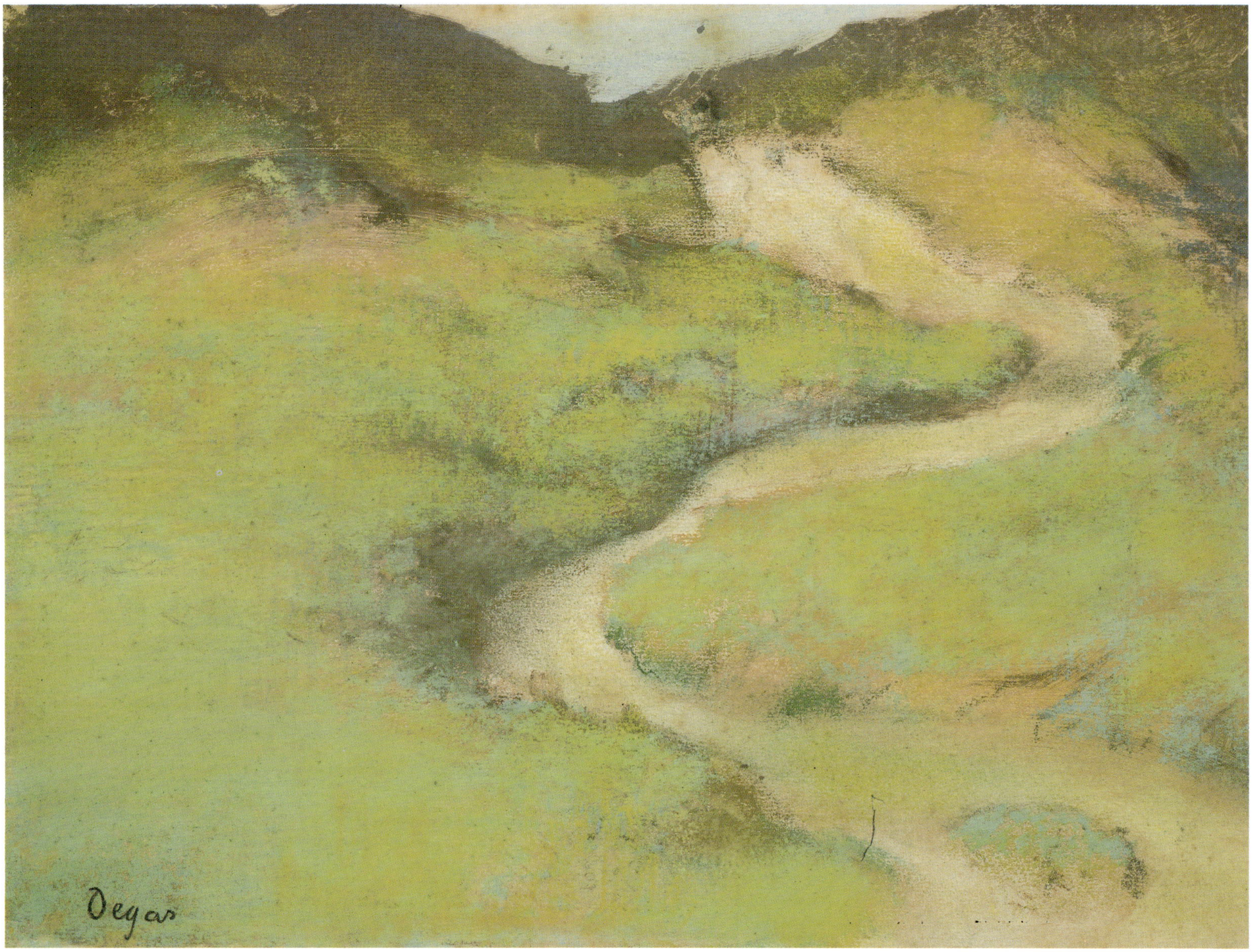

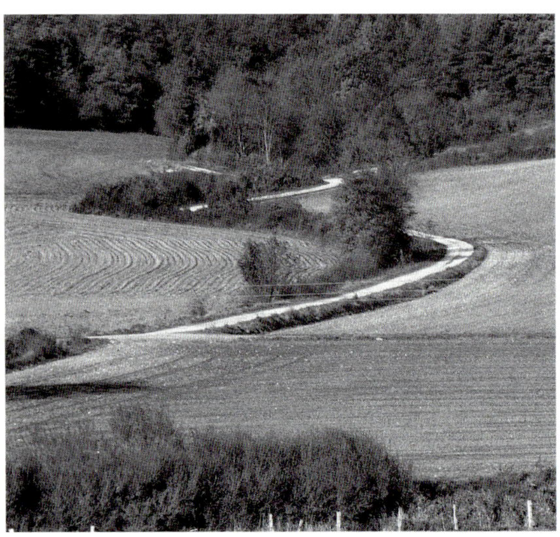

monotype, a whiplash of track bisects the composition into serrated fragments, while the brightness of the road seems to intensify the stark greens and ochres of the vegetation. A twinned pair of such images, of which *Landscape in the Mountains* (fig. 136) was probably the earliest, marks the junction of two or three milk-white roads and again brings animation to the simplest forms with the barest of means.[41] At times resembling streams rather than roads, these spectral paths speak eloquently of the business of travel, hinting at distances to be covered and solitude to be endured. In *Road in the Forest* (fig. 137), an irresolute causeway vanishes into hedges and shadows, as though glimpsed fleetingly from a passing vehicle. Both *Landscape with Rocky Cliffs* (fig. 138) and *Autumn Landscape* (fig. 151) have fragmentary and brightly lit roads in their backgrounds, beckoning the traveller forward and offering relief from the surrounding vastness.

Many other features mentioned by Jeanniot, or evident in the prints themselves, can still be identified on Degas' route. As we would expect in such

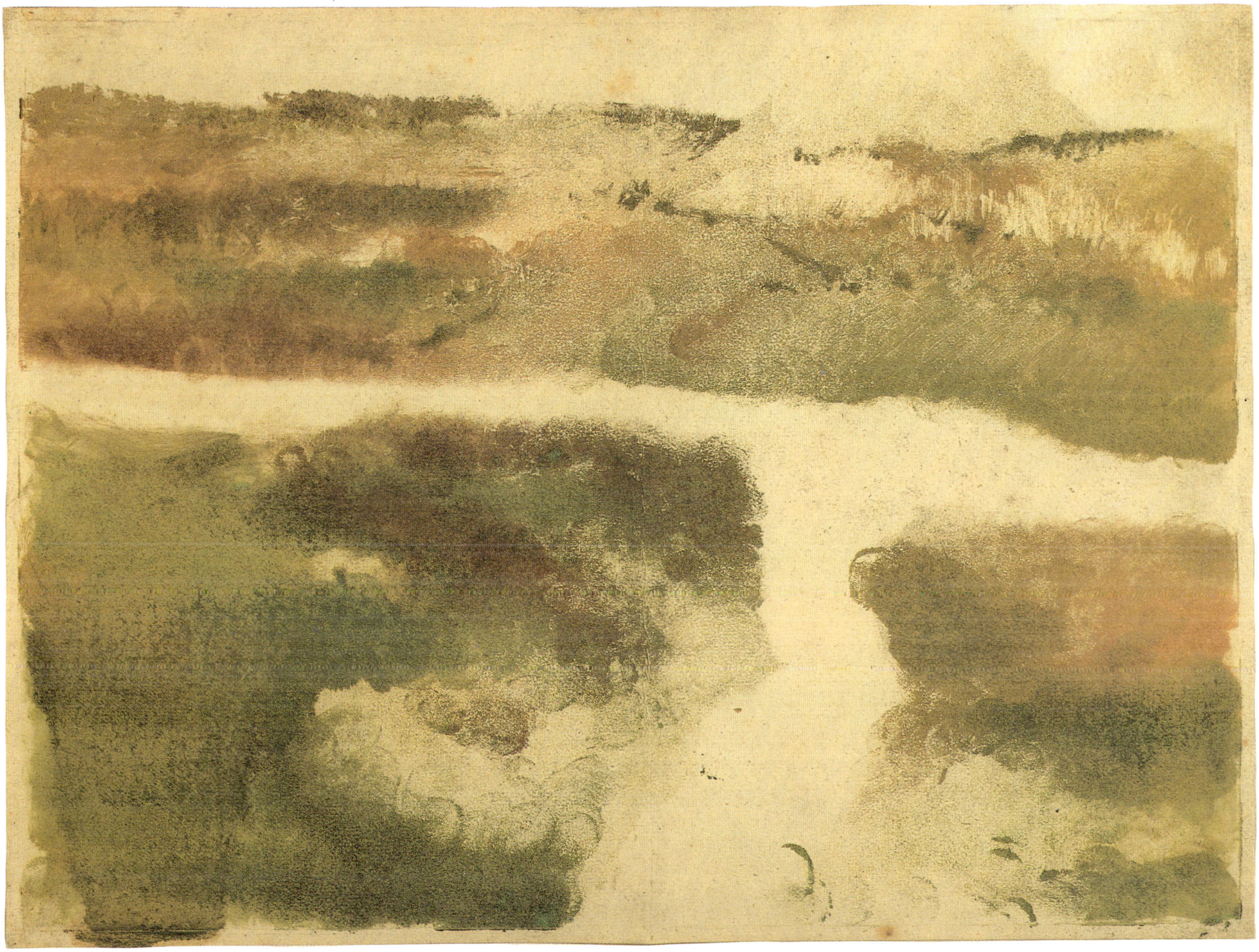

136. *Landscape in the Mountains*, 1890, monotype, 30.4 × 40 (J 289). Los Angeles County Museum of Art.

134 (facing page top). *Pathway in a Field*, 1890, monotype and pastel, 30 × 39.5 (J 286). Yale University Art Gallery, New Haven, Conn.

135 (facing page bottom). A road on Degas' route through Burgundy (taken by the author).

countryside, 'small valleys' and 'fruit trees with black branches' are found in abundance and were duly recorded in a number of monotypes. *Autumn Landscape*, for example, shows the typical rising and falling terrain of the later route, a river valley glinting beneath us and a village such as Aisey-sur-Seine, through which Degas passed, visible amongst the foreground trees. The 'red and brown earth' and 'ruts full of water after the recent downpour' became the virtual subject of *Burgundy Landscape* (fig. 127), and again correspond vividly to arable land near Diénay. While the resemblance between *River Banks* (fig. 132) and the broken bridge at Pont-sur-Yonne has already been noted, such echoes of man-made structures are relatively rare. An exception may be the pair of prints misleadingly entitled *Village in l'Estérel* (fig. 139) and *Estérel Village* (fig. 140). Degas himself seems to have left all his monotypes untitled, and the association of these works with the Massif de l'Estérel, an area near Cannes never visited by the artist, is quite spurious.[42] On the other hand, the distinctive rocky eminence that forms the subject of both pictures, with its suggestion of clustered buildings

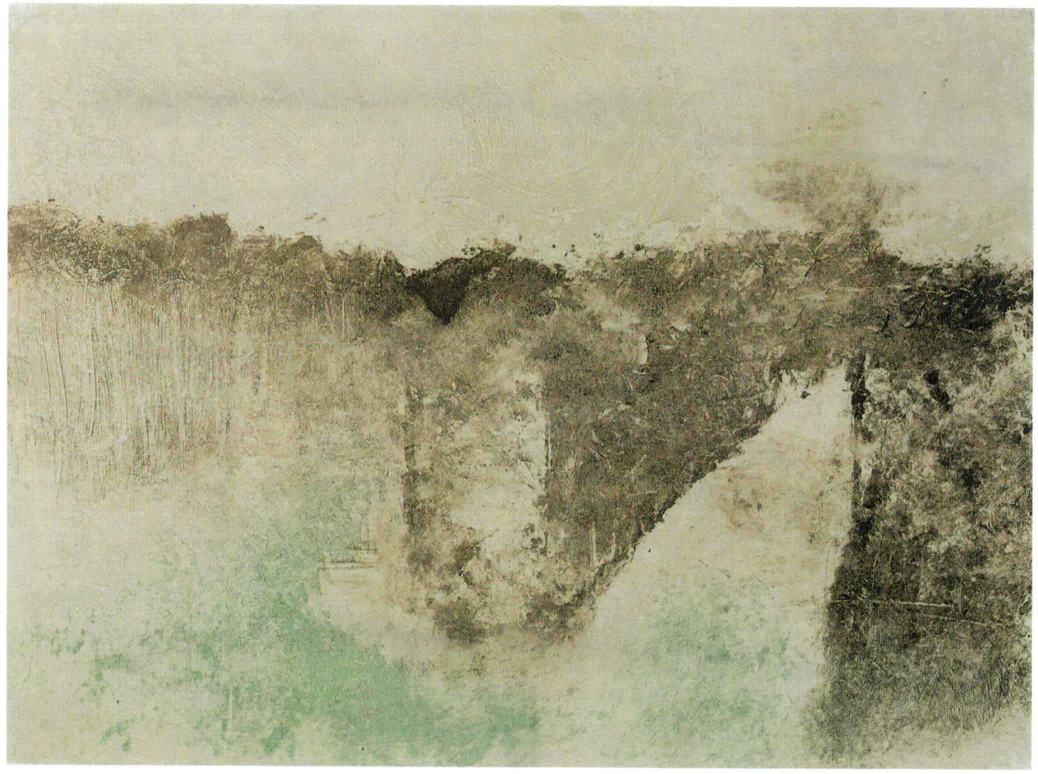

137. *Road in the Forest*, 1890, monotype, 29.9 × 40 (J 292). Fogg Art Museum, Harvard University, Cambridge, Mass., Bequest of Frances L. Hofer.

and a central spire, may well be a memory of the hillside chapel of Saint-Martin-du-Tertre, passed by Degas on the way to Sens (fig. 141). The precipitous incline of the only vertical image in the series, *Landscape with Rocky Cliffs*, in contrast, appears to have no precise equivalent on the route. Grandly spacious and verging on the fantastical, this scene is perhaps best understood as an imaginative response to the valleys and escarpments of the area.[43]

The more apposite title of *Autumn Landscape* prompts us to remember the season at which Degas visited Burgundy. In September and October, the forests of the Côte d'Or are ablaze with fiery colour, their russets and chrome yellows standing out sharply against the still-resonant greens of the pasture. Seasonal mists and fog are also much in evidence, at times softening the contours of the landscape and conjuring up subtle new tonalities (fig. 143). Such effects hardly lend themselves to the precise identification of sites, though once again they seem to have inspired a group of evocative, if more generalised, explorations of colour. The hauntingly crepuscular *Landscape* (fig. 142) recalls many of the wide river valleys and distant escarpments of Degas' itinerary, though its twilight hues transcend the immediate location. In this work, bands of earth-red, olive and dusky purple shimmer against each other, while broadly brushed pigments hint at the mysteries of woodland and undergrowth. A less densely worked image, *Mountain Effect* (fig. 146), seems almost wraith-like, suggesting autumnal tints seen through haze and the partial, uncertain vision of a speeding traveller. At the other extreme, *Green Landscape* (fig. 144) and *Landscape* (fig. 145) explode in sage and apple hues, prompted perhaps by fading stands of poplars and expanses of still-vivid foliage. Imprecise though they are, we should not doubt the degree of resolution of such works in Degas' estimation. *Autumn Landscape* was included in his 1892 exhibition and *Landscape* (fig. 142) was signed and presented to his host at Diénay, Georges Jeanniot.[44]

On arrival at Diénay, Jeanniot tells us, 'Degas was in raptures over the

138. *Landscape with Rocky Cliffs*, 1890, monotype and pastel, 40 × 29 (J 283). Josefowitz collection.

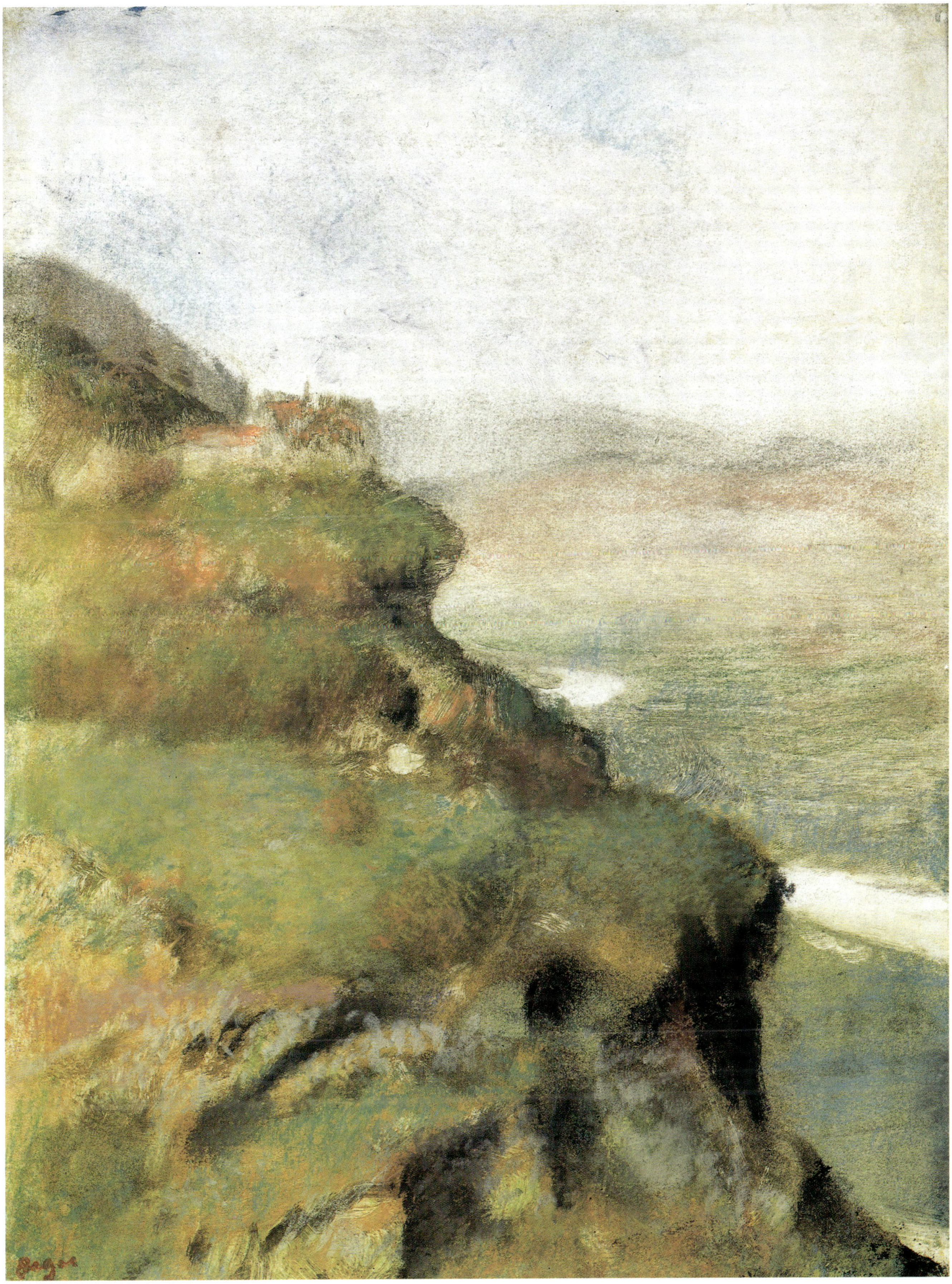

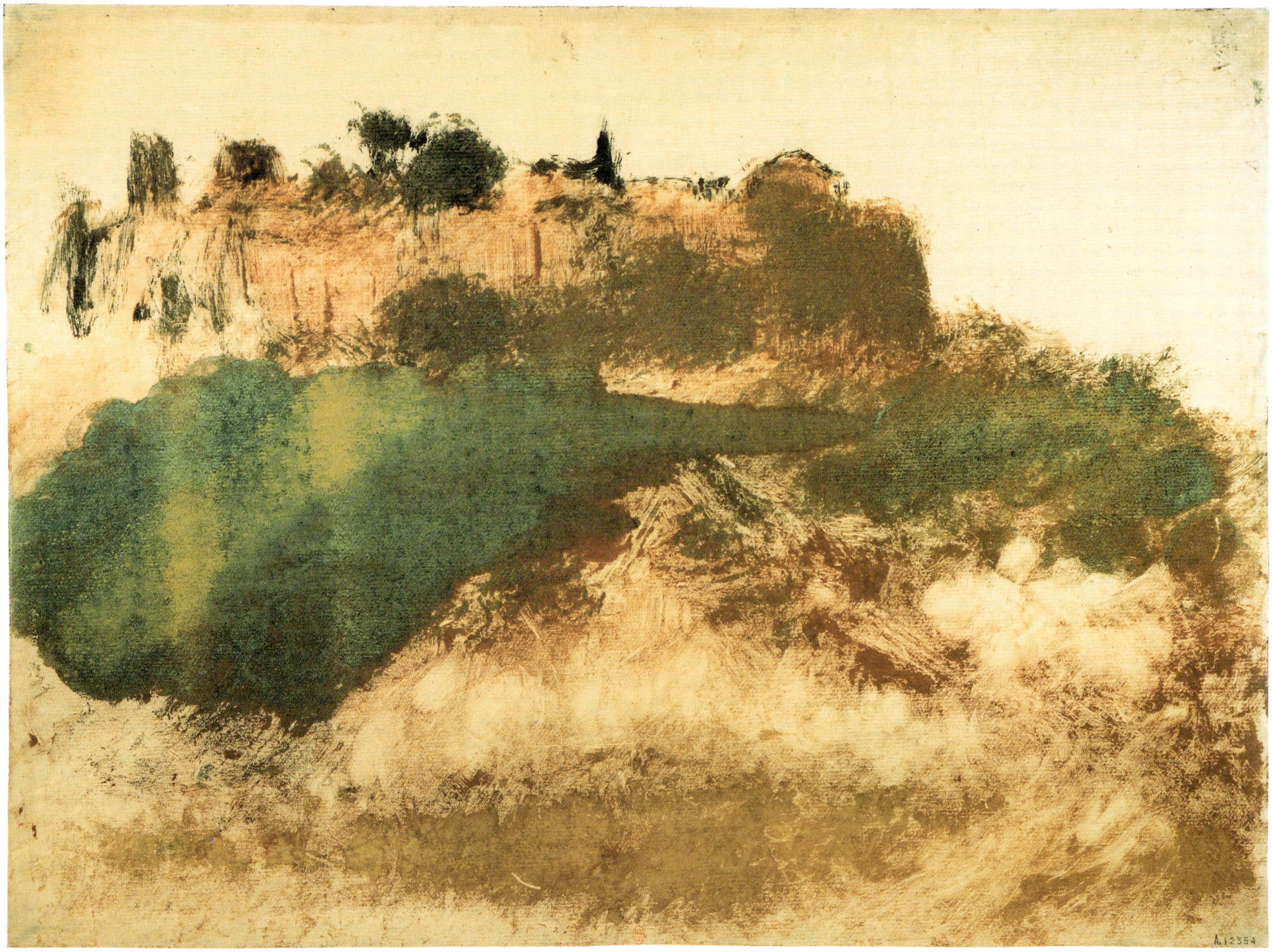

139. *Village in l'Estérel*, 1890, monotype, 30 × 42.5 (J 275). Bibliothèque Nationale, Paris.

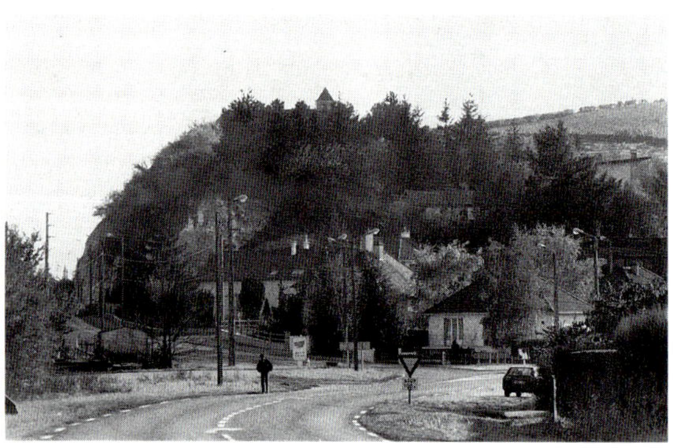

140. Saint-Martin du Tertre (taken by the author).

journey', proceding almost immediately to the studio and announcing: 'I have been wanting for so long to make a series of monotypes.' After inspecting Jeanniot's equipment, he began work, and within 'half an hour, no more', the first print had been pulled. During their stay, 'we would do three or four in a morning', recounts Jeanniot, which would have resulted in fifteen or twenty prints, though a more rarely cited text by the same author puts the figure at thirty. This account comes from a brief manuscript sketch of his own life, written down by Jeanniot for the critic Clément-Janin in 1931. Some measure of the importance of Degas' visit can be gauged from the fact that, in this five-page document, the incident occupies more than an entire page, and that the principal events were still fresh in his mind, some forty years after they had happened. Repeating the tale of the travellers' arrival, Jeanniot went on to decribe Degas at work:

> I can still see him, in my studio, printing on my press the monotypes that were inspired by memories of the landscape; for he made, in front of me,

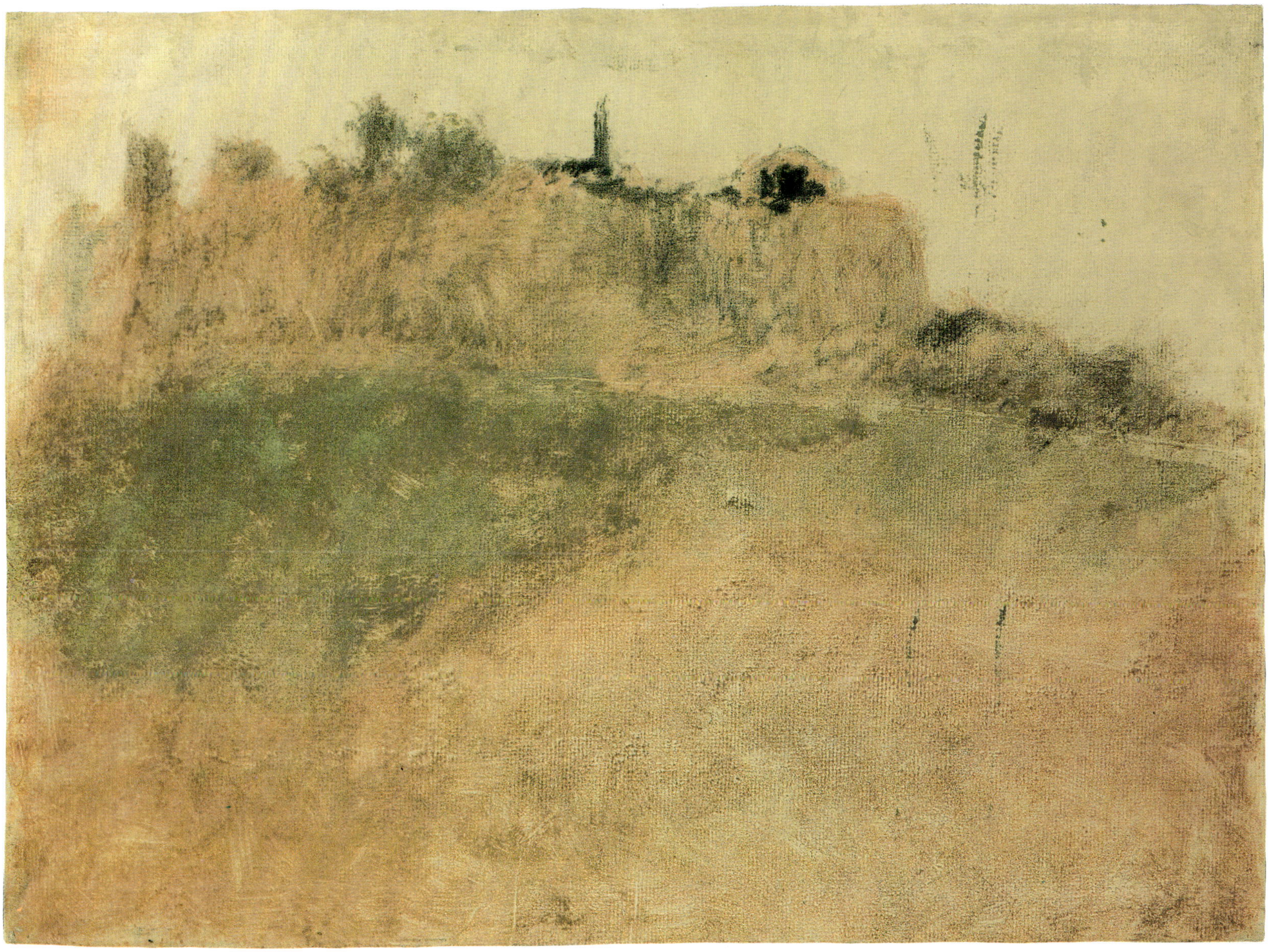

141. *Estérel Village*, 1890, monotype, 30 × 39.9 (J 276). Cleveland Museum of Art, Fiftieth Anniversary Gift of The Print Club of Cleveland.

thirty monotypes, delicious in colour, of an extraordinary fidelity and variety. Once they were printed, he hung them from a line that ran the length of my studio, using clothes pegs. I still have in my painting equipment the cloth pad which he used to apply the colour. When he had finished, he said with a satisfied air, 'So there's thirty-thousand francs for Durand-Ruel . . .'[45]

Vivid though they are, Jeanniot's reminiscences leave a number of practical and historical questions about the making of the monotypes unanswered. Jeanniot, an altogether more conventional artist, seems to have been oblivious to their technical originality, just as he failed to grasp Degas' role as part of a continuing tradition. Strictly speaking, Degas was not the inventor of either the monotype process or the use of colour in monotype printing. The seventeenth-century artist Giovanni Benedetto Castiglione and the English poet and painter William Blake, among others, had explored variants of these procedures, and a number of Degas' contemporaries had made tentative trials in the same direction.[46] However, as Barbara Shapiro has noted, 'it is safe to say that Edgar

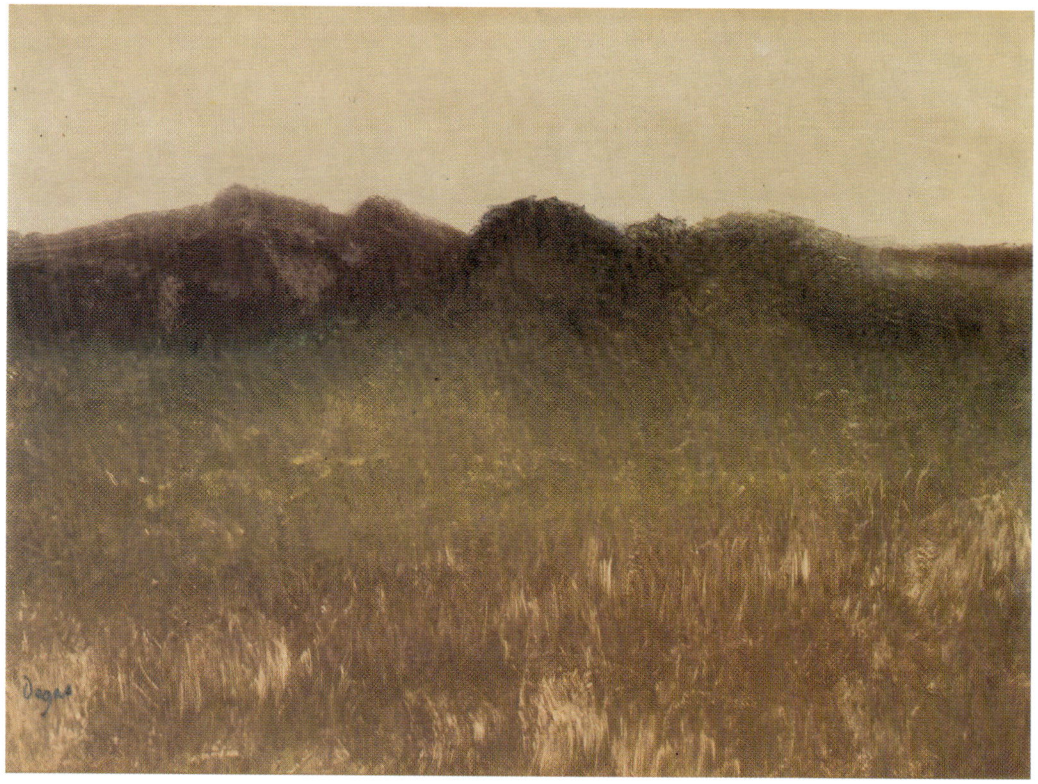

142. *Landscape*, 1890, monotype, 30 × 40 (J 313). Private collection.

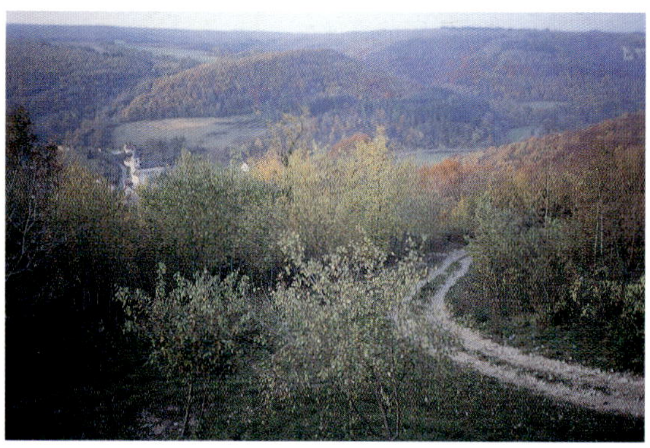

143. Autumnal landscape in the Cote d'Or (taken by the author).

Degas was the greatest innovator and practitioner of the monotype medium in the nineteenth century.'[47] Beginning with his monochrome prints in the late 1870s, Degas had initially transposed the subject-matter and even the style of his other works of art, such as ballet paintings, into the monotype medium. Within a short time, he developed an entirely new range of possibilities, exploiting the sensuousness of monotype ink and its capacities for improvisation and gesture. In his brothel scenes and early prints of the landscape, flourishes of every kind established faces and limbs, textures and conditions of light, all within a palette of monochrome blacks, greys and sepias. Curiously, though he would add pastel or gouache to the surface of these prints, Degas never introduced other hues into the inks themselves. It was not until the autumn of 1890, and Degas' rediscovered wish 'to make a series of monotypes', that he cut himself free from monochrome entirely, pushing the medium into uncharted territory and effectively launching a new era in colour printing.

Several commentators have attempted to define the exceptional character of Degas' colour monotypes and to elucidate the process by which they were made. Paul Lafond, Degas' correspondent at the time of the Diénay excursion, wrote of 'these little panels that are realistic and lyrical at the same time, and of an infinite variety', but skirted round the subject of their fabrication.[48] Denis Rouart, grandson of another intimate friend, devoted an entire chapter of his book, *Degas: à la recherche de sa technique*, to the monotypes, perceptively noting the differences between earlier and later procedures.[49] In the brothel monochromes, for example, Degas would either 'draw' his subject in a series of fluent, calligraphic brushstrokes or cover the plate with a layer of ink, then wipe or scrape away the tone until his design was fixed. Conversely, in his colour landscapes, he never relied on outlines or defined contours, preferring to apply patches of ink directly to the polished plate, then manipulate them with pads of cloth or coarse bristle brushes. Into this still-wet colour, the artist could then

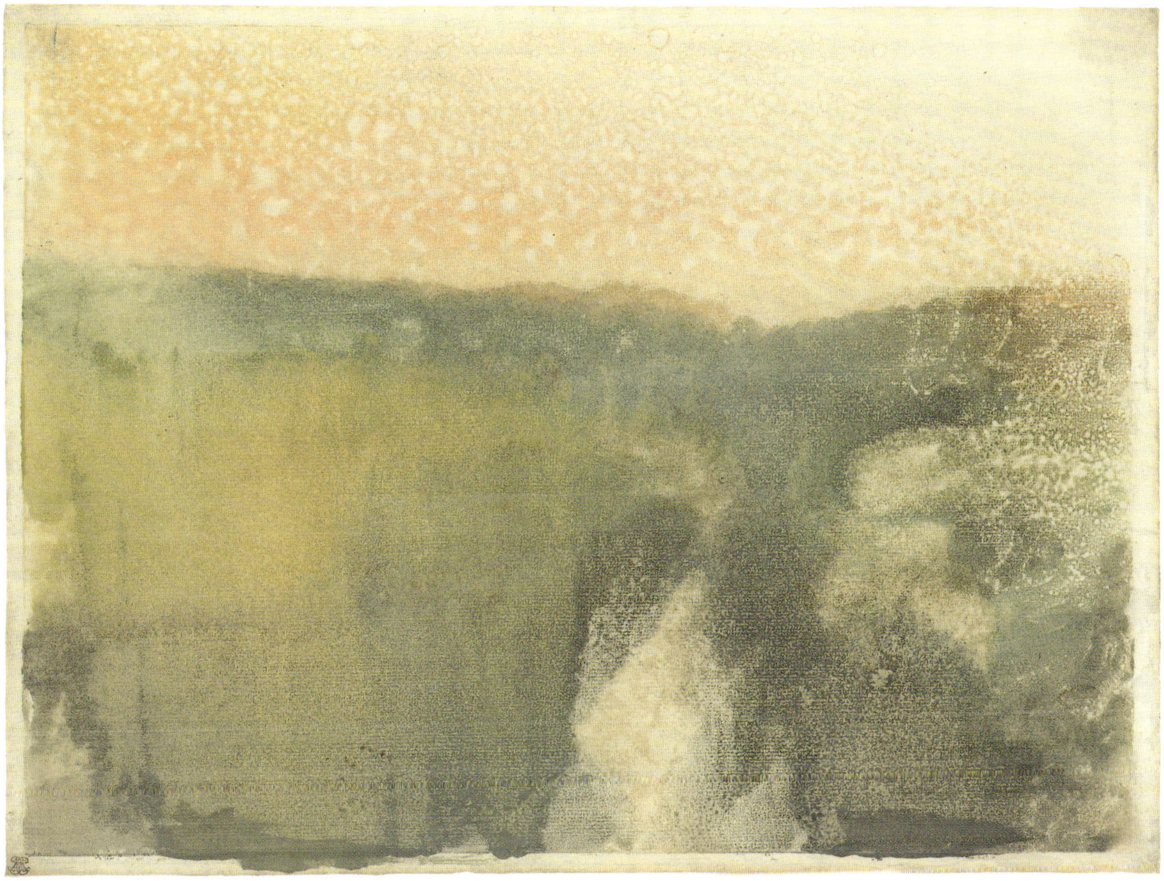

144. *Green Landscape*, 1890, monotype, 30 × 40 (K 2). Collection of Mrs. Bertram Smith.

145. *Landscape*, 1890, monotype, 29.7 × 39.6 (J 305). Private collection.

trace forms with 'the handle of the brush', as Jeanniot noticed, or encourage even greater nebulousness by blending or softening areas of ink. Further colours could be added and new modifications made with whatever tools came to hand, until the ink threatened to dry and the need to print became imperative. Ingeniously, but probably erroneously, in a much later essay Rouart suggested that Degas may have deliberately used old, dried pigments on certain occasions, and even incorporated crushed pastel into his printing surfaces.[50]

In her studies of Degas' monotypes, Eugenia Janis confirmed many of Denis Rouart's observations, while adding refinements and further speculations of her own.[51] Emphasising the tactile engagement of the artist with the inked plate, Janis pointed out that certain images, such as *Landscape in the Mountains* (fig. 136), revealed the application of colour by means of the artist's fingers and thumbs.[52] 'Monotype was an ideal medium for the artist working from memory;' she writes, 'he could smear ink around with his fingers, fashioning curves, contours and masses that became cliffs, roads, mountain lakes, openings and closures without defining specifics. Thus, he began with a generalised statement and defined it gradually. This method was compatible with the process of remembering, since the masses of ink were suggestive and called forth additional details as the work progressed and the artist recalled more.'[53] Unlike Rouart, Janis also noticed the significance of cognate pairs of images, where a fainter second proof of the monotype was pulled from ink remaining on the plate. In such cases, variants of the original scene were inevitably produced, which could be further differentiated or radically transformed as they were heightened with pastel. Other cognate pairs, as Barbara Shapiro has pointed out, could be developed to suggest the same *motif* at different seasons, or perhaps in shifting conditions of weather.[54] There is also some evidence that Degas modified the colour between printings, occasionally dabbing at the membrane of ink before running it through the press a second time.[55]

A print such as *Mountain Effect* (fig. 146) shows the initial stages in the generation of a monotype, uncluttered by later additions or amendments. Ochre and umber have been applied to the metal plate, apparently with crumpled cloths or the bristles of a brush.[56] Certain areas, such as the sky and lower-left foreground, were allowed to remain uncoloured, while the ink of the mountain itself has been further scored and furrowed once on the plate. Choosing a laid paper with a pronounced horizontal 'ribbing', Degas has then applied this to the inked plate, running both through Jeanniot's 'antique press' to produce the first proof. Just visible at the edges of the print are the indented 'plate-marks', where the metal has pressed into the paper, and occasional finger-prints and spots of colour squeezed from the plate's edges. In this example and in such vaporous images as *A Lake in the Pyrenees* (fig. 145*bis*), pigment has been sparingly applied, but in a related monotype, *Autumn Effect in the Mountains* (private collection; J 299), colour has been used in abundance. Here, coarsely spread brownish ink or paint once covered the entire sky, and perhaps the full extent of the picture rectangle. This has then been wiped or roughly brushed away in places, leaving squall-like streaks and an unusually ragged skyline. In both works, mountainous masses take on substance from folds and textures of colour, while the vigour of the artist's manipulations still lingers in their tactility.

145*bis*. *A Lake in the Pyrenees*, 1890, monotype, 29 × 39.6 (J 302). British Museum, London.

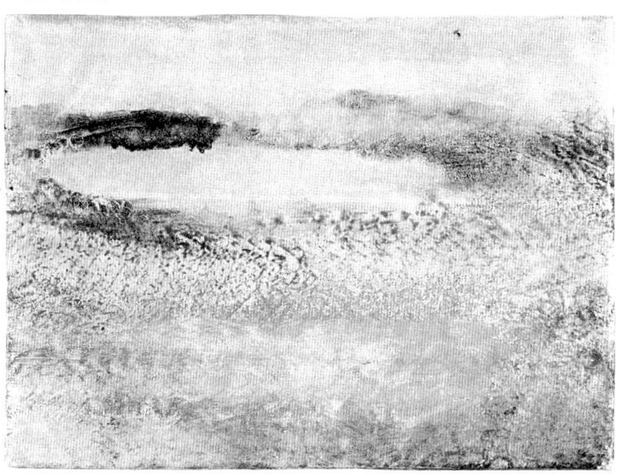

All the original sources, and most subsequent commentaries, are silent on the precise nature of the inks, paints or other colours used by Degas in these monotypes. Careful examination of the prints and attempts to replicate their effects, however, has led to the identification of oil paint as the principal, and probably unique, medium used.[57] Additionally, the known circumstances of the

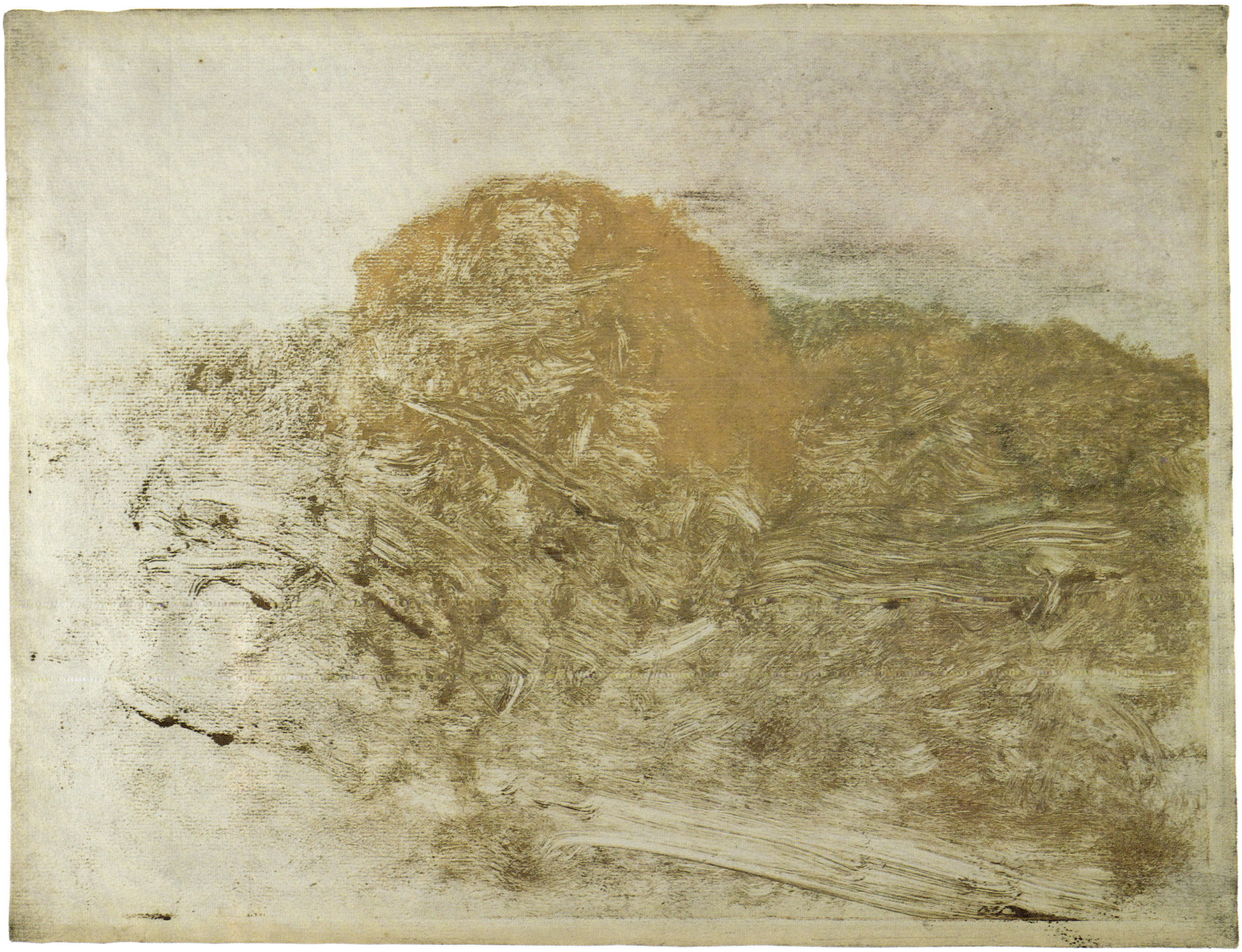

146. *Mountain Effect*, 1890, monotype, 29.9 × 39.5 (J 298). Private collection.

production of the prints argue strongly in the same direction. In his studio at Diénay, Jeanniot worked regularly on his canvases of figures and landscapes and would naturally have had a wide variety of colours, in the form of oil paints, readily available. In 1890, he was also beginning to explore print-making, though all his known proofs of this period are in black and white, as was normal practice.[58] It is most unlikely, therefore, that Jeanniot would have been able to offer Degas a range of coloured printing inks, and even more out of character for Degas to have brought his own. Used straight from the tube, oil paint lends itself to the tacky, textured effects of prints like *Mountain Effect*, though it can also leave 'haloes' of oil on the paper.[59] Slightly diluted with turpentine, in a way much favoured by Degas in other contexts, the same paint will spread more easily and produce smoother areas of colour. Finally, with the addition of a higher proportion of diluent, the paint takes on the fluidity of ink, forming runnels and puddles of free-flowing colour.

Many of the qualities of oil paint used as a monotype-printing medium can be

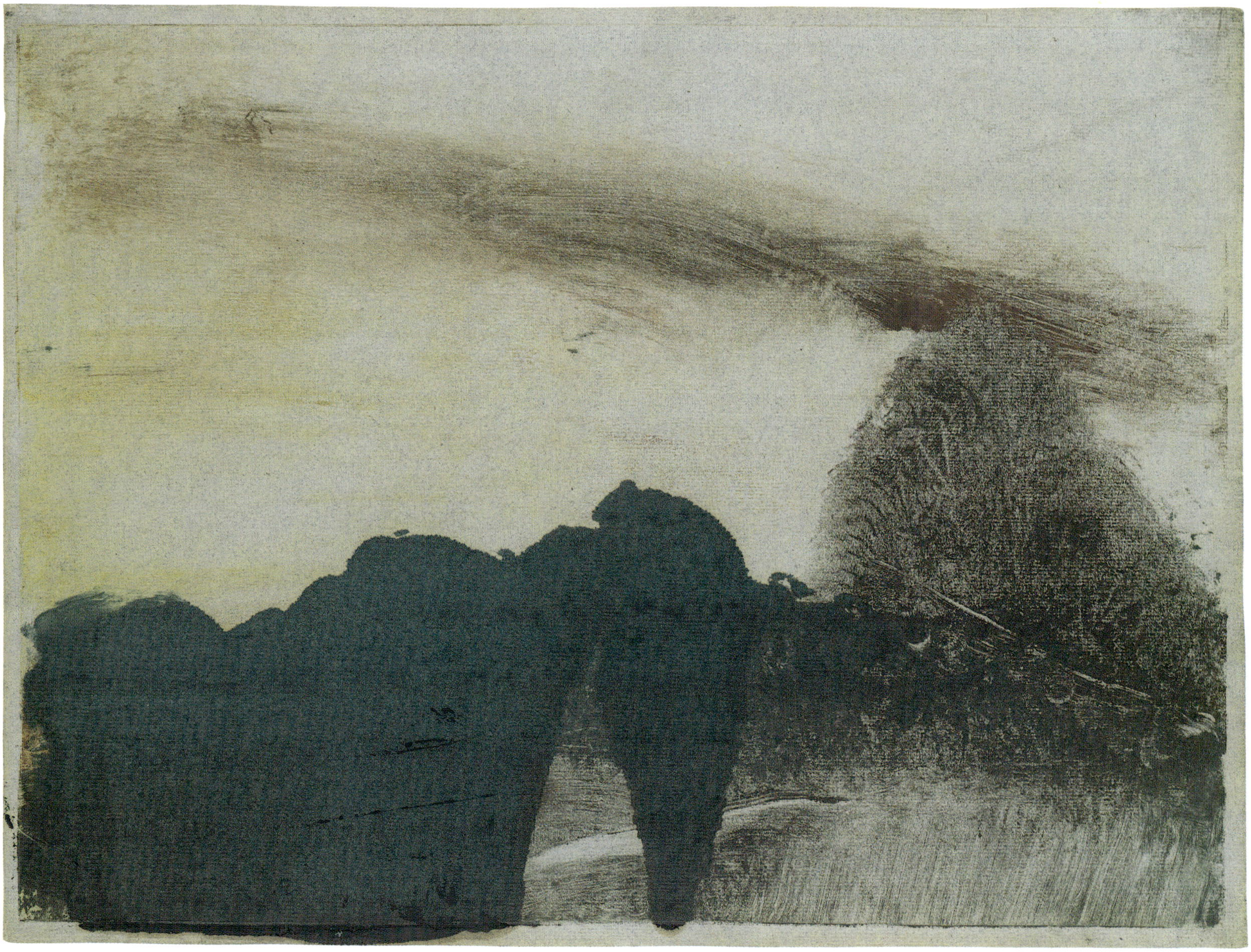

147. *A Wooded Landscape*, 1890, monotype, 29.9 × 40.3 (J 297). Collection of Mrs. Bertram Smith.

seen at their finest in *A Wooded Landscape* (fig. 147). In this finely balanced composition, a delicate sky is set against a firmly stated horizon, while a more ponderous foreground adds gravity and depth to the proceedings. Tinting the upper part of the plate with a soft cloth, perhaps using lightly diluted colour, Degas has wiped away all but a smear of ochre and dull mauve from his twilit sky. Dabs of more viscous grey-green paint were then used to conjure up trees, a hillside and a grassy bank, while paler streaks suggest fingertips and brushes dragged through the oily membrane. Finally, the same green pigment was thinned with turpentine and allowed to spread freely at the lower left, where a dramatic silhouette hints at shadowy hedgerows or rocky outcrops. These curious planes of flat, liquid colour feature in a number of monotypes and have previously eluded explanation. Practical experience has shown that they were formed by a largely uncontrollable process, in which thinned paint was left on the surface of the plate, then spread by the action of the printing press. As plate and paper advanced under the roller, small 'waves' of colour were

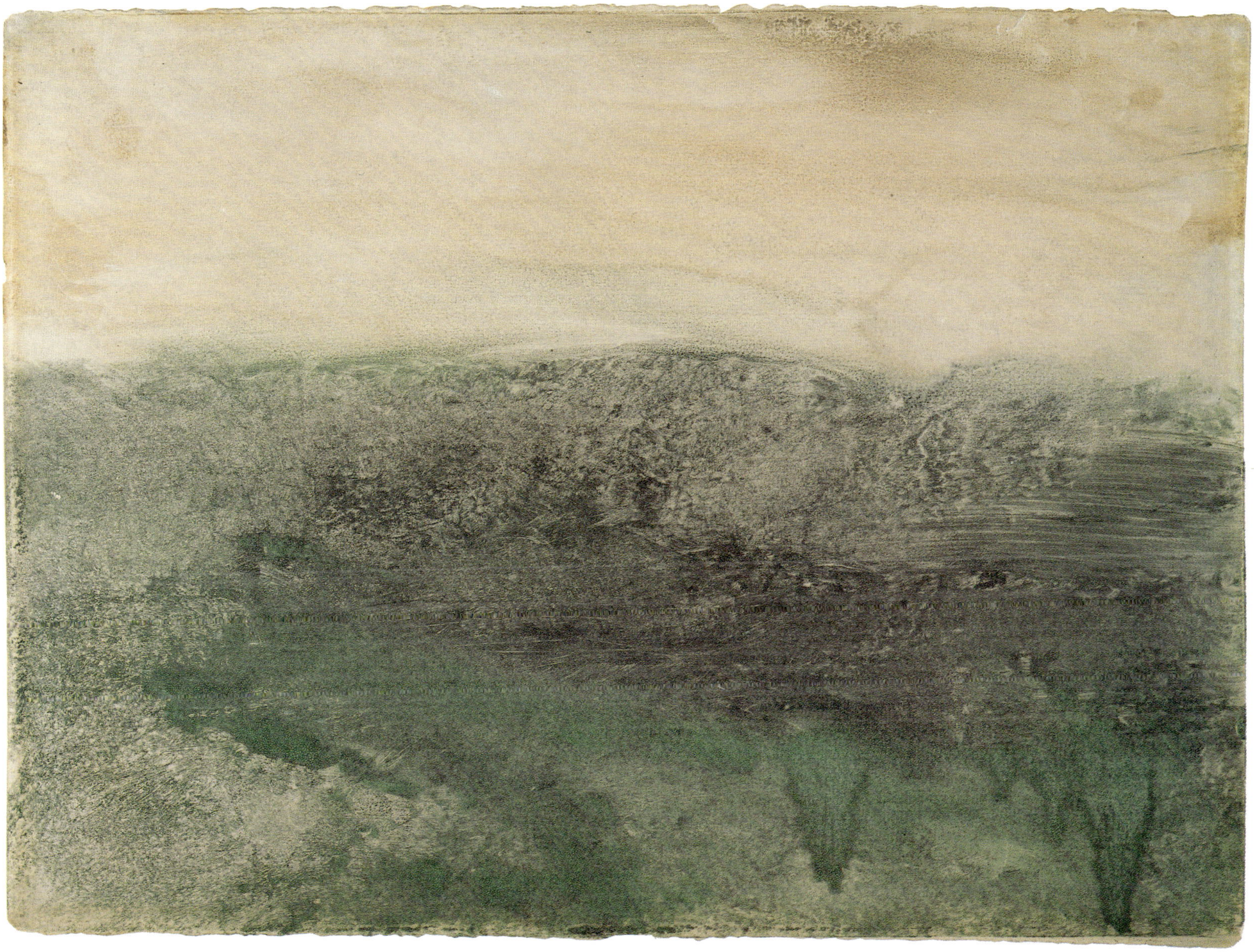

148. *Twilight in the Pyrenees*, 1890, monotype, 28.6 × 38.8 (J 307). Ackland Art Museum, The University of North Carolina at Chapel Hill, Ackland Fund.

pushed forward, sometimes spilling over the edge of the plate and staining the surrounding paper. Though often hidden from view by frames and mounts, this residue can be clearly seen at the lower margin of *A Wooded Landscape*.[60]

Such effects are essentially unpredictable and were almost certainly discovered by accident, at the time Degas made his first colour monotypes. If they occurred only once or twice in his prints, we might put them down to miscalculation and assume that increasing mastery of the medium had led to their disappearance. The fact that he continue to generate such aleatory 'blots', incorporating them into finished prints and exploiting their chance forms in his imagery, should give us pause. By encouraging the random spread of dilute paint across his composition, the artist must have obliterated some of his own carefully defined detail, but also proposed new structures and unrehearsed incidents. As Eugenia Janis has pointed out, these procedures highlighted the suggestiveness of the monotype medium and its capacity for stimulating both the memory and the imagination. The almost random cascade of burnt siena at the left of *Burgundy*

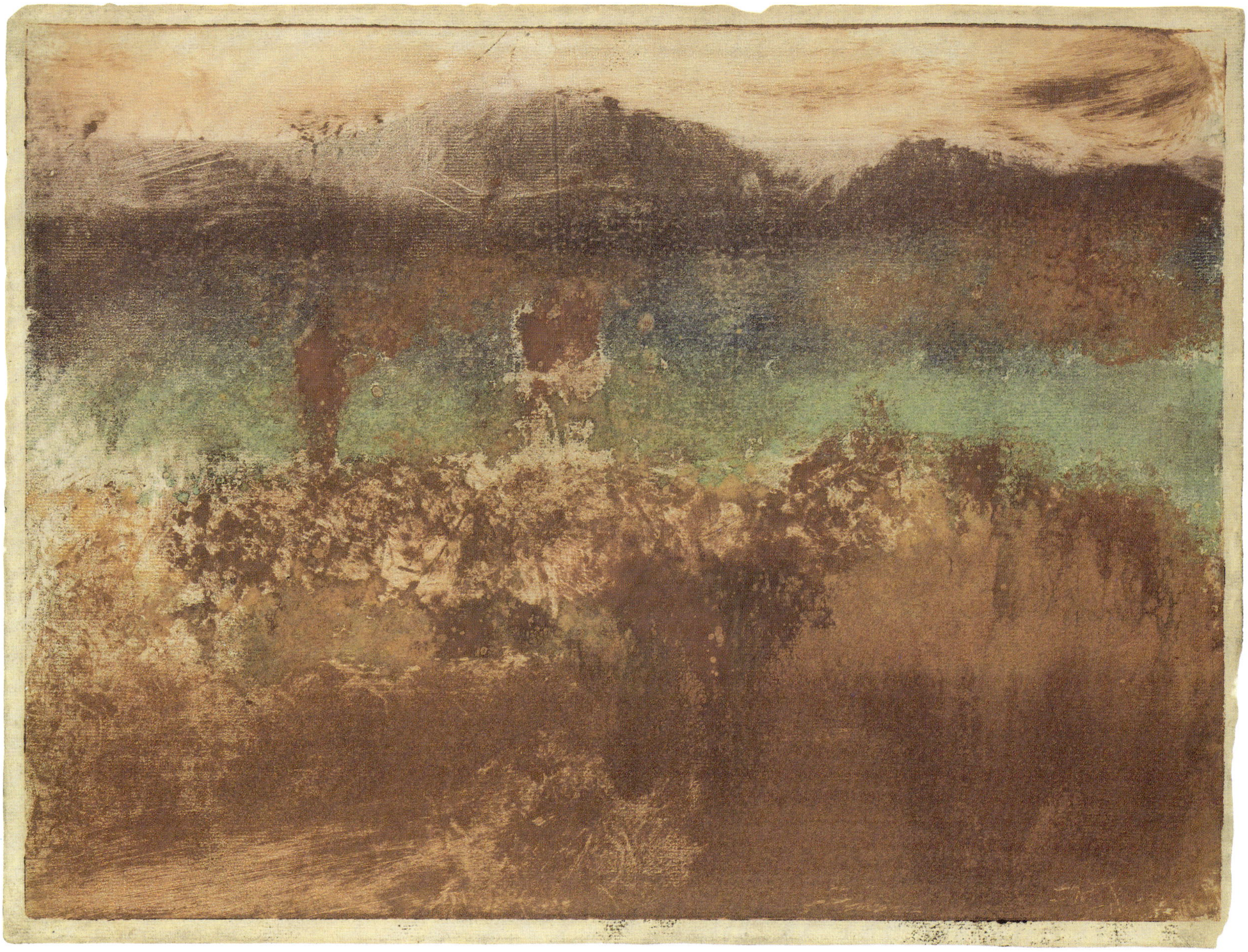

149. *L'Estérel*, 1890, monotype, 30.2 × 40 (J 300). Private collection.

Landscape (fig. 127), for example, is richly expressive of the watery landscapes that Degas is known to have encountered, while the veils of colour in *Green Landscape* might suggest the sunlight that comes between showers. In *Twilight in the Pyrenees* (fig. 148), many surface features seem like the pictorial equivalents of natural events. The broadly washed sky is heavy with moisture, streaked and blotched hillsides hint at blustery storms, and the cascading greens of the foreground speak of swollen streams and damp foliage.

The limits of control and the exploitation of chance are well illustrated in the pairs of cognate monotypes. Even in the hands of a practised printer, the amount of colour left on the plate after a first impression is difficult to predict, and the paleness or virtual invisibility of a second proof is determined by a number of variable factors. These include the viscosity of the ink; the weight, surface quality and dampness of the paper; and the time taken between printings, during which drying will occur. The two linked prints known as *Village in l'Estérel* (fig. 139) and *Estérel Village* (fig. 140) reveal several of these

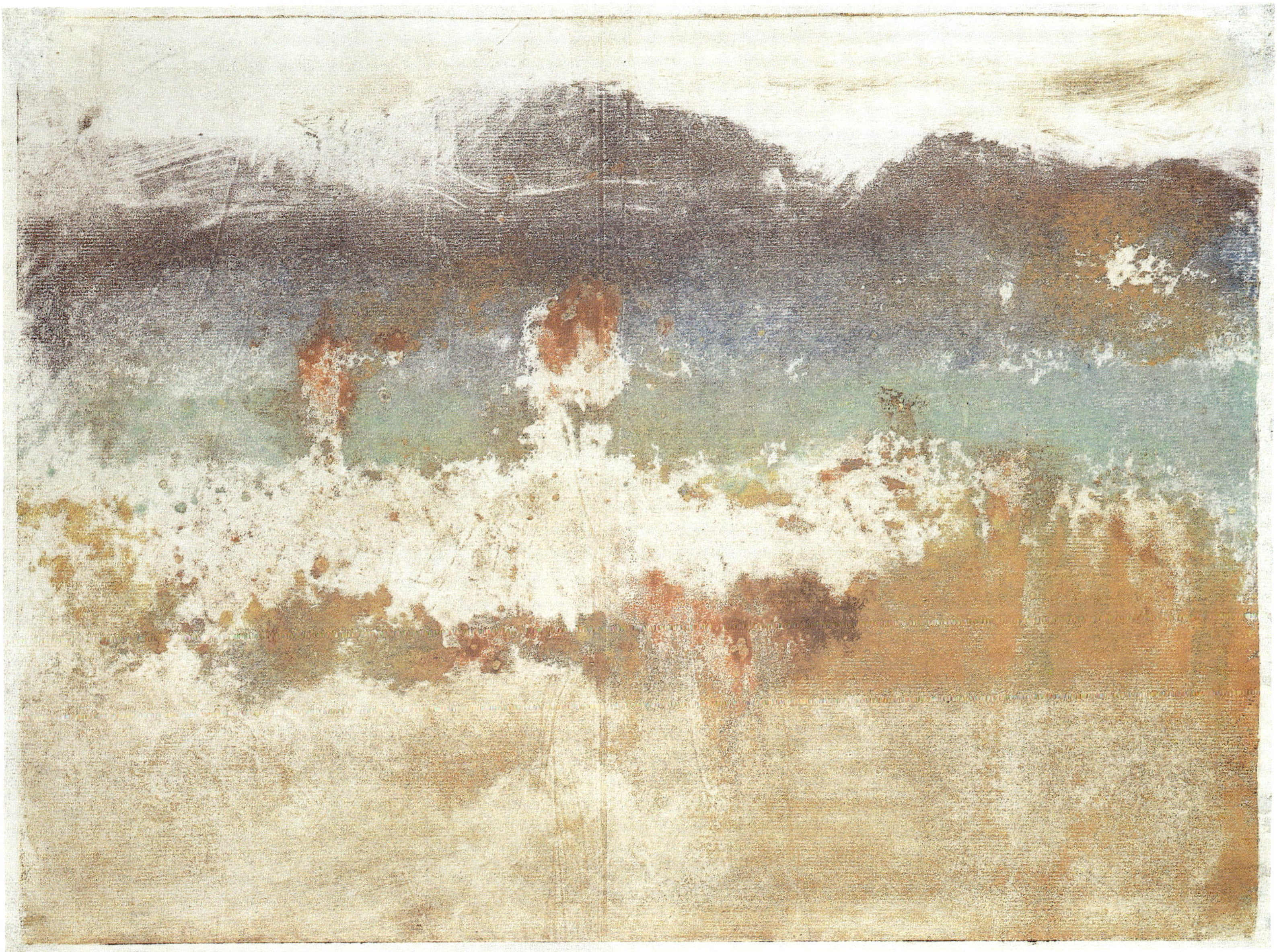

150. *L'Estérel*, 1890, monotype, 30 × 40 (J 301). Norton Simon Museum of Art, Pasadena.

factors at work. The richer tonality of *Village in l'Estérel* shows that it was the earlier of the two impressions, printed while the colour was at its freshest and the paint still fluid enough to spread under the action of the press, forming the yellow-green smear towards the left. Similarly, this print has the sharpest detail, from the crisp brush-mark of the central spire to the abrasively textured rocky escarpment and forestation. Before the printing of its paler companion. *Estérel Village*, Degas seems to have worked again on the inked plate, dabbing on additional areas of colour to reinforce its fading structures. By this stage, much of the precision of the earlier print had become blurred, though the artist has added variety by running a finger or brush-handle across the plate, creating pale paths or tracks. Other cognate pairs demonstrate just as forcefully the temporal constraints of the medium. *L'Estérel* (fig. 149) is majestically designed and stridently coloured, though already shows signs of the crustiness in certain areas of pigment that suggested the use of pastel to Denis Rouart.[61] The second proof, also entitled *L'Estérel* (fig. 150) is markedly paler, pointing to some delay between printings. At its most extreme, forms that were visible in the first print

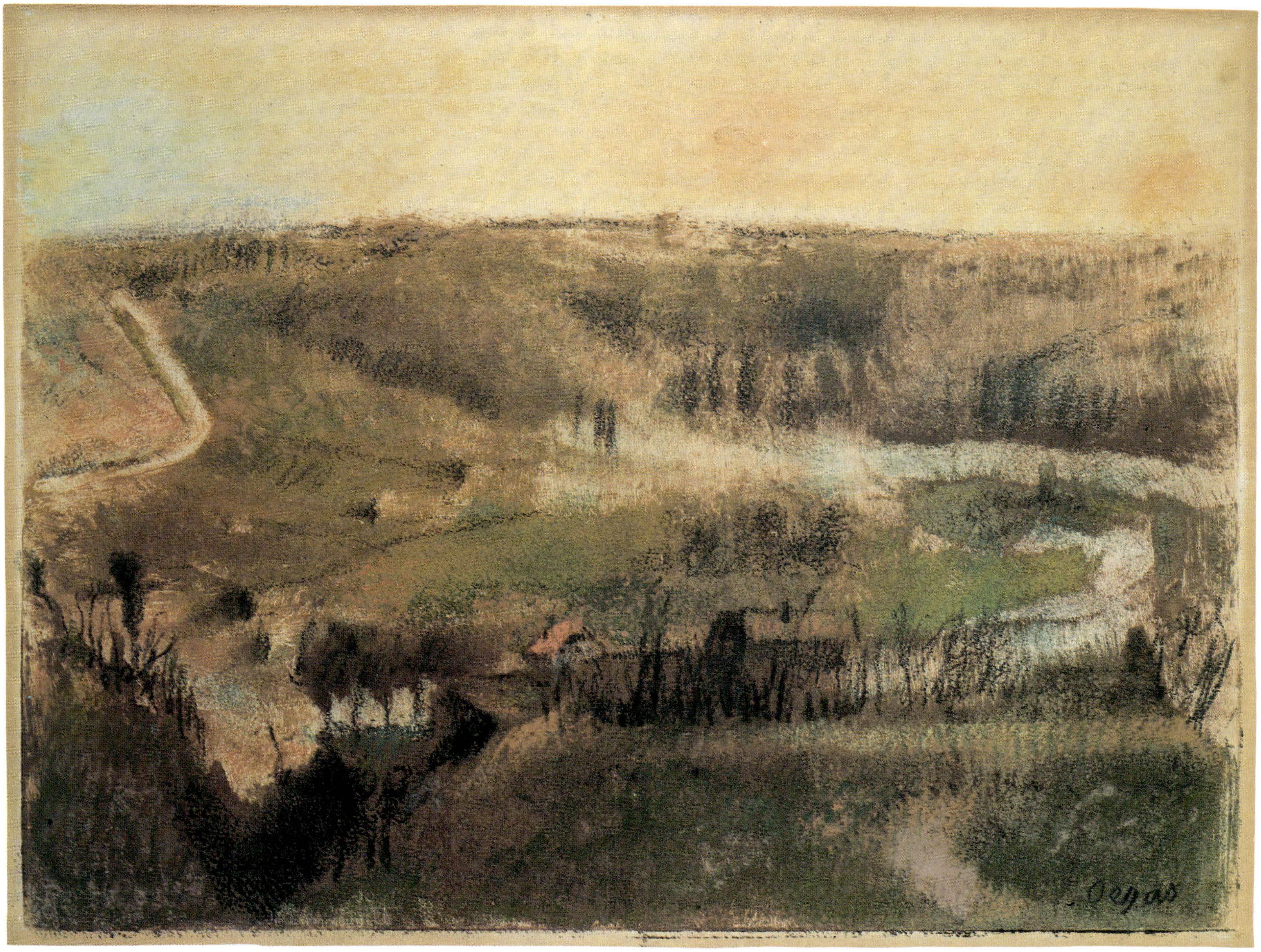

151. *Autumn Landscape*, 1890, monotype and pastel, 30.3 × 40 (J 279). Museum of Fine Arts, Boston, Denman Waldo Ross Collection.

have disappeared, leaving blank or ghostly passages in its delicately abstracted colour.

An even more fundamental disjunction between first and second printings is implicit in the pair of prints *Autumn Landscape* (fig. 151) and *River Banks* (fig. 152), which have been provisionally, but somewhat incompletely, seen as cognates.[62] In the former work, manifestly the denser and therefore the earlier of the two impressions, a dark foreground leads us into a wooded valley, where red-roofed cottages, a glimmering stream and a distantly curving road evoke Jeanniot's account of the ride through Burgundy. After pulling a second proof of this image, the artist decided to enhance both prints with pastel, but not before making a startling and quite literal change of direction. At this point, the second print was *inverted*, transforming the shadowy foreground of *Autumn Landscape* into the wooded backdrop of *River Banks*, and part of its pale stream into a whitewashed cottage. Confronted by two quite different variants of his initial image, one in the original sense, the other upside-down, Degas then set

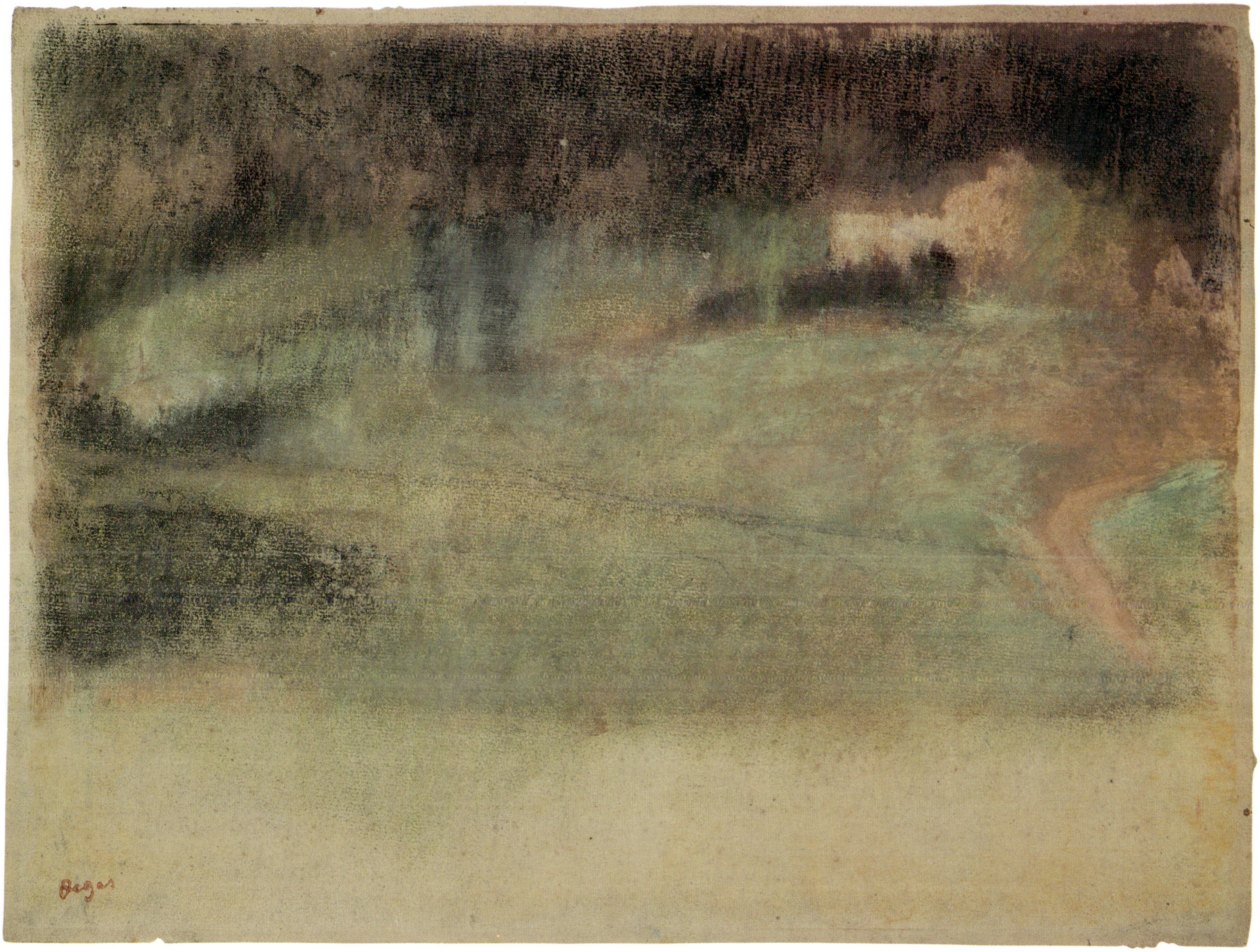

152. *River Banks*, 1890, monotype and pastel, 30 × 40 (J 280). Galerie Fisher, Lucerne.

about developing their respective identities. Using his pastels, he embellished and rationalised his oddly related twins, suppressing such incongruities as the gravity-defying stream in *River Banks*, and changing sky into fields, rivers into paths. The final stage in this extraordinary manoeuvre can be seen in the loop of road which is common to both works, now made to narrow as it approaches the horizon in *Autumn Landscape*, then to converge at its opposite extremity in *River Banks*.

Some of the consequences of this random, serendipitous procedure will be considered in the next chapter, but at this stage its immediate implications for Degas' imagery must be noted. If Jeanniot, Bartholomé and Degas himself are to be believed, the monotypes were made in response to scenes encountered on the artist's recent travels. It follows that, if *Autumn Landscape* was based on one particular scene, its inverted and arbitrarily re-composed cognate *River Banks* could not have been. Following Janis, we might accept that the up-turned image triggered a memory of a different subject, or that it represented a more generalised, less site-specific evocation of the Burgundian landscape. Either case is plausible, but both remind us that the rather literal accounts of Degas' friends should be followed with caution. However they were made, this pair of prints illustrates again the versatility, sometimes approaching a kind of technical anarchy, that the monotype process encouraged. At a practical level, it led to great freedom of execution and even carelessness in the handling of the artist's materials. Many prints have soiled or finger-marked margins and others have clearly been wiped with a sponge or cloth while the paint was still wet, in last-minute adjustments to their surfaces.[63] The very mobility and treacherousness of the medium seems to have attracted Degas, as well as its freedom from established conventions. When he poured turpentine into his colours, scored surfaces with a finger-nail or mischievously transformed a cognate image, Degas was consciously pushing back the frontiers of image-making. As the artist's niece, Jeanne Fevre, noted in another context, 'Degas liked nothing more than difficulty.'[64]

One of the features of monotype that must have appealed to Degas, both in his earlier career and during his visit to Diénay, was the speed with which images could be made. The copper or zinc plate needs no elaborate preparation, its surface is not etched or incised in any way, and once used, can immediately be re-used for another subject, after a rapid cleaning. For the same reasons, a single plate can form the basis of many different images, whose only common feature will be their size. Degas had already exploited this possibility in previous decades, making more than a dozen separate but identically sized monotypes of theatre and cabaret scenes from a single copper surface.[65] Finding himself in Jeanniot's studio in 1890, Degas would have been obliged to repeat the experience, using the limited number of unused plates that came to hand. As a consequence, we would expect the Diénay monotypes to conform to certain sets of dimensions, while other prints made in different circumstances would have distinct shapes and sizes. In this way, Degas' fifty-or-so known colour landscapes might separate themselves into series and sub-groups, each one corresponding to a single originating plate and thus associating itself with a distinct location.

This classification of the monotypes by dimensions, rather than by subject-matter or finish, has not previously been attempted, but its results are both startling and informative (see Appendix 1). Where once we confronted a miscellany of images, we now discover three dominant and precisely defined families, each related by size and format. Allowing for slight variations in habits of measurement and the unreliability of some published information, the great majority of prints fall into one of these three classes.[66] Where they fail to conform, they often turn out to have been mis-catalogued as monotypes.[67] Conversely, when certain landscape pastels share the same dimensions, they have revealed a hidden monotype beneath their familiar surfaces.[68] At its simplest, Degas appears to have used only three separate plates to print the bulk of his monotypes, each of these plates being re-used several times to make a sequence of similarly proportioned images. Other factors, such as paper type, the use of pastel and the scarcity or otherwise of the artist's signature, broadly confirm these clusters, as do the preponderance of subject-matter and imagery. While there are some exceptions, each of which will be discussed in due course, the prints themselves have a pattern of kinship that suggests coherence rather than disparity, evolution rather than stasis.

Numerically, the dominant group of monotypes is that produced from a plate measuring approximately 30 by 40 centimetres, which accounts for more than thirty prints (group A; see Appendix 1). In general, it is also the most

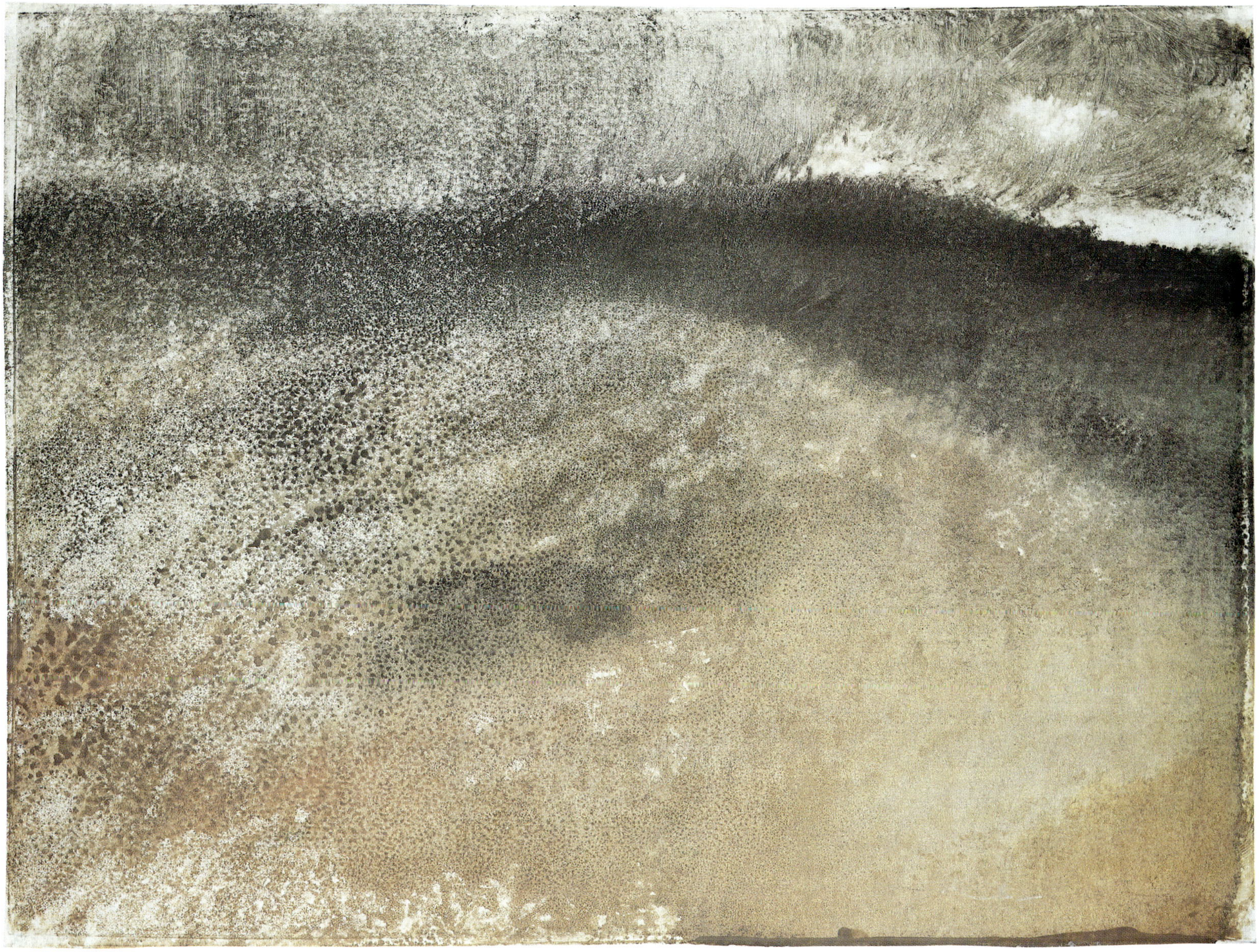

153. *Squall in the Mountains*, 1890, monotype, 30.3 × 39.8 (J 306). Norton Simon Museum of Art, Pasadena.

experimental, or perhaps uncontrolled, sequence of works, showing the greatest incidence of chance effects and a relative lack of finish. Less than half this family, for instance, are developed in pastel and even fewer carry the artist's signature. All the monotypes discussed in the earlier part of this chapter belong to group A and, as we have seen, almost all are consistent with the landscape of Burgundy. Where prints have a known association with Degas' visit to Diénay, such as the *Burgundy Landscape* given to Bartholomé or the *River Banks* belonging to Jeanniot, they also conform to this category. It is difficult to resist the conclusion, therefore, that this family of works was made in Jeanniot's studio, from a single, standard-size plate, in the autumn of 1890.[69] Further corroboration can be found in the exploratory and sometimes unfinished nature of the series, as though they represented the first encounter between artist and medium. Finally, only half a dozen of the group A prints were chosen for the 1892 exhibition at Durand-Ruel's, adding further to their provisional status.

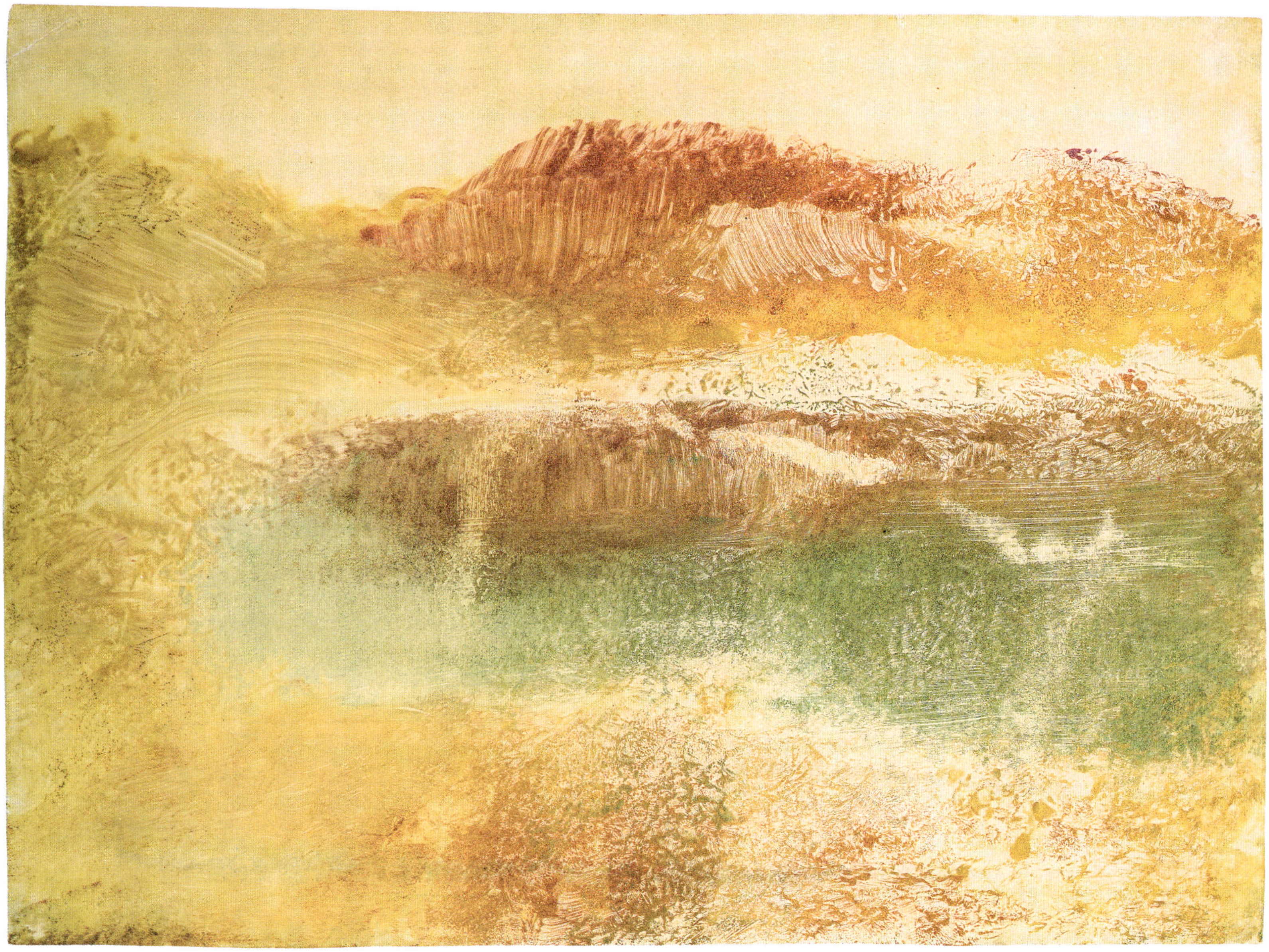

154. *Russet Landscape*, 1890, monotype, 30 × 40 (K 1). Private collection.

The two other landscape families, groups B and C, are smaller in both number and physical size. They are also more assured, showing extensive embellishment in pastel and a high degree of finish. Most remarkably, all but one of the prints in these two groups are signed by the artist and all appear to have been included in the Durand-Ruel show. Each of these factors tends to separate them from Degas' known activity at Diénay, and correspondingly to link them with a second phase of production, such as that described by Daniel Halévy in the summer of 1892. Halévy's account stresses that these prints, too, were based on a period of recent travel, while suggesting that they were executed in Degas' Paris studio, not at some point on his journey. In either case, Degas would have chosen a new copper plate or plates on which to make his landscapes, and new sequences would be expected to emerge. Perhaps with his impending exhibition in mind, Degas seems to have worked more purposefully, enriching his prints with dense skeins of pastel and consciously introducing a more varied repertoire of subject-matter. Inevitably, his rail journeys had

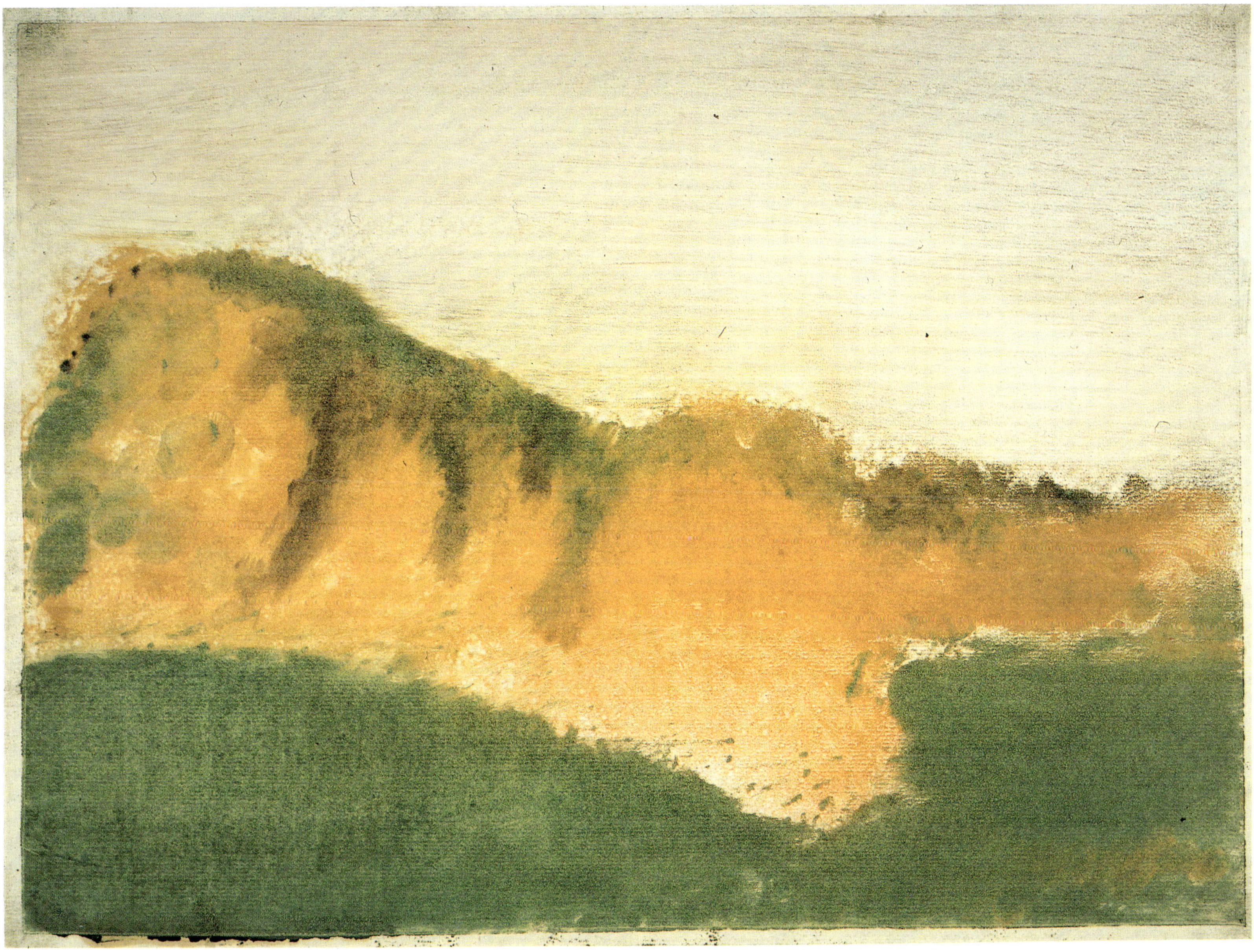

155. *Le Cap Hornu*, 1890, monotype, 29.9 × 40 (J 295). British Museum, London.

brought him up against new kinds of *motifs* and terrain, and it is no surprise to find landscapes quite different from those of the Diénay series. Mountains and lakes, broad vistas and even a volcano, all conspicuously absent from his Burgundian itinerary, make their appearance, as well as humble cornfields and other summery subjects.

Little in Degas' *oeuvre*, however, is as simple as this classification by size would suggest. Intermediate possibilities suggest themselves, such as prints begun at Diénay and transformed with pastel before the Durand-Ruel exhibition, or works from the 1892 phase that recalled earlier, perhaps even Burgundian, *motifs*. Some monotypes from the Diénay series, such as *Squall in the Mountain* (fig. 153) and *Russet Landscape* (fig. 154) may derive their imagery from Degas' travels in the spring and summer of the same year, for example to Switzerland and the Pyrenees.[70] Others from group A, such as *Le Cap Hornu* (fig. 155) and *An Island in the Sea* (fig. 201), cannot be reconciled with the landscape of the Côte d'Or, and seem to anticipate a later interest in imagined topography.[71] This interest is at odds with the assumption that Degas' journeying was the sole source of his subject-matter and reminds us of the exceptional diversity of the prints, rather than their uniformity. Despite this blurring of boundaries, the sub-division of the monotypes helps us to understand their technical history, and focuses attention on Degas' changing priorities. There can be little doubt that most of the dominant group were made at Diénay, printed from a single plate and perhaps knowingly generated as a suite of similarly sized rectangles ('I have been wanting for so long to make a *series* of monotypes', Degas claimed). On the same evidence, we can see them as Degas' first engagement with colour printing, and with the delights and hazards of impulsively applied paint. Finally, the majority of this group appear to have been a response to his surroundings, to the misty valleys, seasonal squalls and autumnal extravagance of 'this admirable Burgundy'.

Why did Degas choose to travel to Burgundy, and why did he wait until the visit to Diénay to embark on his first series of colour monotypes? Though he was familiar with Jeanniot and his wife, their intimacy was not of the same order as that between the artist and the Valpinçons, the Rouarts or the Halévys.[72] As with certain other journeys, Degas may have been glad of the pretext for an outing, as much to appease his 'pitch of travelling excitement' as to seek out the company of his host and hostess. In other respects, the choice of Burgundy and the Côte d'Or was a surprising one. Unlike the resorts of the Channel coast and the spa towns of the Pyrenees, Burgundy had never been a fashionable area, either for family holidays or picturesque excursions. The route taken by Bartholomé and Degas was not covered by the Baedeker guides, and the region was treated with condescension in the travel literature. The Guide Joanne of 1874 had set the tone, announcing that 'Grandiose landscapes are lacking in the *département* of the Côte d'Or, but charming or picturesque sites are not rare.'[73] Illustrating his text with a bleak, rock-strewn hillside (fig. 156), Joanne continued by listing the precipices and defiles, the caverns and cascades the intrepid traveller might encounter, adding that curious stone formations were characteristic of the terrain.[74]

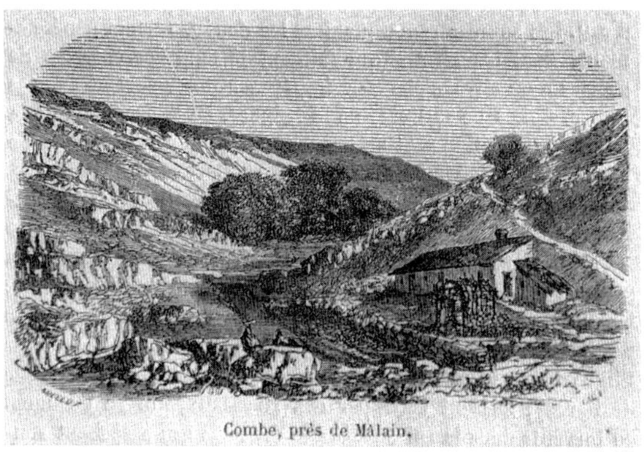

156. Wood engraving from Joanne's *Géographie de la Côte d'Or*, 1874.

Perhaps for the same reasons, Burgundy had been effectively ignored by the celebrated landscape painters of recent and earlier generations. Courbet's home-town of Ornans, some sixty miles to the east, offers the closest comparison, though its broad vistas and plateau-like horizons are topographically distinct. Through family connections, Renoir began to take holidays in the late 1880s at the village of Essoyes, slightly to the north of Degas' route, but again his subject-matter is remote from that of the colour monotypes.[75] While at much the same period, Monet was painting the ravines of the Midi and Cézanne the mountainscape of Provence, Degas seems to have found his own, virtually unpainted stretch of countryside.[76] With an independence that verges on the perverse, Degas chose to base his most important sequence of landscapes on one of the least admired areas of inland France. By doing so, he also avoided what Adolphe Joanne called 'grandiose landscapes', the awesome panoramas and lofty peaks much preferred by guidebook compilers. Degas' anonymous hillsides, rain-sodden fields and blurrs of autumn colour are the antithesis of this repertoire, and seem, wittingly or otherwise, to subvert its premises.

Degas' Burgundy is neither ingratiating nor glamorous, offering few spectacular features and even fewer concessions to human interest. Though he passed through or close to several cathedral towns, he remembered none of their historic sites when making his prints. Unlike his colleague Pissarro, he responded to neither market scenes nor farmsteads, labourers in the fields nor travellers on the road, indeed to no man, woman or child on his route. The scenes he represented might best be called elemental, in the sense already applied to the 1869 pastels. Strips of sky, swathes of woodland and pasture, and broad expanses of road and river make up their compositions, often distributed in block-like, geometric forms. The sheer simplicity of their designs can hardly be exaggerated. A work like *Twilight in the Pyrenees* (fig. 148) shows little more than a featureless land mass against an empty sky, yet its veils of colour hint at erosion and gravity, seasonal change and private solitude.[77] Spatially, such works rely on colour and tone rather than traditional perspective, and balance a concern for two-dimensional pattern with an acknowledgement of depth. In this, and in much of their pictorial radicalism, they belong to a continuing set of preoccupations that have been visible throughout Degas' career. From the empty oil-on-paper skies of his Roman sojourn to the beach-and-ocean studies of Houlgate, and from the monochromes of the 1870s to the monotypes of the early 1890s, these minimal, planar scenes haunt the artist's landscape *oeuvre*. As he once said, memorably and prophetically, to Jeanniot, 'A picture is an original combination of lines and colours that make themselves felt . . .'[78]

The absence of human figures from the monotype landscapes demands further comment. To a limited extent, it can be seen as an expression of the circumstances in which the prints were conceived. When travelling by coach or train, the artist told the Halévys that he 'looked around vaguely', responding to the dominant colours and shifting forms of the passing landscape. Even with his prodigious memory, Degas would hardly have fixed the positions of farm workers or bystanders, let alone faces and localised narratives. Such limitations would normally have been surmounted in the studio, where figures could be added at will; but on this occasion, the emptiness of the terrain suited Degas' purposes. Just as he had cleared the beaches of Normandy to emphasise their breadth and simplicity of form, so the villagers of the Côte d'Or were overlooked in the more timeless spectacle of their surroundings. Both cases are not without poignancy; the desolate promenades of the 1869 pastels remind us of Degas' private unease at this period, as he recovered from entanglements with the Morisot family and explored new techniques and subject-matter. Similarly, the deserted roadways of Burgundy were chosen by an artist who had been 'sad and serious for a long time', though apparently able to enjoy a jocular tilbury ride with his friend.

Further insights into Degas' unpopulated landscapes can be found in his documented attitudes to the countryside. As a confirmed Parisian and one-time *flâneur*, Degas affected an aloofness from the rural scene that could be both comic and contradictory. When visiting Normandy in 1861, he had exclaimed, 'how can anybody live here?', and twenty years later could still be distressed by provincial damp, fresh air and the digestive habits of livestock.[79] Despite such affectations, Degas travelled extravagantly and enjoyed lengthy rural holidays, while apparently maintaining the proprieties of his class. Always correctly dressed, he was photographed in suit, hat and polished shoes during outings at Dieppe in 1885, at Diénay in 1890 and at Ménil-Hubert in 1895.[80] In this sense, Degas was always the city-dweller on vacation, seeing the landscape from a detached and socially selective vantage point. For him, unlike many of his artist contemporaries, the countryside was there to be plundered, to supply colours, forms and ready-made *motifs* which could be transported back to Paris, then made into art. Where Cézanne painted scenes he had known since boyhood,

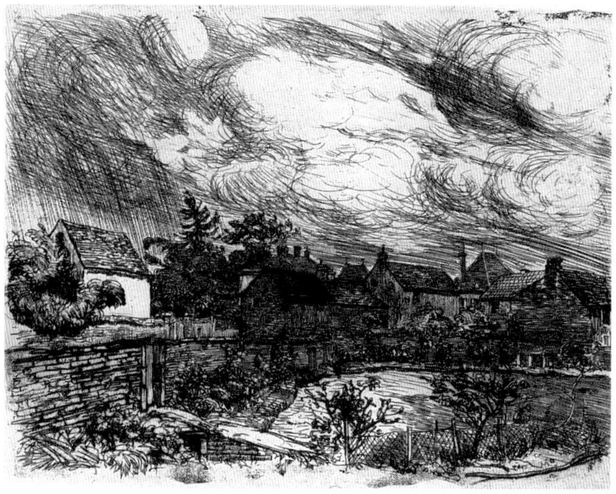

157. Georges Jeanniot, *Entry to Diénay*, 1894, etching. Bibliothèque Nationale, Paris.

158. Georges Jeanniot, *Degas*, 1890, black chalk, 18.8 × 21. Bibliothèque Nationale, Paris.

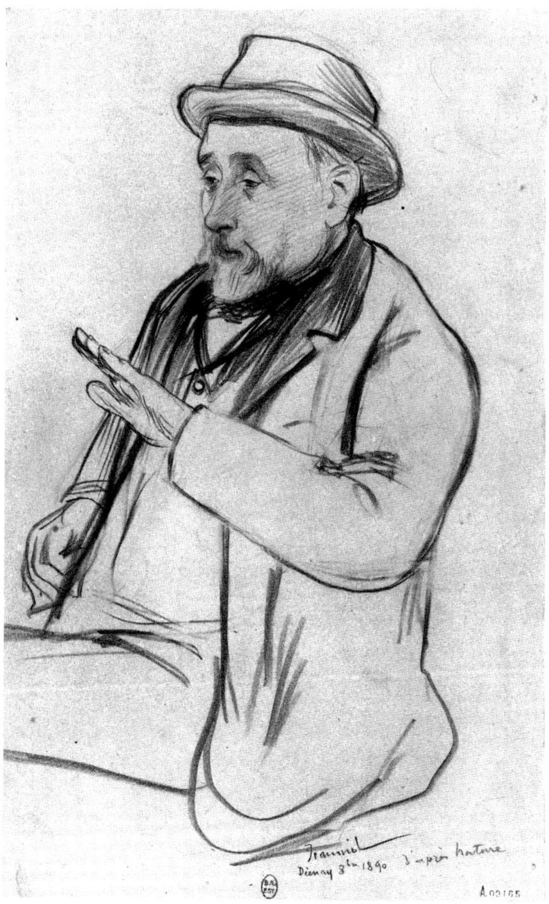

Degas depicted novel experiences and the briefest of visual engagements; where Pissarro found kitchen-gardeners and the labouring poor, Degas saw empty fields. The invisibility of the rural population in Degas' monotypes was, in effect, an extension of his social and political behaviour. Increasingly reactionary in his later years, the artist could admire craftsmen and their dwellings in the city, while looking back to a time 'when everyone stayed in his place and dressed according to his station.'[81] His known contacts with the local population in Burgundy suggest a correct, but somewhat patrician, manner, and confirm his essential lack of interest in rural and provincial encounters.[82]

The distinctiveness of Degas' view of Burgundy is further underlined by contrast with that of his companions and temporary hosts at Diénay. By the time Degas visited him, Georges Jeanniot had already built up a repertoire of local scenery, working in oil paint and a variety of print-making processes. Several of his etchings, such as *Entry to Diénay* (fig. 157), showed the village itself, while a submission to the 1887 Salon, *Banks of the Ignon, Evening*, represented the local river and nearby cottages.[83] As a painter, Jeanniot never achieved great distinction, though his skills in draughtsmanship, caricature and book illustration were sufficient to ensure him a certain celebrity. Some of his earliest work was for the publisher Charpentier, patron of Renoir and Monet, and in the 1890s he made intricate drawings for novels by Zola, Maupassant and Mirbeau.[84] A vivid study of Degas, proudly inscribed 'Diénay, Octobre 1890, d'après nature' (fig. 158), displays his considerable mastery of line, as well as hinting at the older artist's influence over his emergent style. Though often vigorous, Jeanniot's imagery tends towards the literal and the pedantic, insisting on detail at the expense of the *ensemble*. His views of Diénay remind us of the charms of the locality, and of 'the admirable Burgundy' that prompted Degas' journey, even as they stress the remoteness of Degas' own approach to such material. In the colour monotypes, the picturesque *motifs* favoured by Jeanniot were pointedly overlooked, and the village and its inhabitants effectively ignored. So extreme and so contrary were Degas' practices, that they can seem like a rebuke from one generation to another, and perhaps as an object-lesson in print-making, composition and the principles of landscape art.

Degas' approach to Jeanniot's art is in itself instructive. Some fourteen years Degas' junior, Jeanniot had abandoned his career in the army in 1883 to devote himself to painting. Confronted by this relative beginner, and by the evidence of his uncertain talent, Degas took Jeanniot under his artistic wing during excursions to Diénay.[85] Apart from the now-famous monotype session in Jeanniot's attic, the visits included etching lessons, collaborative experiments in print-making and bizarre demonstrations of oil-painting technique, using both landscape and figurative subject-matter.[86] The products of many of these sessions have survived, revealing the unevenness of Jeanniot's skill as well as the occasional peaks of his accomplishment. Not least among these are a group of black-and-white monotypes of military subjects, apparently made under Degas' guidance, which vary in proficiency from the masterful to the frankly feeble.[87] Perhaps to encourage Jeanniot towards greater breadth of handling, Degas also undertook a landscape oil painting while at Diénay, adding his signature and presenting it to his host.[88] Known only through a photograph in the Musée d'Orsay (fig. 159), the composition is consistent with the colour monotypes and features similarly winding roads, undulating hills and softly brushed forms.[89] During one of his painting displays at Diénay, Degas explained his method of laying in the principal masses of such a scene in bold colours: 'It's a useful way of creating, in a short time, an effect of the *ensemble*, because a picture should

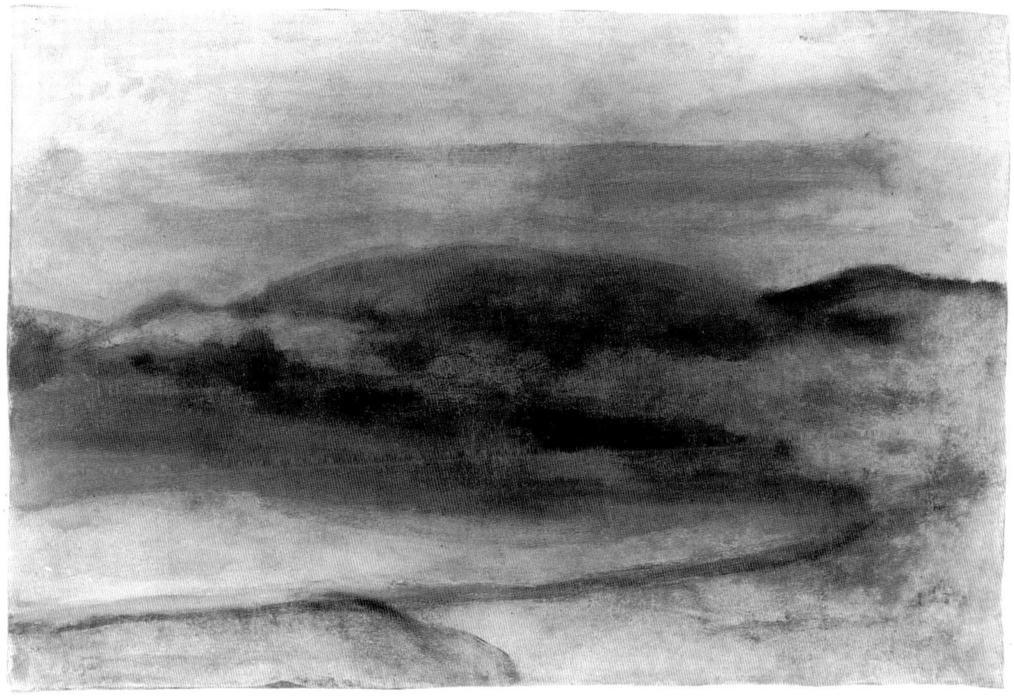

159. *Burgundy Landscape*, *c.*1890, oil on canvas. Location unknown, photo courtesy the Musée d'Orsay, Paris.

only be painted after having made a study in front of nature. It is composed in advance in your mind; the studies that you accumulate just provide you with support, with valuable information.'[90]

The significance for Degas of the small but cultured community at Diénay has been insufficiently explored. Jeanniot's father, also a landscape painter, had been the director of the Ecole des Beaux-Arts at nearby Dijon, and through him Jeanniot had encountered some of the leading artists, photographers, critics and writers of the region. Several of them owned properties at Diénay or enjoyed Jeanniot's hospitality, and most seem to have been invited to meet his distinguished guests in the autumn of 1890. One of Degas' reception party, for example, was Edmond Cousturier, seasonal resident at Diénay and specialist in the history of book illustration and print-making. Cousturier was associated with the periodical *La Revue blanche*, and his wife, the painter Lucie Cousturier, later achieved prominence as a follower of Seurat and the Neo-Impressionists.[91] Another evening, Degas encountered Madame de Fleury, whose low-cut gown both shocked and amused him.[92] Perhaps the most remarkable individual in the Diénay circle, however, was Charles de Meixmoron de Dombasle, early collector of Impressionism, amateur artist, pioneer of photography and tireless advocate of the *pleinairiste* cause.

In the early 1870s, Meixmoron had used his substantial private means to acquire at least ten canvases by Monet, including one of his *Boulevard des Capucines* studies, as well as works by Manet, Boudin, Sisley and Degas himself.[93] Some of this collection was later kept at Diénay and seems to have encouraged his own accomplished, if somewhat derivative, studies of the landscape. Like Jeanniot, he favoured the domestic *motifs* of the village and its environs, producing a Sisley-like canvas of his own château and a study of the parish church that recalls Pissarro.[94] As a photographer, he preceded Degas by a number of years, recalling the classic compositions of an earlier generation while exploring new subtleties of focus and viewpoint.[95] Meixmoron and Degas probably met in September 1890, on the latter's first brief trip to Diénay, prior to the tilbury excursion.[96] Subsequently, Meixmoron's name appears in Degas' correspondence, and it seems that the two artists exchanged information on technical and theoretical matters.[97] At the time of their encounter, Meixmoron had reached a peak of proselytizing activity, publishing his book *Le Paysage d'après nature* in 1890 and soon after a series of popular articles entitled *Le Paysage dans l'atelier*.[98] Broadly speaking, Meixmoron encouraged a practical view of open-air painting, without losing sight of the conceptual challenges it posed. He advised caution in the use of photography as the basis for painting and, like Degas, expressed concern for the 'subordination of details' in the overall design.[99] It may well have been Meixmoron's camera that captured Degas and Bartholomé as they progressed through Diénay in their tilbury, and his example perhaps led to Degas' own experiments with photography later in the decade. Most remarkably, Meixmoron was responsible for a previously unpublished photograph of Degas and two of his companions painting in the open air at Diénay (fig. 160). Distinctively hatted and silver-haired, Degas sits between his colleagues as they solemnly record the local church, for all the world like one of the *pleinairistes* he so energetically despised.

Before we can leave Degas' tour of Burgundy in 1890, we should perhaps complete the circle and return the artist, with his folder of recently finished monotypes, to Paris. Degas and Bartholomé left Diénay on the afternoon of 13 October, travelling now in a south-westerly direction towards Saint-Seine-l'Abbaye, and then northwards again to join their original route at Tonnerre. From the first day of the return trip, the fusillade of letters and witticisms resumed. Writing to Ludovic Halévy, Degas begged him to follow their route on a map, boasting of their progress and expatiating on food and drink they had

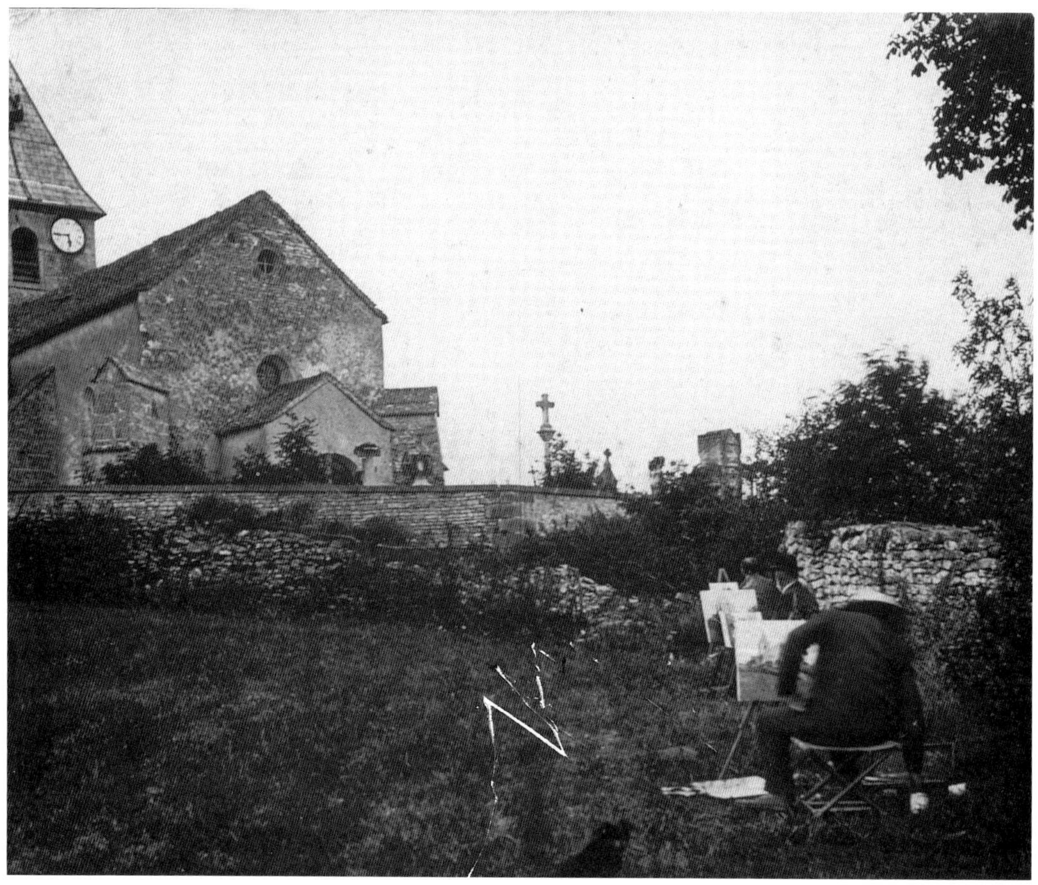

160. Charles de Meixmoron, *Degas and Friends Painting at Diénay*, *c.*1890, photograph. Private collection.

consumed.[100] Insisting that the horse 'knows the direction without a map', Degas proclaimed, 'For the traveller, the beat of the horse's hoofs is sweeter than a woman's footstep.'[101] As they neared Paris, he alerted several friends to their arrival, urging them to meet the tilbury and dine *en route*. Michel Manzi, the draughtsman and print-making impresario, appeared in a carriage, and within hours Jean-Louis Forain had joined the party. Arriving 'on his tricycle in a Garibaldian get-up, he speaks of the destiny of speed', reported Degas, who was soon preparing Halévy for a visit from the 'four assassins'.[102] Once back in his studio, Degas wrote a characteristic note to Jeanniot, sending fond regards to Cousturier, Meixmoron and Mme Jeanniot, while planning future projects and collaborations. This long and only recently discovered letter says much about Degas in his middle years. Wry and affectionate, enthusiastic but deeply enmeshed in practicalities, it outlines a proposed album of prints to which Jeanniot would contribute.[103] Finally, Degas apologised to Jeanniot for their confused experimentation at Diénay, and his 'juggling with pastel and copal varnish', adding, 'forgive me if I played the charlatan a little'.[104]

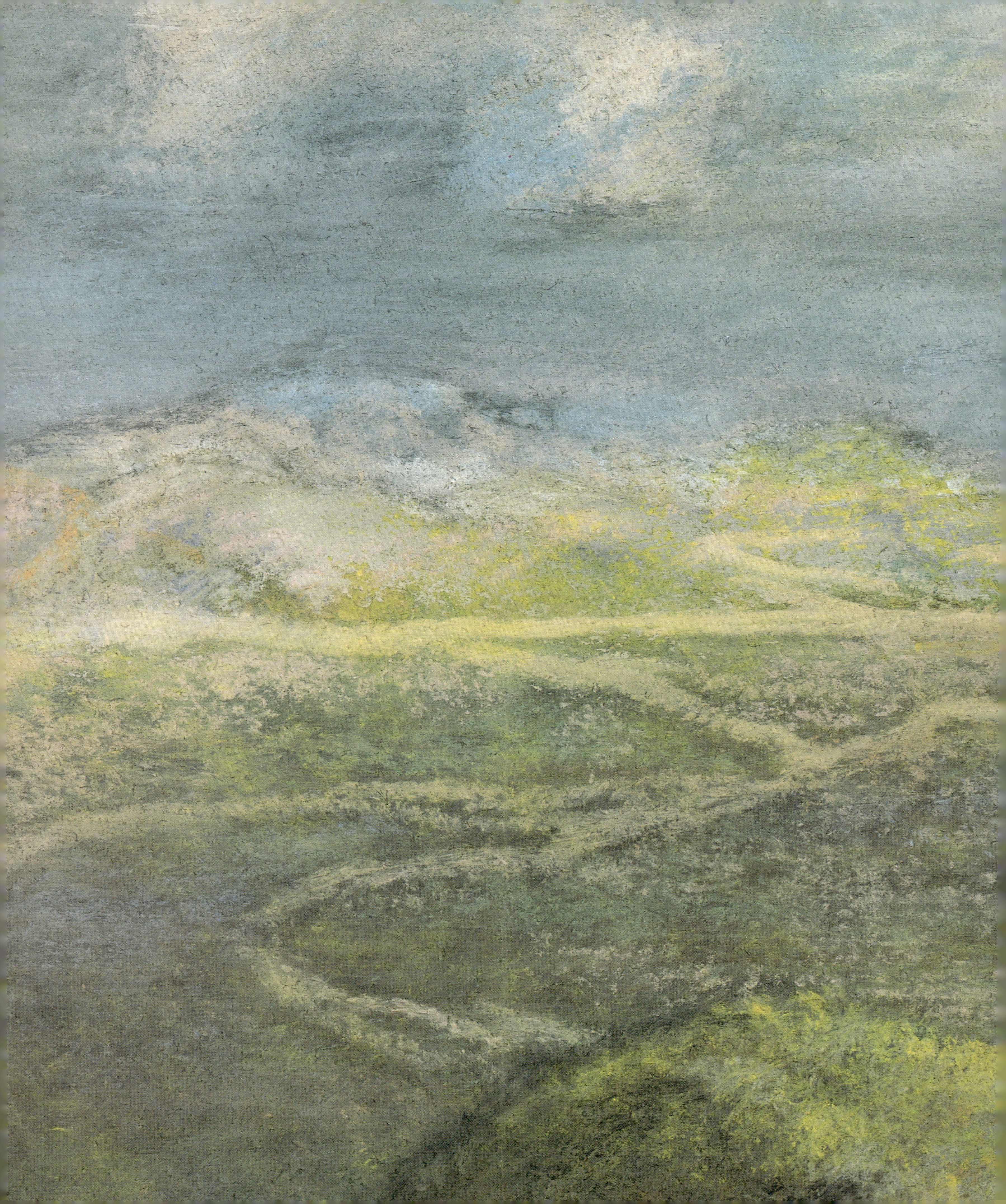

7 The 1892 Exhibition at the Durand-Ruel Gallery

'My dream is to make some landscapes . . .'
(Degas, speaking to Monet, February 1892)

'As you know, Degas never exhibits and it is quite an event to have persuaded him to show a group of new works.'[1] With these oblique and enticing words, Paul Durand-Ruel (fig. 162), the leading dealer in Impressionist paintings in Paris, announced the opening of the latest exhibition at his rue Laffitte premises in November 1892.[2] His note was addressed to the Superintendant of Fine Arts, Henry Roujon, who had recently been instrumental in the purchase of works for the State Collection by both Pissarro and Renoir.[3] Durand-Ruel presumably hoped to cultivate him further, but there is no record of Roujon visiting the gallery or patronising Degas' new work.[4] There is ample evidence, however, of general interest in the exhibition, in the letters of Degas' friends and fellow-artists, in the published responses of critics of various persuasions and in the recollections of those who attended the show. Described by one writer as the 'most extraordinary event of the season', the exhibition soon became the subject of local legend and gave rise to a variety of misapprehensions.[5] The number of works displayed and the medium used have been variously reported, and even the year in which they were shown has been frequently transposed.[6] Durand-Ruel himself was not immune to these solecisms. In his note to Roujon, he summarised the show as 'a most curious collection of twenty-five pastels and watercolours by Degas', though he went straight to the point when describing the exhibition's subject-matter: 'It is', he wrote, 'a series of landscapes.'[7]

By bringing together the accounts of Degas' contemporaries, the archives of the Durand-Ruel gallery and the internal evidence of the works themselves, it has been possible to form a remarkably clear picture of the 1892 exhibition. The researches of Howard G. Lay and Michael Pantazzi have done much to establish the context of the show, while drawing attention to such matters as the presentation and unusual framing of the exhibits.[8] Though no catalogue was produced, enough indications have survived for the majority of pictures to be identified and, in most cases, traced to their modern locations. Behind these relative certainties, however, still lurks the obstinate fact of the exhibition itself and the complex of questions it provokes. Why, after several years of self-imposed and carefully advertised isolation ('As you know, Degas never exhibits'), did the artist allow a show of his recent work? Why did he choose Durand-Ruel's gallery, rather than one of the other dealers who were avid for his products? How did the public respond to the pictures on display, with their colours like 'phosphorus and sulphur' and their surfaces 'like the wings of dragonflies'?[9] And, above all, why did the painter renowned for 'his dancers, his laundresses and his women at their *toilette*' devote the first and only personal exhibition of his lifetime to the subject of landscape?

161. Detail of fig. 199.

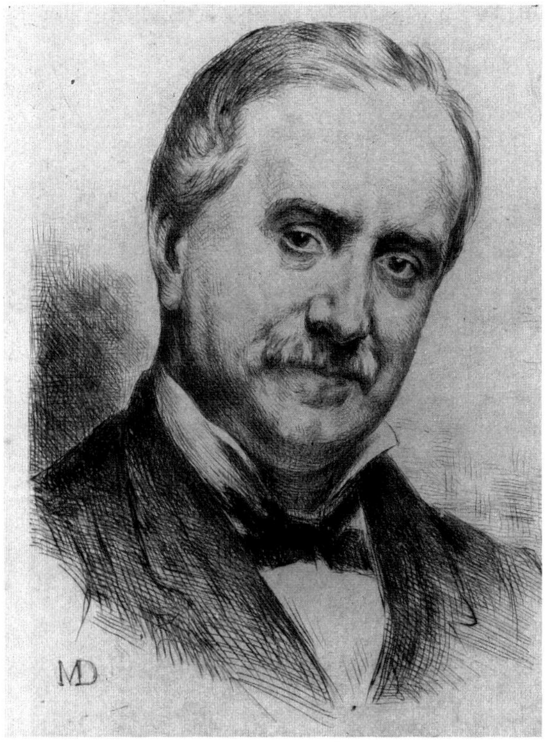

162. Marcellin Desboutin, *Paul Durand-Ruel*, 1882, drypoint, 19.5 × 15. Collection Durand-Ruel, Paris.

The story of Degas' relationship with the exhibition process is long and tortuous, but provides many clues to 'the event of the season' in 1892. As a young man, he had toiled to produce pictures acceptable to the official Salon, only to turn on his judges, as soon as he had gained their approval, with demands for improved conditions of display, then abandoning such occasions altogether. In his thirties, he had actively courted picture-dealers in London, Paris and elsewhere, though success was soon followed by a manipulative, almost aloof, manner with his clients. During the cycle of Impressionist exhibitions, Degas emerged as an energetic organiser of people and policies, shaping the appearance of several of these shows through his attention to installation, lighting and publicity.[10] From the same experience, he learnt the value of selectivity, shrewdly promoting a range of his own subject-matter and occasionally, and rather theatrically, withdrawing work from public display. His failure to produce the advertised *Little Dancer Age Fourteen* in 1880 and his refusal to participate in the exhibition of 1882 reveal this behaviour at its most negative, while the unveiling of the 'suite of nudes' in 1886 demonstrates a continued flair for exposure. Such manoeuverings also remind us that Degas, unlike colleagues such as Sisley and Pissarro, was already selling his work with ease and could afford, when he chose, to exhibit pictures already in private hands, as well as those fresh from the studio.

After the eighth and final Impressionist exhibition of 1886, Degas went through another characteristic about-turn. Once the arch-organiser of Impressionism, he became the enemy of collective shows and joint initiatives; formerly the most loyal of colleagues, he emerged as a solitary, even reclusive, exhibitor; and from being a subtle manipulator of opinion, he became the scourge of critics and even potential collectors. Some of his friends and rivals, among them Renoir and Monet, had already moved to fresh pastures, submitting their work to the once-despised Salon and contracting themselves to single-artist shows with dealers like Georges Petit, Boussod et Valadon and Durand-Ruel. Opportunities abroad had proliferated, and a younger generation that included Gauguin, Seurat and Signac had attracted new admirers and followed new exhibition strategies. Degas rejected all these avenues, eluding an attempt to stage a 'one-man' show in the early 1880s and firmly rejecting an overture from Octave Maus, organiser of 'Le Cercle des XX' in Brussels, in 1888.[11] Durand-Ruel's claim that 'Degas never exhibits', which was echoed soon after by Arsène Alexandre, was, however, only part of the truth.[12] Though his Byzantine reasoning led Degas away from the single-artist show, his work was far from invisible in the Paris art market. For more than a decade, he had been selling pictures to Durand-Ruel, sometimes as individual 'articles', occasionally as batches of a dozen or more items.[13] Other dealers were also acquiring his work and had been able to assemble groups of pictures, even showing them in the form of small-scale exhibitions. In 1888, for example, a second sequence of pastel nudes was shown by Theo van Gogh at Boussod et Valadon, where they were admired by both Gauguin and Berthe Morisot, and the following year a critic could announce that 'M. Van Gogh has at the moment a certain quantity of works by Degas; dancers, studies of women and racecourse scenes.'[14]

Degas' decision to mount a personal show in 1892 does not mark, in any real sense, the end of a state of artistic seclusion, and its significance must be found elsewhere. In the first place, as Durand-Ruel, Alexandre and others emphasised, the exhibition was important in showing recent work, in contrast to the miscellaneous offerings of dealers' displays and even of some of the

Impressionist shows. Never before had Degas put more than twenty brand-new pictures before the public, and never had he presented a 'suite' or 'series' of such extent. In addition, of course, Degas had chosen to step outside his familiar repertoire, not only abandoning the 'dancers, studies of women and racecourse scenes' that were his distinctive territory, but encroaching on the landscape, the preserve of several of his colleagues. Finally, insufficient importance has been attached to the location selected by Degas for his first solo show. Though the artist had been depositing his work with Durand-Ruel for some years, he had never negotiated an exclusive contract with him and at times shared the unease, and even outright hostility, of his fellow-painters towards the gallery's practices.[15] On different occasions, Degas sold work to Bernheim Jeune, Brame, Portier, Vollard, Boussod et Valadon and others, openly taking advantage of their rivalry to raise his prices and assert his independence. More pertinently, a year before his landscape exhibition he had found common cause with Pissarro and Cassatt in their dissatisfaction with Durand-Ruel, planning to sever links with the dealer and take their allegiance elsewhere.[16]

Why, in these circumstances, did Degas opt for Durand-Ruel's gallery in the autumn of 1892? Some of the reason must surely lie in the perceived significance of the rue Laffitte premises, and their recent and conspicuous role in contemporary art. Like every other display sanctioned personally by Degas, the event seems to have been stage-managed to project the artist's view of himself and to redefine his position amongst his peers. In the years immediately preceding his show, the gallery had presented the work of almost all the prominent survivors of Impressionism, as well as some of their more celebrated associates, such as Whistler and Boudin. During 1888, for example, Durand-Ruel had put together a number of mixed displays of the work of Renoir, Pissarro, Morisot, Sisley and Whistler. After one or two lean years, he had then inaugurated a series of individual exhibitions, notably that devoted to Boudin in March 1891, to both Pissarro and Cassatt the following month, to Monet in May and to Renoir in July of the same year. Monet's exhibition had been largely centred on his *Grainstacks*, and the success of this event may have encouraged the dealer to offer further solo shows. In February 1892, another Monet exhibition included the first of his *Poplars* series; in the same month, a selection of Pissarro's work was shown; and in May, a large number of Renoir's paintings, including several recent landscapes, filled the gallery.

The only significant omission from this roll-call of senior Impressionists was that of Degas. Since the last of their group shows in 1886, his work had been seen only sporadically in dealers' displays, and neither Durand-Ruel nor his competitors had managed to interest him in an individual exhibition. To add to his isolation, Degas had also seen the galleries of his principal agent, Durand-Ruel, taken over for the successful promotion of several former colleagues. Most prominent of these was Claude Monet, whose acclaimed and lucrative exhibitions of *Grainstacks* and *Poplars* seemed to have prepared the way for an annual cycle of such shows. For Degas, this precedent was doubly significant. Not only had Monet been identified as his natural rival in earlier decades, but his current success appeared to overlap with the trajectory of Degas' own art. In the 1880s, along with a number of other artists, Degas had begun to explore the possibility of 'families' or 'suites' of images, not least in the 'suite of nudes' shown at the 1886 exhibition. Arriving at Diénay in 1890, he had announced to Jeanniot his wish to make a 'series of landscapes', using a single plate to produce identically sized variants of elemental landscape *motifs*. Like Monet, in a canvas such as *Grainstacks (Snow Effect: Sunlight)* (fig. 163), Degas preferred simple,

165 (facing page top). Title-page of catalogue for Mary Cassatt's 1891 exhibition, Archives Durand-Ruel, Paris.

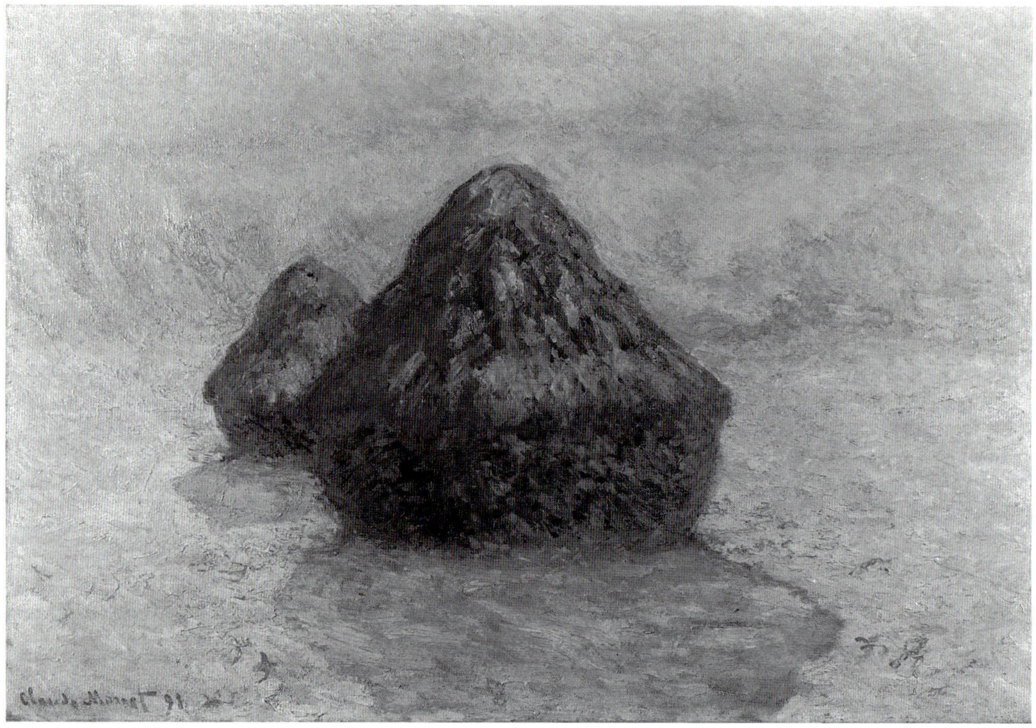

163. Claude Monet, *Grainstacks (Snow Effect: Sunlight)*, 1890–1, oil on canvas, 65.1 × 92.1. National Galleries of Scotland, Edinburgh.

boldly constructed forms, stripped of human and narrative interest and giving maximum licence to the interplay of colour, texture and surface incident. In certain monotypes, most notably the cognate pairs, Degas also invites us to see the image as part of a temporal succession, or a seasonal shift. Finally, Degas must have remembered the circumstances of his own Diénay excursion, as he read the outpourings of Monet's admirers and descriptions of his canvases as 'the uninterrupted flood of changing and interrelated sensations, apparent in the face of a changeless spectacle'.[17]

In early 1892, Degas had good reason to feel chastened by Monet's celebrity and his own absence from Durand-Ruel's exhibition programme. He may reasonably have been encouraged, on the other hand, and may already have been party to, a parallel development at the same gallery. Beginning in January 1889, Durand-Ruel had played host to the first of the annual series of exhibitions of the Société des peintres-graveurs français, nick-named 'les patriotes' by Pissarro, whose foreign birthplace excluded him from their membership. Exhibits ranged widely in technique and manner, from the pedestrian naturalism of Raffaëlli and Jeanniot to the decorations of Rivière and Lucien Pissarro, and from the satires of Steinlen and Forain to the domesticity of Lepère and Maurin. Common to many of these artists, however, was a fascination with the possibilities of colour printing, as opposed to the black-and-white or monochrome processes habitually used by etchers and engravers. Colour had been successfully mastered in commercial lithography and was soon to be exloited to brilliant effect by Toulouse-Lautrec and the Nabis, but it had proved intractable in more orthodox media. Throughout the 1880s, specialist print-makers, such as Félix Buhot, Auguste Délâtre and Henri Guérard, had tinted their plates with single colours or applied a range of inks with their fingers, while multi-block woodcuts had allowed Rivière and others to make the first polychrome landscapes.[18]

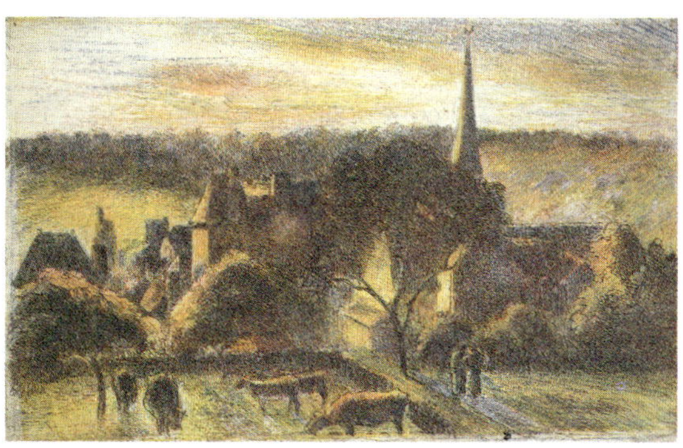

164. Camille Pissarro, *Church and Farm at Eragny*, 1894, colour etching, 15.7 × 24.6. Museum of Fine Arts, Boston, Ellen Frances Mason Fund.

Though never formally allied to the Société, Degas was in touch with most of

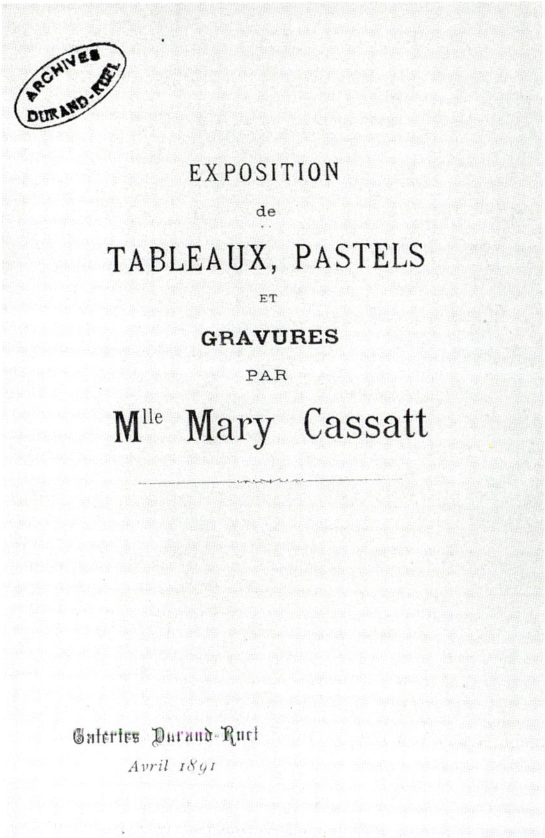

ARCHIVES DURAND-RUEL

EXPOSITION

de

TABLEAUX, PASTELS

ET

GRAVURES

PAR

Mlle Mary Cassatt

Galeries Durand-Ruel

Avril 1891

166. Mary Cassatt, *In the Omnibus*, 1890–1, drypoint with aquatint, 38.4 × 26.7. Worcester Art Museum, Mass., Bequest Mrs. Kingsmill Marrs.

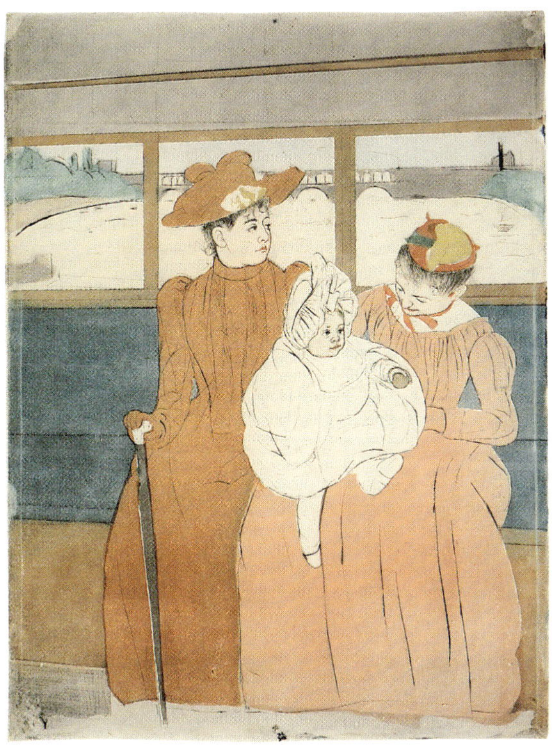

its membership and was held in particular esteem, both as a draughtsman and as a technical pioneer, by many of its adherents. As early as 1880, Degas had discussed his plans for coloured etchings with Camille Pissarro, continuing to share his explorations and even his equipment with the older artist as the years went by.[19] Pissarro's letters provide a touching insight into their collaboration and to his own responses to the colour-printing revolution. Apart from proofing his plates on Degas' press, Pissarro evidently relied on him for criticism and praise, even allowing Degas to make a trial tinted landscape.[20] In the early 1890s, Pissarro printed certain of his images, such as *Church and Farm at Eragny* (fig. 164), as a sequence of colour variants, applying the inks by hand to a previously etched plate.[21] When Degas expressed his enthusiasm for a more restrained attempt, *Meadow and Mill*, Pissarro's delight knew no bounds.[22] Their regard for the work of their younger colleagues, however, was not unequivocal. As early as 1891, Pissarro had found many of the 'attempts at colour engraving' in the exhibition of the *peintres-graveurs* to be 'ugly, dull, tame and commercial', while expressing his frustration at the public's failure to grasp their significance.[23] Whatever their weaknesses, these were original works of art, Pissarro insisted, not just reproductions or displays of technical facility.[24]

The print-making exhibitions at Durand-Ruel's gallery in the winter of 1891 were critical in a number of other respects. Coinciding with the show of the *peintres-graveurs*, Durand-Ruel had arranged smaller displays of the work of both Pissarro and Mary Cassatt, each dominated by their recent graphic output. The two shows were apparently housed in the smaller rooms of the rue Laffitte premises and both attracted considerable comment. Cassatt's was the most prominent, including a small number of paintings and pastels but an entire 'series' of ten new prints, executed in dry-point and aquatint.[25] These prints, which were advertised in an accompanying catalogue (fig. 165), were remarkable in many ways and have remained one of the peaks of Cassatt's achievement. Several pay homage to Degas, using themes and compositional devices familiar from his exhibited *oeuvre*, while imposing upon them Cassatt's distinctive tonalities and almost surgical line. In a plate such as *In the Omnibus* (fig. 166), one of the domestic *motifs* at which Cassatt excelled is presented in a starkly urban setting, while glimpses of a distant landscape remind us of her versatility. Most unforgettably, these prints are richly and elaborately coloured, using a process perfected by Cassatt herself, with the assistance of her printer, Leroy. Pissarro was enthusiastic, delighting in the 'mat tone, fine, delicate, without stains or smudges, with an adorable blue, fresh pinks . . .', and even went to watch Cassatt at work.[26] Though Degas registered one or two doubts, he, too, sprang to her defence, acquiring several prints and a number of working proofs for his own collection.[27] Whatever his reaction, Degas can hardly have missed their extreme accomplishment, nor the bravura resolution of colour and form that held out such promise for the immediate future of print-making.

As a venture into landscape imagery and as a new departure in colour printing, Degas' exhibition in 1892 could hardly have been more timely. From Durand-Ruel's point of view, the exhibition completed the 'stable' of distinguished Impressionist artists who had shown at his gallery in the previous two years and further advertised his dominance of the market. For Degas, it offered a characteristic moment of contrary revelation, reminding critics and fellow-artists of his continuing vitality, while cheerfully upsetting most of their preconceptions about his *oeuvre*. In the galleries where Monet had triumphed with his sequences of *Grainstacks* and *Poplars*, Degas now presumed to show his own 'series of monotypes', each devoted to the landscape and each engaged with a similar 'flood of changing and interrelated sensations, apparent in the face of a changeless spectacle'. Even more impertinently, Degas seemed to take on the entire cohort of *peintres-graveurs*, and perhaps even Pissarro and Cassatt, presenting a sequence of printed, coloured and pastellised images that went further than their most audacious manipulations. In such a context, a number of Degas' activities in the early 1890s suddenly fall into place. His reported remark at the opening of Monet's *Poplars* show, 'my dream is to make some landscapes', becomes more localised and less apparently mischievous.[28] Similarly, Degas' association with prominent experts in the field of print-making, such as Michel Manzi, Edmond Cousturier and Henri Rivière, takes on a more practical significance. Above all, his visit to the *peintre-graveur* Georges Jeanniot at Diénay, with his rural studio and copper plates, Chinese paper and printers' brushes, seems less haphazard, more shrewdly deliberated.

If Degas' 1892 exhibition was a contrived intervention in a self-conscious and competitive *milieu*, the details of its presentation demand an unusually thorough analysis. Reports vary, but it appears that between twenty-four and twenty-six images were shown, the discrepancy being accounted for by lapses of memory and the late inclusion of new works.[29] In the absence of a catalogue, it can be deduced that the show opened in early November, while one of the artist's own letters indicates that it closed two weeks later.[30] Though a fortnight might seem a modest run for such an event, it was by no means unusual; Monet's *Grainstacks* show in the same galleries, for example, had lasted a similar length of time. No record of installation or publicity survives in the Durand-Ruel archives, though circumstantial evidence points to one of the gallery's 'petites salles', where Pissarro and Cassatt had shown, as the location for Degas' display.[31] During the exhibition, Durand-Ruel was at pains to emphasise the modesty of its scale, seeming to whet the appetites of his clients without destroying the myth of a Degas who 'never exhibits'. Writing to a fellow-dealer, he announced: 'Monsieur Degas' exhibition consists of only a few small landscapes in pastel and watercolour that he has authorised me to show to certain collectors. They are not of enough significance to form an exhibition in the true sense of the word: Monsieur Degas would doubtless not approve of one, in any case.'[32]

As far as the pictures in question are concerned, it was Degas himself who inadvertently left behind the most valuable clues to their identity. Following a lifelong habit, the artist appears to have added his signature to the works just before they were exhibited, acknowledging their completion and his own authorship. Of the fifty or so monotypes and related landscapes known today, at least twenty-nine carry Degas' signature, as opposed to the red or black stamp of his studio sale.[33] Two of these signed prints were acquired by Jeanniot and one was presented to Charpentier, leaving us to assume that the remaining twenty-six works were those in Durand-Ruel's 'petite salle'.[34] With one or two exceptions, therefore, where a landscape monotype carries Degas' autograph signature, it must have been hung in the original display, while those without this signature were evidently retained in the artist's studio. Given the nature of the monotypes, we might go further, speculating on the way they were presented on the gallery walls. At least ten of the signed pictures belonged to a pair, consisting of an original proof and a cognate print, and it is difficult to believe that these twinned images were not hung side-by-side.[35] On the same principle, and given the artist's alertness to such matters, we might expect that groups of related *motifs*, such as roads and mountain lakes, would be installed in sequences. Finally, more than one critic pointed out the extremes to which Degas had gone in the framing of his pictures, and we must imagine an idiosyncratic and unexpectedly colourful setting for this most self-effacing 'event of the season'.[36]

How did Degas' audiences react to these two dozen or more landscape monotypes, perhaps arranged in pairs, clusters and sequences? Some, like Arsène Alexandre, were taken aback by their novelty and almost everyone, from Durand-Ruel himself to Degas' close collaborator, Camille Pissarro, was baffled by their unfamiliar technique.[37] Most of all, the first visitors were struck by a quality that has lost none of its force a century later; the range, brilliance and sheer originality of their colour. In some prints, a cool powdery blue or silver-grey might predominate, while in others a preposterous raspberry pink is thrown against bright orange and emerald, or a cuprous green against strident magenta. The small scale of the landscapes seemed to intensify these contrasts, just as it exaggerated the responses and flights of fancy of the critics. One writer noted 'a delicately citron horizon' and an 'almost sumptuous yellow', while others spoke of 'fields the colour of pinkish heather' and a 'blue not seen by vulgar eyes'.[38] Gustave Geffroy exceeded them all, comparing the prints to 'precious sapphires in velvet jewellery boxes', 'tapestries hung in secret boudoirs' and 'colours burnt by the light, disappearing in passages of greenish flame, falling into embers and pink ashes'.[39] Pragmatic as ever, Pissarro recorded that they were 'very curious, a little ungainly, but roughly delicate in tone' and commented on their resemblance to colour prints.[40]

A conspicuous feature of the exhibition was that the monotypes on display, with one solitary exception, had all been worked in pastel and were thus the product of two quite distinct colour processes.[41] In a radical departure from his lifelong habit of working first in monochrome, then superimposing layers of

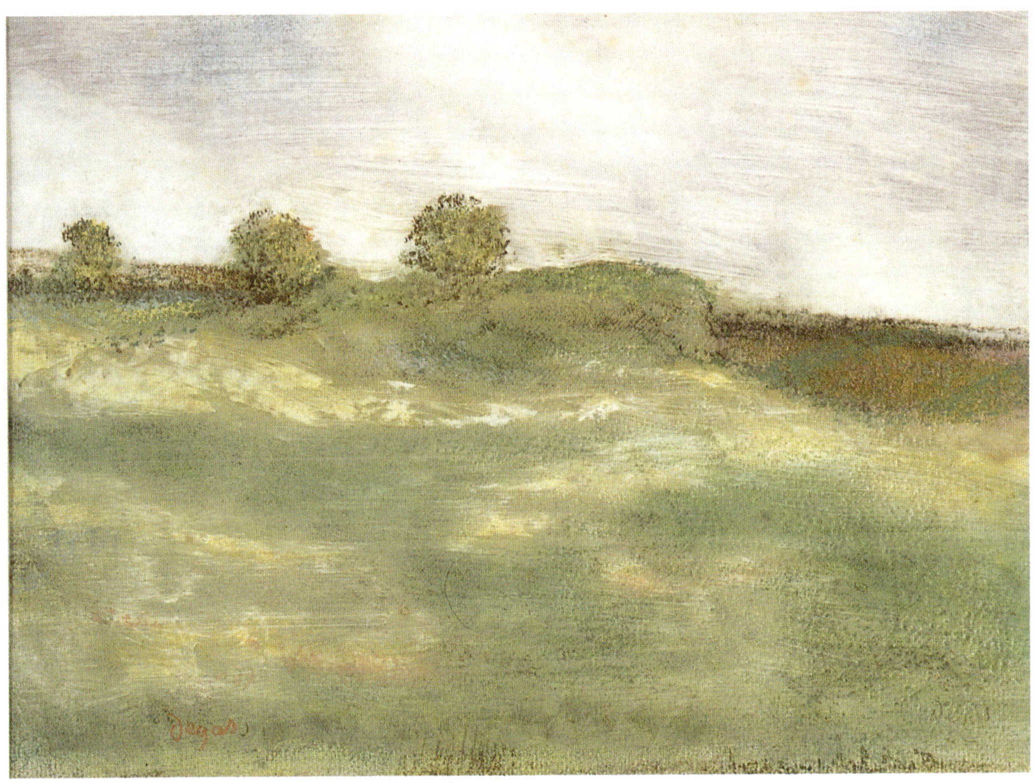

167. *Landscape*, 1892, monotype and pastel, 27 × 36 (J 274). Collection of Mr. Mohammed Al Fayed, Chairman of Harrods.

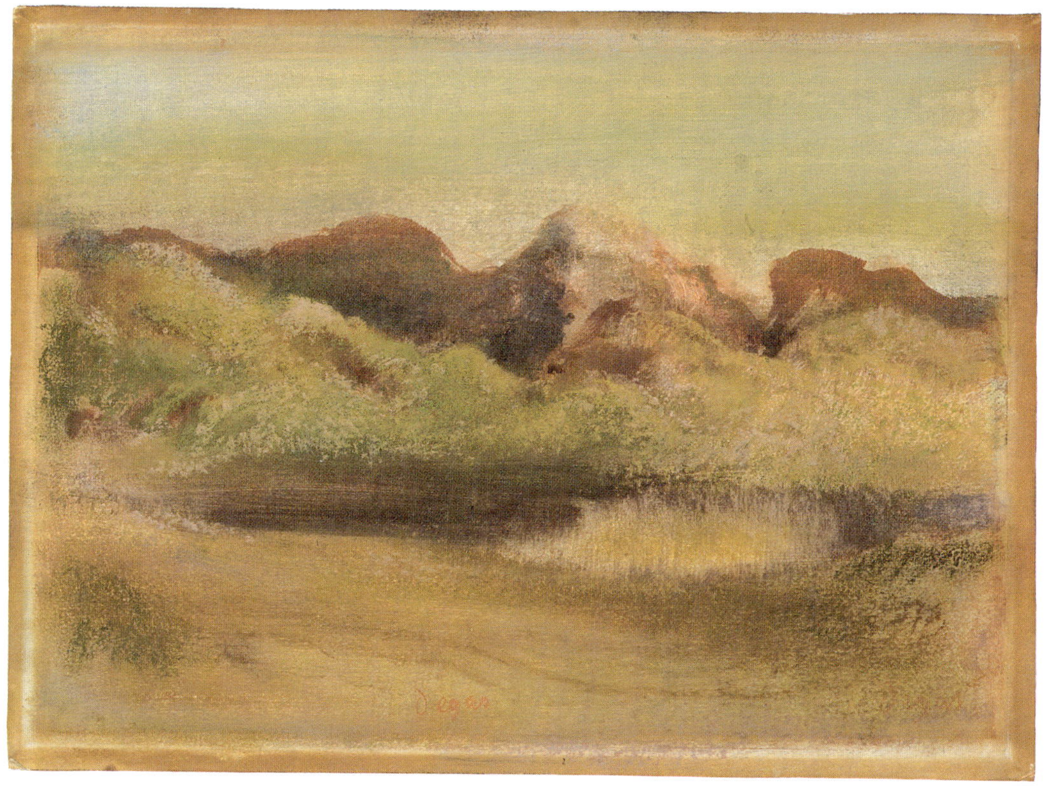

168. *Lake and Mountains*, 1892, monotype and pastel, 24 × 34 (J 304). Private collection, Switzerland.

colour, Degas opted for a chromatic dialogue between upper and lower layers of each image. As the prints made at Diénay show, Degas first established his image in oil paint on a metal plate, then transferred this image onto a sheet of paper as it passed through the press. According to Jeanniot, Degas added strokes of pastel to some of these proofs as soon as they emerged, but it is equally clear that a number of other prints were kept in their original state. Certain of these, such as those given to Bartholomé and Jeanniot, were apparently valued for their intrinsic qualities, while others were retained by the artist for later embellishment. The relationship between this pastel restatement and the original printed image varies a great deal, from landscape to landscape and from group to group. In general, the printed layer in the Diénay group was carefree and experimental, and the pastel additions restrained. In the later series, this balance became more complex, with greater detail and precision in the initial process, followed by a generous overlayer of powdery colour. Pursuing this possibility to its limit, Degas allowed pastel to transform his first conception in certain prints, challenging outlines and swamping earlier forms, and even obliterating the monotype completely.

Two very different prints that were shown in 1892, and probably made in that year, demonstrate the initial stages of the application of pastel. In both *Landscape* (fig. 167) and *Lake and Mountains* (fig. 168), the crisply applied forms of the monotype have been allowed to remain visible within the final composition, resembling brush-marks or sweeps of liquid colour. Where pastel has been applied, it reinforces or enhances a printed landscape feature, rather than attempting to change or conceal it. This is particularly evident in *Landscape*, where the contours of the original image have been faithfully followed and its tones subtly extended by the pastel strokes. In *Lake and Mountains*, on the other hand, the juxtaposition is more combative, most notably in its sequence of colours. The monotype print was originally dominated by earth-reds, purples

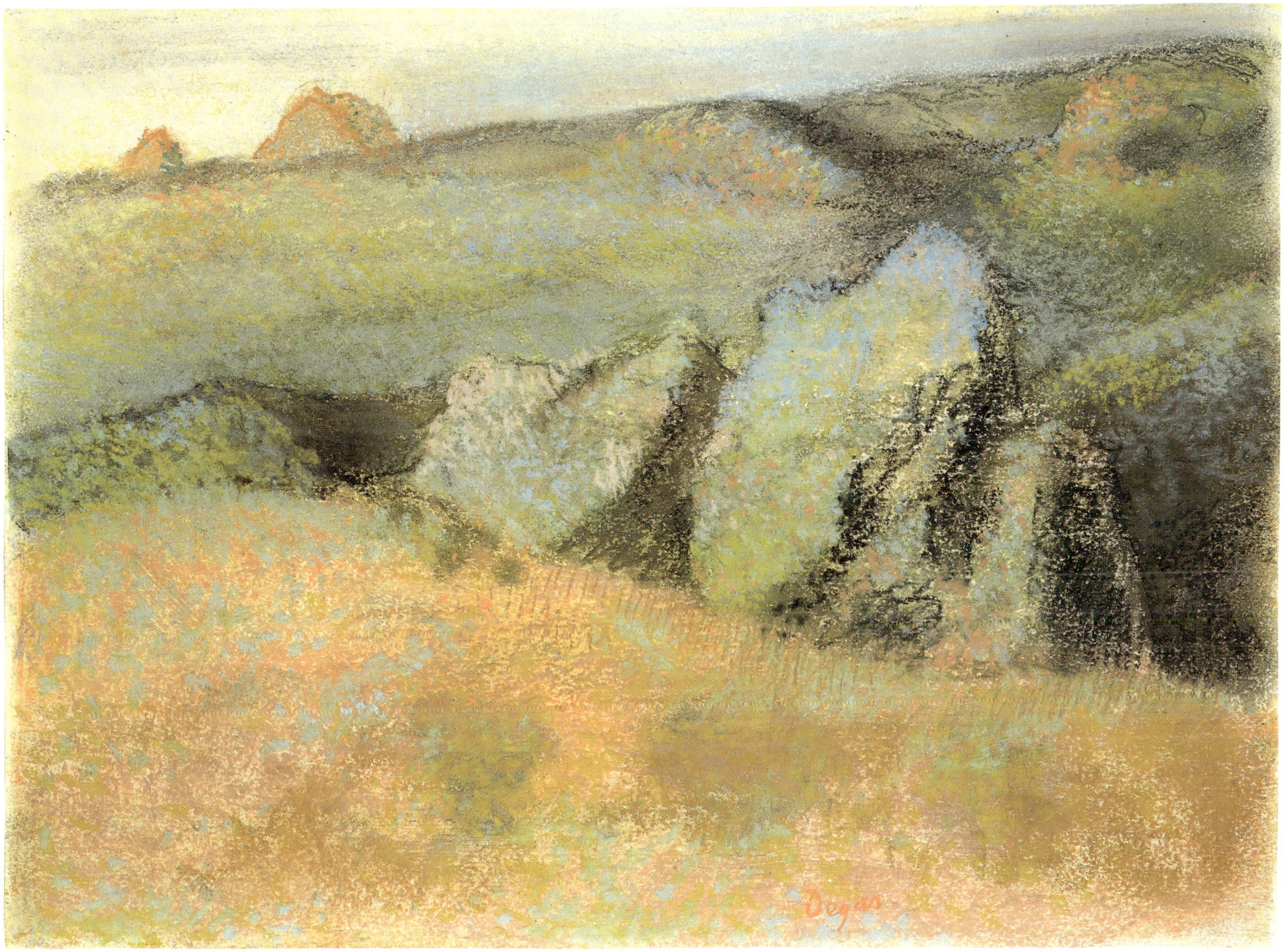

169. *Landscape with Rocks*, 1892, monotype and pastel, 25.7 × 34.5 (J 312). Private collection, photo courtesy Browse & Darby, London.

and dull ochres, some of which continue to define the mountains and lake in the finished work. Over this, the artist has spread flurries of gold and yellow-green pastel, their spring-like extravagance in contrast to the wintery gloom beneath. In places, such layerings of colour suggest the deliberate linking of complementary hues: the daffodil-yellow reflection against the indigo of the lake, for example, or the green vegetation superimposed on a reddish hillside. More commonly, they point to an improvised but animated approach to the picture's surface and to its spatial and descriptive properties. Such improvisation is clearly in evidence in a third print, *Landscape with Rocks* (fig. 169), which takes the sequence of events a step further. The foreground of this work began life as an area of monotype ink or paint, streaked in bright pink from left to right, apparently with a coarse brush. Degas then added stipples and dabs of soft pastel, almost covering his rosy underlayer with dots of sky-blue, greengage-yellow and shadowed brown. To be precise, the effect is one of optical enrichment rather than obliteration, a *pointilliste*-like intensification of colour that is more engaging for its informality.[42]

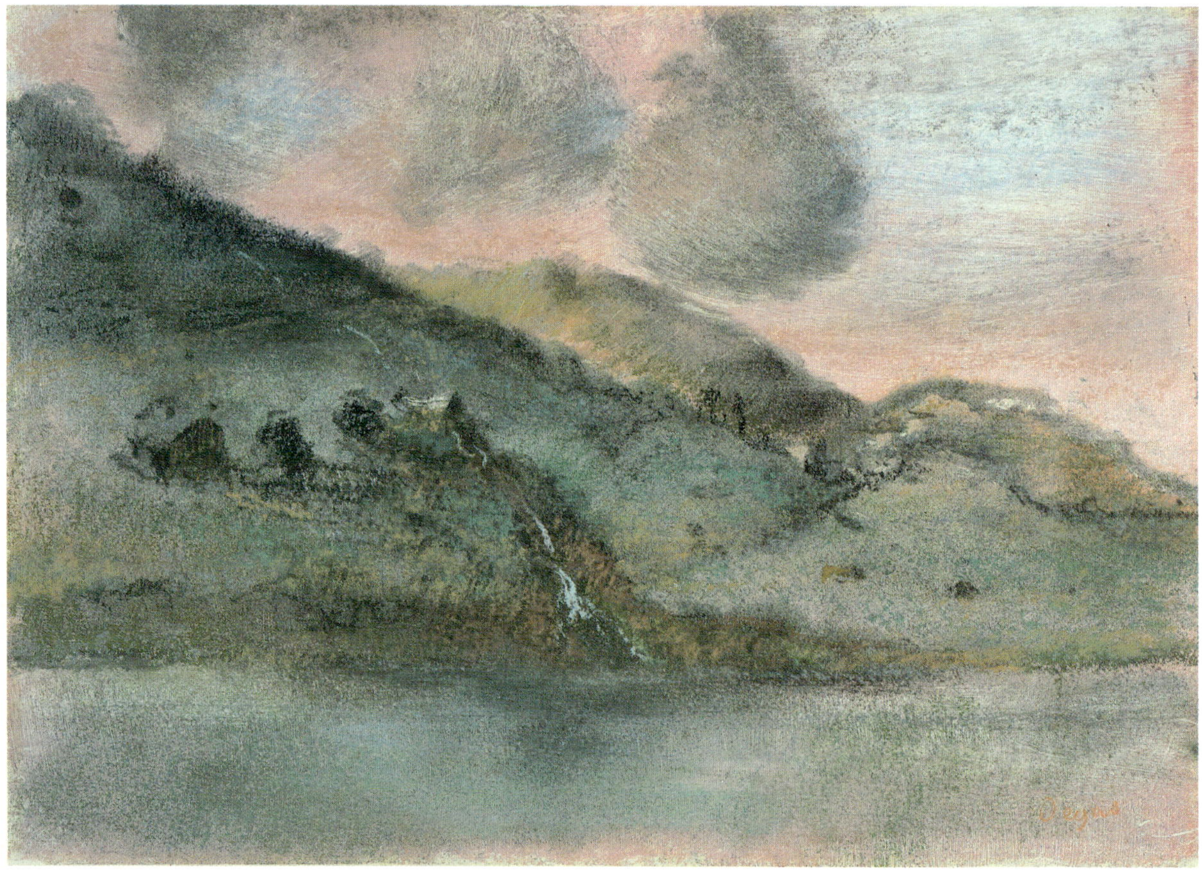

170. *Landscape*, 1892, monotype and pastel, 24.7 × 34.5 (K 5). Private collection.

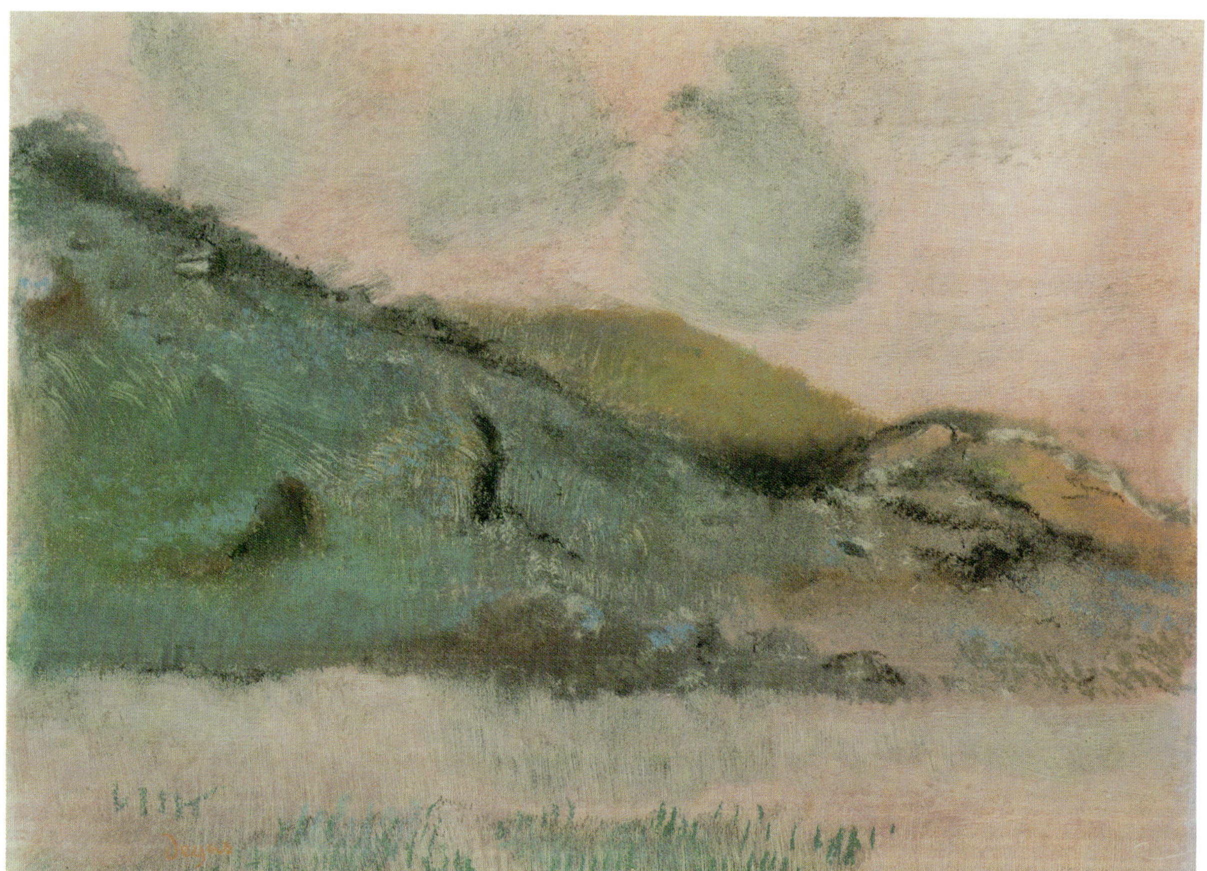

171. *Landscape*, 1892, monotype and pastel, 27 × 36 (J 316). Collection Durand-Ruel, Paris.

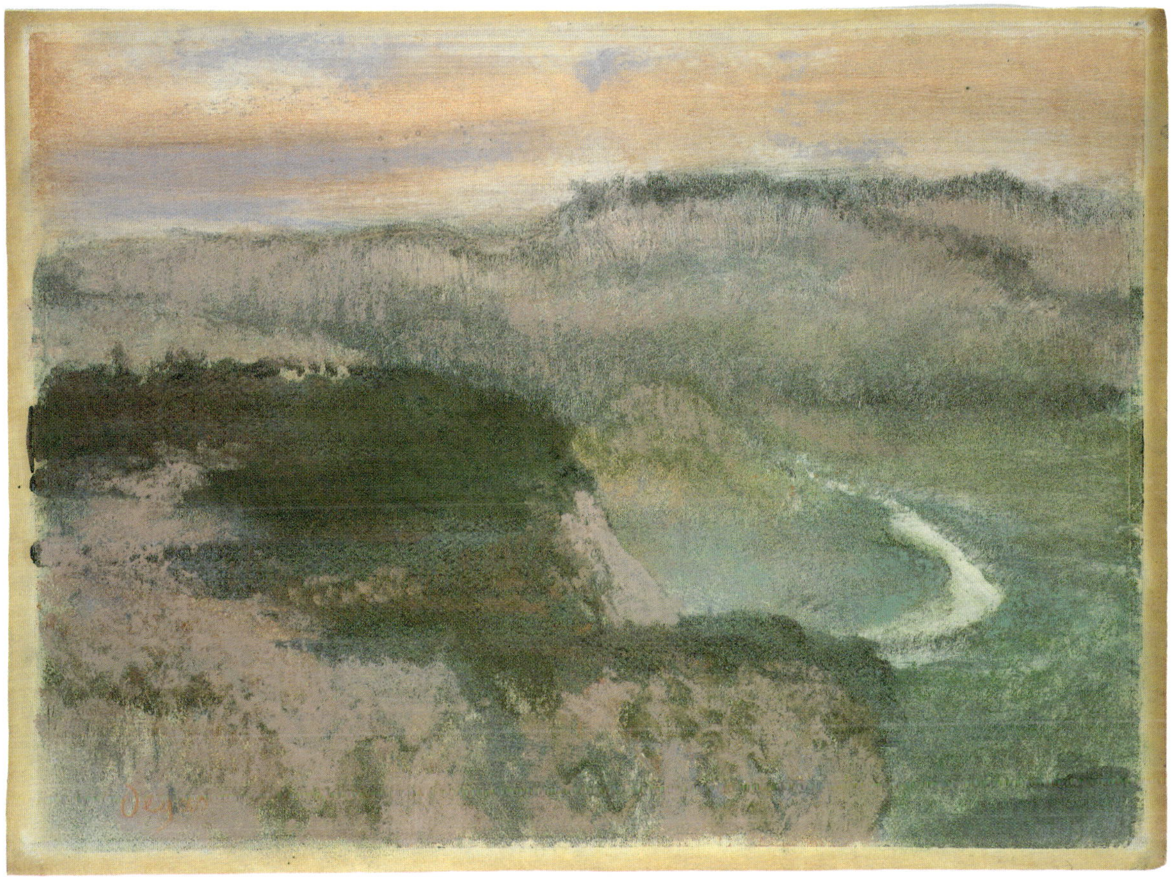

172. *Landscape*, 1892, monotype and pastel, 25.4 × 34.2 (J 284). Museum of Fine Arts, Boston, Denman Waldo Ross Collection.

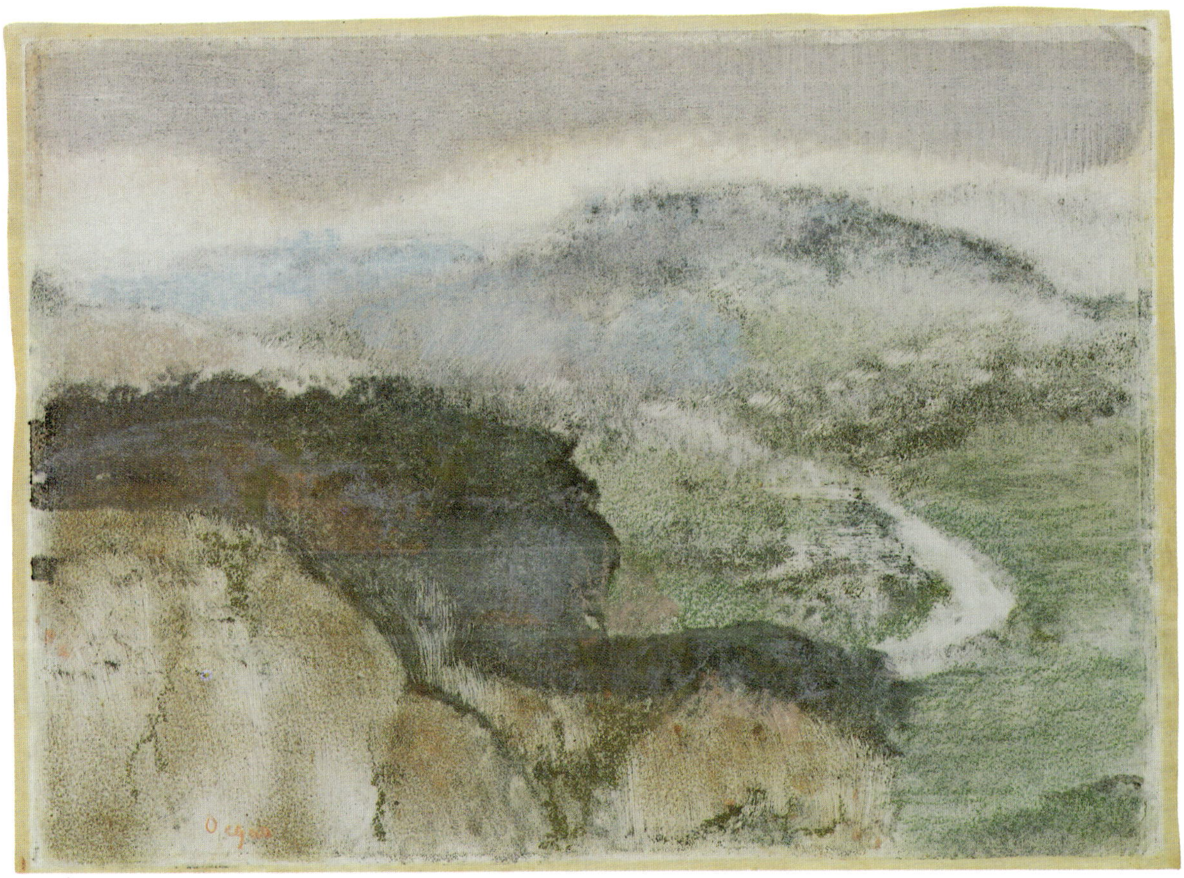

173. *Landscape*, 1892, monotype and pastel, 25.4 × 34 (J 285). The Metropolitan Museum of Art, New York, Purchase, Mr. and Mrs. Richard J. Bernhard Gift, 1972.

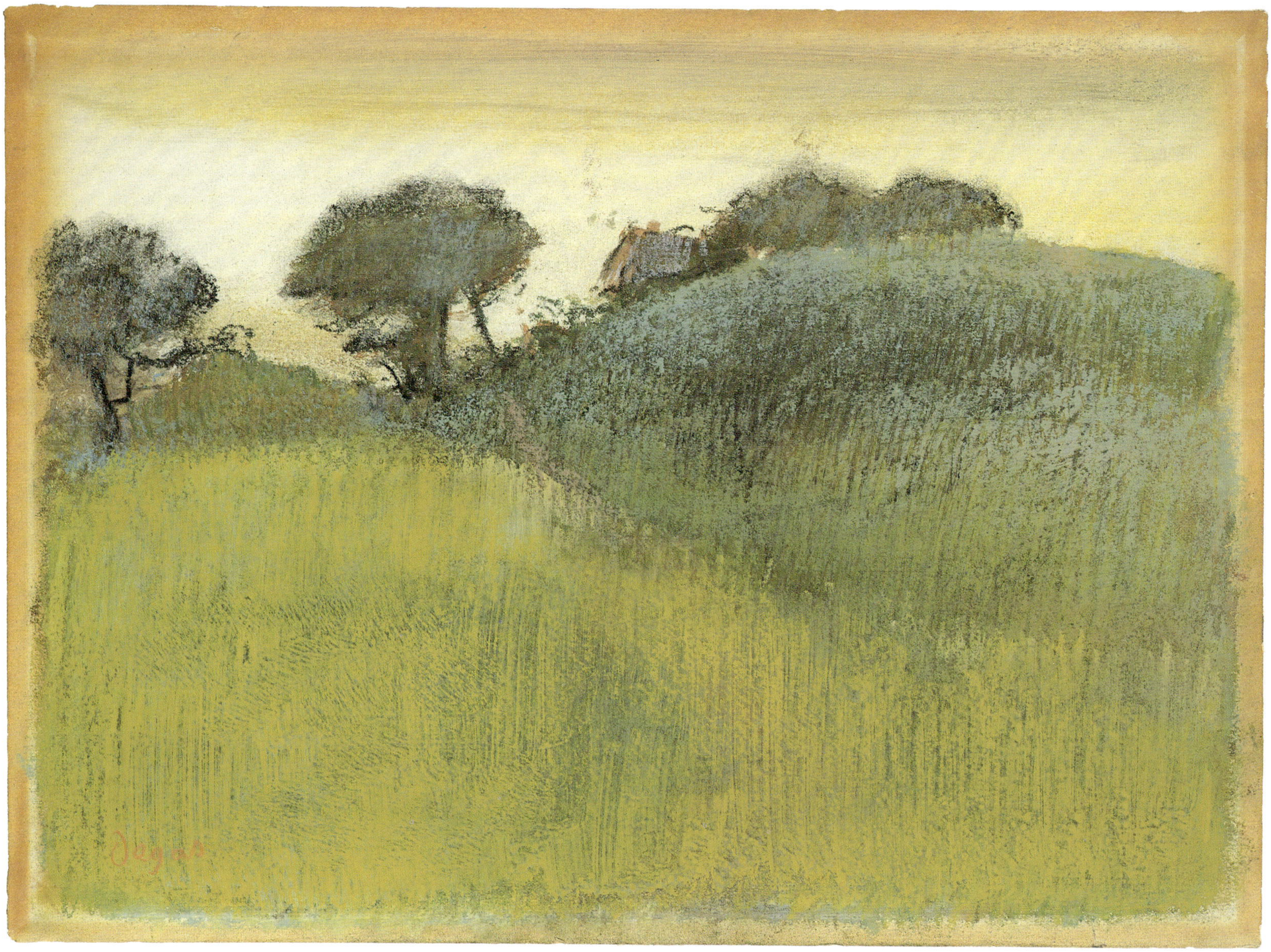

174. *Wheatfield and Green Hill*, 1892, monotype and pastel, 26 × 34 (J 320). Norton Simon Museum of Art, Pasadena.

More direct evidence of transformation through colour can be found in the cognate pairs of prints shown in 1892. One such pair, which has not previously been identified as such, is based on a monotype image of a mountain lake, a descending hillside and a troubled evening sky. As in *Landscape with Rocks*, a lightly brushed pink was first laid down on the metal plate, determining the broad tonality of both compositions. In *Landscape* (fig. 148), this ground note was answered by high-pitched blue and coppery-green pastel, and by resonant ochres in the distant peaks. Its cognate, *Landscape* (fig. 147), seems more muted, as though daylight has faded or a storm passed by. In this print, identical landscape structures have been gently transformed, softened by rubbings and streaks of pastel, and rendered less legible, less descriptive.[43] The most celebrated of all the twinned prints, both simply known as *Landscape*, offer further refinements of this process . The work based on the first proof (fig. 172) has often been described as 'autumnal', the olive greens of its print surface and the dull rose of its pastel overlayer hinting at ripeness and seasonal decay.[44] Its counterpart, (fig. 173), on the other hand, is paler and cooler, and Jean Boggs

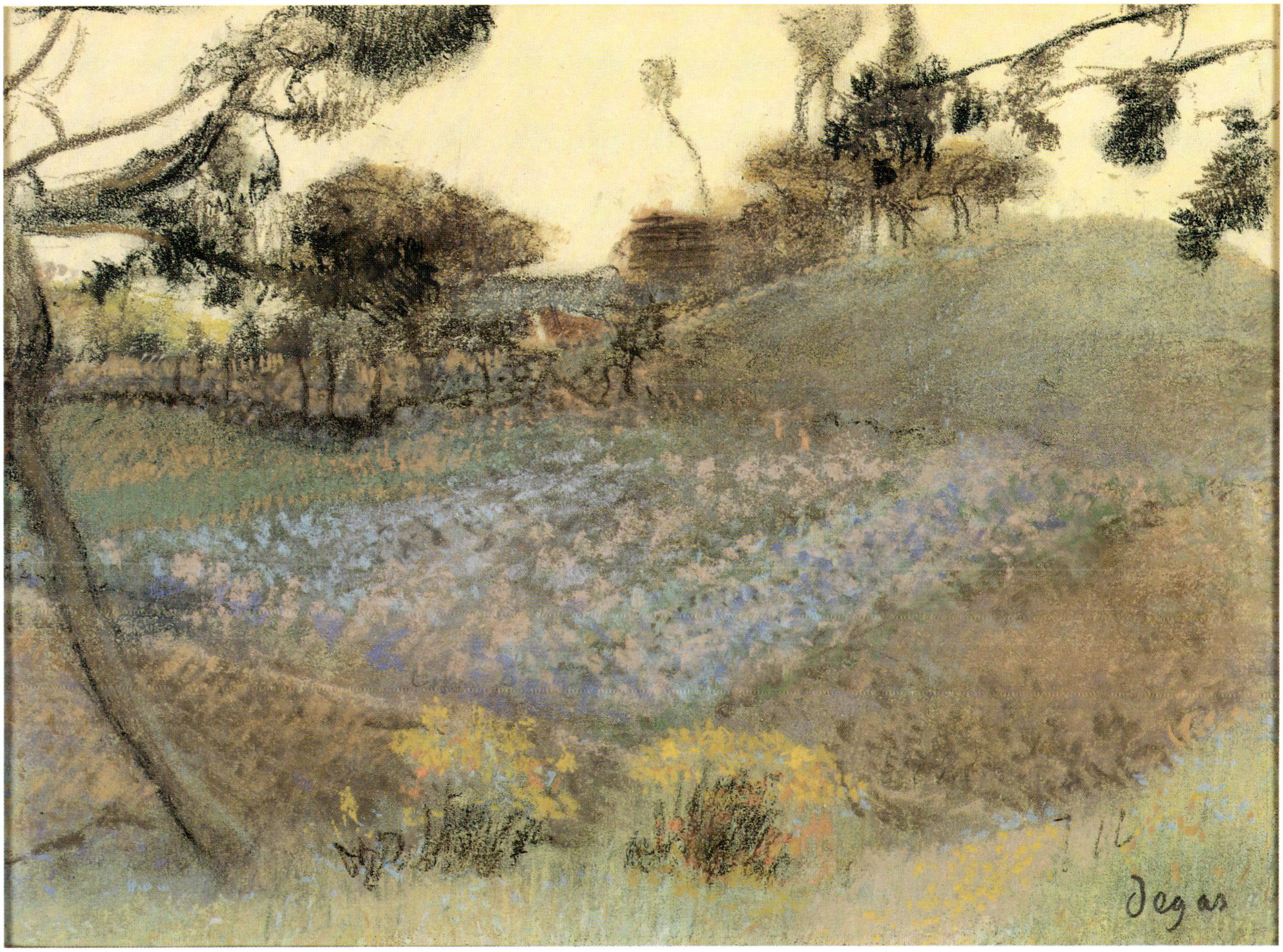

175. *The Field of Flax*, 1892, monotype and pastel, 25 × 34 (J 321). Private collection.

has discovered in it 'a scene of spring'.[45] Significantly, Degas does not insist on the continuity of his subject, wilfully modifying the forms of the foreground with pastel and even intervening in the ink layer between printings.[46] Despite these differences, it is impossible not to see the two images as variants of a single *motif*, perhaps separated by months, as Boggs implies, or by hours or even minutes. Approached in this way, their affinity with Monet's canvases of poplar-trees, exhibited in the same gallery only nine months earlier, is irresistible and could not have been lost on the artists' contemporaries.

At another extreme lies a pair of almost rainbow-hued landscapes, so different in their colouring that they have not formerly been recognised as a cognate pair. Close examination of *Wheatfield and Green Hill* (fig. 174), and *The Field of Flax* (fig. 175) has shown that both were begun over reddish-brown monotypes that depicted a swelling hill, a line of trees and a small central cottage.[47] Working with his pastels, Degas then developed each print into an entirely separate composition, their discrepancies far beyond the vagaries of weather, season or chosen viewpoint. In both cases, the picture surface was densely encrusted with colour, as new forms were introduced and the patterns of the original monotype revised or superseded. The hillside to the right in *Wheatfield and Green Hill*, for example, was first washed in with rust brown and the central field tinted with sage. As the pastel advanced, these areas became green and buttercup-yellow respectively, while the pinkish trees on the horizon were overlaid with deep blue.[48] Though not so drastically recast, *The Field of Flax* has a similarly granular surface that recalls the stages of its evolution. Most surprising are the lavender-blues and floral pinks that suggest a summer garden, and the framing branches of 'russet greenery' that prompted Geffroy, when describing this print, to think of jewel-boxes. So distinct are the two images that only the most sharp-eyed observer would have spotted their kinship, and thus the wit and ingenuity of Degas' performance. In this case at least, the serial notion is given a further twist, while the most basic assumptions of realism are turned on their head.

The complexity of the cognate relationship is further illustrated in a somewhat ill-defined group of prints, at least one of which was shown at Durand-Ruel's gallery. This was *Landscape with Cows* (fig. 176), a work that has generally been catalogued as a pastel, a monotype base not having been discerned.[49] The plot thickens, however, when it is realised that the dimensions of the picture correspond to one of the monotype 'families' of plate sizes, and that a closely related composition, *Landscape by the Sea* (fig. 177), has recently been shown to have a monotype underlayer.[50] The resemblance between the landscape settings of these two images is hardly coincidental and links them to a further pair of identically sized studies, both unfortunately of unknown location.[51] Whatever the sequences and precedents within this group, it is clear that monotype played a role, if only to provide a series of pale cognates for elaboration in pastel. Their subject-matter, on the other hand, deserves further comment. *Landscape with Cows* provides the only animate *motif* so far encountered in the monotypes and reminds us of Degas' continuing debt to Courbet, Millet and perhaps Gauguin.[52] A lost variant with a similarly truncated horse promises comparable delights, and cries out to be reunited with its bovine partner.[53] Adding a final touch of gravity to this group, a dedication in Degas' hand on *Landscape by the Sea* indicates that it was presented to Georges Charpentier, publisher, magazine proprietor and patron of the arts. For several years the employer of Jeanniot, Charpentier evidently shared a number of acquaintances with Degas and was to acquire further works of art from him, including another landscape.[54]

Given the extravagance and subtlety of Degas' use of pastel, and its juxtaposition with complex layers of printed oil paint, are we to see the 1892 landscapes simply as exercises in colour? From the beginning, Degas' audiences seem to have appreciated that these remarkable hues were both experimental and urgently expressive, noting their fusion with timeless subject-matter and a provocative use of form. Several writers identified the rustic, elemental nature of Degas' *motifs*, listing the 'mountains, rivers, fields with cows' or 'a valley, a river, a road, a sky, rolling hills and quarries' that formed the basis of his vision. Another proclaimed: 'Here are plains, here are overhanging peaks and gorges, and here are solitudes', while an anonymous critic spoke of Degas' sense of 'nature, rugged and savage'.[55] Perhaps the most vivid response came from an American visitor, Philip Hale:

> All these sketches represent the strangest, wildest country. They seem to have been done in some mountainous land of volcanic formation. Strange, fantastic-shaped peaks show sharply against the sky, and 'dreadful hollows'

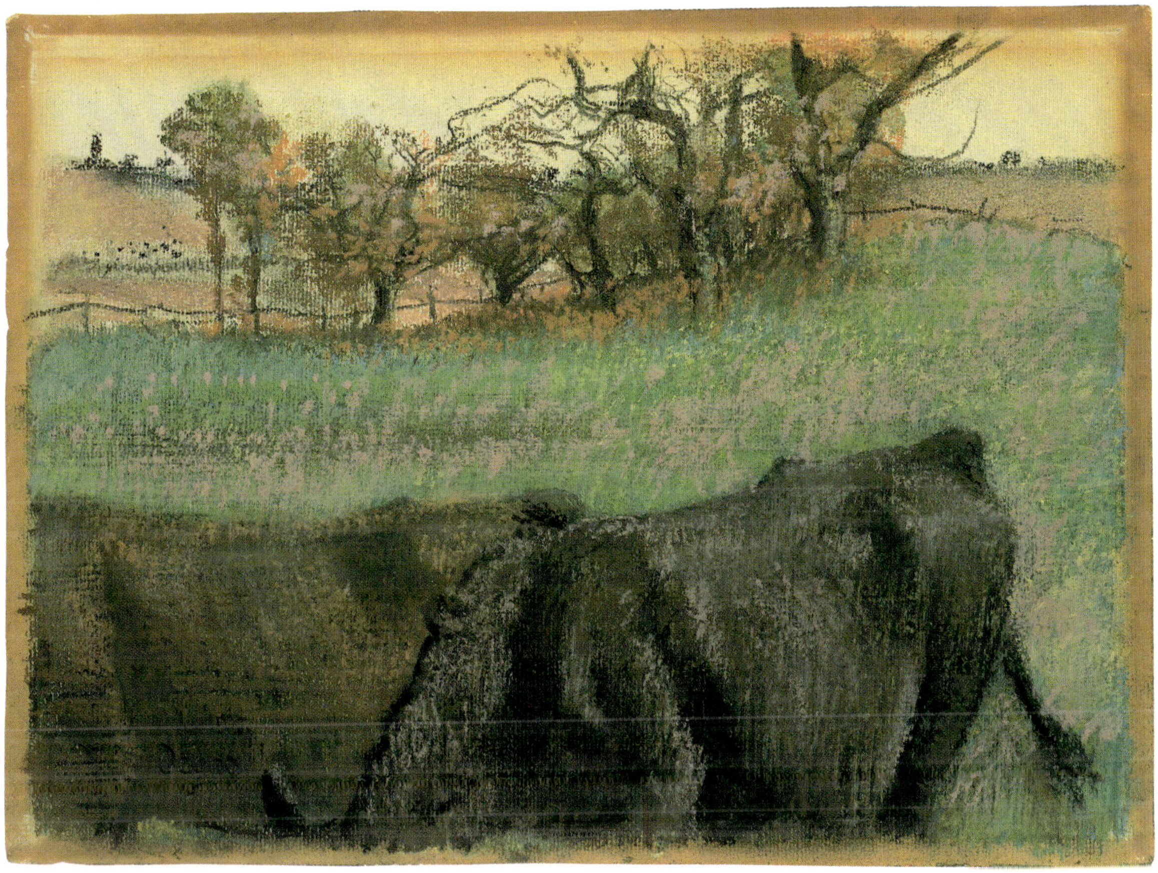

176. *Landscape with Cows*, 1892, monotype and pastel, 26 × 35.5 (K 7). Private collection.

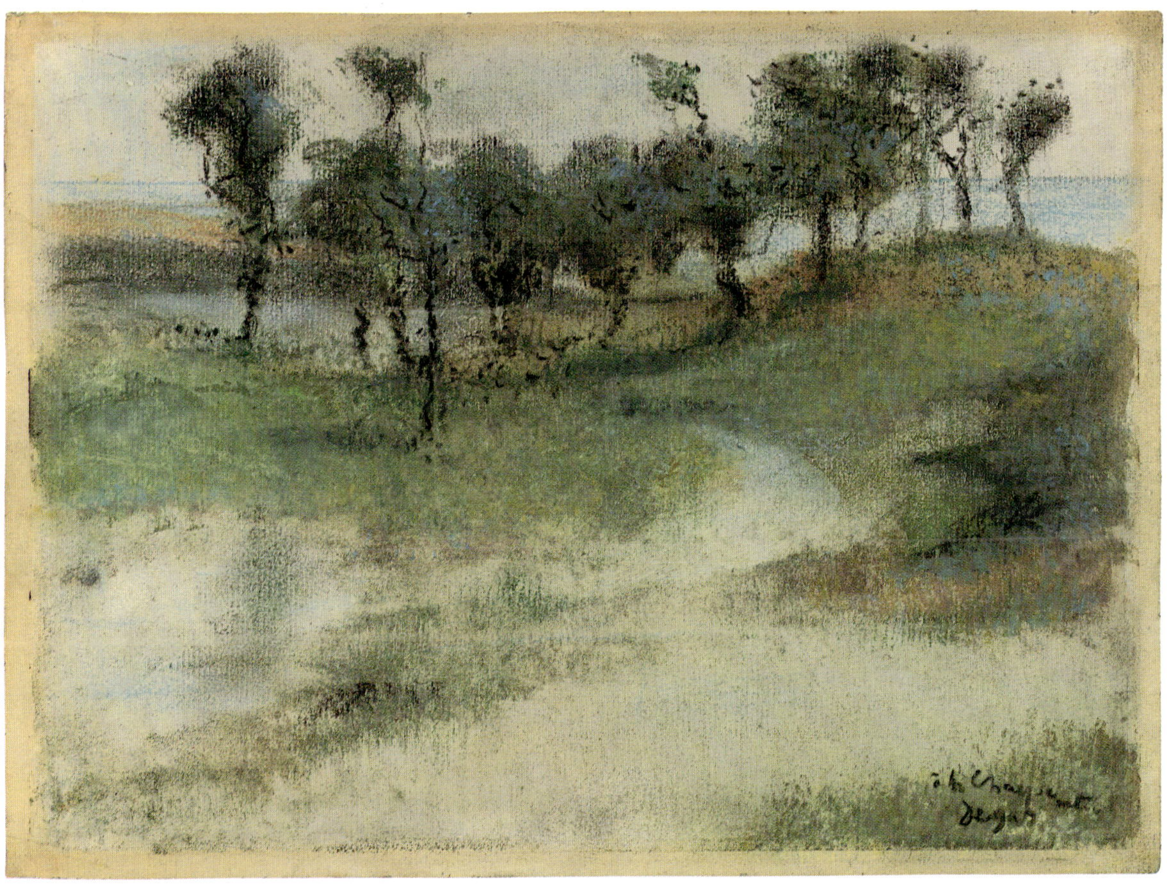

177. *Landscape by the Sea*, 1892, monotype and pastel, 25.2 × 34.4 (K 6). Musée d'Art et d'Histoire, Neuchâtel.

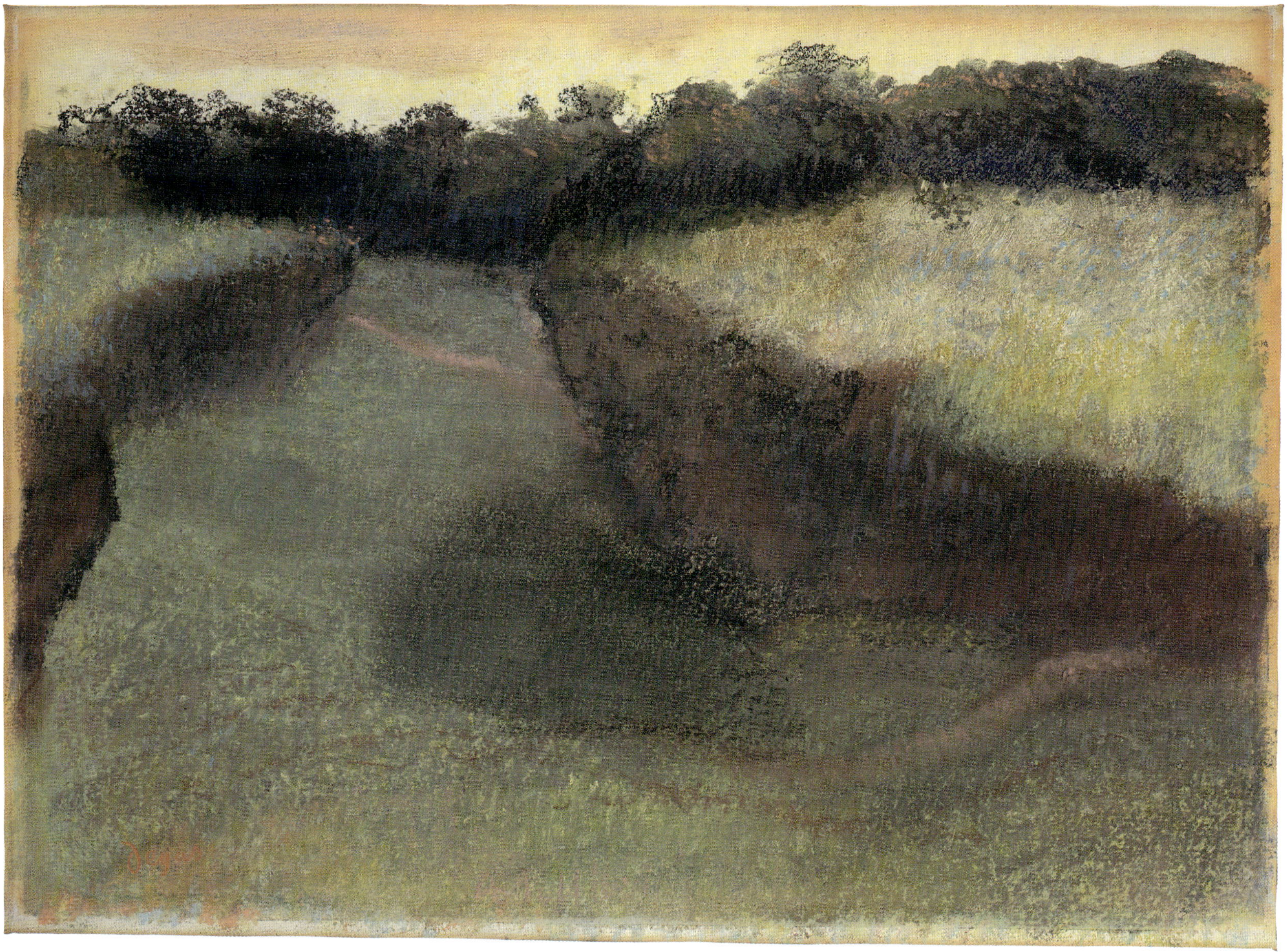

178. *Wheatfield and Line of Trees*, 1892, monotype and pastel, 25 × 34 (J 291). Private collection.

are at their base. Or in some other picture there will be a huge, desolate, dismal plain, like the land of Browning's 'Squat Round Tower', all of red clay, and the grass stamped and crushed; or, in a third, some huge Giant's Causeway, running out into the sea, a mighty causeway not made with hands, nor to be crossed by men. Another is of some deep hollow in the hill, and at its bottom a still pool reflects the grim mountains. Still again, we have a curious wave-like glacier coming down from the purple mountains, through fields bright with flowers, coloured the strange yellow-green of the mimosa.[56]

Several of the monotypes described by Philip Hale can be immediately identified: his 'dismal plain . . . all of red clay' is surely the *Burgundy Landscape* (fig. 127) dedicated to Barthlomé, and his 'Giant's Causeway, running out into the sea' might apply to either version of *Rocky Coast* (figs 185 and 187); *Lake and Mountains* (fig. 168) shows a 'deep hollow' where 'a still pool reflects the grim mountains', and the swelling form at the right in *Wheatfield and Line of Trees* (fig. 178) might have suggested the 'wave-like glacier' descending through

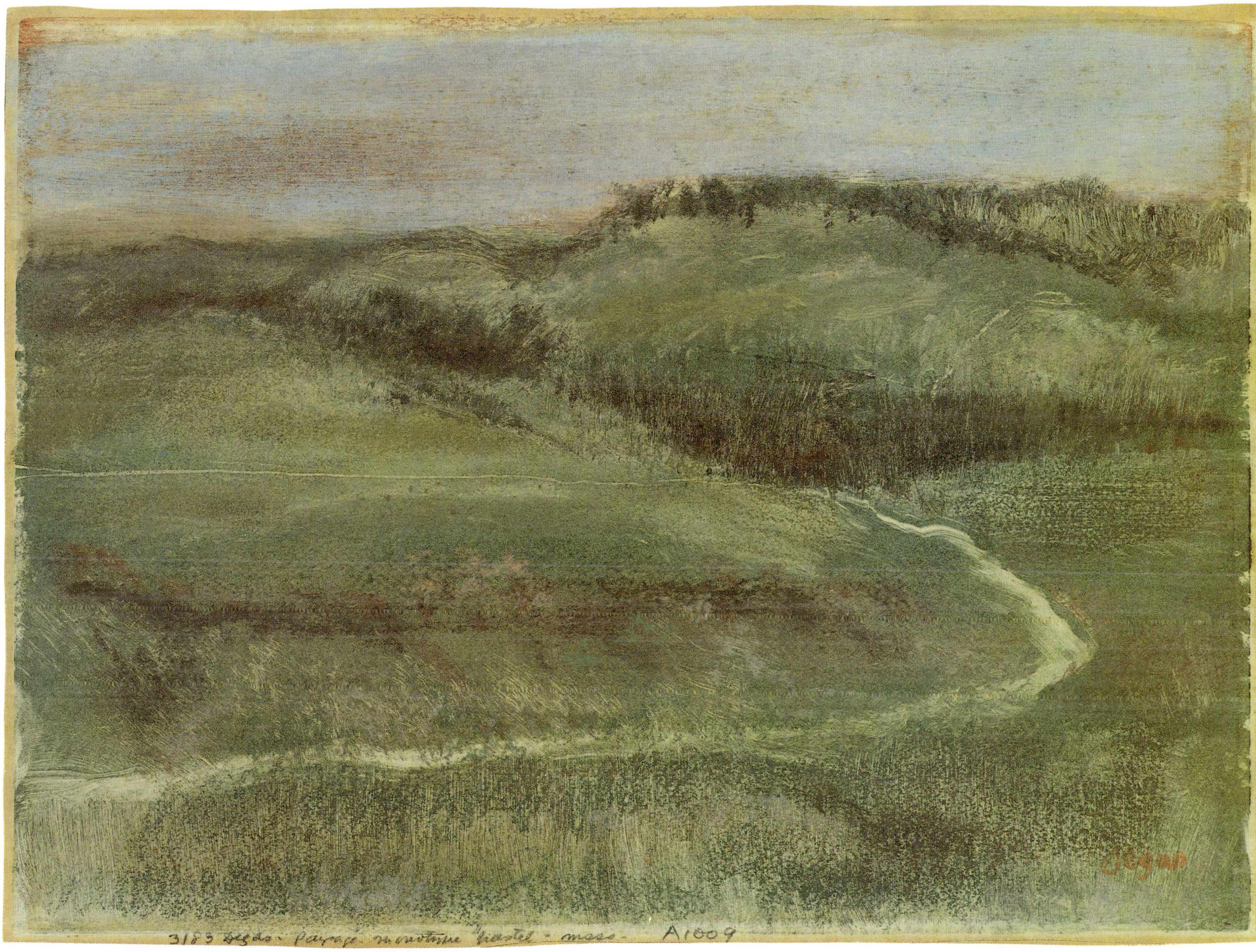

179. *Landscape*, 1892, monotype and pastel, 27 × 36 (J 288). Private collection.

'fields bright with flowers'. Common to all these works, and explicit in Hale's review, is a sense of broad masses and structures powerfully disposed, eloquent of the forces of nature and of the organising intelligence of the artist. As in the Diénay monotypes, many of these images depend on the simplest of geometric arrangements: high, parallel horizons, elliptical roads and the emphatic diagonals of promontories and the verticals of trees. At its most developed, it could result in compositions of a rudimentary simplicity, or perhaps of a supreme refinement. In *Wheatfield and Line of Trees*, for example, three or four blocks of tone converge at the centre, hinting at recession while confining the viewer's attention within the limits of the picture. Each of these blocks has been richly worked, first in monotype and then in hatchings and dabs of pastel, asserting itself as shadow, vegetation or 'fields bright with flowers'. Another recently rediscovered print, *Landscape* (fig. 179), has a similar formal austerity, its swathes of lush greenery subdivided by curving cart tracks, echoing valleys and forestation. Over all, an extraordinary sense of containment prevails, as if the identity of the subjects, the wealth of their colour, and the demands of pictorial design have all been fused and simultaneously resolved.

The extreme formal simplicity of Degas' landscapes and their unorthodox, even exotic, colour had other resonances for his first audience. As we have seen, the monotypes were hung in premises that had been closely linked with the colour-printing revolution, and perhaps in the very galleries where Cassatt's and Pissarro's proofs had recently been shown. Though variously worked in pastel, Degas' pictures conformed to the modest dimensions of framed prints and were generally, if erratically, identified with them.[57] For many visitors at this period, such a display would have been accompanied by another, even more specific, association, and one that several of Degas' contemporaries were at pains to point out. This was with the Japanese wood-block print, one of the most widely collected and influential art forms of the late nineteenth century.[58] Almost all the individuals who showed with the *peintres-graveurs* owed a debt to their Japanese counterparts, ranging from wholesale dependence on their subject- matter to a discreet assimilation of their technical and spatial mastery. More specifically, Pissarro made no secret of his admiration for such artists as Hiroshige, describing him as 'a marvellous Impressionist', and Mary Cassatt had subtitled one of her colour proofs, shown at Durand-Ruel's in 1891, 'Attempt at an imitation of a Japanese print'.[59] In the case of Degas' monotypes, such explanations seem to have been unnecessary. Philip Hale, in the first paragraph of his review, went straight to the point: 'They more resemble a Japanese print of the more expensive sort (such as one buys *chez* Bing), than anything else I can think of', he wrote.[60] Daniel Halévy was even more fulsome: 'The Japanese series is the most beautiful' he reported to his brother, after visiting the show, 'it is Japan, pure Japan, and not the exaggerated and enlarged Japan of Monet and his consorts. The colour is exactly the fresh and brilliant colour of the prints that Manzi has.'[61]

That Degas' landscapes were seen by his contemporaries in the context of Japanese art is graphically illustrated in these responses. Remarkably, this context has not previously been identified, nor has its detailed implications for his techniques or individual prints been examined. As the study of Degas' earlier landscapes has made clear, an awareness of the Japanese achievement was evident in his pictorial vocabulary from the 1860s onwards, and his first acquisitions of Japanese prints may date from that time. Successive waves and ripples of *japonisme* can be charted in later decades, leaving their mark not only in Degas' prints, drawings and pastels but in the writings and imagery of many of his closest associates. During the 1880s, a virtual tide of enthusiasm for all things Japanese gathered momentum, resulting in erudite studies of oriental art on the one hand, and a proliferation of public and commercial exhibitions on the other.[62] In 1887, a display of wood-block prints was held at the Café Tambourin, where they greatly impressed van Gogh; in 1888, there was a similar show at Bing's gallery; the following year, the Universal Exposition included prints in a broad survey of Japanese art, and in 1890 a massive and triumphant exhibition of more than seven hundred works took place at the Ecole des Beaux-Arts.[63] This exhibition caused a considerable stir in Degas' circle, attracting the artist and most of his friends to its opening events and causing Degas, in a typically waspish note to Bartholomé, to satirise its popularity.[64] Pissarro, Morisot, Tissot and Fantin-Latour all attended, and Mary Cassatt, who was currently working on her own colour prints, was moved to acquire several of the exhibits for her own collection.[65]

The *japonisme* of Degas' monotypes, which was so apparent to Philip Hale and Daniel Halévy, needs some elucidation today. At its most brazen, it provided the *motif* for *Vesuvius* (fig. 181), with its unmistakable echoes of Hokusai's *Thirty-six Views of Mount Fuji* and of *Mount Fuji in Clear Weather* (British Museum, London) (fig. 180) in particular. Though slightly less wide than the Hokusai, Degas' image is almost exactly the same height, and its similar purple-blue foreground and roseate volcano seem to offer a Europeanised version of this most celebrated of oriental icons.[66] Other references were more fragmentary or disguised. The pale, serpentine roads that had so captivated Degas in Burgundy were a standard feature of the Japanese repertoire, and such prints as *Pathway in a Field* (fig. 134) must have seemed frankly *japoniste* to his first audiences.[67] Similarly, the 'fantastic-shaped peaks' and 'grim mountains' noticed by Hale, presumably in works like *Lake and Mountains* (fig. 168) and *Landscape* (fig. 183), would have recalled the Japanese fondness for bizarre rock formations, grottoes and ravines.[68] At a further remove, the celebrated use of abrupt or truncated forms in Japanese art, which had inspired some of Degas' most forceful compositions in earlier decades, made a brief reappearance. Described by Boldini as a field 'with cows cut in such a way that all you see is a fragment of spine', *Landscape with Cows* was as structurally audacious as anything in Degas' youthful *oeuvre*.[69]

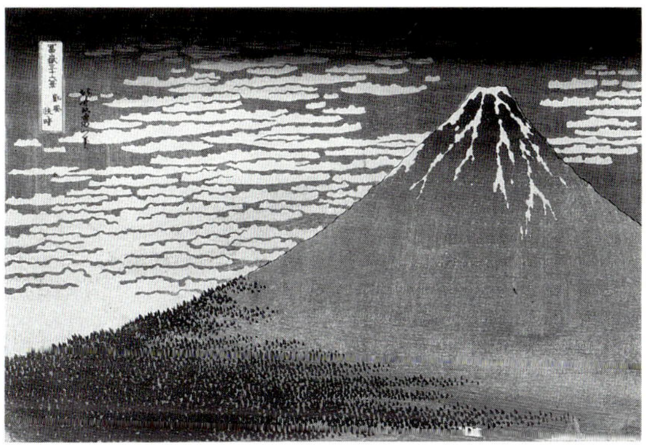

180. Katsushika Hokusai, *Mount Fuji in Clear Weather*, *c.*1830–1, woodblock, 26 × 38.1. British Museum, London.

As Daniel Halévy made clear, however, Degas' affinity with the Japanese tradition was essentially of a more oblique, intuitive kind. Unlike his colleagues Whistler, Tissot and even Monet, to say nothing of print-makers such as Bracquemond, Buhot, Guérard and Rivière, Degas had always stayed aloof from the 'exaggerated Japan' of chrysanthemums and kimonos, fan-waving

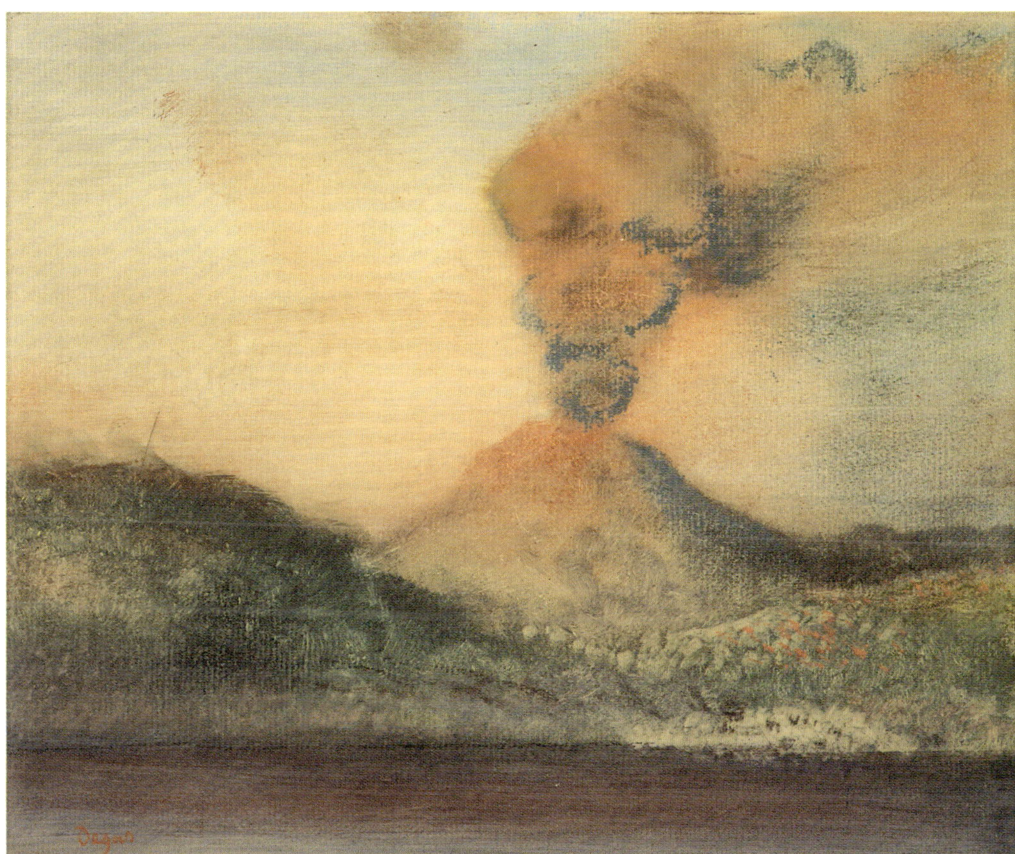

181. *Vesuvius*, 1892, monotype and pastel, 25 × 30 (J 310). Private collection.

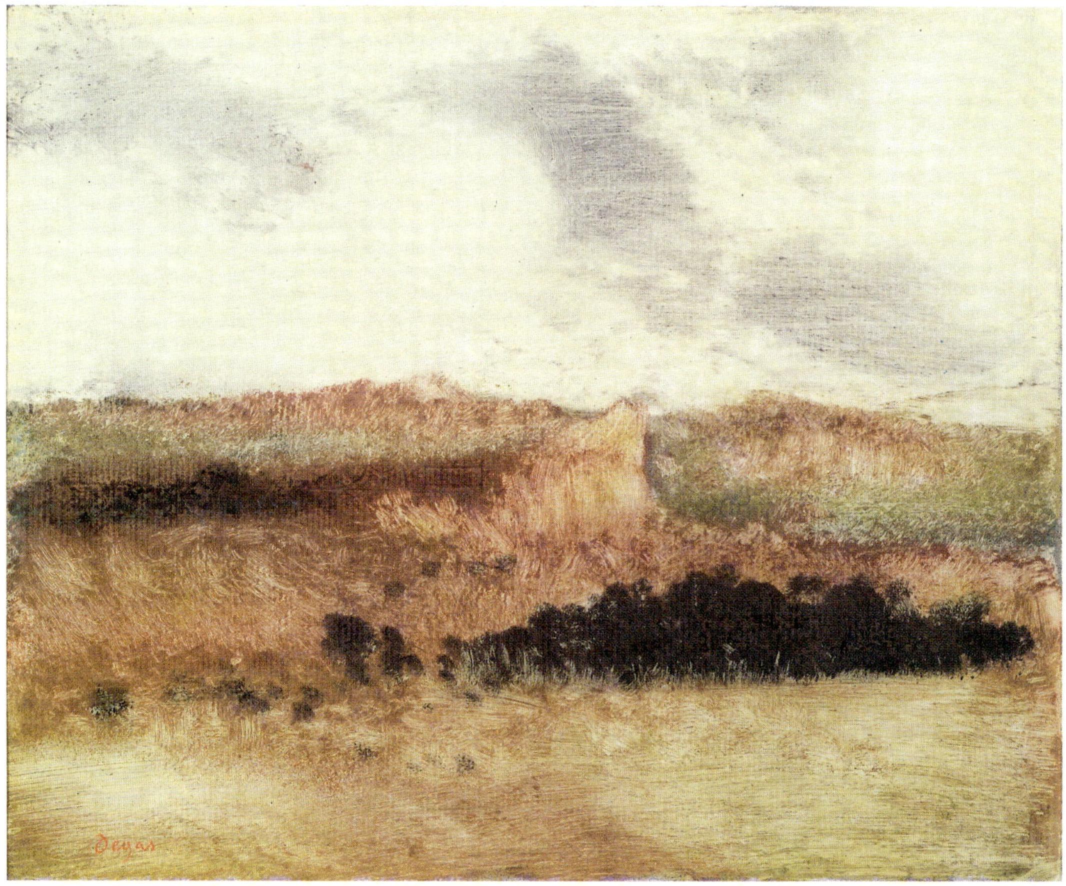

182. *Landscape*, 1892, monotype and pastel, 24.8 × 30 (J 314). Private collection.

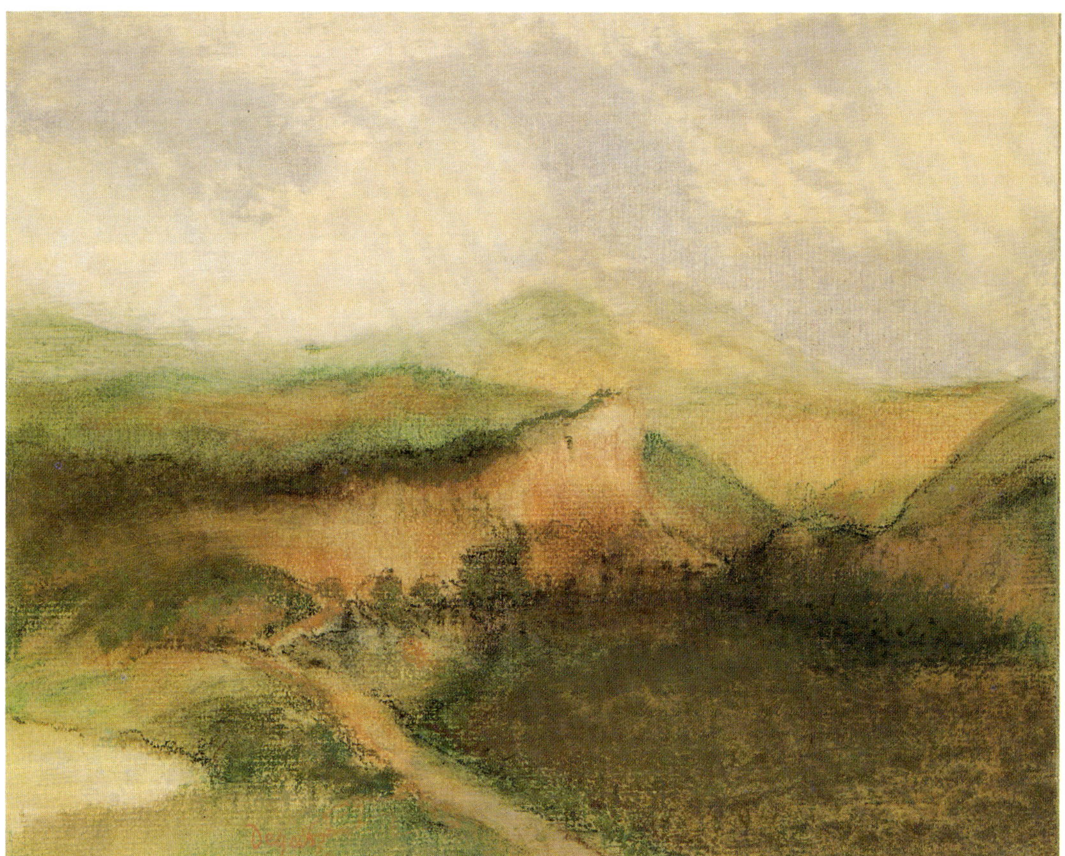

183. *Landscape*, 1892, monotype and pastel, 24.1 × 28.6 (J 278). Private collection.

184. Detail of fig. 174.

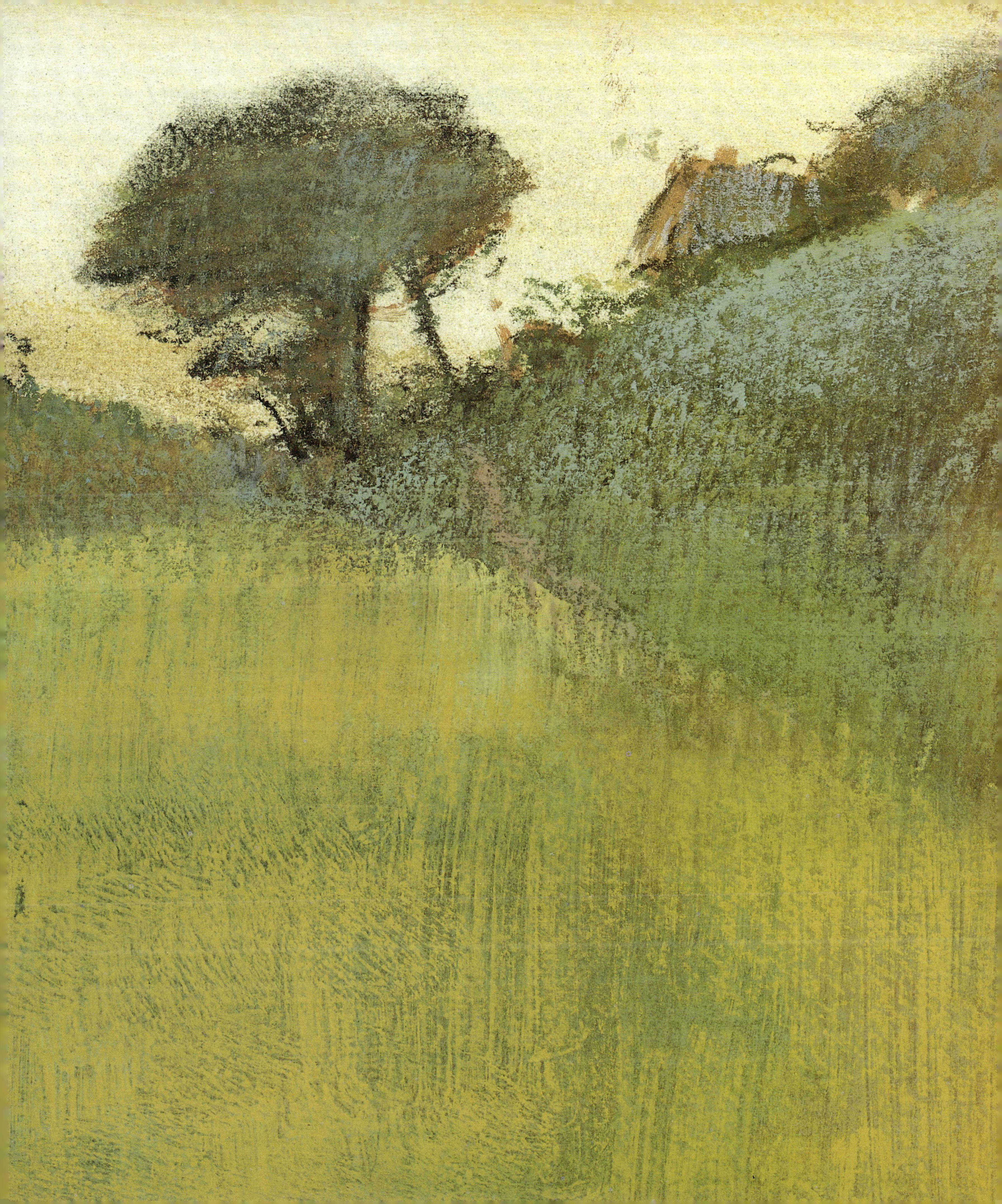

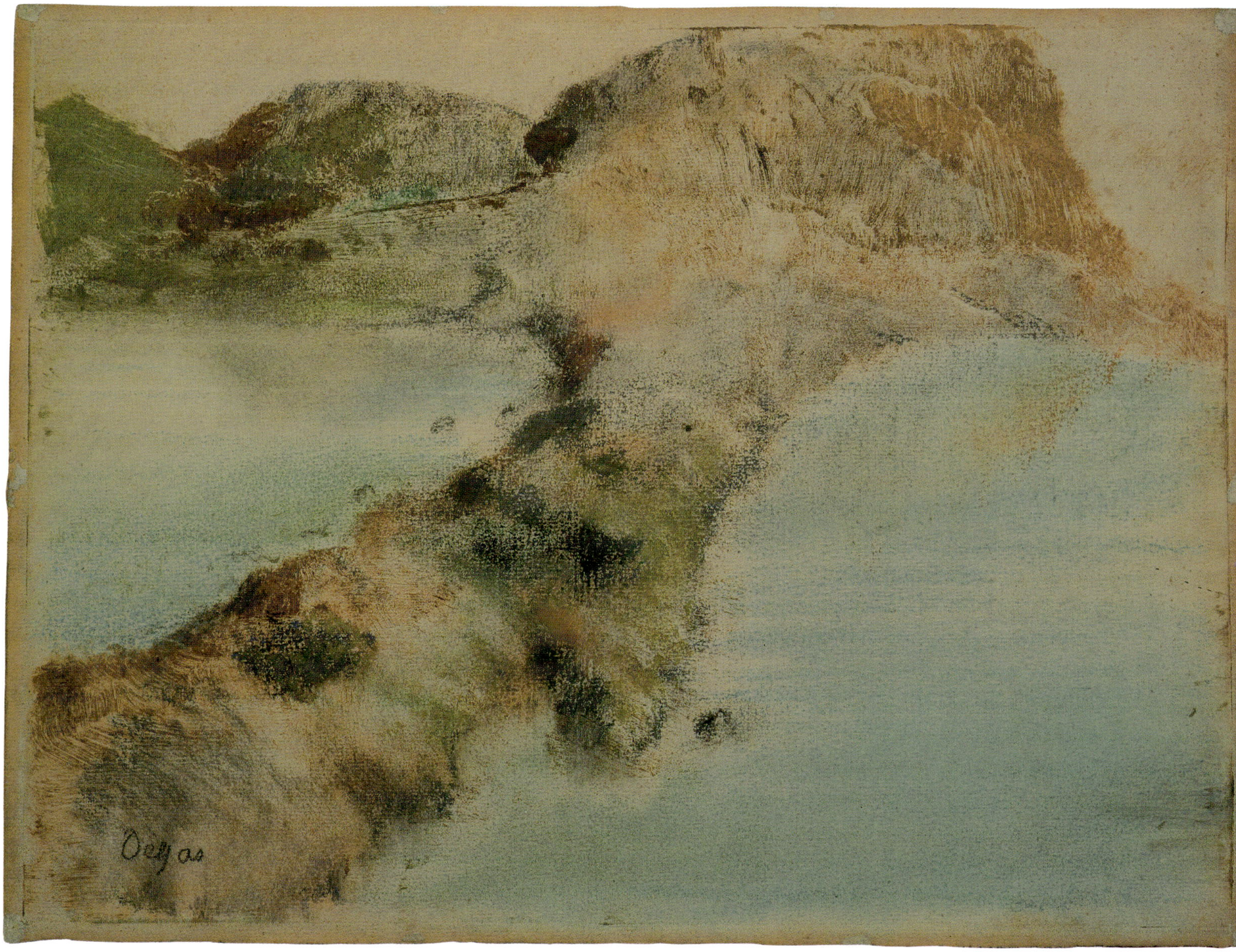

185. *Rocky Coast*, *c.*1890–2, monotype and pastel, 31 × 42 (J 294). Österreichische Galerie, Vienna.

186 (facing page bottom). Katsushika Hokusai, *The Pontoon Bridge at Sano in Winter*, *c.*1834, woodblock, 24.3 × 37.2. British Museum, London.

courtesans and willow-draped bridges. From his earliest contact with their wood-block prints, Degas had responded instinctively to Japanese manipulations of space and design, to their bold pattern-making and their incisive geometry. Apart from his 'fresh and brilliant colour', it was surely this sense of uninhibited, un-European pictorial energy that caught the attention of his admirers. At its simplest, the steep diagonals of *Landscape with Rocky Cliffs* (fig. 138) or *Landscape* (fig. 170) must have brought to mind the angular compositions of Hiroshige and Utamaro, while his delight in zig-zags and oblique structures was evident in roads, rivers and shorelines. More dramatically, the Japanese exploitation of high vantage points, which had again informed Degas' spatial organisation for at least two decades, took flight in several of his exhibited landscapes. Famously summarised in the hovering eagle of Hiroshige's *Plain of Juman-tsubo at Susaki*, the bird's-eye view is implicit in a monotype such as *Landscape* (fig. 183), which has technical links with *Vesuvius*.[70] Here, the observer seems to be suspended above rolling bluffs and hills, as if in a balloon

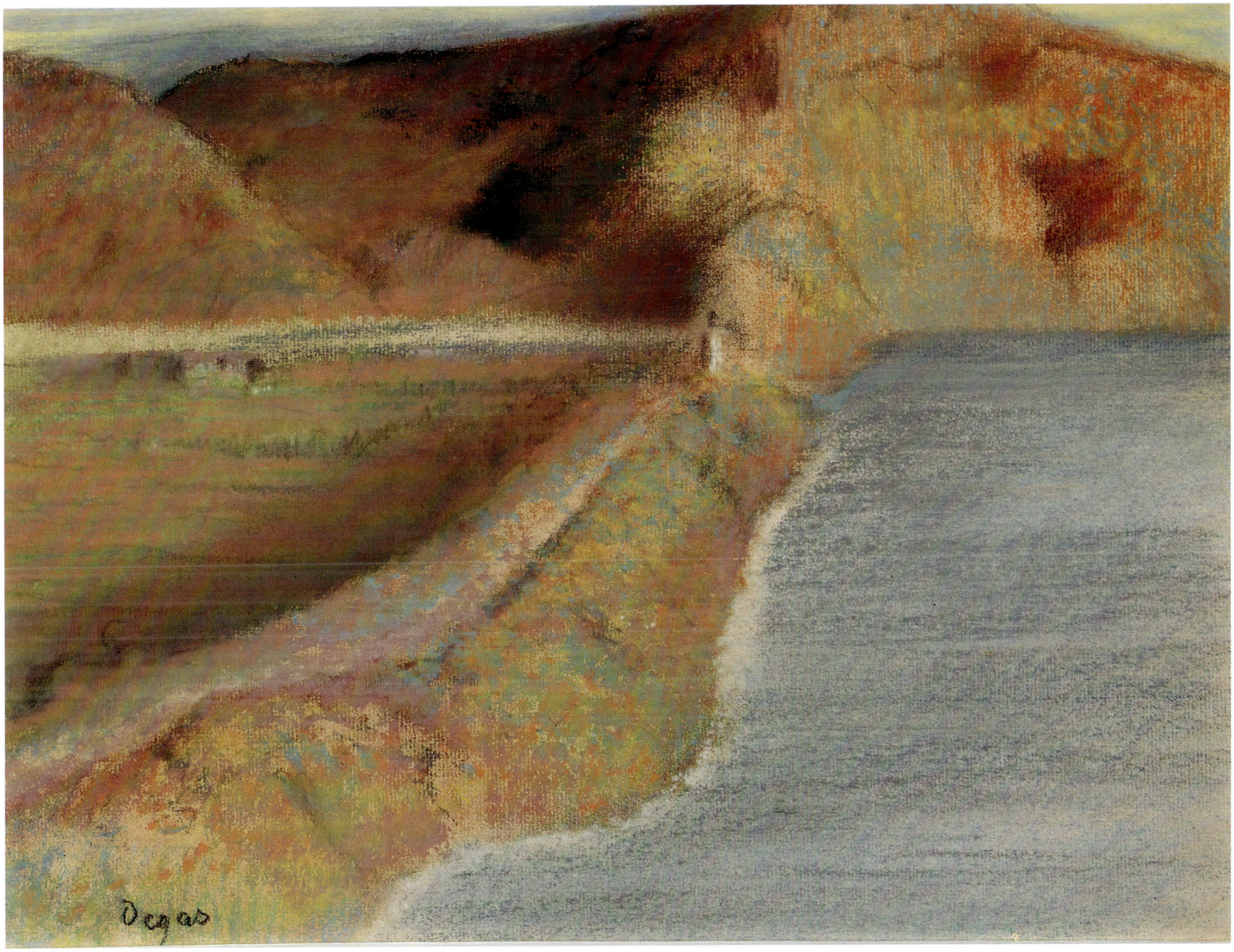

187. *Rocky Coast*, *c.*1890–2, monotype and pastel, 30.5 × 40.9 (J 293). Private collection.

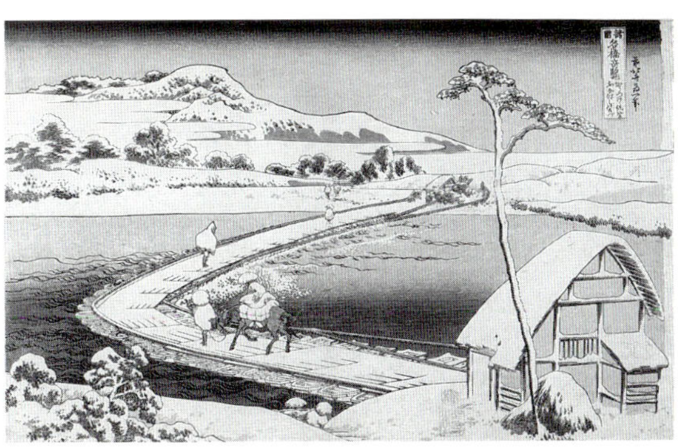

or high on an adjacent peak.[71] Similarly, in another closely related print, *Landscape* (fig. 182), a sense of patterned and subtly stylised remoteness prevails, recalling the spacious vistas of Japanese prints, but without their brittle intensity. As in Hiroshige's image, we are surprised but entranced, distanced but curiously at ease with our surroundings.[72]

Several conventions that are recognisably Japanese come together in the magnificent pair of cognate prints entitled *Rocky Coast* (figs 185 and 187), both signed by the artist and both apparently shown in 1892. In each work, an eccentrically shaped spur of land (Philip Hale's 'Giant's Causeway') juts diagonally across the picture rectangle, animating its formal design and penetrating its space in a single movement. Such oblique, cantilevered structures are frequently found in Japanese wood-block prints and are sometimes linked to strange and celebrated landscape formations.[73] One of the most spectacular is the rising peninsular in Hiroshige's *Ama-na-hashidate*, though a similar principle is at work in the more mundane *Pontoon Bridge at Sano in Winter* by Hokusai (fig. 186). Like many of these works, Degas' two compositions presuppose an elevated point of view, presenting us with a startling, but not wholly improbable, stretch of countryside. In the less heavily worked of the prints (fig. 185), the central form clearly crosses a lake or open waterway, much as in Hiroshige's scene, while its more richly pastellised variant (fig. 187) hints at a domestic landscape, like that of Hokusai. The second of these two monotypes must also have been among the most resonantly coloured in the Durand-Ruel show, with its burning ochres and ripe pinks set against slate-blue water. Again noticeable here is Degas' use of a 'stippling' technique, already encountered in *Landscape with Rocks* (fig. 169) and *Landscape by the Sea* (fig. 177), in which scintillating fragments of sky-blue, orange and green pastel do much to justify Halévy's 'fresh and brilliant' vision of the orient.[74]

The inclusion of cognate pairs in Degas' exhibition may well have added to its *japoniste* appearance for many of his peers. It has often been remarked that Monet's 'series' pictures had their parallels in such collections as Hokusai's *Thirty-six Views of Mount Fuji*, though in Degas' case a more personal and technically appropriate precedent can be found.[75] On the basis of his own studio inventory, it is possible to identify Ando Hiroshige as the object of Degas' greatest admiration among Japanese artists.[76] Represented by almost sixty works in Degas' collection, Hiroshige's name also appears most frequently among the cited sources and inspirations for his landscape repertoire. Known principally for his landscape imagery, Hiroshige had made suites of works that specifically invoked a voyage or a journey through the countryside of Japan.[77] He had also pioneered sequences of prints of a different kind, smaller in extent than Hokusai's and dependent largely on the technology of the workshop. In these sequences, a single set of wooden blocks was used, while the density of the ink and range of colours was varied from one printing to another. As a consequence, the subject or *motif* remained constant, allowing the printer to suggest fluctuations in light and the passage of time through the manipulation of his materials. *Night Rain at Karasaki* (fig. 188) is one such print, belonging to one of Hiroshige's most celebrated landscape series, the *Eight Views of Lake Biwa*. In this variant, the massive central tree has been tinted charcoal-grey, merging with the remorseless verticals of the rain to evoke a gloomy, damp autumn. Other renderings are less heavily inked or variously hued, suppressing the striations of the shower and introducing a rich, spring-like green to the foliage.

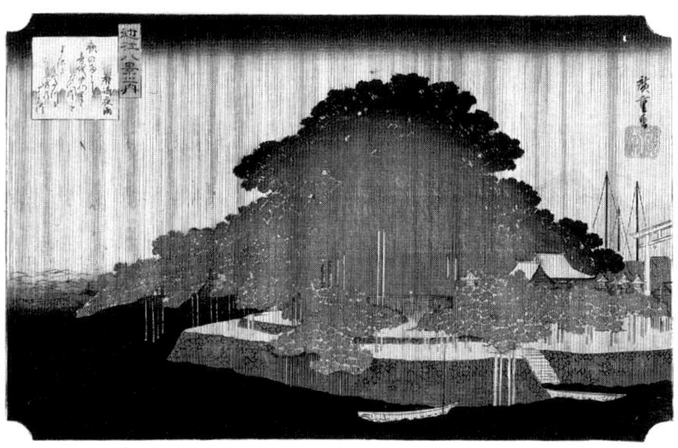

188. Ando Hiroshige, *Night Rain at Karasaki*, *c.*1835, woodblock, 25.7 × 37.9. British Museum, London.

Such shifts of effect from one printing of a landscape subject to another offer the closest of all analogies with Degas' cognate monotypes. They also carry a number of implications, both as exercises in print-making and as depictions of the visible world, that were sympathetic to Degas' evolving attitudes. Hiroshige's *Eight Views of Lake Biwa* drew attention to the uniqueness of each proof, insisting on the personal roles of artist and technician, as well as the responsiveness, even whimsicality, of the wood-block procedure. As such, it contrasted sharply with a view of print-making that was still firmly rooted in Europe, and that had so irritated Pissarro on his visit to the exhibition of the *peintres-graveurs* in 1891. Finding the prints of his contemporaries too impersonal and 'commercial', Pissarro demanded that each work should be seen as an original creation, not just as a mechanical or mass-produced artefact.[78] Like Pissarro and several of their colleagues, Degas, too, had always valued the evidence of the artist's hand, wilfully over-inking his etching plates and refusing to release them as continuous 'editions'.[79] Even in the apparently disciplined Japanese print, eccentricities of touch and simple errors of control seem to have attracted him. The variable graduation of areas of ink, like that in the upper strip of cloud in *Night Rain at Karasaki*, was imitated in certain of his monotypes, while the occasional and accidental streaking of colour in some of Hiroshige's prints may lie behind his own experiments with dribbles and smears.[80]

Returning again to the two proofs of *Rocky Coast*, we can see how Degas has exploited and extended many of these possibilities. The earlier print shows a rocky, inhospitable stretch of country, lightly touched with pastel to suggest sparse vegetation. Using the outlines of the same monotype on his second print, much as Hiroshige had followed the forms of his wood-blocks, Degas then exercised his right to transform the scene. A different palette of colours introduced sunlight and the lushness of summer foliage, while the suppression of its more rugged features hinted at domesticity and cultivation. Unlike Hiroshige, Degas was also able to intervene in the structures of his image, using pastel to smooth the contours of the flower-strewn causeway and subdue the jaggedness of his horizon. In this sense, Degas asserted even more forcefully his independence of print-making rituals, insisting on his right to destroy, as well as to reinvent, the forms present in his proof. Though clearly in sympathy with his Japanese counterpart, Degas at no point followed him or his compatriots slavishly. The highly *japoniste* 'causeway' in *Rocky Coast*, for example, is not insistent in its orientalism, nor festooned with rickshaws, blossoms and pagodas, as it might have been in the work of Degas' followers. Rather, it is seized upon as a dramatic invention, a way of presenting the landscape unexpectedly while retaining its familiarity. As John House has pointed out in a discussion of Monet's 'borrowings', such parallels gave confidence to an artist as he pursued his own solutions, rather than supplying him with ready-made answers.[81] Or in Pissarro's succinct words, written the year after Degas' exhibition, 'those Japanese artists confirm my belief in our vision'.[82]

An illuminating footnote to this story is provided by the figure of Tadama Hayashi, the Japanese art-dealer and expert whose career overlapped with Degas' at many points.[83] Hayashi had arrived in Paris in 1878 and soon established himself as a major importer of Japanese *objets d'art*, selling prints to Cassatt, Monet, Pissarro and Degas, amongst many others. On occasion, he would exchange items from his stock for the paintings and drawings of his customers, gradually building up a wide-ranging collection that included eleven pastels and works on paper by Degas himself.[84] A notable and perhaps surprising feature of Hayashi's collection was the preponderance of landscape paintings, not only by luminaries of the Impressionist movement but by relatively minor figures, many of them friends of Degas, such as Blache, Jeanniot, de Nittis, Rossano and Zandomeneghi.[85] Even less well known is an account, contained in Degas' unpublished inventory, of a painting demonstration by a Japanese artist held in about 1880, at which Hayashi acted as interpreter and Manet, de Nittis and Degas joined the audience.[86] A decade later, Bartholomé produced his sculpture *Mask of Tadamasa Hayashi* (fig. 189), a project he must have begun soon after the tilbury excursion to Diénay.[87] Further evidence of an intimacy between the three men is indicated in Degas' acquisition, at an uncertain date, of a plaster cast of Bartholomé's haunting image of the collector.[88]

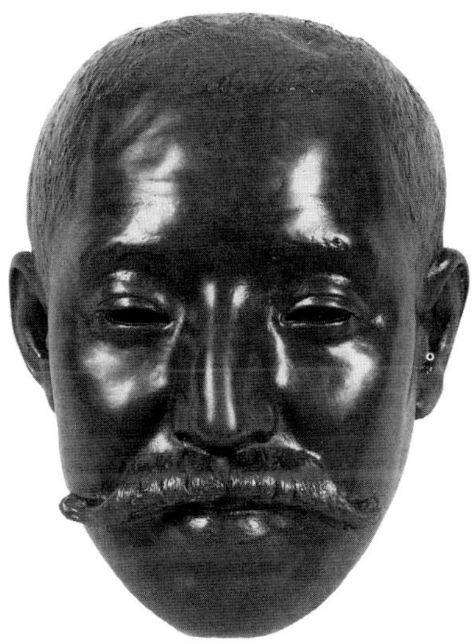

189. Paul-Albert Bartholomé, *Mask of Tadamasa Hayashi*, 1892, bronze. Musée d'Orsay, Paris.

By far the most significant of Hayashi's roles in the present study, however, is as one of the first recorded purchasers of a group of Degas' landscape monotypes. According to Durand-Ruel's stock-book, four landscapes were sold to Hayashi on 23 March 1896, and other records show that they were kept by the Japanese dealer until his death in 1906.[89] Three of the pictures chosen by

Hayashi are highly suggestive in this *japoniste* context. *Pathway in a Field* (fig. 134) has already been singled out as a knowing restatement by Degas of a commonplace wood-block device. Alongside *Landscape with Water* (location unknown; J 290), it also brings to mind the informal geometry of the Japanese print, embracing both the sinuous curves and the grid-like patterns of the landscape. Intriguingly, Hayashi added the first of the two variants of *Rocky Coast* to his collection, perhaps recognising Degas' witty echo of a *motif* from his own native tradition. Finally, Hayashi bought *Landscape* (fig. 197), a remarkable and suggestive confection of cliffs, boulders and a distant road.[90] Though fantastic arrangements of rocks were often depicted by Japanese print-makers, the overt anthropomorphism of this work seems to belong to a European, rather than an oriental, vocabulary.

A less obviously explicable aspect of Hayashi's taste, and of the perceived *japonisme* of the 1892 exhibition in general, was the tendency of Degas' landscapes towards haziness. In contrast to the razor-sharp linearity of the Japanese woodcut, most of the monotypes are granular, unfocused and spatially imprecise, making a virtue of their painterliness and the blurrings of their pastel additions. Hayashi's collection showed a marked predilection for such vagueness, though its predominance in Degas' monotypes caused one or two critics to express their concern. One claimed: 'These are vague landscapes, where one can make out with confidence neither trees, houses nor anything else very definite.'[91] Somewhat later, in his earliest writings on the artist, Paul-André Lemoisne put it more positively, comparing the prints to the oil paintings of Gustave Doré and summarising them as 'vague dream-landscapes, very vaporous, very unreal'.[92] Surprisingly, none of these commentators put forward a comparison that today seems just as compelling as that with Japanese prints or with the landscapes of Doré. In the circles in which Degas moved, a familiarity with the work of J.M.W. Turner was taken for granted, and references to the painter abounded in their correspondence.[93] Some four years before the Durand-Ruel show, Degas and several of his fellow-painters had even composed a letter expressing their appreciation of Turner's achievement, sending it to the Grosvenor Gallery in London on the occasion of an exhibition that included a number of Turner's paintings.[94] At this date, their knowledge of Turner's work was still dominated by his finished oils and watercolours, but signs of an emerging interest in his later and more imprecise imagery are discernible. Camille Groult, a friend of Degas and described by him as 'mad on the English School', already owned Turner's *Landscape with a River and a Bay in the Distance* (Louvre, Paris), a broadly executed canvas from the last decade of the painter's life.[95] Undoubtedly known to Degas, such works may well have encouraged him towards a more diffuse handling, and perhaps suggested the mistiness of such prints as *Landscape* (fig. 173).

The diffuseness of Degas' landscape vision brings us back to the painful subject of the artist's eyesight. On this occasion, we do so with Degas' explicit authority. Following Daniel Halévy's journal, we know that some of the monotypes were prompted by Degas' recent travels, when he had 'stood at the door of the railway carriage, and looked around vaguely'. When asked whether such landscapes might represent 'states of mind', as proposed in the widely read *Journal intime* of Henri-Frédéric Amiel, Degas retorted that, on the contrary, they corresponded to 'states of eyes'.[96] Any ambiguity in Degas' response disappears in Halévy's next journal entry, written shortly before the opening of the Durand-Ruel show. Here Halévy noted, 'His eyes are getting worse and worse, and he wears special glasses which embarrass him very much . . . last month he stopped work completely to get accustomed to his new glasses. He went all alone to Belgium for a week, without reading a single word, not even the railway guides.'[97] Other sources, not least the artist's own letters, confirm that the early 1890s was a period of noticeable deterioration in Degas' visual faculties. After two decades of relative stability, the day-to-day business of seeing had become increasingly burdensome and dispiriting, leading Degas to seek the advice of a prominent ophthalmologist and undertake irksome treatment.[98] In 1891, he confessed: 'I see even worse this winter, I do not even read the newspapers', and added, 'My mind feels heavier than before in the studio and the difficulty of seeing makes me feel numb.'[99]

It is beyond doubt that Degas' landscape monotypes were produced at a time of anxiety about his eyesight and of severe constraints upon his vision. Shortly before the visit to Diénay in 1890, he had described to Bartholomé an excursion to Lourdes, ending with the words: 'with my bad eyes, I missed everything you would have seen'.[100] During their tilbury ride, he wore dark glasses much of the time, a practice that was to become habitual in later years.[101] Both this visit and Degas' railway journeys in 1892 may have been intended as rests for his eyes, though both, paradoxically, were to result in sequences of pictures based on his travels. It is this apparent contradiction that has discouraged a close scrutiny of his condition on the one hand, while generating confusion and misrepresentation on the other. In reality, Degas' eye complaints were acute and diverse, though none prevented him from seeing the world around him. His intolerance of bright light, which had been evident as early as 1871, could be minimised by working in the studio, and his monocular vision was significant only in limited circumstances. More intrusive were the areas of disruption within his visual field, whether the consequence of corneal scarring, a 'blind spot', or other factors. Some of these conditions are known to have produced 'haziness' in front of his eyes, though this was always localised and subject to change.[102] Most importantly, Degas himself insisted that he was not the slave of his vision, a mere passive receptacle for external stimulus. Just as his monotypes contain passages of imprecision and cloudiness that might correspond to the 'vague things' proposed by Halévy, so they also include startling touches of exactitude. These works are the product of a practised hand and a critical mind, as well as a damaged perception. As Degas said bravely in 1891, 'One sees as one wishes to see.'[103]

Another important implication of Halévy's story awaits a thorough examination. In his journal and in other accounts of the same event, it is clear that the landscapes seen 'vaguely' by Degas from railway carriages had been made recently, that is between the summer of 1892 and September of that year.[104] We are obliged, therefore, to imagine at least two sets of monotypes: one made at Diénay in 1890; one completed in Degas' Paris studio in the late summer of 1892; and conceivably others produced in the intervening period. As earlier discussion has suggested, the physical properties of the prints endorse this view, dividing the landscapes into three 'families' that are unified by their size, their subject-matter and their prominence in Degas' exhibition history.[105] The 'family' that is the largest (group A), both in its dimensions and the extent of its membership, is the one most plausibly associated with Diénay. The remaining twenty or so monotypes largely conform to two further plate sizes (groups B and C), and appear to represent the series of recent landscapes announced by Degas at the Halévys' in September 1892.[106] This possibility is strongly reinforced by several shared characteristics in the later groups. All these prints were worked in pastel, many quite heavily, and most of them have highly resolved, almost luxurious surfaces. Crucially, all but one had also been prepared for the forthcoming exhibition in Degas' distinctive manner, by the addition of his signature.

How literally are we to take Degas' claim, as reported by Daniel Halévy, that the landscapes were initiated by glimpses from a speeding train? As with the Diénay monotypes, inspired by a carriage-ride two years previously, many of the later prints lend themselves easily to such an interpretation. Sweeping forms tend to dominate, rather than patiently recorded detail; blurs of pastel hint at urgency and the fleeting glance; and a sense of freshly encountered, almost confrontational, colour pervades the series. A scene such as *Olive Trees against a Mountainous Background* (fig. 190) exemplifies many of these qualities, while raising doubts about their application. If this subject was viewed from a railway compartment, why are some of its elements, such as the foliage and distant mountains, blurred and indistinct, while both the horizon and the foreground tree-trunks are sharply delineated?[107] Are such discrepancies the result of faulty memory, artistic manipulation or an imperfectly, instantaneously perceived *motif*? And finally, where in these months could Degas have seen olive trees and a distinctly mediterranean-looking landscape, to say nothing of a soot-black sea?

During the spring and summer of 1892, Degas had thrown himself into one of the most protracted and uneasy cycles of train travel in this heavily itinerant phase of his life. In March, he journeyed to the extreme south-west of France, to Pau in the Pyrenees, then looped slowly eastwards and northwards through Provence and into Switzerland, to visit his brother in Geneva.[108] By the beginning of August, he was settled at Ménil-Hubert for his annual sojourn with the Valpinçons, staying there for most of the month.[109] Soon afterwards, as Daniel Halévy tells us, he set off for Belgium, travelling alone and returning after a week. As this last visit indicates, much of Degas' journeying was purposeless, or based on the flimsiest of pretexts. At times, it provided an escape from his studio; at others, a solace for his eyes; at some rather abstract level, it also seemed to be linked in Degas' mind with his search for well-being. Six years earlier he had written to Henri Rouart: 'One must continue to look at everything . . . It is the movement of people and things that distracts and consoles us, if there is still consolation to be had for one so unhappy.'[110] More prosaically, Degas' excursions gave him every opportunity to reflect on the nature of his surroundings, on his transient perceptions and on the countryside of his native France. Quite apart from his previous travels, in the early months of 1892 he passed beside mountains and around lakes, through the flat plains of Picardy and the lush valleys of Normandy. Indeed, there are few kinds of terrain in the Durand-Ruel monotypes that Degas would not have encountered, from the Alpine tarns of *Lake and Mountains* to the idyllic rusticity of *Wheatfield and Green Hill*; even the rock-strewn, Italianate vista of *Olive Trees against a Mountainous Background* has its counterparts on his southernmost itinerary.

However widely travelled Degas may have been, and however ingenious our search for his sources, some imponderables remain. Without exception, his contemporaries agree that the monotypes were executed away from the *motif*, dependent above all on Degas' prodigious recollection, his 'memory strong like iron', as Boldini described it.[111] Such a process has its hazards, as well as its practical advantages, and the kind of links with tradition that Degas so valued. As a young man, he had been told by Ingres, 'Never work from nature. Always from memory, or from the engravings of the masters', advice that he passed on to anyone who would listen, among them the young Jeanniot.[112] Degas was

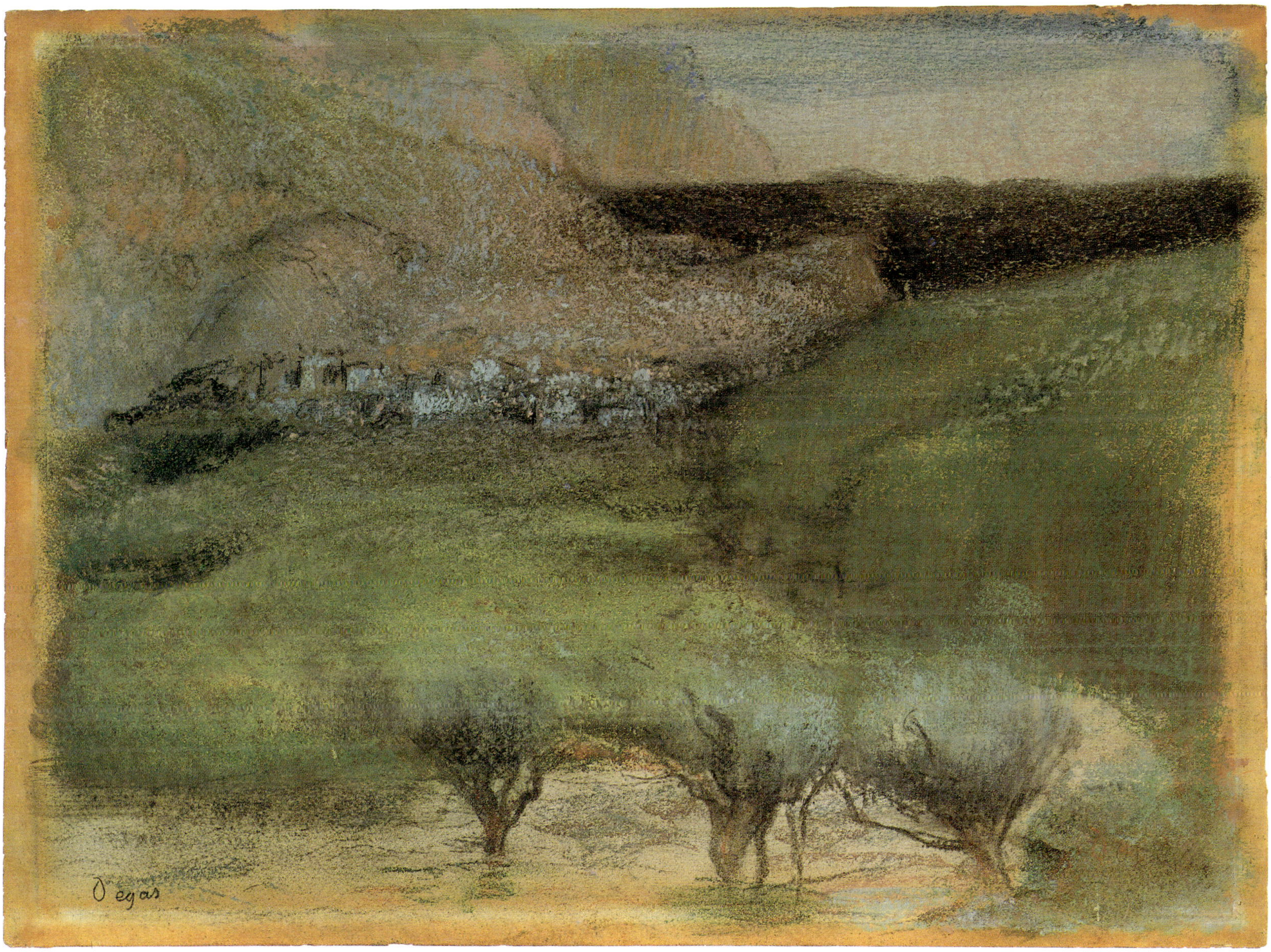

190. *Olive Trees against a Mountainous Background*, 1892, monotype and pastel, 25 × 34 (J 319). Norton Simon Museum of Art, Pasadena.

also said to have admired the memory-training techniques of Lecoq de Boisbaudran, claiming that if he were to set up his own school of art, he would situate the model on one floor while instructing his students to paint on another.[113] Paradoxical though it might seem, Degas insisted with equal vehemence that memory should be combined with a mastery of form, a mastery that came only through drawing directly from the chosen subject. In this respect, his later landscape production was the exception to his own much-proclaimed rule. There is no evidence that Degas studied the countryside of Burgundy or the Pyrenees with pencil and charcoal in hand, or that he carried pastels or watercolours with him on his later railway pilgrimages. No drawings, sketchbook studies or the briefest of *aides-mémoire*, such as those made by Turner while travelling by carriage, have survived for these works.[114] Whatever part memory played in the evolution of the monotypes, it did so entirely unaided.

If we consider a picture such as *Olive Trees against a Mountainous Background* in the light of these speculations, what insight can we gain into the operations of Degas' memory? Accepting that a subject of this kind could have been seen during his summer travels, at the Atlantic coast near Pau, in the Pyrenees or in Provence, it follows that an interval of several weeks would have elapsed before Degas returned to his apartment in Paris. During that time, we must imagine the image locked in his vice-like recollection, then transferred directly and faithfully on to a copper plate in his studio and subsequently rendered more vivid with pastel. Plausible though it is, this model does not stand up to close scrutiny. As in a number of the monotypes, *Olive Trees against a Mountainous Background* shows many signs of revision, not just in its details but in its fundamental structures and pictorial effects. The hill at the right, for example, was once chestnut-brown and was partly bordered by an additional line of trees. At a subsequent stage, Degas covered this entire area in deep green, just as he obliterated many earlier forms in other parts of the composition. Perhaps the most telling detail here is the background, where once the mountains descended without interruption to the fertile valley below. Only at a late stage did Degas add the unexpected segment of black 'sea', transforming his inland valley into a stretch of coastline and dramatically shifting its tonal balance. As if to signal his own vacillation, Degas signed the picture not once, but three times, presumably after each modification: at the left in black graphite and at the right in pencil and in red pastel. In so doing, he seems to have acknowledged that this was not a fixed, precisely recalled image plucked from his memory, but a freely extended and improvised work of art.[115]

Such observations have the effect of distancing some of Degas' imagery from the factual landscape, enhancing the subjective functions of memory and vision, and stressing the role of technique in the definition of his subject-matter. We may still believe that olive trees and sugar-pink mountains, and even an inky ocean, were glimpsed from his railway carriage, but we are not required to accept them as inevitable and documentary components of a single scene. In this sense, 'working from memory' is less like selecting a photograph from a mental filing-cabinet, more like plundering a library of sensual and psychological experiences that could be rearranged at will. Following this analogy, we might argue that the imagery of Degas' monotypes had been stored, edited and sometimes classified with extraneous material, and finally retrieved within the disciplines of the studio. Degas himself accepted the complexity of the memorising process, telling Jeanniot:

> It is very good to copy what one sees; it is much better to draw what you can't see any more but in your memory. It is a transformation in which imagination and memory work together. You only reproduce what struck you, that is to say the necessary. That way, your memories and your fantasy are freed from the tyranny of nature.[116]

In this statement, Degas ingeniously brings together the old and the new. Apart from clear echoes of Ingres, there are signs of familiarity with the essays of Lecoq de Boisbaudran, who similarly linked the functioning of memory and imagination.[117] More surprisingly, Degas seems to open the way to an entirely inventive art, free from the shackles of direct observation.[118]

The idea that nature threatens a tyrannical hold over the artist, and that memory and fantasy are necessary to circumvent it, provides a valuable context for Degas' landscape activity and perhaps for his later career as a whole. On several occasions he reiterated the sentiment: 'A painting requires a little mystery, some vagueness, some fantasy. When you always make your meaning perfectly plain you end up boring people', he claimed.[119] He also asserted his right to work on other kinds of pictures without reference to their subject, revealing that he sometimes continued his pastels of the female nude after the model had left, 'according to my fantasy'.[120] His choice of words provides the proper perspective for his only recorded remark about the Durand-Ruel exhibition. In a letter of December 1892, Degas wrote to his sister Marguerite, recording the further decline of his eyesight and adding, 'I have had a little exhibition at Durand-Ruel of twenty-six imaginary landscapes which has been rather successful.'[121] He had used similar terminology in a reported discussion with Monet about his wish to paint a 'fantasy landscape', and a number of similar phrases soon entered into circulation.[122] The critic of the *Mercure de France* described to his readers 'a series of landscapes by Degas, not studies, but sites that are pleasantly chimerical, recomposed from imagination', and Arsène Alexandre referred to the works as 'reminiscences of nature'.[123] Explaining his use of the word, Alexandre continued: 'I should really have told you that these landscapes, which are very true to life, are not executed from nature: or rather that they are made from nature at second hand: from the nature that the artist has stored away in his head and digested in his imagination.'[124]

The practical consequences of these imaginary procedures have already been seen in action, both in the Diénay monotypes and the later 'families' of prints. At their most disciplined, the brush-marks and dabs of ink in certain of the landscapes were combined with pastel to produce a carefully pre-ordained result. In diluting his colours, however, and allowing them to spread freely across the copper plate, Degas denied himself complete control of his imagery, and even encouraged chance effects and unforeseen structures. Some of these configurations may well have prompted his memory, triggering the mechanisms of recall from previous weeks or even years, allowing him to strengthen and particularise the image as he later worked in pastel. Others seem almost random, at least in their initial stages. The full extent of their arbitrariness can be judged in some of the cognate pairs, where the inverted variant of *Autumn Landscape* (fig. 151) was transmuted into *River Banks* (fig. 152), and in such individual prints as *Landscape with Smokestacks* (fig. 130), in which 'dribbles' of colour have become tree-trunks and bushes. But as with *Olive Trees against a Mountainous Background*, none of their eventual subjects was incompatible with the landscapes Degas had encountered, and all may ultimately derive from the *motifs* 'stored away in his head', as Alexandre put it.

Some of the suggestive, aleatory techniques used by Degas in his landscapes carry this project to the farthest boundaries of realism. His capricious way with brushes and pads of cloth, his puddles of ink and veils of paint, and even his smears and scatterings of pastel, seem to belong to the mid-twentieth century rather than the late nineteenth. Even more eccentrically, certain of the monotypes, such as *Le Cap Ferat* (fig. 191), were composed entirely of thumbprints, a practice that was later to transform a number of the artist's oil paintings.[125] Others find parallels in the experimental, not to say obscure and wayward, practices of his day. Whistler prided himself on the free-flowing 'soup' of paint that preceded many of his paintings, and both George Sand and Victor Hugo evolved their own image-generating alchemy. That used by George Sand, known as 'aquarelle à la dendrite', was a precursor of Max Ernst's *decalcomania*, involving the 'blotting' of areas of wet paint and their elaboration into trees, bushes and landscape forms.[126] Hugo was more various as a graphic artist and more likely to have influenced the 1892 monotypes. An exhibition of Hugo's drawings took place at the Galerie Georges Petit in 1888, accompanied

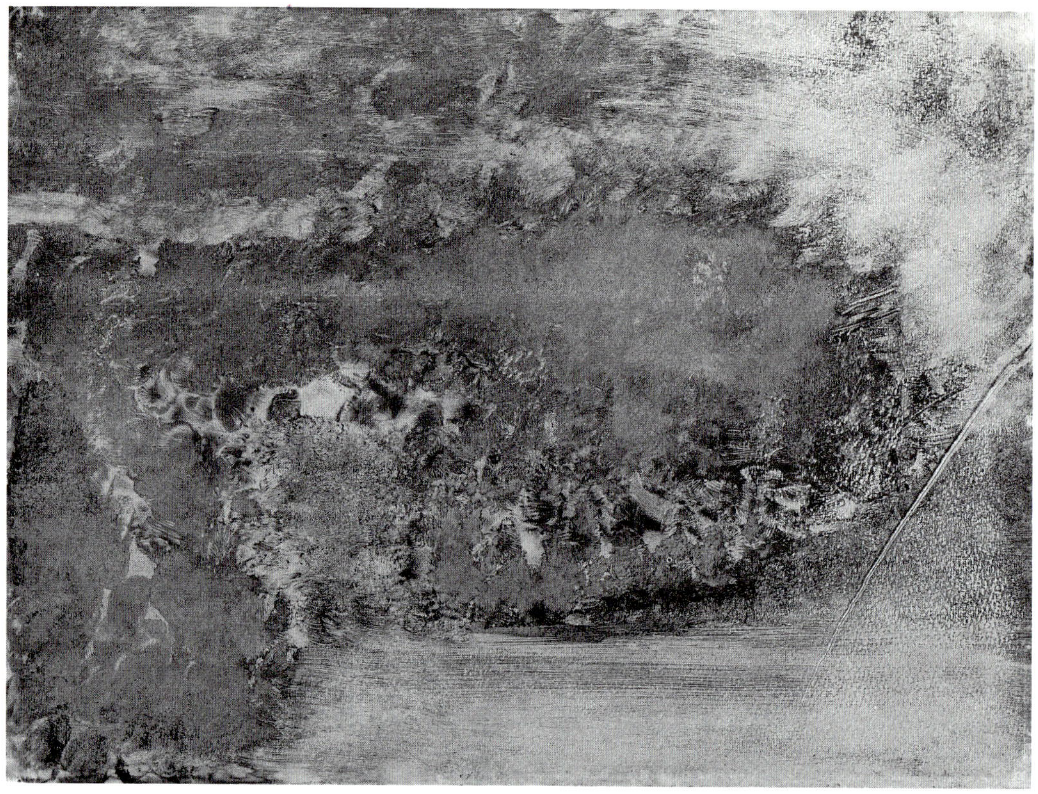

191. *Le Cap Ferrat*, 1892, monotype, 29.7 × 39.9 (J 308). Staatliche Kunsthalle, Karlsruhe.

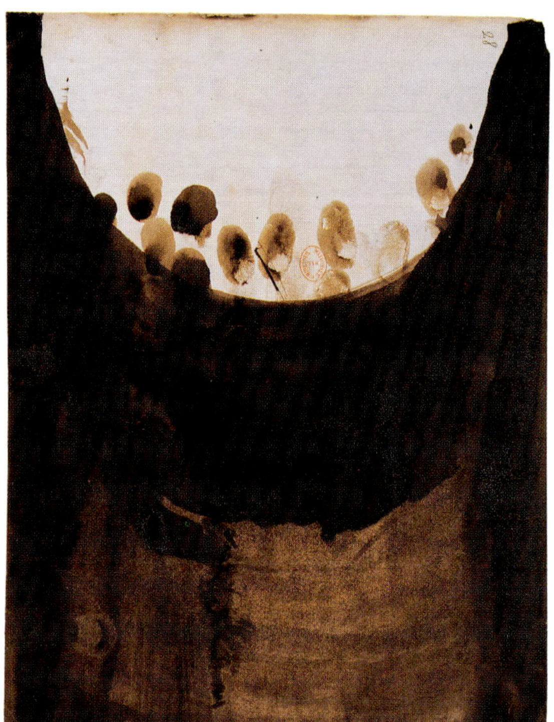

192. Victor Hugo, *Composition with finger-prints*, ink. Bibliothèque Nationale, Paris.

by critical responses to his work from three writers known personally to Degas: Joris-Karl Huysmans, Emile Verhaeren and Albert Wolff.[127] Ranging from the conventional to the technically bizarre, Hugo's work included a large number of topographical studies and images recalled from his travels, such as *Landscapes from a Journey to the Pyrenees*.[128] Though his finished drawings have often been coaxed into the forms of castles, ramparts and stormy skies, many were evidently begun as random blots or spreadings of ink. Even closer to Degas, a lifelong admirer of Hugo, are images like *Composition with Finger-Prints* (fig. 192), which might crucially have stimulated his monotype explorations.[129]

Certain of Degas' monotype landscapes still defy decipherment. *Le Cap Ferrat* is at least as amorphous as Hugo's pen-and-ink washes, swirling around an ill-defined crater or moon-like declivity, its drifts of thumb-marks conjuring up rocks, scrub or volcanic tufa. Defying gravity, *Landscape* (fig. 193) can be read from more than one direction, suggesting trees and a bronze-tinted sunset from one angle, stalagmites or cave formations from another.[130] Neither print was developed by Degas in pastel, and both seem to have been left in a state of heightened suggestiveness, like a Rorschach ink blot or a Hugo wash drawing. Though we know that Degas chose to leave some of his monotypes without pastel re-working, and even signed certain prints in this state, it seems probable that unsigned works like *Le Cap Ferrat* and *Landscape* were destined for subsequent remodelling and clarification.[131] It is equally clear that the artist delighted in the strange and sometimes monstrous forms his experiments threw up, allowing himself to develop them, on occasion, as completely as his more orthodox compositions. In approximately ten of the existing landscapes, hills can be read as swelling limbs or torsos, mounds become breasts and heads, and rocks suggest features and ill-defined extremities. This unexpected aspect of Degas' creativity has yet to be analysed in detail, and seems to have surprised his

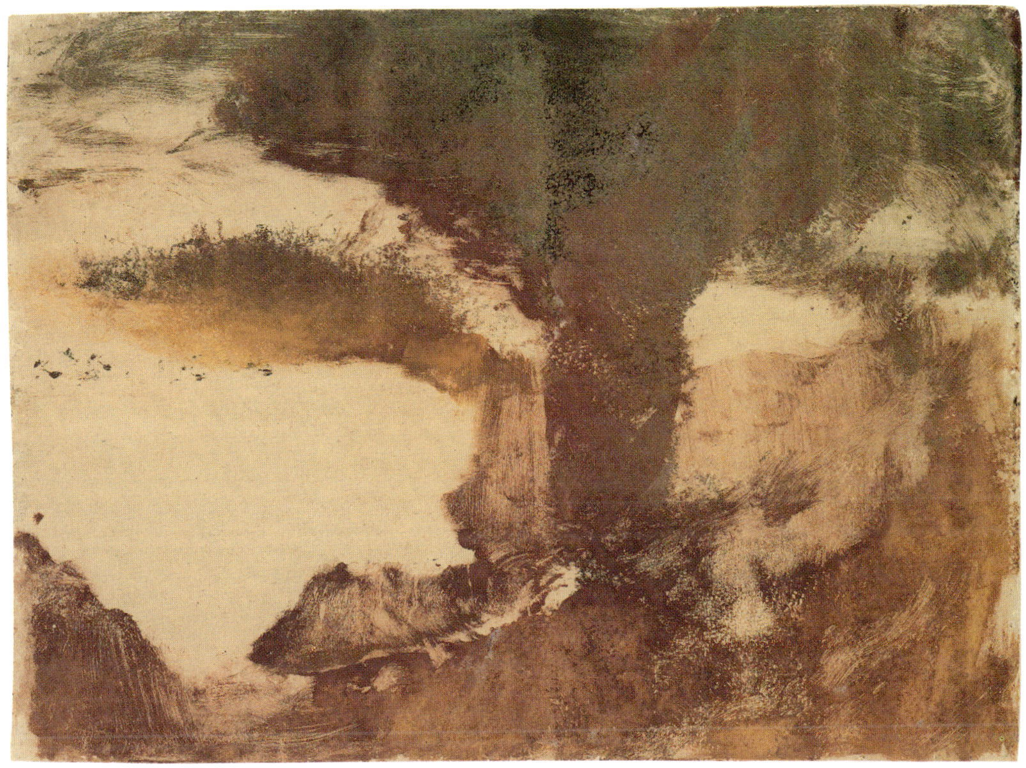

193. *Landscape*, 1890, monotype, 29.9 × 39.9 (J 309). Collection of Phyllis Lambert, Montreal.

original audiences as much as it disconcerts his admirers today. Combining 'a little mystery, some vagueness, some fantasy' in equal parts, these truly 'imaginary landscapes' are amongst the most revealing and under-researched products of his later years.

At the Durand-Ruel show in November 1892, some half-dozen of the exhibited pastels contained anthropomorphic imagery, ranging from the subtly understated and ambiguous to the disarmingly frank. At their most discreet, they offer no more than a hint of complexity or a private pun, of a kind that might amuse a friend or fellow-artist. This category includes the second variant of *Rocky Coast* (fig. 187), a work already rich in allusions of various kinds. While developing its monotype base, Degas seems to have been amused by the resemblance of the central causeway to a pair of legs, such as those stretched out by countless ballerinas in his rehearsal room studies.[132] Using his pastels, he then enhanced this reading of the image, heightening knees, calves and shins without insisting on their legibility. An equally elusive quality was given to *Lake and Mountains* (fig. 168), where the peaks and troughs of the skyline seem less improbable when rotated through ninety degrees. From this angle, a rugged male profile appears, its mountainous nose and beetling brow perhaps reminiscent of one of Degas' companions.[133] In certain monotypes not shown at Durand-Ruel's, it is evident that this punning use of form was established at the printed stage, not just in the later process of elaboration. *Le Cap Hornu, near to Saint-Valéry-sur-Somme* (fig. 155) was never developed in pastel, but remains poised between the contours of the human body and those of the landscape. Quite unlike the stretch of flat country referred to in its title, the image recalls a reclining female figure seen from behind, and once identified as such, resists other interpretations.[134] Similarly, the monotype print *Mountains and Valley* (fig. 194) incorporates a dark head of hair, sinuous back and curving hips in its

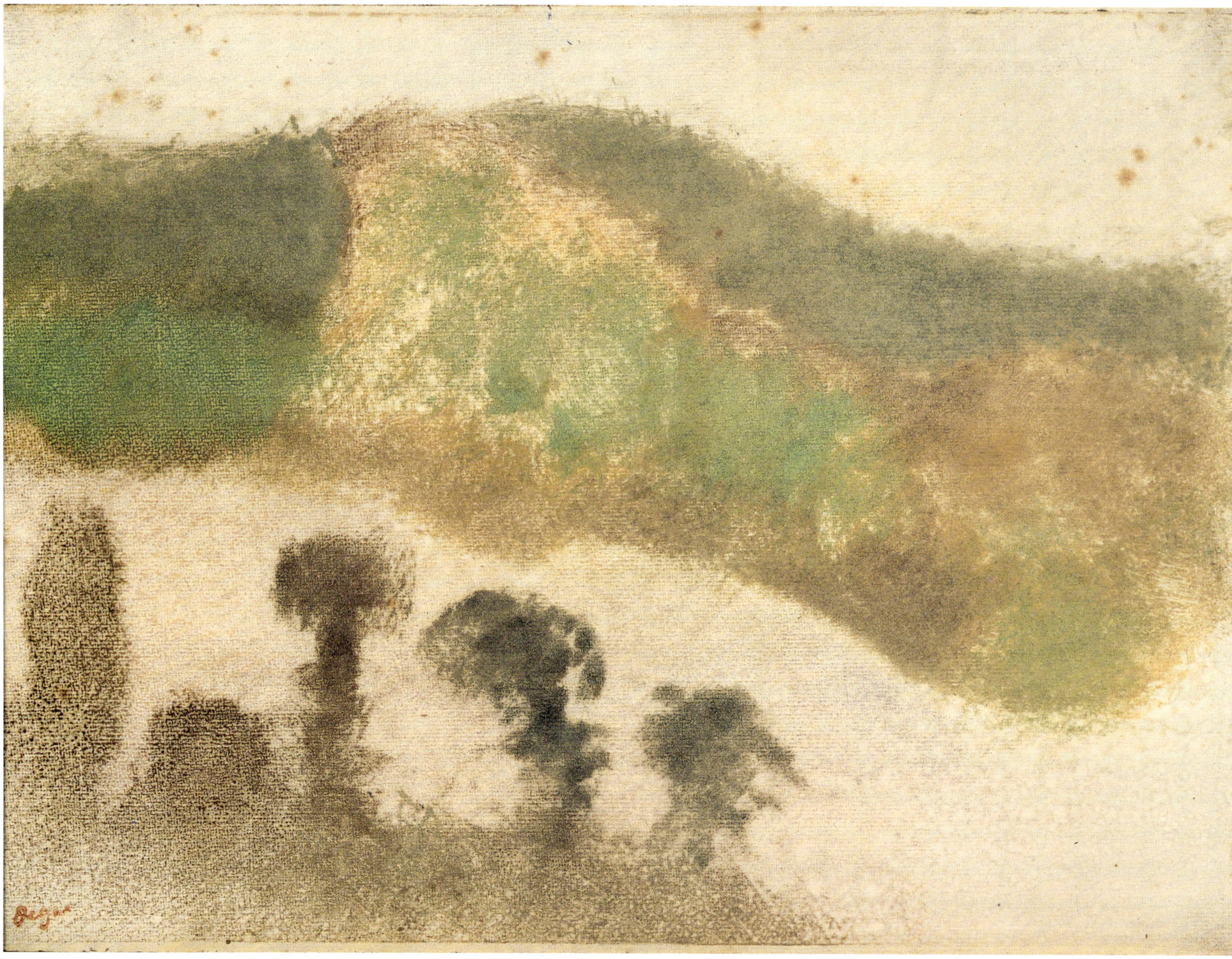

194. *Mountains and Valley*, 1890, monotype, 30 × 40 (J 296). Charles de Montalembert.

principal land mass, and might almost have become a bedroom scene rather than a coastal vista.

The language of anthropomorphism, in both its visual and verbal forms, was part of the common culture of Degas' age, revealing itself in popular illustration and figures of speech, celebrated novels and abstruse feats of draughtsmanship. In his own 1892 landscapes, it was manifestly evident in at least three other works: *Steep Coast* (fig. 199); *Landscape* (fig. 200); and *Landscape* (fig. 197). All three works were extensively enriched with pastel, and all three were signed by the artist prior to exhibition. The first two were also exceptional in their large size and in their lack of a monotype base beneath their pastel crusts.[135] In each case, Degas has had recourse to the most familiar of all anthropomorphic conceits, that of the analogy between the human form and the real or imagined landscape. Reaching back through the grotesqueries of Archimboldo, the *Vexierbilder* of the Mannerists and the wall stains of Leonardo, this tradition was still very much alive in Degas' immediate circle. To cite almost at random, we

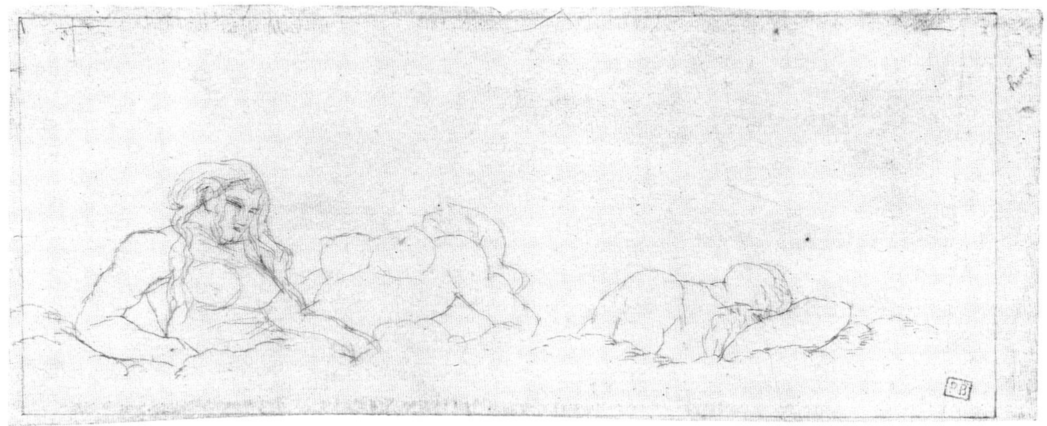

195. Charles Meryon, *Anthropomorphic Cloud Studies (First Version)*, ink, 9.8 × 20.2. Sterling and Francine Clark Art Institute, Williamstown, Mass.

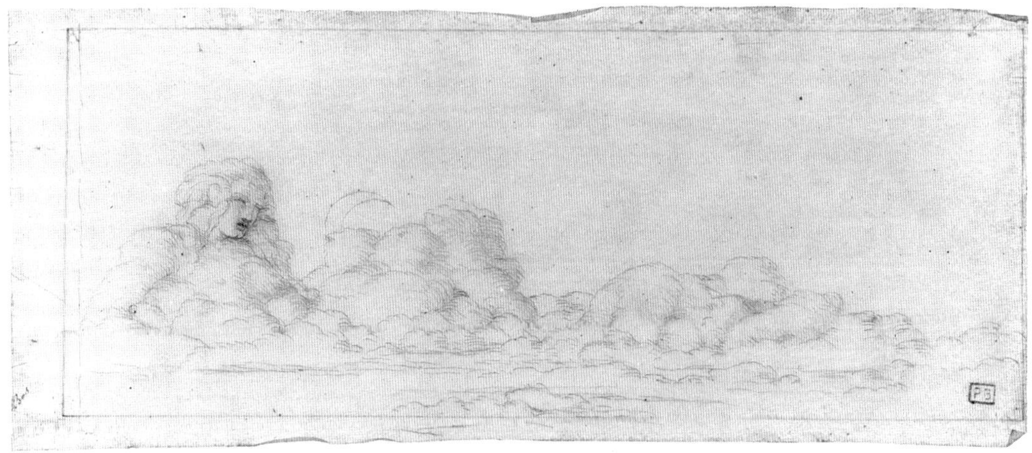

196. Charles Meryon, *Antrhopomorphic Cloud Studies (Second Version)*, ink, 7.9 × 20.2. Sterling and Francine Clark Art Institute, Williamstown, Mass.

find that the same *Journal intime* by Frédéric Amiel compares a mountainous scene to teeth, fangs, pincers and horns, while Degas' novelist friends could be even more explicit.[136] Guy de Maupassant, a great admirer of Degas' art, would occasionally transpose human and topographic forms, writing in *A Woman's Life* of 'the sea, heaving up its gleaming belly heavenwards in an arch, looking like a monstrous bride awaiting the descent of her fiery lover'.[137] In another journal entry, Amiel continued this tendency to see nature in female terms, suggesting that the women of Russia shared the outward features of their native country.[138] Closer to Degas' imaginings, the print-maker Charles Meryon once watched the clouds arrange themselves into muscular female figures, and made a remarkable pair of drawings to record the event (figs 195 and 196).[139] Though Degas could hardly have known them, Meryon's studies also capture the temporal, teasing nature of such formations, which allows the image to slip from one reading to another, then back again, even as we try to grasp their meaning.

Degas' own taste for rhyming or allusive form dates back further than is generally supposed. While travelling by train as early as the 1850s, he had compared the smoke from the locomotive to a horde of galloping horsemen, making a note in his sketchbook and a drawing to illustrate the point.[140] Some years later, he wrote of the resemblance between 'a pebble and a fish, a mountain and a dog's head, clouds and horses', and indulged in the graphic transformation of animals, faces and sexual organs.[141] According to Philip Hale, Degas had a private theory that, 'as poets in all ages have compared the beauties of nature to woman, or *vice versa* (a still lake to a woman's eyes, a woman's hair

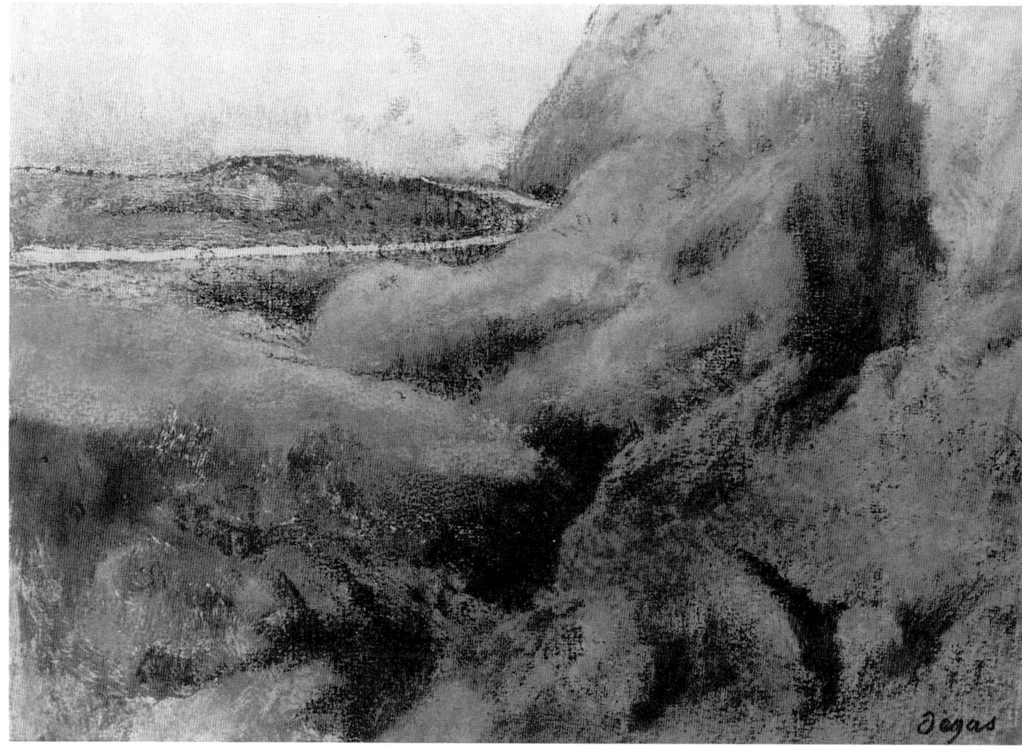

197. *Landscape*, *c.*1890–2, monotype and pastel, 30 × 40 (K 4). Location unknown.

to a river of gold), so the painter, also, should try to reach out and accentuate these resemblances'.[142] Again, the analogy slips unnoticed towards the forms of the female body and implicitly to the language of eroticism. The only monotype in the group under discussion is clearly stated in such terms, conflating the nakedness of a reclining figure with the sensuous openness of the landscape. In *Landscape*, the punning conceits of Degas' youth come to fruition, as he dissolves a boulder into a woman's torso, her limbs into folds of earth and her hair into a plunging cliff-face. Conversely, the woman takes on the massiveness of the rock-strewn hillside, anticipating by almost fifty years the petrified manikins of René Magritte.

Steep Coast is more explicitly sexual, displaying a recumbent female nude of gigantic proportions at her ease on a cliff-top, cushioned by grassy mounds and banks of summer flowers. Here her thighs have become rising hillocks, her breasts distant tumuli, while her hair tumbles down the cliff-face like Hale's evocative 'river of gold'. By softening their outlines, Degas has allowed a certain ambiguity of form, but still brings to mind, wittingly or otherwise, the imagery of Maupassant's 'monstrous bride' and Meryon's cloud-bound phantoms. Behind all these associations, there lurks one of the oldest of cultural devices, that of the female identity of the landscape and its role as earth goddess or earth mother. As Richard Thomson has shown, such traditions were still much in evidence at this period, not least in popular journals and illustrated works of fiction.[143] It is also clear that Degas was aware of such conventions and manipulated them with care, evolving his large and subtly balanced pastel through several stages. He began with a study of the female nude, close in detail to the *Woman Having her Hair Combed* in the Metropolitan Museum of Art, New York.[144] Tilting the figure on its back, he then merged it with a bird's-eye view of sea, cliffs and vegetation, adding layer upon layer of pastel strokes and *pointilliste*-like colour. Even the landscape may have been a knowing device, conceivably directed at the more prosaic *motifs* of Claude Monet: the precipitous incline at the right of the picture, for example, recalls the latter's *Cliffs at Dieppe* (Kunsthaus, Zurich) and the scene has general affinites with his views of Belle-Ile of 1886. If so, the point was not lost on Monet, who is said to have mentioned *Steep Coast* to Theodore Robinson and may have been provoked, in his turn, to introduce suggestive curves into certain of his own later canvases.[145]

The conjunction of painstaking naturalism with pictorial conceit is at its most flamboyant in *Landscape* (fig. 200). Once again, Degas has lavished considerable efforts on the setting, disposing his summer pinks, daisy-yellows and powder-blues across a deep space and insisting on the plausibility of pasture, sky and mossy rocks. Distantly recalling his 1869 pastels, the dune-like horizon and thundery sky bring to mind the coast of Normandy, while the curious network of pale roads may be a reminiscence of the Côte d'Or. The foreground, however, permits no such rationalisation. What at first glance appears as a scattering of boulders and monoliths, soon reveals itself to be something quite different: a monstrous phallus surrounded by glimpses of thigh, knee and hirsute, protruberant belly. Once identified, this cluster of forms exerts a disproportionate hold over the composition and threatens to engulf it entirely, destroying both its pictorial equilibrium and its claims to solemnity. Faced with this challenge, Degas has teased the image into coherence, rhyming adjacent and distant forms even as he delights in their incongruity. But it is colour that comes to his rescue, just as it did in *Steep Coast*, a work that must surely be seen as a pair with *Landscape*.[146] Few landscapes of this period are more densely or more delicately worked, and few establish a more subtle interplay between forms and sensuous surfaces. By continuing his summery palette from foreground to background, Degas has linked the disparate structures of the scene and brought an improbable unity to both image and picture rectangle. Throughout its structure, a rich daffodil-yellow pervades the vast and spacious panorama, linking priapic rocks with undulating dunes, sunny plains with fecund hillside.

198. Le Pierre d'Ampilly-le-Sec (taken by the author).

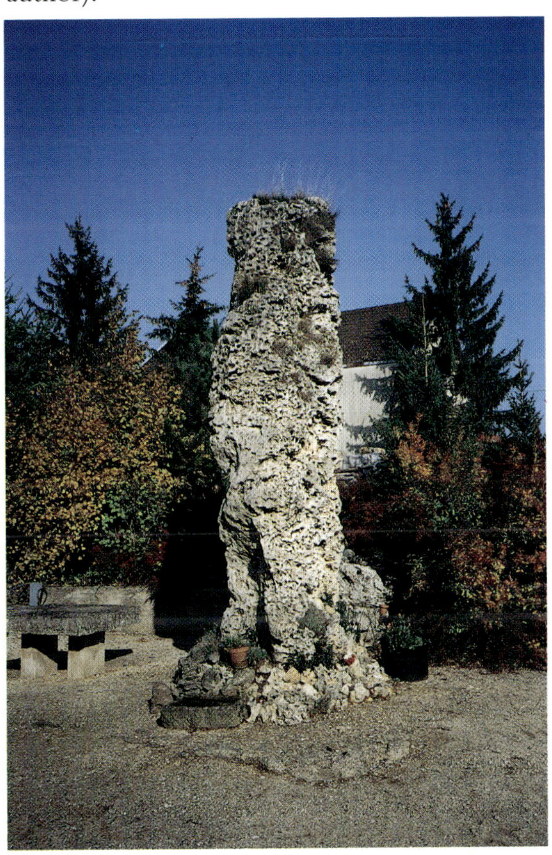

Exceptional in Degas' later *oeuvre*, the allusiveness of *Landscape* again has echoes in the preoccupations of his age and in the less well-known work of his youth. Like most of his peers, Degas had learnt to draw and paint from nude models of both sexes, though his choice of such naked heroes as John the Baptist, David and Goliath, Joseph Bara and the youths of Sparta for his early paintings was less expected.[147] Evidence of an adolescent interest in drawing his own body may be of more relevance here, as is the vexed question of Degas' own sexuality.[148] Historically more immediate are the representations of phallic rocks, standing stones and prehistoric menhirs that were current in Degas' milieu in the 1880s and 1890s. An awareness of such structures, which are found in large numbers in several areas of France, had formed part of the revival of national consciousness in Degas' generation, leading to the publication of the first scholarly studies and the excavation of notable sites. The Côte d'Or, through which Degas and Bartholomé travelled in 1890, was renowned both for its natural rock formations and its ancient monoliths, many of which have a pronounced phallic character.[149] Close to their route, the two artists could have seen such bizarre survivals as the five-metre Pierre d'Ampilly-le-Sec (fig. 198) and perhaps had their attention drawn to others.[150] As with a number of his contemporaries, Degas' receptivity to images of this kind may well have been heightened, paradoxical though it might seem, by his knowledge of Japanese prints. Craggy cliff formations and eroded stone pillars were much admired by Japanese draughtsmen, producing such memorable images as Hiroshige's *Sword-*

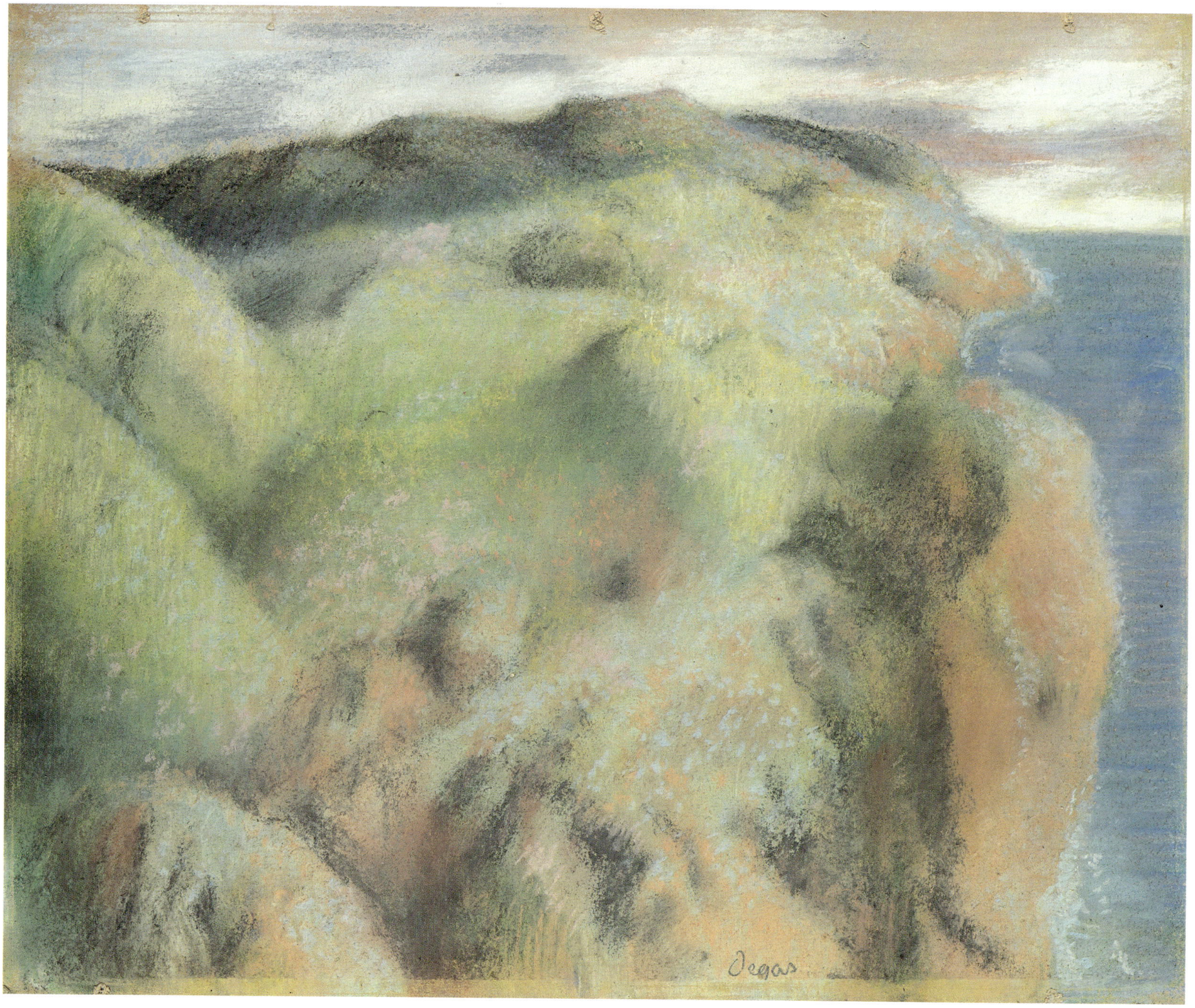

199. *Steep Coast*, *c.*1890–2, pastel, 46 × 54.6 (BR 134), Jan Krugier Gallery.

rocks and his even more suggestive *View of the Bay of Futami*. Monet owned copies of both these prints and clearly had them in mind when making his *Belle-Ile* paintings, while a cliff scene of 1890 by Emile Bernard offers even closer parallels.[151]

It is in the nature of such suggestive, culturally resonant imagery that we should begin to see it everywhere, in places where it is signalled by the artist, in places where it is not, and in the uncertain ground in between. That Degas was intrigued by this speculative hinterland we cannot doubt. Apart from the examples already considered, a number of anecdotes from his later years point to an ironic, almost whimsical approach to form that is at odds with his severe reputation. Several accounts survive of Degas' fascination with found objects,

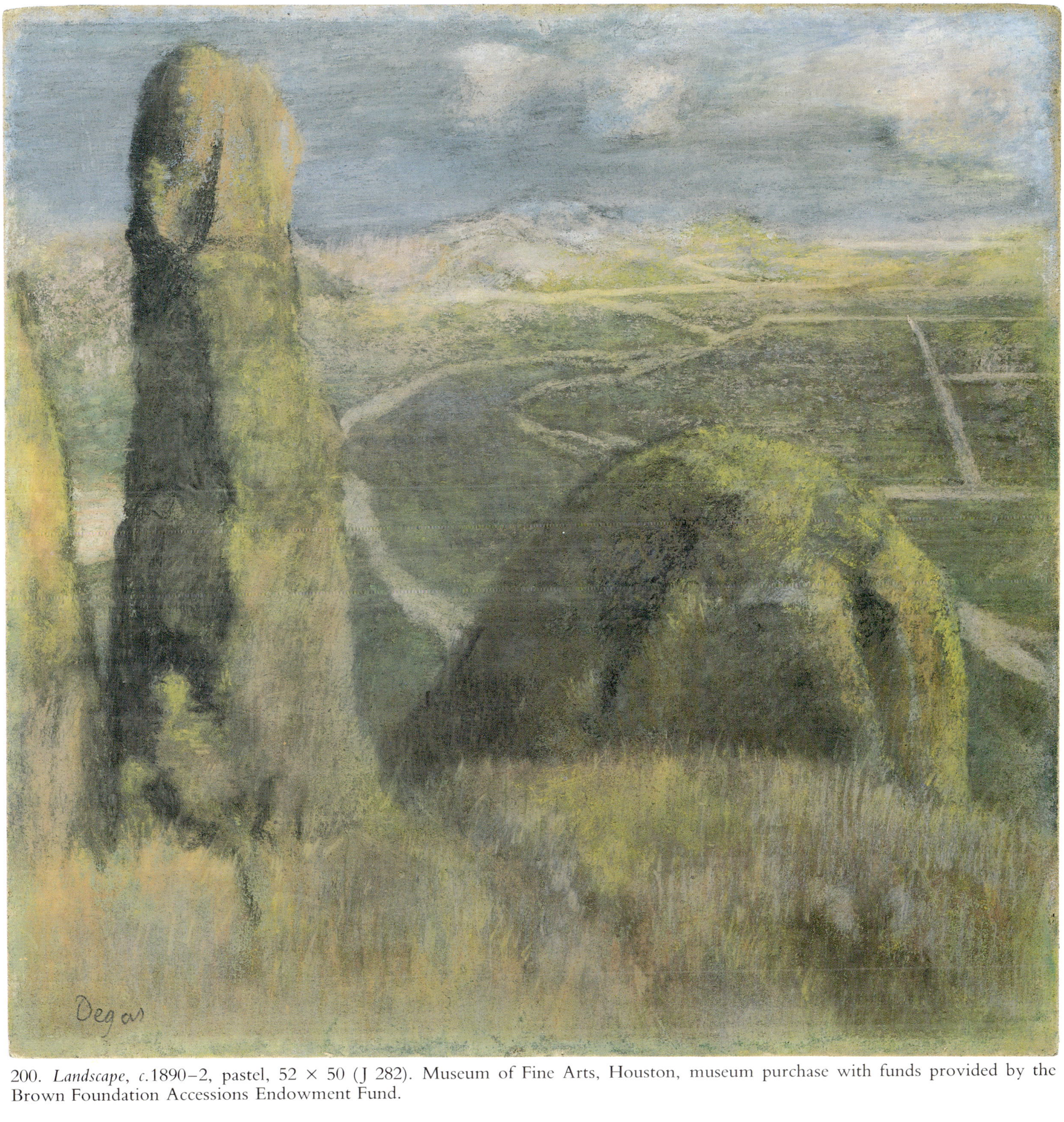

200. *Landscape*, *c.*1890–2, pastel, 52 × 50 (J 282). Museum of Fine Arts, Houston, museum purchase with funds provided by the Brown Foundation Accessions Endowment Fund.

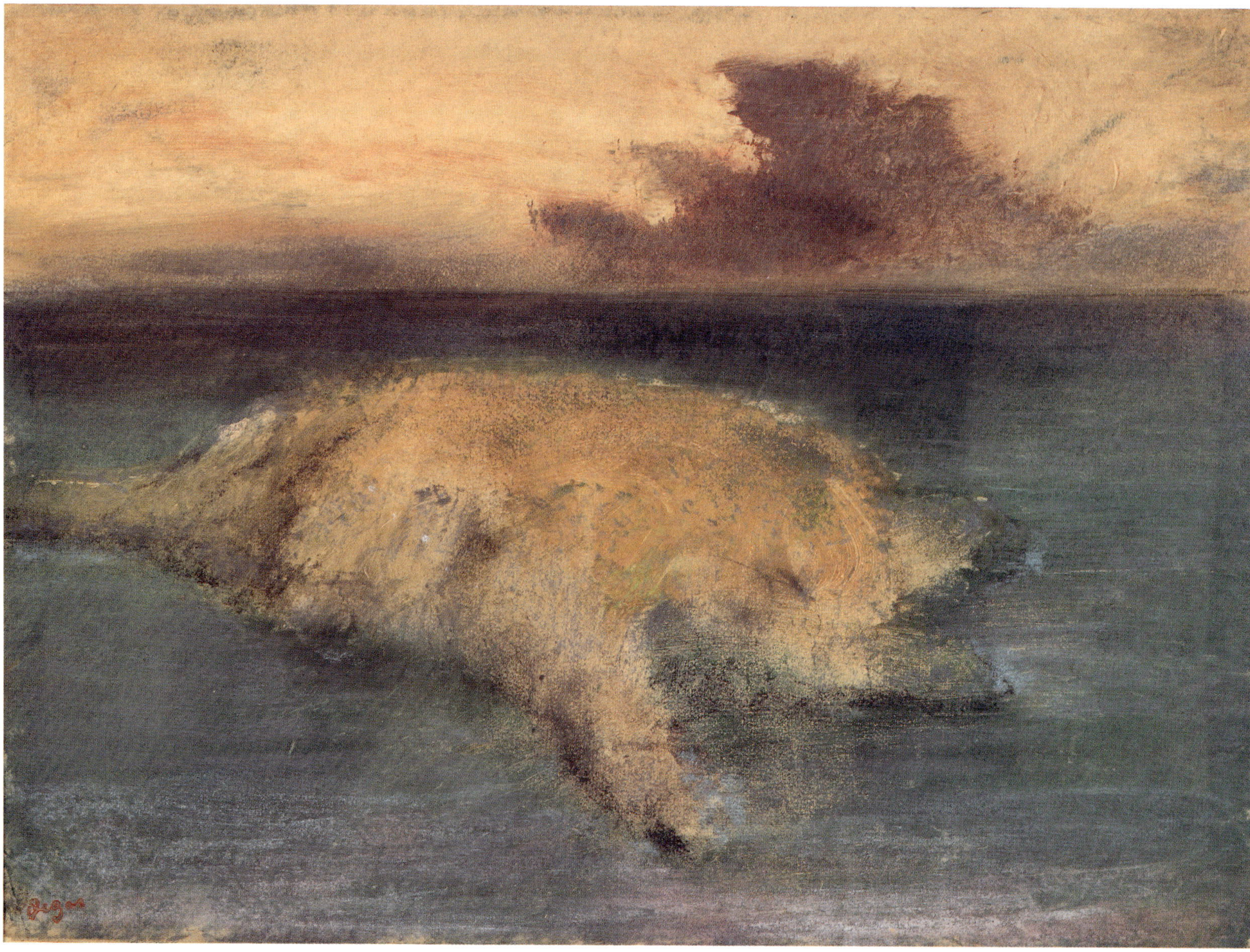

201. *An Island in the Sea*, 1890, monotype and pastel, 30 × 40 (J 311). Charles de Montalembert.

such as stones, coal and crumpled fabric, which would be taken back to his studio and set aside for future transformation.[152] Self-consciously following the precedent of Leonardo and Poussin, Degas would then arrange these humble materials into miniature landscapes or allow them to form random configurations, making 'piled-up boulders' from 'pieces of coke no bigger than a fist', as Paul Valéry put it, and cloudscapes out of handkerchiefs.[153] One piece of stone, retrieved from the street outside his studio while it was under repair, was given the doubly allusive title 'Le Cap de la belle Epaule' and destined to become the basis of a pastel.[154] The outcome is unknown, though a work like *Mountains and Valley* (fig. 194), with its sinuous 'hidden' back and shoulders, may have been evolved in a similar way. Similarly, *Landscape with Rocks* (fig. 146) seems to combine a rock-strewn hillside from the Côte d'Or with a flint-like, or even tooth-like, foreground, suggesting a conflation of several of Degas' sources. A little-known pastel over monotype that was not shown in 1892, *An Island in the Sea* (fig. 201) is equally enigmatic. As a landscape, it appears to recall the islands or rocky outcrops of Brittany or even the Bay of

Naples, seen from above and at a distance. On closer inspection, the central form becomes corporeal, like a tensed animal or a crouching figure, an impression made more haunting by the indigo sea and bruised, angry sky.

How far do such works as *Landscape*, *Steep Coast* and *An Island in the Sea* take us from Diénay, where Bartholomé could recognise in Degas' monotypes 'the places they had gone through, following the gait of the white horse'?[155] By comparison, the prints made during that visit now seem innocent, the late flowering of an Impressionism based on first-hand experience, freshly perceived colour and modest rural encounters. Though Degas rarely planted his easel in the open air, like Monet and Pissarro, and insisted on the liberating, rather than the disabling, functions of memory, those pioneering monotypes related to actual landscapes in a way that was not entirely dissimilar from the work of his colleagues. In contrast, the group of 'imaginary landscapes' included in the 1892 show made a virtue of their remoteness from normality, wittily and irreverently distancing themselves from much current practice. In this sense, the Durand-Ruel exhibition seems like a bravura display of Degas' versatility, and of his fluency in a number of established and topical modes. Between the extremes of *Steep Coast* and a relatively mundane subject like *Autumn Landscape* (fig. 151), the selection of works draws on every aspect of Degas' recent landscape production. His subject-matter embraced mountains and volcanoes, flower gardens and orchards, islands and limb-like causeways; his cognate pairs of prints invoked the 'series' principle and invited comparison with Monet, just as they overturned this principle in some of their juxtapositions; by associating his imagery with memory and the experience of travel, Degas linked certain monotypes with literature and with perceptual theory; his re-workings of Japanese *motifs* were both erudite and abrasively up-to-date; and his technical explorations baffled fellow-artists and critics alike.[156]

Almost every reference to the 1892 monotypes in the art-historical literature has taken for granted that they were a unified, homogeneous set of pictures, made at the same time and for similar reasons. Our study has shown that the reverse was the case, as we have divided the landscapes into geographical and technical groups, and into sequences with differing conceptual implications. We might now go further and suggest that, in addition to displaying Degas' wide-ranging skills, the work in the Durand-Ruel exhibition represented a deliberate critique of the later phases of Impressionism. Certainly, several commentators saw it that way, Arsène Alexandre congratulating Degas on his escape from the 'banalities of Impressionism', and an anonymous colleague noting that 'outdoor research' played no part in his procedures.[157] In certain respects, of course, this response had already become a critical reflex in the late 1880s, as many of Degas' contemporaries re-evaluated their own relationship to the *motif* and came to terms with the complexity of their craft. In another sense, Alexandre's remark was entirely specific. Identifying Degas' show at Durand-Ruel's gallery with the changing fortunes of Impressionism, the critic recognised that it stood as a corrective or rebuke to some of the movement's limitations. Here, the 'banalities of Impressionism' had been replaced by subtle and complex engagement, just as their 'outdoor research' had been overtaken by the dark secrets of the studio. Even when tackling familiar subjects, Degas seemed to insist on their mutability and their subjection to movement and time. Extremes of terrain vied with extremes of sensation, and the boundary between perception and fantasy, so rarely approached by his companions of earlier decades, had been unequivocally crossed.

As Degas' audiences were aware, his colour monotypes offered a dense and seductive range of pictorial possibilities, some recalling the techniques of the past, others linking themselves with the most recondite thought of the new decade. Most prominent in the minds of his younger admirers were the ideals of Symbolism, a movement with which Degas had a complex and much under-researched relationship. Future publications will tease out the affections and animosities, the stylistic sympathies and disjunctions between Degas and his Symbolist colleagues, but the present context allows us to sketch their broad outlines. For the generation of critics that included Alexandre, Mirbeau and Geffroy, the evolution of Degas' work seemed innately sympathetic to their aims, and his recently exhibited pictures appeared receptive to their shifting vocabulary. So different was some of his new imagery, and so changed the language thought appropriate to it, that it was felt necessary to strees its continuity with Degas' previous achievement. Gustave Geffroy, for example, devoted almost a third of his remarkable review to this purpose, explaining that the exhibition 'showed Degas in a new light':

> New, but not unexpected. Degas necessarily remains Degas in front of fields, hills, water, skies. He brings his understanding of the movement and flexibility of bodies to the construction and shaping of the land, to hollowing out ravines and to raising hillocks. He continues to show his perception of harmony by summarising different aspects of nature, just as he disposes his scenes of social life. It is the same eye that sees and the same brain that understands.[158]

Having put his readers at their ease, Geffroy then introduced them to some of the complexity of Degas project, often in language that conveys his familiarity with vanguard thinking. These pictures, he explained, were 'memories of travel', recalled by Degas from 'journeys in the countryside during the months of summer and the months of autumn'.[159] They resulted from 'the passage of man across the scenery of things, and the wish to mark this passage by fixing the forms that so rapidly fade into the distance'.[160] In some of his most sumptuous prose, Geffroy suggested that the landscapes were best understood by analogy, comparing them to richly coloured jewels and carpets, the forms of sleeping women and the wings of exotic insects. Their true subjects, he implied, were 'the beautiful movements and the beautiful repose of matter', as well as the 'green decomposition of advanced civilisations'.[161] Emphasising the prominence of the creative individual as much as the forms of nature, Geffroy concluded: 'A man who is an artist has passed in front of all this, and has brought to life those visions of an instant that, without him, would have remained unknown, born and swallowed up in unconsciousness.'[162]

Geffroy's association of the landscapes with subjectivity, with the passage of time and with the artist's recollection were echoed by other critics and were clearly intended to locate Degas' exhibition in the intellectual climate of the early 1890s. Though not of a theoretical disposition, Degas often found himself in literary, philosophical and even scientific company at this time and reflected some of their interests in his conversation and in the formulations of his art.[163] As Howard Lay first pointed out, many of the issues addressed by Degas' monotypes have specific parallels in the recently published works of both William James and Henri Bergson.[164] Both philosophers argued that experience might be expressed as a stream or continuous flow in time, and both drew attention to the individual's role in selecting and transforming this experience. Bergson's notion of consciousness as a succession of events that 'melt into and permeate one another, without precise outline' had attractive analogies with

210*bis*. Detail of fig. 173.

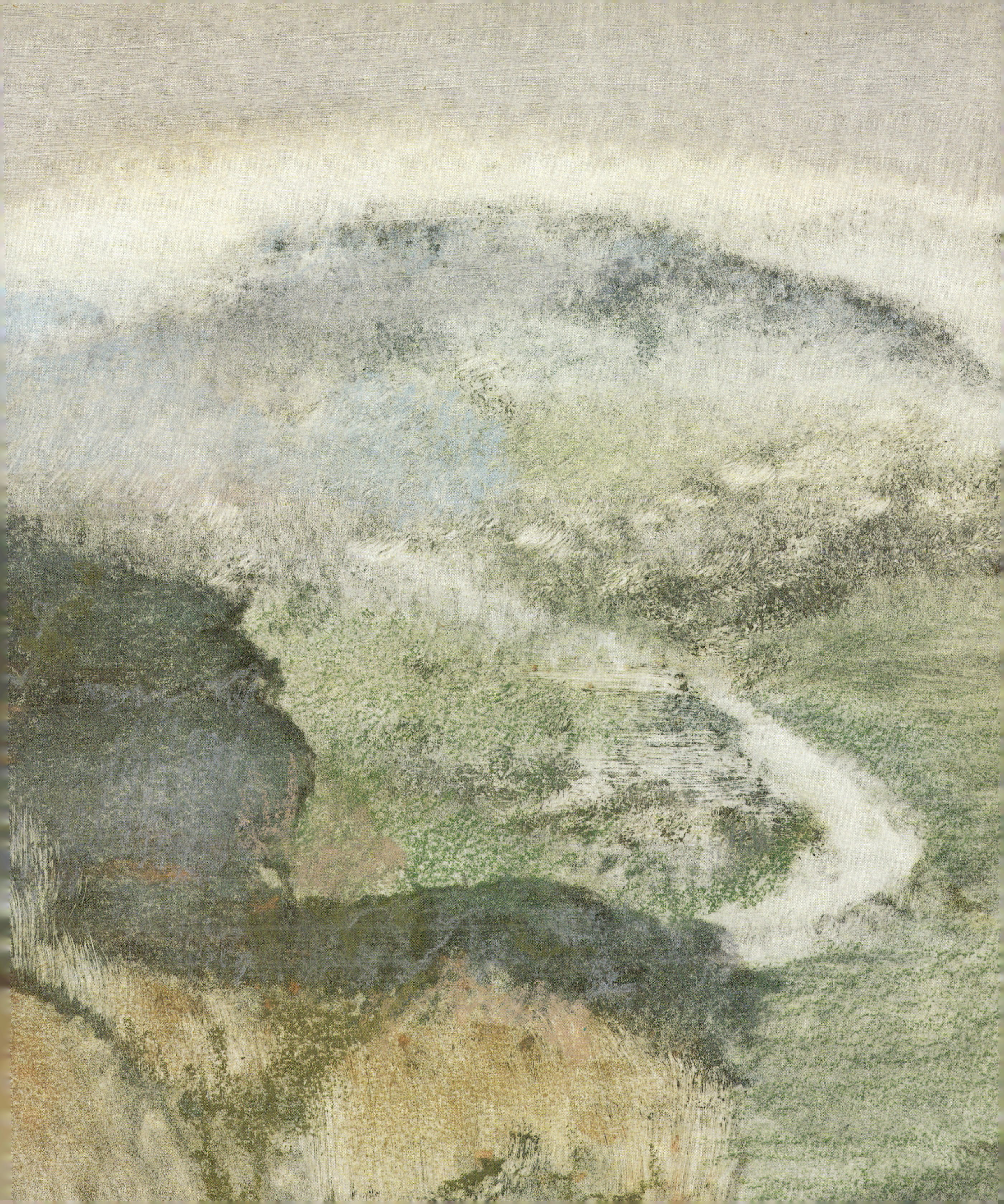

Monet's series paintings and certain of Degas' monotypes, such as the cognate pairs.[165] Equally, his celebration of memory appears sympathetic to Degas' known procedures. According to Bergson, 'matter, as grasped in concrete perception which always occupies a certain duration, is in great part the work of memory', and 'every concrete perception, however short we suppose it, is already a synthesis, made by memory, of an infinity of pure perceptions which succeed each other'.[166]

Our picture of Degas travelling by tilbury through the Côte d'Or, or by train through the Pyrenees, and later synthesising his brief perceptions in a suite of related images, is remarkably consistent with this account. Though there is no certainty that he read Bergson's views, a number of Degas' remarks to his younger colleagues seem to echo their current popularity. Bergson's ambition to 'give up certain habits . . . of perceiving' and to 'find the reality hidden beneath . . . customary images' might have been Degas' own, just as the artist's belief that 'we see what we wish to see' follows that of the philosopher.[167] Paul Valéry, who knew and was influenced by both Degas and Bergson, seems implicitly to acknowledge an affinity between these two heroes of his youth.[168] In his celebrated study of Degas' art, Valéry pondered on the functioning of mind and sight, intelligence and imagination, suggesting that there is 'a kind of structural activity in the eyesight of which habit makes us unaware'.[169] In an even more Bergsonian passage, ostensibly concerned with Degas' attitude to photography, he developed this notion further. Valéry wrote: 'Between the state of vision as mere *patches of colour* and as *things* or *objects*, a whole series of mysterious operations takes place, reducing to order as best it can the incoherence of raw perceptions . . . imposing continuity, connection, and the systems of change which we group under the labels of *space*, *time*, *matter*, and *movement*.'[170]

In the periodical *L'Ermitage*, a critic of the 1892 show went to some lengths to claim Degas for the new subjectivity, welcoming his disdain for anecdote and his delight in transience and the immaterial.[171] *L'Ermitage* had been founded as recently as 1890 and was soon to be dominated by writers of the Symbolist movement, among them the young Paul Valéry. Revealing his own affiliation to the language and imagery of Symbolism, the anonymous and virtually untranslatable critic went on to announce that Degas 'possesses the secret of strange shadows, where the unknown seems to stir, and of certain unknown chiaroscuros, like an astral presence burdened with ghosts, as well as with vague and suggestive colours with which he clouds his figures, so that they loom out of the twilight, pale and haunting like materialised apparitions'.[172] Elsewhere, he notes the 'imaginary tones' and the 'symphonies of muffled sounds' in Degas' landscapes, concluding: 'a subjectivity is reflected in this view of nature. And in front of these transformations, determined by a *self* superb in its tyranny, one must take pity on those laborious reconstructions of physical truth and objective reality.'[173] This curious *mélange* of Bergsonian fugacity and Symbolist individualism was repeated by other reviewers of the same persuasion, though not always in such ornamental language. The principal Symbolist journal, *Mercure de France*, noted 'a series of landscapes by Degas, not studies, but delightfully chimerical scenes, recalled from the imagination'.[174] A number of writers suggested that Degas' pictures were 'Synthetic', recalling not only Bergson's terminology but one of the central precepts of Symbolist theory.[175] Finally, in perhaps the most oblique response to the monotypes, Jean Schmitt urged their affinities with music, in terms that may well have mystified the artist himself.[176]

Like so many of his associations, the links between Degas and the Symbolist movement appear to have been characterised by paradox: on the one hand, he was intimately involved with several of its leading talents, among them Mallarmé and Gauguin, and expressed an active admiration for their art; on the other, he always held aloof from the coteries and the public manifestations of the group, saving his most withering scorn for their extremes of style and behaviour. When Degas mocked the movement's 'young geniuses', when he exploded at their obsession with 'taste', and when he lampooned 'this poetry, this sophistication, and these young men in long frock-coats who talk to women with a lily in their hands', he was attacking the new sensibility at it most attenuated.[177] His opposition becomes more substantial, however, when it is realised that Degas, who was known for his support of young artists, added no pictures by Symbolist painters to his collection.[178] At a time when he was encouraging latter-day Realists and Impressionists like Jeanniot, Forain, Valadon and Braquaval, Degas made no attempt to acquire the works of their Symbolist counterparts; even Eugène Carrière, an artist praised by Degas on a number of occasions, was conspicuous by his absence.[179] Though several commentators have detected parallels between Degas' later style and that of the new generation, substantial links are few and rarely illuminating.[180]

The exception to this rule was, of course, Paul Gauguin, whom Degas had encountered as early as 1879, at the time of the fourth Impressionist exhibition. Their friendship and mutual respect blossomed in the late 1880s, resulting in a period of shared influence and even the exchange of identifiable *motifs* between these two markedly distinct individuals.[181] Degas promoted his young admirer energetically, broadcasting his talents and buying up a substantial collection of Gauguin's wood-block prints, drawings and oil paintings from every stage of his career.[182] Subjects included portraiture and landscape, Tahitian scenes and still lifes, and even Gauguin's copy of Manet's *Olympia*.[183] Some of these works were acquired in the next decade, at sales intended to raise money for the struggling painter, but at least three were bought or exchanged before Gauguin's final departure for Tahiti.[184] Prominent among these was the celebrated canvas of *La Belle Angèle* (Musée d'Orsay, Paris), painted in 1889 and purchased by Degas in 1891, the year preceeding his Durand-Ruel exhibition.[185] Degas' willingness to associate himself with this highly *japoniste* work is characteristic of his brave patronage of the younger artist. Brilliant in colour, audacious in design and dream-like in its juxtaposition of arbitrary forms, *La Belle Angèle* was also one of the most 'Synthetic' of Gauguin's paintings at that date. At the very least, Degas' purchase suggested a modest acknowledgement of Gauguin's recent achievement, at most a willingness to learn from Gauguin's pictorial syntax and apply its lessons to his own language of form.

Degas' significance for Gauguin's early style is well documented and has been analysed in some detail; the opposite case, that of the younger artist's influence on the older, has barely been touched upon.[186] Jean Boggs has pointed to a number of Gauguinesque traits in Degas' landscapes of the later 1890s, but the possibility that Gauguin's example may have radically affected, even initiated, some of the imagery of the 1892 monotypes now presents itself.[187] Given their close association in the late 1880s, it was inevitable that Degas should have encountered Gauguin's current landscape production, in the artist's studio, at the homes of fellow-collectors, or at public exhibitions and sales. In January 1891, for example, he announced at the Halévys' that Gauguin was an artist he 'admired profoundly'; the following month, at the auction sale where he bought *La Belle Angèle*, Degas would have seen about a dozen recent landscapes by

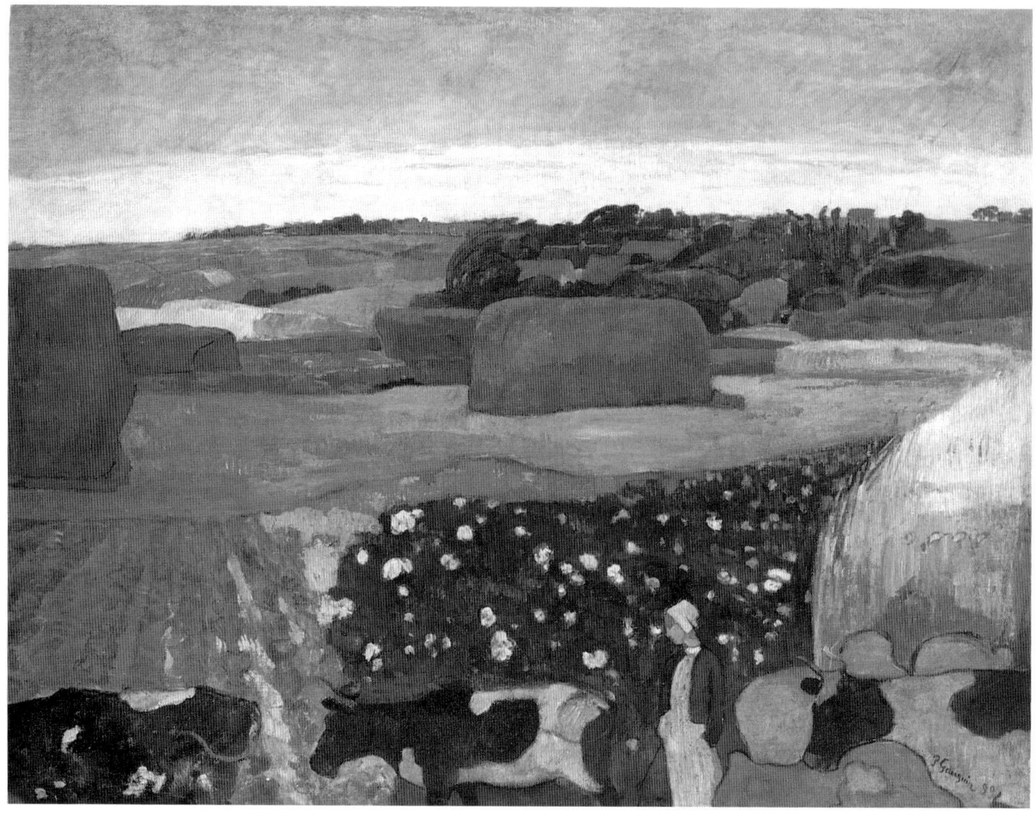

202. Paul Gauguin, *Haystacks in Brittany*, 1890, oil on canvas, 74.3 × 93.6. National Gallery of Art, Washington, D.C., Gift of the W. Averell Harriman Foundation in memory of Marie N. Harriman.

Gauguin, amounting to more than a third of the total works on view.[188] On this and other occasions, Degas would surely have come across the dramatic paintings of Breton scenery completed in 1889 and 1890, such as *Fields by the Sea* (National Gallery of Art, Washington), *Landscape at Le Pouldu* (Nationalmuseum, Stockholm) and *Haystacks in Brittany* (fig. 202). In each of these cases, Gauguin has pushed the horizon to the upper edge of the composition, disposing his coastal forms and rocky inclines in swirling patterns across the canvas, and freely exploring the riches of his palette. Their anticipation of the bold design of Degas' colour monotypes is arresting, and suddenly becomes explicit in the details of individual *motifs*. At least two subjects incorporate the fragmented bodies of cattle in their lower foregrounds, exactly as in Degas' apparently later *Landscape with Cows* (fig. 176), while Gauguin's *Loss of Virginity* (Chrysler Museum, Norfolk, Virginia) of 1890–91, with its ponderously symbolic nude reclining on a rocky promontory, perfectly rehearses the subject of *Steep Coast*. Though these are works in oil on canvas, and though Gauguin's print-making researches lagged behind his mentor's, there is good reason to believe that Degas seized the initiative in his 1892 monotypes, combining his own technical mastery with Gauguin's audacious and occasionally fantastic imagery.

Like Gauguin, Degas was directly involved with a number of leading Symbolist writers, an involvement that reached a peak of significance in the early 1890s. On familiar terms with Heredia, Verhaeren and the young Gide, Degas had the distinction of submitting his own attempts at verse to Stefane Mallarmé and having the finished sonnets admired by Paul Valéry.[189] For all their differences of temperament, Degas and Mallarmé enjoyed a long and fruitful friendship. At various times, Mallarmé commissioned Degas to make an illustration for one of his poems, wrote to the artist in rhyming couplets and posed patiently for one of his most well-known photographs.[190] According to Valéry, Mallarmé also attempted to persuade his friend Henry Roujon, the Superintendant of Fine Arts, to buy one of Degas' pictures for the State, a story that would explain Durand-Ruel's interest in Roujon at the time of the 1892 exhibition.[191] Behind all these incidents, there seems to lie an implicit sympathy between painter and poet, a sympathy which often shows itself in their recorded statements, if not in the forms of their respective creations. At dinner with Berthe Morisot and Mallarmé, Degas declared 'Art is falsehood', adding to his many pronouncements on the need for 'mystery' and 'fantasy' in a work of art at this period, in a way that must have found favour with the company.[192] Conversely, Mallarmé's obsession 'with the notion of an absolute work of imagination', as reported by Valéry, and his belief that a poem should conceal, rather than reveal, its subject, seems strangely applicable to certain of the landscape monotypes.[193] Sharing a delight in the complexity of their craft, a preoccupation with difficulty for its own sake, and a taste for allusion and metaphor, there was much to unite, in Valéry's words, these 'Jansenists of painting and poetry, Degas and Mallarmé'.[194]

It is probably inappropriate to seek a consistent philosophical position, or even a uniform literary taste, in the utterances of a painter, and it is not difficult to find contradictory notions in Degas' letters, aphorisms and documented asides. His art itself is equally various, now marked by precision and rectitude, now grandly ambiguous and wilfully vague. The landscape monotypes produced between 1890 and 1892 could be all of these things, seeming to insist on their diversity as well as their distinction from Degas' previously exhibited work. Far from being an obscure or eccentric event, the Durand-Ruel show was shrewdly timed and widely noticed, announcing to the Parisian art world that the nearly sixty-year-old artist was conversant with, and perhaps a little in advance of, the concerns of his age. Here were exercises in late-Impressionist sensibility, some grouped in Bergsonian sequences that blurred the constraints of time. Here were bravura displays of colour printing, the progeny of the Japanese tradition but already at a questioning distance from it. Some landscapes offered monsters, as fantastic as anything in Gauguin and as formally inventive as a Mallarméan quatrain. On the artist's own testimony, many of their subjects had been prompted by his journeys, by 'looking around vaguely' from trains or consulting the 'paysages imaginaires' of his mind. It was Degas' achievement to bring together such disparate entities, freshly animating the landscape, invigorating current perceptions of nature and giving expression to transience and mobility. Restricted in size and limited in number, these landscapes are nevertheless dense with human and artistic significance. As Barbara Maria Stafford has observed in her monumental study of the representation of travel, by the second half of the nineteenth century an interest in 'physical topography had been replaced with human geography or demography'; in this new order, 'Man assigns nature its character, character is not inherent in nature's aspects', and ultimately we see travel, and implicitly the imagery of travel, 'as a metaphor for art and life'.[195]

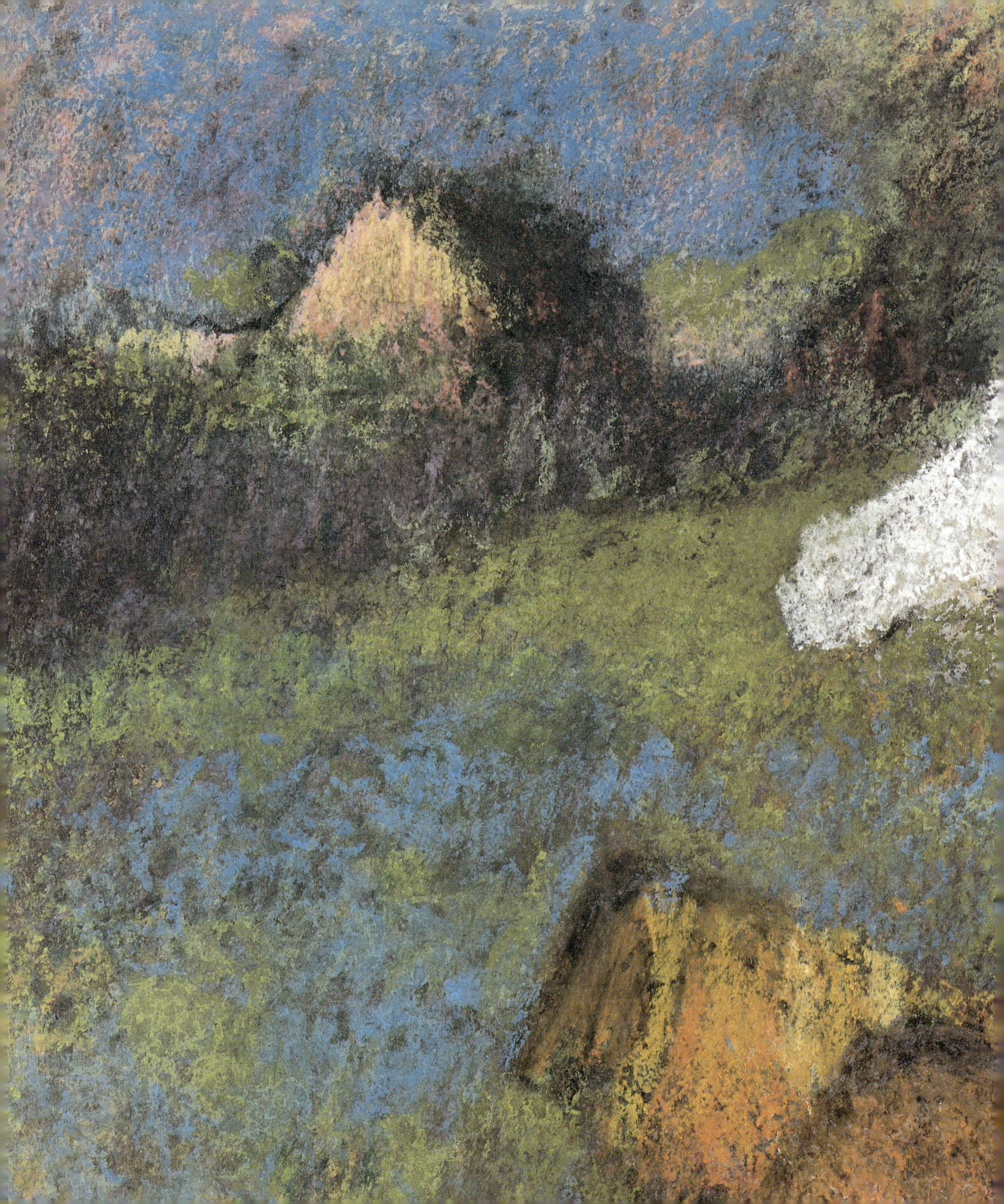

8 After the 1892 Exhibition

'I have just had a little exhibition at Durand-Ruel's . . .'
(Degas, in a letter to his sister)

Soon after the closing of his exhibition of landscape monotypes in November 1892, Degas informed his sister Marguerite, in typically laconic fashion, that it had been received 'rather favourably'.[1] The dozen or so documented responses to the show endorse this modest view, with the solitary and surprising exception of Mary Cassatt, who declared, 'I prefer his landscape when used as background for his figures.'[2] The unfamiliarity of the works, however, seems to have initially discouraged purchasers, and Durand-Ruel took the unusual step of buying almost the entire display for his gallery's stock. Six months after the event, the dealer's ledgers showed that twenty-four pictures, all described simply as 'paysage', had been acquired for the gallery at 1,000 francs each (fig. 204).[3] Soon, Durand-Ruel was taking active steps to place them with collectors both in France and elsewhere. In late 1893, the first of several consignments was dispatched to his recently opened New York premises, and by the end of the following year, almost twenty pictures had crossed the Atlantic.[4] A number of prints appear to have been shown again in Paris in 1894, probably as part of a mixed display, though little is known about the size or significance of this occasion.[5] Meanwhile, the first buyers had come forward: Denman W. Ross of Boston bought *Landscape* (fig. 172) in October 1894 and, three years later, *Autumn Landscape* (fig. 151);[6] at about the same time, Horace and Louisine Havemeyer acquired two, then a further four, landscapes, ranging from the lightly pastellised *Lake and Mountains* (fig. 168) to the richly transformed *Wheatfield and Green Hill* (fig. 174);[7] finally, on 23 March 1896, Tadama Hayashi added four prints to his own collection, bringing the total number of sales from Durand-Ruel's stock to twelve, or approximately half the original group.[8]

By most standards, the 1892 exhibition must be counted a considerable success. It had attracted fellow-artists and friends, writers and representatives of the press, and eventually the patronage of *amateurs* and collectors from near and far. For Degas himself it was something of a mixed blessing. Several of the pictures found permanent homes abroad, and those that remained with Durand-Ruel were apparently not shown again after 1894. As a consequence, the monotypes effectively disappeared from sight, and were remembered partially and inaccurately, if at all, by the artist's first biographers. It was not until Degas' posthumous sales of 1918 and 1919, when the entire contents of his studio were auctioned, that a significant number of landscape prints were again released on to the market. These included works that had been untouched by pastel and perhaps retained for later development, as well as a number of monotypes with extensive pastel re-working.[9] Again, there was a tendency for these challenging images to be kept in obscurity in their new homes, and it was several decades before they became known to the general public. There were honourable and noteworthy exceptions to this pattern. In the first popular illustrated book on

203. Detail of fig. 208.

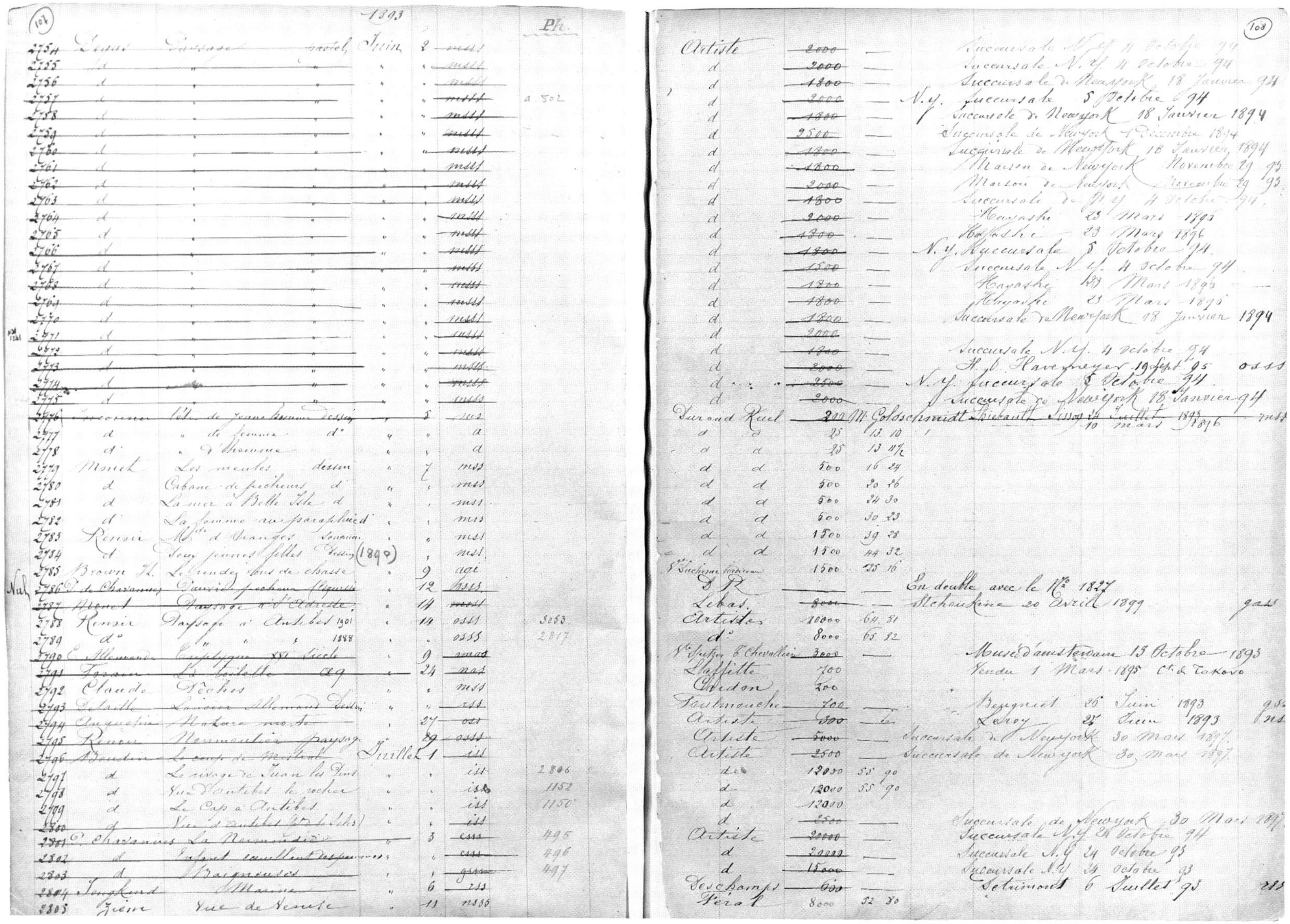

204. Page of Durand-Ruel stockbook for 1893, Archives Durand-Ruel, Paris.

Degas' work, written by George Grappe and published in London and Leipzig in 1909, a black-and-white photograph of *River Banks* (fig. 132) was reproduced among the ballet-dancers, stage scenes and racehorses.[10] Early monographs by both Lemoisne and Lafond made thoughtful reference to the landscapes, and an exhibition at the Galeries Georges Petit in 1924 listed four pastel-over-monotypes in its catalogue.[11]

The progress of Degas' landscapes outside France followed a similarly inconspicuous course. One or two German collectors, such as Max Emden and Hans Werdenbusch, were among the earliest purchasers and the Belvedere Museum in Vienna among the first institutions to acquire prints, the latter becoming the home of Hayashi's *Rocky Coast* after the dealer's death.[12] British taste, as ever, lagged somewhere behind, either through lack of awareness of the works or lack of opportunity to buy them. Despite their generally favourable response to Degas' art, no British critics commented directly on the 1892 show, though Degas' activities as a landscapist were referred to in print.[13] As before, collectors like Arthur Kay, William Burrell and Alexander Reid pursued their acquisitions of pastels and oil paintings by the artist, but it was not until the early twentieth century that the first colour monotype crossed the Channel.[14] This was in 1906, in another of Durand-Ruel's initiatives to open up foreign markets, when *River Banks* (fig. 132) was included in a major London exhibition.[15] Subsequently, the English dealer Percy Moore-Turner added two Degas landscapes to his wide-ranging collection: the gently pastoral *Landscape* (fig. 183) and the more abrasive, nearly abstract *Pathway in a Field* (fig. 134).[16] Moore-Turner provides an intriguing glimpse of progressive British attitudes at this period, and perhaps the first hint of a changing perception of Degas' monotype imagery. He had entered the trade in 1897, working with a number of Parisian dealers before opening the Independent Gallery in London, where he showed uncompromisingly modern pictures by Derain, Friesz and artists of the Bloomsbury circle, among them Vanessa Bell and Duncan Grant.[17] His own taste was catholic, ranging from Gothic Carvings to Old Masters, and from paintings by Corot to drawings by Millet, providing both a sympathetic and an impeccably modernist setting for his two Degas monotypes.[18]

Given the dispersal of the monotypes, it becomes almost impossible to judge their impact on either print-makers or landscapists among Degas' peers. We know that Pissarro, Cassatt, Monet and Boldini saw the exhibition in November 1892, and of the next generation Theodore Robinson and Toulouse-Lautrec were apparently present.[19] As a display of colour printing, it might have been expected to stimulate further research as well as frank emulation, but again the evidence is unclear. A decade or so earlier, Degas had been in the forefront of monotype experimentation, gradually passing on his acquired skills to colleagues like Pissarro, Gauguin and Jeanniot. By the late 1880s, the new medium had become surprisingly widespread, though its use was still largely confined to monochrome inks.[20] With the appearance of the 1892 prints, Degas reasserted his position in the vanguard, not least through his aleatory techniques and his manipulation of a full spectrum of colours, but a number of younger artists were already snapping at his heels. Toulouse-Lautrec made a group of coloured prints at about this time, while a succession of American painters, many of whom had studied in Paris, carried out bravura explorations of the medium.[21] In this context, we need to remember that the majority of monotypes in the Durand-Ruel show were partially or wholly covered in pastel, and seem not to have been identified as prints at first sight by many of their admirers. Even such seasoned technicians as Cassatt and Pissarro described them as pastels, while other observers saw them as watercolours, gouaches and even oil paintings.[22] Today, their mingling of chalky striations with a painterly, yet evidently printed, surface ranks high in our estimate of their achievement, but among Degas' contemporaries, such an obscure and hybrid process made few converts.

In the period immediately after 1892, a scattering of younger artists in Degas' circle began to make landscapes of great simplicity, often using novel print techniques that recalled the qualities of monotype. High horizons and informally geometric compositions were much in evidence, as were stark and rather empty hillsides and rocky coastlines. To some extent, this imagery emerged from a common reservoir of late-Impressionist and Japanese-inspired *motifs*, already familiar from the work of Monet, Gauguin and Degas himself. By this date, however, it had thrown off some of its earlier associations and acquired a maturity of its own. The work of Henri Rivière, client of Tadamasa Hayashi and friend in his later years of Degas, is a case in point.[23] Unashamedly *japoniste* in such series as *Thirty-six Views of the Eiffel Tower*, in the 1890s Rivière became a master colour-printer, producing highly disciplined lithographs and

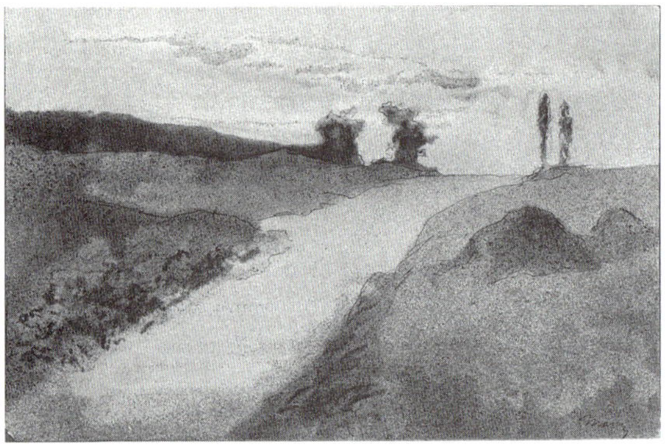

205. Charles Maurin, *Landscape*, *c.*1893, vaporiser watercolour, 31.7 × 48. The Jane Voorhees Zimmerli Art Museum, Rutgers University, New Jersey, Given in memory of Doris E. Brown (1914–1984), the *Home News* art writer, by the *Home News*.

woodcuts of Paris and the Breton landscape. Like Degas, he favoured plunging cliff-tops and suggestive boulders, startling ranges of colour and an austere sense of pattern. Though always more descriptive, some of Rivière's subjects bring Degas strongly to mind and suggest, at the very least, a shared source of inspiration.[24] A less well-known practitioner, Charles Maurin, had even stronger technical affinities with Degas, as well as with his vocabulary of forms. Maurin exhibited at Durand-Ruel's gallery in 1892 with the Société des peintres-graveurs français, shortly before he perfected his 'vaporiser' painting procedure. Analagous to his friend Lautrec's 'spatter' process or to the modern air-brush, Maurin's 'vaporiser' allowed him to build up areas of colour by spraying over prepared masks or silhouettes. In his *Landscape* (fig. 205), made around 1893, he superimposed golds, pinks and purples in successive sprayings, layering his colours and improvising his effects in a way that recalls Degas' studio antics. Even the subject, with its pale road and narrow strip of evening sky, echoes such prints as *Landscape in the Mountains* (fig. 136) and *A Wooded Landscape* (fig. 147), and it is no surprise to find that Degas admired Maurin's work enthusiastically.[25] Less significant as a print-maker, Eugène Carrière produced a number of landscape paintings in the immediate aftermath of Degas' 1892 exhibition which point to a keen admiration for his example. Committed as he was to monochrome, Carrière disregarded the chromatic originality of Degas' prints, but responded instinctively to their serpentine forms, freely brushed tones and elemental vastness. Months after the Durand-Ruel show, Carrière travelled to Brittany, where he produced his monotype-like *Landscape Dedicated to Mme Gabriel Séailles*, painted in oil on board on exactly the scale of certain of Degas' prints. In subsequent years, he worked in Bagnoles-de-l'Orne, Pau in the Pyrenees, and Saint-Valéry-sur-Somme, virtually retracing the steps of his friend and mentor.[26]

206. *Dancers in Salmon-Pink Skirts*, *c.*1897, pastel, 89 × 65 (L 1281). Private collection, photo courtesy Sotheby's.

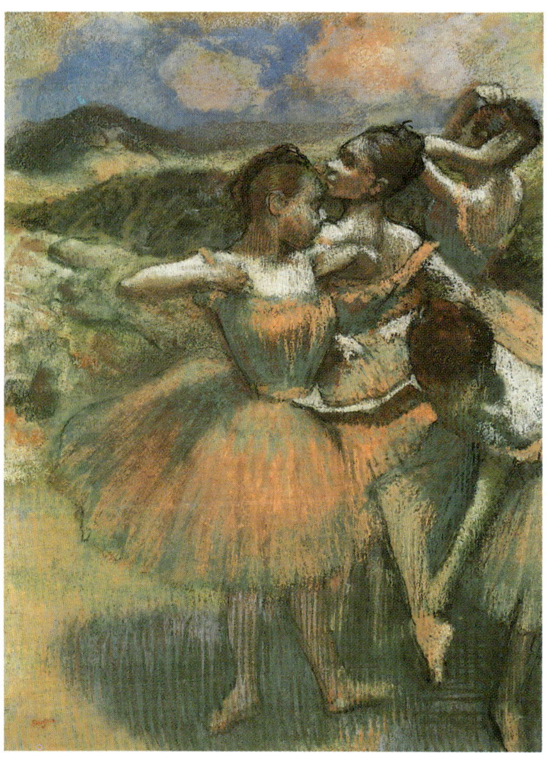

Ultimately, the most significant impact of Degas' landscape monotypes may have been on Degas himself. In no other medium had he luxuriated in colour so freely, allowing paint to flow across his picture surface and mingle with brightly tinted dabbings, smears and thumb-prints. Adding layers of pastel, Degas was able to intensify his hues and heighten his contrasts, blurring areas of texture or conjuring up real and imaginary forms. This sequence of events, which begins with colour and progresses toward drawing and structure, was the converse of the *Ingriste* tradition and of the very axioms that Degas continued to recite. Bizarrely, it was during these years that he claimed, 'I have always tried to urge my colleagues to seek for new combinations along the path of draughtsmanship, which I consider a more fruitful field than that of colour. But they wouldn't listen to me and have gone the other way.'[27] Disregarding his own advice, Degas rooted his monotypes in colour, both practically and imaginatively. Some of them seem to be celebrations of a particular hue, or of the collisions of complementaries or startling new pigments, with draughtsmanship invoked only at the last moment to clarify scale and local incident. Others engage with ambiguity, dissolving contours and flattening perspectives in the most historically treasonable manner. In this sense, they offered a profound challenge to Degas' working practice, not only in his landscapes but in the entire range of his technical and thematic engagement. After forty years of loyalty to his training, drawing seemed to have lost its foothold, and the delights and expressive possibilities of unbridled colour awaited him.

As we now know, Degas was too committed to line and to his own past to renege on his draughtsmanship completely, but his new confidence with colour soon made itself felt. The dance compositions of the mid-1890s, for example,

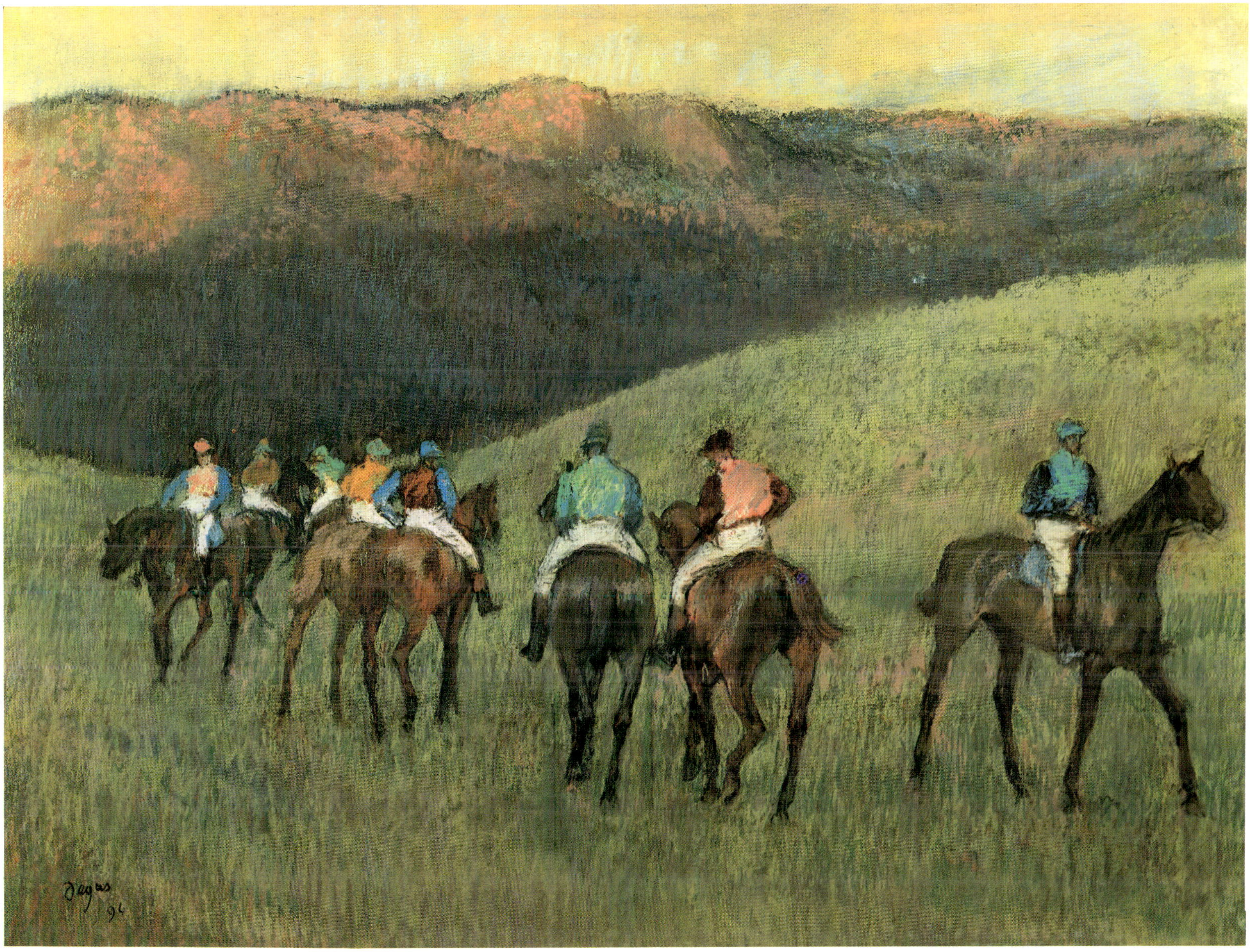

207. *Racehorses in a Landscape*, 1894, pastel, 48.9 × 62.8 (L 1145). Fundación Colleción Thyssen-Bornemisza, Madrid.

were often predicated upon a single dominant hue, perhaps juxtaposed with its complementary, against which the artist's drawing had to compete for survival. Titles such as *Dancers, Pink and Green* and *Blue Dancers* tell their own story, even where they were contrived by the artist's successors.[28] In the pastel *Dancers with Salmon-Pink Skirts* (fig. 206), the indebtedness of these works to the colour monotypes is almost explicit, both in its surface facture and its décor. The clarion call of the tutus is chromatically dominant, echoing through flesh tones and background, and finding its answer in the cooler foreground shadows. Streaks of colour inflect the surface, allowing the tint of the paper and the earlier stages of the pastel to break through, and subtly recalling the depth and transparency of the landscape prints. Finally, a mysterious volcanic hillside looms overall, its ruddy hues harmonising with the warmth of the scene and recalling both Degas' *Vesuvius* (fig. 181) and Hokusai's *Mount Fuji* (fig. 180).

Resonant and sun-filled landscapes were frequently used as settings in the dance pictures of this period, in contrast to their disappearance from Degas' remaining equestrian scenes. A spectacular exception is the pastel *Racehorses in a Landscape* (fig. 207), dated 1894 by the artist, which belongs to the immediate progeny of the Durand-Ruel exhibition.[29] Here, the voluptuous forms of valley and hillside evoke the anthropomorphic dualism of *Steep Coast* (fig. 199) and *Mountains and Valley* (fig. 194), reducing jockeys and racehorses to toy-like miniatures on the back of some monstrous giantess. Far-fetched though this may seem, Degas himself seems to urge the comparison with certain of his monotypes. As in many of these works, the distant mountain-tops have been raised toward the upper edge of the picture, allowing the artist to bathe the horizon in the fiery hues of evening. Speckling and hatching his surfaces with layer upon layer of pastel, Degas has then built up a sensuous crust of colour, granular on the mountains, softer and more down-like in the turf. The landscape itself is remarkably simple, its rhythmic curves recalling such works as *Wheatfield and Green Hill* (fig. 174) and its distant peaks reminiscent of *Lake and Mountains* (fig. 168). Historically, both these prints have the strongest association with *Racehorses in a Landscape*. The latter was bought by Horace Havemeyer from Durand-Ruel in 1895, at precisely the time the Havemeyers were acquiring their formidable group of landscape monotypes.[30] Both *Wheatfield and Green Hill* and the bronze-tinted, alpine *Lake and Mountains* were included in this purchase, reflecting a continuity of taste between monotypes and equestrian scene, as well as an implicit association of their pictorial ambitions.[31]

In practical terms, the landscape monotypes continued to reverberate throughout Degas' studio practice. Always fascinated by the alchemy of the studio and the dialogue between his unorthodox materials, the artist embarked on an exploration of colour that was to preoccupy him until the early twentieth century. Alongside print-making and pastel, Degas applied some of the lessons of his monotypes to the practice of oil painting, spreading brilliant washes of colour over large canvases and building up streaks and scumbles of later brushwork.[32] Like the monotype procedure itself, this departure ran parallel to an interest in Old Master techniques, which was to become one of the obsessions of Degas' old age. Citing Mantegna and Veronese, Titian and Delacroix, Degas would insist that a painting was made in 'a series of operations', each layer of colour leading to the next and each gesture of the hand contributing to the whole.[33] Perhaps from the same source, and again finding confirmation in his print-making, Degas also grew bold in his use of fingers and thumbs.[34] Just as Titian had worked on his later canvases with hands as much as brushes, and Degas had transformed thumb-prints into monotype landscapes, so he now began to attack his oil paintings more directly. In some pictures, notably a pair of interior scenes painted at Ménil-Hubert in 1892, restricted areas are developed in this way, but in a series of major canvases of nudes, ballet-dancers and landscapes, virtually the entire image was built up from the repetitive, disc-like marks of Degas' finger-tips.[35] So entranced was the artist by his new process, that he re-worked a number of earlier paintings, obliterating murky detail in sudden blazes of colour and causing confusion amongst historians.[36] Many of the pictures in question are undated, but there are several reasons for locating the new technique in the period after the first monotypes, and none for placing it earlier.[37]

Colour, exploratory mark-making and the suggestiveness of landscape all come together in one of the finest series of Degas' late career, the *Russian Dancers*. Some twenty charcoal drawings and pastels show a group of exotically

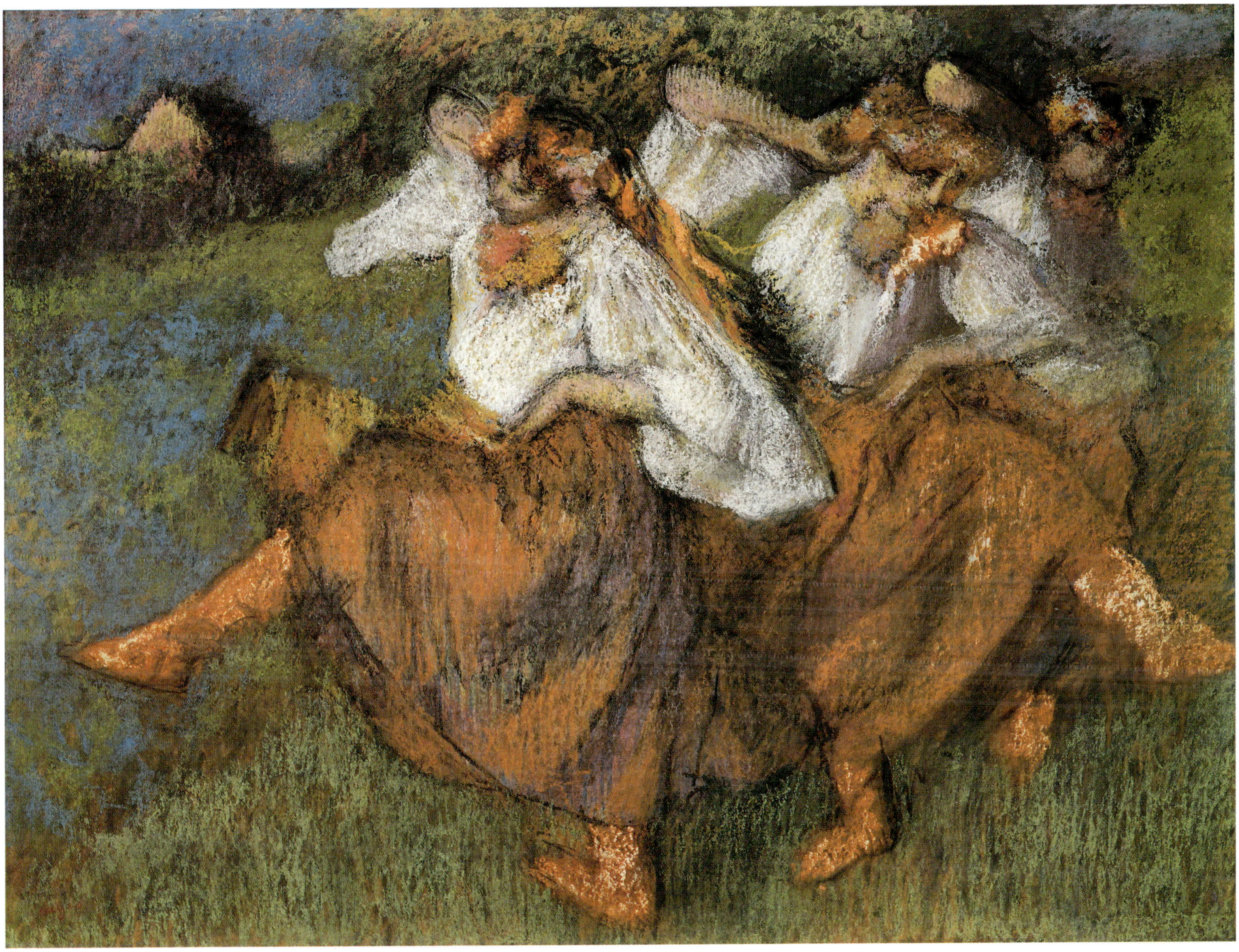

208. *Russian Dancers*, 1899, pastel, 62 × 45.7 (L 1184). Private collection.

clad women in the open air, their orange boots and garlanded hair like flames and glowing coals in the cool pasture.[38] Amongst the most majestic, *Russian Dancers* (fig. 208) reveals the sheer intensity of Degas' procedure. The girls' skirts, for example, were originally drawn over an outline of their legs, and a palette of blues, purples and violets used to tint the fabric. On top of this, further charcoal lines were added, then vigorous strokes of orange-brown to enrich the highlights. Throughout the composition, Degas' moved from line to colour, then colour to line, exhausting his repertoire of hatchings, spirals and flourishes of chalky pigment. In the less finished drawings, it is clear that Degas introduced colour at an early stage, while in other variants the dancers wear lilac, gold, viridian or sky-blue, as if to run the gamut of available hues. Degas himself was proud of this achievement, signing and selling a number of the pictures and describing the still-unfinished works to Julie Manet in 1899 as 'veritable orgies of colour'.[39] Most remarkable in *Russian Dancers* is the highly

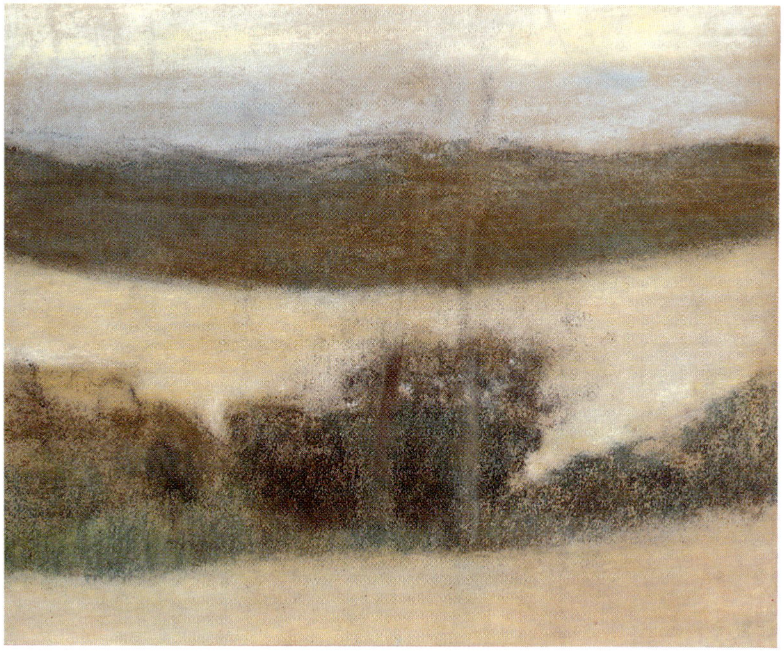

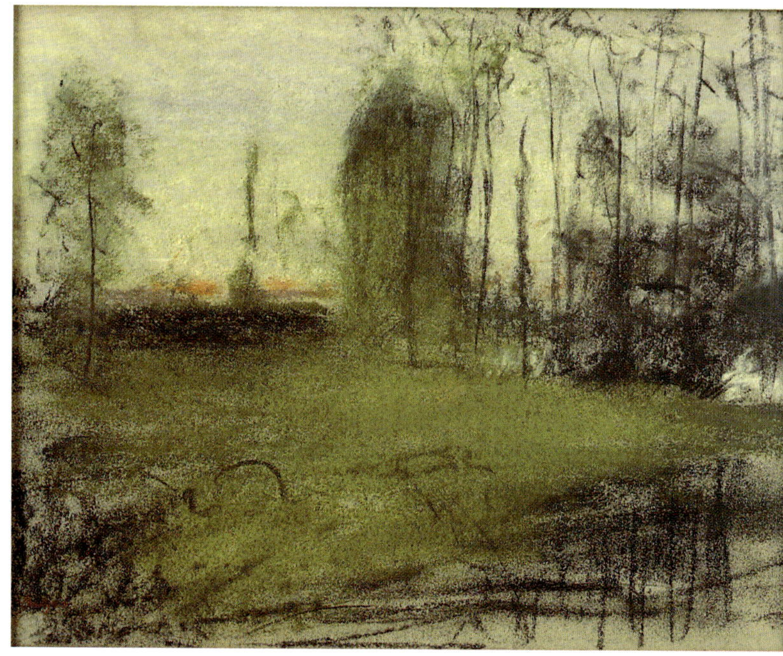

209. *Landscape*, *c.*1893, pastel, 44 × 53 (L 1064). Private collection, photo courtesy Sotheby's.

210. *Meadow beside the Water*, *c.*1893–5, pastel, 26 × 31 (L 282). Private collection.

particularised background, where a distant cottage and a field of blue flowers bring the monotype *The Field of Flax* (fig. 175) vividly to mind.[40] Though technically distinct, it is not too fanciful to see these pastels as grand, latter-day monotypes into which the artist's favourite subject, the female dancer, has mistakenly but magically wandered.

True to past form, and despite the 'rather favourable' reception given to his exhibition of landscape monotypes, Degas did not follow this event with further exercises in the same manner. One or two undated pastels suggest that he may have experimented with similar forms and subjects, while omitting the distinctive printed underlayer of the monotype process. The austerely striated *Landscape* (fig. 209), for example, has all the formal simplicity of the earlier works, though its wintery colouring lacks their many-layered intensity. A pastel dated to the 1870s by Lemoisne, *Meadow beside the Water* (fig. 210) may well be another such venture. Its impetuous charcoal strokes and confident design seem consistent with the artist's maturity, and its brooding, crepuscular tones recall a number of the exhibited monotypes. The site depicted, however, and the circumstances of its execution, remain a mystery, while its vigorous linearity is more reminiscent of Degas' current ballet studies than the 1892 prints. Distinctive as technical essays, these works stand as isolated exceptions, and it was not until the second half of the 1890s that Degas returned whole-heartedly to the landscape. This was in the series of Saint-Valéry-sur-Somme townscapes, where the artist abandoned the precedent of more than four decades, adopting oil paint as his principal medium for a full-scale landscape cycle.

During the intervening period, Degas' relationship with his surroundings returned to its former routines, based on travel, rest-cures and occasional rural reflection. The punishing journeys continued unabated, now overshadowed by illness and the deaths of family and friends. In 1893, he went to Interlaken to be with his sister and her sick husband, and in the following year spent two weeks with the dying Paul Valpinçon, his former host at Ménil-Hubert.[41] Degas' own indifferent health took him to the spa resorts of Cauterets, in the Pyrenees, and Mont-Dore, near Clermont-Ferrand, where Millet had once worked. Some

211. Detail of fig. 207.

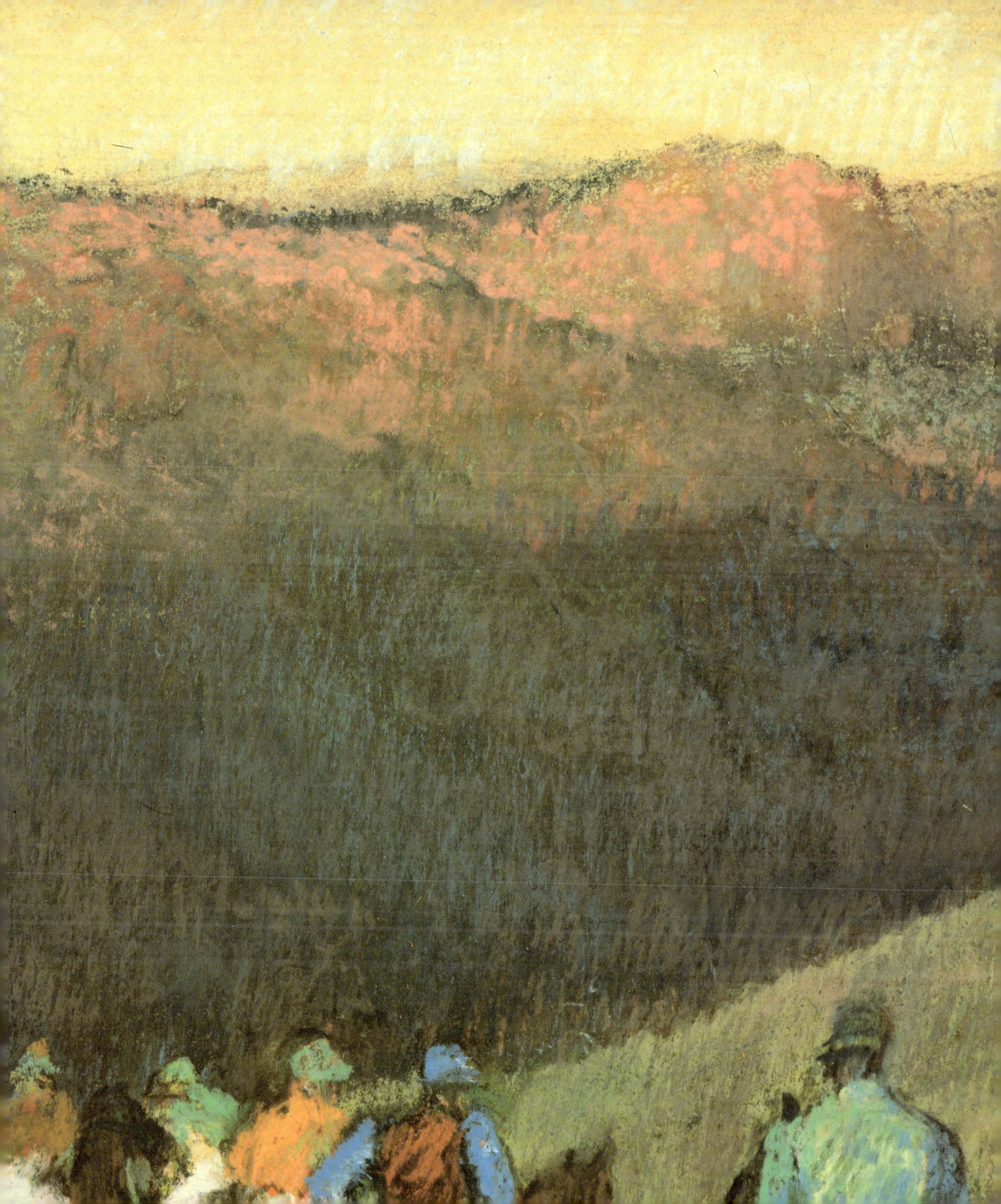

excursions were to the homes of professional colleagues and recalled their former moments of glory. Returning from Switzerland in the summer of 1893, where he wrote, 'It is impossible for me to live far away and not to work', Degas met up again with Bartholomé and made a nostalgic return to the Côte d'Or, to stay with the Jeanniots.[42] The importance of this connection is underscored by a later letter from Jeanniot, written in 1898. Previously unpublished, the note records the imminent arrival of Degas at Diénay, though the outcome of this sojourn is not known.[43] Other expeditions were made to Carpentras, to attend the funeral of Delacroix's pupil, Evariste de Valernes;[44] to Montauban, with Bartholomé again, to enjoy the Ingres Museum;[45] and to Saint-Valéry on the Normandy coast, where Degas' brother, René, had begun to take holidays with his family.[46]

All these journeys would have been taken principally by train, yet none revived in Degas that fascination with glimpses of the landscape, or with his 'states of eyes', that had prompted the 1892 monotypes. His letters, on the other hand, record the artist's continuing concern for his eyesight, as well as the strange contradictions that his disability generated. While planning a trip to Montauban to study the Ingres drawings, he had written, 'Everything is long for a blind man, who wants to pretend that he can see', though he had also announced, months earlier, 'I cannot leave this filthy studio, to which love of glory binds me.'[47] Out of this confusion of hope and physical extremity, another of the most surprising obsessions of his late years was to appear, at some date between 1894 and 1895: Degas' passion for photography.[48] Combining his love for experiment and technical innovation with a lifelong devotion to portraiture; his delight in travel and social exchange with his 'passion for black-and-white'; and his engagement with visual modes in all their complexity, photography became the preoccupation, almost the rage, of the mid-decade. Since his youth, Degas had collected photographs and used them occasionally as source material for his pictures, though the extent of his dependence on their imagery is still hotly debated.[49] What is certain is that his own activities with a camera were confined to the last years of the century, and that Degas' photographs demonstrated, in most known cases, an oblique rather than a direct relationship with his other works of art.

The majority of Degas' fifty or so surviving photographs are studies of friends, though there are documentary records of lost prints of various kinds.[50] Made at a time when the portrait had virtually disappeared from his repertoire as a painter, the photographs of assorted Halévys, Lerolles, Blanches and Valpinçons vary from the orthodox and the symmetrical to the utterly bizarre. Though most were taken indoors, one sequence of prints was devoted to events in the countryside, when Degas and his hosts danced and pirouetted on the terrace outside the château at Ménil-Hubert.[51] Even more inventive are a group of night-time portraits, in which the artist posed members of the Halévy family in the gloom and, in certain cases, made a second and differently angled exposure on the same plate.[52] In such works, phantom limbs and figures emerge from the shadows and commonplace forms take on monstrous significance. Separated from his exhibited landscapes by only two or three years, these pictures recall the anthropomorphism of *Steep Coast* and the associated *Landscape*, as well as Degas' brief flirtation with Symbolism. Other photographs strengthen this conjecture, and suggest further links with the 1892 monotypes. Studies of Bartholomé and his works of sculpture return us to the Diénay visit, itself a much-photographed event that brought Degas into contact with the pioneer photographer, Charles de Meixmoron.[53] Portraits of Mallarmé and

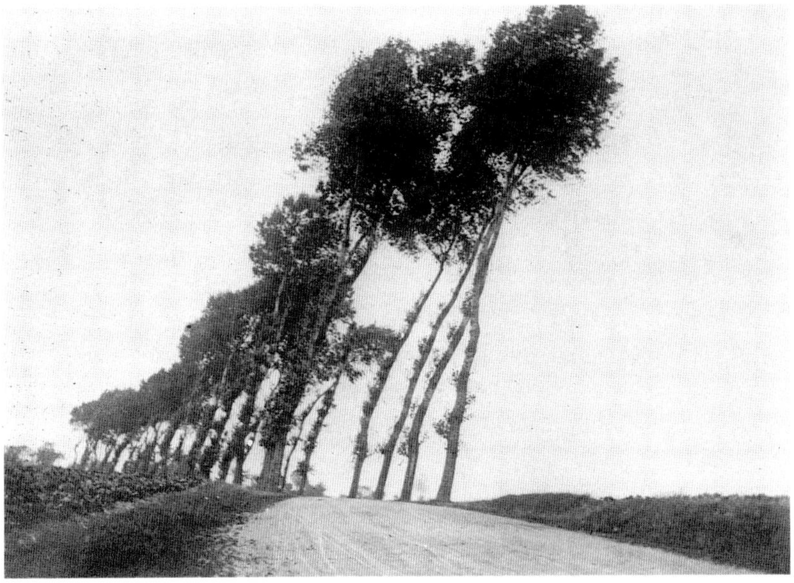

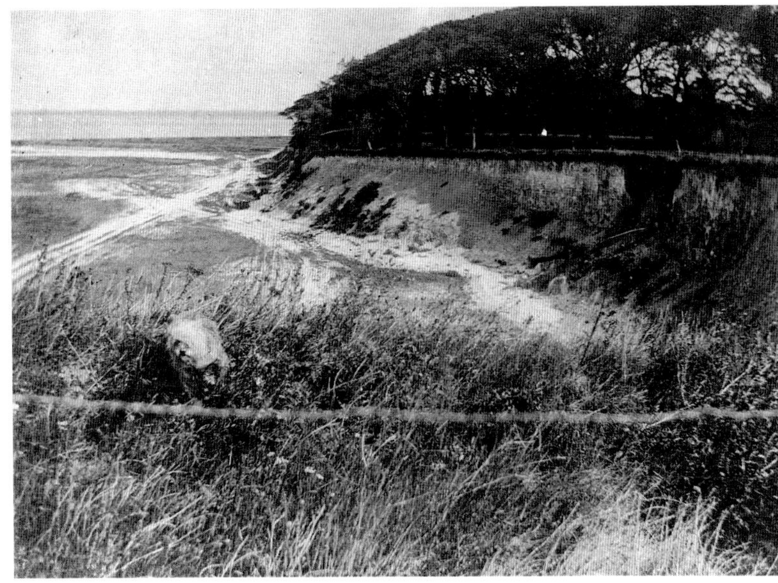

212. *Trees beside a Road*, *c.*1896–8, photograph. Fogg Art Museum, Harvard University, Cambridge, Mass., Gift of Paul J. Sachs. Transferred from the Fine Arts Library.

213. *Cliffs*, *c.*1896–8, photograph. Fogg Art Museum, Harvard University, Cambridge, Mass., Gift of Paul J. Sachs. Transferred from the Fine Arts Library.

Verhaeren remind us of the literary response to the 'paysages imaginaires', and of a reference in a Mallarmé stanza to a Degas photograph.[54] Even a little-known attempt at this period to photograph Whistler, an honorary Symbolist and landscape painter of long acquaintance, seems consistent with Degas' project.[55]

Several contemporary accounts tell us that, during his frenzy for *l'oeil Kodak*, Degas himself made a number of photographs of the landscape. Writing from Mont-Dore in 1895, on a rest-cure that seems to have been distinguished by frantic activity, the artist noted: 'In the evenings I digest and take photographs in the twilight.'[56] Other stories recount his attempts to photograph the moon and make studies of shadows falling on walls, though none of the resulting prints has been traced.[57] Most tantalising of all is a claim by Marcel Guérin, that in Degas' studio 'boxes were found [with] enlargements of photographs of the surroundings of Saint-Valéry, which he had certainly developed himself and which he used for his landscapes, some of them bearing a striking resemblance to the photographs'.[58] No corresponding quantities of prints have ever come to light, though a pair of photographs in the Fogg Art Museum has been traditionally associated with this group.[59] One of these, *Trees beside a Road* (fig. 212), is a strikingly composed but rather bleak confection of horizontals and rising curves, whose site is too generalised to be identified. The other, *Cliffs* (fig. 213), though more particularised, has proved equally difficult to locate in the area around Saint-Valéry and remains similarly enigmatic. Both pictures, on the other hand, have that austerity of composition and resistance to the picturesque, as well as an almost perverse lack of human interest, that has characterised Degas' landscape *oeuvre* from its beginnings. At odds with Guérin's claim, neither of these photographs shows 'a striking resemblance' to the known paintings of Saint-Valéry, though the rhythmic, spindly line of poplars in *Trees beside a Road* has something in common with the trees in *Saint-Valéry-sur-Somme* (fig. 229).

Altogether better documented is another of Degas' obsessive pursuits of the 1890s, that of collecting the work of others. By this stage in his career, he enjoyed a considerable following and was able to command high prices for the works he released on to the market. The response to his Durand-Ruel exhibition is indicative of the new situation. The landscape monotypes were small, based on unfamiliar or challenging subjects, and executed on paper, yet Degas received 1,000 francs for each picture, more than half of which were soon sold. By contrast, Pissarro had reacted with astonishment the previous year when he found that Monet could sell full-size canvases in America for between 4,000 and 6,000 francs.[60] Jeanne Raunay has described Degas' casual way with money and his scorn for those who refused to spend it.[61] As his prices climbed, and as admirers queued up for his 'articles', Degas began to collect in earnest, frequenting the dealers, bidding at auctions and pursuing his latest acquisition with the same passion he brought to print-making and photography. He accumulated literally dozens of works by the twin idols of his youth, Ingres and Delacroix, including folders full of drawings, and paintings both large and small.[62] Among his contemporaries, he tended to exchange or buy a single representative work, though exceptions were made in the case of Manet, with eight canvases, and Gauguin, with ten.[63] Prints, pastels and drawings were bought in abundance, indulging a lifetime's love of draughtsmanship and soon threatening to swamp his apartment. Recognising his addictive habit, Degas showed Daniel Halévy his latest purchases in December 1895: 'Here is my new van Gogh, and my Cézanne: I buy! I buy! I can no longer stop myself!'[64]

There is no direct correlation between Degas' tastes as a collector and his thematic concerns as an artist. Known as 'the painter of dancers', Degas did not cover his walls with pictures of the ballet, nor did he show a preference for studies of the nude, his other definitive *motif*. His acquisitions were catholic and sometimes quixotic, ranging from a battle scene by Delacroix to a *Jupiter* by Ingres, a still life by Manet and a portrait by Renoir, an interior by Jeanniot and a study of children by Bartholomé.[65] Part of this taste, as we have now learned, was a marked responsiveness to the landscape, and it comes as no surprise to find landscape painting as a persistent, though by no means dominant, feature of Degas' collection. True to his youthful enthusiasms, Degas bought no less than seven oils by Corot, notably the superb *Roman Campagna, with the Claudian Aqueduct* (fig. 9) acquired in 1899. His holdings of Delacroix included one of that artist's very few landscape oils, *Landscape, Sunset: Champrosay*, as well as numerous watercolours and drawings of North African and French provincial subjects. Less surprisingly, several of Degas' contemporaries were represented in their capacity as landscapists, though some of the finest practitioners of the genre, such as van Gogh and Cézanne, appear as exponents of the still life or figure. Certain purchases seem to recall Degas' own début as a landscape painter. A fine set of Whistler's *Thames* etchings brings to mind the artistic climate of the 1860s, as does a group of watercolours and pastels by Boudin, including the dramatic *Seashore in Normandy* (fig. 86). Works by Pissarro and Sisley continue this pattern, while the handsome *In a Villa at the Seaside* (Norton Simon Museum, Pasadena) by Berthe Morisot, reminds us of Degas' own visit to the Normandy coast in 1869.

Apart from this element of retrospection, what do Degas' acquisitions tell us about his engagement with the landscape in the 1890s? After his early patronage of Gauguin, Degas continued to buy or exchange works by the Tahitian-based painter, accumulating more than twenty pictures in a diversity of media.[66] His choice of subjects was equally varied, embracing figure studies and still life, outdoor scenes and pure landscapes, amongst them *Martinique Landscape* and *Tahitian, Landscape*.[67] Undaunted by the extremes of Gauguin's latest style and iconography, Degas added the overtly pagan canvas *The Moon and the Earth* (Museum of Modern Art, New York) to his collection, obtaining it directly

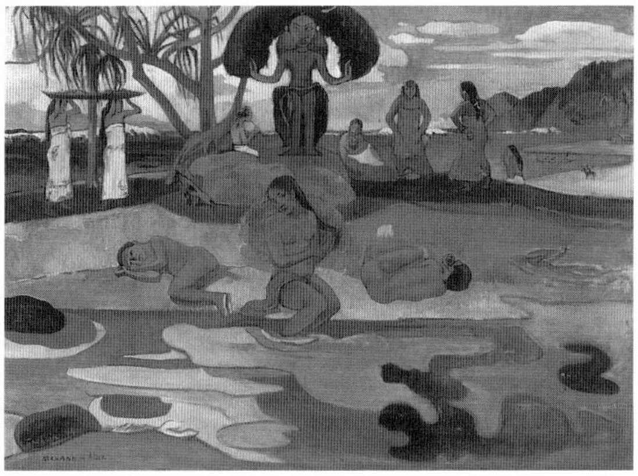

214. Paul Gauguin, *Mehana no atua*, 1894, oil on canvas, 68.3 × 91.5. Art Institute of Chicago, Helen Birch Bartlett Memorial Collection.

from the artist during Gauguin's 1893–5 repatriation.[68] Just as courageous was his purchase of the 1894 *Mahana no atua* (fig. 214), a swirling composition of pinks, oranges and blues that had few equals in audacity or decorative power at this period. Once again, we can only wonder at the impact such works must have made on Degas' apartment walls, and on the sensibilities of his colleagues and visitors.[69] Such pictures carried landscape painting into unexplored territory, both literally and figuratively, opening the subject to the spectator's reverie and the kind of 'fantasy' that Degas had tentatively explored two years earlier. Writing from Tahiti in 1899, in a letter that quotes with approval both Mallarmé and Degas, Gauguin explained his art in terms of music, poetry and the universality of colour, describing them as the outcome of a 'dream of violent harmonies'.[70]

Colours and harmonies with quite different ambitions may have drawn Degas to another of his contemporaries, and one who openly deplored the work of Gauguin: Paul Cézanne. Between 1895 and the turn of the century, Degas acquired at least eight pictures by Cézanne, all of them small but each characteristic of the artist's obsessive themes or expressive pursuits.[71] Portraiture was represented by two fine canvases from earlier decades, the abrasive portrait of Victor Choquet (Virginia Museum of Fine Arts, Richmond) and a resonant study of Cézanne himself, *Portrait of the Artist* (Reinhardt Collection, Winterthur). No less than four still lifes were included, from the minimal *Apples* (Fitzwilliam Museum, Cambridge) to the sumptuous *Apples and Glass* (Kunstmuseum, Basle), showing an unexpected willingness on Degas' part to engage with a theme almost unknown in his own *oeuvre*. Closer to Degas were two nudes, *Bather beside the Water* (Jasper Johns, New York) and *Venus and Cupid* (fig. 215), which show figures in an open coastal setting and a lush woodland glade respectively. Glaringly and perversely absent from this list are examples of Cézanne's pure landscapes. Though Degas certainly knew some of Cézanne's paintings of L'Estaque, Auvers, Aix-en-Provence and Gardanne (fig. 232), and admired both his oil paintings and watercolours, he chose not to add a single example to his collection.[72] As with the work of Monet, the only significant artist from this company who remained unrepresented in Degas' collection, Cézanne's unpopulated studies of mountains, woodland and rocky coasts may have seemed at odds with Degas' public rhetoric, or uncomfortably close to certain of his own rural adventures.

The subject of a group of female nudes in a rustic, arcadian landscape, which occupied so much of Cézanne's energy in his final decade, was to become one of the last major explorations of Degas' career. For once in step with his former Impressionist colleagues, several of whom experienced a similar rediscovery at this period, Degas embarked on an ambitious series of pictures of women bathing, reclining or grooming themselves in the open air.[73] Some sit on apple-green grass, rendered in webs of superimposed pastel, while others linger among trees or frolic in shallow water, accompanied by a dog, a russet cow or a creature that may be a bear.[74] The sheer scale of Degas' project has rarely been spelled out. Apart from preparatory drawings, more than a dozen variants of the theme were initiated, ranging from dense and burnished pastel studies to some of the largest compositions of Degas' career. All but one, a technically alarming pastel on coarse canvas, were executed on paper, several requiring the glueing together of a number of separate sheets to bring them to the required size. Certain pairs and groups have identical dimensions, suggesting that they were made in sequential fashion and were perhaps intended, like the landscape monotypes or the 1886 pastel nudes, to be displayed in this way.[75] Given the

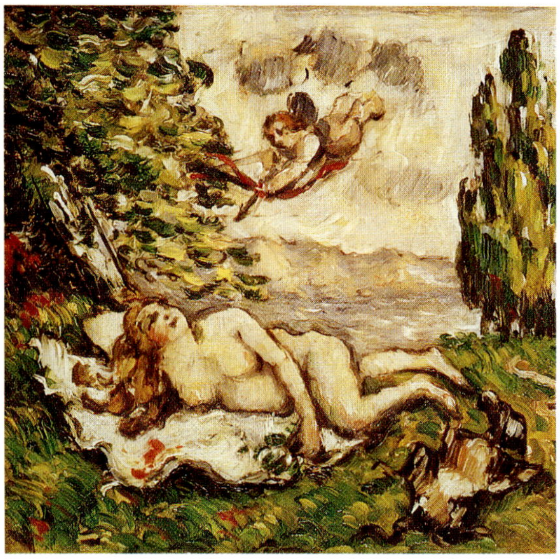

215. Paul Cézanne, *Venus and Cupid*, *c.*1873, oil on canvas, 21 × 21. Private collection.

'rather favourable' reception of his Durand-Ruel exhibition, we should therefore consider that Degas may have planned a second, but sadly unrealised, showing of his latest suite of works, devoted entirely to the pastoral nude. Knowing that Pissarro and Renoir had both sold or exhibited such studies during these years (both at Durand-Ruel's gallery), and that Cézanne's exhibition at Vollard's in 1895 had included the same *motif*, Degas' ever-competitive nature may well have been provoked into such an initiative.[76]

In choosing to carry out, and perhaps to exhibit, a major series of nudes in the landscape, Degas was taking on not only his colleagues and his own past, but the formidable precedent of history. As the artist insisted, his many pastels of bathing women were contemporary restatements of a theme such as Susannah and the Elders, now devoid of biblical and even narrative currency, but still haunted by their allusive past.[77] It is a measure of Degas' ambition and self-presentation that he should have pursued the theme of the nude throughout his career, from his earliest copies and academic canvases to the grandiose pastels of the late 1890s. Youthful studies of Michelangelo's *Battle of Cascina*, Giorgione's *Concert Champêtre* and other canonical works had introduced him to the genre, fixing in his mind the poses and gestures that would resurface in beach scenes and glimpses of the *toilette*.[78] His 1860 oil painting of the *Young Spartans* (fig. 31) exemplifies this progress; originally based on antique reliefs and the classicism of Ingres, it was later repainted as an almost modern confrontation of naked youths, now using models from the streets of Paris.[79] More significant in the present context, the early studies for the *Young Spartans* show a grove of trees and a meandering central stream, their rhythmic forms enveloping the naked protagonists in a way that anticipates the *pastorals* of the 1890s.[80] In subsequent decades, more variants on such ancient devices appeared, some knowing and coy, others aggressive in their modernity. *Beach Scene* (fig. 94) has been compared to Mantegna and to the tradition of the Japanese print, though it remains amongst the most particularised and documentary of all Degas' modern-life bathing subjects.[81] The exceptional *Peasant Girls Bathing in the Sea toward Evening* (fig. 97) seems both pagan and prosaic, and the unequivocally rustic *Girl Drying Herself* (fig. 116) of 1885 is finely poised between antiquity and the rawness of Degas' own age.

The pastoral nudes of the 1890s are, similarly, the product of two fundamental and sometimes conflicting drives in Degas' mature career. Made at a time when the artist still proudly displayed the *Young Spartans* in his apartment, the new series inevitably declared its kinship with the past, while even more clamorously distancing itself from such burdensome associations.[82] The landscape settings for the pastel nudes could hardly be less classical, with no Claudian vistas, Olympian peaks or historically correct architecture, such as the *agora* that once dominated the provocative Spartans.[83] High viewpoints preclude recession and distort perspectives, and our attention is thrust against bare pasture and banal river banks. It is the figures themselves, however, that most loudly declare Degas' independence of tradition. As groups, they lounge and sprawl in inelegant confusion, their torsos, heads and legs repeatedly cropped by the picture rectangle. Individually, they range from the langorous to the comically grotesque, with gross buttocks and spindly limbs following each other in a startling panorama of human particularity. These are neither goddesses nor nymphs, but a familiar cast of laundresses, dancers and artists' models who have escaped from the picture gallery of Degas' earlier decades, now enjoying their rural and curiously anarchic summertime pursuits. More akin to Pissarro's naked peasant girls, who snatch a furtive swim while tending

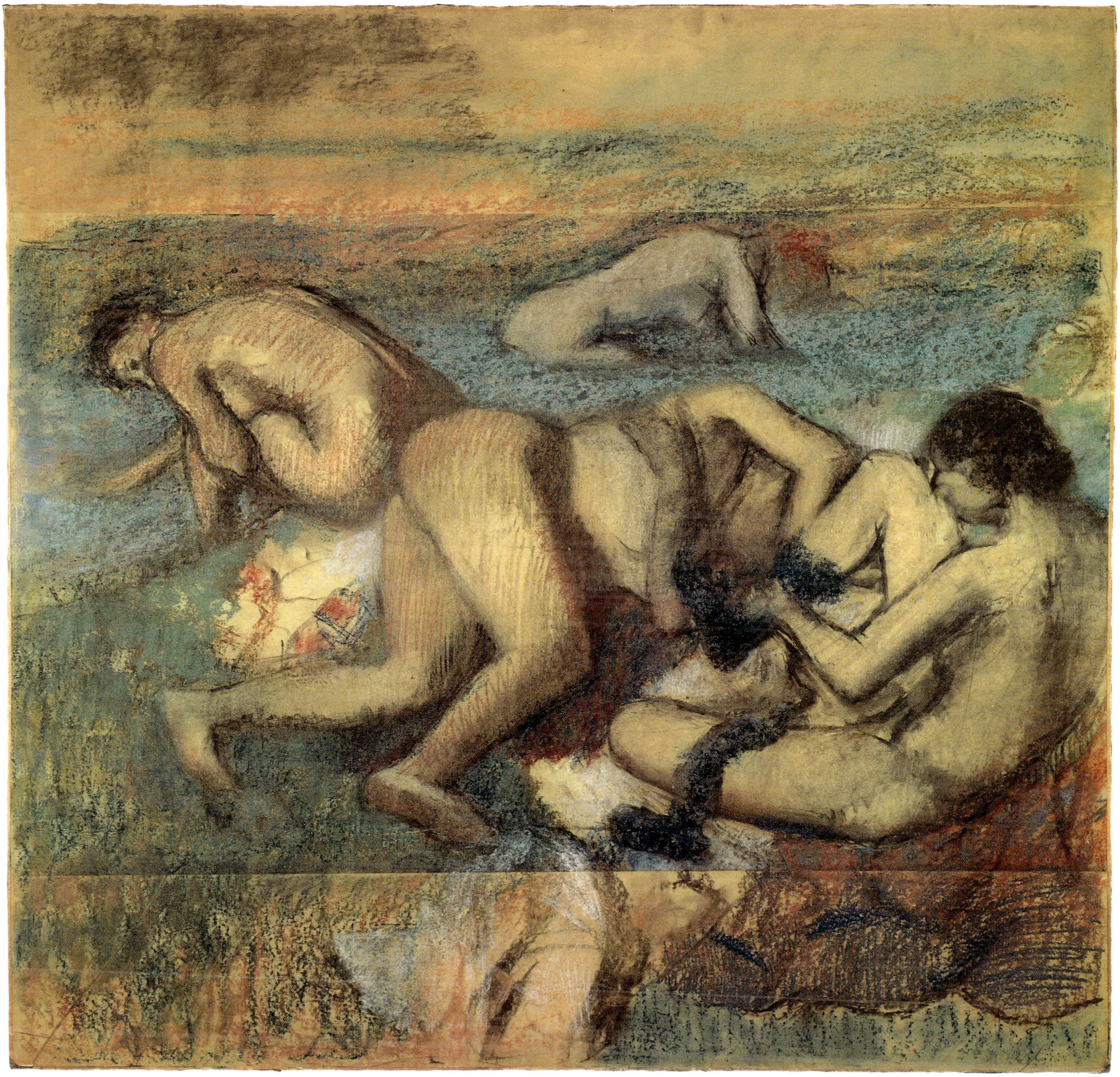

216. *Bathers*, *c.*1895–1905, pastel, 104.6 × 108.3 (L 1079). Art Institute of Chicago, Gift of Nathan Cummings.

their geese, Degas' nudes are remarkable both for their resistance to anecdote and their remoteness from the vocabulary of voyeurism.[84] Equally, they stand apart from the self-conscious, inflated glamour of Renoir's many *Baigneuses* of the same period, as well as the rustic realism of an artist like Lhermitte.[85] Set beside such works, Degas' bathers seem resolutely mundane, though not entirely proof against the artist's erudition. Distant echoes of a Diana and an Eve have been detected, and the foreground nude in *Bathers* (fig. 216), who pulls on a recalcitrant blue stocking, is surely an irreverent reference to Poussin.[86]

Begun soon after Cézanne's 1895 retrospective, which Degas is known to have visited and admired, the new series of bathers offers further evidence of the affinity between these temperamentally distinct individuals.[87] In their earlier years, both artists had indulged a taste for theatricality and extremes of violence in their outdoor scenes of confrontation between the sexes. Certain parallels between works of this period point to a curious, though almost certainly coincidental, identity in their aims. The ravaged, supine nude in the foreground of Degas' *Scene of War in the Middle Ages* (fig. 46), for example, is almost a prefiguration of the pose of the goddess in Cézanne's *Venus and Cupid* (fig. 215), and Degas' later acquisition of this canvas seems to acknowledge a retrospective complicity with his former colleague.[88] Subsequently, both artists chose more innocent-seeming contexts for their nudes, preferring the bathing party and the seaside romp, the matronly gathering and the athletic display. Like Cézanne's, Degas' series is played out by a small cast of figures, many of whom were introduced in other guises as the sequence progressed. Both artists discovered such paradigmatic figures in their own pasts, and both indulged in occasional quotations from existing works of art, more than once turning to the same admired image. In their different ways, the two artists laboured at their separate but sympathetic designs, re-drawing outlines, re-defining forms and striving for a monumentality that would be worthy of their forebears.

Again like Cézanne, Degas accepted the need to work on his nude compositions in the studio, contriving open-air settings from memory and imagination, just as Poussin and Michelangelo had once done.[89] In Cézanne's case, his memories could be recharged through contact with the Provençal landscape, but it is salutary to find Degas expressing a similar need, if only vicariously. Writing to his young admirer Louis Braquaval in about 1896, Degas asked him to make some drawings of trees to help with his latest work, explaining,

> I have begun a large painting in oil, three women bathing in a stream edged with birches. My brother, who knows the countryside like a poacher, always knows right away where to find the birches that I need. I will send you a preliminary outline for this idea, and if you find some trees that will suit my purposes, I would be very pleased if you would make me a sketch or a small study in pastel.[90]

The outcome of this initiative is not recorded, but it seems to coincide with the period of Degas' last paintings of the landscape, made at Saint-Valéry-sur-Somme in the late 1890s.[91] Using such borrowed studies and perhaps memories of the coast, Degas contrived grassy knolls and bathing pools, tree-stumps and an assortment of livestock to surround his ample nudes. Though we are still gently reminded that 'the air you breathe in a picture is not necessarily the same as the air out of doors', touches of precision bring a certain plausibility to his studio-bound narratives.

One of the least eventful backgrounds and one of the most densely worked figure groups were brought together in the extraordinary Chicago *Bathers* (fig. 216).[92] Almost four feet square, this pastel was begun on a horizontal sheet of tracing paper, then extended at top and bottom as Degas' ambitions grew. Within its imposing confines, the artist appears to have summarised many of the themes and practical obsessions of his career; the two background nudes were taken from pastels in his earlier *oeuvre*, where they crouched in bathtubs rather than on timeless river banks;[93] their reclining companion, another distant echo of the figure in *Scene of War in the Middle Ages*, has become a recurring emblem of prostration; and the athletically splayed individual at the right recalls Baptism scenes and Renaissance battles.[94] The subject itself, that of bathers resting beside the water, is equally resonant, harking back to such pioneering works as Degas' *Beach Scene*, and his early association with Boudin, Whistler and Berthe Morisot. Finally, the technique of *Bathers* can be seen as the outcome of decades of experiment, as Degas united line, colour and tapestry-like richness of surface in a triumphant demonstration of picture-making. Lightly shadowed flesh contrasts with the coarseness of turf, limpid water with discarded costume, cool shadow with summery sky, while flourishes and zig-zags of pastel seem to electrify the scene. Even on this large scale, the lessons of the landscape monotypes, with their accretions of colour and extravagances of effect, have not been forgotten.

Like the majority of the late pastoral nudes, *Bathers* was left unfinished and unexhibited, consigned by the artist to the stacks of work in his studio and brought to light only after his death in 1917. In circumstances that are almost entirely undocumented, Degas had embarked on one of the grandest schemes of his maturity, expending considerable energy on its conception and elaboration, and then abandoning it for reasons known only to himself. Some of the pictures, such as the Chicago *Bathers* and the Barnes Foundation's *After the Bath: Three Nude Women* (L 1082), are magnificent in their irresolution, while others, like the Musée d'Orsay's *Bathers* (L 1081), press hard on the heels of the next generation, notably the young Matisse. Undertaken as part of a more general enthusiasm for bather scenes in the mid-1890s, Degas seems to have been discouraged by their scale and their self-generated profusion, or defeated by internal contradictions in his subject-matter. As Cézanne himself was to discover, troupes of naked models remain fundamentally improbable and demand fresh pictorial justifications, and may even be incompatible with the newest demands of painting. Before we rush to find Degas wanting, however, we must remember that his late bathing scenes were almost exactly contemporary with the great *Russian Dancers*, those sumptuous assertions of late maturity. As with the *Russian Dancers*, Degas seems to have planned his *Bathers* as a summary or recapitulation of favourite themes, recalling former glories and revitalising the challenges of earlier decades. Looking back to the figure-in-the-landscape and the idols of his youth, he dreamt of dense configurations of limbs and subtly orchestrated gestures; thinking perhaps of Gauguin, he explored the state of nature, or at least a thoroughly modern state of undress; and remembering his landscape monotypes, he aspired to fuse together colour and space, flesh and foliage.

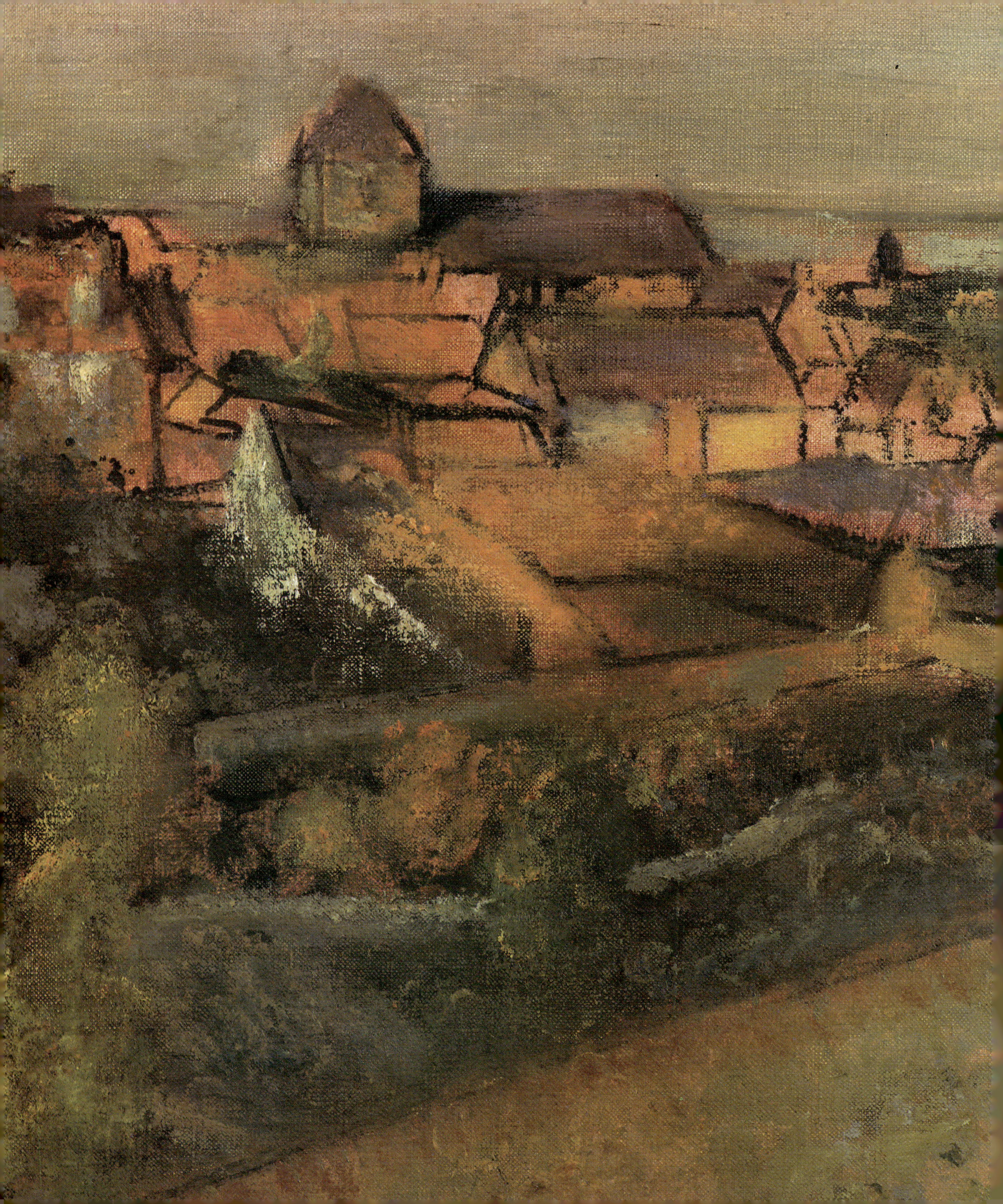

9 Saint-Valéry-sur-Somme

'Were it not for the landscapes I am determined to try,
I should have left.'
(Degas, writing from Saint-Valéry, 1898)

While still in his mid-twenties, the young Degas had made a notebook sketch of the street plan of Saint-Valéry-sur-Somme, a small resort to the west of Abbeville in Picardy.[1] According to Jeanne Raunay, Degas' family took regular holidays in the town when he was a child, and the broad estuary of the Somme and its flat surroundings were among the artist's first experiences of the French landscape. When he later went to visit the Valpinçons at Ménil-Hubert in Normandy, Degas marvelled at the contrast with the coastal scenery, writing in his notebook in 1861: 'It is completely new to me; at St Valéry the countryside seems to me a lot less rich and leafy than here.'[2] Soon after these outings, changes in Degas' family circumstances brought the summer vacations at Saint-Valéry to an end, but the artist and his brother, René, evidently remembered the town with affection. Three decades later, René rented a house there for his own family, and in the late 1890s Degas made several excursions to the coast to stay with his brother or with the painter Louis Braquaval. On one of these visits, in September 1898, Degas wrote to Alexis Rouart: 'Here your letter found me, my dear friend. Were it not for landscapes that I am determined to try, I should have left. My brother had to go back to his newspaper on the 1st, and the landscape (!) kept me here a few days longer. Your brother, will he believe this?'[3] Alexis' brother was, of course, Henri Rouart, lifelong friend of Degas and intransigeant *pleinairiste*. Even at the turn of the century, Degas could still enjoy baiting his old colleague, while relishing the paradox of his own determination to 'try' some landscapes.

The letter of 1898 to Alexis Rouart is almost the only reference by Degas to his last and most underestimated excursion into landscape imagery. Resulting in more than fifteen substantial oil paintings and pastels, this final flourish has gone almost unnoticed by specialists and general public alike, and remains unrepresented in most publications on the artist.[4] With the distinguished exception of a brief essay by Jean Sutherland Boggs, no scholarly attention has been directed at the pictures or their context.[5] Where they have been mentioned, if only in passing, startling claims have been made on their behalf: the influence of Gauguin on one of the canvases has been noted by Jean Boggs;[6] their 'abstracted shapes' have suggested 'proto-Fauvist colour' to Ronald Pickvance;[7] and an anticipation of the forms of Cubism has been proposed by Denys Sutton.[8] As the illustrations in this chapter show, many of the works in question endorse such views, and propose others that challenge our assumptions about the ageing artist. Paint surfaces show signs of radical restructuring and profound shifts of hue and tonality, as though Degas were struggling with new conceptions of picture-making; the stimulus of different kinds of painting, from Turner's late oils to Monet's recent series, and from Pissarro's city views to

217. Detail of fig. 233.

Cézanne's townscapes, can be detected, as can the implications of Degas' experiments with photography; and comparison of the works with the original sites in Saint-Valéry reveals a sometimes scrupulous, occasionally cavalier approach to the *motif*, culminating in a kind of perceptual collage that seems closer to Picasso and Braque than to the art of Degas' peers.

In its salient features, the Saint-Valéry series followed the well-established patterns of Degas' engagement with landscape-making. Like most of his earlier drawings, pastels and monotypes, these pictures were initiated away from Paris and in close proximity to friends, congenial surroundings and the experience of travel. At a distance from his metropolitan disciplines as well as his studio, Degas could revert to the casual improvisation of the Dives-sur-Mer seascapes or the bold experimentation of the Diénay colour prints, tackling new *motifs* and probing old techniques. Such projects also lent themselves to a loosely related series, linked by size, subject-matter and extension in time. In the Saint-Valéry scenes, we are reminded of the peripatetic nature of Degas' landscape activity, as he circled a chosen site, raised or lowered an angle of view, or zoomed in towards a familiar subject. Many of these procedures are effectively autobiographical, defining both the presence of the artist and the peculiarity of his vision. Though self-effacing to an almost debilitating degree, and still as disinclined as ever to populate his landscapes, Degas left his mark on surfaces and structures, tonal registers and schemes of colour. Like the 1869 pastels, these canvases can be silvery and mute, and like the 1892 monotypes they can erupt in rainbow hues; his finger-prints cover entire compositions, as in certain of the monotypes; *hachures* of pastel recall the landscape backgrounds of such works as *Dancers in Salmon-Pink Skirts* (fig. 206) and *Russian Dancers* (fig. 208); and the dialogue between line and colour, as old as the artist's working life, continued its erratic course.

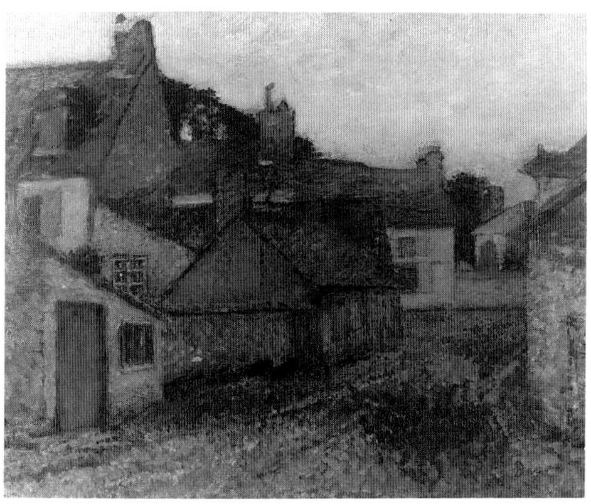

218. *Village Street, Saint-Valéry*, *c.*1896–8, oil on canvas, 50.5 × 61. Location unknown, photo courtesy Marlborough Fine Art, London.

Before examining individual pictures, their status as a group in Degas' later career deserves to be considered. By his own or any other standards, a set of fifteen or more works of art in a variety of media, including twelve in oil on canvas, represents a significant investment of time and professional energy, and more than the passing fancy of one or more seaside excursions. At a time when Degas is widely reported to have abandoned oil painting, he pursued his new ambition over several seasons, returning inventively to some of these canvases and elaborating their surfaces as if they were multi-layered pastels. His satisfaction with the project is shown in his willingness to allow a number of the works into circulation during his lifetime: two were given to, or exchanged with, Louis Braquaval; two were acquired at an unknown date by the artist's niece, Jean Fevre;[9] and a further pair, both of which have escaped the cataloguers' attention, were probably sold by Degas himself.[10] One of these is known only through a black-and-white reproduction, while the other, *Village Street, Saint-Valéry* (fig. 218), carries Degas' signature, the clearest sign of its completion and marketability.[11] As with the pastoral bathers of the 1890s, additional evidence of Degas' consistency and ambition is provided by the dimensions of the works in question. Among the oil paintings, three formats were generally used, one accounting for a series of at least four canvases.[12] Seen together, such a group would have instantly recalled the continuity of his Durand-Ruel monotypes or even the recent installations of Monet's *Pourville* or *Mornings on the Seine* suites, or Pissarro's cityscapes whose dimensions they almost share.[13] Again following the logic of the pastel nudes, it is tempting to imagine Degas as a rival to his contemporaries, planning yet another exhibition of sequential imagery that would confound their expectations.[14]

219. *Village Street*, *c.*1896–8, oil on canvas, 81 × 69 (L 1212). From the Collection of Dr. and Mrs. Julius H. Jacobson II.

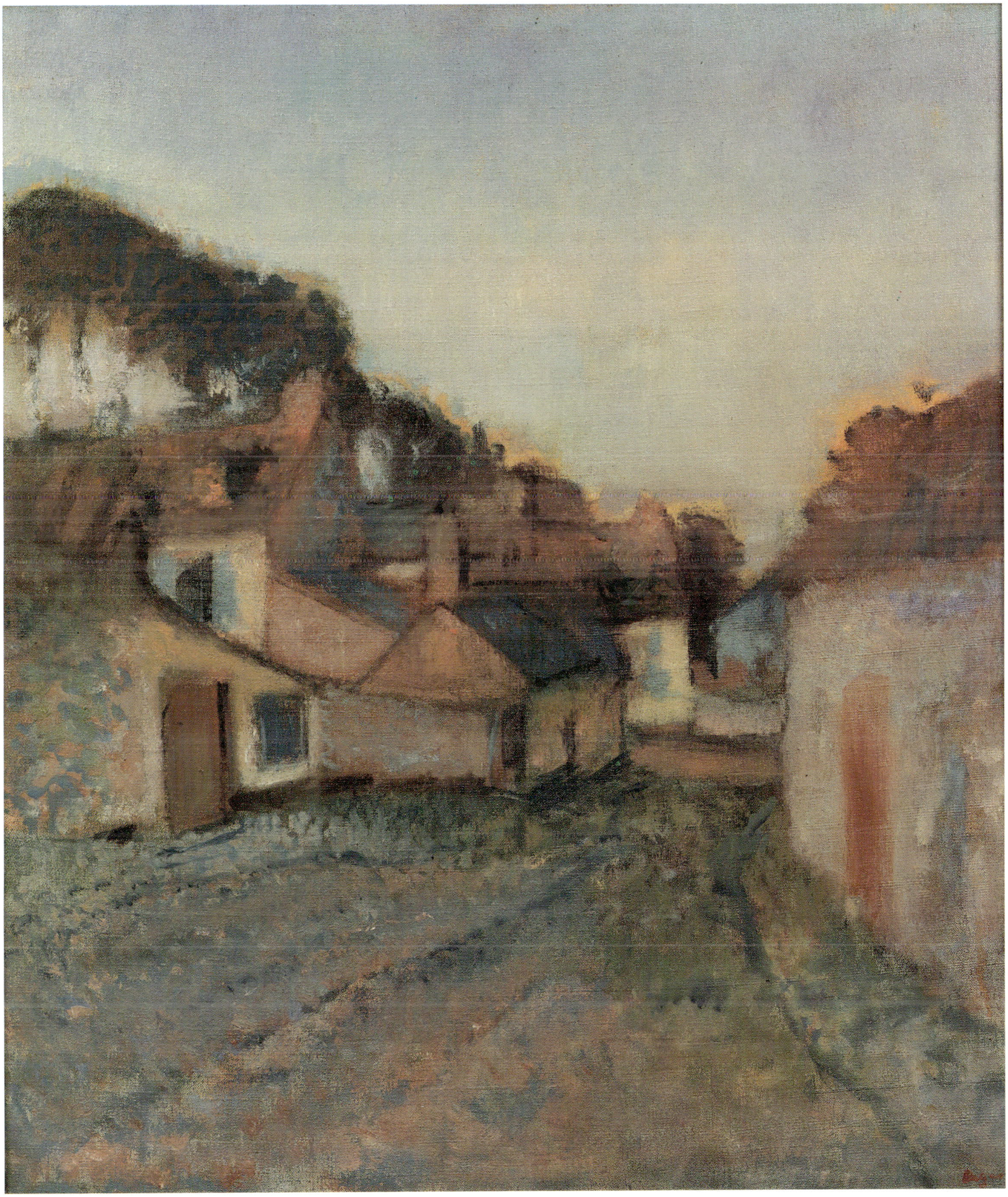

The neglect of the Saint-Valéry pictures by subsequent generations may be attributed in part to Degas' failure to commit himself to such exhibitions, in part to the uncertainty that still surrounds their evolution. Unlike the richly documented landscape monotypes, these works are hardly mentioned in Degas' correspondence, a source that becomes increasingly sporadic and obtuse in his later years. Inevitably, we find ourselves turning to the circumstantial and the secondary, relying on the evidence of the sites themselves and the accounts of Degas' friends, models and fellow-artists. Prominent among the latter was Braquaval, a painter of modest talents who spent part of each summer in a handsome house at the centre of Saint-Valéry.[15] Twenty years younger than Degas, Braquaval had been a pupil of Boudin, another painter who frequented Saint-Valéry and its surrounding beaches and harbours.[16] Degas first met Braquaval in 1895 or 1896, establishing a warm friendship with the young artist, his wife, Julia, and their daughter, Marie-Louise, which was to flourish in annual visits to the coast, domestic gatherings in Paris and a brief but lively correspondence between the two painters.[17] Their affectionate letters included technical advice from Degas to Braquaval and, as we have seen, an unusual request for help with the landscape setting of one of Degas' pastel *Bathers*. It is clear that Degas assumed the role of teacher, even to the extent of collaborating with his *protégé* on at least one canvas.[18] Equally evident is Braquaval's precedence as the painter of Saint-Valéry, and the implication that it was his example that led to Degas' first pictures of the town.

Degas' association with Braquaval was one of a number of relationships with younger or less experienced artists that characterised his later career and had particular significance for his making of landscapes. When he travelled to Diénay in 1890, Degas chose for his companion the minor sculptor Paul-Albert Bartholomé, then elected to make his first monotypes in the presence of the little-known painter Georges Jeanniot. His intimacy with Henri Rouart offered a variation on the same theme, while his professional exchanges with Paul Gauguin, some fourteen years Degas' junior, came closer to mutual respect. With the possible exception of Pissarro, Degas seems to have avoided sharing his landscape activities with the more celebrated practitioners of the day, perhaps nervous of his skills or jealous of his reputation. When in the company of younger admirers, however, he was all confidence and generosity, even as he held forth on a subject and a range of skills that were hardly typical of his own practice. His manner is perfectly captured in an account of Degas' first meeting with Braquaval, recorded in the *Souvenirs anecdotiques* of Jeanne Raunay.[19] Raunay was an opera singer and the wife of a prominent collector of Impressionist art, who became a close friend of Braquaval's daughter during many summers spent together at Saint-Valéry.[20] Describing how Degas would take long walks around the seaside town, Raunay reports his frequent encounters with an unknown young artist, who feverishly drew and painted the surrounding scenery. After watching the artist for some time, Degas introduced himself and began to offer advice to the over-awed beginner. On a subsequent occasion, he was invited to Braquaval's studio, again offering encouragement and criticism in the first of a cycle of inquisitions that were to amount to a virtual apprenticeship, lasting at least six years.[21]

One memorable exchange between master and pupil gives a rare glimpse of Degas the didactic landscapist. According to Jeanne Raunay,

> Degas had invented an instrument to help in composing a picture, which was especially useful for landscapes with wide horizons or for the organisation of

subjects that required a structure, a perspective. It was a small rectangle made from four pieces of wood. At regular intervals, strong metal wires were fixed across its length and breadth, forming squares of equal size. One looked through it, and landscapes and figures would appear to the eye and the mind, already squared up and framed. In the middle of one side, a cord was fixed to a ring so the user could carry it around his neck. This simplified the process of establishing a composition.

Degas rather liked working with a friend on the same canvas. In the countryside, it was a sovereign delight to him, an amusement, a relaxation of the spirit; but he rarely finished the works he began in this way. He enjoyed himself and that was all.

It was in these circumstances that he attempted a large landscape with his friend Braquaval, in Picardy. The two artists were using this very helpful viewing frame; but, as they only had one between them, they were forever swapping it over, and the annoyance of passing it round their necks ten times in succession had made them slightly irritated.

Degas was looking at the picture, which was only sketched in on the canvas; he seemed rather pleased; he was explaining what he had in mind and giving careful, intelligent advice; it was Braquaval who was doing the drawing.

After having a good look, Degas says, 'Give me the grid. There is something in the background, there, on the left, that I don't understand.'

They swap over the grid. Braquaval explains: 'Over there, on the left? But that's a roof with two trees above it.'

Degas: 'I can't see them on the canvas.'

'But yes, they are shown . . . there.'

'On your canvas', Degas answered, 'I can see trees that look fifty centimetres apart, while in reality they are nearly touching.'

'Well yes, its only an indication, an approximation.'

'What, an approximation? An approximation? Well, Sir, I call this approximation a monstrosity; do you hear, a monstrosity.'[22]

Among the many revealing features of this passage are Degas' confident exposition of landscape procedures, his tolerance of Braquaval's *plein-air* tendencies, and his reputed delight in a collaborative work of art. There are some reasons for caution when dealing with Raunay's account, not least her description of the 'grid', which was certainly not invented by Degas. Known to artists since at least the time of Leonardo and Dürer, there is no evidence of its application in Degas' own art and every reason to believe that it was improvised on this occasion for Braquaval, the struggling novice.[23] On the other hand, Degas' instinctive division of the landscapist's labours into two parts still rings true; here Braquaval is responsible for the initial process of drawing, while Degas follows behind with the application of colour. Several years before, in the 1892 landscape monotypes, Degas had made a historic break with this practice, initiating his image in brilliant patterns of oil paint and only later clarifying his forms and heightening them with strokes of pastel. In his collaboration with Braquaval, which was perhaps intended to pass on the precepts of his own early training, Degas reverted to time-honoured practices. Insisting on the need for precise delineation, he trained Braquaval in the use of the Leonardesque 'grid' and reprimanded him for moments of vagueness or inaccuracy. More surprising is the discovery that the pictures made by Degas himself at Saint-Valéry were based on elaborate preliminary drawing, either in the form of separate studies in charcoal and pastel, or as linear underpaintings on his canvases.[24]

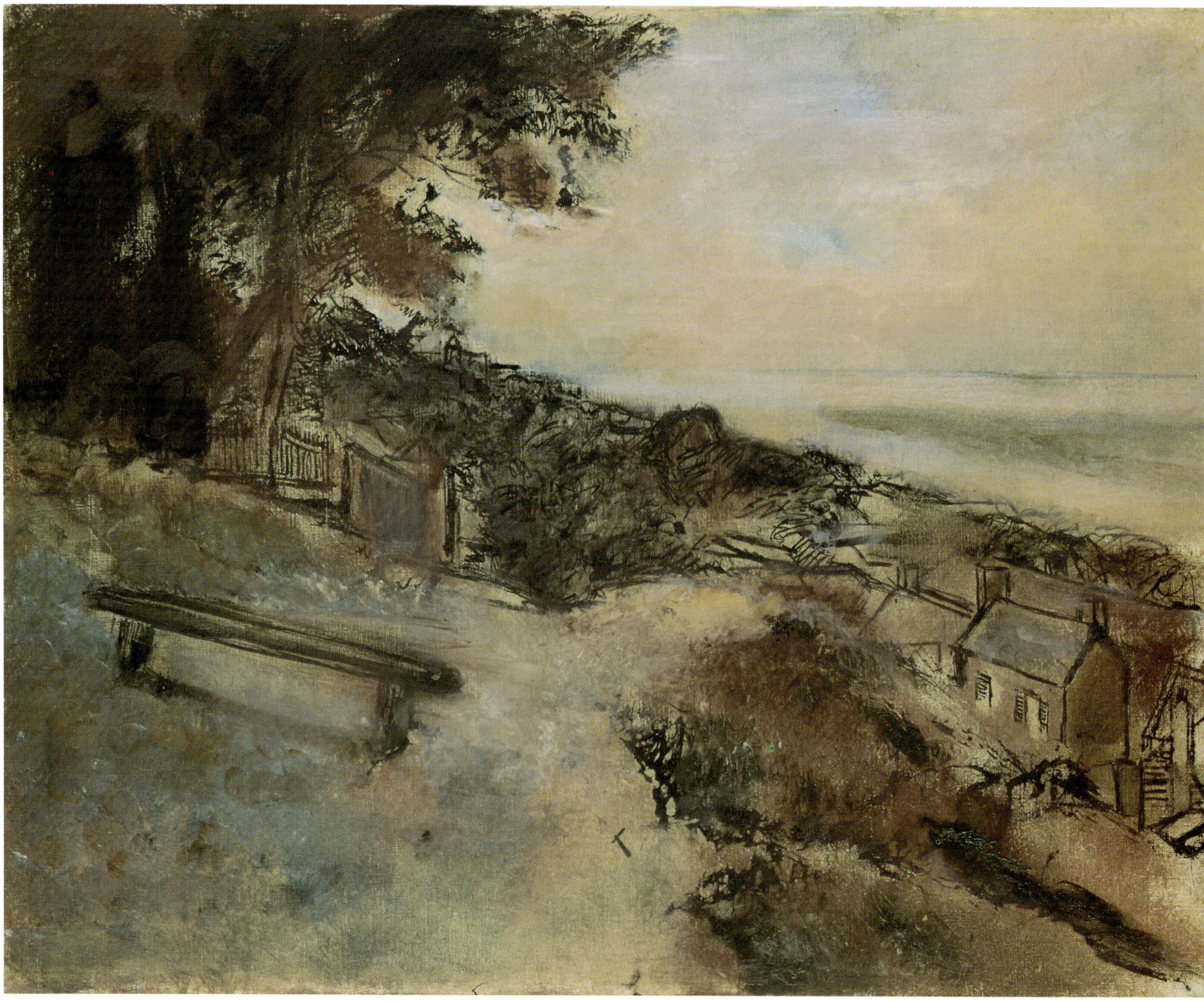

220. *Landscape by the Sea*, *c.*1896–8, oil on canvas, 49 × 59.8 (BR 151). Private collection, courtesy Sotheby's.

The hands of both Braquaval and Degas may be visible in the curious painting *Landscape by the Sea* (fig. 220), which was drafted out in pen and ink on a medium-sized canvas, then developed in flurries of variegated oil colour. The use of ink in preliminary drawings has a distinguished historical pedigree and was perhaps another part of Degas' programme of tuition, though it was largely anachronistic at this period.[25] Degas himself had experimented with the technique in his younger days, making elaborate and highly detailed pen drawings of dance subjects, then applying pastel or thinned oil paint as a secondary process.[26] Significantly, Braquaval was to continue with variations of this procedure for some years. His picture *Market-place at Dunkirk* (Musée de Picardie, Amiens) was executed over a vigorous ink outline, and many of his mature studies of Saint-Valéry, such as *Snow Effect* (fig. 221), have a pronounced

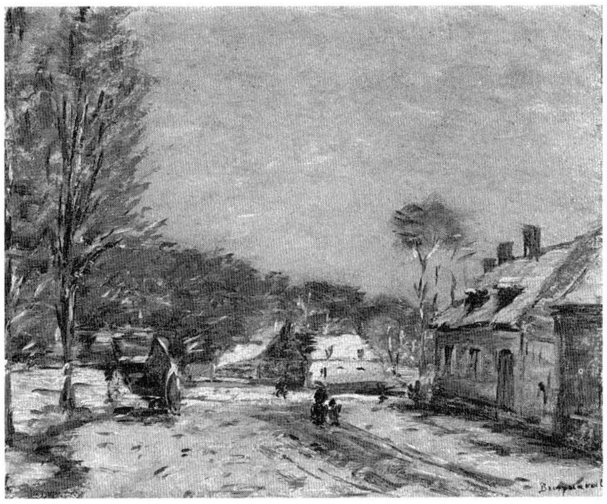

221. Louis Braquaval, *Snow Effect*, oil on panel, 39.5 × 47.5. Musée de Picardie, Amiens.

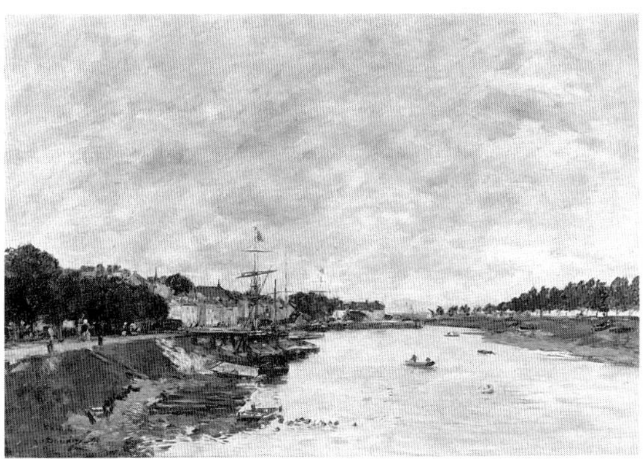

222. Eugène Boudin, *Saint-Valéry-sur-Somme*, 1890, oil on canvas, 66.4 × 85.4. Aberdeen Art Gallery.

linear sub-structure.[27] In *Landscape by the Sea*, the flickering, almost nervous penmanship seems too awkward for Degas himself and may well have been carried out by Braquaval under his new teacher's supervision. Conversely, the imaginative range of tints and the gestural application of paint suggest a more mature technician, here adding colour to an existing monochrome drawing. This and other features of the work correspond closely to Jeanne Raunay's description of their joint venture, allowing us to speculate that *Landscape by the Sea* represents a collaboration between Degas and one of his few documented pupils.[28]

More fundamental issues are raised by the vista of trees, roof-tops and distant estuary in *Landscape by the Sea*. Photographs and postcards made in Saint-Valéry at the turn of the century show an almost identical view, looking out towards the picturesque area known as Le Romerel, situated near the centre of the town (see fig. 223).[29] Though there are inevitable differences of framing and light, the photographs include all the principal elements of the collaborative canvas and even elucidate some of its forms. The tiny pyramidal form beneath the tree, for example, at the point where coastline and horizon converge, is revealed as the tower of the parish church, while the structure at lower left turns out to be a bench for the use of sightseers.[30] What are we to deduce from this evidence? Did Braquaval always work in this way, faithfully transcribing the local scenery? Were Degas' own canvases made from the same kind of subjects, rather than from his memories, his fantasies, or his 'states of eyes'? Did he paint them outdoors, in front of the *motif*, as Braquaval appears to have done? In this case, does the Saint-Valéry series represent Degas' final capitulation to *pleinairisme*, after decades spent mocking its excesses and its celebrated exponents? And, finally, what induced Degas to paint in a town of summer visitors and beauty spots, whose panoramas and seaside views had already been admired, photographed and turned into picture-postcards?

Contrary to first appearances, Degas' decision to make pictures of Saint-Valéry was neither eccentric nor unprecedented. By the time of his encounter with Braquaval, Saint-Valéry-sur-Somme had already become a much-painted town, attracting some of the most celebrated French and British landscape artists of previous generations. Paul Huet, Eugène Isabey, Thomas Shotter Boys and Richard Parkes Bonington had all depicted its waterfront or immediate environs, and Corot had recorded a visit to the area in 1853.[31] Some decades later, it became a favourite *motif* of Boudin, featuring in a Salon submission of 1891 entitled simply *Saint-Valéry-sur-Somme*, and in dozens of somewhat repetitive canvases from his last years.[32] True to their times, both Huet and Bonington had represented the Romantic face of the town, posing colourful fisherfolk on storm-swept beaches and heroic barques beside the Somme estuary. Boudin opted for the distant view, indulging his taste for towering skies and expansive sweeps of harbour. A favoured site was the flat terrain of the lower town, where the newly constructed Abbeville canal (see fig. 223) linked up with the Bay of the Somme, and broad vistas opened out on all sides. Standing with his back to the canal and looking westwards, Boudin had summarised this aspect of the scene in his 1890 canvas, also known as *Saint-Valéry-sur-Somme* (fig. 222). Showing the edge of the town and harbour at the left, Boudin had followed the course of the Somme from the foreground to the open sea beyond, offering a glimpse of the marshes and the Bay of the Somme at the right of his composition.

In reality, Boudin's *Saint-Valéry-sur-Somme* is a highly selective work, showing only one aspect of a topographically diverse and socially fragmented

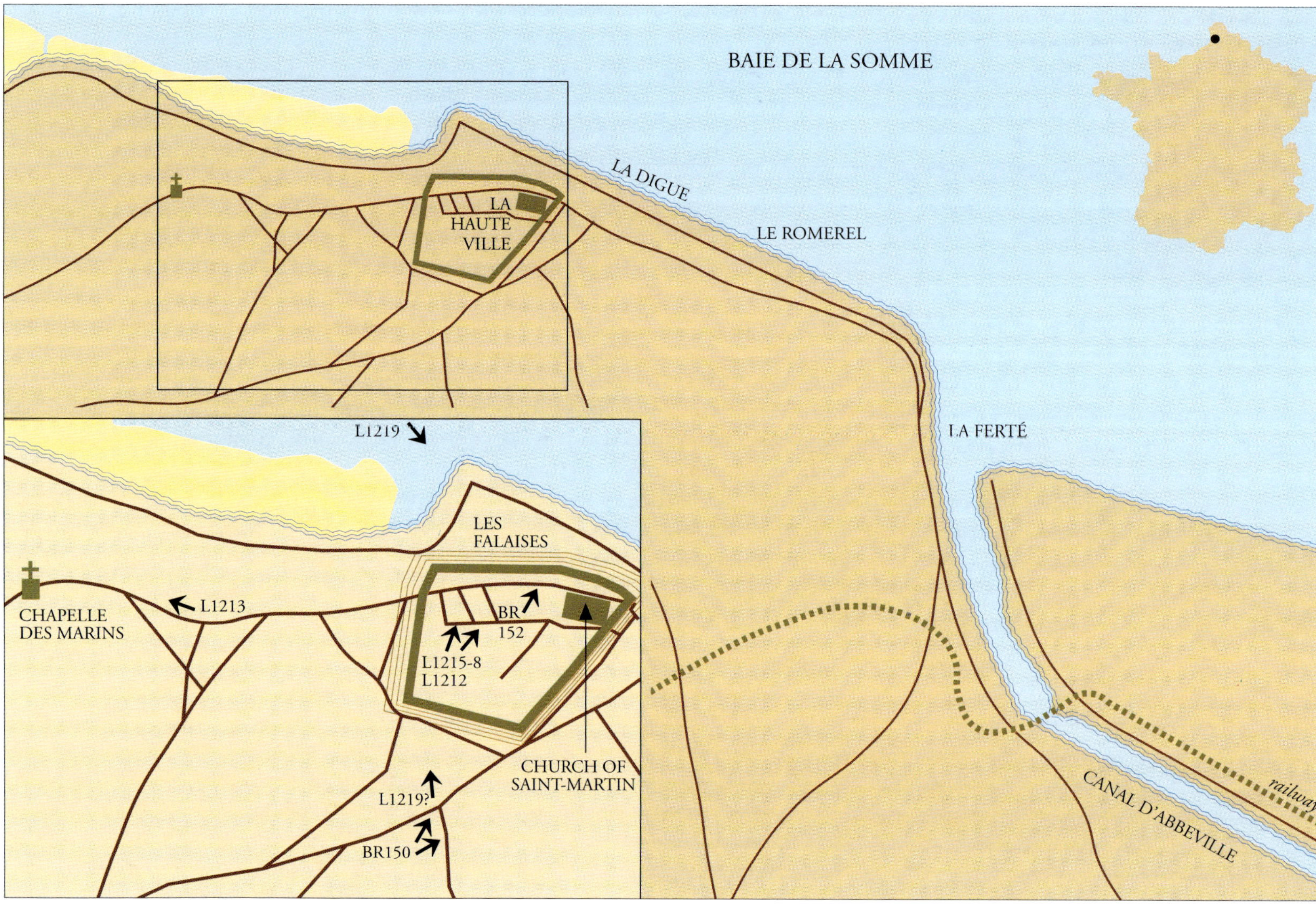

223. Map of Saint-Valéry-sur-Somme. Degas' pictures are identified by Lemoisne catalogue numbers, and arrows indicate their sites or vantage points.

small town. As in all his other pictures of the site, and in most of the paintings of his predecessors, Boudin has emphasised the maritime character of Saint-Valéry, with its harbour, fishing fleet and natural and man-made waterways. By situating himself in or near the lower town, known locally as La Ferté, Boudin has also opted for its modern façades and spectacles, the bustle of its trade and its links with the outside world. Beyond La Ferté, the town continues along the edge of the bay, its unusual crescent-shaped plan leading through a succession of distinct *quartiers*, each with its own history and local significance. First comes a district of shops and working-class housing, prominent today as the commercial heart of the town. Next, a more spacious and wooded area which embraces Le Romerel, where Braquaval and Degas painted *Landscape by the Sea*. At its westernmost limit, the most dramatic shift of all occurs, as visitors are confronted by the towering cliffs and battlements of the old town, or Haute Ville. Built on a cliff-like prominence, this fortified medieval site is centred on a fine gothic church and boasts a tower from the period of the Norman invasion, the remains of a Benedictine abbey and an arch with legendary links to Joan of Arc. Here, too, are the grander mansions and public buildings of Saint-Valéry, as well as the finer private houses, such as the one occupied by Braquaval and his family. Changing yet again, the fortifications finally give way to an agri-

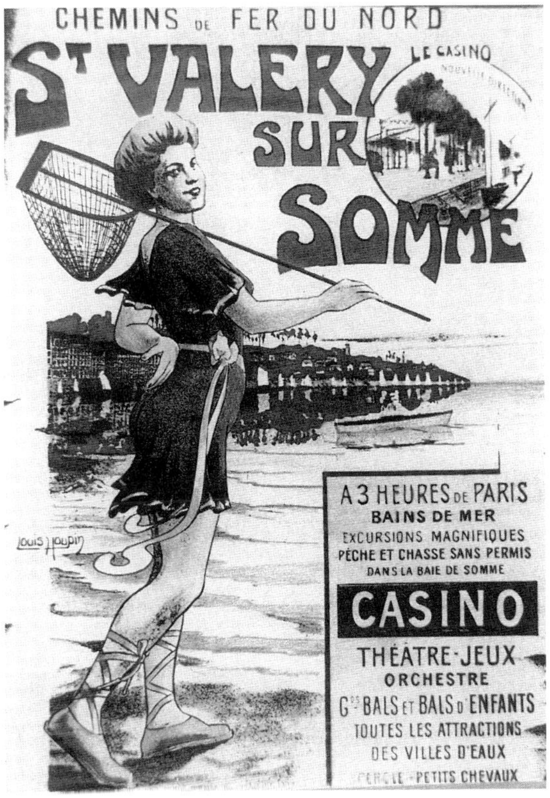

224. Poster of Saint-Valéry. Private collection.

cultural quarter, where modest farms and small holdings lead out into open country.[33]

Though most of these features are visible from the environs of Saint-Valéry, and though many offer a rich vocabulary of forms and prospects to the artist, almost none had been seized upon by Boudin, Huet, Bonington and their itinerant colleagues. In choosing to paint its beaches and fishermen, and even its prosperous modern port, they had effectively disregarded the majority of the town, just as they had overlooked its ancient associations. Most conspicuous among their omissions was the Haute Ville, with its winding streets and traditional houses, and its vertiginous ramparts overlooking the bay (fig. 234). By the time of Degas' later visits, the complex structure of Saint-Valéry had been given a further twist by its development as a seaside resort, complete with promenades, swimming facilities and its own casino (fig. 224). A wide, tree-lined causeway, known as La Digue, had been built between the Haute Ville and La Ferté, and hotels and villas in the latest and most ornamental styles were under construction. We know from Jeanne Raunay's account that Degas liked to walk around the town and can assume from his perambulations and repeated visits that he was familiar with its scattered attractions. We are even told that the artist had a special fondness for taking exercise on La Digue, the principal thoroughfare that linked its scattered *quartiers*.[34] Contrary to our expectations, however, Degas was just as selective as his forbears, though in quite different ways. Beaches and maritime activity do not appear in any of his paintings, nor do La Ferté and the Abbeville canal, formerly so admired by Boudin. Apart from the collaborative *Landscape by the Sea*, the centre of the town is also absent from his imagery, along with the glamorous trappings of the seaside resort. Even the casino and La Digue itself, which would surely have attracted the *peintre du high-life* in his early days, went entirely unrecorded.

All the paintings and pastels made by Degas at Saint-Valéry are linked with the medieval town or Haute Ville, whether as depictions of its streets and buildings, as views from its battlements, or as scenes from its immediate vicinity. Because the town has changed little in the last hundred years, it is possible to go further, identifying precise locations and speculating on their significance for the artist. Inside the fortified town, for example, *Village Street* (fig. 219) shows an obscure cobbled lane close to Braquaval's house, situated half-way between the ruined abbey and the parish church. On either side are ancient walls and cottages, while the steep descent of the path contrasts vividly with the flatness of the lower town. If Degas had positioned himself a little higher, he might have included the Bay of the Somme beyond the painted roof-tops, but in this and a number of similar works, he seems to have chosen to suppress the maritime association. Nearby, another little-used roadway suggested variations on trees, gables and garden walls, culminating in the richly textured oil painting *At Saint-Valéry-sur-Somme* (fig. 226). Looking back towards the Haute Ville, Degas made several studies of the medieval quarter from a distance, notably *View of Saint-Valéry-sur-Somme* (fig. 233). Here he focused on the church of Saint-Martin, with its squat bell-tower and pyramidal roof, a favourite *motif* that recurs in at least four pictures. One of these is *Houses at the Foot of a Cliff* (fig. 236), in which the site is approached from the sea, though once again the ramparts and distant church seem perversely divorced from their watery setting.

The reasons for Degas' exclusive attention to the historic centre of Saint-Valéry can only be the subject of speculation. At their simplest, they may have been practical. Basing himself on Braquaval's house and studio in the old town,

Degas could walk to and from his chosen subjects with ease, checking details and refreshing his memory as each composition demanded. Almost half his surviving pictures depicted sites within a few yards of Braquaval's property, and the rest are only minutes away, suggesting an unusually direct contact between artist and *motif.* On the other hand, Braquaval himself ranged far and wide in his search for subject-matter, and Degas' preferred mode of operation seems more pondered and deliberate than simply pragmatic.[35] As in his excursions to Dives-sur-Mer and the Côte d'Or, the artist's relationship with the landscape could be both intimate and remote, temperamental and nostalgic, using locations and their inhabitants, or rather their lack of them, to express his own unease. At Villers-sur-Mer and Houlgate, he had shunned the *chic* promenades and fashionable streets, finding emblems for his solitude in the deserted headlands and the mundane charms of the Dives waterfront. Travelling to Burgundy in 1890, Degas had followed one of the least glamorous routes on the social circuit, again opting for emptiness and the elemental appeal of the landscape.

By the time of his visits to Saint-Valéry, many of Degas' social and personal mannerisms had become hardened to an almost caricatural degree. Now in his mid-sixties, he was widely seen as aloof and severe, railing against all things modern and denouncing the breakdown of class barriers and norms of behaviour.[36] If his walks along La Digue were a survival of his former *flânerie*, then his decision to avoid the subject-matter of the *bains de mer*, the commercial port and the mercantile quarter was consistent with this latter-day misanthropism. As a visitor to this elaborately stratified town, Degas naturally gravitated to the Haute Ville, turning his back on the modern development of chalets and hotels and taking refuge within the security of the medieval walls. Less precisely, patriotism may also have played its part. During the continuing crisis of the Dreyfus Affair, which coincided with Degas' sojourns at Saint-Valéry, the artist stridently identified himself with the military faction and with the glorious history of France and her people. At Saint-Valéry, he could surround himself with the relics of that past, and with the battlements, church towers and ancient streets that were so expressive of his country's resilience. Predominantly, the old town of Saint-Valéry represented continuity, both in a historic and a personal sense. Jeanne Raunay was emphatic on this point:

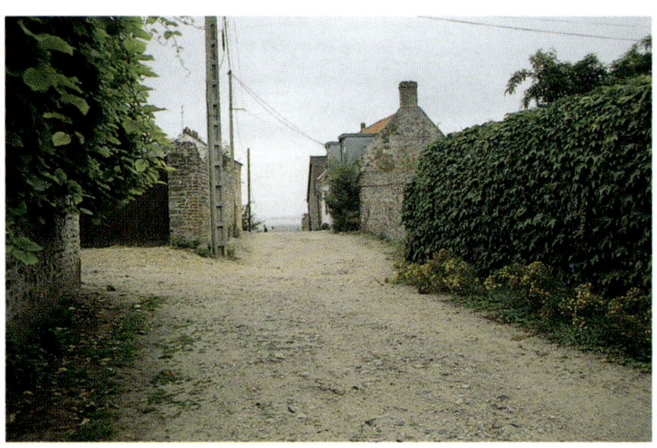

225. La rue de Quesnoy, Saint-Valéry (taken by the author).

> Degas loved to return to this little town where his parents had taken him as a child. He found there everything he had once enjoyed: the sea with all its surprises, roads bordered by old houses, the walls of a ruined tower, a monumental gate under which Joan of Arc had passed; but above all, he would rediscover the first memories of his childhood, and he could recall those he had loved. He liked this region because it was the first he had seen when he returned from Naples, and because the contrast of the two climates was engraved on his childish heart, and on the eyes that would soon develop the confident vision of a painter.[37]

Having chosen the sites that reassured and stimulated him, Degas seems to have set about his paintings of Saint-Valéry in a number of contrasting ways. None of the works is dated and even their sequence is unclear, but the group of four variations on the theme of 'At Saint-Valéry-sur-Somme' is the most technically familiar. Comprising two studies in charcoal and pastel and two oil paintings on canvas, the pictures in the group vary principally in their vantage point and angle of view. *At Saint-Valéry-sur-Somme* (fig. 226) shows a wide and overgrown track, with flanking walls and a distant view of cottages and silhouetted trees. Successive variants advance towards this scene, in a cinematic

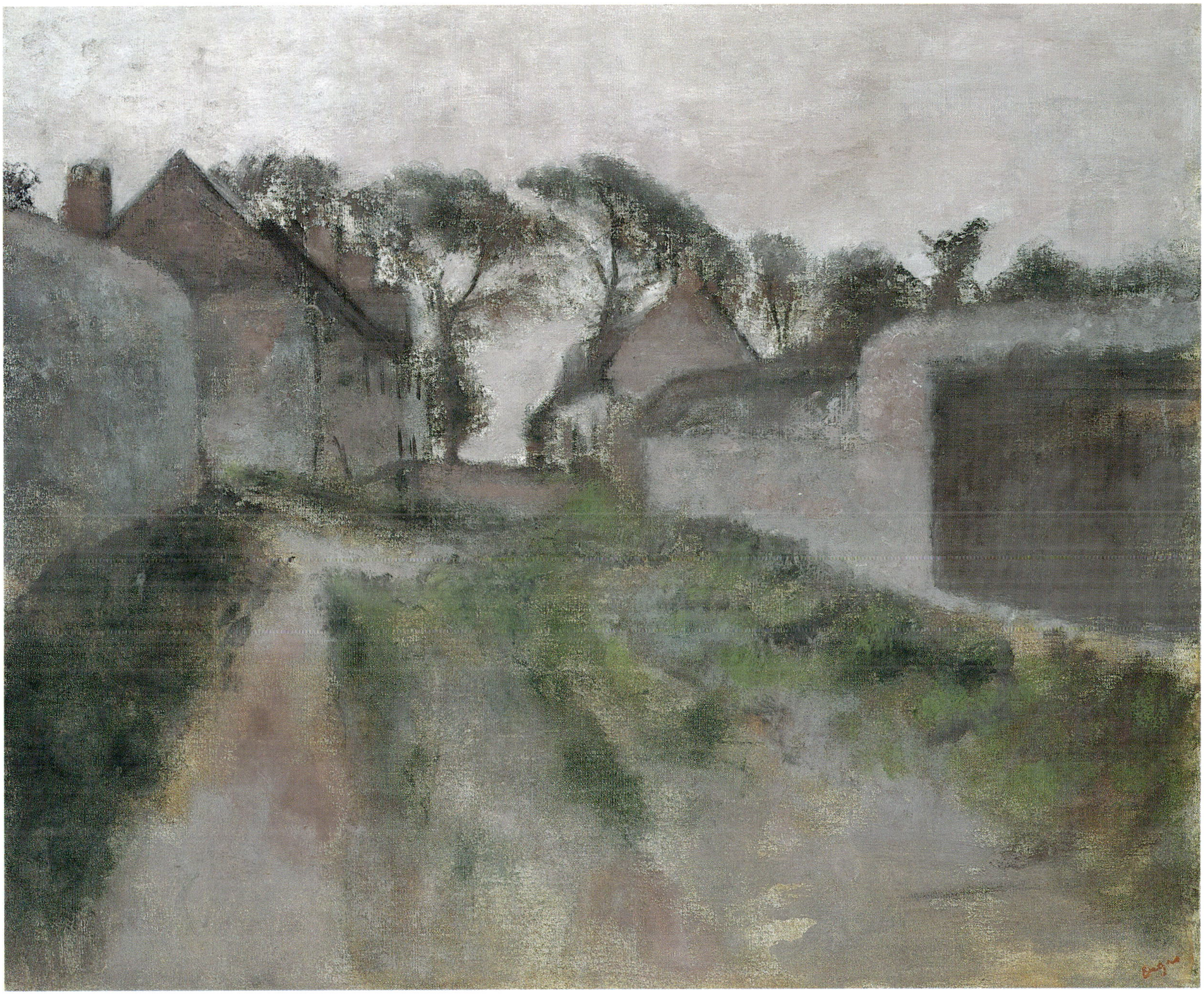

226. *At Saint-Valéry-sur-Somme*, *c.*1896–8, oil on canvas, 67.5 × 81 (L 1215). Ny Carlsberg Glyptothek, Copenhagen.

progression from frame to frame, until in *Entry to the Village* (fig. 227), we find ourselves level with the cottage gables and chimney-stacks. The site in question is immediately identifiable today, on the rue de Quesnoy leading to the rear entrance of Braquaval's house (see fig. 223). A modern photograph (fig. 225) shows its principal features still intact, though the felling of trees and the demolition of a house at the left of the scene has marked the passage of time.[38] In Degas' four pictures, many details of the subject are faithfully recorded, from the distinctive dormer windows and tapering garden wall of the right-hand cottage, down to the modest stone block at the junction of the roads, which still remains in its original place. Such precise, even pedantic fidelity to an outdoor *motif* seems almost shocking in an artist of Degas' reputation, prompting us to ask how it might have come about. The existence of the two charcoal and pastel

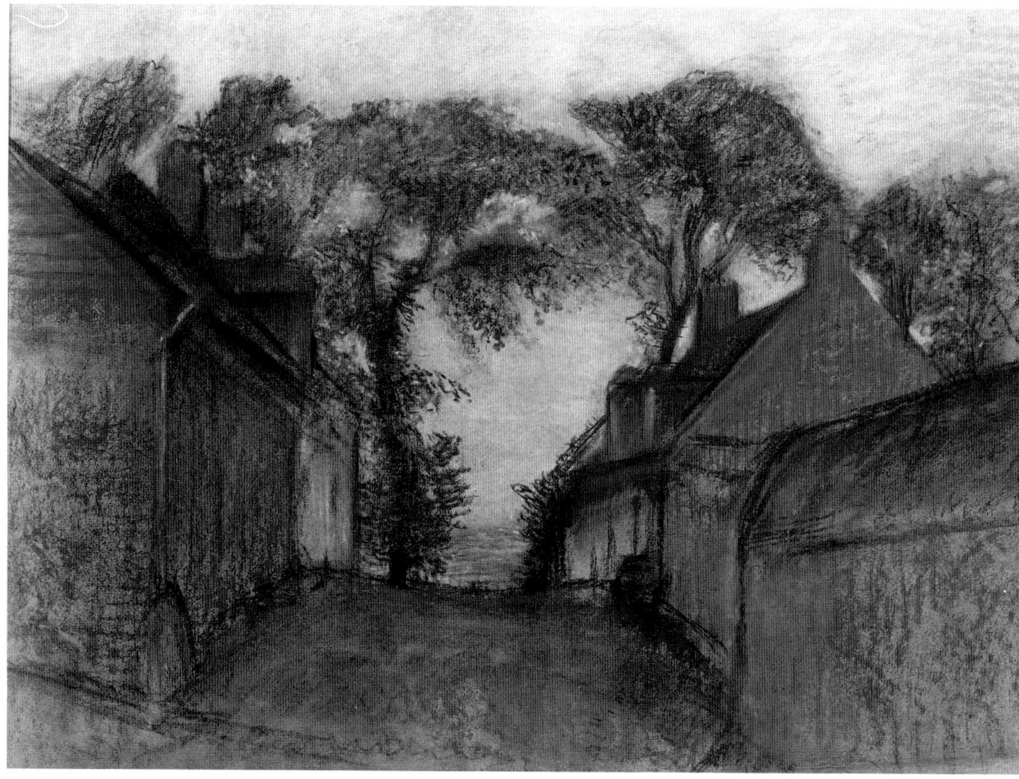

227. *Entry to the Village*, *c.*1896–8, pastel, 49 × 65 (L 1218). Private collection, courtesy Galerie Schmit, Paris.

drawings makes it improbable that Degas' canvases were executed outdoors, while increasing the likelihood that the drawings themselves were *plein-air* studies. Conversely, all four works may have been based on photographs, their pronounced orthogonals and sequential relationship derived from that tantalising box of prints once seen by Marcel Guérin.[39]

What is the real subject of this group of pictures? Though tinged with sentiment for Degas himself, their inoffensive arrangements of walls, trees and roof-tops come dangerously close to banality, devoid as ever of human or animal presences. Were they intended, like *Landscape by the Sea*, as a process of initiation for Braquaval, taking him even more thoroughly through the rituals of drawing, composition and the expressive application of colour? There is certainly no evidence of Braquaval's hand in these works, their extent and concentration pointing to a more sustained engagement on Degas' part with the challenges of picture-making. In both pastels and oil paintings, a subtle dialogue between structure and tonality appears to energise the scene, the artist beckoning his viewers forward into space, then calling us back with delicate textures and surface hues. Each work offers a restatement of this theme, now emphasising the ponderous mass of walls and the tactility of roadways, now hinting at the delicacies of atmosphere. Jean Boggs has drawn attention to the decorative interplay of trees and the geometric forms of the buildings, while stressing the strange beauty of Degas' palette and the breadth of his execution.[40] Linking some of these features with the Fauve painting of the next decade, Boggs also notes the extreme reticence of a picture like *At Saint-Valéry-sur-Somme*. Here it is the close agreement of mauves, lavender-pinks and silver-greys that evokes the 'damp and mournful' subject, hinting once again at solitude and discomfort. Colours have been floated across the canvas, playing off coarse linen against luscious paint, dense shadow against opalescent sky, in a work that gracefully transcends mere description.

228. Detail of fig. 226.

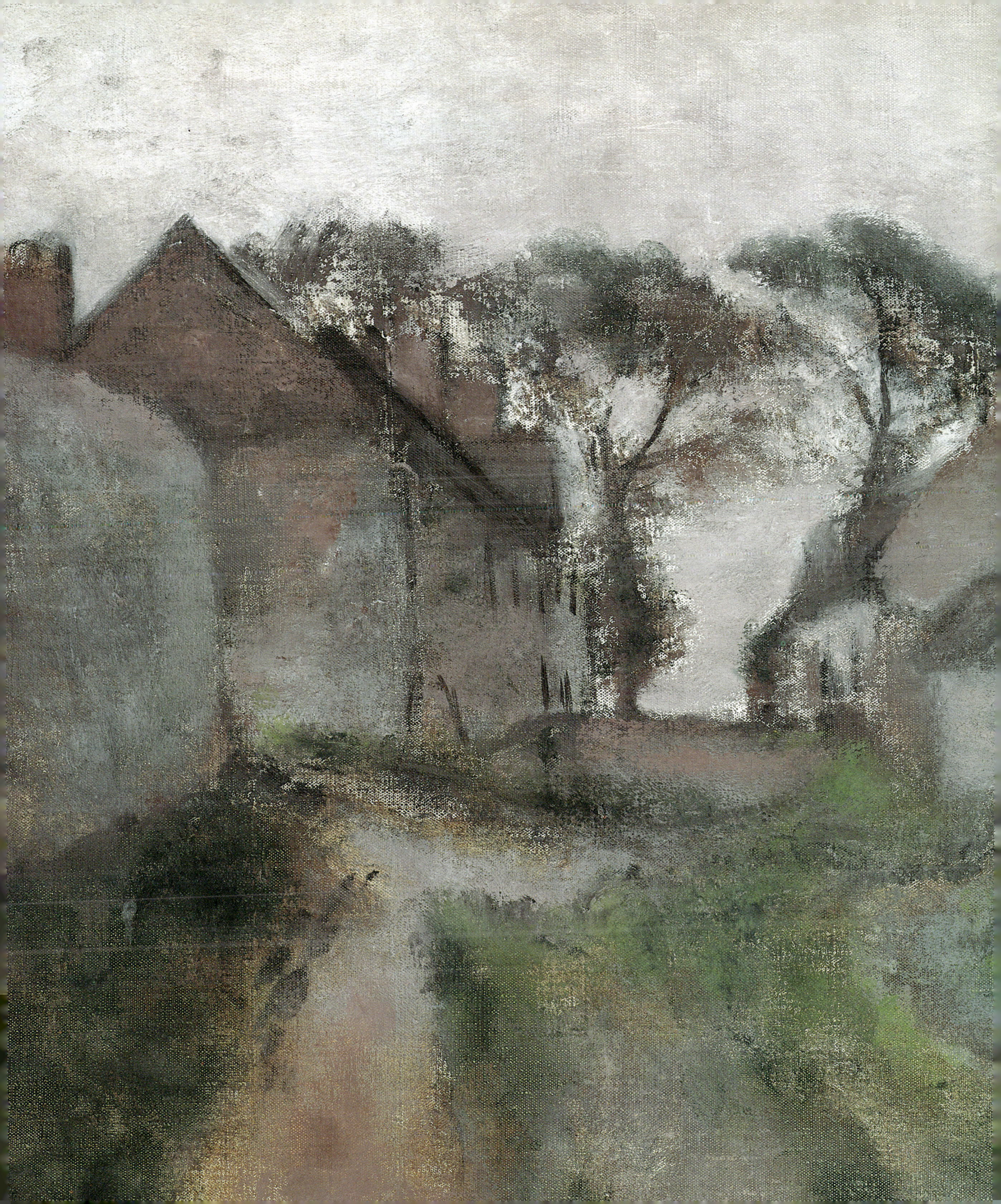

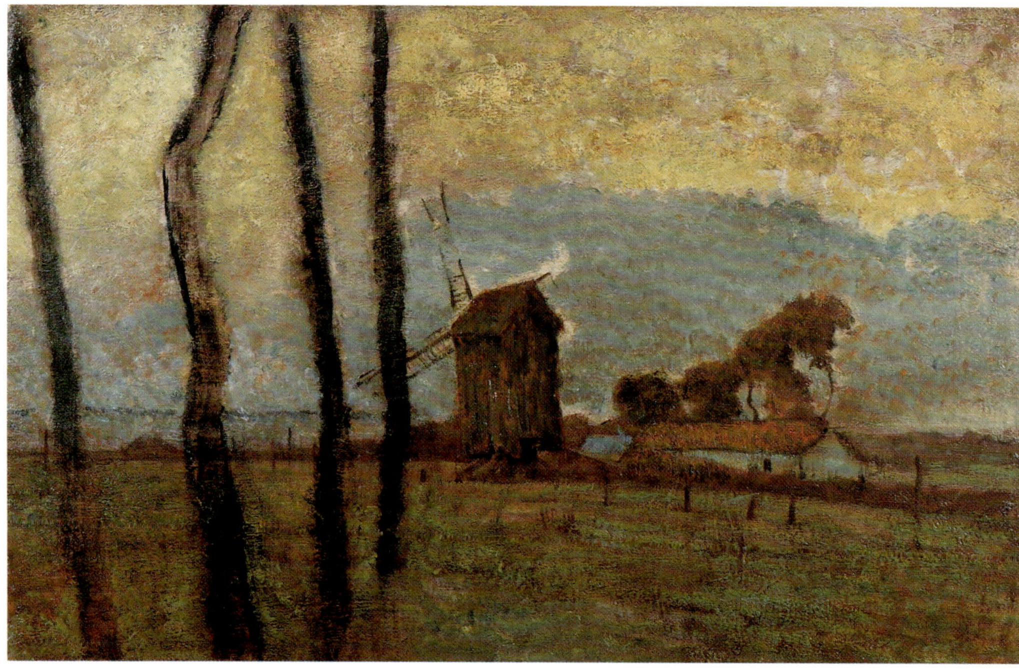

229. *Saint-Valéry-sur-Somme*, *c.*1896–8, oil on canvas, 52.5 × 78 (BR 154). Private collection.

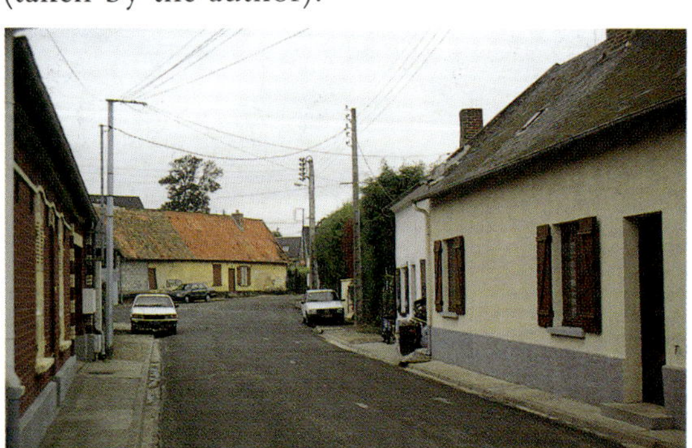

230. The farming quarter of Saint-Valéry (taken by the author).

Rectilinear geometry and autumnal colour characterise two further paintings associated with the Haute Ville, both of which were originally owned by Louis Braquaval. *Landscape* (location unknown; BR 152) shows a view from the ancient ramparts, looking over tree-tops and roofs, and beyond to La Digue and the Bay of the Somme. Dominated by a series of horizontals in landscape and promenade, the picture is saved from severity by answering verticals in foliage, architecture and foreground balustrade. Like several of the Saint-Valéry pictures, *Landscape* adopts a strikingly high viewpoint, directing us from the old town to the new, as we gaze down from the security of Degas' temporary home to the newly built villas beneath.[41] Though we might resist the symbolism of his location, we should again note the inventiveness of Degas' perceptual manoeuvres. In this case, there are no preparatory studies and the evolution of the work, as well as Degas' reasons for choosing to paint on a wooden panel, remain a mystery.[42] The second picture from Braquaval's collection, *Saint-Valéry-sur-Somme* (fig. 229), brings us as close to Degas' photographic sources as the surviving evidence permits. For the first time, a purely rural subject has been selected, presumably from the farming quarter to the west of the town. As in Degas' photograph *Trees beside a Road* (fig. 212), we confront a dramatically cruciform composition, in which a bleak and open horizon strikes against the gaunt uprights of a line of poplars. Enriched by its tapestry-like colouring and densely impasted surface, the canvas still surprises us in its simplicity, calling to mind not only Monet's grid-like *Poplars* but the radicalism of Mondrian and the painters of the Hague school.[43]

Colour takes on a more varied and assertive role in another painting that can be linked with Saint-Valéry's farming community, *Return of the Herd* (fig. 231). Despite the looming forms of the cattle, which represent the only living subjects in the Saint-Valéry series, it is the close-toned ochres, salmon-pinks and honey-browns of their surroundings that linger in the memory. An oppressive evening sky takes up the refrain, hinting at long summer days and the weariness of routine. Such densities of effect have few precedents in Degas' earlier career and

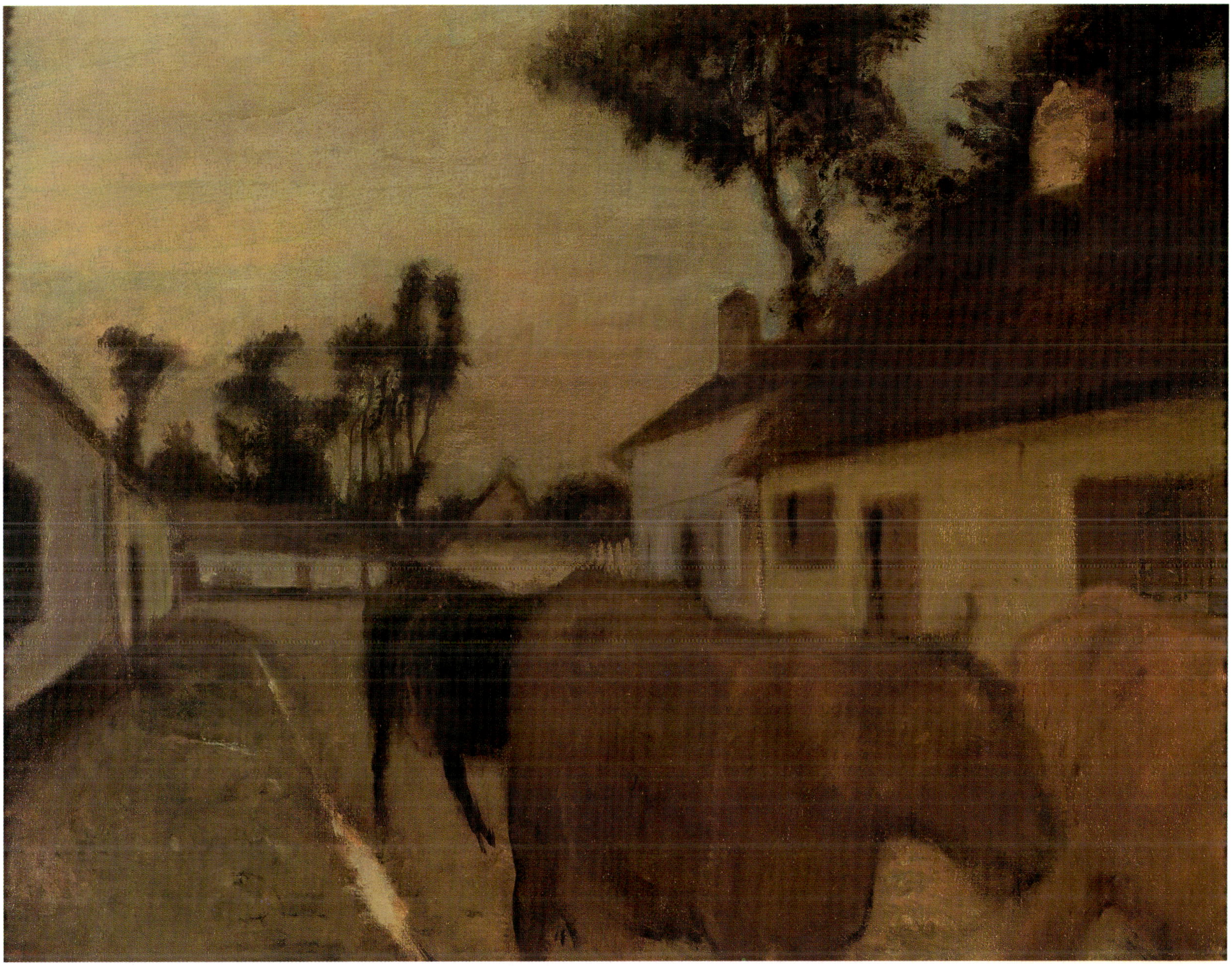

231. *Return of the Herd*, *c.*1896–8, oil on canvas, 73 × 92 (L 1213). Leicestershire Museums, Arts and Records Service.

were clearly the result of considerable labour on this occasion. Where the thickly painted surface permits, the dark lines of an original drawing can be glimpsed, along with washes of orange-brown and a more muted, delicately pink sky.[44] In building up his hues and textures, Degas' seems to have deliberately passed beyond the seductive tones of the twilight, insisting rather on the heaviness and warm familiarity of the scene. Jean Boggs is surely right in seeing the example of Gauguin in this lugubrious image, and even in certain juxtapositions of near-exotic colour.[45] By this date, Degas' had greatly extended his holdings of Gauguin's work, including such landscapes as *Tahitian Landscape* and *Mehana no atua* (fig. 214) amongst his collection of watercolours, wood-block prints and oil paintings by his younger admirer.[46] In a curious sense, *Return of the Herd* seems to combine the subject-matter of Gauguin's Brittany scenes with the intense palette of Tahiti, adding something of Degas' current preoccupation with perspective for good measure. Such a possibility is almost advertised in Degas' truncation of the orange-and-tan cattle, a *motif* shared by his earlier vertiginous *Landscape with Cows* (fig. 176) and such Breton works by Gauguin as *Haystacks in Brittany* (fig. 202).[47]

Less expected, perhaps, is the documentary realism of *Return of the Herd*. Like his picture *At Saint-Valéry-sur-Somme*, the canvas turns out to be a careful rendering of a specific street and identifiable buildings, this time located on the outer limits of the old town. Beyond the western fortifications and close to the ruined abbey, clusters of barns and traditional cottages make up the farming quarter of the Haute Ville, leading eventually to the small Chapelle des marins, just visible at the centre of Degas' picture (see fig. 223). In this modest neighbourhood, single-storey dwellings contrast with the prosperity of the rest of the town, and the rearing of livestock and the growing of vegetables are much in evidence. As a recent photograph shows (fig. 230), many of the houses depicted by Degas' survive to this day, with their low façades and high- pitched roofs, their dark shutters and chocolate-painted doors. Despite some modifications, the long, low farm building in the distance, its frontage parallel to the picture plane, is still recognisable from Degas' painting, and even its ochre walls harmonise with the artist's palette. Made from mud and wattle, most of these structures would have presented earth-coloured or lime-washed faces to the street in Degas' day and go some way towards justifying his chromatic extravagance. Once again, we should be cautious of over-emphasising the significance of such subjects, but Degas' choice of the poorest and least developed quarter of Saint-Valéry, which was also redolent of traditional trades and ways of life, seems nostalgic and wayward at best, regressive at worst.[48]

One of Degas' dominant concerns in the Saint-Valéry paintings was with the complexities and contradictions of pictorial space. In *Return of the Herd*, the cows loom large in the foreground, their heads blurred as though in an ill-focused photograph, and their bulk implicitly bursting from the frame. Conversely, the lines of adjacent buildings fall sharply away into the distance, exaggerating both their own height and the remoteness of the rest of the street. Without the intrusive cattle, the scene resolves itself into a standard perspective scheme, with converging orthogonals and an off-centre vanishing point, of a kind that features repeatedly in other Saint-Valéry canvases. All four versions of *At Saint-Valéry-sur-Somme*, for example, can be seen as explorations of this traditional format, while *Village Street* (fig. 219) and *Village Street, Saint-Valéry* (fig. 218) introduce both curving spaces and descending roadways. Earlier in the decade, Degas had expressed in his letters a wish to master complex perspectives and his frustration with the limited progress he had made.[49] His use of the Renaissance-style 'grid' when instructing Braquaval may have been an offshoot of this preoccupation, just as the extensive drawing beneath his paint surfaces at Saint-Valéry may record related procedures. Most of the surviving paintings were begun as networks of emphatic painted lines, many of which were ruled, using either black or dark-blue oil colour directly on the primed canvas. Over this wiry scaffolding, translucent veils and dense crusts of paint were added, though often with further delineations as the composition progressed. Working from depth to surface, from illusionism to pattern-making, Degas found himself face-to-face with the elements of his craft.

Without subscribing to the more reductive histories of modern painting, it is possible to see in these works a dialogue or confrontation rich in significance for Degas' successors. As his generation knew well, vanishing-point perspective brought with it the benediction of the past, but also the curse of facile illusionism and pictorial inauthenticity. Few of Degas' peers had been willing or able to master the conventional skills of perspective, but for them the expressive and decorative needs of a picture were now in the ascendant. Where pictorial recession was inevitable, it was subverted, heightened or problematised, as in the fractured spaces of Degas' ballet scenes or in Cézanne's stylised recession. The vulgar error that linked this departure with a headlong progress towards abstraction has long since been exposed, but the full implications of the new painterly language have yet to be explored. In Degas' imagery, for example, the majestic interplay of colour and line often holds our attention at the picture surface, but without any systematic denial of three-dimensional form. While his mature compositions tend to occupy shallow, relief-like spaces, the same pictures can revolve around plunging diagonals and overlapping structures, both of which preclude the possibility of flatness. This visual tension is much in evidence in pictures such as *Village Street, Saint-Valéry*, where our progress into the fictive space is arrested by a barrier of houses, then deflected sideways or back to its starting point. In the same work, buildings seem to have been wrenched round into the picture plane, echoing its rectilinear form, and dense agitations of the painted surface with the artist's brushes and fingers remind us of its ultimate physicality.

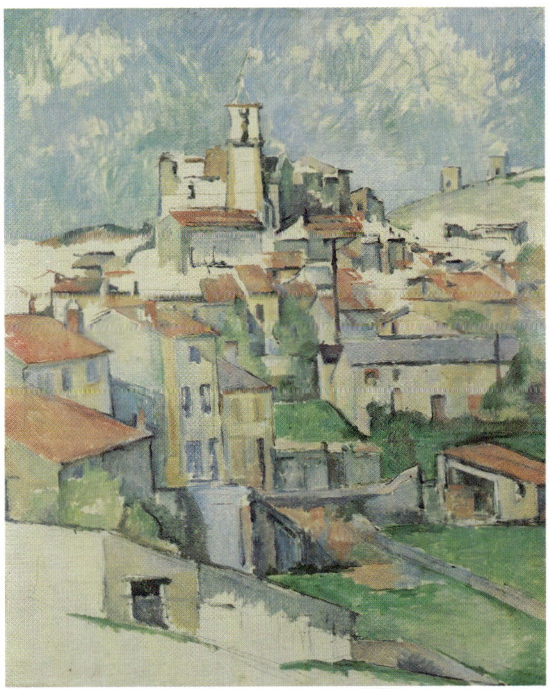

232. Paul Cézanne, *Gardanne*, 1885–6, oil on canvas, 81 × 65. The Metropolitan Museum of Art, New York, Gift of Dr. and Mrs. Franz H. Hirschland, 1957.

To discuss the paintings of Degas in such terms is to invite comparison with the subject-matter and practice of Paul Cézanne, an artist whose work Degas followed closely in the late 1890s. As we have seen, Degas acquired most of his collection of Cézanne's pictures between 1895 and 1898, and shared with him an ambition to make monumental studies of the female nude against trees and beside streams. He was also aware of Cézanne's townscapes, such as his views of L'Estaque, Auvers, Gardanne and Aix-en-Provence, all of which were represented in the 1895 retrospective at Vollard's gallery.[50] One of the less finished of this group of paintings, called simply *Gardanne* (fig. 232), shows the sub-structure of pencilled lines and painted co-ordinates that Cézanne habitually used, and his fusion of colour and form in the later stages of the work. The same picture celebrates the haphazard geometry of the uneven site, playing off façades and roof-tops, rising elevations and sloping terraces in a way that strongly prefigures the paintings of Saint-Valéry. Other studies by Cézanne offer even closer parallels, not least in their plunging foregrounds and terraced streets, and suggest further affinities between the two artists.[51] Both Cézanne and Degas seem to have visually interrogated their subjects at first hand, yet both departed wilfully from the conventions of perspective as occasion demanded. In *Gardanne*, Cézanne delighted in the irregularities of his *motif*, avoiding symmetry and precision just as we know he abhorred their modern counterparts, the straight lines of the streets of Aix and Paris.[52] Without over-stressing their similarities, it is surely inconceivable that Degas' could have overlooked the challenge of Cézanne's town studies, just as it is unimaginable that his own weathered, slightly sombre pictures of Picardy might be mistaken for the Provençal scenes of his near-contemporary.

The extent to which Degas would sometimes take liberties with his urban subject-matter is first encountered in the two versions of *Village Street* (figs 218 and 219). Though contained within contrasting formats and representing different angles of view, the two works are manifestly based on a single corner of the Haute Ville and respect its principal outlines. A comparison of their details, however, shows a sovereign disregard by Degas for the finer points of architecture and the nuances of local topography. Between one picture and another, windows and doors change shape or disappear, a line of trees is

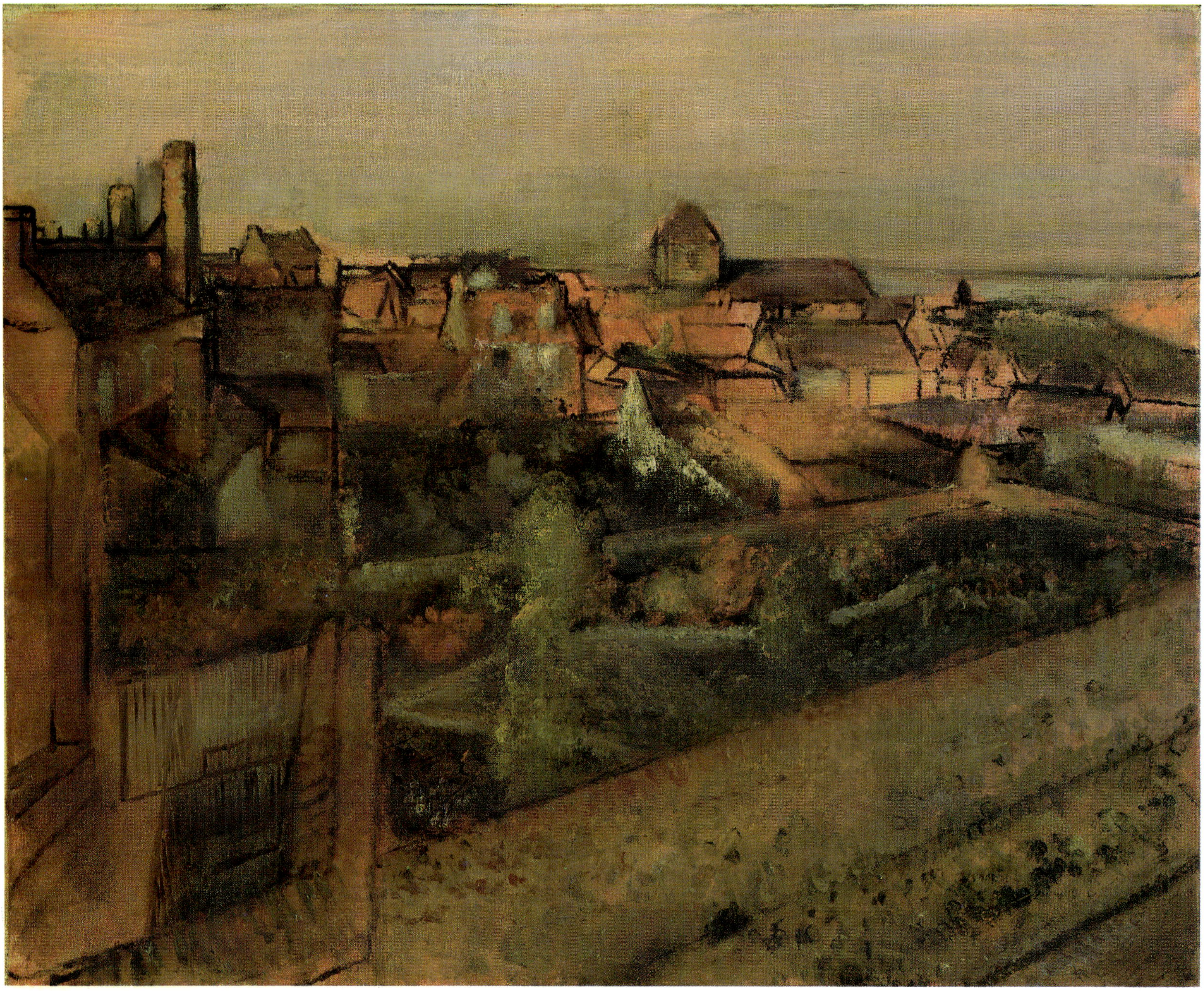

233. *View of Saint-Valéry-sur-Somme*, 1896–8, oil on canvas, 51 × 61 (BR 150). The Metropolitan Museum of Art, New York, The Robert Lehman Collection, 1975.

imperiously axed, and roof-lines and walls take on new orientations to suit altered painterly circumstances. The site in question, which is again adjacent to Braquaval's house, appears to have been extensively remodelled since Degas took note of it, leaving us in some doubt as to the significance of his extemporisations. Of a different order of magnitude, and rather more quantifiable, is the inventiveness of *View of Saint-Valéry-sur-Somme* (fig. 233). Principally derived from a view of the old town from its southern aspect, this canvas shows a huddle of houses around the medieval church, with a glimpse of light on the bay beyond. Today this view can be approximated from the rue au Loups, a small lane leading from the modern D3 road as it rises out of Saint-Valéry in the direction of Cayeux-sur-Mer (see fig. 223). Despite almost a century of rebuilding, most of the elements of Degas' composition can still be seen, including the long, erratically cultivated gardens, the gables and chimney-stacks of barns and dwellings, and even distinctive clumps of trees. Up to this point, the comparison seems straightforward, but from here onwards it demands greater ingenuity. The high, almost aerial prospect of Saint-Valéry in the painting cannot be accounted for from the rue au Loups and presupposes an elevated vantage point, such as that from the three-storey *hôtel* that still stands nearby.[53] More perplexing is the fact that, even from this building, no single viewpoint could embrace all aspects of Degas' scene. If the tower of Saint-Martin is aligned as Degas shows it, the row of shadowy house-backs at the left runs obliquely across our field of vision, not away from us as they appear in the painting. Conversely, if we adopt a position where the houses follow the painting, neither church tower nor the buildings of the old town would fall within the picture rectangle.

These discrepancies have far-reaching and perhaps historic implications. In composing *View of Saint-Valéry-sur-Somme*, Degas appears to have brought together two quite distinct perceptions: the right-hand part of the picture has been viewed and recorded from one angle of view, the left-hand part from another. In themselves, each section is coherent and faithful to its subject, but as a continuous panorama the picture is a fiction. Only by substantially moving his vantage point could Degas' have shifted from one view to another, and only by grafting or fusing these two views together could he have contrived the present composition. So dramatic is this juncture, that the line where right-hand and left-hand elements meet on the canvas surface is still clearly visible, as a dark vertical line about a quarter of the way across the picture rectangle.[54] It is not impossible that photography played a role in this extraordinary process. The distortions of a camera lens might have suggested the realignment of certain peripheral structures, though they would hardly account for the fundamental disruption of the scene. More radically, a collage-like process involving two separate prints, each based on a different view of the subject and then joined or abutted in an arbitrary fashion, would lead to a semblance of the painted image. Just as probable is that Degas' carried the selectivity of his *Village Street* pictures to new extremes, freely editing his subject-matter and even rearranging its principal components.[55] That in doing so he departed from many of the canonical principles of post-Renaissance art, replacing single-point perspective and the sovereignty of the *motif* with a kind of proto-Cubist licence, the modest view of *Saint-Valéry-sur-Somme* has only now revealed.

Any lingering doubts we might have about the perceptual acrobatics of such a picture are laid to rest in one of the most monumental of Degas' Saint-Valéry paintings, *Houses at the Foot of a Cliff* (fig. 236). Here again, two non-contiguous perceptions of the town have been juxtaposed, but in even more extreme and unexpected circumstances. This time, the junction between the two is horizontal, running almost exactly through the centre of the canvas. Above this level, we see a distant prospect of the Haute Ville, with its cliff-like ramparts, its bristling trees and miniature roof-tops, and its church tower catching the evening sun. The same view is recorded in a black-and-white postcard made soon after Degas' visits, showing the battlements from closer quarters and the proliferation of housing that once engulfed the town walls (fig. 234). Both the postcard and the upper part of the painting are depictions of the old town from the north-west, seen either from the extreme limit of the modern promenade or from a boat out in the bay (see fig. 223). Beneath its central dividing line, however, Degas' canvas shows an inexplicable departure from this scene. Here, the artist has painted a grassy bank, a cluster of cottages and, towards the

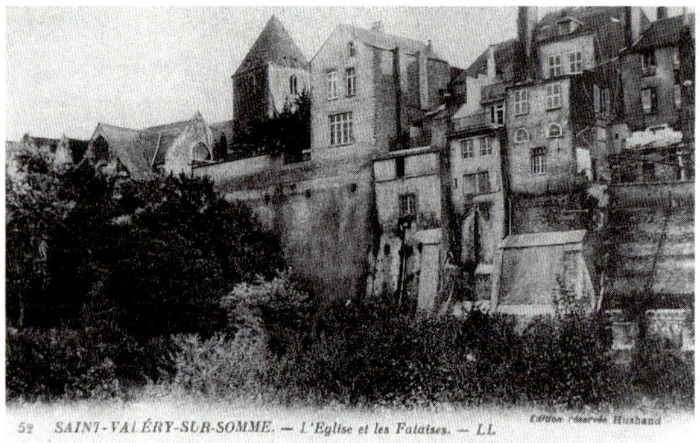

234. Postcard view of the Haute Ville, Saint-Valéry. Private collection.

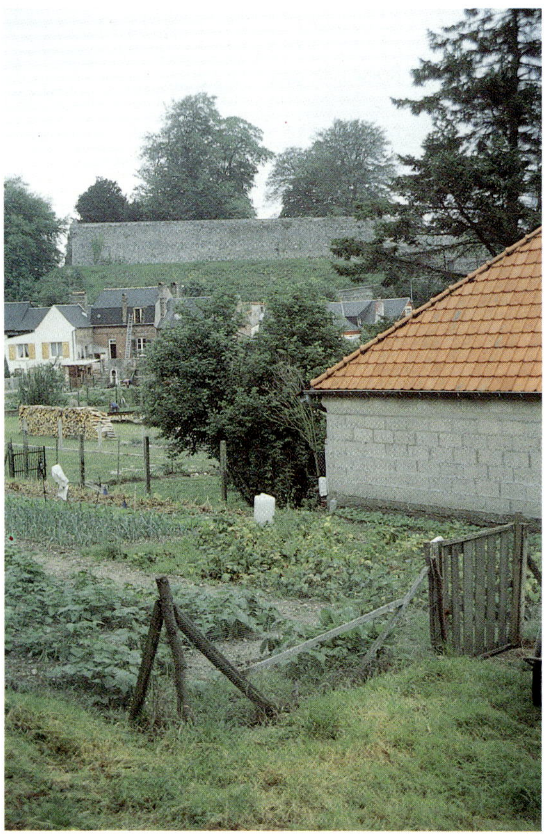

235. The southern ramparts, Saint-Valéry (taken by the author).

236. *Houses at the Foot of a Cliff*, 1896–8, oil on canvas, 92 × 73 (L 1219). Columbus Museum of Art, Ohio, Gift of Howard D. and Babette L. Sirak, The Donors to the Campaign for Enduring Excellence, and the Derby Fund.

left-hand edge of the picture, another church tower basking in the evening light. In the Saint-Valéry that Degas knew, no such features existed on this site, and none is recorded in contemporary maps, plans or photographs.[56] Between the foot of the ramparts and the estuary, only a narrow strip of flat land could be seen, carrying part of the promenade and one or two recently built villas, all quite unlike the modest dwellings in Degas' painting.[57]

When Degas painted *Houses at the Foot of a Cliff*, the level stretch of ground beneath the Saint-Valéry fortifications had little or no resemblance to the scene he composed in the lower half of his canvas. As in *View of Saint-Valéry-sur-Somme*, but on a quite majestic scale, the artist has swept away elements of the existing *motif*, replacing them by others as his fancy dictated. In a further twist to the story, it seems that Degas may have 'borrowed' these new structures from a quite different quarter of the town. At the southern or inland side of the fortifications, within a few paces of the site used to paint *View of Saint-Valéry-sur-Somme*, a comparable group of low-lying cottages still survives, surrounded by trees and grassy slopes (fig. 235). Behind them, the medieval walls rise like the ramparts in *Houses at the Foot of a Cliff* and may have suggested the bizarre conjunction of these two disparate sites. The second sun-lit church has no such justification. Saint-Valéry has only one medieval edifice of this kind, the church of Saint-Martin in the Haute Ville, and Degas had already painted this in its correct position. Undeterred, he seems to have conjured up an additional, phantom version of the original building, complete with a variant of its gabled façade and pyramidal tower, to give extra vitality to this part of the canvas. Adding and subtracting, inventing and preposterously relocating entire sections of the town, Degas painted a Saint-Valéry that existed only in his mind's eye.

Scrutiny of the complex surface of *Houses at the Foot of a Cliff* has cast some light on Degas' creative procedures.[58] Though photography may again have been used, perhaps in the same 'collage' fashion suggested by *View of Saint-Valéry-sur-Somme*, there are few signs of radical disjuncture in the paint layer. As in several other Saint-Valéry canvases, bright stains of colour were first laid down, ranging from warm orange in the lower areas to a surprising green beneath the sky.[59] Perhaps with the techniques of his Venetian predecessors in mind, as so often at this period, Degas' then dabbed and streaked other colours over this ground, allowing occasional glimpses of the earlier layer to remain visible. Painted lines were used to define the forms of houses and tracks, then frequently overpainted and sometimes redrawn. In places, an almost exotic density of paint accumulated, swirling across a Turner-like sky and drifting in elusive pinks, cuprous greens and metallic greys against the shadowy cliff-face. Sharp oppositions of colour abound, with earth-red stroked over leaf-green, gold over lavender, and the blue of the slates juxtaposed with an orange façade.[60] Within such density, there are inevitable shifts of contour and redefinitions of hue, but little to suggest a fundamental change of heart as the composition progressed.[61] Rather, it seems that Degas planned his hybrid image from the beginning, coaxing his newly assembled cast of forms, tints and textures into a gloriously rich ensemble, and proudly asserting his independence of the natural scene.

Such manipulations of the evidence of an artist's senses may seem modest or merely eccentric to a late twentieth-century audience, accustomed as we are to the fragmentations of Cubism and Futurism, the improvisations of Surrealism and the self-referential world of abstraction. In the 1890s, and in the context of an essentially empirical late Impressionism, wholesale dismemberment of the *motif* and its recombination with extraneously gathered material had few

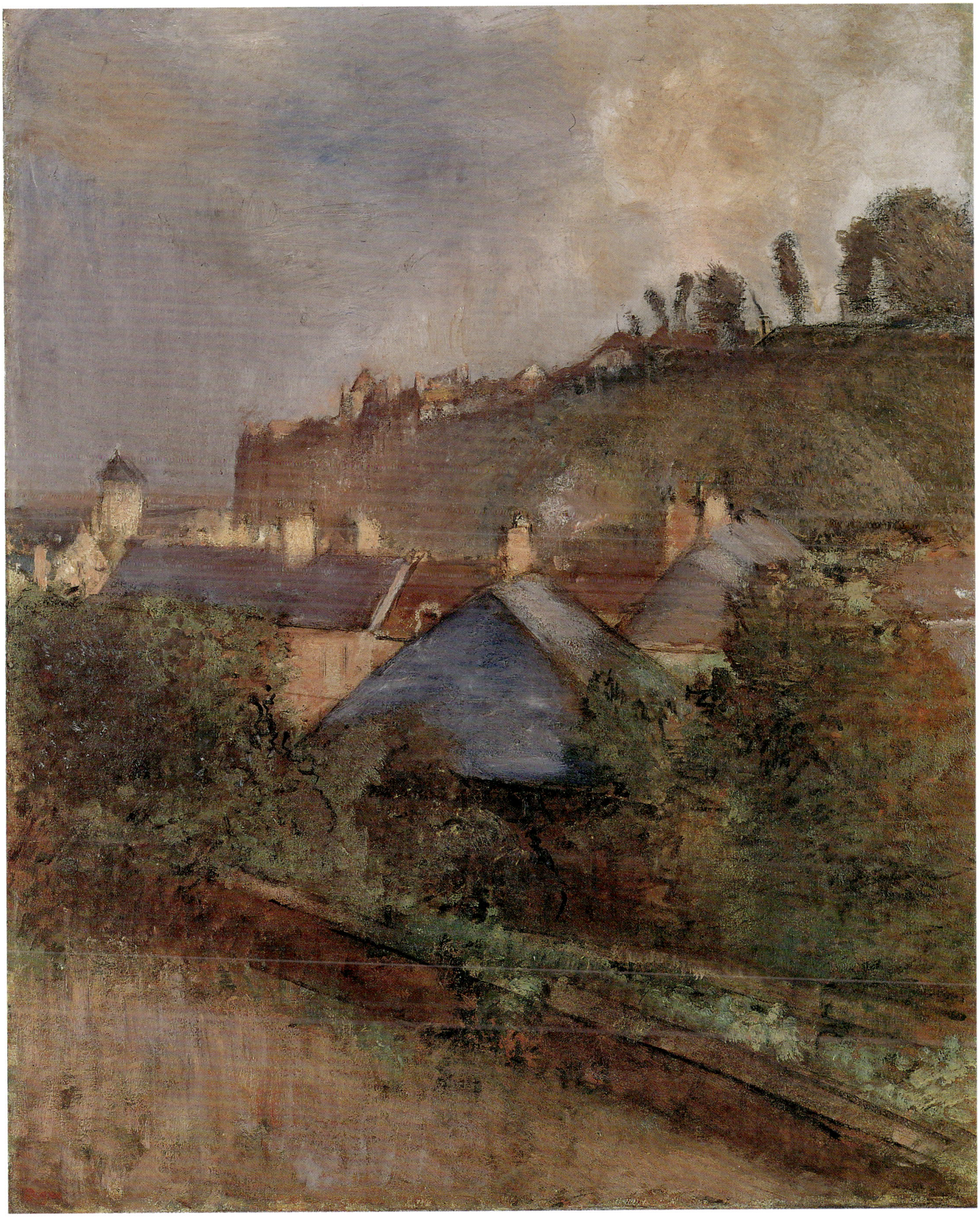

precedents. As we have seen earlier in the decade, Degas' engagement with the landscape had often been characterised by a restless, technically inventive approach to his subject-matter and a relentless questioning of the operations of vision and recollection. When he recomposed his Diénay landscapes from the briefest of memories, when he fused observation and reverie in the 'paysages de fantasie' and when he impatiently guided Braquaval in the use of his Leonardesque 'grid', Degas was exploring both ancient and entirely novel resolutions of the artist's creative quandary. On the one hand, the external world invites scrutiny and pictorial emulation, on the other, its patient transcription rarely satisfies our needs. In their different ways, several of Degas' closest colleagues had probed this dilemma, questioning their own responses to their surroundings and pressing at the limits of representation. Like generations of earlier landscapists, Pissarro would move a road or realign a house to suit his compositions, introducing or eliminating figures, animals and effects of light at will. Cézanne went further, bending parallel walls and marshalling lines of improbably uniform trees, even shifting the position of his eyes when grasping his *motif.* And in his letters, Monet described the 'stubborn encrustations of colours' of his *Rouen Cathedral* paintings as attempts to 'convey what I feel', rather than as mere depictions of what he saw.[62]

Degas is known to have followed the parallel researches of his fellow-painters throughout the 1890s, attending their exhibitions and applauding their advances. Apart from his excited response to Cézanne's 1895 show, where he competed with Renoir for the purchase of a watercolour, Degas may have heard something of Cézanne's practices and methods through their extensive mutual acquaintance.[63] When Monet showed his *Rouen Cathedral* series at Durand-Ruel's in 1895, Degas was amongst those who 'praised them highly', according to the first-hand account of Camille Pissarro.[64] The following year, Pissarro's own display at the same gallery included a group of views of Rouen, many of which were based on high viewing angles, dramatic geometry and abrasive dispositions of streets and roof-tops.[65] Again, Degas was quick to admire them, perhaps remembering such canvases as *Roofs of Old Rouen* when he started work on his Saint-Valéry pictures soon afterwards.[66] Much of this climate of innovation and competitiveness surrounded Degas' last landscape series, and it is difficult not to see such works as *Village Street* and *At Saint-Valéry-sur-Somme* as contributions to a vigorous pictorial debate. Conversely, none of the artists in question seems to have matched Degas' most radical interventions, either in the dramatic visual editing of *View of Saint-Valéry-sur-Somme* or the wholesale rearrangement of the landscape in *Houses at the Foot of a Cliff.* In these pictures, Degas used photographs or fragments of his own perception to reconstitute his vision, combining separate vantage points, discontinuous memories and pure fabrication. At their most pragmatic, his manoeuvres enlivened compositions and brought animation to otherwise placid scenes; at their most audacious, they changed the artist's relationship with the external world.

Not for the first time in Degas' career as a maker of landscapes, the promise of the Saint-Valéry pictures was never fulfilled. The exhibition that might have followed the success of the 1892 monotypes never materialised, and more than half the works remained in the artist's studio, unsigned, unsold and unknown to the world at large.[67] Certain pictures were acquired by those with a personal interest in the story, such as Louis Braquaval, René de Gas and Jeanne Fevre, but the rest were dispersed at the time of the artist's death.[68] In retrospect, it seems most unlikely that the entire sequence of works was made in 1898, the year of Degas' letter to Alexis Rouart, and we must presume that they were

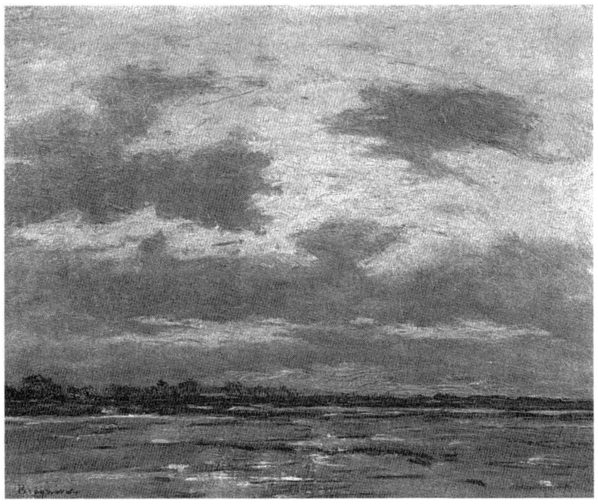

237. Louis Braquaval, *La Baie de Somme*, oil on panel, 37 × 45.8. Musée de Picardie, Amiens.

carried out on successive visits, perhaps beginning in 1896 and lasting until the end of the decade.[69] Correspondence between Degas and the Braquaval family shows that they continued to meet, dine together in Paris and enjoy excursions to the coast as late as 1909, Degas once turning up at Saint-Valéry with the young art-dealer Ambroise Vollard in tow.[70] Degas' encouragement for his younger colleagues persisted, though he can hardly have been gratified by the mannered and pedestrian works that Braquaval began to exhibit, or even his return to the Boudinesque manner of paintings like *La Baie de Somme* (fig. 237).[71] Writing briefly of his own activities at this time, Degas' described to Braquaval his illnesses and eyesight problems, claiming that he was 'unable to leave his studio' but that he continued 'to work obstinately'.[72]

The sequence of Saint-Valéry paintings, pastels and photographs were the last landscapes that Degas made. After the explosion of inventive and expressive landscape-based pictures of the late 1890s, which included the pastoral nudes, the *Russian Dancers* series and the Saint-Valéry works themselves, Degas eliminated this theme from his repertoire, just as he eliminated so many other subjects that survived from his earlier career. During the same decade, he made his last scenes of the racetrack, the last *Laundresses* and almost his final portraits, as if turning his back on the profligacy of youth. Monotype, lithography and etching were also abandoned, each after a final flurry of activity, and no photographs have been found that post-date the Saint-Valéry prints. Beyond the turn of the century, effectively the only subject left in Degas' oeuvre was the single most persistent theme of his career; the female figure. Until about 1912, when he was obliged to move from his Montmartre studio, Degas continued to make images of the dance and studies of preoccupied, lugubrious nudes, working either directly from the model or, as the artist himself admitted, occasionally 'from fantasy'.[73] Though he still travelled, making a perilous journey to Naples in 1906, Degas confined himself increasingly to his studio, preoccupied by his experiments with sculpture and reduced to the most fundamental rituals of his art; 'I trace and retrace' he wrote to Braquaval in 1907.[74]

Degas' last years are still mysterious to us, and the guiding ambitions and concerns of his gravity-defying waxes, his tremulous charcoal drawings and his strident late pastels have yet to be fully articulated. Ill-health and what Sickert called 'the torment that it was to draw' dogged his daily routines, and the deaths of close friend and former colleagues like Henri Rouart and Camille Pissarro lowered his spirits.[75] Though his reclusiveness has often been exaggerated, Degas certainly withdrew from the world of public exhibitions and the competitiveness of the market-place, refusing to lend work to important displays and selling only such items as necessity demanded. The true mystery, perhaps, is that he continued to work at all, cut off from the stimulus and the practical motivations of his middle years. His art became almost alarmingly hermetic, enclosed within the confines of his apartment and within the procedures of tracing, drawing and modelling from the living figure. Still clinging to the precedence of Ingres and Delacroix, even of Michelangelo and Veronese, the artist returned to some of the emblems of his youth, distantly re-working fragments from the *Battle of Cascina*, the *Valpinçon Bather* and the *Entry of the Crusaders into Constantinople*. Conversely, his pictures often advanced towards a complexity and an expressive density that outweighs his earlier achievement. The glorious chromaticism of the *Russian Dancers* and certain of the Saint-Valéry canvases was carried forward into such works as *After the Bath, Woman Drying her Hair* of around 1905;[76] the linear licence of the Chicago

Bathers was taken to new extremes in the charcoal-and-pastel *After the Bath*;[77] and the compositional audacity of such pictures as *Houses at the Foot of a Cliff* found new equivalents in dynamic truncations and fractured spaces.

Surrounded by his own accumulated work and his vast collection of the drawings, prints and paintings of others, Degas spent his last decade as a working artist in a process of recapitulation and entrenchment. On his walls, a portrait by Ingres reminded him of his youth, a landscape by Corot recalled his apprenticeship in Italy, and the *Young Spartans* brought back the faltering start of his professional career.[78] With the exception of the monotypes dispersed after the Durand-Ruel exhibition, most of his own landscapes remained in notebooks, portfolios and in stacks of canvases in his studio, the obscure evidence of a lifetime's clandestine attachment. From his earliest encounters with the work of Claude and Gregoire Soutzo, through his infatuation with Delacroix and the discovery of Boudin, Pollard, Riesener and Hiroshige, landscape had haunted Degas' first decades. In mid-career, his equestrian scenes, beach studies and outdoor portraits had brought him into the closest proximity with his Impressionist colleagues, while defining his distance from them. Endlessly inventive in the studio, if not in the open air, Degas' experiments with colour and the chance generation of form in the 1890 monotypes placed him in the vanguard of the contemporary landscape, and left us with some of his most radical imagery in any medium. Working side-by-side with Pissarro and Gauguin, and at a competitive remove from Monet, Degas explored the coloured print, the fantasy image and the pictorial series, and at a tangent to all of them he pursued the application of photography, and perhaps the photographic collage, in the context of landscape. If he was secretive, he was also astonishingly courageous and innovative, carrying landscape to the very brink of coherence. For Degas, the landscape could be a recreation or a practical discipline, a link with the past and a bridge into the radical future, a pretext for irresponsibility and a challenge to perceptual orthodoxy; at its best, it was all of these things.

Appendix 1 The Complete Colour Monotypes

In this table, all Degas' known colour landscape monotypes are grouped according to the size of the plate from which they were printed. Plate A, measuring approximately 30 × 40 cm, appears to have been used at Diénay in 1890 and corresponds to some of the most experimental prints of the series, the majority of which were not developed in pastel. The remaining plates, B and C, of approximately 25 × 34 cm and 25 × 30 cm respectively, were used probably in 1892 and resulted in two further groups of prints, all of them re-worked in pastel and all but one signed by the artist.

Where possible, the prints have been measured directly by the author or by museum staff; in other cases, the most recently published dimensions have been cited. Where slight variations are evident within a group, they are typically due to imprecise edges on individual images, reliance on 'sight size' rather than plate size, and the loss of plate marks beneath pastel additions.

Catalogue numbers preceded by 'J' refer to Janis 1968; those preceded by 'K' refer to Appendix 2 in this work. Where a monotype has been heightened with pastel or signed by the artist, it is marked by an asterisk. If a print belongs to a cognate pair, the number of its cognate is indicated in the final column.

GROUP	CATALOGUE NUMBER	SHORT TITLE	SIZE	PASTEL	SIGN.	COGN.
A	J 275	*Village in l'Estérel*	30 × 40	–	–	J 276
A	J 276	*Estérel Village*	30 × 39.9	–	–	J 275
A	J 277	*Landscape with Smokestacks*	28 × 40	–	–	–
A	J 279	*Autumn Landscape*	30.3 × 40	*	–	J 280
A	J 280	*River Banks*	30 × 40	*	–	J 279
A	J 281	*River Banks*	30 × 40	*	*	–
A	J 283	*Landscape with Rocky Cliffs*	40 × 29	*	–	–
A	J 286	*Pathway in a Field*	30 × 39.5	*	*	–
A	J 287	*River*	30 × 40	*	–	–
A	J 289	*Landscape in the Mountains*	30.4 × 40	–	–	J 290
A	J 290	*Landscape with Water*	30 × 39	*	*	J 289
A	J 292	*Road in the Forest*	29.9 × 40	–	–	–
A	J 293	*Rocky Coast*	30.5 × 40.9	*	*	J 294
A	J 294	*Rocky Coast*	31 × 42	*	*	J 293
A	J 295	*Le Cap Hornu*	29.9 × 40	–	–	–
A	J 296	*Mountains and Valley*	30 × 40	–	–	–
A	J 297	*A Wooded Landscape*	29.9 × 40.3	–	–	–
A	J 298	*Mountain Effect*	29.9 × 39.5	–	–	–
A	J 299	*Autumn Effect*	30 × 40.2	–	–	–
A	J 300	*L'Estérel*	30.2 × 40	–	–	J 301
A	J 301	*L'Estérel*	30 × 40	–	–	J 300
A	J 302	*A Lake in the Pyrenees*	29.8 × 39.6	–	–	–
A	J 305	*Landscape*	29.7 × 39.6	–	–	–
A	J 306	*Squall in the Mountains*	30.3 × 39.8	–	–	–

GROUP	CATALOGUE NUMBER	SHORT TITLE	SIZE	PASTEL	SIGN.	COGN.
A	J 307	*Twilight in the Pyrenees*	28.6 × 38.8	–	–	–
A	J 308	*Le Cap Ferrat*	29.7 × 39.9	–	–	–
A	J 309	*Landscape*	29.9 × 39.9	–	–	–
A	J 311	*An Island in the Sea*	30 × 40	*	–	–
A	J 313	*Landscape*	30 × 40	–	*	–
A	J 315	*Undulating Terrain*	30 × 40	*	–	–
A	J 317	*Mountainous Terrain*	30 × 40	*	–	–
A	K 1	*Russet Landscape*	30 × 40	–	–	–
A	K 2	*Green Landscape*	30 × 40	–	–	–
A	K 3	*Burgundy Landscape*	30 × 40	–	*	–
A	K 4	*Landscape*	30 × 40	*	*	–
B	J 274	*Landscape*	27 × 36	*	*	–
B	J 284	*Landscape*	25.4 × 34.2	*	*	J 285
B	J 285	*Landscape*	25.4 × 34	*	*	J 286
B	J 288	*Landscape*	25.7 × 34.6	*	*	–
B	J 291	*Wheatfield and Line of Trees*	25 × 34	*	*	–
B	J 303	*Landscape*	27 × 36	*	*	J 304
B	J 304	*Lake and Mountains*	24 × 34	*	*	J 303
B	J 312	*Landscape with Rocks*	25.7 × 34.5	*	*	–
B	J 316	*Landscape*	27 × 36	*	*	K 5
B	K 5	*Landscape*	24.7 × 34.5	*	*	J 316
B	J 319	*Olive Trees . . .*	25 × 34	*	*	–
B	J 320	*Wheatfield and Green Hill*	26 × 34	*	*	J 321
B	J 321	*The Field of Flax*	25 × 34	*	*	J 320
B	K 6	*Landscape beside the Sea*	25.2 × 34.4	*	*	K7/8/9?
B	K 7	*Landscape with Cows*	26 × 35.5	*	*	K6/8/9?
B	K 8	*Ploughed Field . . .*	25 × 34	*	–	K6/7/9?
B	K 9	*Horse beside a Pond*	25 × 34	*	*	K6/7/8?
C	J 278	*Landscape*	24.1 × 28.6	*	*	–
C	J 310	*Vesuvius*	25 × 30	*	*	–
C	J 314	*Landscape*	24.8 × 30	*	*	–

Appendix 2 Additions to the Catalogue of Colour Monotype Landscapes

This appendix is intended to revise and augment the list of colour landscape prints contained in Eugenia P. Janis, *Degas Monotypes: Essay, Catalogue and Checklist*, Cambridge, Mass., 1968. As the present volume makes clear, two works listed by Janis (nos J 282 and J 318) must now be re-classified as pastels, since they lack a monotype base. Conversely, a number of pictures listed as pastels in P.-A. Lemoisne, *Degas et son oeuvre*, Paris 1946–9, have recently been found to have monotype underlayers, and are now catalogued as such. Finally, a small group of works of unknown location appear to have dimensions and other characteristics that link them with the monotype 'families' summarised in appendix 1, and have therefore been provisionally included in the revised list.

1 RUSSET LANDSCAPE *c.*1890 Fig. 154

Monotype in oil colours on buff wove paper. Plate: 29.6 × 39.8 cm. Not signed.

PROVENANCE: Marcel Guérin, Paris; Robert M. Light, Boston: B.C. Holland, Chicago.

EXHIBITIONS: Art Institute of Chicago, 1984 (Supplementary exhibition), no. S.32.

BIBLIOGRAPHY: Adhémar and Cachin 1974, no. 198, p. 280 (illus.).

PRIVATE COLLECTION.

2 GREEN LANDSCAPE *c.*1890 Fig. 144

Monotype in oil colours on beige laid paper. Plate: 30 × 40 cm. Not signed.

PROVENANCE: Marcel Guérin, Paris (collector's stamp lower left).

BIBLIOGRAPHY: Adhémar and Cachin 1974, no. 199, p. 280 (illus.).

PRIVATE COLLECTION, NEW YORK.

3 BURGUNDY LANDSCAPE *c.*1890 Fig. 127

Monotype in oil colours on cream laid paper. Plate: 30 × 40 cm. Signed lower left in red wax crayon, and inscribed *à Bartholomé*.

PROVENANCE: Albert Bartholomé; Robert Le Masle.

EXHIBITIONS: Galerie Durand-Ruel, Paris, 1892; Galeries Georges Petit, Paris, *Degas*, 1924, no. 243 (as 'Le Vallon'); Hayward Gallery, London, *Degas Monotypes*, 1985, no. 26; Grand Palais, Paris, *Degas*, 1988, no. 299; Musée d'Orsay, Paris, *L'Europe des peintres*, 1993.

BIBLIOGRAPHY: Geneviève Monnier, 'Un Monotype Inédit de Degas', *Revue du Louvre*, I, 1973, p. 39; Adhémar and Cachin 1974, no. 201, p. 280 (illus.); Maurice Serullaz, *L'univers de Degas*, 1979, p. 27; Kendall 1987, p. 222.

MUSÉE DU LOUVRE, PARIS.

4 LANDSCAPE *c.*1890 Fig. 197

Pastel over monotype in oil colours, on paper. Plate 30 × 40 cm. Signed lower right.

PROVENANCE: Galerie Durand-Ruel, Paris; Tadamasa Hayashi, Paris; Knoedler and Co., New York; John Quinn, New York; Arthur B. Davies, New York; Katherine D. Murdoch, New York; Sam Salz, New York.

EXHIBITIONS: Galerie Durand-Ruel, Paris, 1892.

BIBLIOGRAPHY: Hayashi 1908, (unpag.); Brame and Reff 1984, no. 136, p. 148 (illus.); Pickvance 1988, p. 253; Mari K. Meller, 'Exercises in and around Degas's classrooms: Part III', *Burlington Magazine*, July 1993, p. 460.

LOCATION UNKNOWN.

5 LANDSCAPE *c.*1892 Fig. 170

Pastel over monotype in oil colours, on greyish-beige wove paper. Cognate of J 316. Plate 24.7 × 34.5 cm. Signed lower right, in red pastel.

PROVENANCE: Shaunaugh Fitzgerald, London.

EXHIBITIONS: Art Institute of Chicago, 1984 (Supplementary exhibition), no. S.33.

PRIVATE COLLECTION.

6 LANDSCAPE BESIDE THE SEA *c.*1892 Fig. 177

Pastel over monotype in oil colours, on buff laid paper. Cognate of K 7, K 8 or K 9?. Plate 25.2 × 34.4 cm. Signed lower right, in black, and inscribed *à M. Charpentier.*

PROVENANCE: Ambroise Vollard, Paris; Yvan and Helene Amez-Droz.

EXHIBITIONS: Galerie Durand-Ruel, Paris, 1892?

BIBLIOGRAPHY: A. Vollard, *Album Degas*, 1914, pl. 53; Lemoisne 1946, no. 632; Musée des Beaux-Arts, Neuchâtel, *Legs Yvan et Helene Amez-Droz*, 1980, p. 29.

MUSÉE DES BEAUX-ARTS, NEUCHÂTEL.

7 LANDSCAPE WITH COWS *c.*1892 Fig. 176

Pastel, presumed to be over monotype in oil colours, on buff laid paper. Cognate of K 6, K 8 or K 9?. Plate 26 × 35.5 cm. Signed lower left in pencil.

PROVENANCE: Galerie Durand-Ruel, Paris: H.O. Havemeyer, New York; Mrs H.O. Havemeyer; Mr and Mrs Horace Havemeyer; Mrs Horace Havemeyer, New York.

EXHIBITIONS: Galerie Durand-Ruel, Paris, 1892; Grand Palais, Paris – National Gallery of Canada, Ottawa – Metropolitan Museum of Art, New York, *Degas*, 1988–9, no. 283; Metropolitan Museum of Art, New York, *Splendid Legacy: The Havemeyer Collection*, 1993, no. 245.

BIBLIOGRAPHY: *H.O. Havemeyer Collection*, New York, 1931, p. 388; Lemoisne 1946, no. 633; Weitzenhoffer 1986, p. 98 and pl. 46.

PRIVATE COLLECTION.

8 PLOUGHED FIELD BORDERED BY TREES *c.*1892

Pastel, presumed to be over monotype in oil colours, on paper. Cognate of K 6, K 7 or K 9?. Plate 25 × 34 cm. Not signed.

PROVENANCE: *Vente IV*, no. 37; Cottevieille, Paris.

BIBLIOGRAPHY: Lemoisne 1946, no. 634.

LOCATION UNKNOWN.

9 HORSE BESIDE A POND *c.*1892

Pastel, presumed to be over monotype in oil colours, on paper. Cognate of K 6, K 7 or K 8?. Plate 25 × 34 cm. Signed bottom left.

PROVENANCE: Durand-Ruel, Paris.

EXHIBITIONS: Galerie Durand-Ruel, Paris, 1892(?)

BIBLIOGRAPHY: Lemoisne 1946, no. 631.

LOCATION UNKNOWN

Notes

Full details of all the works cited can be found in the Bibliography.

References to Degas' notebooks follow the numbering and pagination adopted in Theodore Reff, *The Notebooks of Edgar Degas*, 2 vols, Oxford 1976.

1 The Classical Landscape

1. Loyrette 1991, p. 29.
2. Loyrette 1991, pp. 30–2.
3. Lemoisne 1946, I, p. 29.
4. Lemoisne 1946, I, p. 30.
5. For the history of Degas' notebooks, see Reff 1976 (*Notebooks*), pp. 1–3.
6. Lemoisne 1921, p. 228.
7. Lemoisne 1921, p. 230.
8. Lemoisne 1921, pp. 230–1.
9. See Reff 1976, 'The Landscape Painter Degas might have been'.
10. Reff 1976 (*Notebooks*), notebooks nos 1–6.
11. The identification of the sites of Degas' notebook drawings is indebted to Reff 1976 (*Notebooks*). Though every page is meticulously annotated in volume one of Reff's study, several of the more summary landscape drawings are omitted from the illustrations in volume two.
12. Notebook 3, p. 82.
13. See also notebook 3, pp. 68–70, 74–6, 78, 80, 84 and 86.
14. See Loyrette 1991, pp. 64–5.
15. Exceptions are a study of the vault of Saint-Martin-d'Ainay in notebook 3, p. 94, and a drawing of a Flandrin-like head on p. 20. For the progress of Flandrin's murals, see Foucart 1985, pp. 155–61.
16. See note 13 above.
17. Notebook 4, pp. 68–7.
18. See notebook 4, pp. 20 and 25; notebook 1, pp. 40 and 41.
19. Of particular interest in the present context are the studies of flowers in notebook 2, p. 24, and notebook 4, p. 3; and glimpses of be-hatted and casually dressed fellow-students, perhaps working out of doors, in notebook 2, p. 64, and notebook 5, pp. 39 and 41.
20. See Boime 1971, pp. 34–5. Even Ingres recommended the carrying of sketchbooks for making rapid studies, though without specifying the landscape as a subject; see Delaborde 1870, p. 129.
21. For Degas' relations with Lamothe, see Loyrette 1991, pp. 41–3. Auguste De Gas' disenchantment with Lamothe is implied in a letter to his son; see Lemoisne 1946, I, p. 30.
22. Degas' copies of these works can be found in notebook 2, pp. 30, 54, 59, 79 and 82–3; notebook 19, pp. 49–50.
23. Ingres's *Self-portrait* of 1804 is now in the Musée Condé, Chantilly; for Flandrin, see Foucart 1985, p. 165; for Lamothe, see Loyrette 1984, p. 33.
24. Several accounts of Degas' meetings with Ingres are gathered together in Loyrette 1991, pp. 55–61.
25. Delaborde 1870, p. 148.
26. Delaborde 1870, p. 124.
27. Delaborde 1870, p. 123.
28. Delaborde 1870, pp. 123 and 132.
29. Delaborde 1870, p. 115.
30. See Boime 1971, pp. 8 and 19.
31. A number of drawings by Ingres of landscape subjects can be found in Naef 1971. The discussion of the artist's landscape backgrounds is in Toussaint 1992. I am grateful to Richard Thomson for bringing this article to my attention.
32. Letter to Fantin-Latour; see Bénédite 1905, p. 233.
33. Degas' insistence on drawing is recorded in Sickert 1917, pp. 184–5, and his description of his pastels in Manet 1987, p. 177.
34. Auguste De Gas' remark is in Lemoisne 1946, I, p. 31; see also notebook 15, p. 40.
35. Baudelaire 1955, p. 114; Salon of 1846.
36. Baudelaire 1955, p. 32; Salon of 1845.
37. His admiration for this picture by Corot is in Baudelaire 1955, p. 114; Salon of 1846. The reference to Delacroix's Moroccan scene is in Baudelaire 1955, p. 9; Salon of 1845.
38. Notebook 5, p. 33.
39. Degas' copy is in notebook 6, pp. 3–2; his second discussion with Soutzo is recorded on p. 65.
40. See notebook 8, p. 35; for Soutzo's influence on Degas' taste, see the discussion below.
41. A note made by Degas, apparently in Paris *c.*1860, refers to Soutzo's address; see notebook 13, p. 141. Soutzo's assistance in finding Degas a studio is discussed in Loyrette 1991, pp. 133, 147 and 155.
42. See Lemoisne 1946, I, p. 18, and Reed and Shapiro 1984, p. 2.
43. See Boggs *et al.* 1988, p. 72; for Degas' holdings of works by Soutzo, see the discussion of Degas' inventory below.
44. See notes 47 and 48 below.
45. Loyrette 1991, p. 77. For further information on Soutzo's background and family, see Soutzo 1899.
46. His connection with Nieuwerkerke is noted in Monneret 1987, p. 908, and with Musson in Loyrette 1991, p. 77.
47. The inventory, which is in a French private collection, consists largely of notes on individual works, with occasional reminiscences about the circumstances of their acquisition. In places, the elderly Degas' handwriting is unclear and his syntax resistant to translation. I am indebted to Ann Dumas for drawing my attention to the document and to the owner for permission to quote from it.
48. Cited from entry no. 171 in Degas Inventory.
49. Henri Loyrette's suggestion that Degas' notebook copy from Soutzo was based on an engraving rather than a painting should surely be challenged. Degas' drawing has none of the severity of a print, and suggests rather the softenss and tonal subtlety of an oil painting; see Loyrette 1991, p. 76.
50. Cited in Galassi 1991, p. 67.
51. See, for example, nos 1061–2, 1064–6 in Robaut 1905.
52. Robaut 1905, no. 243.
53. Notebook 18, p. 161.
54. Notebook 4, p. 71.
55. Degas' admiration for Corot is examined in Clarke, July 1991. The story of his 'painting' a Corot is recorded in Fevre 1949, pp. 52–3.
56. Henri Rouart was a keen collector of Corot's paintings and drawings, eventually acquiring his *Bay of Naples with the Castel dell'Ovo*, a picture with the closest affinities to Degas' own Neapolitan *motifs*. The same work was recorded in Degas' portrait of Rouart's daughter Hélène; see Reff 1976 (*Degas: The Artist's Mind*), pp. 138–40, and Gordon 1984, pp. 12–13. The seven Corot canvases owned by Degas are listed in Vente Collection I, nos 16–22.
57. See Vente Soutzo 1870 and Loyrette 1991, p. 77.
58. Works by Marcantonio are listed in notebook 8, p. 71; by Dürer in notebook 23, p. 40; and by Claude in notebook 10, pp. 50–2.
59. See, for example, *Young Man, Seated, in a Velvet Beret, after Rembrandt* (RS 6). Degas' interest in Rembrandt has also been associated with Joseph Tourny, whom he befriended in Italy but met as early as 1855;

see notebook 2, p. 6. For Ingres's views on Rembrandt, see Delaborde 1870, p. 160.

60. The story is recorded in Lemoisne 1946, I, p. 18. It should be noted that Lemoisne linked René's anecdote with Degas' etching *Self-portrait* (RS 8), which is now accepted as a work of his Italian years.
61. Degas' awareness of such books is indicated in notebook 18, pp. 96, 100, 102 and 106; see also Reed and Shapiro 1984, p. 4. The fact that Degas inserted copies of these early etchings into notebook 18 (see pp. 101, 102 and 105) has sometimes been used to date them several years later. However, the awkwardness of the landscape prints contrasts sharply with the delicacy of the *Self-portrait* (RS 8) of 1857 and confirms their earlier date. Delteil specifies that *Greek Landscape* was made under the tuition of Soutzo; Delteil 1919, no. 10.
62. The church is touched in using pencil in state 1, but worked into the plate in state 3; see Reed and Shapiro 1984, pp. 3–4.
63. For a detailed analysis of the different states, see Reed and Shapiro 1984, p. 3.
64. As Reed and Shapiro note, the physical characteristics of this plate link it strongly to the two earlier etchings. Theodore Reff has pointed out, however, that a drawing in a later notebook resembles both the background and the equestrian group in *Sportsman Mounting his Horse*, suggesting a date of c.1859 for this print; see Reff 1976 (*Notebooks*), I, p. 87 (entry for notebook 14A, p. 60).
65. Lemoisne 1946, I, p. 31.
66. Degas made relatively few large-scale copies, but these included two works then attributed to Giovanni Bellini (*Deux têtes d'homme*, L 59, and *Les âmes de purgatoire*, L 67) and pictures by Sebastiano del Piombo (*Sainte Famille*, L 193) and Titian (*Saint Antoine ressuscitant une femme tuée par son mari*, L 54). The other copies are in notebook 13, p. 17; notebook 12, p. 88; and notebook 12, p. 41.
67. Many of these contacts are discussed below. Degas' friendship with the obscure English landscape-painter John Bland is documented in notebook 12, p. 108 and in Degas' letter to Moreau of 21 September 1858; see Reff 1969, p. 281 (where his name is read as Blard). Bland exhibited pictures of Italian scenes at the Royal Academy in 1860 and 1869; see Graves 1970, I, p. 210. His years of study in Paris are traced in Loyrette 1991, p. 53, n. 57, and p. 137, n. 304.
68. Notebook 7, p. 1. The page size is 17.7 × 24.7 cm.
69. Notebook 7, pp. 22, 26, 25, 23 and 19.
70. An inscription on the drawing indicates that it was made at Capodimonte on 10 September 1856.
71. McMullen 1985, p. 51.
72. Other works are listed in Lemoisne 1946, II, nos 47–9; and in Brame and Reff 1984, nos 15–22.
73. Part of the curious history of Degas' landscapes is the propensity of his immediate family for acquiring these works for themselves. At least nine of the oil-on-paper landscapes passed through such collections: the artist's niece, Jean Fevre, owned landscapes from every period of Degas' career, including four of the Roman and Neapolitan series (see Vente Fevre 1934); and René de Gas, the artist's brother, owned seven landscapes of various kinds (see Vente René de Gas 1927).
74. See notebook 19, pp. 6–7.
75. Though variously described, this picture is executed in oil paint on paper mounted on canvas; see Charles de Couessin, 'Technique, transformations dans les toiles de Degas des collections du musée d'Orsay', in Musée d'Orsay 1989, pp. 145–6.
76. For a detailed exploration of this tradition, see Galassi 1991.
77. Valenciennes 1800.
78. Valenciennes 1800, translation from Taylor 1987, p. 253.
79. Valenciennes 1800, translation from Taylor 1987, p. 256.
80. Valenciennes 1800, translation from Taylor 1987, p. 255.
81. For example, Fevre 1949, p. 60. Degas' greater affinity with Valenciennes is proposed in Clarke, July 1991, p. 16.
82. The appearance of the dark, trapezoidal form at the left of this composition recalls certain studies for Degas' *Alexander and Bucephalus* (L 91–3), which the artist was working on during his visit to Naples in 1860; see notebook 18, pp. 104, 125, 151 and 260, and notebook 19, pp. 38 and 58. See also note 136 below.
83. Notebook 4, p. 18.
84. Brettell and McCullagh 1984, p. 17. My thanks are due to Douglas Druick of the Art Institute of Chicago for his kind cooperation in this investigation. Though clear to the naked eye, the landscape is too faint to be visible in a printed reproduction.
85. Claude's picture is no. LV 117 in Roethlisberger 1979.
86. Notebook 7, p. lv.
87. Notebook 10, p. 50.
88. Notebook 10, p. A, has a drawing of goats which is similar to, but not identical with, a detail from Claude's etching *Le chevrier* (Manocci 1988, no. 44). Similarly, Degas' study in notebook 13, p. 73, recalls Claude's print *Le troupeau à l'abreuvoir* (Manocci 1988, no. 16), and his drawing on p. 75 of the same notebook may be an echo of Claude's *Paysage au dessinateur* (Manocci 1988, no. 2).
89. For Corot, see notes 56 above and 91 below. The Ingres drawing is *Vesuvius*, pencil and wash, Musée Ingres, Montauban; no. 867.4303.
90. See National Gallery of Art 1985, no. 78.
91. Degas listed a Corot oil-on-paper *Vésuve* in his own collection (Degas Inventory, no. 23), though this work was not included in his *atelier* sales. The de Nittis is described as *Etude de Vésuve* in Degas Inventory, no. 160, and appears to correspond to *Site d'Italie, paysage montagneuse* in Vente Collection II, no. 73.
92. Reed and Shapiro 1984, nos 6 and 8.
93. Reff 1969, pp. 381 and 383.
94. For comparisons of their drawing, see Pool, May 1964, and Arlette Serullaz, 'Dessins de Degas et des artistes français en Italie (1856–1860). Etude Technique', in Musée d'Orsay 1989, pp. 130–43.
95. The details of a current edition of Poussin's letters are recorded in notebook 11, p. 105. Amongst his many partial and entire copies from Poussin, the full-scale oil of *The Rape of the Sabines* (L 273) in the Norton Simon Museum of Art, Pasadena, is the most dramatic.
96. See Vente Collection I, nos 19 and 20.
97. See Arlette Serullaz, 'Dessins de Degas et des artistes français en Italie (1856–1860). Etude Technique', in Musée d'Orsay 1989, especially plates 11, 12 and 16.
98. See Bittler and Mathieu 1983, nos 764–7, 903–4, 979, 1386–1418.
99. The painting is *View of the Tiber*, dated 1859, Musée Bonnat, Bayonne.
100. The drawing by Delaunay is reproduced in Musée d'Orsay 1989, p. 132. Degas noted Lionnet's name in notebook 11, p. 100, and in letters to Moreau; see Reff 1969, pp. 382 and 383.
101. See Harambourg 1985, p. 236, and Bénézit 1976, p. 684.
102. Notebook 8, p. 39.
103. Notebook 8, p. 37.
104. Notebook 8, p. 36v. The habit of writing dates and colour notes on such drawings is found also in Moreau's contemporary work; see Bittler and Mathieu 1983, nos 1396 and 1418.
105. *Etude de ciel* (BR 17) and notebook 8, p. 66v.
106. *Paysage* (BR 15), *Paysage, effet de soir* (BR 22), *Paysage d'Italie* (L 47) and *Paysage d'Italie* (L 49).
107. *Pont en Italie* (BR 21) and notebook 10, p. 58.
108. For Flandrin, see Foucart 1985, cat. no. 131; for Bonnat, note 99 above.
109. Degas' drawing is inscribed *15 février 1857*; see National Gallery of Art 1985, no. 79.
110. The drawing is *Italian Landscape* (location unknown), inscribed *Tivoli 1857*. It was sold in Vente IV, no. 71b.
111. See notebook 10, pp. 43–6, and note 110 above.
112. Notebook 11, p. 50. Gustave Moreau also travelled from Rome to Florence in 1858, making a number of drawings with brief annotations on them.
113. Notebook 11, pp. 61–2.
114. Notebook 11, pp. 60 and 66.
115. Notebook 11, pp. 78–9.

116. Notebook 11, pp. 95–7.
117. See Pool 1963.
118. For Degas' letters to Moreau, see Reff 1969, pp. 281–6.
119. Reff 1969, p. 282.
120. Reff 1969, p. 283.
121. For Bizet's account, see McMullen 1985, pp. 58–9; that of the Goncourt brothers is contained in Goncourt 1867, where a series of vivid monologues brings to life the dispute between Delacroix and Ingres, and where the life of the Villa Medici is graphically described.
122. For other examples, see note 98 above.
123. The suggestion comes from Loyrette 1991, p. 116. Degas used pastel or chalk in a drawing of November 1857 (Vente IV, no. 71b), made during his visit to Tivoli; see notebook 10, p. 46. Moreau arrived in Rome only days before this event and is unlikely to have influenced its outcome. At this date, Moreau himself seems to have used pastel rarely on his own comparable studies.
124. Reff 1969, p. 281.
125. Reff 1969, p. 283.
126. The movements of Degas' friends at this time are summarised in 'Chronolgy I', in Boggs *et al.* 1988, pp. 50–2. Some of Delaunay's copies made in Venice are included in a notebook in the Louvre (RF 1895), and a number of Moreau's drawings after Carpaccio, Bellini, Titian and others are in the Musée Gustave Moreau, Paris; see, for example, nos 4174, 4178, 4199 and 4222 in Bittler and Mathieu 1983.
127. For Degas' reference to studying the copies brought back by 'the illustrious Lionnet', see Reff 1969, p. 293.
128. Lemoisne 1946, I, p. 31.
129. This letter, dated 30 November, is cited in Lemoisne 1946, I, p. 31.
130. For the copies from Giorgione and Veronese, see Reff 1969, p. 281. The copy from Bellini is L 67 and that from Titian L 54. Degas' study from Titian is undated, but two pencil drawings related to the copy occur in a sketchbook used in the early 1860s; see notebook 19, pp. 244–5. In Reff 1964, p. 250, n. 9, it is pointed out that these studies are pasted in to the notebook and may date from Degas' period at the Ecole des Beaux-Arts, where there was a copy of Titian's painting. While it is true that, during his years in Italy, Degas did not visit Padua (where Titian's picture is located), both Degas' painted copy and the two pencil sketches seem remarkably assured for the date of *c.*1855 suggested by Reff. The possibility that Degas made the copy from some other source, and somewhat later than 1855, should not be ruled out.
131. See notebook 14, p. 12, and notebook 13, p. 95.
132. For Bellini, see L 59; for Veronese, see the uncatalogued painting *The Stage*, fig. 40 in the present volume, and BR 46; for Tintoretto, see BR 34; for paintings associated with Giorgione and Sebastiano del Piombo, see L 193, L 193 *bis* and BR 45; for Carpaccio, see notebook 16, p. 40; for Mantegna, see notebook 18, p. 205, and L 194.
133. Moreau's copy is in pencil and was made in Florence in 1858; see Bittler and Mathieu, no. 4399.
134. There is modest evidence of Degas' interest in Venetian art before his trip to Italy; see, for example, the drawing after Bellini, no. 7 in Adriani 1985.
135. Lemoisne 1946, I, p. 31.
136. The drawings are in notebook 18, pp. 104, 125 and 151; the colour notes are in notebook 19, p. 38. The possibility that *Italian Landscape*, BR 18, with its 'silver sky' and 'milky tone', was a study for this picture has also been considered above; see note 82.
137. For the history of this painting, see Burnell 1969 and Boggs *et al.* 1988, pp. 98–100.
138. The references to Veronese are in notebook 14, p. 1, and notebook 15, p. 40.
139. The evolution of the picture is traced in Finsen 1983 and Loyrette 1984, pp. 162–200. Studies for the composition were begun in Florence, while the canvas was completed in Paris, where it was apparently shown at the Salon of 1867; see Loyrette 1984, pp. 170–1.
140. For the association with Bonnat, see Loyrette 1984, p. 173.
141. See notebook 12, pp. 49–50; notebook 13, p. 16; notebook 12, p. 27.
142. The study of the ship is in notebook 13, p. 5; other Moreau-like subjects are in notebook 13, pp. 4, 7 and 9.
143. The painting was identified in Reff 1976 (*Notebooks*), notebook 12, pp. 40–1.
144. Apart from the sketchbook studies, there is a small drawing of the boar in the Fitwilliam Museum, Cambridge; see Hazlitt, Gooden and Fox 1978, no. 18. The painting in the Uffizi is now regarded as a copy; see Robels 1989, p. 397, no. 308; I and p. 398, no. 805. It is significant that the Snyders composition is dominated by the boar and by frantic figures of hunters and their dogs, whereas Degas' version removes the human narrative and places the animal in a spacious and presumably fanciful rustic setting.
145. The numerous drawings involved are in notebooks 12–16. For a fuller discussion of this transition, see chapter 2.
146. Examples of such letters are cited in Loyrette 1984, pp. 27–31.
147. See Pool 1964, p. 394.
148. See Broude 1987, pp. 71–4.
149. Pictures by these artists were represented in the Demidoff and Troubetzkoy collections.
150. See Broude 1987, pp. 249–64.
151. See Broude 1987, p. 249. The parallels between Boldini's work of this period, especially his sketchbook studies, and that of Degas, are striking; see Dini 1989.
152. See Loyrette 1984, p. 31.
153. Reff 1969, p. 285.
154. Notebook 13, pp. 31 and 51.
155. Baudelaire 1955, p. 264; Salon of 1869.
156. Notebook 19, pp. 8 and 8A.
157. The watercolour is from notebook 19, p. 11, and was used to paint the distant view in *Thérèse De Gas*, L 109.
158. Notebook 18, pp. 110–111A.
159. Notebook 19, pp. 6–19.

2 The Return to France

1. The date is given in Lemoisne 1946, I, p. 39. Notebook 18, in use at this time, includes a reference to a projected portrait of 'la femme de Paul' on p. 96, and a drawing of a male profile, which may be Paul's, on the preceding page. For Degas and the Valpinçons, see Barazzetti 1936 and Pénault 1990. My thanks to Vivien Hamilton for drawing my attention to the latter.
2. Images of the château occur in two pastels (BR 102 and 103), and a sequence of photographs taken by Degas in the 1890s; see Terrasse 1983, nos 40–6.
3. Notebook 18, pp. 161–3.
4. The identification of this picture was made in Reff 1976 (*Notebooks*), notebook 18, p. 161.
5. See notebook 18, p. 162, and notebook 19, pp. 70 and 76.
6. Notebook 18, pp. 169 and 173.
7. Notebook 18, p. 177.
8. *Tree* is no. 273 in Roethlisberger 1968. The collections of the Ecole des Beaux-Arts in Paris included a number of wash drawings by Claude. Degas' copy of Poussin's *The Triumph of Flora* (Vente IV, no. 80c), made at about this time, is also executed in sepia wash; see Boggs *et al.* 1988, no. 28.
9. See the discussion of this painting below.
10. See *Paul Valpinçon*, L 99.
11. For example, notebook 18, pp. 11, 18, 35, 67–9, 147, 154, 202, 207.
12. The story is found in Moreau-Nélaton 1926, I, p. 36.
13. In 1867, Degas exhibited two works entitled *Family Portrait*; in 1869, *Mme Gaujelin*; and in 1870, *Mme Camus in Red* and *Mme Théodore Gobillard*.
14. The landscape of Normandy has been associated with *The Daughter of Jephtha* and *Scene of War in the Middle Ages*, and it has been argued that *Semiramis Building Babylon* makes oblique reference to the rebuilding of Paris; see Boggs *et al.* 1988, p. 92.
15. Degas' visit to the Salon of 1859 with Koenigswater and Lacheurie is described in Loyrette 1984, p. 30. The Paris address of De Courcy is in notebook 21, p. 10v, that of Clère in notebook 16, p. 45.
16. There is a curt reference to Lévy's mural-painting in a letter to Moreau of 26 April 1859; see Reff 1969, p. 285.
17. The copy after Whistler is in notebook 20, p. 17; the addresses of Fantin-Latour and

Tissot are in notebook 21, pp. 17v and 13v, and that of Duranty in notebook 22, p. 211.

18. Pissarro's address first appears in notebook 21, p. 16v; those of Renoir and Bazille occur in notebook 22, pp. 213 and 220. Degas' visits to the Café Guerbois are reported in Lemoisne 1912, p. 36, and Rivière 1935, p. 38.
19. See Spate 1992, pp. 31–40, where Zola's claim that Monet 'cannot paint a landscape without including gentlemen and ladies' is cited.
20. See T. Reff, 'Three Great Draftsmen', in *Degas: The Artist's Mind*, 1976, and Loyrette 1991, pp. 59–63.
21. The letter is quoted in Loyrette 1991, p. 709, n. 30. Copies from Delacroix's works are found in notebook 13, p. 53, and notebook 14, pp. 44 and 59.
22. The reference to Delacroix's painting is in notebook 19, p. 15, and to his colours in notebook 14, p. 1, and notebook 15, p. 6.
23. Other copies from Delacroix are discussed in Fries 1964. Among Degas' friends and acquaintances, Gustave Moreau, Evariste de Valernes and Léon Riesener had all been close to Delacroix.
24. See Johnson 1981–9. Less than five per cent of the total number of paintings have landscape as their principal subject.
25. *Christ on the Lake of Genesareth* was shown in Paris in 1860 and copied by Degas in notebook 16, p. 20A; *Ovid among the Scythians* was in the 1859 Salon, where it was copied by Degas in notebook 18, p. 127; and *Demosthenes Calming the Waters* was visible both as a fresco and as an oil painting in 1860, was referred to by Degas in notebook 19, p. 15, and copied by him in a drawing; see Fries 1964, p. 354.
26. Notebook 19, p. 15.
27. Though sympathetic to Delacroix's image in both style and execution, Degas' copy departs from the original in several respects and appears to be a *tour de force* of drawing from memory. Baudelaire's discussion of the painting is in Baudelaire 1955, p. 249; Salon of 1859.
28. Vente Collection I, no. 141.
29. See Vente Collection I, nos 24–36 and 110–165.
30. See Vente Collection II, no. 95: 2, and Vente Collection I, no. 29.
31. See Vente Collection I, nos 114 and 120, and Vente Collection II, no. 82: 2.
32. See Vente Collection II, nos 90: 1 and 142: 1 and 2.
33. See Vente Collection I, no. 32.
34. Baudelaire 1955, p. 249; Salon of 1859.
35. Baudelaire 1955, p. 250; Salon of 1859.
36. Baudelaire 1955, p. 239; Salon of 1859.
37. Baudelaire 1955, pp. 280 and 276; Salon of 1859.
38. Baudelaire 1955, p. 112; Salon of 1846.
39. Baudelaire 1955, p. 113; Salon of 1846.
40. Baudelaire 1955, p. 117; Salon of 1846.
41. Baudelaire's reviews of the 1859 Salon were published in four instalments in the *Revue Française* in July of that year. In an undated letter from Boulogne-sur-Mer, written probably in 1868 or 1869, Manet asked Degas to return the two volumes by Baudelaire he had lent him; see Boggs *et al.* 1988, p. 57.
42. Baudelaire 1955, p. 283, Salon of 1859.
43. Degas' early acquaintance with Saint-Valéry is recorded also in a roughly sketched map of the town in notebook 14A, pp. 40–1, and in Raunay 1931, p. 274.
44. Guérin 1947, p. 140.
45. Guérin 1947, p. 160.
46. See notebook 18 in Reff 1976 (*Notebooks*) and Reff's more extended introduction to its contents in Guillaud 1984, pp. 225–30. The page size is 254 × 192 mm.
47. See notebook 18, pp. 107–11 and 129.
48. Examples of landscapes from these sources are in notebook 18, pp. 1, 3, 17, 25, 29, 61, 71, 89, 100, 103; the copy from Roberts is on p. 131.
49. See notebook 18, pp. 59, 92, 104, 125, 139, 155 and 192.
50. See notebook 18, pp. 13, 25, 27, 66, 83 and 190.
51. See notebook 18, pp. 11, 17, 133, 159 and 189; the creature on p. 17 is surely an exotic beetle, rather than a tortoise as the cataloguer suggests.
52. See notebook 18, pp. 1, 86, 205, 213, 217, 235 and 241.
53. Baudelaire 1955, p. 232; Salon of 1859.
54. *The Daughter of Jephtha* is based on a story from the Book of Judges; references to Homer and Dante can be found on pp. 106 and 116 respectively. Quotations from George Sand are on pp. 209 and 212, and Degas notes that he is reading Henry Fielding on p. 161.
55. A number of drawings in notebook 18 appear to bridge the gap between the pen-and-ink studies of Normandy and the landscape setting of *The Daughter of Jephtha*; see, for example, pp. 77, 80A and 92.
56. See Burnell 1969.
57. The study is in notebook 12, p. 93; Degas' plan for sky and clouds comes from notebook 16, p. 8.
58. For example, notebook 18, pp. 5, 76–7.
59. Notebook 18, p. 59.
60. For a summary of the notebook studies for *The Daughter of Jephtha*, see Reff 1976 (*Notebooks*), notebook 18, p. 5.
61. Notebook 15, p. 6.
62. The exception is *Scene of War in the Middle Ages*, which was painted quite thinly in oil on paper, and with few modifications.
63. Almost all the subjects of Degas' history pictures have been linked with contemporary issues; see, for example, Boggs *et al.* 1988, pp. 86, 92, 105.
64. Lemoisne 1946, I, p. 42.
65. The resemblance was noted in 1991 by an anonymous visitor to the Galerie du Carrousel in Paris, when the picture was first exhibited.
66. Notebook 14A, p. 36.
67. See notebook 14A, p. 29; notebook 16, p. 23; notebook 18, pp. 24, 39, 41, 57, 129.
68. The drawing is in notebook 19, p. 44. I am indebted to Marianne Feilchenfeldt for leading me to the *Four Willow Trees*.
69. See the earlier studies for the background of the *Young Spartans* in Burnell 1969, and note 55 above.
70. Notebook 18, p. 173.
71. It is plausibly argued by Henri Loyrette in Boggs *et al.* 1988, p. 107, that the painting was finished in 1863.

3 The First Equestrian Landscapes

1. Notable here is the resemblance between the figure at the extreme left of *Scene of War in the Middle Ages* and the subjects of Degas' bather lithographs from the early 1890s, e.g., Reed and Shapiro, nos 61–6; the echoes of the third figure from the left in the late pastel L 1436; and the links between the prostrate nude at the right and the pastoral bathers of the mid-1890s, such as L 1079, L 1080 and L 1083.
2. For example, in notebook, 18, pp. 1 and 5; pp. 13 and 15; pp. 51 and 55; pp. 79 and 83.
3. The profile pony in the foreground of *Semiramis Building Babylon* (L 82) is almost the mirror image, and the exact contemporary, of the carriage horse in *On the Racecourse* (L 77); a similar relationship exists between the principal equestrian groups in *The Gentlemen's Race: Before the Start* (L 101) and *Scene of War in the Middle Ages* (L 124).
4. See notebook 2, pp. 32 and 43; notebook 3, pp. 19 and 28; notebook 6, pp. 65 and 71.
5. Numerous drawings of this kind can be found in notebooks 12 and 13, i.e., those notebooks used shortly before Degas' return to France.
6. Some of Degas' earliest equestrian drawings from his Italian visit, showing the traditional race of riderless horses in Rome, may have been drawn from first-hand experience, though they may also reflect a knowledge of Géricault's images of the same event; see notebook 8, p. 24v, and Vente IV, no. 245c.
7. For Uccello, see Vente IV, no. 92b; for Gozzoli, see Vente IV, no. 91c; for Raphael, see Vente IV, no. 110c; for Rubens, see BR 33; for Van Dyck, see notebook 12, pp. 11 and 72; for Géricault, see notebook 18, pp. 5, 9, 93–4.
8. See, for example, notebook 12, p. 97; notebook 14A, p. 60; notebook 15, p. 5; notebook 18, pp. 13, 21, 25.
9. For Delacroix, see notebook 18, p. 127, and for Géricault, see notebook 13, pp. 61, 63–5, 67, 69, 71, 108, and notes 6 and 7 above; drawings from de Dreux can be

found in notebook 13, pp. 60–1, 65–6, 68, 118–20; those from Meissonier, in notebook 20, pp. 29 and 31; notebook 22, pp. 123 and 127; notebook 23, p. 41.

10. Contributions to this study have been made in Pickvance 1968 and Lipton 1987.
11. See L 50, 75–8, 101; and BR 38.
12. See L 117–19, 121, 140–1, 171, 384.
13. See L 184, 258, 262, 281, 317, 334.
14. The Italian settings of L 50 and BR 38 are demonstrated below. The earliest drawings of racecourse subjects are in notebook 12, pp. 15–16; notebook 13, pp. 61–1, 118–20.
15. For drawings from lithographs by de Dreux, see note 9 above. A group of military and equestrian subjects in the notebooks suggests further links with Fattori; see notebook 12, pp. 68–71, 84, 97, and notebook 13, pp. 78, 114–15, 127. Some drawings of the horse-race can be found in Moreau's work of this period, but their precedence is open to dispute; see Loyrette 1984, p. 34, and Bittler and Mathieu 1983, nos 257, 262, 413, 694.
16. Other studies include BR 16 and 19; notebook 19, pp. 3–19. Virtually the same view forms the subject of Corot's painting *Bay of Naples with the Castel dell'Ovo*, which was later owned by Henri Rouart and pointedly included in Degas' *Portrait of Hélène Rouart in her Father's Study*; see Reff 1975 (*Degas: The Artist's Mind*), pp. 138–9.
17. Notebook 16, p. 20A.
18. Notebook 19, p. 15.
19. Examination of the canvas reveals a complex and somewhat re-worked paint structure. It is clear, however, that both sky and landscape were painted *underneath* the building at the right, which must therefore have been added at a late stage in the picture's evolution. My thanks are due to Judith Durrer and her colleagues at the Kunstmuseum, Bern, for their help in this investigation.
20. See notebook 19, pp. 27, 31 and 33.
21. See notebook 19, pp. 53–7.
22. Notebook 19, p. 58.
23. See *Copie d'après 'La Prise de Constantinople' de Delacroix* (BR 35).
24. The absence of compositional studies for *Promenade by the Sea*, in contrast to their use in *Horses in a Landscape*, might also suggest that it was begun outdoors.
25. Degas was in Naples from 21 March to 2 April 1860; see Boggs *et al.* 1988, p. 53.
26. Other variants on the theme of the two riders, all undated and apparently later, can be found in Vente III, nos 4(iii), 46(iii), and Vente IV, nos 23a, 202a. A similar *motif* also appears in the contemporary work of Moreau; see, for example, Bittler and Mathieu 1983, no. 410.
27. The date can be derived from the fact that *The Gentlemen's Race: Before the Start* (L 101), which must have been close to L 76 before it was repainted, is inscribed *1862*. L 76 seems slightly less experimental, and related drawings can be found amongst studies for *The Daughter of Jephtha*; e.g., notebook 16, p. 38.
28. Lemoisne 1946, II, p. 38.
29. For Géricault, see *The Epsom Downs Derby* (Louvre, Paris). For Manet, see *Courses au Bois de Boulogne* (Witney collection, New York). Berthe Morisot records Manet's claim to have painted this picture, which includes a portrait of Degas in the foreground, from his own collection of English sporting prints; see Adler 1986, p. 164. For a fuller discussion of these issues, see Reff 1982, pp. 129–31.
30. See Selway 1972.
31. Degas' awareness of Guys is discussed in Reff 1976 (*Notebooks*), I, p. 15.
32. See Thomson 1987, pp. 93–5, and Boggs *et al.* 1988, p. 268.
33. See Havercamp-Begemann *et al.* 1964, I, no. 152.
34. For Pollard's picture, see Selway 1972, no. 194.
35. The *motif* of the centrally placed, receding procession of carriages occurs in a number of paintings and prints, among them John Nixon's *Brighton Races* of 1805.
36. For the association of Degas' *At the Races in the Countryside* (L 281) with Normandy and the Valpinçon family, see Boggs *et al.* 1988, p. 15.
37. I am grateful to Richard Thomson for pointing out that the two male figures to left of centre in *On the Racecourse* are derived from a drawing in notebook 18, p. 196. The drawing of Haras-du-Pin is on p. 195 of the same notebook.
38. See notebook 18, pp. 165 and 173.
39. Eunice Lipton's attempt to divide the equestrian pictures into two groups, the 'frieze' mode and the 'unstable' mode, which implicitly appealed to different markets, does not include this early group of paintings, nor does it take account of the presence of both 'modes' in certain canvases; see Lipton 1987, pp. 17–72.
40. Recorded in Moore 1893, p. 37.
41. The watercolour seems to be a version of a now-dismembered oil, portions of which were shown by Manet as separate works; see Harris 1966. In Reff 1982, p. 132, it is calculated that the original oil was *c.*200 cm across.
42. After the exhibition of his oil painting at the Galerie Martinet in 1865, Manet cut up the canvas, presumably because he was dissatisfied with the composition.
43. Lemoisne 1946, no. 119, gives 1864–8, while Henri Loyrette, in Boggs *et al.* 1988, p. 193, suggests 1873. The present argument indicates an original date of *c.*1861–3, with some repainting in 1873.
44. Recent examination of the canvas has shown extensive modification of the picture surface, in which Degas re-painted the rider at the left, scraped away a tree-dominated landscape that may have resembled the Haras-du-Pin studies, and over-painted the sky. Two drawings for riders are also consistent with the early 1860s; see Vente IV, nos 78a and 223a. I am grateful to Manuel Schmit for arranging for me to examine *Leaving for the Hunt*.
45. Large and conspicuous signatures were often used on submissions to the Salon to attract attention to little-known artists. The presence of such a signature on *Leaving for the Hunt* suggests that it may have been intended to accompany the similarly signed *Scene of War in the Middle Ages* to the 1865 Salon.
46. Some of the finely executed detail on its original paint surface, especially in the figures of the riders, is very close to such works as *At the Races: The Start* (L 76) (pl. 53).
47. In Reff 1974, pp. 30–1, one of the drawings here associated with *Leaving for the Hunt* is linked also with *The Morning Ride*.
48. A possible resemblance between the background of *The Morning Ride* and the bay and cliffs at Etretat should also be noted. The deep coffee-coloured surface of this painting appears to be an extreme example of Degas' early interest in monochrome underpainting.
49. The picture is discussed also in Pickvance 1988, p. 79, where it is described as a morning scene.
50. See L 118, 121, 171 and 384.
51. See Vente IV, nos 226b, 237d and 238b; notebook 22, pp. 89, 91 and 96. In Pickvance 1988, p. 79, it is proposed that the picture was intended as a Salon entry.
52. One of the riders may be Hortense Valpinçon, who was born in 1862 and would have been five years old in 1867, when the picture was painted.
53. See Musée du Petit-Palais 1981, no. 305.
54. *Fox in the Snow* was painted in 1860 and shown at the Salon of 1861; see Fernier 1977, no. 263. *Dead Deer*, which has a wooded background very similar to that in Degas' picture, dates from 1855 and was exhibited at the Rond Pont de l'Alma in 1867; see Fernier 1977, no. 159.
55. See Havercamp-Begemann *et al.* 1964, I, no. 157. In Bergot 1990, p. 325, a link with visits to the Valpinçons and a date of 1861–4 is proposed, though similarities with L 171 and the marked influence of Courbet must still favour the later dating.
56. *L'Etang dans la forêt* (L 285) and *Ruisseau sous-bois* (L 286).
57. Bagnoles-de-l'Orne is near Ménil-Hubert in Normandy.
58. See Boggs *et al.* 1988, p. 136, and Musée d'Orsay 1990, p. 67.
59. See Dumas 1988, p. 24, and Charles Stuckey, 'Degas as an Artist: Revised and Still Unfinished', p. 21, in Guillaud 1984.
60. Zola 1970, p. 165.
61. Zola 1970, p. 157.
62. Zola 1970, p. 135.

63. Zola 1970, p. 82.
64. See Reff 1976 (*Degas: The Artist's Mind*), chapters 4 and 5.
65. For the history of the painting, see Boggs *et al.* 1988, pp. 123 and 561–3. An unpublished drawing in notebook 22, p. 61, should also be taken into consideration.
66. The second version is *Fallen Jockey* (Kunstmuseum, Basel; L 141). The suggestion in Boggs *et al.* 1988, p. 561, that this canvas was *begun* in the 1890s as a 'reprise' of the earlier work, is impossible to reconcile with the archaic form of the horse, which is surely among the most awkward of Degas' early equestrian images and is best compared to the 'rocking-horse' figures in the background of such works as L 118 and L 121. Altogether more likely is the possibility, acknowledged in the same catalogue entry, that the Basel picture (which has the same dimensions as *The Steeplechase*) was begun in the mid-1860s, but then set aside for technical or compositional reasons. The vigorously re-worked and perhaps restored surface of the picture today has much the same appearance as a number of Degas' earlier canvases that were later overpainted by the artist.
67. Pickvance 1968, unpag.
68. The print is Pollard's *The Death*, no. 295 in Selway 1972. A faint drawing from this, or a remarkably similar work, is found on a sheet of studies for *The Steeplechase*; see Vente IV, no. 232b.
69. Some landscape forms are indicated on the study for *The Steeplechase* in Vente IV, no. 232b.
70. See Johnson 1981–9, no. 115. There is no record of the exhibition of this work in Degas' lifetime, but a later version exists (Johnson 1981–9, no. 322) and the image became the subject of an etching.
71. The drawings are Vente IV, nos 235a, 237a, 237d; notebook 22, pp. 35, 222.
72. Notebook 21, pp. 31v, 29v and 30.
73. See *Paris Universal Exhibition: Catalogue of the British Section 1867*, and *Exposition Universelle de 1867 à Paris 1867*; though ostensibly based on the same event, these publications show considerable discrepancies of detail. However, all the works noted by Degas can be traced in one or both volumes. The work by Hook entitled *Gamins de la mer* (no. 67), is recorded as belonging to C.P. Mattheiws (*sic*); Matthews is documented as an early owner of the Guildhall *Sea Urchins*. Hook's pictures had previously been admired by Baudelaire at the Salon of 1989; see Baudelaire 1955, p. 220. For Whistler's support of Hook, see Spencer 1984.
74. *Art Journal* 1867, p. 246.
75. *Art Journal* 1867, p. 245.

4 The 1869 Pastels

1. *Gustave Moreau* (Musée Gustave Moreau, Paris; L 178).
2. These and other details of Degas' social and professional life at this period are included in Morisot 1986, pp. 35–8, 43.
3. See notebook 20, p. 17, and notebook 18, p. 109.
4. See chapter 2, note 18.
5. The visit to England is proposed in a letter from Manet of July 1868; see Wilson-Bareau 1991, p. 47. The portrait of Tissot is L 175. Degas recorded the address of Pissarro in notebook 21, p. 16v, that of Boudin in notebook 18, p. 255, and that of Bazille in notebook 22, p. 220.
6. Cézanne's emphasis on figurative subjects during this decade is explored in R. Kendall, 'The Figure in the Landscape', in Kendall 1993.
7. These claims come from McMullen 1985, p. 170, and Boggs *et al.* 1988, p. 154.
8. The association of the series with Manet and Boulogne has an obscure history, but appears to derive from an ambiguous reference in Lemoisne 1946, I, p. 61, for which no authority is cited.
9. See Lemoisne 1946, I, p. 61, and Boggs *et al.* 1988, p. 154.
10. The artist's signature and the date 1869 appear on L 199–205 and L 227; L 238 is signed but undated.
11. According to Lemoisne, L 200 was given by Degas to a 'Dr C . . .'. This was presumably Dr Camus, collector and friend of both Degas and Manet at this period. Degas painted a small portrait of Camus *c.*1868 (L 183) and two large canvases of his wife (L 207 and L 271), one of which was shown at the 1870 Salon. L 238 was acquired at an unspecified date by the dealer Etienne Bignou; by the 1920s, Bignou had assembled an important collection of Degas' work, including several landscapes. All the remaining 1869 pastels, both signed and unsigned, were still in the artist's possession at the time of his death.
12. Pastel had previously been used only in rare sketchbook studies, or in preparatory works for larger pictures, such as *The Bellelli Family* (L 79) or *Semiramis Building Babylon* (L 82). For the story of the Gobillard portrait, see Boggs *et al.* 1988, p. 153.
13. Reff 1968, pp. 87–8.
14. Morisot 1986, p. 41.
15. Morisot 1986, p. 40.
16. Morisot 1986, pp. 36, 38.
17. Morisot 1986, p. 43.
18. The letters included in Morisot 1986 are often incomplete or imprecisely dated. The location of the originals is uncertain.
19. An account of Berthe Morisot's outdoor painting activities at Beuzeval is included in Morisot 1986, pp. 20–1.
20. See Adler and Garb 1987, p. 18, and Morisot 1986, pp. 25–6.
21. After her trip to Brittany, Berthe Morisot was encouraged by her sister Edma to take a holiday. The subjects of one of Berthe's pictures, the Delaroche children, left for Houlgate in August; see Morisot 1986, p. 44.
22. The relationship between their families is described in Morisot 1986, pp. 20–1. Berthe's watercolour of Rosalie Riesener is now in the collection of the Louvre; see Bataille and Wildenstein 1961, no. 612. The meeting at the Salon is recorded in Morisot 1986, pp. 36–7.
23. A letter written by Riesener from Beuzeval, on the occasion of Delacroix's death, is reprinted in Huet 1911, p. 350. For other letters see Viallefond 1955.
24. For Riesener's pictures of Beuzeval, see Couper Gallery 1965, no. 9, and Le Pavillon des Arts 1965, no. 2.
25. Viallefond 1955, p. 40.
26. Vente Collection II, nos 225–38.
27. A number of Huet's studies of the area are reproduced in Heim Gallery 1969.
28. Degas is known to have attended the 1867 exhibition, where Huet's picture was no. 358 in the catalogue; see *Exposition Universelle de 1867 à Paris.*
29. Heim Gallery 1969, no. 79.
30. Huet's paintings of *les vaches noires* include Heim Gallery 1969, no. 23; Degas' representations of the same subject are L 249 and L 253.
31. There is a painting by Huet of Houlgate dated 1869; see Heim Gallery 1969, no. 107.
32. Notebook 23, pp. 149 and 151.
33. The two works were first reproduced side-by-side in Kendall 1987, pp. 86–7. My thanks are due to Andrew Gossett, the designer of that book, for first noticing the connection.
34. The three works are L 200, 246 and 250. Comparable views of jetties at Dives can be seen in contemporary photographs; see Coulon 1986, p. 61.
35. Dunes and beaches are shown in L 222, L 228 and L 243; Cabourg can be seen in the distance in L 203 and L 220; and inland subjects form the basis of L 230–2 and L 238.
36. For a recent discussion of these paintings, see Bomford *et al.* 1990, pp. 120–5.
37. Notebook 23, p. 1.
38. For a discussion of the theme in Impressionist art generally, see Herbert 1988, chapter 6. An early photograph of a train crossing the same stretch of line, also taken from above but looking back towards Dives, is in Coulon 1986, p. 68.
39. See the map on p. 269 of Herbert 1988.
40. Berhaut 1978, nos 149 and 153.
41. Malte-Brun 1882, p. 41.
42. Malte-Brun 1882, p. 42. For the development of the resorts, see Herbert 1988, chapter 7.
43. Photographs of the turn of the century

show the industry, railway and harbour activities at Dives; see Coulon 1986, p. 68.
44. Malte-Brun 1882, p. 41.
45. See Spate 1992, chapter 2, and Brettell 1990, chapter 3.
46. The group of signed and dated works (see note 10 above) contains examples of each kind of image, and certain pastels (e.g., L 202, L 222) combine the qualities of both themes.
47. Notebook 23, pp. 58–9. The word *fleque* in Reff's transcription should read *flaque*.
48. Inscriptions are also found on L 224 and L 246.
49. McMullen 1985, p. 170.
50. Courbet's first series of marine pictures was made at Palavas, on the Mediterranean, in 1854; his second group was made in the mid-1860s, on the Normandy coast.
51. Faunce and Nochlin 1988, p. 158.
52. Bénédite 1905, p. 203.
53. Delacroix's painting is no. 489 in Johnson 1981–9; it was shown at the posthumous sale of the artist's work, by which time it was already well known. Other remarkably spare images of sea and coast, some based on the Normandy area, can be found among Delacroix's watercolours; see Johnson 1991, nos 69–71.
54. Chamfleury 1973, p. 86. Though Degas' views on Chintreuil are not known, his close friend Henri Rouart owned several of Chintreuil's canvases.
55. Hamerton 1867, p. 691.
56. See Getscher 1991, pp. 17–8, 20–2. Whistler's pastels from the late 1860s are technically tentative and largely confined to the human figure.
57. See chapter 2, notes 72–3.
58. In Fernier 1977, fifteen listed landscapes are associated with this exhibition. Ann Dumas argues, however, in Faunce and Nochlin 1988, pp. 157–61, that such precise identification is impossible.
59. Manet's *Le Steam-Boat* was shown; see Cachin *et al.* 1983, no. 86. The Salon included Whistler's *The Thames in Ice* and *Valparaiso*; see Young *et al.* 1980, pp. 15–16, 42–3.
60. Baudelaire 1955, p. 281; Salon of 1859.
61. Baudelaire 1955, p. 281; Salon of 1859.
62. An address is recorded against Boudin's name in notebook 18, p. 255, though it does not correspond with any of the Paris residences of the artist listed for this period in Schmit 1973.
63. Zola 1970, pp. 146–7.
64. Zola 1970, p. 164.
65. Zola 1970, p. 147.
66. Zola 1970, pp. 145, 155.
67. Zola 1970, p. 153.
68. Zola 1970, pp. 164, 155.
69. See chapter 3, note 64.
70. Zola's characterisations of Monet and Pissarro are in Zola 1970, pp. 153 and 148.
71. See Faunce and Nochlin 1988, p. 86, and Monneret 1987, p. 227.
72. See Monneret 1987, p. 139, and Cachin *et al.* 1983, p. 511.
73. For Boudin and Daubigny, see Schmit 1973, p. xxix; for Huet, see note 31 above; for Morisot, see Morisot 1986, p. 41.
74. Degas is described as such in Armstrong 1991, which nevertheless presents a vivid account of his relationship with the theory and practice of Realism.
75. A reference to the artist working on a watercolour 'in full sunlight' occurs in a letter of 1871; see Guérin 1947, p. 12.
76. See Janis 1987 and Heilbrun 1986.
77. Notebook 23, p. 150, lists petty expenses for eight days, apparently in connection with a hotel at Villers, though this period would hardly account for the production of the entire series.
78. Though no preparatory drawings for the pastels exist, some unpublished sketches appear to be linked to the series; see notebook 22, pp. 120 and 125. In adjacent pages of the same notebook, there are also a number of Boudinesque studies of women, apparently posed on the beach; see pp. 107–17. A majority of the pastels was made on two sizes of paper: approximately 32 × 46 cm and 22 × 30 cm; others were made on simple variants, such as half-sheets, of these sizes. The paper is generally warm beige, the warmth of its surface contributing to, or contrasting with, the colours of the pastel drawing. Most of the paper is laid, some sheets showing watermarks, e.g., Canson (L 227 and L 225), Montgolfier (L 204) and Marcel-les-Annon (L 232).
79. Such holes are clearly evident in *Cliffs beside the sea* (L 199) (fig. 73).
80. This effect is rarely visible in photographs, but can clearly be seen at first hand in many of the pastels.
81. Baudelaire 1955, p. 281.

5 Degas and the Impressionist Landscape

1. For the most complete accounts of Degas' participation in the Impressionist exhibitions, see Moffett *et al.* 1986, and Gary Tinterow and Anne Norton, 'Degas aux expositions impressionistes', in Musée d'Orsay 1989, pp. 289–353.
2. Chesneau 1874, p. 2; cited in Riout 1989, p. 63.
3. See, for example, the catalogue of the 1877 exhibition, in Moffett *et al.* 1986, p. 205.
4. Zola 1970, p. 148.
5. See Moffett *et al.* 1986, p. 120.
6. See Moffett *et al.* 1986, pp. 120 and 204.
7. See Cassatt's submissions to the 1879 exhibition, in Moffett *et al.* 1986, p. 267.
8. Though the early critics were not unanimous in praising Degas' draughtsmanship, several commented on his superior grounding in such skills and the accuracy of his observation; for a summary of this criticism, see Moffett *et al.* 1986, pp. 127, 170–6, 216–19.
9. Zola 1970, p. 279.
10. Vollard 1937, p. 56.
11. Vollard 1937, p. 56, and Gide 1947, p. 239.
12. Though the legends of Degas' antipathy to outdoor painting appear in a number of memoirs by his friends, all were published posthumously and all refer implicitly to the last decades of his life.
13. See the discussion of Courbet's influence on these and other paintings in chapters 3 and 4.
14. Guérin 1947, pp. 38–9.
15. Boggs *et al.* 1988, p. 157.
16. The resemblance between the breadth of this work and the eloquent open spaces of Fattori's equestrian paintings is noted in Broude 1987, especially pls 302–3. Close examination of Degas' canvas suggests that some, if not all, the landscape was painted prior to the imposition of the figures, at which stage its affinity with the 1869 pastels would have been evident. The distant hill, for example, can be seen through the body of the seated man and the curved line in the grass at lower left is visible under parts of the carriage.
17. In Boggs *et al.* 1988, p. 160, it is noted that this picture was sold to Durand-Ruel in 1872.
18. Rapid studies for the boats were made in notebook 25, pp. 41 2, perhaps on a visit to Normandy after the Siege of Paris. The figures of the horses are related to a group of drawings in notebook 22, pp. 70–81. A further two paintings, *Chevaux au pâturage* (L 290) and the subsequently reworked *Deux chevaux au pâturage* (L 291), explore variations on this theme. Both L 289 and L 290 play on the *motif* of the linked bodies of a dark and a light animal, a conceit found also in the works of Fromentin, Géricault and others.
19. *At the Races in the Countryside* and *Before the Race* were bought by Faure; see Boggs *et al.* 1988, pp. 158 and 160. Tissot is recorded as the owner of *Horses in the Meadow* in Lemoisne's catalogue entry.
20. *Before the Race* was engraved before being sold to Faure; see Boggs *et al.* 1988, p. 160. *Horses in the Meadow* was later etched by both Degas and Lauzet; see Reed and Shapiro 1984, no. 56. For the exhibition history of *At the Races in the Countryside*, see Boggs *et al.* 1988, p. 158.
21. See Herbert 1988, pp. 155–60.
22. See Moffett *et al.* 1986, p. 120.
23. Chimneys appear in the distance in L 262, L 281, L 317 and the over-painted L 101, and a train features in L 461.
24. The picture was listed in the catalogues of both shows; see Moffett *et al.* 1986, pp. 161 and 204.
25. See Boggs *et al.* 1988, pp. 255–6.
26. Moffett *et al.* 1986, p. 204.
27. This work remained in the artist's posses-

sion; see Vente III, no. 34.

28. Schmit 1973, no. 435.
29. Schmit 1973, no. 510. Further points of contact between the two artists are their remarkably similar sheets of fragmented studies of figures posing in the open air, in Boudin's case executed in watercolour, in Degas', made in *essence*; see, for example, L 259–61.
30. The execution of this work is examined in Bomford *et al.* 1990, pp. 126–31. A similar subject is tackled in Monet's *Camille on the Beach*, Wildenstein 1974–85, no. 161. Monet's occasional use of pastel for outdoor studies should also be noted in the present context.
31. Manet's letters from Boulogne and the paintings associated with his visit are all dated 1868 in Wilson-Bareau 1991, pp. 47–9.
32. At the upper centre of Degas' painting, the pencil outline of a large bathing machine can be clearly seen beneath the paint layer.
33. *Beach Scene* was bought by Henri Rouart; for the history of the other works, see notes 24 and 25 above.
34. See note 24 above.
35. Among several documented examples, *At the Races in the Countryside* (L 281) was painted in 1869, but exhibited in 1874; *Mme Camus en rouge* (L 271) was painted in 1870, shown in the Salon of that year, then included in the 1876 exhibition, as *Portrait, le soir*; *Portrait* (L 163) was painted in 1867, then shown in 1877, where its incompatibility with Degas' other work was noted; see Moffett *et al.* 1986, p. 219.
36. For the rivalry between the two artists, see Loyrette 1991, pp. 219–20, and Morisot 1986, p. 40. Other 'pairs' of pictures are Degas' *Monsieur et Madame Manet* (L 127) and Manet's *Mme Manet au piano*; Degas' *Violinist and Young Woman* (L 274) and Manet's *The Music Lesson*; and the equestrian subjects discussed in chapter 3.
37. *Beach Scene* is painted on three sheets of paper, one of which was reduced in width. The dimensions of the initial sheet are approximately 47 × 31 cm, a format that recurs with slight variations in several of the *essence* studies of the late 1860s, e.g., L 158, L 259–61; *Women Combing their Hair* (L 376) is the same size. Two other related works are painted on a double sheet, i.e., 46 × 62 cm; see L 262 and L 374.
38. This effect is found also in L 153 and L 159, but may have originated in the striped dress of Mlle Fiocre in L 146–7.
39. A similar compositional structure is found in the 1869 *At the Races in the Countryside*. The possibility that Hortense Valpinçon, one of Degas' favourite child models (who was seven years old in 1869), might have posed for the *Beach Scene* should be considered. In this case, the picture may have been prompted by Degas' visit to Ménil-Hubert in 1869, just as *At the Races in the Countryside* was.
40. Wilson-Bareau 1991, p. 47.
41. See Degas' letters to Deschamps and Legros in Reff 1968, pp. 89–90, and to Tissot in Guérin 1947, pp. 29–30.
42. Hook's painting is in need of cleaning, but its original tones may have approximated to Degas' canvas. I am indebted to Jeremy Johnson of the Guildhall Art Gallery for making Hook's picture available to me.
43. Notebook 23, p. 60.
44. It is evident that the surface of *Peasant Girls Bathing in the Sea toward Evening* has been partly repainted by the artist, but its technical history is unclear.
45. Vollard 1937, p. 47.
46. A drawing in the British Museum, *Etude de nu* (Vente IV, no. 289a), is a study for the left-hand bather in *Peasant Girls Bathing in the Sea toward Evening*.
47. All the pictures in the group show evidence of change during their execution. In *Beach Scene*, a bathing machine was pencilled in, then painted over; a further strip of paper was added at the left; and alterations were made to the maid's sleeve. *Nursemaids on the Beach* was manifestly improvised, while *Women Combing their Hair* began life as a brush drawing of three nudes.
48. Manet's preference for painting directly and spontaneously, recorded by eye-witnesses such as Duret, Mallarmé and Jeanniot, is summarised in Wilson 1983, pp. 6–7.
49. See Hertz 1920, p. 20, and Sickert 1917, p. 185.
50. The association of many of Degas' contemporaries with Japanese art has been studied in such works as Ives 1974, Weisberg 1975 and Wichmann 1981. Moreau's interest in these images is demonstrated in his copy of a Kabuki print (Musee Gustave Moreau, no. 975), while the taste of Degas' friend Tillot is recorded in Monneret 1987, pp. 945–6.
51. See Vente Collection Estampes, nos 324–32.
52. Smith 1988, p. 26. Degas' holdings of Hiroshige's prints were grouped together under lots 328 and 329 in Vente Collection Estampes.
53. The remaining two panels of the triptych are similarly unpopulated, with tiny distant boats and high horizons, as in Degas' pastels. The complete work is itself one of a series of three majestic triptychs of panoramic landscapes, entitled *Snow, Moon and Flowers*; see Smith 1988, pp. 148–9.
54. For other examples of Hiroshige's influence, see Weisberg 1975, chapters 1 and 3; for a more combative reading of the evidence, see Varnedoe 1990, chapter 2.
55. Vente Collection Estampes, no. 325.
56. Degas' prints by Toyokuni are referred to in Vente Collection Estampes, no. 330, though their subjects are not specified. The British Museum's copy of the triptych belonged formerly to Degas' friend Tadama Hayashi.
57. Artists as varied as Bazille and Cézanne, Morisot and Monet found themselves grappling with this problem in the 1860s, turning to photography, fashion plates and Japanese art for assistance.
58. See Guérin 1947, pp. 12, 18, 22, 31, 34–5.
59. Kendall 1988. See also Lanthony 1990.
60. The darkness of Degas' studio was noted in Michel 1919, p. 458, and Manet 1987, p. 188.
61. Guérin 1947, p. 12. The correction of 'Château' to 'Châtou' was made in Musée d'Orsay 1989, p. 358.
62. A watercolour of a river scene occurs in notebook 22, p. 11. Another is in the Cabinet des Dessins at the Louvre; see BR 50.
63. Guérin 1947, p. 18.
64. Guérin 1947, p. 31.
65. Degas suffered from largely monocular vision from at least his mid-thirties and complained in later life of a 'blind spot' in one of his eyes. His visual field was erratically blurred, perhaps from corneal scarring, but there is no evidence of colour distortion in his sight.
66. In his maturity, Degas habitually wore tinted spectacles when outdoors. For a summary of his treatment, see Kendall 1988.
67. His habit of working close to his subject, even touching the model to confirm his perceptions, is reported in Michel 1919, pp. 457–60.
68. See Kendall 1988, pp. 183, 188, 190, 196.
69. For example, the incident at Châtou in 1871 (see note 61 above); the letters from Louisiana (see note 64 above); his description of the light at Etretat as 'more Monet than my eyes can stand' (Guérin 1947, p. 70) and the celebrated reference of 1892 to train travel and 'states of eyes' (Guérin 1947, p. 252).
70. Glimpses of gardens and houses can be seen in such pictures as *Children on a Doorstep (New Orleans)* (L 309), and of the landscape in works more uncertainly associated with the visit to America; see Rewald *et al.* 1965.
71. In a letter written shortly before the exhibition, Degas told Tissot, 'My eyes are very bad. The oculist wanted me to have a fortnight's complete rest. He has allowed me to work just a little until I send in my pictures. I do so with much difficulty and the greatest sadness' (Guérin 1947, p. 39). For submissions to the 1874 exhibition, see Moffett *et al.* 1986, pp. 118–23.
72. For Mantz and Chaumelin, see Moffett *et al.* 1986, p. 219 and p. 171 respectively.
73. See Moffett *et al.* 1986, p. 161.
74. See Moffett *et al.* 1986, p. 204.
75. See Moffett *et al.* 1986, p. 267.
76. Zola 1970, p. 337.
77. For Degas' association with Biard, see Guérin 1947, p. 25. For Levert, see Guérin 1947, p. 25; notebook 26, p. 99; notebook 27, pp. 33 and 36; notebook 31, p. 93. For Rossana, see Guérin 1947, p. 54; notebook 31, p. 93.
78. For Tillot, see Guérin 1947, pp. 125 and 136;

notebook 26, pp. 51, 99; notebook 27, p. 36; notebook 31, p. 93; Vente Collection II, no. 68. For Vignon, see Loyrette 1991, p. 397; Vente Collection II, no. 264. For Cazin, see Guérin 1947, pp. 61–2; Vente Collection II, no. 83.

79. For Lepic, see Janis 1968, pp. xvii–iii; Vente Collection II, nos 67 and 216–18. For Rouart, see Moffett *et al.* 1986; the numerous letters in Guérin 1947; Vente Collection II, nos 78 and 238.
80. For de Nittis, see Musée d'Orsay 1989, pp. 419–20, 429, 437; notebook 26, pp. 73, 99; notebook 27, pp. 98, 104A; Loyrette 1991, p. 489; Vente Collection II, nos 71–6 and 224. For Boldini, see Guérin 1947, pp. 134–6; Musée d'Orsay 1989, p. 418. For Zandomeneghi, see notebook 31, pp. 93–4; Loyrette 1991, p. 450. Degas' relations with all three artists are summarised in Matthiesen 1984.
81. Degas' links with Boudin were renewed in the 1890s through their shared pupil Braquaval. His continuing admiration for Boudin is recorded in Jeanniot 1933, p. 287. Evidence for Degas' contact with Berthe Morisot until the time of the latter's death is contained in Morisot 1986, and with Whistler in MacDonald and Newton 1986, pp. 205 and 209.
82. Their meeting is referred to in Rewald 1946, p. 197, and their association first recorded in notebook 21, p. 16v. Pissarro showed in all eight of the Impressionist exhibitions, Degas in seven; see Moffett *et al.* 1986.
83. See Guérin 1947, pp. 56–9, and Reed and Shapiro 1984, pp. xxxix–li.
84. The remark comes from Manet 1953, p. 50. Degas' notorious anti-semitism, which was to lead to his isolation from many Jewish friends, was chiefly evident in his later years.
85. Bailly-Herzberg 1980, p. 204.
86. See Vente Collection I, nos 85–7, 234–5; Vente Collection Estampes, nos 300–11.
87. See Bailly-Herzberg 1980, p. 87, where Pissarro describes its acquisition in 1873. In Degas' inventory, written some twenty years after the event, the artist listed as no. 162, 'Pissarro, *Plaine labourée et carré de choux: sur le devant, ciel mouvementé*, de vers 1875, acheté a Durand-Ruel.' No. 163 is described as '*Sur la Seine, à l'entrée de Bougival*, acheté à la vente de 1874'.
88. Moffett *et al.* 1986, p. 139.
89. These and other similar purchases are recorded in Vente Collection I, Vente Collection II and Vente Collection Estampes. See also notes 77–81 above.
90. Both Monet and Degas were regular visitors to the Café Guerbois in the late 1860s, and active protagonists of the 1874 Impressionist exhibition, though Monet's name does not appear in Degas' notebooks and correspondence until the mid-1870s; see notebook 26, p. 3, and Guérin 1947, p. 43.
91. Critics tended to side with one or other of the two artists. See, for example, Jules Claretie's claim that Degas was 'the most remarkable of all these painters' at the 1874 exhibition, and Duret's characterisation of Monet as 'the Impressionist *par excellence*' in his essay of 1878; see Riout 1989, pp. 74 and 216.
92. Moffett *et al.* 1986, p. 179.
93. Gordon and Forge 1988, p. 11.
94. Guérin 1947, p. 70; Vollard 1937 (*Degas*), p. 46.
95. Sickert 1917, p. 186. Some accounts suggest a more jaundiced view of Monet's later achievement; see Bailly-Herzberg 1986, p. 240, where Degas disparages Monet's pictures as 'beautiful decorations'.
96. A letter of 1885, for example, shows Monet trying to acquire a picture by Degas (Wildenstein 1974–85, letter no. 568); at the time of Degas' death, Monet paid tribute to his achievement (letter no. 2244).
97. See R. Kendall, 'Degas et Cézanne', in Musée d'Orsay 1989, pp. 102–13.
98. See R. Kendall, 'The Figure in the Landscape', in Kendall 1993.
99. See Moffett *et al.* 1986, pp. 118–23, 203–7.
100. Notebook 28, p. 3.
101. Geffroy 1922, p. 136.
102. See Vente Collection I, nos 9–15, 105. For the uncertainty surrounding Degas' acquisition of a Cézanne drawing, see Musée d'Orsay, 1989, p. 113, n. 13.
103. For the echoes of *Venus and Cupid* in Degas' work, see the discussion of his pastoral nudes in chapter 8.
104. Guérin 1947, p. 35.
105. For example, Guérin 1947, pp. 62, 72, 94, 101, 131, 149.
106. Guérin 1947, p. 95.
107. See L 279–80, 284–6, 411–12. The sketch of a cow is discussed in Boggs 1985, pp. 6–7, where its resemblance to a monotype is noted.
108. The view of Etretat is in notebook 35, p. 9, and the sky study is in notebook 32, p. 177. Other landscapes can be found in notebook 26, pp. 78–80; notebook 32, pp. 17–18; notebook 34, pp. 84–5, 88, 91; notebook 37, p. 117.
109. The drawing was sold at Christie's, New York, 17 May 1977, lot 105. The visit is noted in Guérin 1947, p. 101.
110. L 285–6 and L 412–13 are signed; L 510 was signed and sold in 1891 (see Boggs 1985, p. 7); L 411 was acquired during the artist's lifetime by René de Gas.
111. See Janis 1968, nos 260–73.
112. Notebook 30, p. 205.
113. For the dating of the monotypes, see Boggs *et al.* 1988, pp. 257–60.
114. Moffett *et al.* 1986, p. 204.
115. See Janis 1967.
116. Neither work is included in Janis 1968, but both carry the *cachet* of the Degas *ventes* on the reverse.
117. *Place de la Concorde* (private collection, Germany) is L 368.
118. See L 270, 315, 416, 495, 857; L 339 and 888; L 710–12, 825, 879, 1007.
119. See also Kendall and Pollock 1992, pp. 196–7.
120. Moffett *et al.* 1986, p. 452.
121. Moffett *et al.* 1986, p. 44. Degas' portrait of Edmond Duranty (Burrell Collection, Glasgow; L 517) is a self-conscious demonstration of these principles.
122. Significantly, at this date and in this contex Degas made detailed drawings for some of the crowds and pavilions; see L 259–61, and a drawing for the stand in *The False Start* (Yale University Art Gallery; L 258) in a private collection, New York.
123. See L 446, 502–3, 596–7 *bis*, 764 and BR 111. For their possible role as decorations, see Thomson 1987, p. 89.
124. This painting, one of several versions of the subject, is in the Musée de l'Orangerie, Paris.
125. *Before the Race* (Rhode Island School of Design; L 679); *Le Jockey* (Philadelphia Museum of Art; L 1001); *Racehorses* (Carnegie Institute, Pittsburgh; BR 111).
126. Vollard 1937 (*Degas*), p. 87.
127. This important approach to Degas' equestrian scenes has never been studied systematically, though some aspects are covered in Pickvance 1968, Camesasca 1986 and Boggs *et al.* 1988, pp. 402–5, 459–64. In the present instance, the startled animal galloping away from the centre in the *Before the Race* pictures appears to be based on the sculpture *Rearing Horse*, while the standing mounts may derive from *Horse Walking*; see Rewald 1944, nos x and xii.
128. In a conversation of 1897, Degas described how he used his own sculptures of figures and horses as models for his pictures; see Thiébault-Sisson 1921. The moth-eaten remains of a stuffed horse were noted in Degas' studio at the end of his life by Louisine Havemeyer, who claimed that it had been used as a model in *Race Horses and Jockeys*, perhaps a reference to *Racehorses in a Landscape* (L 1145), formerly owned by the Havemeyers; see Havemeyer 1961, p. 247.
129. Guérin 1947, p. 120.
130. Lemoisne's ingenious juxtaposition of L 852 with L 850 is the exception that proves the rule.
131. The pictures are L 340, 400 and 498; see also Boggs *et al.* 1988, pp. 225–30.
132. In Boggs *et al.* 1988, p. 431, the ballet is identified as Meyerbeer's *L'Africaine*.
133. For a summary of identifiable ballets, see Boggs *et al.* 1988, p. 431.
134. See Henri Loyrette, 'Degas à l'Opera', in Musée d'Orsay 1989, pp. 47–63.
135. Moffett *et al.* 1986, p. 45.
136. Millard 1976, p. 121.
137. Riout 1989, p. 347.
138. Riout 1989, p. 347.
139. See, for example, references to Degas in the writings of Mirbeau and Fénéon; Riout 1989, pp. 346, 350 and 396.

140. Riout 1989, pp. 346–7.
141. Apart from the repeated use of words common to both art forms, such as composition, harmony and tone, a critic like Mirbeau applied specifically musical terms to Monet's pictures; see, for example, his description of one canvas as 'symphonically interlinked' in Spate 1992, p. 206.
142. In addition to the works discussed below, the following pastels appear to have been made in this decade; L 510, 635–6, 851, 1053, 1065; BR 102–3.
143. The drawing bears the *cachet* of the Degas *ventes* on the verso, though it is not listed in the printed catalogues.
144. Caillebotte's *Landscape with Restaurant* and *The Artist's House at Petit Genevilliers* (Berhaut 1978, nos 303 and 227) show comparable subjects. The origin of the title of Degas' pastel is not known; Pissarro had worked in Louveciennes in the late 1860s and early 1870s, and the Cassatt family took holidays there in the 1880s.
145. Two landscape fragments on similar paper that may be associated with this period are L 284 and BR 57. Degas chose equally coarse paper for some of his pastels of nudes in mid-decade; see L 765 and L 816.
146. Terrasse 1983, nos 40–6.
147. The provenance is given in Brame and Reff 1984, p. 112. Some similarity between the formal flower-beds and gravelled paths visible in the pastel and the setting of Degas' photographs of Ménil-Hubert (Terrasse 1983, nos 40–6) should also be noted.
148. Degas' habitual use of charcoal underdrawing is discussed in Kendall 1985, pp. 19–27.
149. L 635 and L 636.
150. The two drawings, *Landscape with Fence in the Foreground* and *Landscape with Houses at the Right*, are in the Ashmolean Museum, Oxford. Though unsigned, the latter was included as no. 567 in an exhibition of 1949, when the catalogue recorded that its frame was marked *Atelier Degas*; see Royal Academy 1949, p. 132.
151. Both drawings show the use of pencil prior to the application of ink. For Degas' views on the use of pen and ink, see his advice to Jeanniot in Jeanniot 1933, pp. 293–4, and to Braquaval, in chapter 9 below.
152. Sickert 1947, p. 150. Degas owned an oil painting and a drawing by Millet (Vente Collection I, nos 82 and 231) and four etchings (Vente Collection Estampes, no. 292).
153. The prevalence of this 'dotting' in Millet's prints suggests that the technique may have been derived from his practice as an etcher.
154. May is represented in L 392 and L 499; his collecting is discussed in Loyrette 1991, p. 418. Tillot's association with Millet, Degas and Rouart is summarised in Monneret 1987, pp. 945–6.
155. See Reff 1976 (*Degas: The Artist's Mind*), pp. 138–40, and Gordon 1984, p. 13.
156. See Herbert *et al.* 1976, no. 123. At least fifteen of the drawings in the 1976 Millet exhibition were originally in the collections of May, Tillot or Rouart, and would presumably have been known to Degas.
157. Degas' appreciation of Millet's drawings is recorded in Blanche 1919, p. 278.
158. See Herbert *et al.* 1975, no. 208. For another such sequence, see Herbert 1976, no. 122.
159. For later contacts between Degas and the art of Millet, see Laughton 1991, pp. 193–5.

6 The Visit to Diénay

1. It seems that Degas originally intended to travel alone; see the letter from Bartholomé to Lafond, dated 3 October 1890, in Sutton and Adhémar 1987, p. 166. For Degas and Bartholomé, see Thérèse Burollet, 'Un amicizia paradossale . . . quella di Edgar Degas e dello scultore Albert Bartholomé', in Camesasca 1986.
2. The unpublished Jeanniot correspondence in the Bibliothèque Nationale and the Bibliothèque d'Art et d'Archéologie, Paris, refers to many such visitors.
3. Jeanniot 1933.
4. Jeanniot 1933, p. 289.
5. Jeanniot 1933, p. 290–1.
6. For the history of this work, which was owned by Bartholomé until his death in 1924, see Boggs *et al.* 1988, p. 504.
7. Much of this material is in the Cabinet des Estampes at the Bibliothèque Nationale, Paris. The present location of the pastel by Manzi is unknown.
8. See Janis 1968, Adhémar and Cachin 1974, Lay 1978, Boggs *et al.* 1988, and Pantazzi 1989.
9. Sutton and Adhémar 1987, p. 166, and Guérin 1947, p. 159.
10. Degas' journeys are documented principally in his letters. Useful summaries can be found in the four 'Chronologies' in Boggs *et al.* 1988.
11. Reff 1968, p. 92.
12. This first visit to Diénay is noted in a letter of 26 October 1890 (Guérin 1947, p. 170), but not included in the 'Chronologies' in Boggs *et al.* 1988.
13. In a letter written after a visit to the painter de Valernes, Degas described his friend's studio and the pictures he had seen there; see Guérin 1947, pp. 171–2.
14. His companions at Cauterets are described in Guérin 1947, pp. 148–50, and Sutton and Adhémar, p. 164.
15. The visit to Madrid is recorded in Guérin 1947, pp. 134–6; the favourite Corot is identified in Clarke July 1991; journeys to Montauban are referred to in Guérin 1947, pp. 198–204.
16. See the discussion of BR 102–3 in chapter 5.
17. Guérin 1947, pp. 131 and 149; Sutton and Adhémar 1987, p. 163.
18. See Newhall 1956.
19. Degas' remark is from Guérin 1947, p. 170. The correspondence from the journey is included in Guérin 1947, pp. 153–68, Musée des Beaux-Arts, Nancy 1975, no. 86, and Sutton and Adhémar 1987, p. 166.
20. For other accounts of the monotypes, see below and chapter 7.
21. Jeanniot 1933, p. 290.
22. Champfleury 1973, p. 185.
23. Most famously, at several points in Zola 1977, but also in Maupassant 1972, p. 192. On p. 196 of Maupassant's text, the author describes the experience of seeing the landscape from a moving train.
24. See Jeanniot 1933, p. 299.
25. Guérin 1947, p. 252; translation slightly modified by the author, with reference to the original text in Guérin 1945, pp. 277–8. Evidence that Amiel's remark had achieved some celebrity is provided by Léon Daudet's quotation of the same phrase in Daudet 1992, p. 356.
26. See the analysis of the monotypes as technically and chronologically distinct groups later in this chapter.
27. On the route through Burgundy, for example, Degas passed through towns such as Melun and Sens which supported light industry. For a perceptive discussion of J 277, see Johnson 1984, pp. 34–5.
28. In Jamot 1924, p. 154, the structure is mistaken for a rock. The possibility that the pierced form was intended as a witty reference to Monet's *Etretat* paintings should be considered; I am grateful to Ruth Kendall for this observation.
29. Halévy 1929, pp. 49–50.
30. Guérin 1947, p. 152.
31. The letter to Bartholomé is in Guérin 1947, p. 150; see also the previously unpublished note from Degas to Mme Jeanniot, dated 14 September 1890, in Musée des Beaux-Arts, Nancy 1975, no. 83. I am indebted to Christian Debize for drawing this and other documents concerning the Diénay visit to my attention.
32. Guérin 1947, p. 170, with minor modifications to the translation in the light of the original text in Guérin 1945, p. 177.
33. Lafond 1918, I, p. 139.
34. Guérin 1947, p. 162.
35. Sutton and Adhémar 1987, p. 166; letter from Degas to Lafond.
36. Sutton and Adhémar 1987, p. 166; letter from Bartholomé to Lafond. See also the previously unpublished letter of 5 October 1890, Musée des Beaux-Arts, Nancy 1975, no. 86, where Degas' 'serenity' is remarked upon.
37. Further visits to Diénay are documented in Guérin 1947, p. 186, and an unpublished letter of 27 August 1898, written by Jeanniot; see Bibliothèque Nationale, Départment des manuscrits, Collection Porto Riche, Naf 24962.
38. Guérin 1947, pp. 162 and 165.
39. Though the route can still be traced with

considerable precision, some allowance must be made for the straightening and redirection of roads, and changes in field patterns and land use.

40. Other cases include J 279–80, 283, 286–7, 289–90, 292; K 4, 6.
41. The companion print, the location of which is unknown, is J 290.
42. The titles of Degas' landscape monotypes present a number of vexed questions. All the prints listed in the Durand-Ruel ledgers, which were bought directly from the artist, were described simply as *Paysage*. In common with the rest of Degas' works sold in the *ventes*, however, the prints remaining in the artist's studio after his death were given titles, presumably improvised by the cataloguers. References to L'Esterel and the Pyrenees are therefore likely to have been conjectural, the latter perhaps more inspired than the former.
43. In Kendall and Pollock 1992, p. 154, Richard Thomson points out that this image has a strong resemblance to a wood-engraving of a rock in the shape of a human face, published in *La Nature* in 1899; see Hulten *et al.* 1987, p. 210. Though the date of the illustration precludes a direct influence on Degas' image, such anthropomorphism did play a part in some of his landscape prints; see the discussion of this subject in chapter 7.
44. See Pantazzi 1989.
45. Manuscript in the Bibliothèque d'Art et d'Archéologie, Paris, MS 58488–58492. Part of this account is reproduced in Melot 1974, p. 97.
46. See Metropolitan Museum of Art 1980 for a full discussion of this history.
47. Metropolitan Museum of Art 1980, p. 29.
48. Lafond 1918, II, p. 60.
49. Rouart 1945, pp. 56–63.
50. Rouart, September 1964, pp. 10–11. The same essay was translated for the catalogue of an exhibition of Degas' monotype landscapes at E.V. Thaw, New York, in 1964; see Rouart 1964.
51. Janis 1967 and Janis 1968.
52. See the discussion of no. 71 in Janis 1968.
53. Janis 1973, unpag.
54. Metropolitan Museum of Art 1980, p. 112.
55. Noticed in Metropolitan Museum of Art 1980, p. 112, and in the discussion of other cognate pairs in this chapter.
56. Streaks of purple towards the top right-hand corner may be the residue of an earlier image, imperfectly cleaned from the plate.
57. My thanks are due to Michael and Marianne Howard for the use of their print studio, and for the elucidation of many aspects of monotype print-making that resulted.
58. There are extensive collections of Jeanniot's prints in the Bibliothèque Nationale and the Bibliothèque d'Art et d'Archéologie, Paris. Though he experimented actively with colour printing, such proofs all post-date the Diénay visit; for examples of his later colour work, see Cate and Grivel 1992, nos 100–2.
59. Such 'haloes' of oil are visible on the margins and versos of a number of prints; e.g., J 279, 284, 295, 297, 301.
60. Rouart, September 1964, p. 10, notes the use of turpentine to make 'clots' of colour. Other prints showing similar effects are J 276, 277, 307; K 2, 3. Though these 'puddles' or 'veils' of colour appear to have been allowed to run freely down the plate, the nature of the printing process precludes such an explanation. When liquid colour is subjected to the pressure of the roller, it is forced to spread, advancing across the plate and away from the roller. One consequence of this action is that the form of such a 'veil' indicates the direction in which the plate was printed; i.e., J 297 must have been printed sideways, while J 275 appears to have been placed in the press narrow edge first.
61. Rouart, September 1964, pp. 10–11. Practical experiment suggests that these effects are as likely to have been caused by using stiff or partially dried paint.
62. In Janis 1968, J 280 is described as the second of two impressions, but is reproduced in the same sense as J 279.
63. The latter effect is evident in a number of prints, e.g., J 278, 285, 297, 298, 309, 314, K 3.
64. Fevre 1949, p. 123.
65. The plate used for J 33, *Mlle Becat aux Ambassadeurs*, for example, which measured 16 × 12 cm, was re-used for numerous prints of similar subjects. A plate of similar dimensions formed the basis of several of the monochrome landscapes of this period, while another plate, measuring 16 × 21 cm, generated a second series of such works. Slight discrepancies in their published dimensions are almost certainly due to irregularities in measurement.
66. Some published dimensions appear to be based on sight size rather than plate size, and further discrepancies result from areas of pastel extending beyond the plate mark; see appendix 1.
67. For example, J 282 and 318.
68. See the discussion of K 6 (L 632), K 7 (L 633), K 8 (L 634) and K 9 (L 631) in chapter 7; see also appendix 2.
69. Jeanniot is known to have used plates of this size, which were probably of a standard and commercially available format; see his etching *L'Ouragon*, no. 30A in the Jeanniot collection at the Bibliothèque d'Art et d'Archéologie, Paris.
70. Lemoisne 1946, I, p. 157, suggests a connection with Degas' recent journeys in Mont-Dore or the Pyrenees; see also note 42 above.
71. See chapter 7.
72. Apart from the Diénay excursions, there are very few references to Degas in Jeanniot's correspondence, or to Jeanniot in Degas'. A brief note of 1898 records that the two artists were 'losing contact' (Guérin 1947, p. 208).
73. Joanne 1874, p. 13.
74. Joanne 1874, pp. 13–14. Degas' interest in such bizarre rocks is considered in chapter 7; see also note 43 above.
75. See Renoir 1962, pp. 301 and 312.
76. Monet's visit to the remote village of Fresselines in 1888 has a number of similarities with Degas' excursion. Not only was Monet attracted there by the presence of a Parisian acquaintance, but his rugged and elemental images of the terrain have much in common with the language of Degas' monotypes; see Tucker 1989, chapter 3.
77. The title of this work is written in an anonymous hand in pencil on the verso. It is one of the few monotypes not to have passed through either the 1892 exhibition or the Degas *ventes*, and may therefore have been given away or sold during the artist's lifetime.
78. Jeanniot 1933, p. 281.
79. See Guérin 1947, p. 84.
80. See Boggs *et al.* 1988, pp. 382–3, and Terrasse 1983, nos 4–6.
81. Degas' attitude to the craftsmen of the Marais is recorded in Halévy 1964, p. 53; his remark is in Michel 1919, p. 625.
82. See Guérin 1947, pp. 153, 157, 163, and note 33 above.
83. Jeanniot's painting is reproduced in Palais des Champs-Elysées 1887, no. 1288.
84. For an account of Jeanniot's career, see Alexandre 1903.
85. Some of Degas' teaching is described in Jeanniot 1933, pp. 293–4.
86. An etching entitled *Femme assise dans un jardin*, no. 16B in the Jeanniot collection of the Bibliothèque d'Art et d'Archéologie, is inscribed: *eau-forte executé d'après les conseils de Degas en Septembre 1890 à Diénay*. The aquatint *Trees* (RS 58) was apparently a joint experiment by the two artists.
87. Print no. 4B in the Jeanniot holdings of the Bibliothèque d'Art et d'Archéologie is inscribed in the artist's hand: *Monotype fait d'après les indications de Degas*. Two similar monotypes are nos 39 and 40 in the same collection.
88. According to a written testimonial, the painting was given by Jeanniot to Paul Lanzenberg ('dit Largy, critique d'art à Paris') in about 1930. The same text claims that the authenticity of the work was verified by P.-A. Lemoisne in 1947. Attempts to locate the work among descendants of the family have been unsuccessful; I am most grateful to Anne Roquebert for her help in this search, and for providing a photograph of the work.
89. Its resemblance to *Landscape* (J 288) is particularly marked.
90. Jeanniot 1933, p. 294.
91. Cousturier is printed as Couturier in Guérin 1945, p. 166, and Guérin 1947, p.

161. It is correctly spelled in Jeanniot 1933, p. 289. Further reference to Cousturier and his circle is made in Bailly-Herzberg 1988, p. 17. For Lucie Cousturier, who is listed as the first owner of Seurat's *La Grande Jatte*, see Monneret 1987, p. 157.

92. The individual in question must have been the Marquise de Fleury. She was the mother of Bartholomé's wife, Perie, who had died tragically in 1887. In a letter of 17 October 1890, Degas also reports that he dined with a M. Lemoine at Diénay, though it is not clear what relationship his host had with the other Lemoines and Lemoinnes of the artist's acquaintance. Other friends of the Jeanniots were the Voirin brothers, who collected works by Monet and Sisley, and Clément-Janin, the art critic.

93. For Meixmoron, see Musée des Beaux-Arts, Nancy 1962, Musée des Beaux-Arts, Besançon 1974, Musée des Beaux-Arts, Nancy 1975, Musée des Beaux-Arts, Nancy 1983 and Debize 1984. I am greatly indebted to Christian Debize for bringing some of these publications to my attention.

94. See Musée des Beaux-Arts, Nancy 1975, nos 21 and 23.

95. See Debize 1984.

96. It is clear from the previously unpublished letter of 14 September 1890, in Musée des Beaux-Arts, Nancy 1975, no. 83, that Degas was already acquainted with Meixmoron at this date.

97. Reference to Meixmoron is made in two unpublished letters from Degas to the Jeanniots, Musée des Beaux-Arts, Nancy 1975, nos 90 and 92, and in Guérin 1947, p. 187.

98. Meixmoron 1890 and Meixmoron, Noember 1890.

99. Meixmoron 1890, p. 58.

100. Guérin 1947, pp. 163 and 165.

101. Guérin 1947, p. 163.

102. Guérin 1947, pp. 167–8.

103. The album was to bear the title *Billiards* and was to be 'a humorous treatise on the game', with representations of the gestures made by male and female players, portraits, 'ancient furniture for the sacred game', letters from experts, etc. Whether related to this project or not, both Jeanniot and Meixmoron made pictures of billiards-players, and Degas' technical advice to Jeanniot was offered in the preparation of such a painting; see Jeanniot 1933, pp. 293–4. Though nothing came of the proposed publication, Degas' two paintings of billiard-rooms (L 1114–15) referred to in a letter of 1892 (Guérin 1947, p. 183), may have been intended as his contribution.

104. Musée des Beaux-Arts, Nancy, no. 90.

7 The 1892 Exhibition

1. Letter from Durand-Ruel to Henry Roujon, 10 November 1892; my thanks to Caroline Durand-Ruel Godfroy for permission to reproduce part of the letter in this chapter.
2. The date of this letter has been inaccurately transcribed as September 1892. As Michael Pantazzi has shown, all the circumstantial evidence points to an opening date in early November; see Pantazzi 1989, and note 30 below.
3. For Pissarro, see Bailly-Herzberg 1988, letters of 29 and 30 October and 9, 18 and 29 November 1991. For Renoir, see White 1984, p. 195.
4. Earlier in the year, Roujon had tried to persuade Degas to present a picture to the Luxembourg, using their mutual friend Mallarmé as a go-between; see Guérin 1947, pp. 247–8, and Valéry 1960, p. 31.
5. Alexandre 1892. In a letter of 15 November, Degas reassured Mme de Clermont over her wish to see the exhibition, explaining that she could enter the gallery in the usual way; see Musée d'Orsay 1989, p. 449.
6. For the number of works shown, see Pantazzi 1989, and note 29 below. The exhibition has frequently been dated 1893.
7. See note 1 above.
8. See Lay 1978 and Pantazzi 1989.
9. Geffroy 1894, p. 177.
10. For an account of Degas' approach to these exhibitions, see Moffett *et al.* 1986.
11. See Rewald 1946, p. 604 and Guérin 1947, p. 129.
12. Alexandre followed his announcement of Degas' exhibition with the paradox: 'Degas does not, and never will, exhibit'; see Alexandre 1892.
13. On 25 January 1882, Degas sold twelve studies of dancers to the gallery; Boggs *et al.* 1988, p. 375.
14. For the 1888 show, see Thomson 1988, p. 132, where Gauguin's response is discussed. Morisot's reactions are in Morisot 1986, pp. 152, 165–6. Jules Antoine's remark is cited in Bailly-Herzberg 1986, p. 290.
15. The story of the disaffection of Degas, Pissarro and Cassatt is vividly told in Bailly-Herzberg 1988, pp. 9 and 68.
16. Bailly-Herzberg 1988, p. 68.
17. Geffroy 1891.
18. For a summary of developments in colour printing, see Mathews and Shapiro 1989, pp. 57–85, and Cate and Grivel 1992; see also Fisher and Baxter 1983 and Fields 1983.
19. Guérin 1947, p. 58.
20. A reference to Pissarro's use of Degas' press is in Bailly-Herzberg 1988, p. 56. For the collaboration of the two artists on colour printing, see Cate and Grivel 1992, pp. 18 and 88.
21. Delteil 1923, Pissarro no. 96; dated 1890.
22. Bailly-Herzberg 1988, p. 31.
23. Bailly-Herzberg 1988, p. 55.
24. Bailly-Herzberg 1988, p. 58.
25. See Mathews and Shapiro 1989.
26. Bailly-Herzberg 1988, pp. 55 and 67.
27. Degas' criticisms of Cassatt's work are in Bailly-Herzberg 1988, p. 58. His collection of her prints is listed in Vente Collection Estampes, pp. 10–12.
28. His remark was recorded by Theodore Robinson and was made in February 1892, at the opening of Monet's exhibition of *Poplars* at the Durand-Ruel gallery; see Robinson 'Diary'.
29. In Durand-Ruel's letter to Roujon (see note 1 above), the number given is twenty-five; a letter written by Boldini at the same time mentions 'twenty-four pictures' (see Pantazzi 1989, p. 7); Philip Hale's review refers to 'some thirty' (Hale 1892, p. 326); and in Fevre 1949, p. 102, in a note sent after the exhibition, Degas himself specifies twenty-six works.
30. Michael Pantazzi has pointed out that the exhibition was visited on 7 November, probably its opening day, by the dealer George Lucas; a letter from Degas written on 15 November specifies that the exhibition was due to close 'at the end of the week', i.e., 18 November (Musée d'Orsay 1989, p. 449). Pissarro's reference to Degas' pictures in a letter sent in October suggests that he had seen the works as they were being prepared, not that the exhibition opened during that month; see Bailly-Herzberg 1988, p. 262.
31. Pissarro's use of one of these rooms, where he planned to show twenty-four works (approximately the same number as Degas), is referred to in Bailly-Herzberg 1988, p. 50.
32. Letter to D.C. Thomson of London, dated 16 November 1892, Archives Durand-Ruel, Paris.
33. See appendix 1. The element of uncertainty is due to the unknown location of some of the prints and the inadequacy of existing photographs, as well as the inaccurate classification of such apparently print-based images as L 631 (K 9), L 632 (K 6), L 633 (K 7) and L 634 (K 8).
34. It is conceivable that Jeanniot's prints were loaned to the exhibition and that other signed works were omitted. According to Pantazzi, J 281 and J 313 were first owned by Jeanniot. For Charpentier, see the discussion of K 6 below.
35. For cognate pairs, see appendix 1.
36. The critic Philip Hale noted rather obscurely that Degas' 'little paintings' were displayed 'each in its shadow-box, tinted the dominant colour of the picture' (Hale 1982, p. 326). Unfortunately, none of the pictures has survived with such a frame. An old note on the backboard of J 321, presumably written by Marcel Guérin (who formerly owned the picture), states that 'the frame is that from Degas' exhibition of 24 pastel landscapes at Durand-Ruel's . . .'. The present frame, which does not necessarily correspond to the backboard, is of the conventional moulded and gilt variety. A mat white frame with a dark inner 'box' on

Burgundy Landscape (K 3), which Degas gave to Bartholomé, is perhaps closer to their original appearance.

37. Durand-Ruel's note to Roujon referred to the prints as 'pastels and watercolours' (see not 1 above); Hale claimed that some were executed on canvas, in 'water colours, oils and pastel' (Hale 1892, p. 326); Alexandre guessed at watercolour, gouache and pastel (Alexandre 1892); Pissarro, in Bailly-Herzberg 1988, p. 262, described them as 'pochades au pastel', but noted their resemblance to colour prints.
38. *L'Ermitage* 1892, p. 416 (I am indebted to Richard Thomson for drawing my attention to this review); Alexandre 1892; Hale 1892, p. 326.
39. Geffroy 1894, pp. 176–7.
40. Bailly-Herzberg 1988, p. 262.
41. The exception is K 3. Two of the exhibits, J 281 and BR 134, were entirely executed in pastel and have no monotype base.
42. This distinctive 'speckling' of touches of pastel occurs on a number of the works shown; see, for example, J 281–2, J 291, J 293, J 321, BR 134, K6–9. The possibility that Degas may have briefly experimented with Seurat's application of colour is considered in Kendall 1985, p. 23.
43. The detail of the distant houses and rooftops is present in the monotype layer, showing that the subject was determined with some precision at this preliminary stage.
44. For example, in Metropolitan Museum of Art 1980, p. 112.
45. Boggs *et al.* 1988, p. 504.
46. Examination of the paint layer in both prints has shown that Degas re-worked certain areas, such as the sky, before pulling the second proof. In J 284, the sky is dominated by horizontal striations in dull pink; in J 285, by vertical marks in mauve.
47. My thanks are due to Philip Conisbee and Sara Campbell for helping me with access to these two works.
48. Some darker forms, apparently trees, were once clearly visible at the right.
49. The presence of this subject in the exhibition was noted by Boldini; see note 29 above. Though the weight of probability favours a monotype origin for this work, the most careful scrutiny of the picture (in its frame) has yet to reveal traces of the original print.
50. I am grateful to Mr and Mrs Paul Josefowitz for calling my attention to this picture, and to Walter Tschopp and Nicole Quellet for facilitating my examination of it. Monotype traces are evident in many areas of the image and plate-marks are visible on at least three edges.
51. Both L 631 (K 9) and L 634 (K 8) are recorded by Lemoisne as having the dimensions 25 × 34 cm, and both are based on a similar landscape with steep foreground, high horizon and bedraggled hedge. In all probability the works represent two sets of cognate prints, or conceivably a single pair with (very uncharacteristic) working drawings.
52. For Courbet, see Pantazzi 1989, p. 12; for Millet, see, amongst others, *Watering Cows*, Museum of Fine Arts, Boston; for Gauguin, see the discussion below.
53. L 631.
54. A similar dedication appears on L 413 and a drawing of *c.*1898, *Femme s'essuyant*. As these inscriptions follow a similar pattern and appear to have been added at the same time, it is probable that the pictures were acquired in the late 1890s (Charpentier died in 1901). However, Degas is recorded at a dinner with Charpentier in 1892 (see Morisot 1986, p. 188) and again in 1894 (see Sutton and Adhémar 1987, p. 171, n. 2).
55. See Schmitt 1894, Alexandre 1892 and *L'Ermitage* 1892, p. 415.
56. Hale 1892, p. 326.
57. See notes 60 and 61 below, and Pissarro's observation, in Bailly-Herzberg 1988, p. 262, that the landscapes resembled coloured prints.
58. Most of Degas' prints correspond closely and perhaps deliberately to the standard dimensions of the woodblock print (the *Oban*), approximately 35 × 25 cm; see Strange 1983, p. 10, and Smith 1988, p. 15.
59. Bailly-Herzberg 1988, p. 309, and Mathews and Shapiro 1989, p. 19.
60. Hale 1892, p. 326.
61. Loyrette 1991, p. 563.
62. See Ives 1974, Weisberg 1975, Wichmann 1981 and Meech-Pekarik 1982.
63. For the 1890 exhibition, see Weisberg 1975, p. 55, and Mathews and Shapiro 1989, pp. 62–8.
64. Guérin 1947, p. 146. In the same letter, Degas notes that he has dined with Mary Cassatt at the Fleurys, parents of Mme Bartholomé, and refers to a recent meeting with the print-maker Manzi.
65. For Pissarro, see Bailly-Herzberg 1986, p. 351; for Morisot, see Morisot 1986, p. 174; for Cassatt, Tissot and Fantin, see Mathews 1984, p. 214.
66. Degas' print measures 25 × 30 cm, Hokusai's 26 × 38.1 cm.
67. Such roads occur in numerous prints by Hiroshige, Harunobu and others, but are perhaps most vividly exemplified in a page of Hokusai's sketchbook, which provides a compelling precedent for Degas' composition; see Michener 1958, p. 137.
68. Apart from Hokusai's views of Mount Fuji, Hiroshige's *Oyashirazu Cliff, Echigo* is typical of an entire genre of such imagery.
69. See note 26 above.
70. Both prints have the same dimensions and belong to the small 'family' of plates, group C; see appendix 1. Similarities in colour, paper and technique suggest that they were made in close proximity to each other.
71. In Lemoisne 1945, I, p. 157, the analogy with views from an aeroplane is proposed.
72. In each of the three prints discussed, which together make up group C, the 'streaking' of their skies seems to show an awareness of similar effects in Japanese woodblocks.
73. Hiroshige's fondness for such rising diagonals, which can take the form of roadways, bridges, tree-trunks and spurs of land, is one of the most pronounced characteristics of his prints. An angled causeway similar to that in *Rocky Coast* can be found in Hiroshige's *Fan Design: The Usui Pass and Kumagai Embankment*, reproduced in Strange 1983, p. 92.
74. See note 42 above.
75. See House 1986, p. 58.
76. Vente Collection Estampes, under *Hiroshige*: no. 328 ('Landscapes; forty-two items, mostly by Hiroshige') and no. 329 ('Monkeys, Various birds, Flowers, Fish, Crawfish, Landscapes; fifteen drawings, many brushed with watercolour'). For a more sceptical view of Hiroshige's influence, see Varnedoe 1990, pp. 53–76.
77. Most celebrated of these was the sequence of fifty-five landscapes seen on a journey along the Tokaido road; see Strange 1983, ch. 5.
78. Bailly-Herzberg 1988, p. 58.
79. The exception to this rule was the projected journal Le Jour et la nuit, in which Degas, Cassatt, Pissarro and others planned to publish their prints. For technical and temperamental reasons, the journal never appeared.
80. See notes 46 and 72 above.
81. House 1986, p. 58.
82. Bailly-Herzberg 1988, p. 309.
83. For Hayashi, see Meech-Pekarik 1982, pp. 96–7; Aitken and Delafond 1987, pp. 21–2; Pickyance 1988, pp. 252–4.
84. See Hayashi 1908.
85. Hayashi owned oils by Monet, Pissarro, Sisley, Renoir and Guillaumin, as well as works on paper by Cassatt, Manzi, Boudin and others; see Hayashi 1908, where a number of these pictures are reproduced.
86. Degas Inventory, no. 174.
87. See Musée d'Orsay 1990, p. 159. An exhibition of Bartholomé's work was held at the Durand-Ruel gallery in 1890. The finished bronze of Hayashi is dated 1892.
88. Degas Inventory, no. 4. Hayashi's collection included an etched portrait of Degas by Manzi; see Hayashi 1908.
89. I am again grateful for the generous cooperation of Mme Caroline Durand-Ruel Godfroy in this investigation, not least for allowing the reproduction of the pages from the gallery stockbook where Hayashi's purchases are recorded. The identities of the four prints can be deduced from Hayashi 1908 and his posthumous sale catalogues.
90. The print was later in the collection of the New York dealer Sam Salz, but no record of its sale has survived.
91. Schmitt 1894. Hayashi's taste for the nebulous imagery of the landscapist and friend

of Degas, Charles Blache, is an extreme case in point.
92. Lemoisne 1912, p. 80.
93. See, for example, Bailly-Herzberg 1988, pp. 84 and 218, and other cases cited in Broude 1991, pp. 57 and 63.
94. Cited in Gage 1987, p. 244, n. 33. My thanks to Richard Thomson for bringing this reference to my attention. The exhibition in question included eleven oils by Turner, most of them early, and was entitled *British Art 1737–1837*.
95. Degas' remark is in an undated letter to Whistler; see MacDonald and Newton 1986, p. 205. His connections with Groult are documented in Guérin 1947, pp. 61 and 83, and Reff 1968, p. 90. Though he is unlikely to have known about them, Turner's 'colour beginnings' offer a fascinating precedent for some of Degas' landscape monotypes.
96. The conversation is recorded in Guérin 1947, pp. 251–2. The first volume of Amiel's journal was published in Geneva in 1882, the second in 1884. Amiel had been Professor of Moral Philosophy at the Geneva Academy, and his volumes of religious, literary and moral reflections, which had often been stimulated by travel, were widely popular in Europe. See also chapter 6, note 25.
97. Guérin 1947, p. 253.
98. In August 1891, Degas had an appointment with the celebrated ophthalmologist Dr Edmund Landolt; see Guérin 1947, p. 177, and Kendall 1988, p. 187.
99. Guérin 1947, p. 174.
100. Guérin 1947, p. 148.
101. Degas' dark glasses can be seen in the photographs of himself and Bartholomé *en route* in chapter 6, and in a photograph taken in a garden at Diénay; see Musée des Beaux-Arts, Nancy 1975, no. 91.
102. For accounts of this aspect of Degas' sight, see Guérin 1947, p. 96, and Fevre 1949, p. 138.
103. Halévy 1964, p. 58.
104. In Halévy's journal entry for September 1892, Degas specifies that the prints were made 'this summer'; Guérin 1947, pp. 251–2. See also Halévy's account of the same event in Halévy 1929, pp. 49–50.
105. See appendix 1.
106. Certain other characteristics unite images within the groups: e.g., the marks of a bevelled edge can be seen on some of the images printed with plate B.
107. For a discussion of imagery seen from trains in the context of Monet, see Spate 1992, p. 102.
108. See the recently published letter of March 1892 in Boggs *et al.* 1988, p. 487, and the undated letter (1892?) in Fevre 1949, p. 94.
109. Guérin 1947, pp. 181–3.
110. Guérin 1947, p. 117.
111. See Pantazzi 1989, p. 7. Other testimonials to Degas' memory can be found in Jeanniot 1933, p. 290, and Fevre 1949, p. 60.
112. See Valéry 1960, p. 35, and Jeanniot 1933, p. 158.
113. Though it is often cited with great solemnity, Lecoq's 'system' depended on little more than regular practice in drawing from memory; Lecoq de Boisbaudran 1862 expands this principle to book length. Lecoq's address was written down by Degas in the early 1880s; see notebook 34, p. 7.
114. The highly peripatetic Turner offers interesting parallels with Degas' travels. In 1802, for example, Turner made a carriage journey from Paris to Fontainebleau, Sens, Joigny and Auxerre (close to Degas' route in 1890) and eventually to Geneva (see Wilkinson 1974, p. 38).
115. Degas' habit of signing certain works of art more than once first appears earlier in his career, in such pictures as *Woman with Chrysanthemums* (L 125) and *The Gentlemen's Race: Before the Start* (L 101), where it is associated with a modification or reworking of an earlier image. In the present case, it appears to suggest second (or third) thoughts about a recently completed picture.
116. Jeanniot 1933, p. 158.
117. Lecoq de Boisbaudran 1862, p. 21.
118. Georges Braque's practice of painting his landscapes indoors, away from the *motif*, in the years immediately preceding Cubism, was similarly presented as an attempt to break the stranglehold of nature.
119. Jeanniot 1933, p. 281.
120. Jeanniot 1933, p. 170.
121. Fevre 1949, p. 102.
122. See Robinson 'Diary', and note 28 above.
123. 'R.G.' 1892, p. 374; Alexandre 1892.
124. Alexandre 1892.
125. The technique was first described in the context of Degas' oil painting in Rouart 1945, pp. 44–50.
126. See Fauchereau 1991.
127. See Georgel 1974, unpag.
128. Georgel 1974, no. 12.
129. According to Daniel Halévy's journal, Degas was reading Victor Hugo in 1890; see Halévy 1960, p. 41. Hugo is listed among Degas' five favourite poets in Fevre 1949, p. 117.
130. The possibility that Degas recalled in some of these works the legendary rock formations of Burgundy, which included a number of caves and grottoes, is discussed in chapter 6 and below. J 309 belongs to monotype group A and thus appears to have been one of several imaginative studies (among them J 295, J 296, J 311 and K 4) either made on the 1890 Diénay visit or elaborated subsequently.
131. Both J 313 and K 3 were signed and given to friends, without pastel additions.
132. For example, Vente II, no. 324; L 844 *bis*; and *Dancer Adjusting her Tights*, Fitzwilliam Museum, Cambridge.
133. The bushy beard and pronounced nose of Bartholomé, evident in contemporary photographs, might have been Degas' target. It seems highly probable that Degas was aware of such images as the anonymous *Enigmatic Landscape*, a lithograph of *c.*1830–40 that ingeniously merges a similar male profile with a rocky horizon line; see Hulten *et al.* 1987, p. 209. My thanks to Peter Brookes for drawing my attention to this image.
134. Cap Hornu is a small and almost featureless area of low-lying ground to the west of Saint-Valéry-sur-Somme.
135. Careful examination of both works has failed to reveal any evidence of monotype printing. Significantly, the dimensions of both pastels are also quite distinct from the monotype groups in appendix 1.
136. Amiel 1885, II, p. 5. See also Stafford 1984, pp. 15, 23 and 417.
137. Maupassant 1972, p. 33. The novel was first published in 1883.
138. Amiel 1885, I, p. 97.
139. See Haverkamp-Begemann *et al.* 1964, nos 254 and 255.
140. Notebook 13, p. 34.
141. Notebook 22, pp. 24, 75, 76; notebook 23, p. 147.
142. Hale 1892, p. 326.
143. Thomson 1988, pp. 203–5, and Kendall and Pollock 1992, pp. 154–5.
144. See Thomson 1987, pp. 110–11.
145. In Robinson 'Diary'; Monet's swelling, torso-like studies of the cliffs at Dieppe of 1897 have distinct anthropomorphic echoes.
146. Though not quite identical in size, the two pastels vary substantially from the rest of the series, but from each other only by a few centimetres. Both are executed on a rough, fibrous paper, unlike the monotypes, and there are close affinities in their imagery and facture.
147. See L 8, L 21, L 73 and L 114.
148. Though the owner of the legs in notebook 1, p. 41, is uncertain, the naked thigh and knee seen from above in notebook 3, p. 47, which curiously anticipates the subject of J 282, can only be the artist's.
149. See Vachon (n.d.), where *Monuments du paganisme en Côte-d'Or* (1891) is cited. It is notable that a number of these standing stones have allusive titles, often referring to animals or parts of the body; see, for example, *La Cheval Gris* at Chambain and *Les Dents de Chien* (which recalls J 312) at Saint-Aubin.
150. This stone is considered to be a naturally occurring monolith, though man-made examples are also found in the region.
151. Aitken and Delafond 1987, nos 130 and 148; see Bernard's *Vertical Cliffs on the Coast of Brittany near Le Pouldu* (private collection) and *Cliffs at Yport*, 1892 (Luthi 1982, no. 342).
152. Valéry 1960, p. 43, and Guérin 1947, p. 252.
153. Valéry 1960, pp. 43–4.
154. Guérin 1947, p. 252.

155. Jeanniot 1933, p. 290. See note 130 above for the group of anthropomorphic landscapes begun at Diénay, though perhaps developed later.
156. It is noticeable that none of the visitors who recorded their reactions to the exhibition made a correct identification of the medium used (see note 37 above). This may be explained partly by the unfamiliarity of the colour monotype process, partly by the concealment of the monotype by layers of pastel.
157. Alexandre 1892 and *L'Ermitage* 1892, p. 415.
158. Geffroy 1894, pp. 175–6.
159. Geffroy 1894, pp. 175 and 177.
160. Geffroy 1894, p. 178.
161. Geffroy 1894, pp. 176–8.
162. Geffroy 1894, p. 178.
163. Little is known of Degas' reading habits, though he expressed something of the curiosity and his age in intellectual matters. Several of his acquaintances and patrons were doctors, his close friend Henri Rouart was an engineer, and Degas himself became an experimental photographer. On at least two occasions, Degas showed awareness of specialist research; he noted a recent issue of *La Nature*, containing articles on Marey and Muybridge, in notebook 31, p. 81; and referred to the findings of Liebreich, published in the *Proceedings of the Royal Institution*, in a conversation at the Halévys' (see Kendall 1988, p. 183, n. 26).
164. Lay 1978, pp. 145–6; see also Hamilton 1975. Bergson's *Time and Free Will* was published in 1889, his *Matter and Memory* in 1896.
165. Bergson 1910, p. 104. For Monet and Bergson, see Tucker 1989, p. 101.
166. Bergson 1913, pp. 237–8.
167. Bergson 1913, p. 241; Halévy 1960, p. 69.
168. See 'Henri Bergson et la Philosophie' in Lefèvre 1926, pp. 77–9.
169. Valéry 1960, p. 45.
170. Valéry 1960, p. 41.
171. *L'Ermitage* 1892; unsigned review.
172. *L'Ermitage* 1892, p. 415.
173. *L'Ermitage* 1892, p. 416.
174. 'R.G.' 1892, p. 374.
175. The phrase is used in *L'Ermitage* 1892, p. 415; Geffroy 1894, p. 177; and in a brief reference to the Degas landscape exhibition in Bouyer 1894, p. 94. Thanks to Richard Thomson for drawing my attention to the latter.
176. Schmitt 1894.
177. Degas' remarks are found in Bailly-Herzberg 1988, p. 113, and Halévy 1960, pp. 96 and 109.
178. This observation is made in Loyrette 1991, p. 618.
179. Degas' responses to Carrière are recorded in Halévy 1960, p. 68–9, and Vollard 1937 (*Degas*), p. 36.
180. See Lay 1978, p. 146, and Boggs *et al*. 1988, pp. 502, 536.
181. See Belinda Thomson 1987, especially pp. 57–63, 85–6; Thomson 1988, pp. 170–1; Françoise Cachin, 'Degas et Gauguin', in Musée d'Orsay 1989, pp. 115–27.
182. Degas' acquisitions are listed in Vente Collection I, nos 40–9, 177; Vente Collection Estampes, nos 123–8.
183. See Vente Collection I, nos 42, 45, 43, 48 and 46.
184. In Degas Inventory, the artist specifies that no. 71 ('Defile au bord de la mer et danse baigneux') was bought from Gauguin himself in December 1894, and no. 73 ('Paysage de la Martinique, cases, nègres sous les arbres; a gauche, à l'horizon moulin à vent') was exchanged with Manzi 'after the first sale'. No. 75 ('Petite nature morte, Mandoline sur un tapis, etc.') was exchanged with the artist at an unspecified date.
185. In Degas Inventory, no. 72 ('La Belle Angèle') is said to have been bought 'at the first sale . . . before his departure for Tahiti'.
186. For Gauguin's borrowings from Degas, see note 181.
187. Boggs *et al*. 1988, p. 568.
188. Halévy 1960, p. 61.
189. See Valéry 1960, pp. 28–31, 62; Gide 1947; Degas' photograph of Verhaeren is in Terrasse 1983, no. 62.
190. For Degas and Mallarmé, see Loyrette 1991, pp. 547–52; the photograph, a copy of which once belonged to Paul Valéry, is Terrasse 1983, no. 12.
191. Valéry 1960, p. 31.
192. Valéry 1960, p. 84.
193. Valéry 1960, p. 28.
194. Valéry 1960, p. 102.
195. Stafford 1984, pp. 470–6.

8 After the 1892 Exhibition

1. Fevre 1949, p. 102.
2. Mathews 1984, p. 240.
3. In addition to these twenty-four, K 3 would have been returned to its dedicatee, Bartholomé, and Degas himself kept J 310, which reappeared in Vente II, no. 199. Only a few landscapes can be identified from the details given in the Durand-Ruel records, though it is tempting to assume that the two works with the highest prices were the pair of large pastels, J 282 and BR 134.
4. See the entries in the Durand-Ruel stock-book. It appears that these works were 'sold' to the New York branch, then 'bought back' on return.
5. Schmitt 1894 is written as a review of a current show.
6. The records of the Museum of Fine Arts in Boston, to whom the pictures were donated, show that J 284 was bought by Ross from the New York gallery on 17 November 1894, and that J 279 was acquired in 1897.
7. The Havemeyers' name appears against no. 2773 in the Durand-Ruel list, with the date of sale as 19 September 1895. For a detailed account of the Havemeyers' purchases, see Weitzenhoffer 1986, p. 98, and Freylinghuysen *et al*. 1993, pp. 214–15 and 334–7. The Havemeyers eventually owned J 291, J 304, J 319, J 320 and K 56.
8. Hayashi's purchases are clearly indicated as nos 2764–5 and 2768–9 in the Durand-Ruel ledger. From Hayashi 1908 and other sources, they can be identified as J 286, J 290, J 294 and BR 136.
9. Individual lots were Vente II, no. 199, and Vente II, pp. 38–45. Some prints appear to have been sold as mixed lots, *hors catalogue*.
10. Grappe 1909, pl. 51.
11. Petit 1924. Titles vary a little from later usage, but the works on show appear to have been J 286, J 293, J 316 and J 321.
12. Emden acquired J 282; Werdenbusch bought J 303 before 1900; Hayashi died in 1906 and his sale took place in 1913.
13. See P.G. Hamerton, 'The Present State of the Fine Arts in France: Impressionism', 1891, in Flint 1984, p. 100.
14. See Fowle 1992.
15. A label on the back of J 281 reads 'Exposition Londres 1906 no. 66'. This presumably refers to the exhibition of the International Society, held at the New Gallery from January to March 1906.
16. Their dates of acquisition are not known. Moore-Turner was also the owner of the painting *Dancer* (L 973) and eventually acquired Cézanne's *Venus and Cupid*, formerly the property of Degas. A number of other nineteenth-century works from Moore-Turner's collection were loaned to an exhibition in London in 1949; see Royal Academy 1949.
17. These notes on Percy Morre-Turner have been kindly augmented by Jon Whitely of the Ashmolean Museum, the institution to which much of his collection was bequeathed. Moore-Turner's career is also discussed in Sutton 1972.
18. Most aspects of the collection were represented in the bequest to the Ashmolean Museum of 1951; see the museum records for that year.
19. See chapter 7; Toulouse-Lautrec's familiarity with the landscapes is revealed in Joyant 1926, p. 192.
20. Metropolitan Museum of Art 1980, pp. 29–39 and 93–139.
21. Metropolitan Musseum of Art 1980, pp. 138–9, and 40–8, 142–89.
22. See chapter 7, note 37.
23. See Fields 1983; Rivière was commissioned to make murals for Hayashi's Tokyo appartment.
24. For example, Rivière's *Baie de la Fresnaye* of 1891, his *Etude de vague* of 1892, and his *La Falaise* of 1897.
25. For Maurin, see Goldschmidt Gallery 1986 and Cate and Boyer 1986; Degas' views are recorded in Vollard 1936, p. 127.

26. Carrière's landscape activities are summarised in Bantens 1990, pp. 84–94.
27. Sickert 1917, pp. 184–5.
28. L 1149 and L 1014; the former is dated 1894, and the latter belongs to the same period.
29. Its association with the landscape monotypes was suggested in Boggs *et al.* 1988, p. 511 and developed in Boggs and Maheux 1992, p. 132.
30. See Boggs *et al.* 1988, p. 511 and Freylinghuysen *et al.* 1993, pp. 337–8.
31. For the purchase of the monotypes, see note 7 above.
32. Degas' experiments with under-painting in bright colour can be seen in such works as L 1128 and L 1231, and in several of the Saint-Valéry landscapes; for his advocacy of green grounds, now linked with Old Master technique, see Valéry 1960, pp. 94–7.
33. Valéry 1960, pp. 6 and 50.
34. See Rouart 1945, pp. 44–50, where the link with the Old Masters is made. Rouart notes the use of finger-painting in the Saint-Valéry landscapes, but does not trace the technique to its origin in Degas' monotypes.
35. The Ménil-Hubert interiors are L 1114 and L 1115. Among the most conspicuous examples of Degas' new technique are L 1104 and L 1014.
36. Canvases re-worked in this way include L 587, L 839 and L 1013.
37. Degas' extensive use of finger-painting almost certainly derives from his experience of the colour monotype in 1890 and 1892. Though occasional and partial finger marks were present in the monochrome prints of the 1870s, they were not used to build images systematically, as they were in such monotypes as J 289 and J 308. None of the oil paintings re-worked with the artist's fingers (see notes 35 and 36 above) is securely detable before 1890, on either documentary or stylistic grounds, and it would seem reasonable to locate all such technical experiments in the period after the first colour monotypes. For Degas' concurrent interest in the finger-painting activities of Titian, see note 34 above.
38. L 1181–93; see also Boggs *et al.* 1988, pp. 581–5.
39. Manet 1987, p. 177; journal entry for 1 July 1899.
40. In both monotype and pastel, the flowers may be the lavender blue of flax blossoms.
41. Guérin 1947, p. 186, and Fevre 1949, p. 93.
42. Guérin 1947, pp. 186–8.
43. The letter is dated 27 August 1898 and is in the Porto Riche collection, p. 201, Naf 24962; Bibliothèque Nationale, Paris.
44. Sutton and Adhémar 1987, p. 173.
45. Guérin 1947, p. 198.
46. Guérin 1947, pp. 210–11, and Sutton and Adhémar 1987, p. 173.
47. Guérin 1947, pp. 199 and 195.
48. See Newhall 1956; Hoctin 1960; Pickvance 1970; Terrasse 1983; Eugenia Parry Janis, 'Edgar Degas' Photographic Theatre', in Guillaud 1984, pp. 451–86; Boggs *et al.* 1988, pp. 535–40; and Françoise Heibrun, 'Sur les photographies de Degas', in Musée d'Orsay 1989, pp. 159–80.
49. In addition to the works cited in note 48, see the more contentious viewpoints of Varnedoe, January 1980, Varnedoe, May 1980 and Varnedoe 1990, ch. 3.
50. Missing photographs include those taken at Mont-Dore described in Newhall 1956; the landscapes of Saint-Valéry recorded in Guérin 1947, p. 210, n. 1; and the portrait of Whistler referred to in MacDonald and Newton 1986, p. 209.
51. Terrasse 1983, nos 40–5.
52. See Terrasse 1983, nos 17 and 18, and Boggs *et al.* 1988, pp. 535–40.
53. For Bartholomé, see Terrase 1983, nos 58–9; for Meixmoron, see chapter 6.
54. Terrasse 1983, nos 11, 12 and 62; the Mallarmé lines are cited in Boggs *et al.* 1988, p. 536.
55. An undated letter from the 1890s sent by Degas refers to some 'mediocre' proofs of 'the model', Whistler; see MacDonald and Newton 1986, p. 209.
56. Guérin 1947, p. 210.
57. Musée d'Orsay 1989, p. 174, and Hoctin 1960, p. 36.
58. Guérin 1947, p. 210, n. 1.
59. Terrasse 1983, nos 60–1. Terrasse associates them erroneously with Saint-Valéry-en-Caux rather than Saint-Valéry-sur-Mer. His text specifies that the photographs were loaned by Marcel Guérin to the Degas exhibition in Philadelphia in 1936, when Guérin described them as coming from Degas' studio.
60. Bailly-Herzberg 1988, p. 55.
61. Raunay 1931, p. 624.
62. Degas' acquistions by both artists are listed in Vente Collection I, Vente Collection II and Vente Collection Estampes; see also, Anne Roquebert, 'Degas collectionneur', in Musée d'Orsay 1989, pp. 65–85.
63. See Vente Collection I, nos 72–9, and nos 40–9.
64. Halévy 1960, p. 86.
65. Vente Collection I, nos 26, 61, 75, 88, 70, 5.
66. Vente Collection I, nos 40–9, 177; Vente Collection Estampes, nos 123–8.
67. Vente Collection I, nos 45 and 47.
68. Vente Collection I, no. 40, and Degas Inventory, no. 79.
69. Vente Collection I, no. 43, and Degas Inventory, no. 71.
70. Malingue 1946, p. 216.
71. See Richard Kendall, 'Degas et Cézanne', in Musée d'Orsay 1989, pp. 103–13.
72. Degas is known to have visited Cézanne's 1895 exhibition at Vollard's gallery, where all these subjects were represented; see Manet 1987, p. 76, and Vollard 1937 (*Cézanne*), p. 53.
73. L 1070–83; L 1174; Vente IV, no. 251.
74. For a discussion of their imagery, see Boggs *et al.* 1988, pp. 554–60.
75. For example, L 1077 and L 1081 measure 70 × 70 cm, while L 1078 and L 1082 are both approximately 60 × 74 cm.
76. Renoir showed at Durand-Ruel in 1896 and 1898; for Pissarro's nudes, see Thomson 1990, pp. 85–92; for Cézanne's 1895 exhibition, see Vollard 1937 (*Cézanne*), p. 53.
77. See Halévy 1960, pp. 159–60.
78. Notebook 8, p. 39v; notebook 9, p. 17; notebook 10, p. 65; notebook 18, p. 35.
79. See the discussion of this picture in chapter 2, and in Douglas Druick, 'La petite danseuse et les criminels: Degas moraliste', in Musée d'Orsay 1989, pp. 225–50.
80. See Burnell 1969.
81. For the comparison with Mantegna, see Smith 1982; with Japanese prints, see chapter 5.
82. For the evidence that Degas showed the *Young Spartans* in his apartment, see Boggs *et al.* 1988, p. 98.
83. This building is evident in the early studies reproduced in Burnell 1969 and elsewhere, but can also be glimpsed, in the form of an over-painted pediment or platform, beneath the final paint layer of the finished picture.
84. For Pissarro's pictures from the mid-1890s of comparable subjects, see Thomson 1990, pp. 85–92.
85. See Lhermitte's pastel *The Bather* of 1907, in the Glasgow Art Gallery and Museum.
86. The association with Diana and Eve is made in Boggs *et al.* 1988, p. 558. In Brettell and McCullagh 1984, p. 190, the foreground nude is linked with a figure from Michelangelo's *Battle of Cascina*, which Degas had studied as a young man (see note 78 above). While this is plausible, it may be significant that Poussin, who himself borrowed this figure from Michelangelo for his *Baptism*, placed a conspicuous blue stocking on her raised foot, just as Degas has done. Degas could not have seen either of the two original versions of Poussin's composition, since they were both in English private collections at this time, but he might have responded to one of the many copies in circulation.
87. In Krumrine 1990, p. 273, it is estimated that ten bather compositions were included in Cézanne's exhibition.
88. The same *motif* occurs in the two pastels L 854 and L 855.
89. The circumstances in which Degas' pastels were executed are not known, but it is clear from the works themselves that several were recombinations of existing poses, and that their landscape backgrounds were developed as the pictures progressed.
90. Boggs *et al.* 1988, p. 557.
91. The picture referred to by Degas may have been *Bathers* (Vente IV, no. 254), a large canvas showing nudes among willow-like

trees, begun in charcoal but never worked in oil.

92. See Brettell and McCullagh 1984, pp. 188–91, for a stimulating discussion of this picture.
93. Similar figures appear in L 818, L 891, L 1120 and L 1139.
94. See notes 86 and 88 above.

9 Saint-Valéry-sur-Somme

1. Notebook 14 A, p. 40.
2. Notebook 18, p. 161.
3. Guérin 1947, p. 210.
4. The pictures are L 1212–19, BR 150–4, and two uncatalogued works; *Village Street, Saint-Valéry* (location unknown), reproduced in the present chapter; and an untitled painting of rooftops and foliage, illustrated in Vasselle 1960, p. 11.
5. Boggs *et al.* 1988, pp. 566–8.
6. Boggs *et al.* 1988, p. 568.
7. Pickvance 1988, p. 143.
8. Sutton 1986, p. 301.
9. BR 152 and 154 were first owned by Braquaval. BR 150 and 151 appeared in Vente Fevre 1934 as nos 135 and 110, where both were described as having the 'timbre d'Atelier' on the reverse, indicating that they were acquired after the artist's death.
10. See note 4 above.
11. The picture, which has been untraced since the 1950s, is reproduced in colour as the frontispiece to Dunlop 1954.
12. L 1213 and L 1219 are 73 × 92 cm; L 1212 and L 1215 are 81 × 69 cm; L 1216, BR 150, BR 151 and *Village Street, Saint-Valéry* are 50 × 61 cm.
13. At the 1898 exhibition of Monet's pictures at Petit's gallery, several canvases measured 73 × 93 cm or 81 × 92 cm; see, for example, Wildenstein 1974–85, nos 1435, 1477, 1479, 1480, 1481, 1482, 1499. Pissarro's exhibition at Durand-Ruel's in the same year included groups of canvases with the dimensions 55 × 64 cm, 65 × 81 cm and 74 × 91; see Brettell and Pissarro 1992, nos 60, 63, 65, 68, 69, 73.
14. Degas' admiration for the later 'series' exhibitions of his peers is well documented; see notes 64 and 66 below.
15. The house still exists; it was occupied by Braquaval and his family from 1893 to 1919.
16. For Boudin's association with Saint-Valéry, see the discussion below.
17. In Boggs *et al.* 1988, p. 566, the date of their meeting is given as 1896, but in Musée d'Orsay 1989, p. 388, the year 1897 is suggested. However, in Fevre 1949, pp. 92 and 96, two letters from Degas make it clear that he had stayed in Saint-Valéry in 1895. A letter from Boudin of 1896 established that Braquaval had already met Degas by this date; see Sutton and Adhémar 1987, p. 180. Degas' familiarity with Braquaval in 1896 is shown in a note of 12 May, where he addresses the younger painter as 'mon cher'; the more formal openings of subsequent letters are surely facetious. Their correspondence is reprinted in Musée d'Orsay 1989, pp. 388–400 and 421.
18. BR 151.
19. Raunay 1931, pp. 274–7 and 472–3.
20. See Loyrette 1991, p. 601.
21. Raunay 1931, pp. 276–7.
22. Raunay 1931, pp. 472–3.
23. For illustrations of such devices and a history of their application, see Kemp 1990, pp. 170–3.
24. The drawings L 1214, L 1217 and L 1217 appear to anticipate paintings of the same subjects. The surfaces of canvases such as L 1213, L 1219 and BR 150 show extensive painted lines beneath later applications of colour.
25. The practice of drawing in charcoal, then 'fixing' the required lines with pen and ink, was widely recommended in practical treatises of the Renaissance and earlier.
26. See, for example, L 400 and L 498.
27. Both these works were executed on wooden panel. Degas may have been inspired by Braquaval's example, or dependent on the materials in the younger artist's studio, when he painted BR 152 on panel
28. The first documented owner of the picture was Jeanne Fevre; see Vente Fevre 1934, no. 151, and note 9 above.
29. See Mallet 1985, p. 105.
30. This vantage point remains largely unchanged today. The bench, occupied by two girls who survey the scene, can be seen in a photograph in Mallet 1985, p. 105.
31. For Huet, see Delteil 1911, no. 67; for Bonington and Shotter Boys, see Noon 1991, nos 35 and 119; for Corot, see Robaut 1905, I, p. 150, and IV, p. 335.
32. Other groups of paintings of Saint-Valéry follow Robaut 1905, nos 1948 and 3246.
33. Most of these features, recorded in turn-off-the-century photographs, are illustrated in Mallet 1985.
34. Raunay 1931, p. 275.
35. For Braquaval's range of subjects, see Braquaval 1922.
36. See, for example, Jeanniot 1933, p. 299, and Michel 1919, p. 625.
37. Raunay 1931, p. 274.
38. The façade of this house is still visible, integrated into the modern wall.
39. See Guérin 1947, p. 210, and the analysis of these photographs in chapter 8.
40. Boggs *et al.* 1988, p. 567.
41. None of the late-nineteenth century houses beneath the ramparts corresponds precisely to Degas' painting, though several have generic resemblances. The turn-of-the-century photograph of the ramparts reproduced in the present chapter reminds us that the unobstructed view from this site, which is such a feature of the town today, was largely obscured by housing in Degas' time. The vantage point used for BR 152 may have been the garden of a house at the western corner of the battlements, which still has a cast-iron railing of the kind visible in Degas' painting.
42. But see note 27 above.
43. See, for example, Whitworth Art Gallery 1980, nos 54, 56, 57, 60.
44. I am grateful to Julia Collieu and her colleagues for assisting my examination of this work.
45. Boggs *et al.* 1988, p. 568.
46. See chapter 8, notes 66–9.
47. The looming or cropped animal seems to have taken on an almost talismanic, or perhaps ironic, significance for Degas, linking the different phases of his career and marking affinities with Millet, Courbet, Gauguin and the Japanese print; see chapter 7, note 52, and the references to Gauguin's *Haystacks in Brittany* in the same chapter.
48. Degas' admiration for houses in the working-class area of the Marais, in Paris, is documented in Guérin 1947, p. 242.
49. Guérin 1947, p. 183.
50. See Vollard 1937 (*Cézanne*), p. 53.
51. The watercolour *Rue dans un village*, *c.*1885, offers a particularly close parallel.
52. Gasquet 1926, p. 18.
53. The façade bears the date 1847; its upper windows may well have provided the varied viewpoints necessary for Degas' picture.
54. For this and many other observations on the Saint-Valéry pictures and their sites, I am indebted to Mollie Sayer.
55. Further evidence of Degas' manipulations can be found on the canvas surface, where signs of earlier drafting, erasures and subsequent repainting can still be seen. For this picture, see also Boggs *et al.* 1988, p. 567, and Metropolitan Museum of Art 1986, no. 23.
56. See Mallet 1985. The area of land in question had been recently reclaimed from the sea by the building of the embankment making up the Digue.
57. Photographs from the second half of the nineteenth century show the area devoid of housing. Another impression of the site can be gained from BR 152, where the artist has looked down on the flat ground and newly built villas below the ramparts.
58. My thanks are due to Roger Clisby and his colleagues at the Columbus Museum of Art for their kind co-operation in this investigation.
59. These stains are visible to the naked eye at the edges of the canvas.
60. As noted at several points in this study, such multi-layered effects bring together Degas' experiments with oil paint, pastel and monotype, as well as his fascination with Old Master technique. Such juxtapositions of complementary colours also remind us of Degas' interest in this subject, which was never systematic, but also never casual.
61. Some areas of painting 'wet-over-dry'

point to a return to the canvas after a period of time, perhaps even on a later visit to Saint-Valéry. The area of densest activity is across the centre of the canvas, where the boundary of cliff-top and sky has been revised more than once. There is insufficient evidence, however, to support the possibility of a radical restructuring of the composition in successive campigns.

62. Letters of 4 April 1893 and 28 March 1893; see Wildenstein 1974–85.
63. Manet 1987, p. 76. In addition to fellow-artists such as Monet and Pissarro, Degas and Cézanne were both in touch with younger contemporaries like Geffroy, Vollard and Denis.
64. Rewald 1943, p. 270.
65. See Brettell and Pissarro 1992, no. 31.
66. Rewald 1943, p. 289.
67. L 1212–19 were all included in the *ventes*.
68. Braquaval owned BR 152 and BR 154; René de Gas acquired L 1216 (see Vente René de Gas 1927, no. 82); Jeanne Fevre owned BR 150 and BR 151 (see note 9 above).
69. The association of Julie Manet's 1897 reference to certain of Degas' landscapes with the Saint-Valéry pictures is surely mistaken (Boggs *et al.* 1988); Manet's description of 'sweeping lines of hills' and 'green meadows and yellow trees' seems closer to the colour monotypes, which she might have seen as a fourteen-year-old in 1892, or later at Durand-Ruel's.
70. The last dated letter is in Musée d'Orsay 1989, p. 399; the incident with Vollard is reported in Vollard 1937 (*Degas*), p. 50.
71. See Braquaval 1922.
72. Musée d'Orsay 1989, p. 394.
73. Jeanniot 1933, p. 170.
74. Musée d'Orsay 1989, p. 398.
75. Sickert 1947, p. 154.
76. L 1424.
77. L 1382.
78. The Ingres is recalled in Sickert 1917, p. 186, the Corot in Valéry 1960, p. 20, and the evidence concerning the *Young Spartans* is summarised in Boggs *et al.* 1988, p. 98.

Bibliography

Abbreviations for the standard catalogues of Degas' works used in the text are as follows:

L Lemoisne 1946
BR Brame and Reff 1984
J Janis 1968
RS Reed and Shapiro 1984
K Kendall, the present volume. See appendix 2

Adhémar, Jean, 'Un monotype de Degas au Cabinet des Estampes', *Gazette des Beaux-Arts*, 1964, pp. 372–6.

Adhémar, Jean, and Françoise Cachin, *Degas, The Complete Etchings, Lithographs and Monotypes*, London 1974.

Adler, Kathleen, *Manet*, Oxford 1986.

Adler, Kathleen, and Tamar Garb, *Berthe Morisot*, Oxford 1987.

Adriani, Götz, *Degas: Pastels, Oil Sketches, Drawings*, London 1985.

Aitken, Geneviève, and Marianne Delafond, *La Collection d'estampes japonaises de Claude Monet à Giverny*, Paris 1987.

Alexandre, Arsène, 'Chroniques d'aujourd'hui', *Paris*, 9 November 1892.

Alexandre, Arsène, 'Jeanniot', *Figaro Illustré*, March 1903, pp. 1–24.

Amiel, Henri-Frédéric, *Journal Intime*, Geneva 1882. English version: *Amiel's Journal: the Journal intime of Henri-Frédéric Amiel*, 2 vols, London 1885.

Armstrong, Carol, *Odd Man Out; Readings of the Life and Work of Edgar Degas*, Chicago and London, 1991.

Art Journal (anon.), 'Paris International Exhibition', *Art Journal*, 1867, pp. 245–7.

Bailly-Herzberg, Janine (ed.), *Correspondance de Camille Pissarro:* I: *1865–1885*, Paris 1980.

Bailly-Herzberg, Janine (ed.), *Correspondance de Camille Pissarro:* II: *1886–1890*, Paris 1986.

Bailly-Herzberg, Janine (ed.), *Correspondance de Camille Pissarro:* III: *1891–1894*, Paris 1988.

Bailly-Herzberg, Janine (ed.), *Correspondance de Camille Pissarro:* IV: *1895–1898*, Paris 1989.

Bantens, Robert, *Eugène Carrière: The Symbol of Creation*, New York 1990.

Barazzetti, Suzanne, 'Degas et ses amis Valpinçon', *Beaux-Arts*, 21 August 1936, pp. 1 and 4; 4 September, pp. 1–2.

Bataille, M.-L., and G. Wildenstein, *Berthe Morisot*, Paris 1961.

Baudelaire, Charles, *The Mirror of Art*, Oxford 1955.

Bénédite, Léonce, 'Whistler', *Gazette des Beaux-Arts*, XXXIII, 1905, pp. 496–511; XXXIV, 1905, pp. 143–233.

Bénézit, E., *Dictionnaire critique et documentaire des peintres, sculpteurs, dessinateurs et graveurs . . .*, 10 vols, Paris 1976.

Bergot, François, 'Edgar Degas, "Renard mort, sous-bois"', *Revue du Louvre*, 4, 1990, p. 325.

Bergson, Henri, *Time and Free Will: An Essay in the Immediate Data of Consciousness*, Paris 1889, English edition; London 1910.

Bergson, Henri, *Matter and Memory*, Paris 1896. English edition, London 1913.

Berhaut, Marie, *Caillebotte, sa vie et son oeuvre*, Paris 1978.

Bernadac, Christian, *George Sand: Dessins et aquarelles 'les montagnes bleus'*, Paris 1992.

Bittler, Paul, and Pierre-Louis Mathieu, *Catalogue des dessins de Gustave Moreau*, Paris, 1983.

Blanche, Jacques-Emile, *Propos de peintre: de David à Degas*, Paris 1919.
Boggs, Jean Sutherland, 'Degas at the Museum: Works in the Philadelphia Museum of Art and John G. Johnson Collection', *Bulletin of the Philadelphia Museum of Art*, LXXXI, no. 346, spring 1985.
Boggs, Jean Sutherland, Douglas Druick, Henri Loyrette, Michael Pantazzi and Gary Tinterow, *Degas*, Paris, Ottawa and New York 1988–9.
Boggs, Jean Sutherland, and Anne Maheux, *Degas Pastels*, London 1992.
Boime, Albert, *The Academy and French Painting in the Nineteenth Century*, New Haven and London 1971.
Boisbaudran, Horace Lecoq de, *The Training of the Memory of the Artist*, trans. L.D. Luard, London 1911.
Bomford, David, Jo Kirby, John Leighton and Ashok Roy, *Art in the Making: Impressionism*, London 1990.
Bouyer, Raymond, *Le Paysage dans l'Art*, Paris 1894.
Braquaval, Louis (intr. Albert Besnard), *Oeuvres de Braquaval*, Paris, 1922.
Brame, Philippe, and Theodore Reff, *Degas et son oeuvre: A Supplement*, New York 1984.
Brettell, Richard, and Suzanne F. McCullagh, *Degas in the Art Institute of Chicago*, Chicago 1984.
Brettell, Richard, *Pissarro and Pontoise*, New Haven and London 1990.
Brettell, Richard, and Joachim Pissarro, *The Impressionist and the City: Pissarro's Series Paintings*, Dallas, Philadelphia and London 1992–3.
Broude, Norma, *The Macchiaioli: Italian Painters of the Nineteenth Century*, New Haven and London 1987.
Broude, Norma, *Impressionism: A Feminist Reading*, New York 1991.
Burnell, Devin, 'Degas and his "Young Spartans Exercising"', *Art Institute of Chicago Museum Studies*, 4, 1969, pp. 49–65.
Cachin, Françoise, Charles Moffett and Michel Melot, *Manet*, Paris 1983.
Camesasca, Ettore, *Degas scultore*, Florence 1986.
Cate, Phillip Dennis, and Patricia Eckert Boyer, *The Circle of Toulouse-Lautrec*, New Brunswick 1986.
Cate, Phillip Dennis, and Marianne Grivel, *From Pissarro to Picasso: Colour Etching in France*, Paris 1992.
Champfleury, Jules, *Le Réalisme*, ed. Geneviève and Jean Lacambre, Paris 1973.
Chesneau, Ernest, 'A côté du Salon, le plein air. Exposition du Boulevard des Capucines', in *Paris Journal*, 7 May 1874, p. 2.
Clarke, Michael, *Corot and the Art of Landscape*, London 1991.
Clarke, Michael, 'Degas and Corot', *Apollo*, July 1991, pp. 15–20.
Coulon, Bernard, *Promenades en Normandie avec un guide nommé Marcel Proust*, Conde-sur-Noireau 1986.
Couper Gallery, London, *Léon Riesener: From Romanticism to Impressionism*, London 1965.
Curry, David Park, *James McNeill Whistler at the Freer Gallery of Art*, Washington 1984.
Daudet, Léon, *Souvenirs et Polemiques*, Paris 1992.
Debize, Christian, 'Charles de Meixmoron, l'éveil de la sensation optique', *Gazette des Beaux-Arts*, July-August 1984, pp. 33–44.
Degas Inventory, *Manuscript inventory of Degas' collection of paintings*, private collection, Paris.
Delaborde, Henri, *Ingres: sa vie, ses travaux, sa doctrine*, Paris 1870.
Delteil, Loys, *Paul Huet: le peintre-graveur illustré*, VII, Paris 1911.
Delteil, Loys, *Degas: le peintre-graveur illustré*, IX, Paris 1919.
Delteil, Loys, *Pissarro, Sisley, Renoir: le peintre-graveur illustré*, XVII, Paris 1923.
'Diénay' (pseud.), 'Georges Jeanniot', *La Lorraine Artiste*, no. 42, 18 October 1891, pp. 661–4.
Dini, Piero, *Boldini Macchiaiolo con 156 disegni inediti dai taccuini di Casa Banti*, Turin 1989.
Dumas, Ann, *'Mlle. Fiocre' in Context: A Study of 'Portrait de Mlle. E.F. . . .' à propos du ballet "La Source"*, Brooklyn 1988.
Dunlop, R.O., *Landscape Painting: Ma Yuan to Picasso*, London 1954.
Dunlop, Ian, *Degas*, London 1979.
L'Ermitage (anon.), 'Galerie Durand-Ruel: Paysages de M. Degas; Oeuvres de Lépine',

L'Ermitage, v, no. 12, December 1892, pp. 415–16.
Exposition Universelle de 1867 à Paris: Catalogue Général Publié par la Commission Impériale, 2 vols, Paris 1867.
Fauchereau, Serge, *Peintures et dessins d'écrivains*, Paris 1991.
Faunce, Sarah, and Linda Nochlin, *Courbet Reconsidered*, Brooklyn 1988.
Fernier, Robert, *La vie et l'oeuvre de Gustave Courbet: catalogue raisonné*, 2 vols, Lausanne and Paris, 1977.
Fevre, Jeanne, *Mon Oncle Degas*, Geneva 1949.
Fields, Armond, *Henri Rivière*, Salt Lake City 1983.
Finsen, Hanne, *Degas og Familien Bellelli*, Ordrupgaard 1983.
Fisher, Jay McKean, and Colles Baxter, *Félix Buhot, Peintre-Graveur: Prints, Drawings and Paintings*, Baltimore 1983.
Flint, Kate (ed.), *Impressionists in England: The Critical Reception*, London 1984.
Forrer, Matthi, *Hokusai*, London and Munich 1991.
Foucart, Jacques, *et al.*, *Hippolyte, Auguste et Paul Flandrin: Une fraternité picturale au XIXe siècle*, Paris 1985.
Fowle, Francis, 'Impressionism in Scotland: An Acquired Taste', *Apollo*, December 1992, pp. 374–9.
Freylinghuysen, Alice C., *et al.*, *Splendid Legacy: The Havemeyer Collection*, New York 1983.
Fries, G., 'Degas et les maîtres', *L'Art de France*, IV, 1964, pp. 352–7.
'R.G.' (Rémy de Gourmant), 'Choses d'art', *Mercure de France*, v, December 1892, p. 374.
Gage, John, *J.M.W. Turner: 'A Wonderful Range of Mind'*, New Haven and London 1987.
Galassi, Peter, *Corot in Italy*, New Haven and London 1991.
Gasquet, Joachim, *Cézanne*, Paris 1926.
Geffroy, Gustave, 'Exposition Claude Monet', *L'Art dans les deux mondes*, 9 May 1891.
Geffroy, Gustave, *La Vie artistique*, Ième série, Paris 1894.
Geffroy, Gustave, *Claude Monet: sa vie, son oeuvre*, Paris 1924.
Georgel, Pierre, *Drawings by Victor Hugo*, London 1974.
Getscher, Robert H., *James Abbott McNeill Whistler: Pastels*, London 1991.
Gide, André, *The Journals of André Gide*, I, London 1947.
Goldschmidt, Lucien, Gallery, *Charles Maurin: The Vaporiser Watercolours*, New York 1986.
Goncourt, Edmond and Jules de, *Manette Salamon*, Paris 1867.
Gordon, Dillian, *Hélène Rouart in her Father's Study*, London 1984.
Gordon, Robert, and Andrew Forge, *Degas*, London 1988.
Grappe, Georges, *E.M. Degas*, London and Leipzig 1909.
Graves, Algernon, *The Royal Academy of Arts: A Complete Dictionary of Contributors and Their Work from Its Foundation in 1769 to 1904*, 8 vols, London 1905; reprinted in 4 vols, London 1970.
Grunchec, Philippe, *Les concours des Prix de Rome*, 2 vols, Paris 1986.
Guérin, Marcel (ed.), *Lettres de Degas*, Paris 1945.
Guérin, Marcel (ed.), *Degas Letters*, Oxford 1947.
Guillaud, Maurice (ed.), *Degas: Form and Space*, Paris 1984.
Hale, Philip, 'Art in Paris', *Arcadia*, I, no. 16, 15 December 1892, p. 326.
Halévy, Daniel, *Degas parle*, Paris 1960; English translation, *My Friend Degas*, Middletown 1964.
Halévy, Daniel, *Pays Parisiens*, Paris 1929.
Hamerton, Philip Gilbert, 'Pictures of the Year: IX', *The Saturday Review*, 1 June 1867, p. 691.
Hamilton, George Heard, 'The Philosophical Implications of Impressionist Landscape Painting', *Bulletin of the Museum of Fine Arts, Houston*, VI, no. 1, Spring 1975, pp. 2–17.
Harambourg, Lydia, *Dictionnaire des Peintres Paysagistes Français au XIXe*, Neuchâtel 1985.
Harris, Jean C., *Manet's Racetrack Paintings*, *Art Bulletin* XLVIII, 1966, pp. 78–82.
Havemeyer, Louisine, *Sixteen to Sixty: Memoirs of a Collector*, New York 1961.
Haverkamp-Begemann, E., S.D. Lawder and C.W. Talbot, *Drawings from the Clark Art Institute*, 2 vols, New Haven 1964.
Hayashi, Tadamasa, *Catalogue of the Collection of Tadamasa Hayashi*, Tokyo 1908.

Hazlitt, Gooden and Fox, *Selected Works from the Andrew Gow Bequest*, London 1978.
Heilbrun, Françoise, *Photographie* I: *Les paysages des impressionistes*, Paris 1986.
Heim Gallery, London, *Paintings by Paul Huet (1803–1869) and some Contemporary French Sculpture*, London 1969.
Herbert, Robert, *Impressionism: Art, Leisure, and Parisian Society*, New Haven and London 1988.
Herbert, Robert, Roseline Bacou and Michel Laclotte, *Jean-François Millet*, Paris 1975.
Herbert, Robert, Roseline Bacou and Michel Laclotte, *Jean-François Millet*, London 1976.
Hertz, Henri, *Degas*, Paris 1920.
Hoctin, Lucie, 'Degas photographe', *L'Oeil*, May 1960, pp. 37–43.
House, John, *Monet: Nature into Art*, New Haven and London 1986.
Huet, Paul, *Paul Huet (1803–1869), d'après ses notes, sa correspondance, ses contemporains*, Paris 1911.
Hugo, Victor, *Oeuvres Complètes*, 18 vols, Paris 1969; vol. XVIII: *Dessins et Lavis*.
Hulten, Pontus, *et al.*, *The Archimboldo Effect*, London 1987.
Ives, Colta, *The Great Wave: The Influence of Japanese Woodcuts on French Prints*, New York 1974.
Jamot, Paul, *Degas*, Paris 1924.
Janis, Eugenia P., 'The Role of the Monotype in the Working Method of Degas', *Burlington Magazine*, CIX, no. 766, January 1967, pp. 20–7, and CIX, no. 767, February 1967, pp. 71–81.
Janis, Eugenia P., *Degas Monotypes: Essay, Catalogue and Checklist*, Cambridge, Mass., 1968.
Janis, Eugenia P., 'An Autumnal Landscape by Edgar Degas', *The Metropolitan Museum of Art Bulletin*, XXXI, no. 4, Summer 1973, unpag.
Janis, Eugenia P., *The Photography of Gustave le Gray*, Chicago 1987.
Jeanniot, Georges, 'Souvenirs sur Degas', *Revue Universelle*, LV, no. 14, 15 October 1933, pp. 152–74, and LV, no. 14, 1 November 1933.
Joanne, P., *Dictionnaire Géographique et Administratif de la France*, 7 vols, Paris 1890–1905.
Joanne, Adolphe, *Géographie du département de la Côte d'Or*, Paris 1874.
Johnson, Deborah J., and Eric M. Zafran, *From the Age of David to the Age of Picasso*, Providence, R.I., 1984.
Johnson, Lee, *The Paintings of Eugène Delacroix*, 6 vols, Oxford 1981–9.
Johnson, Lee, *Eugène Delacroix: Paintings, Drawings and Prints from North American Collections*, Metropolitan Museum of Art, New York 1991.
Joyant, Maurice, *Henri de Toulouse-Lautrec: 1864–1901*, 2 vols, 1926–7.
Kemp, Martin, *The Science of Art*, New Haven and London 1990.
Kendall, Richard (ed.), *Degas 1834–1984*, Manchester 1985.
Kendall, Richard, *Degas By Himself*, London 1987.
Kendall, Richard, 'Degas and the Contingency of Vision', *Burlington Magazine*, CXXX, no. 1020, March 1988, pp. 180–97.
Kendall, Richard, *Degas: Images of Women*, Liverpool 1989.
Kendall, Richard, and Griselda Pollock (eds), *Dealing With Degas*, London 1992.
Kendall, Richard (ed.), *Cézanne and Poussin: A Symposium*, Sheffield 1993.
Krumrine, Mary Louise, *Paul Cézanne: The Bathers*, London 1990.
Lafond, Paul, *Degas*, 2 vols, Paris 1918–19.
Lanthony, Phillipe, 'La malvision d'Edgar Degas: Pathographies 110', *Médecine et Hygène*, XLVIII, 1990, pp. 2382–401.
Laughton, Bruce, *The Drawings of Daumier and Millet*, New Haven and London 1991.
Lay, Howard G., 'Degas at Durand-Ruel, 1892: the landscape monotypes', *The Print Collector's Newsletter*, IX, no. 5, November–December 1978, pp. 142–7.
Lecoq de Boisbaudran, François, *Education de la mémoire pittoresque*, Paris 1862.
Lefèvre, Frédéric (ed.), *Entretiens avec Paul Valéry*, Paris 1926.
Lemoisne, Paul-André, *Degas*, Paris 1912.
Lemoisne, Paul-André, 'Les carnets de Degas au Cabinet des Estampes', *Gazette des Beaux-Arts*, April 1921, pp. 219–31.
Lemoisne, Paul-André, *Degas et son oeuvre*, 4 vols, Paris 1946–9.
Lewison, Florence, 'Theodore Robinson and Claude Monet', *Apollo*, September 1963, pp. 208–11.
Lhôte, Jean-Marie, 'Discours imprononcable quoique méthodique à propos d'un episode mal connu de la jeunesse de Degas', *Bizarre*, no. 26, 1962.

Lipton, Eunice, *Looking Into Degas: Uneasy Images of Women and Modern Life*, Berkeley 1987.

Loyrette, Henri, *Degas*, Paris 1991.

Loyrette, Henri, *Degas e l'Italia*, Rome 1984.

Luthi, Jean-Jacques, *Emile Bernard: Catalogue raisonné de l'oeuvre peint*, Paris 1982.

Macdonald, Margaret, and Joy Newton, 'Letters from the Whistler Collection (University of Glasgow)', *Gazette des Beaux-Arts*, December 1986, pp. 201–14.

Malingue, Maurice (ed.), *Paul Gauguin: Letters to His Wife and Friends*, Paris and London 1946.

Mallet, Robert (ed.), *Saint-Valéry d'hier: Vie quotidienne à Saint-Valéry de 1866 à 1940*, Abbeville 1985.

Malte-Brun, V.-A., *Calvados: géographie, histoire, statistique, administration*, 1882.

Manet, Edouard, *Manet raconté par lui-meme et par ses amis*, Lausanne 1953.

Manet, Julie, *Growing up with the Impressionists: The Diary of Julie Manet*, London 1987.

Mannocci, Lino, *The Etchings of Claude Lorrain*, New Haven and London 1988.

Mathews, Nancy Mowll (ed.), *Cassatt and Her Circle: Selected Letters*, New York 1984.

Mathews, Nancy Mowll, and Barbara Stern Shapiro, *Mary Cassatt: The Color Prints*, New York 1989.

Matthiesen, Stair Sainty, *Three Italian Friends of the Impressionists: Boldini, De Nittis, Zandomeneghi*, New York 1984.

Maupassant, Guy de, *A Woman's Life*, Harmondsworth 1972.

McMullen, Roy, *Degas: His Life, Times and Work*, London 1985.

Meech-Pakarik, Julia, 'Early Collectors of Japanese Prints and the Metropolitan Museum of Art', *Metropolitan Museum Journal*, XVII, 1982, pp. 93–118.

Meixmoron, Charles de, 'Le paysage dans l'atelier', *La Lorraine Artiste*, no. 29, 30 November 1890, p. 337 *et seq.*

Meixmoron, Charles de, *Le paysage d'après nature*, Nancy 1890.

Melot, Michel, *L'estampe impressioniste*, Paris 1974.

Metropolitan Museum of Art, *The Painterly Print: Monotypes from the Seventeenth to the Twentieth Centuries*, New York 1980.

Metropolitan Museum of Art, *French Masterpieces: XIX and XX Century Paintings and Drawings from the Robert Lehman Collection*, Copenhagen 1986.

Michel, Alice, 'Degas et son modèle', *Mercure de France*, 16 February 1919, pp. 457–78, 623–39.

Michener, James A., *The Hokusai Sketchbooks: Selections from the Manga*, Tokyo 1958.

Millard, Charles W., *The Sculpture of Edgar Degas*, Princeton 1976.

Miquel, Pierre, *Paul Huet: de l'aube romantique à l'aube impressioniste*, Paris 1962.

Moffett, Charles S., *et al.*, *The New Painting: Impressionism 1874–1886*, Geneva 1986.

Monneret, Sophie, *L'Impressionisme et son époque*, 2 vols, Paris 1987.

Monnier, Geneviève, *Musée du Louvre; Musée d'Orsay. Cabinet des dessins: pastels du XIXe siècle*, Paris 1985.

Moore, George, *Modern Painting*, London 1893.

Moreau-Nélaton, Etienne, *Manet raconté par lui-même*, 2 vols, Paris 1926.

Moreau-Nélaton, Etienne, 'Deux heures avec Degas', *L'Amour de l'Art*, XII, July 1931, pp. 267–70.

Berthe, Morisot, *The Correspondence of Berthe Morisot*, ed. Denis Rouart, London 1986.

Musée des Beaux-Arts, Besançon, *Charles de Meixmoron, un Impressioniste, 1839–1912*, Besançon 1974.

Musée des Beaux-Arts, Nancy, *Charles de Meixmoron 1839–1912*, Nancy 1962.

Musée des Beaux-Arts, Nancy, *Impressionisme en Lorraine*, Nancy 1975.

Musée des Beaux-Arts, Nancy, *Photographes et photographie d'art*, Nancy 1983.

Musée d'Orsay, Paris, *Degas Inédit*, Paris 1989.

Musée d'Orsay, Paris, *De Manet à Matisse: sept ans d'enrichissements au Musée d'Orsay*, Paris 1990.

Musée du Petit-Palais, Paris, *Catalogue sommaire illustré des peintures*, 2 vols, Paris 1981.

Naef, Hans, *Ingres in Rome*, Washington, D.C., 1971.

National Gallery of Art, Washington, D.C., *Master Drawings from Titian to Picasso: The Curtis O. Baer Collection*, Washington, D.C., 1985.

Newhall, Beaumont, 'Degas, Amateur Photographer: Eight Unpublished Letters by the Famous Painter Written on a Photographic Vocation', *Image*, v, no. 6, June 1956, pp. 124–6.

Noon, Patrick, *Richard Parkes Bonington: 'On the Pleasure of Painting'*, New Haven and London 1991.
Pantazzi, Michael, 'The Event of the Season: Monsieur Degas Exhibits', unpublished lecture 1989.
Palais des Champs-Elysées, Paris, *Salon de 1887: catalogue illustré, peinture et sculpture*, Paris 1887.
Paris Universal Exhibition of 1867: Catalogue of the British Section, London 1867.
Pavillon des Arts, Le, *Léon Riesener 1808–1878*, Paris n.d. [1965].
Pénault, Pierre-Jean, 'Monsieur Degas à la campagne', *Pays d'Auge*, June 1990, pp. 2–16.
Galeries Georges Petit, *Exposition Degas: au profit de la ligue franco-americaine contre le cancer*, Paris 1924.
Pickvance, Ronald, *Degas' Racing World*, New York 1968.
Pickvance, Ronald, *Degas, pastels and drawings*, Nottingham 1969.
Pickvance, Ronald, 'Degas as a photographer', *Lithopinion*, January 1970, pp. 73–9.
Pickvance, Ronald, *Edgar Degas*, Tokyo 1988.
Pool, Phoebe, 'Degas and Moreau', *Burlington Magazine*, CV, June 1963, pp. 251–6.
Pool, Phoebe, 'The History Pictures of Edgar Degas and their background', *Apollo*, October 1964, pp. 306–11.
Pool, Phoebe, 'Some Early Friends of Edgar Degas', *Apollo*, May 1964, pp. 391–4.
Randall, Lillian M.C., *The Diary of George A. Lucas, an American Art Agent in Paris 1857–1909*, 2 vols, Princeton 1979.
Raunay, Jeanne, 'Degas, souvenirs anecdotiques', *La Revue de France*, 15 March 1931, pp. 262–82; 1 April 1931, pp. 469–83; 15 April 1931, pp. 619–32.
Reed, Sue Welsh, and Barbara Shapiro, *Edgar Degas: The Painter as Printmaker*, Boston 1984.
Reff, Theodore, 'Degas's Copies of Older Art', *Burlington Magazine*, CV, June 1963, pp. 241–51.
Reff, Theodore, 'New Light on Degas's Copies', *Burlington Magazine*, CVI, June 1964, pp. 250–9.
Reff, Theodore, 'Some Unpublished Letters of Degas', *Art Bulletin*, L, no. 1, March 1968, pp. 87–93.
Reff, Theodore, 'More Unpublished Letters of Degas', *Art Bulletin*, LI, no. 3, September 1969, pp. 281–9.
Reff, Theodore, 'Works by Degas in the Detroit Institute of Arts', *Bulletin of the Detroit Institute of Arts*, LIII, no. 1, 1974.
Reff, Theodore, 'The Landscape Painter Degas might have been', *Art News*, January 1976, pp. 41–3.
Reff, Theodore, *The Notebooks of Edgar Degas*, 2 vols, Oxford 1976.
Reff, Theodore, *Degas: The Artist's Mind*, New York 1976.
Reff, Theodore, *Degas: A Master among Masters*, New York 1976.
Reff, Theodore, *Manet and Modern Paris*, Washington, D.C., 1982.
Reff, Theodore, 'Cézanne et la perspective: quelques remarques à la lumière de documents nouveaux', *Revue de l'Art*, no. 86, 1989, pp. 8–15.
Renoir, Jean, *Renoir, My Father*, London 1962.
Rewald, John, *The History of Impressionism*, New York 1946.
Rewald, John (ed.), *Camille Pissarro: Letters to His Son Lucien*, New York 1943.
Rewald, John, *Degas, Works in Sculpture: A Complete Catelogue*, New York 1944.
Rewald, John, *et al.*, *Edgar Degas: His family and friends in New Orleans*, New Orleans 1965.
Rewald, John, *Paul Cézanne: The Watercolours*, London 1983.
Riout, Denis (ed.), *Les écrivains devant l'impressionisme*, Paris 1989.
Rivière, Georges, *Monsieur Degas, Bourgeois de Paris*, Paris 1935.
Robaut, Alfred, *L'oeuvre complet de Eugène Delacroix*, Paris 1885.
Robaut, Alfred, *L'oeuvre de Corot*, 4 vols, Paris 1905.
Robels, Hella, *Frans Snyders: Stilleben und Tiermaler, 1579–1657*, Munich 1989.
Robinson, Theodore, 'Diary', manuscript in Frick Art Reference Library, New York.
Roethlisberger, Marcel, *Claude Lorrain: The Paintings*, 2 vols, New York 1979.
Rouart, Denis, *Degas: à la récherche de sa technique*, Paris 1945.
Rouart, Denis, *Nine Monotypes by Degas*, New York 1964.
Rouart, Denis, 'Degas: paysages en monotype', *L'Oeil*, September 1964, pp. 10–15.

Royal Academy of Arts, London, *Catalogue of an Exhibition of Landscape in French Art, 1550–1900*, London 1949.
Schmit, Robert, *Boudin*, 3 vols, Paris 1973.
Schmit, Galerie, *Exposition Degas*, Paris 1975.
Schmitt, Jean E., 'Choses d'art', *Le Siècle*, 5 October 1894.
Selway, N.C., *The Golden Age of Coaching and Sport, As Depicted by James Pollard*, Leigh-on-Sea 1972.
Sickert, Walter, 'Degas', *Burlington Magazine*, November 1917, pp. 183–91.
Sickert, Walter, *A Free House*, London 1947.
Smith, Alistair, *Second Sight*, London 1982.
Smith, Lawrence, *Ukiyoe: Images of Unknown Japan*, London 1988.
Soutzo, Nicolas, *Mémoires de prince Nicolas Soutzo, grand-logothète de Moldavie, 1897–1871*, Vienna 1899.
Spate, Virginia, *The Colour of Time: Claude Monet*, London 1992.
Spencer, Robin, 'Whistler and James Clarke Hook', *Gazette de Beaux-Arts*, July–August 1984, pp. 45–8.
Stafford, Barbara Maria, *Journey into Substance: Art, Science, and the Illustrated Travel Account, 1760–1840*, Cambridge, Mass., 1984.
Strange, Edward, *Hiroshige's Woodblock Prints: A Guide*, New York 1983.
Sutton, Denys, *Nocturne: the Art of James McNeill Whistler*, London 1963.
Sutton, Denys (ed.), *The Letters of Roger Fry*, 2 vols, London 1972.
Sutton, Denys, *Edgar Degas: Life and Work*, London 1986.
Sutton, Denys, and Jean Adhémar, 'Lettres inédites de Degas à Paul Lafond et autres documents', *Gazette des Beaux-Arts*, CIX, no. 1419, April 1987, pp. 159–80.
Taylor, Joshua, *Nineteenth Century Theories of Art*, Berkeley, Los Angeles and London, 1987.
Terrasse, Antoine, *Degas et la photographie*, Paris 1983.
Thiébault-Sisson, François, 'Degas sculpteur par lui-même', *Le Temps*, 23 May 1923.
Thomson, Belinda, *Gauguin*, London 1987.
Thomson, Richard, *The Private Degas*, London 1987
Thomson, Richard, *Degas: the Nudes*, London 1988.
Thomson, Richard, *Camille Pissarro: Impressionism, Landscape and Rural Labour*, London 1990.
Toussaint, Hélène, 'Les fonds de portraits d'Ingres: peintures à fond de paysage', *Bulletin du Musée Ingres*, nos 63–4, 1991.
Tucker, Paul, *Monet in the '90s: The Series Paintings*, New Haven and London 1989.
Vachon, Patrice, *Côte-d'Or: de Menhirs en Dolmens*, Dijon n.d.
Valenciennes, Pierre-Henri de, *Elemens de perspective pratique à l'usage des artistes . . .*, Paris 1820.
Valéry, Paul, 'Degas Dance Drawing', in *Degas Manet Morisot*, Princeton 1960.
Varnedoe, Kirk, 'The Artifice of Candour: Photography and Impressionism Reconsidered', *Art in America*, January 1980, pp. 66–78.
Varnedoe, Kirk, 'The Ideology of Time: Degas and Photography', *Art in America*, May 1980, pp. 96–110.
Varnedoe, Kirk, *A Fine Disregard: What Makes Modern Art Modern*, London 1990.
Vasselle, P., 'Degas paysagiste à Saint-Valéry-sur-Somme', *Les lettres françaises*, no. 832, 7 July 1960, pp. 1 and 11.
Vente I, *Catalogue des tableaux, pastels et dessins par Edgar Degas . . .*, Paris, May 1918.
Vente II, *Catalogue des tableaux, pastels et dessins par Edgar Degas . . .*, Paris, December 1918.
Vente III, *Catalogue des tableaux, pastels et dessins par Edgar Degas . . .*, Paris, April 1919.
Vente IV, *Catalogue des tableaux, pastels et dessins par Edgar Degas . . .*, Paris, July 1919.
Vente Collection I, *Catalogue des tableaux modernes et anciens . . . composant la collection Edgar Degas . . .*, Paris, March 1918.
Vente Collection II, *Catalogue des tableaux modernes . . . faisant partie de la collection Edgar Degas . . .*, Paris, November 1918.
Vente Collection Estampes, *Catalogue des estampes anciennes et modernes . . . composant la collection Edgar Degas*, Paris, November 1918.
Vente Estampes, *Catalogue des eaux-fortes, vernis-moux, aqua-tintes, lithographies et monotypes par Edgar Degas . . .*, Paris, November 1918.
Vente René de Gas, *Catalogue des Tableaux, Pastels, Aquarelles, Dessins, Gravures par*

Edgar Degas . . ., Paris 1927.
Vente Fevre, *Catalogues des Tableaux, Aquarelles, Pastels, Dessins, Estampes, Monotypes par Edgar Degas . . .*, Paris 1934.
Vente Soutzo, *Catalogue d'estampes anciennes . . . formant la collection de feu M. le prince Gregoire Soutzo*, Paris 1870.
Viallefond, Geneviève, *Le peintre Léon Riesener, 1808–1878, sa vie, son oeuvre, avec des extraits d'un manuscrit inédit d'artiste*, Paris 1955.
Vollard, Ambroise, *Recollections of a Picture Dealer*, Boston 1936.
Vollard, Ambroise, *Paul Cézanne, his Life and Art*, New York 1937.
Vollard, Ambroise, *Degas, An Intimate Portrait*, New York 1937.
Weisberg, Gabriel, *et al.*, *Japonisme: Japanese Influence on French Art 1854–1910*, Cleveland 1975.
Weitzenhoffer, Frances, *The Havemeyers: Impressionism comes to America*, New York 1986.
White, Barbara Ehrlich, *Renoir: His Life, Art and Letters*, New York 1984.
Whitworth Art Gallery, Manchester, *Mondriaan and The Hague School*, Manchester 1980.
Wichmann, Siegfried, *Japonisme*, London 1981.
Wildenstein, Daniel, *Claude Monet: biographie et catalogue raisonné*, 4 vols, Paris 1974–85.
Wilkinson, Gerald, *The Sketches of Turner R.A. 1802–20: Genius of the Romantic*, London 1974.
Wilson, Michael, *Manet at Work*, London 1983.
Wilson-Bareau, Juliet, *Manet By Himself*, London 1991.
Young, Andrew McLaren, *et al.*, *The Paintings of James McNeill Whistler*, 2 vols, New Haven and London, 1980.
Zola, Emile, *Mon Salon: Manet: Ecrits sur l'art*, Paris 1970.
Zola, Emile, *La Bête Humaine* (English translation, Leonard Tancock), London 1977.

Directors' Acknowledgements

Degas Landscapes

The Metropolitan Museum of Art
21 January–3 April 1994

The Museum of Fine Arts, Houston
24 April–3 July 1994

The Metropolitan Museum of Art and the Museum of Fine Arts, Houston, are honored to present this exhibition of relatively unknown work by one of the most famous artists in the western tradition. Justly celebrated for his innovative depictions of the human figure, Edgar Degas is often seen as a painter who cared little for landscape, preferring the gaslight of a Parisian interior to the sunlit fields favored by his Impressionist colleagues Pissarro or Monet. Presenting works from Degas' student days in Italy in the 1850s to his maturity four decades later, this exhibition reveals more than ever before his real love of landscape and his intensely personal vision of the natural world.

The exhibition has been organized by George Shackelford of the Museum of Fine Arts, Houston, and Colta Ives of the Metropolitan Museum of Art, who have been advised throughout by Richard Kendall, author of this splendid volume. We are grateful to them, and to the staffs of our two museums, for bringing this project to such a rich and compelling conclusion. We would like to thank also the following people who were particularly helpful in the organization of the exhibition and the preparation of this publication: Thereza Crowe, Douglas Druick, Sheila Lee, Gillian Malpass, Lisa Moore, Emily Neff, Ashley Scott, and Barbara Stern Shapiro.

Presentation of the exhibition in Houston has been made possible by Max and Isabell Smith Herzstein. Curatorial travel and research for the exhibition have been supported by a grant from The Apollo Foundation for the Arts.

We are grateful, above all, to the museums and collectors who have lent to the exhibition. Their generosity has made it possible for us to assemble an unprecedented survey of Degas' landscape works, one that will greatly enlarge our understanding of the artist's multifaceted career.

Philippe de Montebello
Director
The Metropolitan Museum of Art
New York

Peter C. Marzio
Director
The Museum of Fine Arts,
Houston

Checklist of the Exhibition

NOTE: The abbreviated references included in these entries refer to the catalogues of Degas' works compiled by P.-A. Lemoisne (L), Eugenia Janis (J), Jean Adhémar and Françoise Cachin (AC), and to the catalogue of monotypes compiled by Richard Kendall, which is found in Appendix 2 of this book (K).

1 *Italian Landscape Seen through an Arch* [fig. 15]
1856
Oil on paper mounted on canvas
37 × 32 cm
Private collection
(L 48: *Paysage d'Italie vu par une lucarne*)

2 *View of Mount Vesuvius* [fig. 22]
*c.*1856
Pencil on white laid paper
26 × 36.8 cm
Curtis O. Baer Collection

3 *Roman Landscape* [fig. 28]
1857
Pencil on pinkish paper
27 × 43.8 cm
The Museum of Fine Arts, Houston, museum purchase with funds provided by the Sarah Campbell Blaffer Foundation

4 *Italian Landscape* [fig. 20]
*c.*1857–8
Oil on paper
22.8 × 31.1 cm
Browse & Darby, London
(BR 18: *Paysage d'Italie*)

5 *The Convent of Santa Trinita dei Monti Seen from a Tower of the Villa Medici* [fig. 17]
*c.*1858
Oil on paper, mounted on canvas
21.4 × 28.2 cm
Private collection
(L 47bis: *Paysage. Vue de Rome*)

6 *Landscape Study from Veronese* [fig. 44]
*c.*1859–60
Oil on paper, mounted on canvas
25.5 × 18.5 cm
Private collection, courtesy Galerie Schmit, Paris

7 *Promenade beside the Sea* [fig. 48]
*c.*1860
Oil on canvas
22.5 × 32.5 cm
Private collection
(BR 38: *Promenade au bord de la mer*)

8 *Horses in a Landscape* [fig. 50]
*c.*1860
Oil on canvas
54 × 64 cm
Kunstmuseum, Bern
(L 50: *Chevaux dans un paysage*)

9 *At the Races: The Start* [fig. 53]
*c.*1860–2
Oil on canvas
32 × 46 cm
Fogg Art Museum, Harvard University, Cambridge, MA, Bequest of Annie Swan Coburn
(L 76: *Aux courses, le départ*)

10 *Four Willow Trees* [fig. 45]
*c.*1863–5
Pencil and watercolour
38 × 26 cm
Private collection

11 *Leaving for the Hunt* [fig. 57]
*c.*1863–5 and 1873
Oil on canvas
69 × 88.5 cm
Private collection, courtesy Galerie Schmit, Paris
(L 119: *Le Départ pour la chasse*)

12 *The Morning Ride* [fig. 58]
1865–8
Oil on canvas
81 × 65 cm
Detroit Institute of Arts, Founders' Society Purchase, Ralph Harman Booth Bequest Fund
(L 118: *La Promenade à cheval*)

13 *Rocks in a Wood at Bagnoles-de-l'Orne* [fig. 62]
*c.*1867
Watercolour
22 × 19 cm
Musée du Louvre, Département des Arts Graphiques, Fonds du Musée d'Orsay, Paris
(L 191: *Rochers sous-bois à Bagnoles-de-l'Orne*)

14 *Rocks and Trees at Bagnoles-de-l'Orne* [fig. 63]
*c.*1867
Watercolour
25 × 20 cm
Syndics of the Fitzwilliam Museum, Cambridge
(L 192: *Sous-bois à Bagnoles-de-l'Orne*)

15 *Beside the Sea* [fig. 66]
1869
Pastel
24 × 31 cm
Private collection, courtesy Galerie Schmit, Paris
(L 205: *Au bord de la mer*)

16 *Fishing Boats Moored at the Entrance to a Port* [fig. 75]
1869
Pastel
23 × 33 cm
Private collection
(L 251: *Bateaux de pêche amarrés a l'entrée d'un port*)

17 *On the Cliff* [fig. 76]
1869
Pastel
33 × 46 cm
Private collection, Paris
(L 232: *Sur la falaise*)

18 *Cliffs beside the Sea* [fig. 77]
1869
Pastel
23 × 31 cm
Private collection, courtesy Galerie Schmit, Paris
(L 239: Falaises au bord de la mer)

19 *Beach at Low Tide* [fig. 79]
1869
Pastel
30 × 46 cm
Von der Heydt-Museum, Wuppertal
(L 249: *Plage à marée basse*)

20 *Houses on a Cliff* [fig. 80]
1869
Pastel
31 × 47 cm
Wadsworth Atheneum, Hartford, Connecticut, Bequest of Anne Parrish Titzell
(L 247: *Maisons sur une falaise*)

21 *Houses on Cliffs Surrounding a Bay* [fig. 81]
1869
Pastel
32 × 48 cm
Private collection, New York
(L 252: *Maisons sur des falaises contournant une baie*)

22 *Beach at Low Tide* [fig. 82]
1869
Pastel
22 × 31 cm
Private collection, New York
(L 234: *Plage à marée basse*)

23 *Seascape at Sunset* [fig. 85]
1869
Pastel
21.5 × 30 cm
Dr. and Mrs. John Robertson
(L 240: *Marine, soleil couchant*)

24 *The Beached Boat* [fig. 87]
*c.*1869
Pastel
23 × 32 cm
Private collection
(L 250: *Bateau echoué*)

25 *Horses in the Meadow* [fig. 91]
1871
Oil on canvas
32 × 40 cm
Janet Traeger Salz
(L 289: *Chevaux dans la prairie*)

26 *Women Combing their Hair* [fig. 97*bis*]
*c.*1875
Oil on paper mounted on canvas
32.3 × 46 cm
The Phillips Collection, Washington, D.C.
(L 376: *Femmes se peignant*)

27 *Beside the Sea* [fig. 106]
*c.*1877–9
Monotype
12 × 15.8 cm
Private collection
(J 264: *Au bord de la mer*; AC 181)

28 *Factory Smoke* [fig. 107]
*c.*1877–79
Monotype
11.9 × 16 cm
The Metropolitan Museum of Art, New York, The Elisha Whittelsey Collection, The Elisha Whittelsey Fund, 1982
(J 269: *Fumées d'usines*; AC 182)

29 *A Family out Walking* [fig. 109]
*c.*1877–9
Monotype
15.8 × 21.3 cm
Private collection
(J 263: *La Famille en promenade*; AC 179)

30 *Rest in the Field* [fig. 108]
*c.*1877–9
Monotype
21.2 × 16 cm
Sterling and Francine Clark Art Institute, Williamstown, Massachusetts
(J 265: *Repos dans les champs*; AC 178)

31 *The Road* [fig. 110]
*c.*1877–9
Monotype
11.8 × 16.1 cm
National Gallery of Art, Washington, D.C., Rosenwald Collection
(J 266: *La Route [chemin et arbres]*; AC 175)

32 *The Rising Road* [fig. 111]
*c.*1877–9
Monotype
11.7 × 16 cm
Museum of Fine Arts, Boston, Horatio Greenough Curtis Fund
(J 267: *Le Chemin montant*; AC 177)

33 *Moonrise* [fig. 112)
c. 1877–9
Monotype
11.9 × 16.1 cm
Sterling and Francine Clark Art Institute, Williamstown, Massachusetts
(J 270: *Lever la lune*; AC 182)

34 *The River* [fig. 113]
*c.*1877–9
Monotype
8.9 × 17.3 cm
Museum of Fine Arts, Boston, Katherine Bullard Fund
(J 272: *La Rivière*; AC 180)

35 *The Little Valley* [fig. 114]
*c.*1877–9
Monotype
11.9 × 16 cm
Bibliothèque Nationale, Paris

36 *The Valley* [fig. 115]
*c.*1877–9
Monotype
11.9 × 16 cm
Bibliothèque Nationale, Paris

37 *Landscape with House, Figures and Fountain* [fig. 107*bis*]
*c.*1878
Monotype
17.8 × 22.2 cm
Trustees of the British Museum, London
(J 271; AC 172: *Château et jet d'eau*)

38 *Avenue du Bois de Boulogne* [fig. 106*bis*]
*c.*1878
Monotype
12.1 × 15.9 cm
Syndics of the Fitzwilliam Museum, Cambridge
(J 260; AC 53)

39 *Conversation*
*c.*1889
Pastel
54 × 66 cm
Private collection, courtesy Galerie Schmit, Paris
(L 1007: *La Conversation [Deux femmes causant au bord d'un chemin]*)

40 *Landscape with Smokestacks* [fig. 130]
1890
Monotype and pastel
28 × 40 cm
Mr. and Mrs. Daniel Searle
(L 1054: *Paysage*; J 277)

41 *River Banks* [fig. 132]
1890
Monotype and pastel
30 × 40 cm
Private collection
(L 1042: *Bords de rivière*; J 281)

42 *Pathway in a Field* [fig. 134]
1890
Monotype and pastel
30 × 39.5 cm
Yale University Art Gallery, New Haven, Connecticutt
(L 1046: *Sentier dans la prairie*; J 286)

43 *Landscape in the Mountains* [fig. 136]
1890
Monotype
31.1 × 41 cm
Los Angeles County Museum of Art
(J 289: *Paysage dans la montagne*; AC 194)

44 *Village in l'Estérel* [fig. 139]
1890
Monotype
30 × 42.5 cm
Bibliothèque Nationale, Paris
(J 275: *Village dans l'Estérel*; AC 191)

45 *Estérel Village* [fig. 141]
1890
Monotype
30 × 39.9 cm
The Cleveland Museum of Art, Fiftieth Anniversary Gift of The Print Club of Cleveland
(J 276; AC 191a)

46 *Landscape with Rocky Cliffs* [fig. 138]
1890
Monotype and pastel
40 × 29 cm
Josefowitz collection
(L 1043: *Rochers au bord d'une rivière*; J 283)

47 *Landscape* [fig. 142]
1890
Monotype
30 × 40 cm
Private collection
(L 1063: *Paysage*; J 313; AC 200: *Paysage au ciel clair*)

48 *Green Landscape* [fig. 144]
1890
Monotype
30 × 40 cm
Collection of Mrs. Bertram Smith
(AC 199: *Paysage vert*; K 2)

49 *Landscape* [fig. 145]
1890
Monotype
29.7 × 39.6 cm
Private collection
(J 305: *Paysage*; AC 196)

50 *Mountain Effect* [fig. 146]
1890
Monotype
29.9 × 39.5 cm
Private collection
(J 298: *Effet de montagne*; AC 188)

51 *A Wooded Landscape* [fig. 147]
1890
Monotype
29.9 × 40.3 cm
Collection of Mrs. Bertram Smith
(J 297: *Forêt dans la montagne*; AC 187)

52 *Twilight in the Pyrenees* [fig. 148]
1890
Monotype
28.6 × 38.8 cm
Ackland Art Museum, The University of North Carolina of Chapel Hill, Akland Fund
(J 307: *Le Crépuscule sur les Pyrenées*; AC 185)

53 *L'Estérel* [fig. 149]
1890
Monotype
30.2 × 40 cm
Private collection
(J 300: *L'Estérel*; AC 186)

54 *Squall in the Mountains* [fig. 153]
1890
Monotype
30.3 × 39.8 cm
Norton Simon Museum of Art, Pasadena
(J 306: *Bourrasque dans la montagne*; AC 197)

55 *Le Cap Hornu* [fig. 155]
1890
Monotype
29.9 × 40 cm
Trustees of the British Museum, London
(J 295: *Le Cap Hornu près St. Valéry-sur-Somme*; AC 192)

56 *Landscape* [fig. 193]
1890
Monotype
29.9 × 39.9 cm
Collection of Phyllis Lambert, Montreal
(J 309: *Paysage*; AC 190)

57 *Mountains and Valley* [fig. 194]
1890
Monotype
30 × 40 cm
Charles de Montalembert
(L 1057: *Montagnes et vallon*; J 296)

58 *An Island in the Sea* [fig. 201]
1890
Monotype and pastel
30 × 40 cm
Charles de Montalembert
(L 1061: *Un Îlot en pleine mer*; J 311)

59 *A Lake in the Pyrenees* [fig. 145*bis*]
1890
Monotype
29 × 39.6 cm
Trustees of the British Museum, London
(J 302; AC 193: *Un lac dans les pyrenées*)

60 *Rocky Coast* [fig. 187]
c. 1890–2
Monotype and pastel
30.5 × 40.9 cm
Private collection
(L 1059: *Côte rocheuse*; J 293)

61 *Steep Coast* [fig. 199]
c. 1890–2
Pastel
46 × 54.6 cm
Jan Krugier Gallery
(BR 134: *Paysage*)

62 *Landscape* [fig. 200]
c. 1890–2
Pastel
52 × 50 cm
The Museum of Fine Arts, Houston, museum purchase with funds provided by the Brown Foundation Accessions Endowment Fund
(J 282; BR 127: *Paysage*)

63 *The Field of Flax* [fig. 175]
1892
Monotype and pastel
25 × 34 cm
Private collection
(L 1041: *Le Champ de lin*; J 321)

64 *Landscape* [fig. 182]
1892
Monotype and pastel
24.8 × 30 cm
Private collection
(L 1039: *Paysage*; J 314)

65 *Lake and Mountains* [fig. 168]
1892
Monotype and pastel
25 × 34 cm
Private collection, Switzerland
(L 1048: *Lac et montagnes*; J 304)

66 *Landscape* [fig. 173]
1892
Monotype and pastel
25.4 × 34 cm
The Metropolitan Museum of Art, New York, Purchase, Mr. and Mrs. Richard J. Bernhard Gift, 1972
(L 1044: *Paysage*; J 285)

67 *Wheatfield and Green Hill* [fig. 174]
1892
Monotype and pastel
26 × 34 cm
Norton Simon Museum of Art, Pasadena
(L 1034: *Champ de blé et colline vert*; J 320)

68 *Landscape by the Sea* [fig. 177]
1892
Monotype and pastel
25.2 × 34.4 cm
Musée d'Art et d'Histoire, Neuchâtel
(L 632: *Paysage*; K 6)

69 *Wheatfield and Line of Trees* [fig. 178]
1892
Monotype and pastel
25 × 34 cm
Private collection
(L 1035: *Champ de blé et ligne d'arbres*; J 291)

70 *Landscape* [fig. 179]
1892
Monotype and pastel
25.7 × 34.6 cm
Private collection
(L 1037: *Paysage*; J 288)

71 *Vesuvius* [fig. 181]
1892
Monotype and pastel
25 × 30 cm
Private collection
(L 1052: *Le Vésuve*; J 310)

72 *Landscape* [fig. 183]
1892
Monotype and pastel
24.1 × 28.6 cm
Private collection
(J 278: *Paysage*)

73 *Village Street* [fig. 219]
*c.*1896–8
Oil on canvas
81 × 69 cm
From the Collection of Dr. and Mrs. Julius H. Jacobson II
(L 1212: *Rue de village*)

74 *View of Saint-Valéry-sur-Somme* [fig. 233]
*c.*1896–8
Oil on canvas
51 × 61 cm
The Metropolitan Museum of Art, New York, The Robert Lehman Collection, 1975
(BR 150: *Le Village, Saint-Valéry-sur-Somme*)

75 *At Saint-Valéry-sur-Somme* [fig. 226]
*c.*1896–8
Oil on canvas
67.5 × 81 cm
Ny Carlsberg Glyptothek, Copenhagen
(L 1215: *A Saint-Valéry-sur-Somme [Entrée de village]*)

76 *Return of the Herd* [fig. 231]
*c.*1896–8
Oil on canvas
73 × 92 cm
Leicestershire Museums, Arts and Records Service
(L 1213: *La Rentrée du troupeau*)

77 *Houses at the Foot of a Cliff* [fig. 236]
1896–8
Oil on canvas
92 × 73 cm
Columbus Museum of Art, Ohio: Gift of Howard D. and Babette L. Sirak, The Donors to the Campaign for Enduring Excellence, and the Derby Fund.
(L 1219: *Maisons au Pied d'une Falaise*)

78 *Three Jockeys*
*c.*1900
Pastel on tracing paper laid down on board
49 × 62 cm
The Metropolitan Museum of Art, New York, Partial and promised gift of Mr. and Mrs. Douglas Dillon, 1992

Index

Pages with illustrations are *italicised*